Broňa Brejová (Ed.)

ITAT 2016: Information Technologies—Applications and Theory
Proceedings

Conference on Theory and Practice of Information Technologies
Tatranské Matliare, Slovakia, September 15-19, 2016

ITAT 2016: Information Technologies—Applications and Theory (Proceedings)
Tatranské Matliare, Slovakia, September 15-19, 2016
Broňa Brejová (Ed.)
Cover design: Róbert Novotný
Cover photograph: Jordi Masague (CC BY-SA 2.9)
Publisher: CreateSpace Independent Publishing Platform, 2016
ISBN 978-1537016740

Also published online by CEUR Workshop Proceedings vol. 1649
http://ceur-ws.org/Vol-1649/
Series ISSN 1613-0073

http://www.itat.cz/

Introduction

This volume contains papers from the 16th ITAT conference, which took place on September 15-19, 2016 in Tatranské Matliare, Slovakia. ITAT is a computer science conference with the primary goal of presenting new results of young researchers and doctoral students from Slovakia and the Czech Republic. The conference serves as a platform for information exchange within the community, and also provides opportunities for informal meetings of the participants in a mountainous regions of the Czech Republic and Slovakia. The traditional topics of the conference include software engineering, data processing and knowledge representation, information security, computational intelligence, theoretical foundations of computer science, distributed computing, natural language processing, and computer science education. The conference accepts papers describing original previously unpublished results, reports of significant work in progress, as well as reviews of topics of special interest to the conference audience.

The conference program this year included the main track, four specialized workshops and three invited lectures. All refereed papers in these proceedings were reviewed by at least two anonymous referees; further details including the program committees can be found in the introduction to the main track and individual workshops. Some workshops featured presentations submitted only as abstracts; these were not refereed. This volume also contains abstracts of three invited lectures by Michal Valko (INRIA Lille, France), Jiří Materna (Seznam.cz), and Ľuboš Buzna (University of Žilina, Slovakia).

I would like to thank all workshop organizers, program committee members, anonymous referees, invited speakers, and authors of the submitted papers for contributing to the scientific program of ITAT 2016. I also want to thank to the dedicated groups of organizers from the P. J. Šafárik University in Košice for organizing this conference every year.

Broňa Brejová
Comenius University in Bratislava
Chair of the Program Committee

Steering Committee

Peter Vojtáš, Charles University, Prague (chair)
Martin Holeňa, Czech Academy of Sciences
Tomáš Horváth, P. J. Šafárik University in Košice
Tomáš Vinař, Comenius University in Bratislava
Filip Zavoral, Charles University, Prague

Organizing Committee

Peter Gurský, P. J. Šafárik University in Košice (chair)
Tomáš Jakab, P. J. Šafárik University in Košice
Ľubomír Antoni, P. J. Šafárik University in Košice

Contents

Workshop on Algorithmic and Structural Aspects of Complex Networks and Applications (WASACNA 2016) 195

Invited talk

Refereed papers

Abstracts

Algorithmic Aspects of Finding Semigroups of Partial Automorphisms of Combinatorial Structures (AAFSPACS 2016) 235

Abstracts

ITAT 2016 Main Track

The main track of the ITAT conference accepts contributions in all areas of computer science. Since 2013, the conference also features specialized thematic workshops in several topics previously represented in the main track of the conference. As the focus of the conference shifts to these workshops, the number of submission to the main track decreases. This year the main track had six submissions, four of which were accepted based on anonymous reviews from at least two independent members of the program committee. I would like to thank to the authors of the submitted papers and to all program committee members for their contribution to the ITAT conference.

Broňa Brejová
Comenius University in Bratislava
Chair of the Program Committee

Program Committee

Broňa Brejová, Comenius University in Bratislava (chair)
David Bednárek, Charles University, Prague
Mária Bieliková, Slovak University of Technology in Bratislava
Jiří Dokulil, University of Vienna
Martin Holeňa, Czech Academy of Sciences
Tomáš Horváth, P. J. Šafárik University in Košice
Daniela Chudá, Slovak University of Technology in Bratislava
Jozef Jirásek, P. J. Šafárik University in Košice
Jana Katreniaková, Comenius University in Bratislava
Rastislav Královič, Comenius University in Bratislava
Michal Krátký, VŠB - Technical University of Ostrava
Věra Kůrková, Czech Academy of Sciences
Markéta Lopatková, Charles University, Prague
Dana Pardubská, Comenius University in Bratislava
Martin Plátek, Charles University, Prague
Karel Richta, Charles University, Prague
Gabriel Semanišin, P. J. Šafárik University in Košice
Roman Špánek, Czech Academy of Sciences
Ondrej Šuch, Matej Bel University, Banská Bystrica
Tomáš Vinař, Comenius University in Bratislava
Jakub Yaghob, Charles University, Prague
Filip Zavoral, Charles University, Prague

Sequential Learning on Graphs With Limited Feedback
(Invited Talk)

Michal Valko

INRIA Lille – Nord Europe, France
michal.valko@inria.fr

In this talk, we investigate the structural properties of certain sequential decision-making problems with limited feedback (bandits) in order to bring the known algorithmic solutions closer to a practical use including, online influence maximization or sequential recommender systems. To address these structured settings, we can always ignore the graph and use known algorithms for multi-armed bandits. However, their performance scales unfavorably with the number of nodes N, which is undesirable when N means a thousand of sensors or a million of movies. We describe several graph bandit problems and show how to use their graph structure to design new algorithms with faster learning rates, scaling not with N but with graph-dependent quantities, often much smaller than N in real-world graphs.

Michal Valko absolvoval magisterské štúdium informatiky na FMFI UK v Bratislave, doktorandské štúdium ukončil na University of Pittsburgh v oblasti machine learning a habilitáciu v sequential machine learning obhájil na École Normale Supérieure de Cachan. Od roku 2011 pôsobí ako vedecký pracovník v tíme SequeL na Francúzskom národnom inštitúte pre informatiku a aplikovanú matematiku - Inria. Hlavnou oblasťou jeho výskumu je machine learning, kde sa špecializuje na metódy, ktoré minimalizujú objem dát, ktoré treba poskytnúť algoritmom predtým, než začnú byť užitočné.

ITAT 2016 Proceedings, pp. 3–10
ISBN 978-1537016740, © 2016 M. Kratochvíl

Compiling functional code for system-level environment

Miroslav Kratochvíl[1]*

Department of Software Engineering, Charles University in Prague
kratochvil@ksi.mff.cuni.cz

Abstract: Compilation of programming languages based
on λ–calculus to standalone, low-level machine code involves a challenge of removing automatic memory management that is usually required for supporting implicit allocations produced by currently available compilers. We
propose a compilation approach that is able to convert
pure, lazily-evaluated functional code to machine code
suitable for running on bare hardware with no run-time
support, and describe a Haskell-like programming language that demonstrates feasibility of the new method. Using the proposed approach, the missing ability to directly
control the hardware and memory allocation may be added
to purely functional languages, which otherwise have several advantages over traditional procedural languages, including easier verification and parallelization.

1 Introduction

Ideas from functional programming have always been influencing more traditional imperative programming languages. Apparent simplicity and expressiveness of
λ–based constructions is reflected both in new features of
some languages (notably the new functionality of C++11)
or in whole new languages (Clojure, Rust, partially also in
Swift or Nim). Functional languages, on the other hand,
are being improved to acquire the benefits of languages
with more direct control of resulting machine code, which
may be required for reaching performance, efficiency, or
binary compatibility goals — there has been much research aiming to make the high-level constructions more
efficient, concerning e.g. memory allocation efficiency
[7], type unboxing for performance [18] and various inlining methods.

We push both of these developments to one of possible
meeting points — we demonstrate a language that satisfies the requirements from the system-level languages by
having similar (mostly compatible) resulting code, execution and memory management model as C or C++, while
supporting functional programming paradigms, type systems, syntax, and many practical programming constructions from Haskell and similar languages.

Major challenges. Such combination may easily lead to a
direct contradiction, as the phenomena common in functional languages imply the need either for garbage collection or for other, possibly even more complicated run-time
processing:

- Variables of recursive types (like lists and trees), that
  form a highly valued building block of functional
  programming, are quite difficult to be implemented
  efficiently without some kind of automatic deallocation decision. Common example of such decision
  may be seen in automatic handling of two singly-
  linked list objects that share a common 'tail'.

- A quite common technique in functional programming — generating functions on runtime by partial
  application and passing them around as first-class
  objects — is impossible in minimalist system-level
  conditions, as any code generator (or, equivalently, a
  compiler) can not be a part of the language runtime.
  Similar problem arises with code that implies need
  for lazy evaluation, which, if it can not be removed
  by inlining at compile time, is usually supported by
  run-time allocation of *thunks* in automatically managed memory.

- Arbitrarily deep recursion, a common method to run
  loops in functional programming, is usually supported by unbounded automatic allocation of a stack-
  like structure. In system-level programming, the programs and all recursion must fit into a standard, limited and unmanaged program stack segment.

Viability of a new language. The main motivation for creating a new language is to explore the possibilities that
arise from the expressive power of a purely functional language applied to a full stack[1] of code that runs on bare
hardware. The benefits may include easier high-level optimization and simplified static analysis.

In particular, performing partial evaluation of the functional code is a computationally easy, well developed and
very effective method of optimization [20]. The lack of
side effects (or correct embedding of side effects in a tan-
gible construction) also simplifies derivation of semantic
meaning of the code by reducing amount of variables that
affect how the code is run.

Moreover, functional languages do not reflect any of
the traditional paradigms that the system-level programming languages inherited: They are not designed specifically for register-based machines, nor uniprocessors, nor
for sequential code execution[2], not even for preservation

---

*This work was supported by the grant 11562/2016 of the Charles
University Grant Agency.

[1]We indirectly refer to the valuable property of C-like languages,
that all dependencies of C (esp. the standard library) can again be written
only in C.

[2]Any code that touches a common system-level primitive directly is
almost necessarily sequential.

of call conventions and code structures shared by program parts. We consider lack of those properties a crucial benefit for simplification of automatic code processing, significant both for further elimination of variables affecting derivation of high-level optimization possibilities and, more notably, for automatic parallelization of code, as the compiler is not forced to perform a potentially sub-optimal decomposition of sequentially written code into paralellizable fibers.

Explicitly specified procedures and calls in block-structured code often represent some semantic value (like an API for module separation) that is unimportant or even harmful for resulting program structure — non-existence of any explicit code-structuring syntax leaves the choice of the call convention and separation of the code into subroutines on the compiler, which may produce better program while leaving the source semantically clean and readable.

We are further motivated by the recent high-performance results achieved by the language-centric functional programming approach, most notably the cache-oblivious memory allocation [2] or the generative approach to code parallelization [22].

1.1 Related research

We highlight several compilers that target a similar set of goals:

PreScheme — a language by Kelsey [15] is based on a compiler that transforms a simplified version of Scheme language to machine code. The approach chosen by authors is to completely replace all recursive types in the runtime with vectors, and to forcibly inline all code, so that no code-generating β–reductions present at runtime. As in other Scheme implementations, all evaluation is always eager and sequential structure of code is preserved.

Habit — a project of Portland State university HASP group [10] that states a need for similar system-programming language. Most recent publications from the project discuss the language features and provide a clear specification for implementation. To the best of our knowledge, no implementation of Habit is available yet.

Rust — a relatively new language that exploits techniques similar to linear types to stay both very efficient with memory allocations and safe against programmer errors. Compilation method and execution model chosen by Rust is similar to ours, with the exception of the imperative Rust syntax and the fact that the Rust runtime needs a garbage collector to work with recursive types from its standard library.

Swift — a recent product of Apple shows corporate interest in small, fast languages that reduce the memory-management overhead and include functional-programming improvements (notably pattern matching and a shifted view on classes, represented e.g. by Swift protocols and improved enumerated types).

Important theoretical result about evaluation methods, the fact that pure and eager functional languages can be shown inferior in terms of performance to languages that are either lazily evaluated or allow side-effects, was discussed by Bird, Jones and De Moor [1]. The low-level target environment of our language can not support lazy evaluation directly (although, in the code, the programmer can use lazy evaluation for any construction); we therefore must allow some well-contained amount of side effects.

We make extensive use of the knowledge that was gathered during the GHC development. Discussed compilation and optimization methods are usually based on the methods used to compile Haskell, as described for example in GHC Internals [13].

1.2 Approach

As a main goal we construct a simple language to demonstrate that there is no technical obstacle that would make system-level programming in a purely functional language impossible. To solve the aforementioned problems with run-time dependency on automatic memory management, we make following design choices:

- Recursive types are replaced by pointed types. We discuss the reasons and effects of this removal in section 2.3. As in C, management of all memory except the stack is done by programmer (directly or indirectly using library code) through pointed types or constructions based on them.

- Deep functional recursion is allowed, but it is replaced with tail recursion at all tail-call positions. Such trivial approach is used successfully in many compilers, including the GHC. See section 2.4 for details.

- Our main contribution is the method to run lazy evaluation without heap allocation of thunks. We store the thunks *in program stack* and apply them to function bodies that were modified at compile time to expect them as arguments, passed to them by a standard calling convention. We describe a fast, deterministic inference-based algorithm that converts functional code to such equivalently-behaving non-lazy form in section 2.2. Note that our solution works without any partial evaluation technique that is usually exploited for this purpose, but maintains the code in a form that is still able to be optimized and transformed by standard inlining algorithms.

For demonstration purposes, we only provide a simple type system (Hindley-Milner with several extensions) and rely on the LLVM compiler framework to generate platform-specific code. Results are presented in section 3.

Although there is currently no guarantee that resulting programming language will be practical, we believe that low-level programming languages with high levels of abstraction are currently very favorable[3] and current development is producing a lot of small languages inspired by functional programming that target low-level goals (e.g. the Nim language), in which our resulting language could fit easily. Still, its main purpose is to serve as a future testbed for optimization and automatic parallelization techniques.

2 Language internals

The language is constructed similarly as other pure functional languages. We tightly follow the standard definition structure and functional syntax known from Haskell, with some simplifications (e.g. the syntax for type classes and related constructions is unnecessary for our purpose). Upon compilation, source code is type-checked, rewritten to non-polymorphic non-lazy equivalent, functions are lifted to form top-level blocks, and partially evaluated to certain extent for optimization.

The testing compiler finally emits a pack of LLVM intermediate code with several functions (e.g. `main`) exported to serve as entry points. LLVM framework is then used to compile the almost-machine LLVM code to an object file (or executable) of the target platform. Using LLVM as "assembly" allows us to simplify the compiler in three ways: We do not have to care about register allocation, spilling and raw stack operations, program can be easily linked with any code the LLVM bytecode is able to link with (notably any library that follows the C calling conventions, including the C standard library), and we can use the vast library of already-available low-level optimizations that can be run on LLVM bytecode.

2.1 Evaluation

In our case, the compilation of function evaluation is principally similar to that used in GHC — the function definitions that were optimized and lifted to top-level are compiled to form code blocks that obey a machine-level calling convention, and the machine code is generated for them. In contrast to GHC, our resulting code can only use a set of primitives applicable to system-level environment, notably it can not implicitly access any memory other than on the program stack. The two cases when GHC uses such allocation are the handling of boxed or recursive types (which we disallowed) and allocation of thunks for lazy evaluation, which must be worked around.

Lazy evaluation Instead of thunk allocation in the STG[4] data structure, we will use a structure that is of predictable size and stored completely on stack. The only problematic part of such *static thunk* is its "meaning", or, technically, a description of the function that will evaluate the thunk. As the concept of function objects has no straightforward assembly-level representation, we replace it by a code address of a previously-prepared compiled function (or simply a "function pointer" to code generated at compile time) that is able to compute the actual result of the thunk. Rest of the static thunk consists of a tuple of the argument values that are expected by the pointed function on evaluation.

In resulting situation, the compiler must solve following new tasks:

- It has to ensure that the code is ready for passing the thunks around as function arguments or return values instead of simple values.

- It has to prepare thunk-evaluating functions for all occurrences of thunks in the code.

For example, consider this simple functional code:

```
f a = (+) a
g a b = a b
h a = g (f a) a
```

We will ignore the fact that any reasonable compiler would choose inlining with a far better result, and generate static thunks for demonstration. We progress as follows:

1. We will first derive the types of the code. Given initial basis $\Gamma \ni (+ : \mathbb{N} \to \mathbb{N} \to \mathbb{N})$, usual type inference would output following type assignments for the code: $f : \mathbb{N} \to \mathbb{N} \to \mathbb{N}$, $g : \mathbb{N} \to \mathbb{N} \to \mathbb{N} \to \mathbb{N}$ and $h : \mathbb{N} \to \mathbb{N}$.

   Instead, we reflect the need to see which functions must be called lazily and modify the type system to allow such expression. Specifically, the typing inferred for f is $f : \mathbb{N} \to \textbf{thunk}(\{\mathbb{N}\}, \mathbb{N} \to \mathbb{N})$.

   The type expression means that f returns a thunk that can be used as a function of type $\mathbb{N} \to \mathbb{N}$ and already carries one argument of type $\mathbb{N}$ that will be passed to evaluating function. We will show how to derive such information later.

2. From that, the compiler sees that f must be called lazily, and creates an eagerly evaluable function that can be referenced from the thunk:

   ```
   f_eager t1 t2 = (+) t1 t2
   ```

3. It correspondingly translates the "inner" call (`f a`) in h to a thunk represented as a tuple $(\texttt{address\_of(f\_eager)}, \texttt{a})$.

---

[3]This knowledge was gained by looking at the statistical distribution of programming languages used in software packages installed on an average Debian Linux system. [19]

[4]Spineless Tagless G-Machine, the structure used to store all implicitly allocated data of programs compiled by GHC.

4. To translate the outer call, a new version of g, called g_eager that accepts a tuple in the above form as a second argument, is generated, and h is rewritten:

```
g_eager (fptr,a) t3 = fptr a t3
h a = g_eager (f_eager,a) a
```

Resulting code now does not contain any lazy evaluation.

Overhead of static thunks. Compared to code inlining that would trivially solve the aforementioned example, static thunks may potentially present significant runtime overhead arising from the necessity to transfer function pointers and (possibly bulky) thunk data through the stack structures (such behavior may manifest as appearance of functions with surprisingly many arguments), and from the possibility that the thunk may get evaluated more than once. In our view, the first case is a counterweight to a similar situation present with inlining process — inlining may produce a program that runs faster, but usually for the price of code size. Allocating thunks produces possibly smaller code (because the compiler is not forced to inline all partial applications), but the required data transfers and indirections add overhead and reduce execution efficiency.

Compared to thunks allocated on heap, our approach profits from the simplicity of stack allocation, which is usually handled by one-instruction modification of a CPU register. General-purpose heap allocators may require hundreds of instructions and possibly produce several CPU cache misses.

Strictness. Strict method of evaluation is a common optimization in compilers of lazy functional languages, as it is usually cheaper to actually evaluate the result than to allocate the thunk and possibly re-evaluate it on each usage[5]. There are practical methods that automatically determine which results should be evaluated strictly, including the one from Haskell [12] or OCaml [24].

Our approach is simpler — because the need to produce specialized code with additional data transfers may impose significant performance overhead, we consider all calls strict by default, allowing lazy evaluation only when needed (i.e. where inlining was unable to remove it) or on programmer's choice.

Effect of strict evaluation on correctness. The common argument against strict evaluation — that it may prevent the program from halting — holds here. Moreover, our work with pointed types may cause a program crash if the statements are not evaluated in exact order (e.g. a null-pointer check followed by a dereference is a common construction, but may get evaluated in a reverse order if both parts were arguments of one function). We argue that our environment is not affected by those kinds of errors — all potentially harmful side effects (especially the out-of-stack

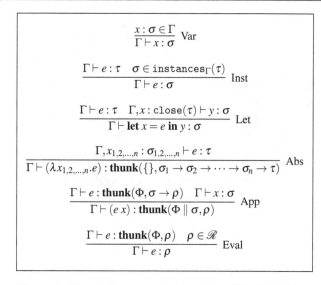

Figure 1: Type inference rules based on Hindley-Milner type system. The original abstraction and application rules are modified to augment the simple function types with information about all possible thunk-evaluating functions.

memory operations) are contained in a monad environment, and we provide syntax for marking lazy code that the programmer can use to avoid possible infinite loops of eager evaluation.

2.2 Type system

The language is typed statically by a Hindley-Milner-style type inference as described by Damas and Milner [5]. While we use several non-trivial practical extensions (notably the statically defined overloading in a manner similar to that of Kaes [14] and support for recursion without explicit handling of the fixpoint operator) we only describe the minimal extension of the system that informs the compiler about the requirements for removing lazy evaluation. See Figure 1 for the modified inference rules.

In the figure, the functions instances and close are used exactly for the purposes of the original system — close introduces the $\forall$-polymorphism (to create a polytype), and instances$_\Gamma$ removes it, by describing a set of new possible monotype instances with fresh type variables free in the basis Γ.

The information stored in a **thunk** covers

- the actual type of the function the thunk represents at current place

- one list of argument types for each thunk-evaluating function that must be able to get arguments required for its evaluation from this thunk.

Syntactically, the situation is described as follows. The structure:

$$\mathbf{thunk}\left(\{(\tau_1, \tau_2, \ldots, \tau_n), (\sigma_1, \ldots), \ldots\}, \rho\right)$$

---

[5]With the exception of popular counterexamples, including long lists that get only first few items instantiated.

describes a thunk that returns (possibly functional) type ρ, and stores enough arguments to be evaluated either by function of type $\tau_1 \to \tau_2 \to \cdots \to \tau_n \to \rho$, or $\sigma_1 \to \cdots \to \rho$, etc. Argument lists can be empty, in that case we write them as . Operation $\Phi \parallel \sigma$ in the figure produces a new set of argument lists, containing all lists from Φ with σ appended on the end.

Such set-based construction is necessary to overcome the possible incompatibility of thunks that can arise from a code similar to this:

```
succ :: N -> N
if :: Boolean -> a -> a -> a
f = succ
g x = (+) x
h a b = if a f (g b)
```

Because underlying code can not prepare the result of h for evaluation by derived thunk-evaluating functions of either f or g, it is necessary for the thunk to be universal. Its universal type is decided as $\mathbf{thunk}(\{,(\mathbb{N})\}, \mathbb{N} \to \mathbb{N})$. Consecutive application of a value of type $\mathbb{N}$ to the result of h produces $\mathbf{thunk}(\{(\mathbb{N}), (\mathbb{N}, \mathbb{N})\}, \mathbb{N})$, which can be readily evaluated — the argument lists exactly correspond to the argument lists of succ and (+). Note that it is not necessary to mark which argument list is going to be used on evaluation, as that information is also (implicitly) present in the code of the associated pointed function.

Unification of the thunk descriptions, required for the inference system to work, is done structurally in the type part, and by set union in the argument list. In our implementation, set union is handled by working with the set contents as with an separate object external to actual unification process, storing only a variable-like reference. Technical details are omitted.

There is a chance for non-determinism introduced in rules Abs and Eval, as it is not clear for the compiler whether e.g. the thunk should be evaluated on spot or passed down unmodified; or whether successive λ-abstractions should be converted to a single thunk or multiple smaller thunks that would eventually get evaluated successively. For our purpose, we use early evaluation of every thunk in the Eval case by completely disallowing already-evaluable thunks, and the all-at-once thunk construction in the Abs case. Such approach satisfies our requirements on the compiler; other alternatives were not considered as they bring "additional laziness" of the evaluation and measurement of their effect is not in the scope of this paper.

Thunk storage. Given a deterministic storage method, the size required for thunk structure can be computed at compile-time for any thunk type. Thunks can therefore be passed around as traditional function arguments and return values without any need for dynamic memory management.

Exact order in which the arguments are stored in the thunk is completely arbitrary, as long as the basic operations (addition of a new argument, set unification and extraction of any complete argument list) stay deterministic.

An easily implementable example is a tuple with just enough fields of every type so that each argument list can fit in, stored in tail-aligned order to allow easy addition of a newly applied argument to list tails.

Function specialization. After inference, function bodies specialized for thunk processing are created by a very gratifying side effect of the overloading resolution algorithm: In the same way in which e.g. an arithmetic function is specialized to support both integer and floating-point arguments, it can also be specialized to support thunks values. The difference in the code is then created on the place of the "invisible" application operator, instead of the more traditional place of an arithmetical operator.

2.3 Recursive types

Recursive types, such as auto-allocated lists and trees, form a basic building block of many current functional languages. Their removal in our language is justified by the addition of pointed ("reference") types that, like in other languages, are able to replicate the functionality to a practical extent. While other solutions for replacing the need for automatic deallocation exist (like the linear type systems), our choice is supported by following considerations:

- Almost all primitives used by a system-programming language require some computation with memory addresses (e.g. the system calls).

- Usage of first-class references is a fairly standard method to define complicated data structures.[6]

- Inclusion of pointers does not prohibit the possibility of future addition of automatic memory management by the programmer, just as with garbage collectors for C/C++ [3].

- All memory operations can be contained in a monad to produce a pure language. This can be further exploited to provide some automatic safety of memory operations, but forces the programmer to use complicated syntax for trivially-looking tasks.

As we are not aware of any officially recognized syntax that would allow to directly use pointers in a purely functional language, we reuse the sizeOf, peek and poke primitives from Haskell FFI library [4], that shares a similar set of goals. Allocation and deallocation functions are linked from standard C library, having type signatures alloc :: IO (Ptr a) and free :: Ptr a -> IO ().[7]

---

[6] Moreover, naive data structure implementations in pure languages suffer from a fatal inefficiency resulting from the need to constantly re-allocate immutable data. In those cases, non-trivial constructions such as the zipper [11] are required to produce effective code.

[7] alloc can decide about allocation size from previous type inference.

2.4   Recursion

The common model for transforming functional recursion to loops using tail calls fits our scheme with one exception — unbounded, non-tail recursion along a data structure will cause stack overflow much earlier than in a common functional language, where the "stack" structure is allocated dynamically on heap and the actual system stack holds only rarely-expanding structures. In case of Haskell, infinite non-tail recursion will cause a regular memory depletion error, stack overflows can happen only on evaluation of deeply-nested thunk values.[8]

The risk of unwanted stack overflows can be mitigated syntactically: Whenever the compiler would emit code that calls some function recursively using a non-tail call, i.e. when there is a loop in call graph that contains at least one non-tail call edge, it may abort the compilation and require the programmer to syntactically acknowledge the acceptance of the risk (or existence of some functionality that alleviates it) with a keyword at call site.

3   Implementation and results

Our demonstrational compiler is implemented as an expansion of the `tlc` compiler written in C++ [17]. We measure its performance in two ways: First, to measure the general performance of our approach, we compare the speed of simple implementations of two algorithms that solve relatively common problems with other compilers. Next, performance overhead of a synthetic case of static thunk usage is tested on a small program that runs an equivalent of standard Haskell `foldl` function on a list structure.

The exact test problems for first comparison are:

- Insertion of 2^{20} pseudo-random elements into a binary search tree, and

- 2^{28} rounds of TEA cipher [23].

We have created simple implementations of both test algorithms in C, Haskell and in our testing language, and compared the execution speed of the code produced by each compiler. The measurements are shown in the figure 2. Results show almost identical running times for C and our language, and some overhead for the code produced by Haskell compiler. The tiny speedup over C++ in one case was determined to be a product of complete inlining of the functional code; it was no longer measurable after forcibly inlining the C++ code by hand to a form with similar structure as the assembly produced by `tlc`

Next, thunk overhead was measured on the `foldl` function used to sum elements in a prepared linked-list structure with pseudo-random numbers. The function was run

---

[8]The nice example given on Haskell Wiki [9] exploits the properties of lazy implementation of `scanl`: Code `print $ last $ scanl (+)` `[0..1000000]` is killed in older GHC implementations as the stack gets filled by the back-references to unevaluated list elements.

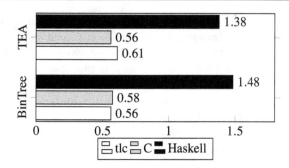

Figure 2: Performance results for the test programs, lower is better. Values are average run time in seconds over 100 runs.

repeatedly on a list that fitted in the CPU L3 cache. Fully inlined, specialized `foldl` was able to process one list element on average in around 4.152ns, `foldl` that was passed a thunk that contained the adding function took 4.548ns. Several (less than 10) extra 8-byte arguments passed with the thunk increased the processing time of one element by around 0.1ns each.

We consider the overhead of indirection less than 10% in a pathological stress-test a good result, and do not expect real applications to suffer serious performance problems. Overhead of passing reasonably-sized thunk contents around seems similarly inconsequential.

All tests were measured on Intel®Core™i5-4200M CPU at 2.50GHz, used C compiler was standard Debian GCC of version 5.3.1-19, Haskell compiler was GHC version 7.10.3.

3.1   Drawbacks and unsolved problems

The main drawbacks of the new language originate in the new combination of system-level problems with purely functional syntax. Suitable solutions for some problems listed below are not yet established, and are slightly more interesting as a question of language design than of actual compiler functionality. We present the most interesting problems as open questions:

Destructors. Finding a good spot for automatic release of resources held by local variables is not very straightforward in a functional language, as the concept of imperative code blocks that correspond to variable validity in C-like languages is not extensible to the monad environment.

A related approach that merely prevents the programmer from forgetting to deallocate a structure (thus creating a memory leak) is the bracketing pattern, known for example from Python as the `with` construction, or as `bracket` from Haskell `Control.Exception` library. For our purpose, bracketing is composable with monads [8] to form an illusion of variable-holding program-blocks that resemble well-accepted syntax from procedural programming.

Similar problems arise with temporary data structures required for sub-results of certain operations: For instance, the multiplication of 3 matrix objects (a*b*c) usually implicitly allocates space for sub-result (a*b). In a functional environment, * has to be replaced by some monadic construction to allow access to impure primitives (e.g. heap memory operations) required to allocate the space for sub-results.

Pointers to stack. A common method to allocate and deallocate a small structure needed for communication with a system- or a library-call is to allocate it dynamically on the stack and only pass a pointer; a great example of such structure is struct timeval. In a functional language, careless usage of such pointer may lead to a program crash — because the stack management does not necessarily correspond to variable scope as in C-like languages, no dependency that would hold the structure in place until is implicitly materialized and the pointer may easily become dangling.

List processing. Easy list traversal and recursive structure comprehension is one of the main features of the functional programming languages. Similar functionality may also exist in a low-level language that forbids the (required) recursive types: Pattern matching on list structures, as known from Haskell, can be also applied to pointers. Common functional allocation of list structures (e.g. the well-known function pattern that returns list tail with a new prepended head) can be either replaced by allocation-free generators similar to Data.Traversable, or redesigned to work on STL-like list structures that are implicitly allocated by well-hidden language construction.

4   Conclusion

We have presented a new method to compile a pure functional language to low-level code suitable for system-programming. Main improvement, described in section 2.2, is the inference algorithm that allows to transform lazily-evaluated functional code to a form that does not require automatic memory management for run-time allocation of thunks. Resulting compiler is comparably simple, fast, and produces code that does not require any run-time support, shows no significant performance drawbacks when compared to code generated by current C compilers, and allows basic usage of high-level constructions known from current functional languages.

While the language is not yet very pleasant to work with, mainly because of the drawbacks that are mentioned in section 3.1 and lack of well-developed standard library, the code of the test programs is concise, shows no unnecessary complexity, are is readily comprehensible by any functional-aware programmer. Moreover, as described in section 2, the language allows direct linking with many existing libraries through standardized calling conventions, which may be easily exploited for further applications.

4.1   Future research

Apart from the demonstration of the original goal, the new language opens possibilities to apply high-level optimization methods to programs that intend to run on bare hardware, possibly yielding better results than the optimizers of Haskell that are encased in a pre-defined scheme of memory management, or the optimizers of C++ which are constrained by aliasing problems arising from impurity of the language.

An example of approaches that aggressively modify and restructure the subroutine structure of the program is the work of Danvy and Schultz [6] that shows beneficial impact of possibly non-deterministic combination of argument dropping, lifting and inlining. Similarly, purity of the code allows for a more efficient elimination of common sub-expressions and repeated code. Practical impact of both techniques is yet to be measured.

Newly added program control possibilities, mainly the memory-related primitives described in section 2.3, create many new chances for programmer errors. While current type checkers can discover many errors on compilation, more complicated type systems or verification approaches could be able to check e.g. actual memory safety or related constraint satisfaction. We hope to implement and test the ideas from the Sage language [16] that allows automatic addition of runtime checks for constraints that the compiler was not able to satisfy by static checking; or some of the work of Roorda [21], which allows to use a quite powerful concept of pure type systems in a practical environment.

References

[1] Richard Bird, Geraint Jones, and Oege De Moor. More haste, less speed: lazy versus eager evaluation. *Journal of Functional Programming*, 7(05):541–547, 1997.

[2] Guy E Blelloch and Robert Harper. Cache efficient functional algorithms. *Communications of the ACM*, 58(7):101–108, 2015.

[3] Hans Boehm, Alan Demers, and Mark Weiser. A garbage collector for C and C++, 2002.

[4] Manuel MT Chakravarty, Sigbjørn Finne, F Henderson, Marcin Kowalczyk, Daan Leijen, Simon Marlow, Erik Meijer, Sven Panne, S Peyton Jones, Alastair Reid, et al. The Haskell 98 foreign function interface 1.0, 2002. *Available onlin e: http://www. cse. unsw. edu. au/ chak/haskell/ffi.*

[5] Luis Damas and Robin Milner. Principal type-schemes for functional programs. In *Proceedings of the 9th ACM SIGPLAN-SIGACT symposium on Principles of programming languages*, pages 207–212. ACM, 1982.

[6] Olivier Danvy and Ulrik P Schultz. *Lambda-dropping: transforming recursive equations into programs with block structure*, volume 32. ACM, 1997.

[7] Damien Doligez and Xavier Leroy. A concurrent, generational garbage collector for a multithreaded implementation of ML. In *Proceedings of the 20th ACM SIGPLAN-SIGACT*

symposium on Principles of programming languages, pages 113–123. ACM, 1993.

[8] Cale Gibbard. Bracket pattern. `https://wiki.haskell.org/Bracket_pattern`, 2008. Accessed: 2016-05-10.

[9] Stack Overflow - Haskell Wiki. `https://wiki.haskell.org/Stack_overflow`. Accessed: 2015-12-21.

[10] The High Assurance Systems Programming Project HASP. *The Habit Programming Language: The Revised Preliminary Report*. Department of Computer Science, Portland State University Portland, Oregon 97207, USA, November 2010.

[11] Gérard Huet. The zipper. *Journal of functional programming*, 7(05):549–554, 1997.

[12] Kristian Damm Jensen, Peter Hjæresen, and Mads Rosendahl. Efficient strictness analysis of Haskell. In *Static Analysis*, pages 346–362. Springer, 1994.

[13] SL Peyton Jones, Cordy Hall, Kevin Hammond, Will Partain, and Philip Wadler. The Glasgow Haskell compiler: a technical overview. In *Proc. UK Joint Framework for Information Technology (JFIT) Technical Conference*, volume 93, 1993.

[14] Stefan Kaes. Parametric overloading in polymorphic programming languages. In *ESOP'88*, pages 131–144. Springer, 1988.

[15] Richard A Kelsey. Pre-Scheme: A Scheme dialect for systems programming, 1997.

[16] Kenneth Knowles, Aaron Tomb, Jessica Gronski, Stephen N Freund, and Cormac Flanagan. SAGE: Unified hybrid checking for first-class types, general refinement types, and dynamic (extended report), 2006.

[17] Miroslav Kratochvíl. Low-level functional programming language. Master's thesis, Charles University in Prague, 2015.

[18] Xavier Leroy. Unboxed objects and polymorphic typing. In *Proceedings of the 19th ACM SIGPLAN-SIGACT symposium on Principles of programming languages*, pages 177–188. ACM, 1992.

[19] Avery Pennarun, Bill Allombert, and Petter Reinholdtsen. Debian popularity contest, 2012.

[20] Simon Peyton Jones and Simon Marlow. Secrets of the glasgow haskell compiler inliner. *Journal of Functional Programming*, 12(4-5):393–434, 2002.

[21] J-W Roorda and JT Jeuring. Pure type systems for functional programming. 2007.

[22] Michel Steuwer, Christian Fensch, Sam Lindley, and Christophe Dubach. Generating performance portable code using rewrite rules. 2015.

[23] David J Wheeler and Roger M Needham. TEA, a tiny encryption algorithm. In *Fast Software Encryption*, pages 363–366. Springer, 1994.

[24] Hirofumi Yokouchi. Strictness analysis algorithms based on an inequality system for lazy types. In *Functional and Logic Programming*, pages 255–271. Springer, 2008.

ITAT 2016 Proceedings, pp. 11–17
ISBN 978-1537016740, © 2016 V. Kuboň, M. Lopatková, T. Hercig

Searching for a Measure of Word Order Freedom

Vladislav Kuboň[1], Markéta Lopatková[1], and Tomáš Hercig[2,3]

[1] Charles University in Prague, Faculty of Mathematics and Physics,
Institute of Formal and Applied Linguistics
[2] Department of Computer Science and Engineering, Faculty of Applied Sciences,
University of West Bohemia, Univerzitní 8, 306 14 Plzeň, Czech Republic
[3] NTIS—New Technologies for the Information Society, Faculty of Applied Sciences,
University of West Bohemia, Technická 8, 306 14 Plzeň, Czech Republic
{vk,lopatkova}@ufal.mff.cuni.cz , tigi@ntis.zcu.cz

Abstract: This paper compares various means of measuring of word order freedom applied to data from syntactically annotated corpora for 23 languages. The corpora are part of the HamleDT project, the word order statistics are relative frequencies of all word order combinations of subject, predicate and object both in main and subordinated clauses. The measures include Euclidean distance, max-min distance, entropy and cosine similarity. The differences among the measures are discussed.

1 Motivation

The question of different features of natural languages has been engrossing theoretical linguists for hundred of years. They have been studying various language characteristics and classifying natural languages according to their properties, giving arise of a language typology, see esp. [1] and [2], or [3], to mention also the Czech tradition. These investigations led to a system of four basic language types, namely isolated, agglutinative, inflectional and polysynthetic languages.

Theoretical linguists have introduced an extensive list of relevant language features, a summary can be found, e.g., in the World Atlas of Language Structures (WALS) [4]. We will focus one particular phenomenon, word order of natural languages. While the classification of languages cannot be based upon a single phenomenon, the word order characteristics seems to belong among important features both for theoretical research and for practical natural language applications.

Languages are typically classified according to the degree of word order freedom to (more or less) fixed word order and free word order languages. The former type is often exemplified by English, where a word order position encodes a syntactic function (e.g., the first noun in an indicative sentence, having prototypically the function of subject, is followed by a predicative verb and a noun with the object functions); this property typically correlates with under-developed flection. The later type can be exemplified by Czech, where a syntactic function is encoded by morphological case marking [5], and word order expresses an information structure.

From the practical point of view, a freedom of word order to a great extent correlates with a parsing difficulty of a particular natural language (a language with more fixed word order is typically easier to parse than a language containing, e.g., non-projective constructions). On top of that, modern unsupervised methods of natural language processing might also profit from investigations of a similar kind as we present in this paper. If researchers would have an exact information about the properties of a language which they want to process using unsupervised methods, this knowledge might help them to choose an adequate processing method and/or to properly set its parameters.

The examination of a natural language typology have been traditionally based upon a systematic observation of linguistic material. However, linguistic research is in completely different position now: linguistic observations can be based on large amount of language data stored in corpora which have been growing not only in size but also in complexity of annotation during the last decade.

Moreover, several attempts to propose an unified annotation scheme – let us mention at least Stanford Dependencies and Stanford Universal Dependencies [6, 7, 8],[1] Google Universal Tags [9], Universal Dependencies [10],[2] – make it possible to use existing corpora for different languages.

In this paper we exploit the annotation developed in the frame of the HamleDT project (Harmonized Multi-Language Dependency Treebank [11]).[3]

We have already presented a study where we focused on word order properties of HamleDT treebanks and the languages ranking – we used a simple max-min distance based on a distribution of sentences among all variants of the word order. Here we re-calculate the results of the experiments described in [12] using standard measures like Euclidean distance, entropy, and cosine similarity.

In the remaining sections of the paper we are first going to introduce the data and tools used for the experiment, section 3 describes the setup of the experiment, section 4 presents the results and the final section discusses the conclusions and possible directions for future work.

---

[1] http://nlp.stanford.edu/software/stanford-dependencies.shtml
[2] http://universaldependencies.org/
[3] https://ufal.mff.cuni.cz/hamledt

2   Available Data Resources and Tools

HamleDT (Harmonized Multi-Language Dependency Treebank, [11])[4] is a compilation of existing dependency treebanks (or dependency conversions of other treebanks), transformed so that they all conform to the same annotation style. These treebanks as well as searching tools are available through a repository for linguistic data and resources LINDAT/CLARIN.[5]

2.1   Corpora

HamleDT integrates corpora for several tens of languages. Wherever it is possible due to license agreements, the corpora are transformed into a common data and annotation format, which enables a user – after a very short period of getting acquainted with each particular treebank – to search and analyze comfortably the data of a particular language.

The HamleDT family of treebanks is based on the dependency framework and technology developed for the Prague Dependency Treebank (PDT),[6] i.e., large syntactically annotated corpus for the Czech language [15]. Here we focus on the so-called analytical layer, describing a surface sentence structure (relevant for studying word order properties). Unfortunately, due to various technical and licensing restrictions, it was not possible to use all treebanks contained in HamleDT. Thus our effort focusses on 23 treebanks with available annotation on this syntactic layer, which still represent a wide variety of languages having various word-order properties.

As an example, Figure 1 shows three dependency representations for an English sentence in the HamleDT format.[7] Tables 1 and 2 provide an overview of the languages and the size of the corpora examined in our experiment.

2.2   Querying Tool

The advantage of using a common annotation framework for multiple treebanks also has a very useful consequence – instead of developing tailor-made searching tools we can apply a common tool to all treebanks we are analyzing. In the case of HamleDT, we can use the PML-TQ [16] search tool,[8] originally developed for processing the data from PDT.

Having the treebanks in the common data format and annotation scheme, the PML-TQ framework makes it possible to analyze the data in a uniform way. A typical user

---

[7]Data of each treebank in HamleDT are distributed in three annotation schemes – (a) the transformation of the treebank to the praguian style (used in PDT; leftmost in Figure 1), (b) the original annotation format of the given treebank (or its dependency transformation in case of non-dependency treebanks; in the middle of Figure 1), and (c) the transformation of the treebank to the Universal Dependencies style (rigthmost in the figure).

[8]https://lindat.mff.cuni.cz/services/pmltq/

interested in monolingual data can use PML-TQ in an interactive way. Such approach would, of course, not work for our set of 23 treebanks, therefore we have used a command line interface which PML-TQ also provides. This interface makes it possible to create scripts that process a specified set of treebanks automatically.

Let us now give an example of a PML-TQ query used in our analysis. It counts sentences having an SVO word order in the main clause.

```
a-node $p :=
[ depth() = "1", id ~ "prague",
  afun = "Pred", tag ~ "^V",
  1x a-node
    [ afun = "Sb" ],
  1x a-node
    [ afun = "Obj" ],
  a-node
    [ afun = "Sb", ord < $p.ord ],
  a-node
    [ afun = "Obj", ord > $p.ord ] ];
>> give count()
```

The query searches data annotated in the praguian style (id ~ "prague") for sentences containing verbs (tag ~ "^V") with the analytical function of a predicate (afun = "Pred") at the depth of one level below the technical root of the tree (depth() = "1"; i.e., this query focuses on the word order in main clauses, excluding coordinated predicates and disregarding also subordinate clauses). There must be exactly one subject and one object directly depending on the predicate (for the subject: 1x a-node [afun = "Sb"]), the subject must precede the verb (afun = "Sb", ord < $p.ord), and the object must follow it (afun = "Obj", ord > $p.ord). The result of the query is the count of such sentences (>> give count()). The visualization of the PML-TQ query can be found in Figure 2.

3   The Experiment

In order to avoid possible bias caused by a combination of too many language phenomena in complicated sentences, we have decided to exclude all sentences containing coordinated predicates, subjects or objects from our experiment. The phenomenon of coordination is to some extent "orthogonal" to that of word order (especially in dependency-based approaches to a language description); thus the results might have been negatively influenced if coordination of verbs or the coordination of its direct dependents would be allowed.

In this experiment, we have focused on "full" structures, i.e., sentences with core syntactic structure consisting of subject, predicate and object. We have created several queries aiming at a thorough investigation of the phenomenon of the mutual position of these syntactic units.

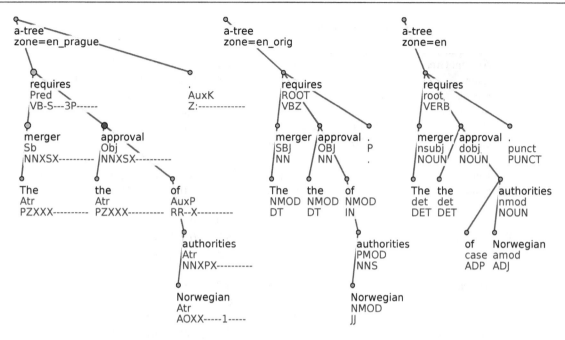

Figure 1: Three dependency representations of the sentence "The merger requires the approval of Norwegian authorities." in HamleDT 3.0. It is also one of the results of the query from Figure 2; nodes matching the query are slightly enlarged (in the left tree, nodes "requires", "merger" and "approval").

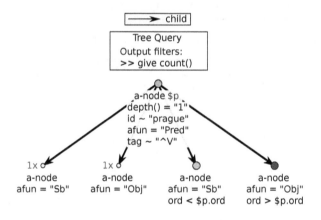

Figure 2: Visualization of the PML-TQ query

We have counted sentences for all six possible combinations (SVO, OVS, VSO, VOS, SOV, OSV), separately for main clauses and for subordinated clauses Table 1 and Table 2.

4   Comparison of Measures

The results presented in Tables 1 and 2 may serve as a basis for an estimation of a degree of word order freedom of individual languages. A typical mutual position of a subject, a predicate and an object constitutes one of the basic typological characteristic of a natural language. The problem of measuring the degree of word order freedom cannot be, of course, reduced only to this phenomenon, the freedom of word order of other sentence elements should proba-

bly be taken into account as well. Our decision to base the estimation on just these three constituents has several reasons. First of all, these constituents are present in a vast majority of sentences, they constitute a certain backbone of every sentence. Second, they are also relatively easily identifiable in all treebanks, regardless of the original annotation schemes. Although the HamleDT treebanks provide uniform annotation, the transformation of less frequent language phenomena from various languages may provide results which are not as uniform as we would like them to be. Last but not least, the three main constituents are located on top of the dependency tree, they do not require overly complex queries which might bring additional bias into the experiment.

The number we are looking for would describe how far is the distribution of individual variants of word order from the ideal absolutely free order of the main constituents. It is obvious that the languages with the highest degree of word order freedom would demonstrate the most equal distribution of sentences among all variants of the word order described in our tables, i.e., the frequency of all variants of the order of subject, verb and object will be equal to 16.66% (let us denote this "ideal vector" as Y)[9]. The difference between an actual distribution vector of each particular language from our table and this ideal vector then expresses the difference in word order freedom.

There are several measures which we can use for these

---

[9]The equal frequency of all variants actually means that there are probably no grammatical rules which would prefer any order of constituents over the others.

Treebank	Number of sentences	Number of matches	SVO (%)	OVS (%)	VSO (%)	VOS (%)	SOV (%)	OSV (%)
Ancient Greek	21,173	1,648	24.6	21.1	5.1	5.2	27.2	16.8
Latin	3,473	395	25.1	6.8	8.6	4.1	41.3	14.2
Slovak	63,238	7,794	47.8	22.9	5.5	8.0	12.2	3.6
Slovenian	1,936	182	47.8	25.3	4.4	2.2	17.0	3.3
Czech	87,913	16,862	51.2	21.4	9.6	10.0	5.8	2.0
German	40,020	18,617	49.8	12.0	35.2	2.8	0.2	0.0
Tamil	600	132	0.0	6.8	0.0	0.0	59.1	34.1
Dutch	13,735	2,646	60.4	15.5	23.5	0.4	0.2	0.1
Spanish	17,709	5,569	61.3	20.4	1.0	0.5	16.5	0.4
Bengali	1,279	307	21.5	9.8	0.0	0.0	61.6	7.2
Romanian	4,042	1,132	62.1	12.9	0.4	0.8	23.6	0.2
Catalan	16,786	5,921	65.5	15.3	0.2	0.5	18.2	0.3
Polish	8,227	1,645	71.4	11.5	4.9	5.3	4.1	2.8
Telugu	1,600	254	2.4	3.9	0.0	0.0	69.7	24.0
Russian	34,895	6,194	72.2	15.2	1.6	3.5	4.2	3.4
Arabic	7,664	1,203	22.4	0.2	74.1	3.3	0.0	0.0
Turkish	5,935	802	3.2	13.3	0.6	0.1	79.2	3.5
Portuguese	9,359	2,879	80.7	9.1	1.9	5.1	3.1	0.2
Persian	12,455	2,480	15.9	0.2	0.1	0.0	81.1	2.8
English	18,791	8,585	83.1	7.3	0.3	0.0	0.0	9.2
Japanese	17,753	138	0.0	0.0	0.0	0.0	85.5	14.5
Estonian	1,315	359	85.5	4.7	7.8	1.1	0.8	0.0
Hindi	13,274	1,490	3.0	0.1	0.0	0.0	93.4	3.5

Table 1: Relative frequencies for word order variants in the main sentence in 23 studied languages.

Treebank	Number of sentences	Number of matches	SVO (%)	OVS (%)	VSO (%)	VOS (%)	SOV (%)	OSV (%)
Ancient Greek	21,173	2,133	22.3	16.3	3.5	2.1	38.0	17.9
Latin	3,473	595	25.5	6.6	3.7	2.7	44.4	17.1
Slovak	63,238	6,354	54.0	14.8	3.1	4.2	12.2	11.7
Slovenian	1,936	137	30.7	28.5	5.1	2.2	8.8	24.8
Czech	87,913	11,849	60.2	12.2	4.8	4.9	10.4	7.6
German	40,020	9,655	14.9	0.7	8.2	0.3	70.0	6.0
Tamil	600	44	0.0	0.0	0.0	0.0	68.2	31.8
Dutch	13,735	1,155	8.7	0.4	1.8	0.1	73.4	15.5
Spanish	17,709	9,227	55.0	13.6	0.4	0.4	21.9	8.7
Bengali	1,279	54	1.9	3.7	0.0	0.0	81.5	13.0
Romanian	4,042	15	60.0	26.7	0.0	13.3	0.0	0.0
Catalan	16,786	8,612	50.6	16.6	0.1	0.7	23.3	8.7
Polish	8,227	331	71.9	6.9	2.1	2.1	10.6	6.3
Telugu	1,600	34	2.9	0.0	0.0	0.0	73.5	23.5
Russian	34,895	4,152	68.7	13.0	1.9	5.0	4.9	6.4
Arabic	7,664	1,816	48.3	0.1	17.4	34.2	0.0	0.0
Turkish	5,935	264	1.5	0.4	0.0	0.0	91.7	6.4
Portuguese	9,359	2,623	76.0	1.7	1.1	3.6	11.8	5.8
Persian	12,455	882	10.7	0.0	0.0	0.0	84.6	4.8
English	18,791	6,830	96.9	0.1	0.0	0.0	0.0	3.0
Japanese	17,753	538	0.0	0.0	0.0	0.0	70.6	29.4
Estonian	1,315	33	57.6	9.1	3.0	3.0	18.2	9.1
Hindi	13,274	1,374	0.3	0.0	0.0	0.0	95.5	4.2

Table 2: Relative frequencies for word order variants in subordinated sentences in 23 studied languages.

calculations.[10] Let us start with the simplest one, the max-min measure (marked as M_1 in the subsequent text):

$$M_1 = \max_{i \in 1,..n} x_i - \min_{i \in 1,..n} x_i$$

This measure has a value 0 for the ideal vector. The higher its value, the more fixed seems to be the word order of that particular language. The main advantage of this measure is its ability to reduce n-dimensional vectors into two dimensions only (leaving aside all four other values), thus enabling simple graphical representation. The same property also constitutes the greatest disadvantage of this measure, i.e. its insensitivity to subtle differences in distribution of values among the four variants which were actually left aside.

The second measure is the standard Euclidean distance between two vectors (marked as M_2 in the subsequent text):

$$M_2 = \|X - Y\| = \sqrt{\sum_{i=1}^{n} (x_i - y_i)^2}$$

In this formula, the symbol X represents the distribution of word order variants of a given language and Y is the "ideal vector" with equal distribution of frequencies. The Euclidean distance is more precise than M_1 because it reflects all six variants of the word order.

The third measure, very often used for measuring the similarity of two vectors in information retrieval, is the cosine similarity (marked as M_3 in the subsequent text):

$$M_3 = \frac{\sum_{i=1}^{n} (x_i \times y_i)}{\sqrt{\sum_{i=1}^{n} (x_i)^2} \times \sqrt{\sum_{i=1}^{n} (y_i)^2}}$$

Actually, because both M_2 and M_3 represent a distance between two vectors (although measured by different means and providing numerically different values), their results with regard to the estimation of word order freedom would be very similar, the main difference being the order of the numerical values of M_2 and M_3. While the values of M_2 are decreasing with the growing word order freedom, the values of M_3 are increasing.

Because M_2 and M_3 are in principle quite similar, let us therefore use one more measure which is also quite natural and widely used, namely the entropy (marked as M_4 in the subsequent text):

$$M_4 = -\sum_{i=1}^{n} P(x_i) \ln P(x_i)$$

The values $P(x_i)$ are the probabilities of individual word order variants. Because we do not know the exact probabilities, we are going to use their relative frequencies from Tables 1 and 2. The entropy is maximal for the equal distribution of relative frequencies (probabilities), minimal for

---

[10]Actually, the word *measure* should not be understood as a strictly mathematical term. The cosine similarity is not a measure in a mathematical sense, it does not have all properties required by the mathematical definition of the term *measure*.

an absolutely deterministic system which has only one acceptable type of the word order. In other words, the higher is the entropy for a particular language, the higher is its degree of word order freedom.

The results obtained for all four measures are presented in Tables 3 and 4. In order to enable an easier comparison of individual measures, we are presenting also the rank of all languages with regard to their degree of word order freedom for each particular measure. The ranks then show how similar the measures are. In both tables, the order of languages corresponds to their rank according to the M_1 measure applied to main sentences.

Table 3 shows the rank of individual languages with regard to the word order freedom calculated according to all measures mentioned above. It was calculated on main sentences with "full" structure, i.e. main sentences containing both subject and (exactly one) object, and although the rank according to each individual measure differs (with the exception of M_2 and M_3 which provide, not surprisingly, an absolutely identical rank), the highest rank always belongs to the two classical languages, Latin and Ancient Greek, closely followed by three Slavic languages (Slovak, Slovenian and Czech) and German. The languages with the most fixed word order are, according to all measures, English, Japanese, Estonian and Hindi.

When comparing both tables, we may notice some substantial differences in the word order freedom rank for main and subordinated clauses. We may identify two distinctive groups of languages which exhibit a relatively big rank shift. The languages with substantially higher degree of the word order freedom in subordinated clauses are Arabic, Catalan and Estonian. The languages with exactly opposite property are Bengali, German and Dutch. In case of Dutch we may recall the famous examples of phenomena exceeding the expressive power of context-free languages, namely the subordinated clauses such as *...dat Jan Piet de kinderen zag helpen zwemmen* (... that Jan saw Piet help the children swim) where the Dutch syntax requires a very strict order of words. Also in German, the word order in subordinated clauses follows much stricter rules than in the main ones. In this respect, the results obtained through our experiment correlate with the syntactic rules of the language.

5 Final Remarks and Conclusion

Although the results presented in this paper support to a relatively great extent the intuitive comprehension of the notion of word order freedom of "big" European languages, there are at least two aspects of our experiment which are, according to our opinion, quite interesting. The first one is the fact that our experiment is based solely on data, publicly available in syntactically annotated corpora. Thanks to this fact the experiment does not require the knowledge of, or even the familiarity with all the languages under investigation. On the other hand, some of

Treebank	M_1	Rank	M_2	Rank	M_3	Rank	M_4	Rank
Ancient Greek	27.18	1	0.2145	1	0.8852	1	1.6320	1
Latin	41.27	2	0.3166	2	0.7902	2	1.5134	2
Slovak	47.82	3	0.3744	3	0.7370	3	1.4273	3
Slovenian	47.80	4	0.3978	4	0.7162	4	1.3357	5
Czech	49.19	5	0.4052	5	0.7098	5	1.3714	4
German	49.76	6	0.4693	6	0.6563	6	1.0830	6
Tamil	59.09	7	0.5508	11	0.5955	11	0.8608	14
Dutch	60.24	8	0.5259	8	0.6132	8	0.9761	10
Spanish	60.89	9	0.5269	9	0.6125	9	1.0135	9
Bengali	61.56	10	0.5227	7	0.6155	7	1.0453	7
Romanian	61.93	11	0.5398	10	0.6032	10	0.9743	11
Catalan	65.53	12	0.5650	12	0.5856	12	0.9291	13
Polish	68.63	13	0.6037	13	0.5602	13	1.0231	8
Telugu	69.69	14	0.6154	14	0.5528	14	0.8101	15
Russian	72.18	15	0.6179	15	0.5512	15	0.9509	12
Arabic	74.15	16	0.6590	16	0.5267	16	0.6805	18
Turkish	79.05	17	0.6931	17	0.5075	17	0.7219	17
Portuguese	80.51	18	0.7047	18	0.5013	18	0.7352	16
Persian	81.09	19	0.7189	19	0.4938	19	0.5780	20
English	83.13	20	0.7337	20	0.4862	20	0.5857	19
Japanese	85.51	21	0.7652	22	0.4707	22	0.4138	22
Estonian	85.52	22	0.7571	21	0.4746	21	0.5673	21
Hindi	93.42	23	0.8416	23	0.4365	23	0.2935	23

Table 3: Ranks of individual languages for word order variants in the main sentence for all four measures.

Treebank	M_1	Rank	M_2	Rank	M_3	Rank	M_4	Rank
Ancient Greek	35.91	2	0.2954	2	0.8100	2	1.5034	2
Latin	41.68	3	0.3622	3	0.7479	3	1.4092	3
Slovak	50.88	6	0.4215	4	0.6956	4	1.3645	4
Slovenian	28.47	1	0.2840	1	0.8208	1	1.5149	1
Czech	55.35	9	0.4810	9	0.6470	9	1.2862	5
German	69.69	13	0.5959	12	0.5651	12	0.9586	12
Tamil	68.18	12	0.6320	14	0.5425	14	0.6254	18
Dutch	73.33	16	0.6359	15	0.5402	15	0.8314	15
Spanish	54.62	8	0.4584	6	0.6650	6	1.1902	8
Bengali	81.48	19	0.7181	19	0.4941	19	0.6276	17
Romanian	60.00	10	0.5312	10	0.6093	10	0.9276	13
Catalan	50.53	5	0.4233	5	0.6941	5	1.2345	7
Polish	69.79	14	0.6093	13	0.5566	13	0.9980	11
Telugu	73.53	17	0.6559	18	0.5284	18	0.6702	16
Russian	66.81	11	0.5760	11	0.5782	11	1.0734	9
Arabic	48.35	4	0.4629	7	0.6614	7	1.0267	10
Turkish	91.67	21	0.8234	21	0.4442	21	0.3409	21
Portuguese	74.91	18	0.6558	17	0.5284	17	0.8639	14
Persian	84.58	20	0.7498	20	0.4781	20	0.5252	20
English	96.88	23	0.8791	23	0.4211	23	0.1441	23
Japanese	70.63	15	0.6468	16	0.5336	16	0.6054	19
Estonian	54.55	7	0.4650	8	0.6597	8	1.2757	6
Hindi	95.49	22	0.8642	22	0.4271	22	0.1946	22

Table 4: Ranks of individual languages for word order variants for subordinate sentences for all four measures.

the corpora contained in the HamleDT set are too small to constitute a reliable source of information about the properties of a given language. However, this obstacle can be easily overcome in the future with the growing size and number of treebanks available under a common annotation scheme.

The second interesting aspect is the comparison of measures which give in principle very similar results and thus they support the claim that the phenomenon of word order freedom may be quantified practically by any reasonably selected measure. In other words, it is not necessary to develop any specialized measures just for this particular purpose, it is enough if we use the well known ones, such as the Euclidean distance or entropy.

Grant support

The work on this project was partially supported by the LINDAT/CLARIN project of the Ministry of Education, Youth and Sports of the Czech Republic (project LM2015071).

This work was also supported by the project LO1506 of the Czech Ministry of Education, Youth and Sports and by Grant No. SGS-2016-018 Data and Software Engineering for Advanced Applications.

This work has been using language resources and tools developed and/or stored and/or distributed by the LINDAT/CLARIN project of the Ministry of Education, Youth and Sports of the Czech Republic (project LM2015071).

References

[1] Saussure, F.: Course in General Linguistics. Open Court, La Salle, Illinois (1983) (prepared by C. Bally and A. Sechehaye, translated by R. Harris).

[2] Sapir, E.: Language. An Introduction to the Study of Speech. Harcourt, Brace and company, New York (1921) (http://www.gutenberg.org/files/12629/12629-h/12629-h.htm).

[3] Skalička, V.: Vývoj jazyka. Soubor statí. Státní pedagogické nakladatelství, Praha (1960)

[4] Dryer, M.S., Haspelmath, M.: The World Atlas of Language Structures Online. Harcourt, Brace and company, Leipzig (2005-2013) Available online at http://wals.info, Accessed on 2015-06-28.

[5] Futrell, R., Mahowald, K., Gibson, E.: Quantifying Word Order Freedom in Dependency Corpora. In: Proceedings of the International Conference on Dependency Linguistics (Depling 2015), Uppsala, Sweden, Uppsala University (2015)

[6] de Marneffe, M.C., MacCartney, B., Manning, C.D.: Generating typed dependency parses from phrase structure parses. In: Proceedings of LREC 2006. (2006)

[7] de Marneffe, M.C., Manning, C.D.: The Stanford typed dependencies representation. In: COLING Workshop on Cross-framework and Cross-domain Parser Evaluation. (2008)

[8] de Marneffe, M.C., Dozat, T., Silveira, N., Haverinen, K., Ginter, F., Nivre, J., Manning, C.: Universal Stanford Dependencies: A cross-linguistic typology. In: Proceedings of LREC 2014. (2014)

[9] McDonald, R., Nivre, J.: Characterizing the errors of data-driven dependency parsing models. In: Proceedings of EMNLP-CoNLL 2007. (2007)

[10] Nivre, J., de Marneffe, M.C., Ginter, F., Goldberg, Y., Hajič, J., Manning, C., McDonald, R., Petrov, S., Pyysalo, S., Silveira, N., Tsarfaty, R., Zeman, D.: Universal dependencies v1: A multilingual treebank collection. In: Proceedings of the 10th International Conference on Language Resources and Evaluation (LREC 2016), Portorož, Slovenia, European Language Resources Association (2016)

[11] Zeman, D., Dušek, O., Mareček, D., Popel, M., Ramasamy, L., Štěpánek, J., Žabokrtský, Z., Hajič, J.: HamleDT: Harmonized multi-language dependency treebank. Language Resources and Evaluation **48** (2014) 601–637

[12] Kuboň, V., Lopatková, M., Mírovský, J.: Analysis of Word Order in Multiple Treebanks. In: Proceedings of CICLing 2016. LNCS, Berlin Heidelberg, Springer-Verlag (2016)

[13] Lopatková, M., Kuboň, V.: Free or FixedWord Order: What can Treebanks Reveal? In Yaghob, J., ed.: Information Technologies – Applications and Theory, Prague, Charles University in Prague (2015) 23–29

[14] Kuboň, V., Lopatková, M.: Word-order analysis based upon treebank data. In Sidorov, G., Galicia-Haro, S., eds.: MICAI 2015: Advances in Artificial Intelligence and Soft Computing, Part I. Volume 9413., Berlin / Heidelberg, Springer (2015) 47–58

[15] Bejček, E., Hajičová, E., Hajič, J., Jínová, P., Kettnerová, V., Kolářová, V., Mikulová, M., Mírovský, J., Nedoluzhko, A., Panevová, J., Poláková, L., Ševčíková, M., Štěpánek, J., Zikánová, Š.: Prague Dependency Treebank 3.0. Charles University in Prague, MFF, ÚFAL, Prague (2013) (http://ufal.mff.cuni.cz/pdt3.0/).

[16] Pajas, P., Štěpánek, J.: System for Querying Syntactically Annotated Corpora. In: Proceedings of the ACL-IJCNLP 2009 Software Demonstrations, Suntec, Singapore, Association for Computational Linguistics (2009) 33–36

ITAT 2016 Proceedings, pp. 18–25
ISBN 978-1537016740, © 2016 M. Macko, M. Králik, B. Brejová, T. Vinař

OB-Fold Recognition Combining Sequence and Structural Motifs

Martin Macko, Martin Králik, Broňa Brejová, and Tomáš Vinař

Faculty of Mathematics, Physics and Informatics, Comenius University in Bratislava
Mlynská dolina, 842 48 Bratislava, Slovakia
martin.macko1@gmail.com, brejova@dcs.fmph.uniba.sk, vinar@fmph.uniba.sk

Abstract: Remote protein homology detection is an important step towards understanding protein function in living organisms. The problem is notoriously difficult; distant homologs can often be detected only by a combination of sequence and structural features.

We propose a new framework, where important sequence and structural features are described by the user in the form of a descriptor, and the descriptor is then used to search a database of protein sequences and score potential candidates. We develop algorithms necessary to support such search using support vector machines and discrete optimization methods. We demonstrate our approach on the example of the telomere-binding OB-fold domain, showing that not only we can distinguish between Telo_bind family members and negatives, but we also identify proteins from related protein families carrying similar OB-fold domains.

Prototype implementation of the descriptor search software is available for Linux operating system at http://compbio.fmph.uniba.sk/descal/

1 Introduction

Remote homology detection is a key to understanding the role of individual proteins in living organisms. This problem is notoriously difficult; the most commonly used tools build profiles from groups of related proteins, representing preferred amino acids at individual loci (e.g. [1, 6, 24]). However, distant homologs are difficult to detect by sequence alone, since the function of a protein is largely determined by its 3D structure. Methods combining structural and sequence-based elements can therefore achieve higher sensitivity [29, 19, 17, 4].

A similar problem is encountered in search for RNA genes, where considering secondary RNA structure is essential to finding distant homologs of known genes. In addition to fully-automated systems for such tasks [9], success was achieved by tools allowing expert human users to handcraft motif descriptors representing the most important features of the target RNAs [8, 5, 22, 28, 21]. Such descriptors specify restrictions on the base-pairing structure of the target RNA (characterizing important secondary structure features), as well as sequence constraints in the form of regular expressions (characterizing important conserved functional sites).

In this work, we propose to extend such descriptor-based approach to protein homology search. However, proteins do not have an equivalent of the simple deterministic rules for RNA base-pairing, and sequence constraints are more naturally written in the form of profiles rather than simple regular expressions. For these reasons, our approach combines techniques from machine learning (support vector machines), probabilistic modeling (sequence profiles), and manual selection of important structural features.

In particular, as the first step, the user creates a descriptor characterizing the most important sequential and structural features of a given protein or a protein family. In the second step, we use our algorithm to score individual proteins (e.g., all proteins in a particular organism) based on how well the descriptor fits these proteins; the score combines sequential features, secondary structure features, and interactions between individual structural elements. Finally, the candidate proteins can be ordered based on this score and the highest scoring candidates will be considered as homologs of the original protein.

Consider an example of the telomere binding OB-fold protein CDC13 in *Saccharomyces cerevisiae*. The important structural elements of this protein have been well characterized [18] and are outlined in Fig. 1. Secondary structure of the telomere-binding OB-fold domain is composed of five β-strands and two α-helices. The β-strands form a typical β-barrel structure. Even though large sequence divergence is typical for this domain, several sequence sites are strongly conserved. To search for putative CDC13 homologs in various species, we propose to describe all these features in a single descriptor, as shown in Fig. 2. By screening a protein database and scoring individual proteins based on this descriptor, we can see that relevant homologs (those containing telomere binding domain) are scored the highest, the proteins from related families have moderate scores, and unrelated proteins have generally low scores (Fig. 5). Thus, the highest scoring proteins are potential candidates for functional homologs of CDC13 in other species.

The paper is organized as follows. First, we describe general framework of descriptors characterizing sequence and structural features of a protein domain and illustrate it on the telomere-binding OB-fold domain. An important feature of these descriptors is identification of potential bonded β-strands. We have developed a support vector machine based classifier for this task. Next, we describe two algorithms for descriptor search in protein sequences. Finally, we evaluate our method on the example of telomere-binding OB-fold proteins, as outlined in the previous paragraph.

2 Methods

2.1 Protein Domain Descriptors

To search for occurrences of a known protein domain, we propose to characterize the domain in the form of a descriptor inspired by descriptors used in RNA structure search [10, 21]. The main idea is to divide the whole domain into segments corresponding to secondary structure elements; these segments have fixed order along the sequence. Each segment is characterized by the minimum and maximum allowed length and the secondary structure class (α-helix, β-strand or coil). For each segment, it is also possible to provide a short sequence motif in the form of a position-specific scoring matrix (PSSM). An important aspect is the ability to specify interactions between distant segments of the protein. In our descriptor, we allow specification of hydrogen bonds between individual β-strand segments which can be parallel or anti-parallel; we also specify the minimum number of hydrogen bonds.

Most constraints specified by the descriptor are soft; we allow arbitrary consecutive placement of descriptor segments on the query protein subject only to the length constraints. Each such alignment of the descriptor to the protein obtains a score according to the scoring scheme described below, and the score of the protein is the score obtained by the best alignment. All examined proteins are then ranked by their scores, and the user can examine selected proteins from the top of the list, or choose a suitable cutoff score for protein classification.

The scoring scheme consists of three components which are combined to the overall score by a linear combination with suitable weights. The first component measures the agreement of the desired secondary structure elements with the predicted secondary structure of the query protein. The score s_j of segment j placed at positions $k \ldots \ell$ is the sum $s_j = \sum_{i=k}^{\ell} \ln(p_i + 0.5)$, where p_i is the posterior probability of the desired secondary structure type at position i. In this way, we prefer alignments that agree with the predicted secondary structure, while at the same time we tolerate unavoidable errors in the secondary structure prediction.

The methods for estimating posterior probabilities of each position in the protein being either α-helix, β-sheet, or a coil have been previously developed, and we use PSIPRED [13] to estimate them.

The second component of the score evaluates the agreement of the sequence with the specified sequence motif in each segment. The motif is given by a PSSM containing a log-odds score for every amino acid at each position within the motif. We use PSSMs extracted from strongly conserved regions of PFAM profiles. In general, the motif is shorter than the minimum segment length, and we use

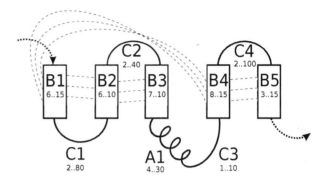

Figure 1: Cartoon representation of the descriptor for the telomere-binding OB-fold domain from Fig.2. Boxes represent β-strands, dotted lines are the required hydrogen bonds. Each segment is annotated with its minimum and maximum allowed length.

the score of the best-scoring ungapped alignment of the PSSM within the particular sequence segment.

Finally, the third score component characterizes the propensity of two β-strands to form hydrogen bonds (we call such β-strands *interacting*). In the next section, we describe a sequence-based classifier that estimates whether two amino acids are likely to form a hydrogen bond in the context of two interacting β-strands; we denote the resulting score for positions i and j as $\text{bond}(i, j)$. For a pair of segments required to interact through k parallel hydrogen bonds, we find positions i and j within the segments such that the score $m_{i,j} = \sum_{\ell=0}^{k-1} \text{bond}(i + 2\ell, j + 2\ell)$ is maximized. (We proceed similarly for anti-parallel interacting β-strand segments.) Note that orientation of amino acids in a β-strand typically alternates, and therefore we skip one position between adjacent bonds. Even though a β-strand as a whole can interact with two other β-strands, we require that each amino acid is involved in at most one hydrogen bond.

Figures 1 and 2 show an example of a descriptor for the telomere binding OB-fold domain. The descriptor contains ten segments, out of which five are β-strands and one is an α-helix. Six of the segments contain sequence motifs corresponding to strongly conserved sections of the Pfam model for the Telo_bind domain. The descriptor also specifies anti-parallel interactions between β-strands forming a β-barrel.

2.2 SVMs Recognizing Interacting β-strands

An important part of the descriptor language is the ability to specify the pattern of hydrogen bonding between individual β-strands that are possibly quite distant in the primary sequence. The use of β-strand interactions has been shown to improve the accuracy of fold recognition in β-strand rich proteins [17, 4]. Several grammar-based methods for recognition of hydrogen bond structure of β-sheets were proposed in the context of protein structure prediction [16, 27, 3]. Another approach to predicting

```
B1|C1|B2|C2|B3|A1|C3|B4|C4|B5
B1: 6 15 B1_LOGO
C1: 2 80
B2: 6 10 B2_LOGO
C2: 2 40 C2_LOGO
B3: 7 10 B3_LOGO
A1: 4 30
C3: 1 10
B4: 8 15 B4_LOGO
C4: 2 100 C4_LOGO
B5: 3 15
- B1 B2: 3
- B2 B3: 3
- B4 B5: 3
- B1 B4: 3


***********LOGO_DEFINITIONS*************
B1_LOGO: [5]
1.4737  0.5703  1.4760  1.1420  ...
1.5272  0.8311  1.2353  1.2990  ...
-0.6192 -0.2024 0.5459  -1.0728 ...
1.1771  0.8718  2.0237  -0.0035 ...
1.0375  0.8607  1.8582  1.3712  ...
B2_LOGO: [3]
-0.7001 -0.7778 -0.9399 0.4729  ...
0.4238  1.1190  0.6647  -0.3823 ...
-1.1356 -0.6612 -0.3739 -1.4812 ...
C2_LOGO: [6]
-1.2004 -1.2746 -1.0686 -1.5443 ...

...

B3_LOGO: [6]
1.4816  1.4929  0.9900  1.1481  ...

...
```

Figure 2: A descriptor of the telomere binding OB-fold protein domain (see also Fig.1). The first line shows the order of individual segments along the sequence and the desired secondary structure of the segments (B for β-strands, A for α-helices, C for coils). The second section contains for each segment its length constraints and an optional PSSM identifier. The third section describes interactions between individual β-strands. Finally, the last section describes PSSMs (each line corresponds to one position and contains 20 log-odds scores of individual amino acids; most numbers were omitted).

the topology of β-sheets and interstrand β-residue pairings uses neural networks [2].

We have created two classifiers to determine if two putative β-strands are likely to form hydrogen bonds, one for parallel and one for anti-parallel strands. The input to each classifier consists of two sequence windows of length 5. The classifier estimates whether the middle amino acids in these windows are likely to form a hydrogen bond with each other. The classifier has the form of a support vector machine (SVM) [26]. We first convert the two sequence windows to a numerical feature vector of length

201. Each sequence position is represented by 20 binary features. One of these features is always set to one and the remaining 19 features are set to zero, depending on the encoded amino acid.

The last feature is the log-odds score for the interaction of the two middle amino acids. In particular, by using our training set, we have estimated frequencies $f_{a,b}$ with which pairs of amino acids a and b occur among hydrogen bonds between interacting β-strands, and frequencies f_x with which amino acids x occur in β-strands individually. If the two amino acids in the middle of the evaluated windows are a and b, then the log-odds score will be defined as $s_{a,b} = \log \frac{f_{a,b}}{f_a f_b}$.

To create a training set, we clustered sequences in the PDB database [23] to clusters with 90% sequence similarity by software CD-Hit [15]. From each cluster we have selected only one sequence for further processing, thus obtaining a representative sample of the proteins in the database. (Without this preprocessing, we would over sample from few large clusters of very similar proteins.)

In addition to the sequence and to the secondary structure annotations (all of which is contained in the PDB database), we also need to determine hydrogen bonds in selected sequences. These were calculated using Jmol Viewer [11]. A positive sample is a pair of sequence windows of length 5 taken from two beta strands of the same protein that have their middle amino acids connected by a hydrogen bond and that have at least one other hydrogen bond between endpoints of the two windows. Parallel or anti-parallel orientation of the windows is determined based on this second bond. A negative sample is a pair of windows from two different β-strands in the same protein that are not connected by any hydrogen bond.

We have selected a random subset of 160,000 positive and 766,239 negative samples for the anti-parallel model and 86,887 positive and 434,435 negative samples for the parallel model. Testing sets for both models contained 15,000 positive and 75,000 negative samples and did not overlap the training set.

By using a small validation set that did not overlap the training or testing set, we have explored a variety of kernels for the SVM by using software SVM-light [12]. Fig.3 shows the accuracy of the models with different SVM kernels. Our final choice was the polynomial kernel of degree 7.

2.3 Descriptor Alignment as an Integer Linear Program

We will call the task of finding the best placement of individual descriptor segments on the query protein sequence the *descriptor alignment problem*. Since the scoring scheme includes long-range interactions between segments, and the positions of interacting segment pairs within the descriptor are not constrained, this problem is NP-hard, similarly to protein threading [14] and RNA descriptor search with pseudoknots [20].

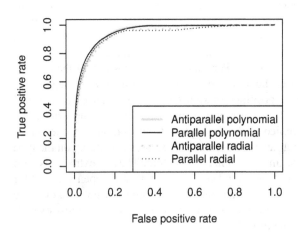

Figure 3: Accurracy of SVM models hydrogen bonds between parallel and antiparallel β-strands. Polynomial kernel of degree 7 used in this work is compared with radial kernel with parameter 0.3.

We therefore formulate the problem as an integer linear program (ILP) and use existing ILP solvers (CPLEX) to find the optimal solution. For simplicity, we show only formulation for parallel interacting β-strands; antiparallel strands are analogous. Our formulation uses the following binary variables:

- Variable x_{is} indicates whether position i is covered by segment s.

- Variable m_{is} indicates whether position i is the starting position of the motif alignment within segment s.

- Variable y_{isjt} indicates whether positions i and j are the first in a chain of hydrogen bonds between (parallel) interacting segments s and t.

- Variable p_{ist} indicates whether position i is involved in a hydrogen bond between segments s and t.

We add hypothetical segments 0 and $m+1$ that fill the gap at the beginning and at the end of the sequence, but do not contribute to the score. The goal of the optimization is to maximize the score for the alignment given by the variables:

$$\sum_{i,s}(e_{is}x_{is}+f_{is}m_{is})+\sum_{i,j,s,t}g_{isjt}y_{isjt}$$

Coefficients e_{is}, f_{is}, and g_{isjt} are precomputed according to the scoring function, including the weights of individual components. The optimization is subject to linear constraints shown in Figure 4. Constraints P_1-P_3 ensure that all the segments are placed consecutively and in the correct order onto the protein sequence. The length of segment is constrained by L_1. The motif occurences must be placed within their corresponding segments (constraints

$$
\begin{array}{ll}
(P_1) & \forall i : \sum_s x_{is} = 1 \\
(P_2) & \forall i \geq 1, s \geq 1 : x_{is} - x_{i-1,s} \leq x_{i-1,s-1} \\
(P_3) & \forall i \geq 1 : x_{i,0} \leq x_{i-1,0} \\
(L_1) & \forall s : \text{lower}_s \leq \sum_i x_{is} \leq \text{upper}_s \\
(M_1) & \forall s : \sum_i m_{is} = 1 \\
(M_2) & \forall i,s : m_{is} \leq x_{is} \\
(M_3) & \forall i,s : m_{is} \leq x_{i+\text{mot\_len}_s-1,s} \\
(B_1) & \forall i,s,j,t, 0 \leq \ell < b_{st} : y_{isjt} \leq x_{i+2\ell,s} \\
(B_2) & \forall i,s,j,t, 0 \leq \ell < b_{st} : y_{isjt} \leq x_{j+2\ell,t} \\
(B_3) & \forall s,t : \sum_{i,j} y_{isjt} = 1 \\
(S_1) & \forall i,s,t : p_{ist} = \sum_{\ell=0}^{b_{st}-1}\sum_j y_{i-2\ell,s,j,t} \\
(S_2) & \forall i : \sum_{s,t} p_{ist} \leq 1
\end{array}
$$

Figure 4: Linear constraints in the integer linear program for the descriptor alignment problem. In these constraints, s and t are segments, i and j are positions in the sequence, lower$_s$ and upper$_s$ are bounds on the segment length, mot_len$_s$ is the motif length, b_{st} is the number of hydrogen bonds between s and t.

M_1-M_3). The hydrogen bonds between a pair of interacting segments s and t must also lie within these segments (constraints B_1-B_3). Finally, each amino acid can be involved in at most one hydrogen bond (constraints S_1, S_2).

We have tested variants of this ILP formulation for several proteins. Short positive examples can be typically solved within minutes. However, the running time for negative examples was usually quite high, and therefore we were not able to complete more extensive tests with this approach. Instead, we propose a dynamic programming algorithm for a slightly simplified version of the problem as described in the next section.

2.4 Efficient Dynamic Programming Algorithm

Since the descriptor alignment problem is NP-hard for general conformation of interacting segment pairs, we will solve a special case where the interactions within the descriptor are limited. In particular, if segments s_1 and s_2 interact, we do not allow any interactions for segment s such that $s_1 < s < s_2$. Interacting pairs form chains of the form $(s_1, s_2), (s_2, s_3), \ldots, (s_{k-1}, s_k)$, and different chains occupy disjoint regions of the descriptor. The descriptor in Fig.2 does not satisfy this restriction because segments B_2 and B_3 interact, and they lie within interacting pair (B_1, B_4). If we remove pair (B_1, B_4), the remaining interactions satisfy the restriction and form two chains $[(B_1, B_2), (B_2, B_3)]$ and $[(B_4, B_5)]$.

We will show that under this restriction, the alignment problem can be solved optimally in polynomial time by dynamic programming. First, we will consider two simpler problems. If there are no interactions in the descriptor, we can use straightforward dynamic programming as follows. Let $A[s, t]$ be the score of the best alignment of the first s segments of the descriptor, where last of them ends at the sequence position t. This value can be computed using the values for the first $s-1$ segments ending at positions $t' < t$: $A[s,t] = \max_f A[s-1,f-1] + S[s,f,t]$. In this formula, $S[s,f,t]$ is the segment score for segment s extending from position f to t. This score includes the secondary structure and sequence motif scores, combined with appropriate weights.

We will now extend this dynamic programming to the case where we allow restricted interaction configurations as described above. However, we will not enforce the condition that a single amino acid can only be used in a single hydrogen bond. To accommodate interactions, we need to include the score for the best placement of hydrogen bonds between interacting segments. Let $B[s,f',t',f,t]$ be the interaction score between segment s and its interaction partner $s' < s$ if s extends from f to t and s' extends from f' to t'. This score is precomputed by finding the highest scoring position of hydrogen bonds within the two segments. In order to incorporate such interaction scores to our dynamic programming, we need to increase the dimension of matrix A to keep track of the position of s'.

If segments s_1 and s_2 interact and s is a segment such that $s_1 \leq s < s_2$, we say that s_1 is an *open segment* for s. Under our restriction on descriptors, each segment s has at most one open segment. We can define the subproblem of the dynamic programming $A[s,t,f',t']$ as the score of the best alignment of the first s segments of the descriptor, where segment s ends at position t and the open segment for s starts at f' and ends at t'. We compute this value from values for $s-1$, distinguishing the following four cases.

In the first case, s interacts with two other segments s_1 and s_2, where $s_1 < s < s_2$. Then s is its own open segment, and therefore s starts at f' and ends at $t' = t$. We maximize over possible values f'' and t'' that represent start and end of segment s_1 (which is the open segment for $s-1$): $\max_{f'',t''} A[s-1,f'-1,f'',t''] + S[s,f',t'] + B[s,f'',t'',f',t']$.

In the second case, s interacts with one segment s_1, where $s_1 < s$. Then s does not have an open segment, and we only consider values $f' = t' = \perp$. We maximize over all possible values of f, f'' and t'', where f'' and t'' represent start and end of segment s_1, and f is the start of segment s: $\max_{f'',t'',f} A[s-1,f-1,f'',t''] + S[s,f,t] + B[s,f'',t'',f,t]$.

In the third case, s interacts with one segment s_2, where $s_2 > s$. Again, s is its own open segment, and therefore we require $t = t'$. On the other hand, $s-1$ does not have an open segment, and thus we do not need to maximize over any values, obtaining the equation $A[s,t,f',t'] = A[s-1,f'-1,\perp,\perp] + S[s,f',t]$.

The last case occurs when s does not interact with any segment. It may have an open segment $s' < s$, which is then also the open segment for $s-1$, or it does not have any open segment, which means that $f' = t' = \perp$. We maximize over all possible starts f of segment s: $\max_f A[s-1,f-1,f',t'] + S[s,f,t]$.

Finally, we further extend our algorithm to enforce that each amino acid is involved in at most one hydrogen bond. Let (s_1,s_2) and (s_2,s_3) be two interacting pairs of seg-

ments sharing segment s_2. When choosing bond positions for (s_2,s_3), we need to know which positions were already used for bonds in (s_1,s_2) and thus cannot be used again. To do this, we introduce new parameter b' into our table $A[s,t,f',t',b']$. Parameter b' is the position of the first hydrogen bond within the open segment s_1 of segment s. Other positions in s_1 used by bonds can be determined based on the required number of bonds and orientation specified in the descriptor. Computation of values in table A needs to distinguish six cases depending on the type of segment s, similarly as before. The two extra cases arise from the need to keep track whether the open segment for segment $s-1$ has restricted positions or not. We omit the full recurrence, which can be derived by carefully extending the formulas above.

The running time of the algorithm is $O(nmf\ell^4)$, where n is the length of the protein sequence, m is the number of segments in the descriptor, ℓ is the maximum segment length, and f is the maximum flexibility of interacting pairs defined as the difference between the smallest and the largest possible distance between their ends t and t'.

2.5 Implementation Details

To compute interaction scores, we need to run the SVM predictor for all pairs of windows of length 5 that can be covered by interacting β-strands. In the worst case, the number of such pairs grows quadratically with the protein length, although in practice the flexibility of the descriptor is limited, thus bounding achievable distance of these pairs. Nonetheless, computation of all required SVM values was the most time-consuming part of the dynamic programing solution. Therefore we have added a heuristic rule which allows hydrogen bonds only between amino acids that have posterior probability of β-strand secondary structure from PSIPRED at least 0.5. This rule has dramatically lowered the computation time. As we will see in the next section, many negative examples do not have enough potential placements for hydrogen bonds, and as a result, no alignment of the descriptor is possible. On the other hand, this situation happens only very rarely for positive examples.

Our scoring scheme allows us to assign different weights to the three components. Ideally, these weights would be optimized to improve the prediction accuracy. For simplicity, we have used weight 1 for secondary structure and sequence motifs and weight 2 for interactions. The weight of interactions was increased because values produced by the SVM were relatively small compared to the overall score.

In order to comply with constrains imposed by the dynamic programming, we omit the interaction between segments B_1 and B_4 from the descriptor of the OB-fold protein domain shown in Fig.2. After computing solution for the reduced descriptor with the dynamic programming, we simply try every possible position for the B_1-B_4 interaction and include the best one in the overall score.

3 Results

To evaluate our descriptor approach, we have used the descriptor in Fig.2 and our dynamic programming algorithm to recognize proteins containing the telomere-binding OB-fold domain. Note that in the dynamic programming, we omit some of the interacting pairs to make the problem tractable. Even though part of the score corresponding to missing interactions is later added to the final score, the alignment of the descriptor obtained by the dynamic programming may not be optimal.

We have randomly selected 50 proteins with telomere-binding OB-fold domain annotated in Pfam (Pfam domain PF02765 Telo_bind). We have also randomly chosen 50 SWISS-PROT proteins not associated with the PF02765 family as a negative sample. Finally, we have selected four other families from the OB-fold clan: RNA polymerase Rpb8 family (PF03870 Rpb8), single-strand binding protein family (PF00436 SSB), tRNA binding domain (PF01588 tRna_bind), and eukaryotic elongation factor 5A hypusine (PF01287 elF-5a). From each of these four families, we have randomly chosen 20 proteins.

The results are summarized in Fig.5. Our descriptor can reliably recognize Telo_bind proteins from the negative samples. Only three negative samples had score higher than 20, with the largest score 38.9. Two positives scored less than 35, additional two proteins were filtered out in the secondary-structure filtering. HMMer [7] achieved perfect separation between Telo_bind and negatives (Fig.5c), but this comparison is not fair since the annotation of protein domains in Pfam is based on the same profile HMM which was used in this test, and therefore it is not surprising that it achieves perfect classification.

Our goal is, however, to search for distant homologs that cannot be reliably recognized by Pfam profiles. The descriptor search is able to recognize proteins from related families that also contain OB-folds, and yet at the same time, it is possible to distinguish them quite successfully from Telo_bind proteins. On the other hand, HMMer results cannot distinguish these four additional families from negatives (compare Fig.5b and c). These results suggest that it is sensible to use the descriptor search to locate distant homologs, examining the resulting candidates in order of the assigned scores. This can be especially beneficial when sequence-based methods (such as HMMer) fail to find any matches.

Pot1 and CDC13 are OB-fold telomere binding proteins that bind single-stranded telomere overhang and are key players in telomere maintenance. It has been a long standing question, which protein performs this crucial role in the pathogenic yeast *Candida albicans* and related species. No homolog could be found by common sequence-based methods [25]. Yu *et al.* [30] have demonstrated that a short protein (Uniprot ID Q5AB98) associates with telomere DNA and regulates telomere lengths. They postulate that this is the missing ortholog of CDC13. Search with our descriptor against this protein produced score of 32.8,

which is on the low end of the range for Telo_bind and well within range of other OB-fold containing families. Note that search for Pfam domains in this protein does not return any significant matches.

4 Conclusion

In this paper, we have introduced a framework of combining sequence and structural information in search of distant protein homologs. Important sequence and structural features of a given protein or a protein family are first manually selected and described in the form of a descriptor which is then used to search a database of protein sequences and score potential candidates.

We have demonstrated the use of our framework on the telomere-binding OB-fold domain. Based on the description of the *S. cerevisiae* CDC13 protein by Mitton-Fry *et al.* [18], we have created a descriptor that includes the information on the secondary structure elements, interaction of individual β-strands, and highly conserved sequence motifs. We have developed an algorithm that allowed us to score individual proteins with this descriptor, and we have demonstrated that not only the descriptor search was able to distinguish between Telo_bind family members and negative examples, but it also identified proteins from related families containing similar domains.

There are many avenues for further research in this area. First, even though our algorithms are universal, we have mostly targeted the features required to support CDC13 distant homolog search. There are many other features that could be included within the same algorithmic framework (e.g., more flexible sequence motifs, irregular hydrogen bond configurations, flexible distances between individual elements), while others would require development of new algorithms (e.g., more complex interaction models between segments).

The experience from a similar RNA search framework suggests that writing sensitive and specific descriptors is a long iterative process. Our Telo_bind descriptor is only the first attempt at this task, further examination of results could suggest which features are perhaps less important and could be omitted, and which new features should be included instead. Continuing this work could lead to a discovery of telomere binding OB-fold proteins in species where these proteins are yet unknown, and also to greater understanding of importance of individual features of this protein. Development of additional tools supporting such research would be of great interest.

The scoring function of the descriptor alignment to a protein is a linear combination of several components. The overall score is optimized globally, however, the weights controlling individual contributions of the components were chosen ad hoc. Systematic choice of these constants, perhaps through machine learning methods, could lead to higher accuracy.

One obstacle to a wider deployment of our current

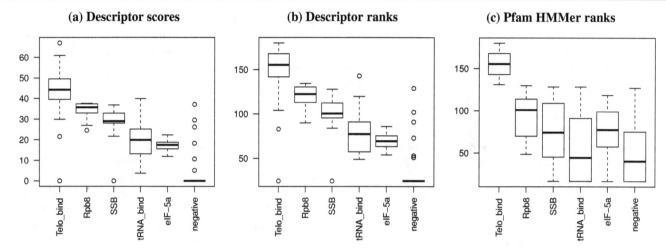

(a) Descriptor scores   **(b) Descriptor ranks**   **(c) Pfam HMMer ranks**

Figure 5: Recognizing a variety of OB-fold families using the OB-fold descriptor and HMMer search with the Pfam model of the Telo_bind domain. Each box plot shows score or rank distributions for one method within different OB-fold families and negative samples. Both the descriptor and the Pfam model can reliably distinguish between telomere binding OB-fold proteins and negative samples. Descriptor approach can, however, also identify proteins from related protein families that also contain an OB-fold domain.

search tool is its running time. The alignment of the descriptor to a single protein requires anything between couple of seconds to several hours. In the dynamic programming, we have sacrificed information provided through one of the β-strand interactions, and we have further restricted the search space by discarding segment positions that did not match the secondary structure constraints well. Yet, we believe that these relaxations changed the final result very little. Perhaps further heuristic relaxations and approximations could lead to a faster search tools.

Finally, one could imagine that efforts towards assembling a database of descriptors characterizing common protein functions could lead to a better and faster functional annotation of newly sequenced species.

Acknowledgements. This research was funded by APVV grant APVV-14-0253 and VEGA grants 1/0719/14 (TV) and 1/0684/16 (BB).

References

[1] Altschul, S. F., Madden, T. L., Schaffer, A. A., Zhang, J., Zhang, Z., Miller, W., and Lipman, D. J. (1997). Gapped BLAST and PSI-BLAST: a new generation of protein database search programs. *Nucleic Acids Res*, **25**(17), 3389–3392.

[2] Cheng, J. and Baldi, P. (2005). Three-stage prediction of protein β-sheets by neural networks, alignments and graph algorithms. *Bioinformatics*, **21**(suppl 1), i75–i84.

[3] Chiang, D., Joshi, A., and Searls, D. (2006). Grammatical representations of macromolecular structure. *Journal of Computational Biology*, **13**(5), 1077–1100.

[4] Daniels, N. M., Hosur, R., Berger, B., and Cowen, L. J. (2012). SMURFLite: combining simplified Markov random fields with simulated evolution improves remote homology detection for beta-structural proteins into the twilight zone. *Bioinformatics*.

[5] Eddy, S. R. (1996). RNABob: a program to search for rna secondary structure motifs in sequence databases. unpublished.

[6] Eddy, S. R. (2009). A new generation of homology search tools based on probabilistic inference. *Genome Inform*, **23**(1), 205–211.

[7] Eddy, S. R. (2011). Accelerated Profile HMM Searches. *PLoS Comput Biol*, **7**(10), e1002195.

[8] Gautheret, D., Major, F., and Cedergren, R. (1990). Pattern searching/alignment with RNA primary and secondary structures: an effective descriptor for tRNA. *Comput Appl Biosci*, **6**(4), 325–331.

[9] Griffiths-Jones, S., Bateman, A., Marshall, M., Khanna, A., and Eddy, S. R. (2003). Rfam: an RNA family database. *Nucleic Acids Res*, **31**(1), 439–441.

[10] Jimenez, R. M., Rampasek, L., Brejova, B., Vinar, T., and Luptak, A. (2012). Discovery of RNA motifs using a computational pipeline that allows insertions in paired regions and filtering of candidate sequences. *Methods Mol Biol*, **848**, 145–148.

[11] Jmol (2012). Jmol: an open-source Java viewer for chemical structures in 3D. www.jmol.org.

[12] Joachims, T. (1999). Making large-scale SVM learning practical. In B. Schölkopf, C. Burges, and A. Smola, editors, *Advances in Kernel Methods - Support Vector Learning*. MIT-Press.

[13] Jones, D. T. (1999). Protein secondary structure prediction based on position-specific scoring matrices. *J Mol Biol*, **292**(2), 195–202.

[14] Lathrop, R. H. (1994). The protein threading problem with sequence amino acid interaction preferences is NP-complete. *Protein Eng*, **7**(9), 1059–1068.

[15] Li, W. and Godzik, A. (2006). Cd-hit: a fast program for clustering and comparing large sets of protein or nucleotide sequences. *Bioinformatics*, **22**(13), 1658–1659.

[16] Mamitsuka, H. and Abe, N. (1994). Predicting location and structure of beta-sheet regions using stochastic tree grammars. *ISMB-94*, pages 276–284.

[17] Menke, M., Berger, B., and Cowen, L. (2010). Markov random fields reveal an N-terminal double beta-propeller motif as part of a bacterial hybrid two-component sensor system. *Proc Natl Acad Sci U S A*, **107**(9), 4069–4074.

[18] Mitton-Fry, R. M., Anderson, E. M., Theobald, D. L., Glustrom, L. W., and Wuttke, D. S. (2004). Structural basis for telomeric single-stranded DNA recognition by yeast Cdc13. *J Mol Biol*, **338**(2), 241–245.

[19] Nielsen, M., Lundegaard, C., Lund, O., and Petersen, T. N. (2010). CPHmodels-3.0–remote homology modeling using structure-guided sequence profiles. *Nucleic Acids Res*, **38**(Web Server issue), W576–581.

[20] Rampasek, L. (2011). RNA structural motif search is NP-complete. In *Studentska vedecka konferencia FMFI UK, Bratislava*, pages 341–348.

[21] Rampasek, L., Jimenez, R. M., Luptak, A., Vinar, T., and Brejova, B. (2016). RNA motif search with data-driven element ordering. *BMC Bioinformatics*, **17**(1), 216.

[22] Reeder, J., Reeder, J., and Giegerich, R. (2007). Locomotif: from graphical motif description to RNA motif search. *Bioinformatics*, **23**(13), i392–400.

[23] Rose, P. W. *et al.* (2011). The RCSB Protein Data Bank: redesigned web site and web services. *Nucleic Acids Res*, **39**(Database issue), D392–401.

[24] Sadreyev, R. I. and Grishin, N. V. (2008). Accurate statistical model of comparison between multiple sequence alignments. *Nucleic Acids Res*, **36**(7), 2240–2248.

[25] Teixeira, M. T. and Gilson, E. (2005). Telomere maintenance, function and evolution: the yeast paradigm. *Chromosome Res*, **13**(5), 535–538.

[26] Vapnik, V. N. (1995). *The Nature of Statistical Learning Theory*. Springer.

[27] Waldispühl, J., Berger, B., Clote, P., and Steyaert, J. (2006). Predicting transmembrane β-barrels and interstrand residue interactions from sequence. *PROTEINS: Structure, Function, and Bioinformatics*, **65**(1), 61–74.

[28] Webb, C.-H. T., Riccitelli, N. J., Ruminski, D. J., and Luptak, A. (2009). Widespread occurrence of self-cleaving ribozymes. *Science*, **326**(5955), 953.

[29] Xu, J., Li, M., Kim, D., and Xu, Y. (2003). RAPTOR: optimal protein threading by linear programming. *J Bioinform Comput Biol*, **1**(1), 95–117.

[30] Yu, E. Y., Sun, J., Lei, M., and Lue, N. F. (2012). Analyses of Candida Cdc13 orthologues revealed a novel OB fold dimer arrangement, dimerization-assisted DNA binding, and substantial structural differences between Cdc13 and RPA70. *Mol Cell Biol*, **32**(1), 186–188.

ITAT 2016 Proceedings, pp. 26–33
ISBN 978-1537016740, © 2016 M. Plátek, K. Oliva

Redukční analýza A-stromů s minimalistickými omezeními.*

Martin Plátek[1] a Karel Oliva[2]

[1] MFF UK Praha, Malostranské nám. 25, 118 00 Praha, Česká Republika
martin.platek@ufal.mff.cuni.cz
[2] UJČ ČAV Praha, Letenská, 118 00 Praha, Česká Republika
oliva@ujc.cas.cz

Abstrakt: Tento příspěvek navazuje na náš loňský příspěvek na ITATu. Zpracovává novým způsobem redukční analýzu na A-stromech, které jsou formalizací stromů, zpracovaných metodikou pro analytickou rovinu Pražského závislostního korpusu (PDT). Redukční analýza A-stromů sestává z minimálních korektních redukcí, které používají pouze elementární operace delete a shift.

Hlavním cílem je vyvinout formální prostředky, které by exaktně zachycovaly lingvisticky pozorované minimalistické vlastnosti jednotlivých parametrů stromové redukční analýzy stromů ve formátu PDT a dovolily následně realizovat podobná pozorování na různých přirozených, či umělých jazycích.

Pomocí pozorování lingvistického typu upřesňujeme strukturálně-složitostní vlastnosti A-stromů se závislostmi a koordinacemi. Zvýrazňujeme vlastnosti, kterými se závislosti a koordinace liší.

1 Úvod

V této práci zavádíme a studujeme exaktní pojem (úplné) redukční analýzy A-stromů (URAS). A-stromy modelují stromy analytické roviny Pražského závislostního korpusu (PDT). URAS obsahuje všechny korektní redukce, které lze zařadit do lingvisticky korektní (manuální) redukční analýzy na A-stromech. URAS používá operace delete a shift a jeho redukce jsou minimalizovány s ohledem na počet těchto operací. Postupně zavádíme různé další omezující parametry, které je možno minimalizovat a užívat pro jemnější aproximace lingvisticky intuitivní redukční analýzy. Zavádíme tříčlennou škálu stability pro omezené URAS. Za korektní omezené URAS považujeme ty, co jsou stabilní alespoň v tom nejslabším smyslu. Stabilita pomáhá hledat spodní odhady pro intuitivní redukční analýzu. Typ stability určuje větší či menší vzdálenost od neomezené URAS.

Zavedené pojmy používáme pro klasifikaci pozorování lingvistického typu. Pozorujeme množiny A-stromů, které odpovídají českým větám a jsou zpracovány metodikou analytické roviny PDT. Odkrýváme tak řadu strukturálních vlastností takovýchto A-stromů. Povšimněme si, že prezentovaná pozorování jsou smysluplná a netriviální na konečných i nekonečných jazycích (množinách). To je ve spojitosti s lingvistikou velmi užitečné. Prezentujeme strukturální pozorování a nekombinujeme je (zatím) s pozorováními statistického typu.

1.1 Neformální úvod do redukční analýzy.

V této sekci neformálně představujeme redukční analýzu A-stromů se závislostmi a s koordinacemi. Redukční analýzou českých vět a jejímu modelování se zabýváme již delší dobu. Jako základní variantu redukční analýzy předkládáme úplnou redukční analýzu A-stromů (URAS). Navazujeme na články z minulých let (viz [2, 1, 3]). Při zavádění variant redukčních analýz zvýrazňujeme jejich minimalistický charakter.

URAS je založena na postupném zjednodušování A-stromu po minimálních krocích. URAS definuje všechny možné posloupnosti větných redukcí – každá redukce spočívá ve *vypuštění* několika uzlů, nejméně však jednoho uzlu analyzovaného A-stromu. V A-stromě vypouštíme tak, abychom z A-stromu získali opět A-strom a každá cesta v novém A-stromě byla podposloupností cesty v původním A-stromě. Viz např. obrázky z příkladu 1. V některých redukcích může být kromě vypuštění použita operace *shift*, která přesune nějaký uzel na novou pozici v A-stromě.

V našich lingvistických pozorováních budeme rozlišovat vypouštění listů a vypouštění vnitřních uzlů. Kořeny se v URAS nevypouští. Intuitivně i v URAS u většiny závislostních jevů stačí používat vypouštění listů. Ukážeme, že redukce koordinací v PDT s vypouštěním listů nevystačí.

Metoda URAS je popsaná následujícími zásadami:

(i) URAS je složena z jednotlivých redukcí; redukce používají operace dvou typů : (1) vypuštění (delete) a (2) přesun (shift); To znamená, že tvary jednotlivých slov (i interpunkčních znamének), jejich morfologické charakteristiky i jejich syntaktické kategorie se nemění během jednotlivých redukcí.

(ii) Struktura, která je korektním A-stromem, musí být korektním A-stromem i po redukci.

(iii) Redukce nepatří do předem vytipované množiny zakázaných redukcí. Příkladem zakázané redukce je vynechání samotného zvratného ´se´.

(iv) Uvažujeme jen nezmenšitelné redukce, t.j. vynecháme-li z libovolné redukce jednu či více

*Příspěvek prezentuje výsledky dosažené v rámci projektu agentury GAČR číslo GA15-04960S.

operací, nastane porušení principu zachování gramatické správnosti (ii) nebo redukce se stane zakázanou a tím poruší princip (iii).

(v) URAS obsahuje všechny možné redukce splňující zásady (i) až (iv).

URAS tvoří základ, z kterého budeme odvozovat další varianty redukční analýzy, tak aby odpovídaly některým typům lingvistické (minimalisticé) intuice. Tento záměr budeme rozvíjet především ve formální části.

V následujících odstavcích nejprve uvedeme jeden příklad ilustrující URAS. Příklad se týká jen redukcí, které zjednodušují závislosti. Později budou následovat příklady, týkající se koordinací. Příklady nejprve poslouží pro úvod do problematiky, později (ve výsledkové části) jako separační příklady pro taxonomii redukčních analýz. A-stromy na obrázcích v našich příkladech jsou oproti stromům z PDT trochu zjednodušené. Za prvé: neobsahují identifikační uzel, který nenese žádnou syntaktickou informaci a neodpovídá žádnému slovu věty. Za druhé: značka 'Coord' je nahrazena značkou 'Cr' a za třetí vynecháváme morfologické značky.

Všimněme si, že korektní A-strom zcela určuje jednu korektní českou větu i s jejím korektním značkováním.

Příklad 1. *Zde ilustrujeme URAS k větě (1). Nevypouštíme zvratnou částici se, neboť vypuštění pouhé zvratné částice považujeme za zakázanou redukci. Zde vůbec nepoužíváme shift.*
(1) Rozhodl.Pred se.AuxT dnes.Adv odstoupit.Sb ..AuxK

Obrázek 1 reprezentuje schema větné redukční analýzy (tzv. UPRA). Isomorfní (velmi podobné) schema mají URAS A-stromů $T1_1$ a $T1_2$ z obrázku 2. Obrázek 1 zde zastupuje i tato schemata.

V jednotlivých redukcích URAS A-stromu $T1_1$ se vypouštějí jen listy, tedy redukcemi nevznikají nové hrany. U $T1_2$, při redukci položky 'odstoupit.Sb', se vypouští vnitřní uzel A-stromu, tedy vzniká nová hrana a to v tomto případě signalizuje změnu významu. To není žádoucí.

Vznikne tak strom $T1_3$, viz obr. 3. Doplňme, že $T1_1$ a $T1_2$ lze redukovat na $T1_4$ a $T1_3$ lze také redukovat na $T1_5$. Obrázky těchto redukcí jsme vynechali. K tomuto příkladu patří ještě obrázek 4, zobrazující redukci $T1_4$ na $T1_5$.

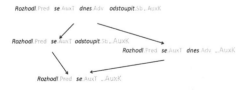

Obrázek 1: UPRA věty (1).

2 Formalizace redukční analýzy.

Zde zavedeme obecné formální pojmy, které mohou sloužit k formulaci redukčních vlastností jak závislostních

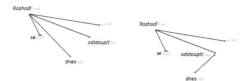

Obrázek 2: A-stromy $T1_1$ a $T1_2$ nad větou (1).

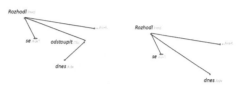

Obrázek 3: Redukce $T1_2$ na $T1_3$.

stromů přirozených jazyků, tak i podobných struktur u programovacích a dotazovacích jazyků. V podsekcích, prezentujících pozorování lingvistického typu, se budeme věnovat formulaci redukčních vlastností stromů analytické roviny PDT. Značka $\subset$ znamená v celém příspěvku vlastní podmnožinu.

Formalizace redukční analýzy analytických stromů se neobejde bez formalizace lexikální analýzy.

2.1 Formalizace lexikální analýzy

Při formalizaci lexikální analýzy rozlišujeme tři konečné množiny slov a značek. Σ_p označuje tzv. vlastní slovník [1], který obsahuje jednotlivé slovní formy a interpunkční znaménka daného jazyka. Σ_c označuje tzv. kategoriální seznam, tedy množinu syntakticko-morfologických značek. Hlavní slovník $\Gamma \subseteq \Sigma_p \times \Sigma_c$ reprezentuje zjednoznačněnou lexikální analýzu daného jazyka.

Projekce z Γ^+ do Σ_p^* resp. do Σ_c^* přirozeně definujeme pomocí homomorfismů: *slovníkovým homomorfismem* $h_p :$ $\Gamma \to \Sigma_p$ a *kategoriálním homomorfismem* $h_c : \Gamma \to \Sigma_c$: $h_p([a,b]) = a$ a $h_c([a,b]) = b$ pro všechny $[a,b] \in \Gamma$.

Příklad 2. *V našich pozorováních analytické roviny PDT pracujeme s hlavním slovníkem označeným jako Γ_{PDT}, Σ_{pPDT} označuje vlastní slovník a Σ_{cPDT} označuje kategoriální seznam značek, užívaných v PDT.*

Obrázek 4: Redukce $T1_4$ na $T1_5$.

---

[1] Index p při označení abecedy se vztahuje na anglickou verzi, kde se používá slovo proper

Výše definované pojmy ilustrujeme na příklade, který vychází z příkladu 1.

{ *Rozhodl, se, dnes , odstoupit, . }* $\subset \Sigma_{pPDT}$,

{ *Pred, AuxT, Adv, Sb, AuxK}* $\subset \Sigma_{cPDT}$,

{ *[Rozhodl,Pred], [se,AuxT],*

[dnes,Adv], [odstoupit,Sb], [.,AuxK]} $\subset \Gamma_{PDT}$.

Jednotlivým položkám hlavního slovníku z tohoto příkladu přiřazujeme jména (b_1 atd.), která budeme v dalších příkladech užívat jako zkratky.

b_1= *[Rozhodl,Pred]*, b_2=*[se,AuxT]*, b_3= *[dnes,Adv]*,
b_4=*[odstoupit,Sb]*, b_5=*[.,AuxK]*.

V abecedě kategorií v tomto příkladě jsou využity jen jednoduché závislostní kategorie (ne všechny). Kategorie mohou být složené z více značek. Kategorie pro koordinace budou obsahovat značky 'Cr', nebo 'Co'.

Věty v našich příkladech končí sentinelem (ukončením věty), který se během redukční analýzy ani nevypouští, ani nepřesunuje. Je to [.,AuxK].

2.2 R-seznamy a A-stromy.

V následující části budeme reprezentovat věty pomocí tzv. R-seznamů a jejich syntaktické struktury pomocí A-stromů. R-seznamy a A-stromy jsou datové typy, vhodné pro používání operací delete a shift. Na R-seznamech a A-stromech zavádíme uniformním způsobem redukce, založené právě na operacích delete a shift. Redukční seznamy (R-seznamy) zjemňují pojem řetězu a A-stromy nesou více informace než R-seznamy. A-strom a R-seznam se skládají z uzlů, které v PDT reprezenují výskyty lexikálních jednotek (slov, interpunkčních znamének a jejich značek) v príslušné větě.

V A-stromu jsou pomocí stromové struktury reprezentovány syntaktické vztahy, pomocí R-seznamu, jež je součástí každého A-stromu, je reprezentováno pořadí slov.

R-seznam. Nechť I je konečná množina přirozených čísel, Γ konečná abeceda a $V \subseteq (I \times \Gamma)$, kde V reprezentuje totální zobrazení množiny I do Γ. Nechť *ord* je úplné uspořádání množiny V. Říkáme, že *ord* je redukčním seznamem (R-seznamem) na Γ. Zapisujeme ho jako seznam prvků z V. Prvky R-seznamu označujeme jako uzly. Množinu R-seznamů, která vznikla všemi možnými uspořádáními množiny V, označujeme jako *ord*(V).

Nechť $u \in V$, pak $u = [i,a]$, kde $i \in I$, $a \in \Gamma$. Říkáme, že i je *indexem uzlu u*. Slouží k jednoznačné identifikaci uzlu. Říkáme, že a je *symbolem uzlu u*.

A-strom. A-strom nad Γ je trojice $s = (V,E,ord)$, kde (V,E) je orientovaný strom, jehož (maximální) cesty začínají v listech a končí v kořeni, V je konečná množina jeho uzlů, $E \subset V \times V$ konečná množina jeho hran a *ord* $\in$ *ord*(V). Říkáme, že *ord* je R-seznamem A-stromu s. Píšeme $R(s) = ord$.

Projekce. Je-li $ord = ([i_1,a_1],\cdots,[i_n,a_n])$, tak $w = a_1 \cdots a_n$ je řetěz (resp. věta), který označujeme $Str(s) = w$

nebo $Str(ord) = w$, a říkáme, že w je řetězem (projekcí) A-stromu s nebo řetězem (projekcí) R-seznamu *ord*.

Normalizace. Říkáme, že A-strom $s = (V,E,ord)$ (R-seznam *ord*) je *normalizovaný*, pokud *ord* má tvar $ord = ([1,a_1],[2,a_2],\cdots,[n,a_n])$. *Normalizace* A-stromu $s = (V,E,ord)$ je takový normalizovaný A-strom $s_1 = (V_1,E_1,ord_1)$, pro který (V,E) a (V_1,E_1) jsou izomorfní a $Str(s) = Str(s_1)$. Všimněme si, že normalizace A-stromu je jednoznačně daná.

Ekvivalence. Dva A-stromy (R-seznamy) jsou ekvivalentní, pokud mají stejnou normalizaci. Ekvivalentní A-stromy často nebudeme rozlišovat.

Operace shift a delete zavedeme tak, že převedou A-strom na A-strom.

Delete. Operace $dl(i)$ vyřadí z množiny V a z R-seznamu *ord* uzel tvaru $[i,a_i]$ a získá tím množinu V_1 a R-seznam ord_1. Z A-stromu $s = (V,E,ord)$ operace $dl(i)$ udělá A-strom $s_1 = (V_1,E_1,ord_1)$ tím, že vyřadí uzel tvaru $[i,a_i]$ jak z množiny V, tak z R-seznamu *ord*. Dále vyřadí z E všechny dvojice hran tvaru $([j,a_j],[i,a_i])$ a $([i,a_i],[k,a_k])$ (pokud existují). Každou takovou dvojici hran nahradí v E_1 jedinou hranou tvaru $([j,a_j],[k,a_k])$. Viz příklad 3.

Shift. Operace $sh(i,j)$ přesune v R-seznamu *ord* uzel s indexem i před uzel s indexem j. Vytvoří tak nový R-seznam ord_2. Provedeme-li operaci $sh(i,j)$ na A-strom $s = (V,E,ord)$, získáme tím A-strom $s_2 = (V,E,ord_2)$. Operace shift mění v A-stromě pouze R-seznam, tedy slovosled. Viz příklad 4.

Poznámka. Připomeňme si, že operace mají být voleny tak, že posledním uzlem trvale zůstává sentinel.

2.3 URAS (Úplná redukční analýza A-stromu).

Zavádíme URAS s možností regulace pomocí množiny (významově) zakázaných redukcí. Příkladem zakázané redukce A-stromů z PDT, je vynechání předložky z předložkové vazby, či vynechání samotné zvratné částice.

Značení. Nechť Γ je konečná abeceda. $T(\Gamma)$ značí množinu všech A-stromů na Γ. Nechť $\mathsf{T} \subseteq T(\Gamma)$. Říkáme, že T tvoří T-jazyk na Γ. Množinu R-seznamů $R(\mathsf{T}) = \{R(t) \mid t \in \mathsf{T}\}$ nazýváme R-jazykem T-jazyka T. Analogicky, jazyk $Str(\mathsf{T}) = \{Str(t) \mid t \in \mathsf{T}\}$ nazýváme Str-jazykem T. Nechť $Z \subset \{(s,t) \mid s,t \in \mathsf{T}\}$ je daná množina zakázaných redukcí na T. Označíme $Str(Z) = \{(Str(s),Str(t)) \mid (s,t) \in Z\}$ a $R(Z) = \{(R(s),R(t)) \mid (s,t) \in Z\}$.

Redukce. Nyní zavedeme k T-jazyku T a dané množině zakázaných redukcí Z redukce typu $\vdash_{\mathsf{T}}^{Z}$. Nechť s,t jsou A-stromy. Říkáme, že s je přímo redukovatelné na t podle T a Z a píšeme $s \vdash_{\mathsf{T}}^{Z} t$ pokud:

- $s,t \in \mathsf{T}$ a $|Str(s)| > |Str(t)|$ a (s,t) není ze Z;
- t je získáno z s provedením množiny operací vypuštění (deletů) Dl a následně postupným provedením shiftů z uspořádané množiny Sh. Dl je povinně neprázdná, Sh může být prázdná.

- Libovolný uzel je přesouván pomocí Sh maximálně jednou.
- **Operační nezmenšitelnost redukce.** Pokud bychom vynechali při aplikaci na s jednu nebo více operací z Dl nebo z Sh, získali bychom A-strom z takový, že $z \notin \mathsf{T}$, nebo $(s,z) \in Z$.
- Jako $DL(s,t)$ označujeme množinu uzlů A-stromu s, vypuštěnou během redukce $s \vdash_T^Z t$ a říkáme, že je DL-množinou redukce $s \vdash_T^Z t$. O Sh říkáme, že je SH-sekvencí redukce $s \vdash_T^Z t$.

Doplňující pojmy. Reflexívní a tranzitívní uzávěr relace $\vdash_T^Z$ označujeme $\vdash_T^Z *$. Částečné uspořádání $\vdash_T^Z$ přirozeně definuje

- $T_{\vdash_T^Z}^0 = \{v \in \mathsf{T} \mid \neg\exists u \in \mathsf{T} : v \vdash_T^Z u\}$ - množina neredukovatelných A-stromů T-jazyka T.
- $T_{\vdash_T^Z}^{n+1} = \{v \in \mathsf{T} \mid \exists u \in T_{\vdash_T^Z}^n : u \vdash_T^Z v\} \cup T_{\vdash_T^Z}^n$, $n \in N$ - množina A-stromů z T, které je možné zredukovat na neredukovatelný A-strom z T posloupností URAS-redukcí délky nanejvýš $n+1$.

URAS. Pro A-strom $s \in \mathsf{T}$ a zakázanou množinu Z nazveme URAS$(s,\mathsf{T},Z) = \{u \vdash_T^Z v \mid s \vdash_T^Z *u\}$ (úplnou) redukční analýzou s podle T a Z.

Větev. Nechť $B = (s_1, s_2, \cdots, s_n)$ je posloupnost A-stromů taková, že $s_1 \vdash_T^Z s_2$, $s_2 \vdash_T^Z s_3$, $\cdots$, $s_{n-1} \vdash_T^Z s_n$ a $s_n \in T_{\vdash_T^Z}^0$.
Říkáme, že B je větví URAS(s,T,Z) a n je její délka.

DL-sekvence a DL-charakteristika. Nechť Dl_i je Dl-množinou redukce $s_i \vdash_T s_{i+1}$ pro $1 \leq i < n$ a Dl_n je množinou uzlů A-stromu s_n.
Píšeme $Dl(B) = (Dl_1, Dl_2, \cdots, Dl_{n-1})$ a říkáme, že $Dl(B)$ je DL-sekvencí větve B.
Množina $Ch(B) = (\{Dl_1, Dl_2, \cdots, Dl_{n-1}\})$ je DL-charakteristikou větve B.
DL-charakteristika a DL-sekvence se liší tím, že u DL-charakteristiky nezáleží na pořadí redukčních množin, ale u DL-sekvence ano.
Vidíme, že pro $1 \leq i < j < n$ jsou Dl_i a Dl_j disjunktní.

2.4 Algebraické vlastnosti závislostí a koordinací u analytických stromů PDT.

Touto podsekcí začíná výsledková část příspěvku. Předkládáme výsledky dvou typů. Nejčastěji prezentujeme lingvistická pozorování, formulovaná pomocí zavedeného aparátu. Získali jsme je (neúplným) procházením materiálu z PDT. K pozorováním jsme nenašli žádné výjimky a nevěříme, že se nějaké najdou. Pozorování by měla být podnětem ke (korpusově lingvistické) diskusi.

Druhým typem výsledků jsou tvrzení a důsledky matematického charakteru. Vycházejí z rozboru prezentovaných (lingvistických) příkladů a z vlastností zavedeného aparátu.

T_P v následujícím textu označuje množinu korektních A-stromů s koordinacemi a závislostmi, zpracovaných metodikou analytické roviny PDT. Rozhodnout o tom, zda daný A-strom patří do T_P, by měli umět lidé (lingvisté, anotátoři), ovládající češtinu a metodiku PDT.

ZP označuje množinu zakázaných redukcí pro analytickou rovinu PDT.

Příklad 3. *Tento příklad navazuje na příklady 1 a 2. Obsahuje formalizaci A-stromů $T1_2$ a $T1_3$ a tím i popis redukce $T1_2 \vdash_{T_P}^{ZP} T1_3$:*
$T1_2 = (V_2, E_2, ord_2)$, *přičemž*
$V_2 = \{[1,b_1], [2,b_2], [3,b_3], [4,b_4], [5,b_5]\}$
$E_2 = \{([2,b_2],[1,b_1]), ([3,b_3],[4,b_4]), ([4,b_4],[1,b_1]),$
$([5,b_5],[1,b_1])\}$,
$ord_2 = ([1,b_1],[2,b_2],[3,b_3],[4,b_4],[5,b_5])$
$T1_3 = (V_3, E_3, ord_3)$, *přičemž*
$V_3 = \{[1,b_1],[2,b_2],[3,b_3],[5,b_5]\}$
$E_3 = \{([2,b_2],[1,b_1]), ([3,b_3],[1,b_1]), ([5,b_5],[1,b_1])\}$
$ord_3 = ([1,b_1],[2,b_2],[3,b_3],[5,b_5])$
Vidíme, že $T1_2$ je normalizovaný a že $T1_3$ normalizovaný není, protože vznikl z $T1_2$ vypuštěním uzlu $[4,b_4]$.

Následují strukturální pozorování A-stromů z T_P. Pozorování odrážejí syntaktické vlastnosti českých vět a anotátorskou metodiku pro analytickou rovinu PDT. Naše příklady tato pozorování ilustrují.

Pozorování 1. *Nechť s je A-strom z T_P. Všechny větve URAS(s,T_P,ZP) mají stejnou délku.*

Pozorování 2. *Nechť s je A-strom z T_P, který neobsahuje koordinace (tj. značky 'Cr' a 'Co'). Všechny větve URAS(s,T_P,ZP) mají nejen stejnou délku, ale i stejnou DL-charakteristiku. Navíc URAS(s,T_P,ZP) obsahuje jediný neredukovatelný A-strom. Tedy URAS(s,T_P,ZP) lze považovat za (algebraickou strukturu zvanou) svaz.*

Pozorování 3. *Nechť s je A-strom z T_P, který neobsahuje koordinace a r_1, r_2 jsou dvě různé redukce z URAS(s,T_P,ZP). Platí, že r_1 a r_2 mají disjunktní DL-množiny.*

Pozorování 4. *Nechť s je A-strom z T_P, který obsahuje koordinaci alespoň tří členů. Existují dvě větve URAS(s,T_P,ZP) s různou DL-charakteristikou.*

Pozorování 5. *Nechť s je A-strom z T_P, který obsahuje koordinaci alespoň tří členů. Existují dvě redukce z URAS(s,T_P,ZP), které nemají disjunktní DL-množiny. Průnik těchto DL-množin obsahuje uzel se spojkou nebo čárkou se značkou "AuxX".*

Předchozí dvě pozorování jsou ilustrovány příkladem 4.

Tvrzení 1. *Existuje $t \in T_P$, jehož URAS obsahuje více než jeden neredukovalený A-strom.*

Předchozí tvrzení lze dokázat pomocí A-stromu k větě 'Přišel, viděl, zvítězil.'.

2.5 UPRA (úplná větná redukční analýza.)

Abychom mohli dát do souvislosti URAS se starším pojmem, větnou redukční analýzou, zavádíme úplnou větnou redukční analýzu (UPRA), viz [3]. Do UPRA vstupuje věta ve formě R-seznamu. UPRA zavádíme zcela analogicky jako URAS.

Redukce. Mějme jazyk L a R-seznam u takový, že $Str(u) \in L$. Říkáme, že u je R-seznamem k jazyku L a píšeme $u \in R(L)$. Nechť $U \subset \{(u,v)|u,v \in R(L)\}$ je daná množina zakázaných redukcí.

Zavedeme k $R(L)$ a dané U redukce $\succ_L^U$. Nechť $u, v \in R(L)$. Říkáme, že u je redukovatelné na v podle L a U a označujeme $u \succ_L^U v$, pokud:

- $|Str(u)| > |Str(v)|$ a (u,v) není z U;
- R-seznam v je získán z u provedením množiny operací vypuštění (deletů) Dl a následně postupným provedením shiftů z uspořádané množiny Sh. Dl je povinně neprázdná, Sh může být prázdná.
- Libovolný uzel je přesouván pomocí Sh maximálně jednou.
- **Operační nezmenšitelnost redukce.** Pokud bychom vynechali při aplikaci na u jednu nebo více operací z Dl nebo z Sh, získali bychom R-seznam z takový, že $Str(z) \notin L$, nebo $(u,z) \in U$.
- Jako $Dl(u,v)$ označujeme množinu uzlů R-seznamu u, vypuštěnou provedením množiny deletů Dl a říkáme, že $Dl(u,v)$ je DL-množinou redukce $u \succ_L^U v$. O Sh říkáme, že je SH-sekvencí redukce $u \succ_L^U v$.

UPRA. Nechť $w \in R(L)$ a $U \subset \{(u,v)|u,v \in R(L)\}$ je daná množina zakázaných redukcí. UPRA$(w,L,U) = \{u \succ_L^U v \,|\, w \succ_L^U {}^* u\}$ nazveme úplnou redukční analýzou w k jazyku L a množině nekorektních redukcí U.

Zbývající potřebné pojmy pro UPRA lze zavést zcela analogicky jako pro URAS.

2.6 Nesouvislosti a stabilita redukcí.

Zavádíme dvě míry nesouvislosti redukcí, které se vzájemně doplňují. S ohledem na tyto a další míry zavádíme několik typů stability pro URAS, které nám dovolí klasifikovat omezená URAS jako stabilní, nebo nestabilní. Stabilita URAS pro jednotlivé A-stromy je formálním kriteriem pro lingvistickou adekvátnost redukční analýzy, s ohledem na daná omezení. Budeme hledat maximální omezení taková, která zachovávají alespoň nejslabší typ stability. Následuje několik formálních definic.

Graf redukce. Mějme redukci $s \vdash_T^Z t$, kde $s = (V, E, or)$, a její DL-množinu $DL(s,t)$. Píšeme $G(s,t) = (DL(s,t), \{(a,b) \in E | a,b \in DL(s,t)\})$ a říkáme, že $G(s,t)$ je DL-grafem redukce $s \vdash_T^Z t$.

Počet komponent redukce. Nechť i je počet komponent DL-grafu $G(s,t)$. Budeme psát, že $pk(s,t) = i$ a říkat, že i je počet komponent redukce $s \vdash_T^Z t$.

URAS s omezeným počtem komponent. Nechť i je přirozené číslo. Označíme jako URAS$(s,T,Z; pk \leq i)$ podmnožinu URAS(s,T,Z), která obsahuje všechny redukce z URAS(s,T,Z), které nemají více komponent než i.

Vidíme, že neredukovatelné stromy v URAS$(s,T,Z; pk \leq i)$ mohou být pro některá i jiné (větší), než ty z URAS(s,T,Z).

Říkáme, že URAS$(s,T,Z; pk \leq i)$ je pro dané i T-stabilní, pokud URAS$(s,T,Z; pk \leq i)$ = URAS(s,T,Z).

Říkáme, že URAS$(s,T,Z; pk \leq i)$ je pro dané i CH-stabilní, pokud množina charakteristik URAS$(s,T,Z; pk \leq i)$ a URAS(s,T,Z) je stejná.

URAS$(s,T,Z; pk \leq i)$ je pro dané i Mn-stabilní, pokud každý neredukovatelný strom z URAS$(s,T,Z, pk \leq i)$ je i neredukovatelným stromem URAS(s,T,Z).

Požadavky na stabilitu jsou seřazeny od nejsilnější k nejslabší. Nahlédneme, že stejně můžeme užívat zavedené typy stability pro další typy redukčních omezení.

Počet komponent je jednou přirozenou mírou nesouvislosti redukce A-stromu. Budeme používat ještě jednu míru nesouvislosti redukce, která měří velikost mezer mezi komponentami. Následují další formální definice.

Velikost mezer v redukci. Jako $Sv(s,t)$ budeme označovat nejmenší souvislý (bez ohledu na orientaci) podgraf A-stromu s, který obsahuje DL-graf $G(s,t)$. Nechť j je počet uzlů, které obsahuje $Sv(s,t)$ navíc oproti $G(s,t)$. Píšeme $ns(s,t) = j$ a říkáme, že redukce $s \vdash_T^Z t$ má velikost mezer j.

URAS s omezením na velikost mezer. Nechť i je přirozené číslo. Označíme jako URAS$(s,T,Z : ns \leq i)$ podmnožinu URAS(s,T,Z), která obsahuje všechny redukce z URAS(s,T,Z), které nemají velikost mezer větší než i.

Omezení můžeme i skládat. Např. URAS$(s,T,Z; pk \leq i, ns \leq j)$ = URAS$(s,T,Z; pk \leq i) \cap$ URAS$(s,T,Z; ns \leq j)$.

Množiny stromů stabilní s ohledem na omezení. Budeme používat následující typy značení pro množiny A-stromů splňující daná omezení.

Např. TRAS$(T,Z; pk \leq 1, ns \leq 0;$ T-st $) = \{t \in T|$ URAS$(t,T,Z; pk \leq 1, ns \leq 0)$ je T-stabilní $\}$.

Analogicky TRAS$(T,Z; pk \leq 1;$ CH-st $) = \{t \in T|$ URAS$(t,T,Z; pk \leq 1)$ je CH-stabilní $\}$. Podobně budeme popisovat množiny A-stromů z T parametrizované dalšími omezeními a různými typy stability ze škály T-stabilní, CH-stabilní, Mn-stabilní.

2.7 Rozlišení závislostí a koordinací pomocí (ne)souvislosti.

Předchozí pojmy a následující příklady využijeme k formulaci nových pozorování o PDT.

Příklad 4. *Tento příklad ilustruje redukce vícenásobných koordinací a použití grafově nesouvislé redukce v URAS.*

(3) Je.Pred dědou.Obj.Co ,.AuxX otcem.Obj.Co a..Cr strýcem.Obj.Co..AuxK

Na obrázku 5 vidíme schema *UPRA* věty *(3)* podle stromu $T3_1$, jazyka T_P a prázdné zakázané množiny. Schema stejného tvaru má i schema URAS A-stromu $T3_1$. Věta *(3)* obsahuje trojnásobnou koordinaci předmětů. Povšimněme si, že dalšímu zjemnění schematu zabraňují kategorie *(značky)*, použité podle vzoru PDT. Značka 'Cr' znamená koordinující symbol *(slovo)*, 'Co' značí koordinované slovo, či symbol. Schematu na obrázku odpovídají redukce A-stromů, které jsou reprezentovány obrázky 4 až 8. Všechny tři redukce A-stromu $T3_1$ vypouštějí *(při zjednodušování trojnásobné koordinace na dvojnásobnou)* dva nesouvisející listy *(podstromy)*. Třetí redukce navíc používá *shift*. Zbývající redukce dvojnásobných koordinací se realizují postupným vypouštěním listů, které tvoří souvislý úplný podstrom.

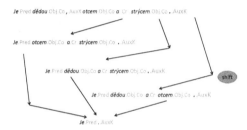

Obrázek 5: UPRA věty *(3)* podle $T3_1$.

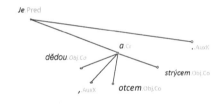

Obrázek 6: A-strom $T3_1$.

Obrázek 7: $T3_2$ a $T3_3$ vzniklé redukcemi z $T3_1$.

Snadno ověříme z definic následující tvrzení.

Tvrzení 2. *Vidíme, že*
$URAS(T1_1, T_P, ZP; pk \le 1)$ *je T-stabilní,*
$URAS(T3_1, T_P, ZP; pk \le 2)$ *je T-stabilní a*
$URAS(T3_1, T_P, ZP; pk \le 1)$ *není Mn-stabilní.*

Obrázek 8: Vlevo $T3_4$, vzniklý redukcí z $T3_1$ a vpravo $T3_5$ vzniklý redukcemi z $T3_2$, $T3_3$ a $T3_4$.

Z předchozích tvrzení vyplývá následující důsledek.

Důsledek 1. *Vidíme, že*
$TRAS(T_P, ZP, pk \le 1; T\text{-}st) \subset TRAS(T_P, ZP; pk \le 2; T\text{-}st)$

Následují výsledky našeho pozorování T_P, které se týkají nesouvislostí.

Pozorování 6. *Nechť $s \in T_P$. URAS$(s, T_P, ZP; pk \le 2)$ je T-stabilní.*

Pozorování 7. *Nechť $s \in T_P$ je A-strom bez koordinací. URAS$(s, T_P, ZP; pk \le 1)$ je T-stabilní.*

Pozorování 8. *Nechť $s \in T_P$ je A-strom s alespoň trojnásbnou koordinací. URAS$(s, T_P, ZP; pk \le 1)$ není Mn-stabilní.*

Poznámky k předchozímu pozorování. Podobně jako u $T3_1$, každá alespoň trojnásobná koordinace z PDT vyžaduje alespoň jednu redukci se dvěma komponentami. Pokud povolíme redukce s maximálně jednou komponentou, bude každý neredukovatelný strom z URAS$(s, T_P, ZP; pk \le 1)$ minimálně o jednu nevykonanou redukci větší, než příslušný neredukovatelný strom z URAS(s, T_P, ZP).

Pozorování o velikosti mezer jsou analogická pozorováním o počtu komponent. Důležité pozorování je, že koordinace dovolují redukcím jen velikost mezer rovnou jedné a stromy bez koordinací dovolují redukcím jen jedinou komponentu.

Pozorování 9. *Vypozorovali jsme, že*
$TRAS(T_P, ZP, ns \le 0; T\text{-}st) = TRAS(T_P, ZP; pk \le 1; T\text{-}st),$
$TRAS(T_P, ZP; ns \le 1; T\text{-}st) = TRAS(T_P, ZP, pk \le 2; T\text{-}st)$
$= T_P.$

Pozorování 10. *Nechť $s \in T_P$ je A-strom bez koordinací. URAS$(s, T_P, ZP; ns \le 0)$ je T-stabilní. Vidíme, že i URAS$(s, T_P, ZP; pk \le 1, ns \le 0)$ je T-stabilní.*

Pozorování 11. *Nechť $s \in T_P$ je A-strom s alespoň trojnásobnou koordinací. Platí, že URAS$(s, T_P, ZP; ns \le 0)$ není Mn-stabilní.*

2.8 URAS s omezeními míry (ne)listovosti.

Snažíme se minimalizovat při redukcích změny hran *(změny významu)*, takže se snažíme redukovat stromy bez koordinací tak, že vypouštíme v jistém pořadí jen listy. Pojmy zaváděné v tomto odstavci zavádíme za dvojím účelem. Prvním účelem je dát prostředky pro formální aproximaci intuitivní redukční analýzy stromů bez koordinací. Druhým účelem je exaktně zachytit fakt, že redukce vložených koordinací nutně používají vypuštění vnitřního uzlu a charakterizovat složitost tohoto faktu. Při redukci vložených koordinací se význam redukovaného stromu nijak nemění.

Nechť o je nějaké uspořádání množiny Dl, kde Dl je DL-množinou nějaké redukce A-stromu s. Pak říkáme, že o realizuje Dl na s. Píšeme $o \in ord(Dl, s)$.

IN-stupněm operace $dl(i)$ na A-stromě s nazveme počet hran z E vcházejících do uzlu $[i, a_i]$. Všimněme si, že delete uzlu $[i, a_i]$ má IN-stupeň 0 právě tehdy, pokud $[i, a_i]$ je listem A-stromu s.

Uvažujme různé realizace množiny Dl, kde Dl je DL-množina na s. V různých realizacích Dl na s může mít $dl(i) \in Dl$ různou hodnotu svého IN-stupně, neboť $dl(i)$ může být prováděna na různých A-stromech.

Omezíme se jen na neklesající realizace DL-množin v redukcích, neboť realizace vypouštějící jen listy musí být neklesající. Budeme využívat faktu, že ke každé redukci existuje neklesající realizace.

Značení. Říkáme, že $o \in ord(Dl, s)$ je neklesající a píšeme $o \in Nord(Dl, s)$, pokud $o = (dl(i_1), dl(i_2), \cdots, dl(i_n))$ a $IN(dl(i_1)) \leq IN(dl(i_2)), \cdots, IN(dl(i_{n-1})) \leq IN(dl(i_n))$. Píšeme $IN(o) = (IN(dl(i_1)), IN(dl(i_2)), \cdots, IN(dl(i_n)))$.
Nechť $o \in Nord(Dl, s)$, první prvek z o je $dl(i)$, poslední prvek z o je $dl(j)$. Budeme psát $MinIN(o) = IN(dl(i))$ a $MaxIN(o) = IN(dl(j))$.

URAS se spodní mírou (ne)listovosti. Označíme jako $URAS(s, T, Z; MinIN \leq i)$ podmnožinu $URAS(s, T, Z)$, která obsahuje všechny redukce z $URAS(s, T, Z)$, které mají neklesající realizaci o s $MinIN(o) \leq i$.

URAS s horní mírou (ne)listovosti. Označíme jako $URAS(s, T, Z; MaxIN \leq i)$ podmnožinu $URAS(s, T, Z)$, která obsahuje všechny redukce z $URAS(s, T, Z)$, které mají neklesající realizaci o s $MaxIN(o) \leq i$.

2.9 Závislosti, vložená koordinace a (ne)listovost.

Příklad 5.   *Tento příklad ilustruje redukce vložených koordinací.*

(5) Pracujeme.Pred.Co a.Cr.Co myslíme.Pred.Co i..Cr jednáme.Pred.Co..AuxK

Na obrázku 9 vidíme schema UPRA věty (5) podle T5₁, T_P a ZP. Věta (5) je věta s vloženou koordinací. A-stromy odpovídající redukcím jsou na obrázcích 10 až 12. Vložená koordinace se v A-stromě T5₁ zjednodušuje tak, že se vyjme jedna hrana s řídícím uzlem se značkou 'Cr.Co'. To odpovídá dvěma redukcím v UPRA z obrázku . Vidíme, že tyto redukce vypouštějí jeden list a jeden vnitřní uzel do kterého vchází jediná hrana.

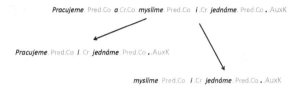

Obrázek 9: UPRA věty s vloženou koordinací.

Obrázek 10: T5₁

Tvrzení 3. *Pro pro čistě závislostní strom T1₁ z příkladu 1 platí, že $URAS(T1_1, T_P, ZP; MaxIN \leq 0)$ je T-stabilní.*

Tvrzení 4. *Pro čistě závislostní strom T1₂ z příkladu 1 platí, že $URAS(T1_2, T_P, MaxIN \leq 0)$ není T-stabilní, ale je Mn-stabilní. Navíc $URAS(T1_2, T_P, MinIn \leq 1, MaxIN \leq 1)$ je T-stabilní.*

Důsledek 2. *Vidíme, že*

- *$TRAS(T_P, ZP; MaxIN \leq 0; T\text{-st})$*
  $\subset TRAS(T_P, ZP; MaxIN \leq 1; T\text{-st}).$

- *$TRAS(T_P, ZP; MinIN \leq 0; T\text{-st})$*
  $\subset TRAS(T_P, ZP; MinIN \leq 1; T\text{-st}).$

Pozorování 12. *$TRAS(T_P, ZP; MinIN \leq 1; T\text{-st}) \subset T_P$.*

Tvrzení 5. *Pro T5₁ z příkladu 5 platí, že $URAS(T5_1, T_P, ZP; MinIN \leq 0)$ je T-stabilní, $URAS(T5_1, T_P, ZP; MaxIN \leq 0)$ není Mn-stabilní a $URAS(T5_1, T_P, ZP; MinIN \leq 0, MaxIN \leq 1)$ je T-stabilní.*
T5₁ nese koordinaci vloženou do koordinace. Vidíme, že platí T5₁ $\in TRAS(T_P, ZP; MinIN \leq 0, MaxIn \leq 1; T\text{-st})$

Pozorování 13. *Nechť $t \in T_P$ nese koordinaci vloženou do koordinace. Platí, že $URAS(t, T_P, ZP; MaxIN \leq 0)$ není Mn-stabilní.*

Důsledek 3. *Vidíme, že*

- *$TRAS(T_P, ZP; MaxIN \leq 0; T\text{-st})$*
  $\subset TRAS(T_P, ZP; MinIN \leq 0; MaxIn \leq 1; Mn\text{-st})$

- *$TRAS(T_P, ZP; MinIN \leq 0; MaxIn \leq 1; Mn\text{-st})$*
  $\subset TRAS(T_P, ZP; MinIN \leq 1; MaxIn \leq 1; Mn\text{-st})$

Obrázek 11: $T5_2$, vzniklé redukcí z T5₁.

Obrázek 12: $T5_3$, vzniklé redukcí z $T5_1$.

- $TRAS(T_P,ZP;MinIN \leq 1,MaxIn \leq 1; Mn\text{-}st\ ) \subseteq T_P$.

Poznámka. Pro každé $t \in T_P$, které jsme pozorovali, bylo URAS$(t,T_P,ZP;MinIN \leq 1)$ Mn-stabilní. Neumíme odhadnout, zda existuje A-strom $t \in T_P$ takový, že URAS$(t,T_P,ZP;MinIN \leq 1)$ není Mn-stabilní, tedy zda TRAS$(T_P,ZP,MinIN \leq 1,MaxInPc \leq 1;$ Mn-st $) = T_P$.

2.10 Konzistence URAS a UPRA nad PDT

L_P značí množinu korektních českých vět (jen) s koordinacemi a závislostmi, která je korektně značkovaná metodikou analytické roviny PDT. Připomeňme, že T_P označuje množinu všech korektních A-stromů s koordinacemi a závislostmi, zpracovaných metodikou analytické roviny PDT. ZP označuje množinu zakázaných redukcí na T_P.

Následuje pozorování o konzistenci mezi URAS na T_P a UPRA na L_P.

Podle našich pozorování a naší notace platí, že $L_P = Str(T_P)$, $R(L_P) = R(T_P)$ a $UP = R(ZP)$.

Pozorování 14. *Nechť' $s \vdash_{T_P}^{ZP} t$, pak $R(s) \succ_{L_P}^{UP} R(t)$. Nechť' $s,t \in T_P$ a $R(s) \succ_{L_P}^{UP} R(t)$, pak $s \vdash_{T_P}^{ZP} t$.*

Předchozí pozorování formuluje vlastnost konzistence mezi UPRA a PRAS. Říká, že A-stromy z PDT jsou konstruovány v souladu s větnou redukční analýzou. Toto pozorování je naším základním pozorováním analytické roviny PDT. Přirozeně všechny zde prezentované příklady na URAS a UPRA splňují podmínky konzistence mezi URAS a UPRA.

2.11 Další omezení a výhledy do budoucna.

Následující omezení mají, na rozdíl od předchozích podobnou platnost pro URAS i pro UPRA.

URAS s omezením na počet deletů. Nechť' i je přirozené číslo. Označíme jako URAS$(s,T,Z : dl \leq i)$ podmnožinu URAS(s,T,Z), která obsahuje všechny redukce z URAS(s,T,Z), které nemají počet deletů větší než i.

URAS s omezením na vzdálenost vypouštěných uzlů. Nechť' k je přirozené číslo. Označíme jako URAS$(s,T,Z : ds \leq k)$ podmnožinu URAS(s,T,Z), která obsahuje všechny redukce z URAS(s,T,Z), které nemají vzdálenost mezi vypouštěnými uzly (podle uspořádání v R-seznamu) větší než k.

Příklad 6. *Uvažujme formální jazyk $L_1 = \{a^n b^n | n > 0\}$. Každému slovu (větě) tohoto jazyka přiřadíme A-strom t_n následujícím způsobem:*

a) kořenem t_n bude nejlevější a,

b) z každého a, které není kořenem vede hrana do jeho levého souseda,

c) z i-tého b vede hrana do i-tého a. Jiné hrany t_n neobsahuje.

Budiž $T_1 = \{t_n | n > 0\}$. Vidíme, že TRAS$(T_1,\emptyset;dl \leq 2, ds \leq 2, pk \leq 1, MaxIn \leq 0; T\text{-}st) = T_1$.

Předchozí rovnost dává strukturálně-složitostní charakteristiku T-jazyka T_1. Zmenšením kteréhokoliv parametru buď' rovnost ztrácíme, nebo zmenšení parametru nemá smysl.

Následující tvrzení není těžké nahlédnout.

Tvrzení 6. *Ke každému $k \in \mathbb{N}$ existuje regulární jazyk L, takový, že pro libovolný T-jazyk T takový, že $Str(T) = L$ platí, že TRAS$(T,\emptyset;ds \leq k, Mn\text{-}st) \neq T$.*

Podobné tvrzení platí pro bezkontextové jazyky, které nejsou regulární.

Poznamenejme, že v následujícím zřejmém tvrzení mají označení UPRA$(u,L,\emptyset;ds \leq k)$ a Mn-stabilita analogický význam jako pro URAS.

Tvrzení 7. *Ke každému bezkontextovému jazyku L existuje $k \in \mathbb{N}$ takové, že pro libovolné $u \in R(L)$ platí, že UPRA$(u,L,\emptyset;ds \leq k)$ je Mn-stabilní.*

Předchozí příklad a tvrzení uvádíme, abychom poukázali na souvislosti našich lingvistických pozorování T_P a formální teorií (nekonečných) jazyků. Vidíme, že z pohledu formální redukční analýzy, nejsou A-stromy z T_P příliš složité. Přesto jsme (na základě lingvistického folklóru) očekávali jednodušší a uniformější výsledky.

V budoucnu plánujeme zavést míry neprojektivity a řetězové nesouvislosti založené na redukční analýze a konfrontovat tyto míry s PDT. Očekáváme, že se ukáže souvislost těchto měr s časovou složitostí redukční analýzy.

Reference

[1] Markéta Lopatková, Jiří Mírovský, and Vladislav Kuboň. Gramatické závislosti vs. koordinace z pohledu redukční analýzy. In *Proceedings of the main track of the 14th Conference on Information Technologies - Applications and Theory (ITAT 2014), with selected papers from Znalosti 2014 collocated with Znalosti 2014, Demanovska Dolina - Jasna, Slovakia, September 25 - 29, 2014.*, pages 61–67, 2014.

[2] Martin Plátek, Dana Pardubská, and Markéta Lopatková. On minimalism of analysis by reduction by restarting automata. In *Formal Grammar - 19th International Conference, FG 2014, Tübingen, Germany, August 16-17, 2014. Proceedings*, pages 155–170, 2014.

[3] Martin Plátek, Dana Pardubská, and Karel Oliva. Redukční analýza a pražský závislostní korpus. In *Proceedings ITAT 2015: Information Technologies - Applications and Theory, Slovensky Raj, Slovakia, September 17-21, 2015.*, pages 43–50, 2015.

Slovenskočeský NLP workshop (SloNLP 2016)

SloNLP is a workshop focused on Natural Language Processing (NLP) and Computational Linguistics. Its primary aim is to promote cooperation among NLP researchers in Slovakia and Czech Republic.

The topics of the workshop include automatic speech recognition, automatic natural language analysis and generation (morphology, syntax, semantics, etc.), dialogue systems, machine translation, information retrieval, practical applications of NLP technologies, and other topics of computational linguistics.

In the second year of the workshop, 11 submissions were received and 8 of them accepted. Authors of two rejected papers chose to present an abstract of their work.

Rudolf Rosa
Petra Barančíková
Charles University in Prague
Workshop organizers

Program Committee

Petra Barančíková, Charles University, Prague
Vladimír Benko, Slovak Academy of Sciences
Ján Genči, Technical University of Košice
Aleš Horák, Masaryk University, Brno
Markéta Lopatková, Charles University, Prague
David Mareček, Charles University, Prague
Rudolf Rosa, Charles University, Prague
Alexandr Rosen, Charles University, Prague

ITAT 2016 Proceedings, p. 36
ISBN 978-1537016740, © 2016 J. Materna

Aplikace strojového učení ve fulltextovém vyhledávání
(pozvaná přednáška)

Jiří Materna

Seznam.cz

Velká část veřejných informací je dnes k dispozici na internetu v elektronické podobě. Ve většině případů však neznáme přesné umístění odpovědí na naše otázky a jsme zvyklí pro jejich nalezení používat internetové vyhledávače jako jsou Seznam nebo Google. Zatímco v době vzniku prvních vyhledávačů se pro nalezení nejrelevantnějších odpovědí používaly jednoduché algoritmy a pravidlové systémy, dnes už se téměř ve všech částech vyhledávače využívá síly a robustnosti strojového učení.

Zajímá vás, jak moderní vyhledávače fungují a jaké problémy je ve fulltextovém vyhledávání třeba řešit? V této přednášce si představíme obecnou architekturu fulltextového vyhledávače a zaměříme se na vybrané aplikace strojového učení ve vyhledávání. Typickými příklady jsou porozumění dotazu, řazení výsledků nebo využití hlubokých neuronových sítí pro zpracování textové i obrazové informace.

Jiří Materna vystudoval obor informatika na Fakultě informatiky Masarykovy univerzity, kde také získal doktorát v oboru Umělá inteligence a počítačová lingvistika. Od roku 2008 je zaměstnán ve společnosti Seznam.cz, kde nyní zastává pozici vedoucího výzkumného oddělení. Je zakladatel a spoluorganizátor konference Machine Learning Prague, mentorem podnikatelského akcelerátoru StartupYard a autorem blogu o strojovém učení www.mlguru.cz. Mezi jeho odborné zájmy patří strojové učení, zpracování přirozeného jazyka, information retrieval, statistika a obecně řešení těžkých problémů z oblasti informatiky s aplikacemi v běžném životě.

ITAT 2016 Proceedings, pp. 37–41
ISBN 978-1537016740, © 2016 J. Chaloupka

Automatic Symbol Processing for Language Model Building in Slavic Languages

Josef Chaloupka

The Institute of Information Technology and Electronics,
Technical University of Liberec, Studentska 2, 461 17, Liberec, Czech Republic
josef.chaloupka@tul.cz,
WWW home page: https://www.ite.tul.cz/speechlabe/

Abstract: When we want to adapt an existing automatic speech recognition system to a new language, we need a large corpus of texts to create a lexicon, a language model and a database of annotated recordings to train an acoustic model. Usually the texts in the corpus (or in annotations) contain not only words but also some other symbols, mainly strings of digits, special characters and some frequent abbreviations of units. The common feature of all these symbols is that there is not a straightforward correspondence between their printed form and the spoken one. The main goal of this work was to develop efficient tools for automatic translation of symbols or symbolic terms to words for almost all Slavic languages. In this paper we present the research of the basic elements and the production rules in Slavic languages which was used for design of our universal text pre- and post-processing tools.

1 Introduction

The systems for automatic continuous speech recognition are developed for different languages at present. Most of these systems use for classification an acoustic model (AM) together with a language model (LM) and a lexicon [1, 2]. It is necessary to have a large audio database with audio recordings and text transcriptions for the training of AM. We also need large text corpora for the calculation of LM. The problem is that very often some special symbols occur in transcribed text or in text corpora very often [3]. There are about 2 to 5% of such cases in our text data. In many cases, the symbols include strings of digits, special characters (%, €, $, ...) or some frequent abbreviations of physical units (km, kg, °C, ...).

When we build a lexicon, these symbols are usually omitted. In case of digits, it would be impossible to have all their combinations in the vocabulary. As to the other symbols, it would be impractical to keep both abbreviated and full forms there. In inflected languages, the problem is even more complex. A digit or a string of them can be translated into several different words or word combinations, depending on the context. The word corresponding, e.g. to digit '2', could be either cardinal or ordinal number, it can change its suffix according to the gender and case of the related word (typically a noun), it can be a part of a decimal number, etc. For the symbols similar rules apply.

A straightforward solution to this problem does not exist. In non-inflected languages (e.g. in English), this is often solved by a translation table (for the symbols) or a translation generator (for the digit strings). This approach is sometimes used also for the inflectional languages together with some simplified (e.g. majority based) rules. It is also possible to ignore the symbols and just skip them during the LM calculation. The latter approach has several risks, though. The most dangerous one is that some words may never appear in the text form (e.g. 'Celsius' or some less frequent names of numbers) and therefore they will not be included in the lexicon, and hence they cannot be recognized by the ASR (Automatic Speech Recognition) system. And this may happen also when they are in the lexicon but not (or just poorly) represented by the LM. Since the digits and the terms represented by the frequent symbols play an important role in the information carried by speech, it is necessary to find an appropriate solution to this problem.

2 Motivation and Context of our Research

Recently, we have been developing a multi-lingual broadcast monitoring system that employs an ASR technology we had built previously [4]. In a rather short period we need to build language specific modules (lexicons, LMs and AMs) for more than 10 languages. As all of them belong to the Slavic family, our task is some-what easier because we can benefit several facts. All the Slavic languages are more or less related and share many common features, they use similar patterns in grammar and in morphology and what is very important, they can be mutually understood – at least to some extent and after a short reading and listening training.

For each language, we need to solve the same or very similar tasks, and the symbol and digit processing is one of them. Therefore, we decided to design a set of universal transcription tools that will allow to avoid routine tasks that would be otherwise repeated for each language. We have defined the following goals for the transcription: They should be able to generate basic (and with some extensions also several declined) text forms of cardinal numbers. The same should be available also for ordinal numbers. A special tool should process digit strings that specify dates and years, and another tool will process numbers with a decimal point. The last type of tools should be focused on the most frequent abbreviations (physical units, currencies, etc.).

If we want to design and use the tools efficiently, we need to find the patterns and features that are com-mon either for all Slavic languages or at least for some of them (CZ – Czech, SK – Slovak, PL – Polish, RU – Russian, BY – Belarusian, UA – Ukrainian, HR – Croatian, RS – Serbian, SL – Slovenian, BG – Bulgarian and MK – Macedonian). These Slavic languages have been selected because we have designed and implemented a complex system for automatic broadcast programs transcription for these languages [5, 6, 7] or we are modifying the system for them (UA, BY). The resulting recognition rate of our transcription system is over 80% for all the mentioned languages. It is a relatively good result but we are continuously improving the transcription system for each Slavic language.

After that we need to define the basic elements (primitives) and the production rules, which will allow us to translate almost any digit string, any date and year, or any decimal number to the correct text form in each of the given languages. The tools are essential for several practical tasks, namely:

- To ensure that the words usually represented by their symbols appear in the lexicon.

- To translate symbols and symbolic terms to words (text pre-processing) and when needed also back to symbols (post-processing).

- To enhance the LM by adding translated forms into the corpus. The enhancement can be done also by generating randomly chosen digit and symbol strings using the rules and patterns applicable for each language.

- To enhance acoustic model training by better and more correct annotation of speech data, employing the transcription tools and allowing them to use alternative, minor or even colloquial rules of transcription and pronunciation.

3   Symbol to Text Translation

In this work, symbol to text translation is solved for cardinal, ordinal, decimal numbers or dates or for a cardinal/decimal number in combination with an abbreviation.

3.1   Cardinal Numbers

The first task was to find how to convert a string of digits to a word representation for different Slavic languages (SLang). This task is relatively easy in English but it is more complicated for SLang. The words for numbers one and two (+ three, four in SK) are inflected by gender - gender dependent (GD), other numbers from 3 (5 in SK)

to 9 are gender independent (GI). It would be possible to generate numbers from eleven to nineteen (number 1-9 + teen) or tens (10, 20, . . .), which are formed by adding 'ten' to the end of the digit root or hundreds (100, 200, . . .), which are formed the same way as the tens by adding the suffix hundred. But we work with them like with specific words because there are several exception in different SLang. Only SK and SL have the least exceptions and we can generate hundreds without exception. Several different patterns (systems of rules) are in SLang for numbers from twenty-one to ninety-nine:

- DU: the ten 'D - Decade' comes first, then the Unit 'U'

- D_U: the same as the first one but the space '_' is between the D and U

- D_&_U: the spaces and word 'and - &' (e.g. CZ - a, PL - i, SL - in) are between D and U

- U&D: U comes first, then D, joined together by the word 'and - &'.

Only the patterns which are being used most often in single SLang are shown in Table 1. We know that in different SLang there are also alternative (or minor) patterns for conversion of digits (21 - 99) to word numbers (e.g. CZ - U&D) but we have not considered them in this work.

Table 1: Cardinal number patterns

Numbers	Pattern	Language
1, 2	GD	All
3, 4	GD	SK
21-99	D_U	CZ, RU, UA, BY, PL
	DU	SK
	D_&_U	HR, RS, BG, MK
	U&D	SL
hundreds	-	-
thousands	3F	CZ, PL, RU, UA, BY, HR, RS
	2F	BG, MK
	1F	SK, SL
millions	3F	CZ, SK, PL, RU, UA, BY, SL
	2F	HR, RS, BG, MK
milliards	3F	CZ, SK, PL, RU, UA, BY, HR, RS, SL
	2F	BG, MK

The conversion of numbers larger than a thousand is once again specific. Being gendered, all the Higher Scale Names (HSN - thousands, millions, milliard, . . .) follow the declension rules in different SLang. They are three main patterns for the conversion of HSN:

- 3F: three different word forms (1 HSN, 2-4 HSN and more than 4 HSN, e.g. CZ - jeden milion (one million), dva miliony (two millions), pět milionů (five millions)).

- 2F: two different word forms (1 HSN, more than 1 HSN)

- 1F: one word form (without declension)

Several large-number naming system exist for numbers greater than million. We are using the long scale (LS) and short scale (SS) systems in the Europe. In the LS, every new term greater than million is one million times bigger than the previous term (e.g. billion means a million millions) and every new term greater than million is one thousand times bigger than the previous term in the SS (e.g. billion means a thousand millions). The LS is used in CZ, SK, PL, HR, RS and the SS system in RU, UA, BY, BG and MK but with one exception: milliard in the LS system is billion in the SS system. Slavic countries with the SS system use the word milliard (from LS) instead of billion. Other names for higher numbers are from the SS system (trillion, quadrillion, . . .). The strings of digits with values higher than milliard are very rare in our text corpora therefore they are not solved in this work.

The patterns (Table 1.) and a list of words representing the names of numbers are necessary for the conversion from strings of digits to words or for generation of numbers for training LM of any SLang. The list of words of numbers is larger than in English but it is still relatively small, e.g. we need only 49 words for the generation of any cardinal number from zero to several milliards in CZ.

3.2 Ordinal Numbers

The ordinal numbers are presented in text (in almost all SLang) by strings of digits where dot '.' is the last character. The exception is ordinal number (without dot) in date, see chapter 3.4. Two patterns exist for translation of strings of digits to words if the string is higher ordinal number, e.g. 21.:

- AO: All word number forms are Ordinal (e.g. PL - dwudziesty pierwszy (twentieth first))

- LO: only Last member is Ordinal, other words are cardinal numbers (e.g. HR - dvadeset i prvi (twenty and first)))

Other rules for combination of words in ordinal numbers are the same as for cardinal numbers. The combination of digits and abbreviation are used for writing of ordinal numbers in English language very often, e.g. 1st - first. Similar writing pattern appears in text in RU, BY and MK , e.g. RU - 1-й (первый - first). We solved it in RU (BY, MK) by simple lookup table. In other SLang, the combination of digits and abbreviation doesn't exist or it is very rare.

Table 2: Ordinal number patterns

Pattern	Language
AO	CZ, SK, PL
LO	RU, UA, BY, HR, RS, SL, BG, MK

3.3 Decimal Numbers

Two main decimal marks (separator) are used to separate the Integer part (I) from the Fractional part (F) of a decimal number. The decimal comma is used as decimal mark in all SLang. Only in HR language can be found in text corpuses decimal comma or decimal point. The decimal comma is read as whole (w) (e.g. SL - cela), comma (c) (e.g. HR - zarez) or as and (&) (e.g. PL - i). The word - name of the last digit's place value (DN) can be used in decimal number conversion (e.g. tenths, hundredths, thousandths, ten-thousandths, hundred-thousandth, millionth).

The patterns for translation of decimal numbers (digits) to words are as follows:

- W_w_F(DN): e.g. CZ - dvě celé šest setin - two whole six hundredths

- W_&_F(DN): e.g. PL - dwa i sześć setnych - two and six hundredths

- W_w_&_F(DN): e.g. BG - два цяло и шест стотни - two and six hundredths

- W_c_F: e.g. MK - два запирка нула еден - two comma zero six

The alternative patterns for decimal numbers (digits) conversion exist in several SLang, e.g. pattern W_w_&_F in UA and PL. But only main patterns are used in our transcription system at present.

The word whole (e.g. SL – cela) and DN are inflected in SLang. There are three word forms for word whole in CZ and SK, two word forms in RU and SL and only one in BG. In SK and CZ, the number placed before the comma is followed by the first word form for numbers ending by one, by the second word form for numbers from two to four and the third word form for all other numbers. In RU and SL, it is first word form of word whole for numbers ending in one and second word form for other words. Inflection of words DN is more complicated. There are several different exceptions here, so we have a special list of DN words for the group of numbers for each SLang.

Table 3: Decimal number patterns

Pattern	Language
W_w_F(DN)	CZ, SK, RU, SL
W_&_F(DN)	PL, UA, BY
W_w_&_F(DN)	BG, (PL), (UA)
W_c_F	HR, RS, MK

The last exception in SLang (which use word 'whole' in decimal numbers) is that the most common form for reading a decimal number beginning by zero is to read only the fractional part (F) together with DN, e.g. CZ - 0,21 - dvacet jedna setin - twenty one hundredths.

3.4 Dates and Years

The date occurs frequently in text corpora in the form of strings of digits, e.g. 8. 5. 1945, or in a combination of strings of digits with the name of the month, e.g. PL - 8 maja 1945. The main format of date is day-month-year in all SLang. We decide that some strings are date if two strings of digits followed by dots (ordinal numbers) are next to each, e.g. 8. 5., or if the string of digit precedes the name of the month. In different SLang a string of digits preceding a dot precedes the name of the month (CZ, SK, HR, RS, SL), e. g. CZ - 8. května, or we have only a string of digits without a dot (PL, RU, UA, BY, BG, MK), e.g. PL - 8 maja. It is necessary to know that string of digit without dot before the name of the month is still an ordinal number. Latin-derived names of months are used in SK, RU, RS, SL, BG, MK; a set of older names for the months that differs from the Latin month names is used in CZ, PL, UA, BY, HR.

In our tools, we solve the day together with the month and year separately. There are two possible readings of date strings in SLang, e.g. '1. 1.' - 'first first' or 'first January'. The words for ordinal numbers are inflected by case (N - nominative, G - genitive, ...) in the first approach ('first first'). There isn't any inflection by case in BG and MK, therefore the words stay in their basic form (B_B). There are three possible patterns, e.g.:

- G_N: e.g. CZ - prvního (first - genitive) první (first - nominative)

- N_N: e.g. PL - pierwszy (first - nominative) pierwszy (first - nominative)

- G_G: e.g. HR - prvog (first - genitive) prvog (first - genitive)

- B_B: e.g. BG - първи (first) първи (first)

Pattern G_N occurs in CZ, SK, N_N in PL, G_G in HR, RS and B_B in BG and MK. Otherwise, the first approach is very rare or unusual in other SLang and the second approach is more common.

Both words, the ordinal number presenting day and the name of month, are in genitive in the second approach ('first January') in SLang (without BG and MK - they don't have cases). The ordinal number has to be in nominative if the name of month is in nominative, but this approach is less common in all SLang.

The string of digits is detected as a year in the text if: 1) the name of the month precedes, 2) two short (1 - 31(12)) ordinal numbers precede, 3) some form of word year (or

abbreviation, e.g. BG - г.) precedes or follows the string. The year is usually cardinal (CZ, SK, SL) or ordinal number (PL, RU, UA, BY, HR, RS, BG, MK). There are several exceptions for the transcription of the date and the year in different SLangs therefore our tools use only the main patterns (forms).

CZ has one specific: years above one thousand and below two thousand are read as multiples of the word one hundred, e.g. 1900 - devatenáct set - nineteen hundred.

3.5 Combination of digits and abbreviation

The last task was to translate a string of digits followed by an abbreviation to words in the text. In our case, the abbreviation were special characters '€', '$' or '%' and abbreviations of physical units 'km', 'l', 'kg', '°C' or 'm/s'. This task is relatively easy. The number (a string of digits) before the abbreviation is a cardinal number and there are three (3F) or two (2F) word forms of abbreviation. The first word form is in combination with number one, second for numbers from two to four and third for numbers higher than four in 3F, e.g. SL - en kilometer (one kilometer), dva kilometra (two kilometers), pet kilometrov (five kilometers). In 2F, the first word form is for abbreviation in combination with number one (singular) and second word form is for numbers higher than one (plural). Pattern 2F is the same as in English. There are several exceptions for the inflection of some abbreviations in pattern 3F or 2F in different SLang. For example, the word euro ('€') isn't inflected in PL, RU, UA, BY, BG, MK and pattern 2F (not 3F) is used in HR and RS.

Table 4: Inflection of abbreviation with combination of digit string

Pattern	Language
3F	CZ, SK, PL, SL, RU, UA, BY, HR, RS
2F	BG, MK

4 Discussion and Practical Applications

We have developed the universal program tool for translating symbols (mainly digits) and symbolic terms to words (text pre-processing) and back (post-processing). The pre(post)-processing from this tool is used on our databases (text corpora or annotated audio recordings) to train AM or calculating LM. This tool is also possible to use as a random or interval generator of word strings (cardinal, ordinal, decimal numbers or dates or cardinal/decimal numbers with abbreviation). The generator is useful for re-training LM. The input to this tool is a XML file for different SLangs and several parameters which are represented by the patterns described above. All important information for transcription is saved in the XML file, e.g. 1 – one, 2 – two, 1. – first, 2. – second ...

Example for CZ: CZ.XML –F T D_U GD 2 AO W_w_F -DN Yes -ZERO Yes -Year 11 CN

where: [-F T] Function: T translation, G generator, [GD 2] digits 1 and 2 are not transcribed – we cannot solve transcription of GD cardinal numbers at present, [–Year 11 CN] year is cardinal number (CN) and 11 indicates that years above 1000 and below 2000 are read as multiples of the word one hundred. Parameter 10 is set for all other SLangs, [-DN Yes] parameter for decimal numbers – the name of the last digit's place value is used, e.g. 0,25 - nula celá dvacet pět setin, [-DN No] e.g. nula celá dvacet pět, [-ZERO Yes] parameter for decimal numbers – first word is zero for 0,..., e.g. nula celá dvacet pět setin, [-ZERO No] e.g. dvacet pět setin.

It is very easy to generate word strings from minor patterns by parameter settings in different SLangs. The translation tool is available on-line: http://kvap.tul.cz/slavic_symbols.php and it is still being improved by the help of native speakers.

5 Conclusion and Future Work

We have defined several patterns for the translation of any digit string in texts of almost all Slavic languages. The digit strings are a cardinal, ordinal, decimal number or date or it is a number in combination with abbreviation. The rules are relatively complex but we have focused primarily on the main patterns because we need it for building systems for the automatic transcription of broadcast programs. The people speak mainly formal and they use official patterns in their speech. Our text corpora mostly consist from news and there is formal language too. The patterns described in this paper are used to develop tools for translation of symbols to words in pre-processing and also in post-processing of text. The main application area for these tools is the enhancement of language models or improvement of speech data annotation for training the acoustic model. The tools have been designed and implemented in the same way for all Slavic languages. Only the patterns as parameters and lexicon are changed for each Slavic language in the tools.

We would like to find the probability of alternative or minor patterns in our audio recordings in the near future. These alternative patterns will be used for random generation of words from symbols in the process of language model re-training. The main patterns will still be used for symbol to word translation in text pre- or post-processing because otherwise the resulting error rate could be possibly higher than improvements by translation tools.

6 Acknowledgments

The research described in this paper was supported by the Technology Agency of the Czech Republic (project no. TA04010199).

References

[1] Chong, T., Y., Banchs, R. E., Chng, E., S., Li, H.: TDTO Language Modeling with Feedforward Neural Networks. In Proc. of Interspeech 2015, Dresden, Germany, p. 1458-1462, 2015.

[2] Loof, J., Gollan, C., Ney, H.: Cross-language bootstrapping for unsupervised acoustic model training: Rapid development of a Polish speech recognition system. In Proc. of Interspeech 2009, UK, p. 88-91, 2009.

[3] Vasserman, L., Schogol, V., Hall, K.: Sequence-based Class Tagging for Robust Transcription in ASR, In Interspeech 2015, p. 473-477, 2015.

[4] Nouza, J., Cerva, P., Kucharova, M.: Cost-Efficient Development of Acoustic Models for Speech Recognition of Related Languages, In Radioengineering, vol. 22, no. 3, p. 866-873, ISSN 1210-2512, 2013.

[5] Cerva, P., Nouza, J., Silovsky J.: Study on Cross-Lingual Adaptation of a Czech LVCSR System towards Slovak. Springer Verlag, Vol. 6800, p. 81-87, 2011.

[6] Nouza, J., Cerva, P., Zdansky, J., Kucharova, M.: A study on adapting Czech automatic speech recognition system to Croatian language. In Proc. of Elmar 2012. Zadar (Croatia), p. 227-230, 2012.

[7] Nouza, J., Cerva, P., Safarik, R.: Cross-Lingual Adaptation of Broadcast Transcription System to Polish Language Using Public Data Sources, In LTC 2015, Poland, p. 181-185, ISBN 978-83-932640-8-7, 2015.

ITAT 2016 Proceedings, pp. 42–47
ISBN 978-1537016740, © 2016 T. Jelínek

Partial accuracy rates and agreements of parsers: two experiments with ensemble parsing of Czech

Tomáš Jelínek

Charles University, Prague, Czech Republic
Tomas.Jelinek@ff.cuni.cz

Abstract: We present two experiments with ensemble parsing, in which we obtain a 1.4% improvement of UAS compared to the best parser. We use five parsers: MateParser, TurboParser, Parsito, MaltParser a MST-Parser, and the data of the analytical layer of Prague Dependency Treebank (1.5 million tokens). We split training data into 10 data-splits and run a 10-fold cross-validation scheme with each of the five parsers. In this way, we obtain large parsed data to experiment with. In one experiment, we calculate partial accuracy rates of each parser according to a list of parameters, which we then use as weights in a combination of parsers using an algorithm for finding the maximum spanning tree. In the other experiment, we calculate success rates for agreements of parsers (e.g. Mate+MST vs. Turbo+Malt), and use these rates in another combination of parsers. Both experiments achieve an UAS above 90.0% (1.4% higher than TurboParser), the experiment with accuracy rates achieves better LAS.

1 Introduction

For some tasks in NLP (such as corpus annotation, creation of gold standard using human corrected parser output etc.), the accuracy of dependency parsing is far more important than parsing speed. For such cases, ensemble parsing (the combination of several parsers) may do the best job. In this paper, we present two experiments with ensemble parsing, in which we obtain a 1.4% improvement of UAS compared to the best parser. We use five parsers and the data of the analytical layer of Prague Dependency Treebank. We run a 10-fold cross-validation scheme over the training data with each of the five parsers. In this way, we obtain large parsed data to experiment with. In one experiment, we calculate partial accuracy rates of each parser (e. g. the proportion of correct attachments of a token with a given POS to another token), which we then use as weights in a combination of parsers. In another experiment, we calculate a success rate for agreements of parsers (e. g. Mate+MST vs. Turbo+Malt), and use these rates in another combination of parsers.

We focus only on Czech, as our main goal is to create a well parsed Czech treebank, but we plan to test our approach on other languages, in subsection 6.3 we enumerate the steps necessary to reproduce our experiments on other languages.

Similar experiments with ensemble parsing have been performed, e. g. [3] and [2] for the first experiment and [10] for the second one.

2 Parsers and data

In our experiments with ensemble parsing, we use five dependency parsers: TurboParser [6], a dependency parser included in Mate-tools [1] (MateParser), Parsito [9], MaltParser [8] and MSTParser [7]. The experiments are based on the data from the analytical layer of Prague Dependency Treebank[4] (PDT: 1.5 million tokens, 80.000 sentences). PDT data are split into training data (1.170.000 tokens), development test data (dtest, 159.000 tokens) and evaluation test data (etest, 174.000 tokens). We performed morphological tagging of the data using the Featurama tagger[1] with a precision of 95.2%. One of the parsers, Mate-tools, does its own tagging, with a slightly lower precision of 94.1%.

In the two following sub-sections, we describe two steps we take before the training of the parsers and parsing in order to improve parsing accuracy. They are not directly related to the subject of this paper, but they influence the results of the experiments.

2.1 Text simplification tool

In previous experiments with parsing, we found out that parsing accuracy can be significantly increased by reducing the variability of the text.

In the process of training, the parsers create a language model based on the training data. Because of phenomena like valency the parsers cannot rely on morphological tags only, they need to consider lemmas (and occasionally forms) of the tokens. But the data are sparse, in PDT 45% of lemmas occur only once and many more Czech lemmas are completely out-of-vocabulary. Consequently, the model formed by the parser is incomplete which limits the quality of parsing new text.

We have devised (see [5]) a partial solution to this problem: a text simplification tool. In many syntactic constructions, the choice of any lemma inside a group of words yields the same dependency tree: *president Clinton / Bush / Obama declared*. We identify members of about fifty

The work has been supported by the grant 16-07473S (Between lexicon and grammar) of the Grant Agency of the Czech Republic.

---

[1]See http://sourceforge.net/projects/featurama/.

such groups of words with identical syntactic properties and replace them with one representative member for each group. The text loses information (kept in a backup file), but the reduced variability facilitates parsing. Both training and new data are simplified. The variability of lemmas in text is reduced by approx. 20%, resulting in an increase of parsing accuracy of 0.5–1.5% (some parsers, e. g. Malt, benefit more from text simplification than others, e. g. MST). Mate-tools lemmatizes and tags the text itself, and therefore it could not use our simplification: only a limited simplification of the raw data (based mostly on word forms) is performed.

2.2 MWE identification and replacement

We use a list of multi-word expressions with suitable syntactic properties and replace them in the text (both training data and new text to be parsed) by one proxy item. This replacement can be only if either there cannot be any tokens dependent on any member of the MWE, or it is known to which token of the MWE each dependent token has to be attached. Our list of MWEs includes compound words, e. g. compound prepositions such as *v souvislosti s* 'relating to', phrasemes/idioms (*ležet ladem* 'lie fallow') and multi-word named entities (*Kolín nad Rýnem* 'Cologne upon the Rhein').

2.3 Parsing the training data

In order to obtain detailed information on the behavior of the parsers, we parse all the training data (1.2 million tokens) using a 10-fold cross-validation scenario (the training data are split into 10 parts, we use 90% as training data and 10% as test data in 10 iterations) with each of the five parsers. Using these data, we test two approaches to ensemble parsing.

2.4 Parsing the test data

All five parsers were also trained on the whole training data (1.2 M tokens) and used to parse PDT dtest and etest data (approx. 150.000 tokens each). The output of the parsers was then merged in one file to allow experiments with ensemble parsing. Table 1 shows the accuracy of the parsers on PDT etest data. Four accuracy measures are shown: UAS and LAS (unlabeled and labeled attachment score for single tokens), SENT_U and SENT_L (unlabeled and labeled attachment score for the whole sentences). TurboParser achieved the best UAS score (88.63%), but performed only slightly better than MateParser, which has all four scores very high (TurboParser has comparatively poor labeled scores).

3 Analysis of merged parsed data

The results of the parsing by the five parsers of all the data (train data, dev. test, eval. test) are merged in three files.

Table 1: Accuracy of the parsers (etest)

	UAS	LAS	SENT_U	SENT_L
Mate	88.58	83.09	45.87	33.77
Turbo	88.63	82.37	44.86	28.75
Malt	86.74	81.32	42.40	32.68
Parsito	86.71	81.42	41.81	32.65
MST	86.41	79.30	38.93	24.64

We use merged train data to gather information on the behaviour of parsers for the purpose of the ensemble parsing experiments, dev. test is used for fine-tuning both approaches, eval. test is used for final testing.

In this section, we provide a brief analysis of the parsed data based on the dev. test. We count how frequently the parsers agree among one another and what the accuracy corresponding to the occurrences is when a given number of parsers agree. We calculate a hypothetical floor and ceiling for the accuracy rates (UAS, LAS etc.) of any ensemble parsing experiment using these data. We detect and count potential cycles in the data.

3.1 Agreements and disagreements of parsers

In the dev. test data, we calculate how often any given number of parsers agree on a dependency relation (unlabeled scores) or on a dependency relation and a dependency label (labeled scores), then we calculate the accuracy rate of the dependency relation chosen by the highest number of parsers. For example, we find 8330 tokens for which any three parsers agree on one dependency relation and two other parsers agree on another one ("3+2" in Table 2), and the proportion of correct tokens chosen by three parsers in these 8330 tokens is 56.95%.

Table 2 and 3 present these statistics for unlabeled and labeled relations, respectively. The first column indicates the size (number) of agreeing groups of parsers ("5" means all parsers agree, "2+2+1" means two parsers agree on one dep. relation, other two parsers agree on another one, one parser has chosen a third possible dependency relation). The second column shows the number of such occurrences in dev. test data. The third column shows the accuracy, i. e. the portion of correct dep. relations chosen by the highest number of parsers; for "2+2+1" and "1+1+1+1+1", the number expresses the accuracy of a random choice (number of occurrences when at least one of the two pairs or five individual parsers is correct divided by two or five, respectively).

For 88.68% of the tokens, four or five parsers agree on an unlabeled dependency relation, with an unlabeled accuracy rate of 94.99%.

For labeled agreements, the parsers disagree more frequently and the accuracy is lower, but for the majority of tokens, 83.24%, four or five parsers agree, with a labeled accuracy of 92.59%.

Table 2: Unlabeled agreements of parsers (dtest)

Agree	Occurrences	Accuracy
5	123751	97.32
4+1	17215	78.32
3+2	8330	56.95
3+1+1	4515	58.51
2+2+1	2830	35.38
2+1+1+1	2003	35.90
1+1+1+1+1	318	14.33

Table 3: Labeled agreements of parsers (dtest)

Agree	Occurrences	Accuracy
5	111083	95.90
4+1	21237	75.31
3+2	10221	54.59
3+1+1	7058	54.61
2+2+1	4117	33.57
2+1+1+1	4133	32.71
1+1+1+1+1	1113	11.16

3.2 Floor and ceiling

We calculate a hypothetical floor and ceiling for any ensemble parsing experiment using these data: the floor is the worst possible outcome of any experiment (every token, for which at least one parser has an incorrect dep. relation (or label) is considered incorrect), the ceiling is the best possible outcome (if at least one parser has found the correct dep. relation, the token is counted as correct).

We calculate also the floor and ceiling for a simple combination of parsers, in which the dependency relation (or a labeled dep. relation) for which the most parsers agree is always taken. Only if all parsers disagree or two pairs of parsers disagree, the incorrect attachments are counted for the floor of the combination and correct attachments (if any) are counted for the ceiling of the combination.

In neither case, the cycles formed are counted or resolved, therefore the numbers do not reflect accurately the possibilities of a real ensemble parsing experiment.

Table 4 shows the accuracy rates for the floor and ceiling of any experiment and of a simple combination. The

Table 4: Floor and ceiling for ensemble parsing (dtest)

	UAS	LAS	SENT_U	SENT_L
Floor any	75.76	67.02	25.95	16.84
Floor comb.	89.34	83.86	46.29	33.46
Ceiling comb.	90.75	85.99	48.74	36.12
Ceiling any	95.72	92.55	69.03	55.27

difference in accuracy measures between the floor and the ceiling of the simple combination is small, because a decision has to be made only for approx. 2% of the tokens (when all five parsers disagree or two pairs of parsers and one single parser each choose a different dep. relation).

3.3 Potential cycles

We calculate also the number of sentences, where a combination of the results of the five parsers may form a cycle. If any unlabeled dependency relation proposed by any parser can be chosen, the cycles can form in 46.35% of the sentences. For the simple combination described above, a cycle can form in 8.76% of sentences.

4 Ensemble parsing using partial accuracy rates

Our first approach to ensemble parsing is based on the observation (experimentally confirmed) that each parser tends to make consistently the same types of mistakes when using similar training and testing data. Using parsed training data, we determine the strengths and weaknesses of each parser and use them as additional input when combining the parses of new sentences.

4.1 Partial accuracy rates

Based on the parsed training data, we calculate partial accuracy rates for each parser, comparing parsed data with the gold standard. These rates are calculated as the ratio of correct attachments (and labels, in case of labeled rates) of tokens with a given morphosyntactic parameter (e. g. POS) in the total number of such tokens, partial accuracy rates have values between 0 and 1. For example, an accuracy rate 0.92 calculated for the MateParser for the unlabeled parameter POS2POS with the value "NV" means that among all dependency relations with nouns as dependent tokens and verbs as governing tokens, 92% are correct. Twelve parameters are calculated using more or less fine-grained morphosyntactic and syntactic parameters: overall accuracy of the parsers, POS of the dependent token and POS of the governing token, the distance between the dependent and the governing tokens (11 intervals: distance 0/root, 1, 2–3, 4–6, 7–10, 11 and more, dependent to the left or to the right), POS and more detailed morphological properties of the dependent token (subtype of POS and case). There are approx. 1400 values altogether for each parser (7000 values in the table of partial accuracy rates).

Table 5 presents a fraction of the table of partial accuracy rates: two values of the unlabeled parameter POS2POS calculated for all five parsers. The value "NA" indicates nouns attached to adjectives, as in *plný ryb* 'full of fish', "NV" denotes nouns attached to verbs, e. g. *chytil rybu* 'he caught a fish'.

4.2 Ensemble parsing using the MST algorithm

These partial accuracy rates (of a chosen parameter or combination of parameters) are used as weights of edges in ensemble parsing, where all five parses of a sentence

Table 5: Example of partial accuracy rates

Parser	parameter	un/lab	value	e. rate
Malt	POS2POS	UAS	NA	0.769
Mate	POS2POS	UAS	NA	0.796
MST	POS2POS	UAS	NA	0.757
Parsito	POS2POS	UAS	NA	0.741
Turbo	POS2POS	UAS	NA	0.810
Malt	POS2POS	UAS	NV	0.898
Mate	POS2POS	UAS	NV	0.921
MST	POS2POS	UAS	NV	0.894
Parsito	POS2POS	UAS	NV	0.903
Turbo	POS2POS	UAS	NV	0.909

Table 6: Tests of parameters for ensemble parsing (dtest)

Parameter	un/lab	exp.	UAS	LAS	SENT_U	SENT_L
MateParser			88.62	83.11	45.91	33.79
2POS	LAS	1	88.82	83.62	41.70	31.47
DIST	UAS	2	89.67	84.09	46.01	32.98
ALL	LAS	1	89.74	84.43	47.20	34.17
POS	LAS	4	89.82	84.53	47.22	34.20
POSCASE	LAS	2	90.02	84.76	47.51	34.54
POS2POS	UAS	6	90.07	84.83	47.61	34.78

are merged into one oriented graph. If some parsers agree on an edge (dependency relation), the sum of the accuracy rates of the parsers is used. An exponent can be also included in the calculation of weights: it raises the accuracy rate to the power of the chosen number (e. g. 0.741^6), increasing the differences between good and bad error rates, as suggested in [3].

We use Chu-Liu-Edmonds' algorithm to find the maximum spanning tree in the graph (see [2], p. 526), determining the best outcome of the combination of dependency parses of any sentence according to the chosen parameter. If parsers agree on a dependency relation, but disagree on a dependency label, weights (labeled, even if unlabeled parameter is chosen for edges) are also used to determine the best label.

Using PDT dtest data, we run a series of experiments with various parameters and combinations of parameters to determine the best parameter and exponent to use for the calculation of weights.

The results vary between the baseline (MateParser) and a 1.4/1.7% increase in UAS/LAS. Table 6 shows six examples of ensemble parsing using PDT dtest data, with various parameters (UAS/LAS and exponent for the best results with the given parameter are chosen). The first column indicates the parameter used, the second one indicates whether labeled or unlabeled attachments were used to calculate error rates, the third column presents the exponent. LAS, UAS, SENT_U and SENT_L scores are shown. The accuracy scores of MateParser are included in the table as baseline.

"ALL" parameter reflects the overall accuracy of each parser (UAS or LAS score). "2POS" parameter is based on POS of the governing token. "POS" parameter is based on POS of the dependent token. "POS2POS" combines both. "POSCASE" uses POS of the dependent token and its case. "DIST" parameter expresses the distance between the governing and dependent tokens (see subsection 4.1). For each parameter (and some of their combinations), 18 tests of ensemble parsing were run, with labeled and unlabeled accuracy rates and exponents of 1 to 9 (in our tests, higher exponents than 9 never led to an increase in accuracy).

The best results were obtained with the parameter POS2POS, unlabeled, with the exponent 6. For some combinations of two or more parameters (for example, POS:LAS+POSSUBPOS:LAS, with exp. 4 achieves an accuracy of 89.83 / 84.55 / 47.24 / 34.26), we did get better than average results, but no such combination has achieved better accuracy in all categories than the POS2POS parameter.

5 Ensemble parsing using agreements of parsers

Our second approach to ensemble parsing stems from the observation of the interaction of parsers. Using the parsed training data, we calculate how reliable parsers are in the task of assigning dependency relations to tokens, when they agree or disagree with other parsers. We sort pairs and triples of parsers by their accuracy and use this piece of information to choose the dependency relation determined by the most reliable combination of parsers. A similar (simpler) approach was proposed in [10].

5.1 Accuracy rates of agreements of parsers

We start with a file containing the training data parsed by all five parsers, the same way as in the case of our first approach with error rates. From these data, we calculate a reliability rate (accuracy) of "agreements" of parsers, i.e. of instances when two or more parsers agree on a prediction of a dependency relation for a token and some other parsers disagree.

We count the number of occurrences when a group of parsers (or just one single parser) chooses a dependency relation for a token and another group agree on another (or the others disagree), and the number of occurrences when such a choice is correct. For example, there are approx. 10.000 cases when Mate, Turbo and MST agree on a dependency relation for a token and Malt and Parsito agree on another one. In 62.8% of such cases, the choice of the three parsers is correct (identical to the gold standard). So the "agreement" accuracy of Mate+Turbo+MST versus Malt+Parsito is 62.8%. There are 7.000 cases when Mate, Turbo and MST agree, and Malt and Parsito each choose another dependency. In 61.2% of such cases, the choice of the three parsers is correct. The "agreement" accuracy of Mate+Turbo+MST versus Malt and Parsito (not agreeing) is 61.2%.

Table 7 presents a part of the table recording the accuracy of "agreements" of parsers. Scores for unlabeled relations are presented (first column). The second column indicates which parsers agree on a dependency relation, the third column shows the agreement or disagreement of the other parsers. The fourth column shows the accuracy score, i. e. the ratio of correct dependency relations among all occurrences of this combination of agreements. The fourth column presents the number of occurrences. The table is sorted by accuracy.

Table 7: Accuracy of "agreements" of parsers

Un/lab	Parser(s)	Other parsers	Accuracy	Occurr.
UAS	all agree	none	97.16	867999
...		...	...	...
UAS	Malt+MST+Parsito	Mate+Turbo	47.25	5543
UAS	Mate+Turbo	Malt+Parsito|MST	46.96	2329
UAS	Mate+Turbo	Malt+MST|Parsito	45.71	1426
UAS	Mate+Turbo	Malt+MST+Parsito	44.70	5543
UAS	Mate+Turbo	Malt|MST|Parsito	44.53	2237
UAS	Mate+Turbo	Malt|MST+Parsito	44.34	1449

When using unlabeled dependency relations, any three parsers agreeing outperform any pair of parsers. With labeled dependencies, one pair of parsers, Mate+Parsito, has slightly better results when opposing the other three agreeing parsers.

5.2 Ensemble parsing using agreements of parsers

We sort agreements of parsers by their reliability and use this information in a combination of parsers. In new sentences (test data) parsed with all parsers, we detect for each token, which parsers agree and which disagree, and we choose for each token one dependency relation which has the highest "accuracy of agreement" value, for example, if Malt+MST+Parsito chooses one dependency relation for the given token and Mate+Turbo chooses another one, we choose the dependency indicated by the three parsers.

Should any cycle occur in the output of the combination of parsers, the algorithm assigns a new governing token to the member of the cycle with the lowest value of agreements of parsers.

Unlabeled and labeled reliability of agreements of parsers can be applied. If unlabeled scores are used, first the dependency relation is determined, then the dependency label is chosen amid the labels proposed by parsers which initially agreed on the dependency relation according to labeled agreement scores. If labeled scores are used, dependency relation and dependency label are treated together from the start.

Table 8 shows the results of both approaches (labeled and unlabeled agreement scores).

Table 8: Accuracy of combinations of parsers (dtest)

	Un/lab	UAS	LAS	SENT_U	SENT_L
Agreements	LAS	88.58	80.89	46.07	29.62
Agreements	UAS	90.11	80.55	47.67	28.53

The procedure using unlabeled accuracy scores of agreements of parsers has better results in UAS, and the difference between the LAS scores is low. The approach using unlabeled agreements has very good unlabeled results (UAS, SENT_U), but comparatively poor labeled results (LAS, SENT_L).

6 Results

In this section, we summarize the results of our experiments, we present our baseline and an hypothetical ceiling, and we discuss parsing speed.

6.1 Etest results

As the baseline for our results, we use the accuracy of MateParser which has a slightly lower UAS than TurboParser, but its labeled scores are far better. We calculate a hypothetical floor and ceiling for the accuracy of the combination of our five parsers (see 3.2). Table 9 shows the results of our two experiments with ensemble parsing. UAS, LAS, SENT_U and SENT_L scores are presented. The best settings for our ensemble parsing methods (tuned up on the dtest data) were tested on PDT etest data.

Table 9: Accuracy of combinations of parsers (etest)

	UAS	LAS	SENT_U	SENT_L
Floor	74.52	65.33	26.54	17.61
MateParser	88.58	83.09	45.87	33.77
Error rates	90.04	84.77	47.57	34.70
Agreements	90.07	81.91	47.61	30.65
Ceiling	95.51	92.18	69.36	55.71

A 1.5% improvement in UAS and a 1.7% improvement in SENT_U (unlabeled attachment score for the whole sentences) compared to the baseline was achieved by both ensemble parsing methods. As for labeled scores, the approach using error rates attained a 1.7% LAS and a 0.9% SENT_L improvement, whereas the method using agreements of parsers has worse labeled results than the baseline (but better than the average of the parsers). The reason for this difference lies probably in the more sophisticated way in which dependency labels are chosen by the method with error rates, which reflects better the strengths of the parsers in the domain of dependency labels. The method of dealing with cycles in the experiment with the agreements of parsers is perhaps also to blame, in the future, we plan to use a maximum spanning tree algorithm, too.

6.2 Speed

We claimed in the introduction that parsing speed is not important for some tasks in NLP, such as corpus annotation. It can still be an issue when the data to be parsed are large, even if most of the process can be parallelized.

We measured the speed of all five parsers and of the program handling the combination of parsers on an Intel Xeon E5-2670 2,3GHz machine on the PDT etest data (approx. 8.000 sentences), using a single thread mode. Table 10 shows both speed (in sentences per second) and parsing time (in seconds per sentence) for the five parsers we used and for our ensemble parsing tools.

Table 10: Speed of parsers and ensemble parsing tools

Parser	Speed (sent/s)	Parsing time (s/sent)
MateParser	2.08	0.48
TurboParser	8.33	0.12
MaltParser	0.47	2.12
Parsito	16.67	0.06
MSTParser	11.11	0.09
Ensemble error rates	25	0.04
Ensemble agreements	50	0.02

The speed of the whole process of ensemble parsing in our experiments was determined by the speed of the slowest parser (MaltParser), which needs 3x more time per sentence than all the other parsers together. The merging of outputs of parsers and their combination (a perl program) requires only a negligible amount of time. Excluding the slowest parser would increase parsing speed considerably, but it would significantly decrease parsing accuracy (only 0.2% UAS, but almost 1.0% SENT_L), it would be therefore better to try to replace MaltParser by another parser, faster, but with good results in ensemble parsing. MaltParser trained with *liblinear* algorithm instead of *libsvm* is faster, but with far worse results in parsing PDT data.

6.3 Applicability to other languages

We did not test our approach on other languages because of a lack of time and computational resources, we intend to do that in the future. The most important points in the procedure are: optimize four or five parsers, parse training data using 10-fold cross-validation, gather information about the behavior and quality of the parsers from parsed training data. Then train all parsers again using training data and parse train data, merge parsing results and use the previously gathered information (using morphosyntactic parameters or agreements of parsers) in ensemble parsing as weights using an algorithm for finding a maximum spanning tree.

A 10-fold cross-validation over the whole data is also possible, but it would require a great amount of computational resources, as it would necessitate 110 cycles of training and parsing multiplied by the number of the parsers used.

7 Conclusion

In this paper, we have presented two methods of ensemble parsing which both achieve a significant (1.4%) increase in unlabeled attachment score compared to the best parser used. The approach using error rates calculated for each parser as weights in a combination of parsers using an algorithm for finding the maximum spanning tree in an oriented graph attains also very good labeled scores (1.7% increase in LAS).

References

[1] B. Bohnet, J. Nivre, "A Transition-Based System for Joint Part-of-Speech Tagging and Labeled Non-Projective Dependency Parsing," in Proceedings of EMNLP 2012, 2012.

[2] N.D. Green, Improvements to Syntax-based Machine Translation using Ensemble Dependency Parsers (thesis). Faculty of Mathematics and Physics, Charles University, Prague, 2013.

[3] N.D. Green, Z. Žabokrtský, "Hybrid combination of constituency and dependency trees into an ensemble dependency parser" in Proceedings of ACL 2012, 2012.

[4] J. Hajič, "Complex Corpus Annotation: The Prague Dependency Treebank," in Šimková M. (ed.): Insight into the Slovak and Czech Corpus Linguistics, pp. 54–73. Veda, Bratislava, Slovakia, 2006.

[5] T. Jelínek, "Improving Dependency Parsing by Filtering Linguistic Noise," in Proceedings of TSD 2013, 2013.

[6] A.F.T. Martins, M.B. Almeida, N.A. Smith, "Turning on the Turbo: Fast Third-Order Non-Projective Turbo Parsers," in Proceedings of ACL 2013, 2013.

[7] R. McDonald, F. Pereira, K. Ribarov, J. Hajic, "Non-projective Dependency Parsing using Spanning Tree Algorithms," in Proceedings of EMNLP 2005, 2005.

[8] J. Nivre, J. Hall, J. Nilsson, "MaltParser: A Data-Driven Parser-Generator for Dependency Parsing," in Proceedings of LREC 2006, 2006.

[9] M. Straka, J. Hajič, J. Straková, J. Hajič jr., "Parsing Universal Dependency Treebanks using Neural Networks and Search-Based Oracle," in Proceedings of TLT 2015, 2015.

[10] D. Zeman, Z. Žabokrtský, "Improving Parsing Accuracy by Combining Diverse Dependency Parsers," in Proceedings of IWPT 2005, 2005.

ITAT 2016 Proceedings, pp. 48–55
ISBN 978-1537016740, © 2016 L. Lenc, T. Hercig

Neural Networks for Sentiment Analysis in Czech

Ladislav Lenc[1,2] and Tomáš Hercig[1,2]

[1] Department of Computer Science and Engineering, Faculty of Applied Sciences,
University of West Bohemia, Univerzitní 8, 306 14 Plzeň, Czech Republic
[2] NTIS—New Technologies for the Information Society, Faculty of Applied Sciences,
University of West Bohemia, Technická 8, 306 14 Plzeň, Czech Republic
nlp.kiv.zcu.cz
{llenc,tigi}@kiv.zcu.cz

Abstract: This paper presents the first attempt at using neural networks for sentiment analysis in Czech. The neural networks have shown very good results on sentiment analysis in English, thus we adapt them to the Czech environment. We first perform experiments on two English corpora to allow comparability with the existing state-of-the-art methods for sentiment analysis in English. Then we explore the effectiveness of using neural networks on four Czech corpora. We show that the networks achieve promising results however there is still much room for improvement especially on the Czech corpora.

Keywords: Sentiment Analysis, Neural Networks, Czech

1 Introduction

The current approaches to sentiment analysis in English explore various neural network architectures (e.g. [1, 2, 3]). We try to replicate the results shown in [1] and adapt the proposed architecture to the sentiment analysis task in Czech – a highly inflectional Slavic language. To the best of our knowledge, neural networks have not been used for the sentiment analysis task in Czech.

The goal of aspect-based sentiment analysis (ABSA) is to identify the aspects of a given target entity and estimate the sentiment polarity for each mentioned aspect, while the general goal of sentiment analysis is to detect the polarity of a text. In this work we will focus on polarity detection on various levels (texts, sentences, and aspects).

In recent years the aspect-based sentiment analysis has undergone rapid development mainly because of competitive tasks such as SemEval 2014 - 2016 [4, 5, 6].

Aspect-based sentiment analysis firstly identifies the aspects of target entity and then assigns a polarity to each aspect. There are several ways to define aspects and polarities.

The definition of the ABSA task from SemEval 2014 distinguishes two types of aspect-based sentiment: aspect terms and aspect categories. The whole task is divided into four subtasks.

- **Aspect Term Extraction (TE)** – identify aspect terms.

```
Our server checked on us maybe twice during the
entire meal.
→ {server, meal}
```

- **Aspect Term Polarity (TP)** – determine the polarity of each aspect term.

```
Our server checked on us maybe twice during the
entire meal.
→ {server: negative, meal: neutral}
```

- **Aspect Category Extraction (CE)** – identify (predefined) aspect categories.

```
Our server checked on us maybe twice during the
entire meal.
→ {service}
```

- **Aspect Category Polarity (CP)** – determine the polarity of each (pre-identified) aspect category.

```
Our server checked on us maybe twice during the
entire meal.
→ {service: negative}
```

The later SemEval's ABSA tasks (2015 and 2016) further distinguish between more detailed aspect categories and associate aspect terms (targets) with aspect categories.

The current ABSA task - SemEval 2016 [6] has three subtasks: Sentence-level (SB1), Text-level (SB2) and Out-of-domain ABSA (SB3). The subtasks are further divided into three slots. The following example is from the training data (including the typographical error).

- **1) Aspect Category Detection** – identify (predefined) aspect category – entity and attribute (E#A) pair.

```
The pizza is yummy and I like the atmoshpere.
→ {FOOD#QUALITY, AMBIENCE#GENERAL}
```

- **2) Opinion Target Expression (OTE)** – extract the OTE referring to the reviewed entity (aspect category).

```
The pizza is yummy and I like the atmoshpere.
→ {pizza, atmoshpere}
```

- **3) Sentiment Polarity** – assign polarity (positive, negative, and neutral) to each identified E#A, OTE tuple.

```
The pizza is yummy and I like the atmoshpere.
→ {FOOD#QUALITY - pizza: positive,
   AMBIENCE#GENERAL - atmoshpere: positive}
```

In this work we will focus on the sentiment polarity task on aspect-level and document-level[1] for Czech and English. In terms of the SemEval 2014 task it is the *Aspect Term Polarity* and *Aspect Category Polarity* (TP and CP) subtasks. In terms of the SemEval 2016 task it is the *Sentence-level Sentiment Polarity* subtask.

Our main goal is to measure the difference between the previous results and the new results achieved by neural network architectures.

2 Related Work

2.1 Sentiment Analysis in Czech

Initial research on Czech sentiment analysis has been done in [7, 8, 9, 10]. However they used only small news datasets and because of the small data size no strong conclusions can be drawn.

The first extensive evaluation of Czech sentiment analysis was done by Habernal et al. in [11]. Three different classifiers, namely Naive Bayes, Support Vector Machines and Maximum Entropy classifiers were tested on large-scale labeled corpora (Facebook posts, movie reviews, and product reviews). In [12] they further experimented with feature selection methods.

Habernal and Brychcin [13] used semantic spaces (see [14]) created from unlabeled data as an additional source of information to improve results. Brychcin and Habernal [15] explored the benefits of the global target context and outperformed the previous unsupervised approach.

The first attempt at aspect-based sentiment analysis in Czech was presented in [16]. This work provides an annotated corpus of 1244 sentences from the restaurant reviews domain and a baseline ABSA model. Hercig et al. [17] extended the dataset from [16], nearly doubling its size and presented results using several unsupervised methods for word meaning representation.

The work in [18] creates a dataset in the domain of IT product reviews. This dataset contains 200 annotated sentences and 2000 short segments, both annotated with sentiment and marked aspect terms (targets) without any categorization and sentiment toward the marked targets. Using 5-fold cross validation on the aspect term extraction task (TE) they achieved 65.79% F-measure on the short segments and 30.27% F-measure on the long segments.

2.2 Neural Networks and Sentiment Analysis

First attempt to estimate sentiment using a neural network was presented in [19]. The authors propose using Active Deep Networks which is a semi-supervised algorithm. The network is based on Restricted Boltzmann Machines. The approach is evaluated on several review datasets containing an earlier version of the movie review dataset created

by Pang and Lee [20]. It outperforms the state of the art approaches on these datasets.

Ghiassi et al. [21] use Dynamic Artificial Network for sentiment analysis of Tweets. The network uses *n*-gram features and creates a Twitter-specific lexicon. The approach is compared to Support Vector Machines classifier and achieves better results.

Socher et al. [2] utilizes a Recursive Neural Tensor Network trained on the Stanford Sentiment Treebank (SST). The network is tested on the binary sentiment classification and on the fine-grained (continuous number from 0 to 1) sentiment polarity scale. It outperforms the state of the art methods on both tasks.

A Deep Convolutional Neural Network is utilized for sentiment classification in [3]. Classification accuracies of 48.3% (5 sentiment levels) and 85.7% (binary) on the the SST dataset are achieved.

Several papers propose more general neural networks used for NLP tasks that are tested also on sentiment datasets. One of such methods is presented in [1]. A Convolutional Neural Network (CNN) architecture is proposed and tested on several datasets such as Movie Review (MR) dataset and SST. The tasks were sentiment classification (binary or 5 sentiment levels), subjectivity classification (subjective/objective) and question type classification. It proved state-of-the-art performance on all datasets.

In [22] a Dynamic Convolutional Neural Network is proposed. A concept of dynamic k-max pooling is used in this network. It is tested on sentiment analysis and question classification tasks.

The authors of [23] propose two CNNs for ontology classification, sentiment analysis and single-label document classification. Their networks are composed of 9 layers out of which 6 are convolutional layers and 3 fully-connected layers with different numbers of hidden units and frame sizes. They show that the proposed method significantly outperforms the baseline approaches (bag of words) on English and Chinese corpora.

3 Data

In this work we use two types of corpora:

- Aspect-level for the ABSA task and

- Document-level for the sentiment polarity task.

The properties of these corpora are shown in Table 1. The English Aspect-level datasets come from the SemEval ABSA tasks. Although we show properties of the datasets from previous years, we report results only on the latest datasets from the SemEval 2016.

We do not use the Czech IT product datasets because of its small size and because no results for the sentiment polarity task have been reported using these datasets so far. The Czech Facebook dataset has a label for bipolar sentiment which we discard, similarly to the original publication.

---
[1]For the English RT dataset and Czech Facebook dataset it can be also called the sentence-level.

Table 1: Properties of the aspect-level and document-level corpora in terms of the number of *sentences*, *average length* of sentences (number of words), and numbers of *positive*, *negative*, *neutral* and *bipolar* labels.

Aspect-level Sentiment Dataset	Sentences	Average Length	Positive	Negative	Neutral	
English 2016 Laptops train + test	3.3k	14	2.1k	1.4k	0.2k	
English 2016 Restaurants train + test	2.7k	13	2.3k	1k	0.1k	
English 2015 Restaurants train + test	2k	13	1.7k	0.7k	0.1k	
Czech Restaurant reviews	2.15k	14	2.6k	2.5k	1.2k	
Czech IT product reviews short	2k	6	1k	1k	–	
Czech IT product reviews long	0.2k	144	0.1k	0.1k	–	
Document-level Sentiment Dataset	Sentences	Average Length	Positive	Negative	Neutral	Bipolar
English RT Movie reviews	10.7k	21	5.3k	5.3k	–	–
Czech CSFD Movie reviews	91.4k	51	30.9k	29.7k	30.8k	–
Czech MALL Product reviews	145.3k	19	103k	10.4k	31.9k	–
Czech Facebook posts	10k	11	2.6k	2k	5.2k	0.2k

For all experiments we use 10-fold cross validation in cases where there are no designated test and train data splits.

4 System

The proposed sentiment classification system can be divided into two modules. The first one serves for data preprocessing and creates the data representation while the second one performs the classification. The classification module utilizes three different neural network architectures. All networks use the same preprocessing.

4.1 Data Preprocessing and Representation

The importance of data preprocessing has been proven in many NLP tasks. The first step in our preprocessing chain is removing the accents similarly to [12] and converting the text to lower case. This process may lead to loss of some information but we include it due to the fact that the data we use are collected from the Internet and therefore it may contain grammatical errors, misspellings and could be written either with or without accents. Finally, all numbers are replaced with one common token. We also perform stemming utilizing the High Precision Stemmer [24].

The input feature of the neural networks is a sequence of words in the document represented using the one hot encoding. A dictionary is first created from the training set. It contains a specified number of most frequent words. The words are then represented by their indexes in the dictionary. The words that are not in the dictionary are assigned a reserved "Out of dictionary" index. An important issue is the variable length of classified sentences. Therefore, we cut the longer ones and pad the shorter ones to a fixed length. The padding token has also a reserved index. We use dictionary size 20,000 in all experiments. The sentence length was set to 50 in all experiments with document-level sentiment. We set the sequence length to 11 in the aspect-level sentiment experiments.

4.2 CNN 1

This network was proposed by Kim in [1]. It is a modification of the architecture proposed in [25]. The first layer is the embedding one. It learns a word vector of fixed length k for each word. We use $k = 300$ in all experiments. It uses one convolutional layer which is composed of a set of filters of size $n \times k$ which means that it is applied on sequence of n words and the whole word vector (k is the length of the word vector). The application of such filters results in a set of feature maps (results after applying the convolutional filters to the input matrix). Kim proposes to use multiple filter sizes ($n = 3, 4, 5$) and utilizes 100 filters of each size. Rectified linear units (Relu) are used as activation function, drop-out rate is set to 0.5 and the mini-batch size is 50. After this step, a max-over-time pooling is applied on each feature map and thus the most significant features are extracted. The selection of one most important feature from each feature map is supposed to ensure invariance to the sentence length. The max pooling layer is followed by a fully connected softmax layer which outputs the probability distribution over labels. There are four approaches to the training of the embedding layer:

- **1)** Word vectors trained from scratch (randomly initialized)

- **2)** Static word2vec [26] vectors

- **3)** Non-static vectors (initialized by word2vec and then fine tuned)

- **4)** Multichannel (both random initialized and pretrained by word2vec).

The hyper-parameters of the network was set on the development set from SST-2 dataset[2]. We use identical configuration in our experiments to allow comparability. We implemented only the basic – randomly initialized version of word embeddings. Figure 1 depicts the architecture of the network.

---

[2]Stanford Sentiment Treebank with neutral reviews removed and binary labels

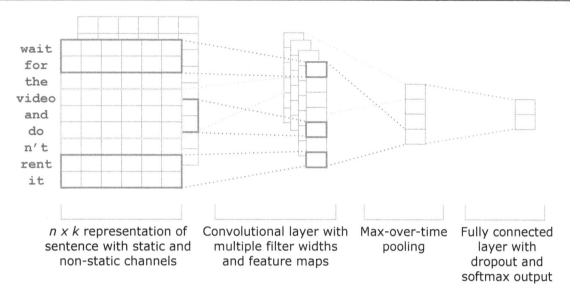

n x k representation of sentence with static and non-static channels

Convolutional layer with multiple filter widths and feature maps

Max-over-time pooling

Fully connected layer with dropout and softmax output

Figure 1: Architecture of the convolutional network CNN1

4.3 CNN 2

The architecture of this network was designed according to [27] where it is successfully used for multi-label document classification.

Contrary to the work of Kim [1] this network uses just one size of the convolutional kernels and not the combination of several sizes. The kernels have only 1 dimension (1D) while Kim have used larger 2 dimensional kernels. It was proven on the document classification task that the simple 1D kernels give better results than the 2D ones.

The input of the network is a vector of word indexes as described in Section 4.1. The first layer is an embedding layer which represents each input word as a vector of a given length. The document is thus represented as a matrix with l rows and k columns where k is the length of embedding vectors. The embedding length is set to 300. The next layer is the convolutional one. We use n_c convolution kernels of the size $l_k \times 1$ which means we do 1D convolution over one position in the embedding vector over l_k input words. The size k is set to 3 (aspect-level sentiment) and 5 (document-level sentiment) in our experiments and we use $n_c = 32$ kernels. The following layer performs max pooling over the length $l - l_k + 1$ resulting in n_n $1 \times k$ vectors. The output of this layer is then flattened and connected with the output layer containing either 2 or 3 nodes (number of sentiment labels). Figure 2 shows the architecture of the network.

4.4 LSTM

The word sequence is the input to an embedding layer same as for the CNNs. We use the embedding length of 300 in all experiments. The word embeddings are then fed to the recurrent LSTM layer with 128 hidden neurons. Dropout rate of 0.5 is then applied and the final state of the

LSTM layer is connected with the softmax output layer. The network architecture is depicted in Figure 3.

4.5 Tools

We used Keras [28] for implementation of all above mentioned neural networks. It is based on the Theano deep learning library [29]. It has been chosen mainly because of good performance and our previous experience with this tool. All experiments were computed on GPU to achieve reasonable computation times.

5 Experiments

Results on RT movie dataset [30] (10662 sentences, 2 classes) confirm that our implementation works similarly to the original (see Table 2).

Table 2: Accuracy on the English RT movie reviews dataset in %.

Description	Results
Kim [1] randomly initialized	76.1
Kim [1] best result	**81.5**
CNN1	77.1
CNN2	76.2
LSTM	61.7
Confidence Interval	±0.8

We further performed evaluation on the current SemEval 2016 ABSA dataset to allow comparison with the current state-of-the-art methods. These results (see Table 3) show that the used neural network architectures are still quite far from the finely tuned state-of-the-art results. However we need to remind the reader that our goal was

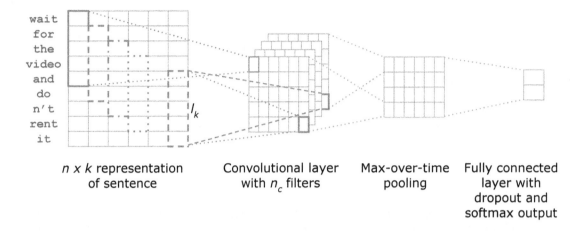

Figure 2: Architecture of the convolutional network CNN2

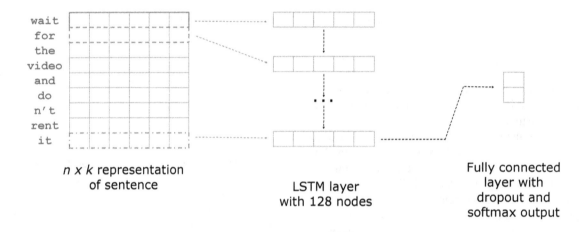

Figure 3: Architecture of the LSTM network

not to achieve the state-of-the-art results, but to replicate network architectures that are used for sentiment analysis in English as well as some networks utilized for other tasks in Czech.

Results on the Czech document-level datasets are shown in Table 4. For the CSFD movie dataset, results are much worse than the previous work. We believe that this is due to the number of words used for representation. We used 50 words in all experiments and it may not suffice to fully understand the review. This is supported by the fact that the global target context [15] helps to improve the results by 1.5%.

We applied three types of neural networks to the term polarity (TP) and class polarity (CP) tasks and evaluated them on the Czech aspect-level restaurant reviews dataset. The results in Table 5 show markedly inferior results compared to the state-of-the-art results 72.5% for the TP and 75.2% for the CP tasks in [17]. Best results are achieved using the combination of words and stemms as input.

The inputs of the networks are one-hot vectors created from words in the context window of the given aspect term. We used five words in each direction of the searched aspect term resulting in window size 11. We do not use any weighting to give more importance to the closest words as in [17].

For statistical significance testing, we report confidence intervals at α 0.05.

CNN1 and CNN2 present similar results although the average best performance is achieved by the CNN2 architecture. The LSTM architecture consistently underperforms, we believe that this is due to the basic architecture model.

6 Conclusion and Future Work

In this work we have presented the first attempts to classify sentiment of Czech sentences using a neural network. We evaluated three architectures.

We first performed experiments on two English corpora mainly to allow comparability with existing work for sentiment analysis in English.

Table 3: Accuracy on the English SemEval 2016 ABSA datasets in %.

Description	Restaurants	Laptops
SemEval 2016 best result	**88**	**82**
SemEval 2016 best constrained	**88**	75
CNN1	78	68
CNN2	78	71
LSTM	72	68
Confidence Interval	±3	±3

Table 4: F-measure on the Czech document-level datasets in %.

Description	CSFD Movies	MALL Products	Facebook Posts
Supervised Machine Learning [11]	78.5	75.3	**69.4**
Semantic Spaces [13]	**80**	**78**	-
Global Target Context [15]	**81.5**	-	-
CNN1 stemmed	70.8	74.4	**68.9**
CNN2 stemmed	71.0	75.5	**69.4**
LSTM stemmed	70.2	73.5	67.6
Confidence Interval	±0.3	±0.2	±1.0

Table 5: Accuracy on the Czech aspect-level restaurant reviews dataset in %. W denotes words, S stemms and $W+S$ the combination of these inputs.

Description \ Features	Term Polarity			Class Polarity		
	W	S	W+S	W	S	W+S
CNN1	65	66	**67**	65	66	68
CNN2	64	65	66	67	68	**69**
LSTM	61	62	62	65	65	64
Confidence Interval	±2	±2	±2	±2	±2	±2

We have further experimented with three Czech corpora for document-level sentiment analysis and one corpus for aspect based sentiment analysis. The experiments proved that the tested networks don't achieve as good results as the state-of-the-art approaches. The most promising results were obtained when using the CNN2 architecture. However, regarding the confidence intervals, we can consider the performance of the architectures rather comparable.

The results show that Czech is much more complicated to handle when determining sentiment polarity. This can be caused by various properties of Czech language that differ from English (e.g. double negative, sentence length, comparative and superlative adjectives, or free word order). Double or multiple negatives are grammatically correct ways to express negation in Czech while in English double negative is not acceptable in formal situations or in writing. Thus the semantic meaning of sentences with double or multiple negatives is hard to determine. In English comparative and superlative forms of adjectives are created by adding suffixes[3] while in Czech suffixes and prefixes are used. Informal texts can contain mixed irregular adjectives with prefixes and/or suffixes thus making it

harder to determine the semantic meaning of these texts. The free word order can also cause difficulties to train the models because the same thing may be expressed differently.

However, it must be noted that the compared approaches utilize much richer information than our basic features fed to the neural networks. The neural networks were also not fine-tuned for the task. Therefore we believe that there is much room for further improvement and that neural networks can reach or even outperform the state-of-the-art results.

We consider this paper to be the initial work on sentiment analysis in Czech using neural networks. Therefore, there are numerous possibilities for the future work. The obtained results must be thoroughly analysed to identify cases where the neural networks fail. An interesting experiment would be sentiment analysis on Czech data automatically translated to English. One possible direction of further improvement is utilizing word embeddings to initialize the embedding layer. We also plan to experiment with neural networks on the other two tasks of aspect based sentiment analysis – aspect term extraction and aspect category extraction. Another perspective is to develop new neural network architectures for sentiment analysis.

---

[3]excluding irregular and long adjectives

Acknowledgements

This work was supported by the project LO1506 of the Czech Ministry of Education, Youth and Sports and by Grant No. SGS-2016-018 Data and Software Engineering for Advanced Applications. Computational resources were provided by the CESNET LM2015042 and the CERIT Scientific Cloud LM2015085, provided under the programme "Projects of Large Research, Development, and Innovations Infrastructures".

References

[1] Kim, Y.: Convolutional neural networks for sentence classification. arXiv preprint arXiv:1408.5882 (2014)

[2] Socher, R., Perelygin, A., Wu, J.Y., Chuang, J., Manning, C.D., Ng, A.Y., Potts, C.: Recursive deep models for semantic compositionality over a sentiment treebank. In: Proceedings of the conference on empirical methods in natural language processing (EMNLP). Volume 1631., Citeseer (2013) 1642

[3] dos Santos, C.N., Gatti, M.: Deep convolutional neural networks for sentiment analysis of short texts. In: COLING. (2014) 69–78

[4] Pontiki, M., Galanis, D., Pavlopoulos, J., Papageorgiou, H., Androutsopoulos, I., Manandhar, S.: SemEval-2014 Task 4: Aspect based sentiment analysis. In: Proceedings of the 8th International Workshop on Semantic Evaluation (SemEval 2014), Dublin, Ireland, Association for Computational Linguistics and Dublin City University (August 2014) 27–35

[5] Pontiki, M., Galanis, D., Papageorgiou, H., Manandhar, S., Androutsopoulos, I.: Semeval-2015 task 12: Aspect based sentiment analysis. In: Proceedings of the 9th International Workshop on Semantic Evaluation (SemEval 2015), Association for Computational Linguistics, Denver, Colorado. (2015) 486–495

[6] Pontiki, M., Galanis, D., Papageorgiou, H., Androutsopoulos, I., Manandhar, S., AL-Smadi, M., Al-Ayyoub, M., Zhao, Y., Qin, B., Clercq, O.D., Hoste, V., Apidianaki, M., Tannier, X., Loukachevitch, N., Kotelnikov, E., Bel, N., Jiménez-Zafra, S.M., Eryiğit, G.: SemEval-2016 task 5: Aspect based sentiment analysis. In: Proceedings of the 10th International Workshop on Semantic Evaluation. SemEval '16, San Diego, California, Association for Computational Linguistics (June 2016)

[7] Veselovská, K., Hajič jr., J., Šindlerová, J.: Creating annotated resources for polarity classification in Czech. In Jancsary, J., ed.: Proceedings of KONVENS 2012, ÖGAI (September 2012) 296–304 PATHOS 2012 Workshop.

[8] Steinberger, J., Lenkova, P., Kabadjov, M., Steinberger, R., van der Goot, E.: Multilingual entity-centered sentiment analysis evaluated by parallel corpora. In: Proceedings of the 8th International Conference Recent Advances in Natural Language Processing. (2011) 770–775

[9] Steinberger, J., Ebrahim, M., M., E., Hurriyetoglu, A., Kabadjov, M., Lenkova, P., Steinberger, R., Tanev, H., Vázquez, S., Zavarella, V.: Creating sentiment dictionaries via triangulation. Decision Support Systems 53 (2012) 689—694

[10] Veselovská, K., Hajič jr., J.: Why words alone are not enough: Error analysis of lexicon-based polarity classifier for Czech. In: Proceedings of the 6th International Joint Conference on Natural Language Processing, Nagoya, Japan, Asian Federation of Natural Language Processing, Asian Federation of Natural Language Processing (2013) 1–5

[11] Habernal, I., Ptáček, T., Steinberger, J.: Sentiment analysis in Czech social media using supervised machine learning. In: Proceedings of the 4th Workshop on Computational Approaches to Subjectivity, Sentiment and Social Media Analysis, Atlanta, GA, USA, Association for Computational Linguistics (June 2013) 65–74

[12] Habernal, I., Ptáček, T., Steinberger, J.: Supervised sentiment analysis in Czech social media. Information Processing & Management 50(5) (2014) 693–707

[13] Habernal, I., Brychcín, T.: Semantic spaces for sentiment analysis. In: Text, Speech and Dialogue. Volume 8082 of Lecture Notes in Computer Science., Berlin, Springer-Verlag (2013) 482–489

[14] Brychcín, T., Konopík, M.: Semantic spaces for improving language modeling. Computer Speech & Language 28(1) (2014) 192 – 209

[15] Brychcín, T., Habernal, I.: Unsupervised improving of sentiment analysis using global target context. In: Proceedings of the International Conference Recent Advances in Natural Language Processing RANLP 2013, Shoumen, Bulgaria, INCOMA Ltd. (September 2013) 122–128

[16] Steinberger, J., Brychcín, T., Konkol, M.: Aspect-level sentiment analysis in Czech. In: Proceedings of the 5th Workshop on Computational Approaches to Subjectivity, Sentiment and Social Media Analysis, Baltimore, MD, USA, Association for Computational Linguistics (June 2014)

[17] Hercig, T., Brychcín, T., Svoboda, L., Konkol, M., Steinberger, J.: Unsupervised methods to improve aspect-based sentiment analysis in Czech. Computación y Sistemas (in press)

[18] Tamchyna, A., Fiala, O., Veselovská, K.: Czech aspect-based sentiment analysis: A new dataset and preliminary results. Proceedings of the 15th conference ITAT 2015 (2015) 95–99

[19] Zhou, S., Chen, Q., Wang, X.: Active deep networks for semi-supervised sentiment classification. In: Proceedings of the 23rd International Conference on Computational Linguistics: Posters, Association for Computational Linguistics (2010) 1515–1523

[20] Pang, B., Lee, L., Vaithyanathan, S.: Thumbs up?: sentiment classification using machine learning techniques. In: Proceedings of the ACL-02 conference on Empirical methods in natural language processing-Volume 10, Association for Computational Linguistics (2002) 79–86

[21] Ghiassi, M., Skinner, J., Zimbra, D.: Twitter brand sentiment analysis: A hybrid system using n-gram analysis and dynamic artificial neural network. Expert Systems with applications 40(16) (2013) 6266–6282

[22] Kalchbrenner, N., Grefenstette, E., Blunsom, P.: A convolutional neural network for modelling sentences. arXiv

preprint arXiv:1404.2188 (2014)

[23] Zhang, X., LeCun, Y.: Text understanding from scratch. arXiv preprint arXiv:1502.01710 (2015)

[24] Brychcín, T., Konopík, M.: Hps: High precision stemmer. Information Processing & Management **51**(1) (2015) 68–91

[25] Collobert, R., Weston, J., Bottou, L., Karlen, M., Kavukcuoglu, K., Kuksa, P.: Natural language processing (almost) from scratch. The Journal of Machine Learning Research **12** (2011) 2493–2537

[26] Mikolov, T., Chen, K., Corrado, G., Dean, J.: Efficient estimation of word representations in vector space. (2013) arXiv preprint arXiv:1301.3781.

[27] Lenc, L., Král, P.: Deep neural networks for Czech multi-label document classification. In: International Conference on Intelligent Text Processing and Computational Linguistics, Konya, Turkey (April 3 - 9 2016)

[28] Chollet, F.: Keras. https://github.com/fchollet/keras (2015)

[29] Bergstra, J., Breuleux, O., Bastien, F., Lamblin, P., Pascanu, R., Desjardins, G., Turian, J., Warde-Farley, D., Bengio, Y.: Theano: a cpu and gpu math expression compiler. In: Proceedings of the Python for scientific computing conference (SciPy). Volume 4., Austin, TX (2010) 3

[30] Pang, B., Lee, L.: Seeing stars: Exploiting class relationships for sentiment categorization with respect to rating scales. In: Proceedings of the ACL. (2005)

ITAT 2016 Proceedings, pp. 56–62
ISBN 978-1537016740, © 2016 D. Mareček

Twelve Years of Unsupervised Dependency Parsing

David Mareček

Institute of Formal and Applied Linguistics, Faculty of Mathematics and Physics
Charles University in Prague, Malostranské nám. 25, 118 00, Prague, Czech Republic
marecek@ufal.mff.cuni.cz

Abstract: In the last 12 years, there has been a big progress in the field of unsupervised dependency parsing. Different approaches however sometimes differ in motivation and definition of the problem. Some of them allow using resources that are forbidden by others, since they are treated as a kind of supervision. The goal of this paper is to define all the variants of unsupervised dependency parsing problem and show their motivation, progress, and the best results. We also discuss the usefulness of the unsupervised parsing generally, both for the formal linguistics and for the applications.

1 Introduction

Dependency parsing is one of the traditional tasks in natural language processing. It gets a tokenized sentence as input (in most cases, individual tokens (words) are labelled by part-of-speech (POS) tags), and produces a rooted dependency tree, in which the nodes correspond to words and edges correspond to syntactic relations between the words.

Rule-based approaches of dependency parsing were suppressed by the statistical dependency parsers, which achieved better quality compared to the human annotations. Important milestones in dependency parsing were the CoNLL shared tasks in 2006 [4] and 2007 [22]. They provided about 20 treebanks of different languages available in the same format. This became the standard for measuring quality of dependency parsers in fact up to now. [1]

At the same time, there were efforts to develop a parser that does not need any annotated data. The unsupervised parsers infer the dependency structures based on language- and tagset-independent properties of dependency trees, which is mainly the low entropies of the governing-dependent word pairs and low entropies of the word fertilities (number of dependents).

One general motivation is to be able to parse languages for which no annotated treebanks exist. Less sound motivation is to create a dependency structure which better suits a particular NLP application, e.g. machine translation.

This is a survey paper about unsupervised dependency parsers. Since different approaches have different moti-

vations, allow to use different kinds of data and different amount of knowledge about them, they cannot be compared because of different degree of (un)supervision. The aim of this paper is to cluster the approaches to several groups in which they are comparable and to show the most important ones together with the results.

The paper is structured as follows: In Section 2, we define different unsupervised parsing problem settings and summarize the motivations and advantages. Section 3 describes different evaluation measures developed for unsupervised parsers. In Section 4, we go through the works done in this field and describe the most important approaches. In Section 5, we compare the results across data, parsers, and languages. Section 6 discusses generally the usefulness of unsupervised parsing methods in linguistics and in applications. Section 7 concludes.

2 Problem Settings

Some unsupervised parsing approaches use different kinds of data for the grammar inference than others. What is used in one is treated as not allowed kind of supervision in another. We therefore categorize the approaches into four groups. They are described in the following subsections and sorted from the least unsupervised (more data and knowledge) to the most unsupervised (less data and knowledge).

2.1 Using supervised POS tags and some knowledge about them

In the first group of approaches, there are parsers that need the sentences labelled by supervised POS tags, i.e. by a manually designed tagset. On top of that they also somehow utilizes the knowledge about the tagset. For example, they know which tags are used for verbs and therefore treat them differently through the grammar inference. This is the main difference from the second group (Section 2.2) and it is sometimes considered as a bit of cheating. If we know the meaning of the POS tags, we could easily build a simple rule-based parser, which would definitely not be unsupervised. This also relates to so-called delexicalized parsing, where the parser is trained on a different language with the same POS tagset and the model can then be used for languages without treebanks. This is however beyond the scope of this paper. The approaches we assigned to this group however use only a bit of such knowledge that help the inferred structures to be in a required shape.

---

[1]In recent years, many researchers work on a project called Universal Dependencies [21], a collection of treebanks for many languages (51 treebanks and 40 languages in its current version 1.3), where the morphological and dependency annotation styles are unified across the languages.

2.2 Using supervised POS tags without any knowledge about them

The majority of works describing unsupervised dependency parsing utilize supervised POS tags without any knowledge about them. In other words, the parsers take the POS tags only as labels without any meaning. It is a bit strange not to tell the parser anything, for example: "ADJ are adjectives and often depends on the following NOUNs", if there is such possibility, however allowing it would bring the parsers to the first group (Section 2.1) whose unsupervisedness is sometimes disputable.

Nevertheless, what is more strange, is the usage of supervised POS tags. The POS tags carry a lot of syntactic information. Imagine a sequence of POS tags "ADJ NOUN VERB PREP ADJ NOUN". You would easily build the most probable dependency tree. The motivation of this problem setting may be:

1. We want to compare supervised and unsupervised parsers operating on the same tagset.

2. We want to evaluate an unsupervised parser and, in the future, we will use the unsupervised word classes instead of the supervised tags on low-resourced languages and hope that it will work as well.

3. We have a language without treebank and we have a POS tagger. However, we are not able to find the meaning of POS tags used.

The third option is rather hypothetical. We always find someone who speaks that language or have a parallel corpus from which we could get basic meanings of individual words and tags.

It is also worth to mention that almost all the experiments and evaluation in the papers were done using gold standard POS tags, i.e. the POS tags assigned manually by human annotations. This is not surprising. While the qualities of unsupervised parsers are substantially lower than the qualities of supervised parsers, it is not worthy to make experiments also with the predicted POS tags.

2.3 Using unsupervised POS tags

The lower attention was given to fully unsupervised parsers using unsupervised POS tags (words classes). The only source they use is raw text. The motivation is obvious here: If we want to analyze a language without any manually annotated resources, we need exactly this approach. Other motivation could be the need of having different structures from that present in annotated treebanks. Majority of works here used the same parser as for supervised POS tags (Section 2.2) and obtain the unsupervised POS tags by some of the best word clustering tools available.

2.4 Direct parsing from raw text without POS tags

The last setting we describe is unsupervised parsing from raw texts. Here we do not use any POS tags or word classes. The only units the parser plays with are the words. The results should be theoretically compared with the previous category (2.3), where unsupervised word clustering is used. However, the word classes are typically inferred on much larger text corpora than dependency trees are. This approaches use therefore much less data for the inference and that is why we assign them into a separate category. Such approaches would be the most elegant way of parsing, however, they naturally achieve very poor results.

3 Parsing Evaluation

The unsupervised parsing approaches sometimes differ also in evaluation metrics. The standard attachment score is sometimes found too strict to evaluate the inferred structures and therefore new, more tolerant metrics, are designed. The following three evaluation metrics exists:

1. **Directed attachment score** (unlabeled attachment score[2]) is a standard metric for measuring dependency parsing quality. It is a percentage of words correctly attached to their parents. It does not allow even the slightest local structural differences, which might be caused just by more or less arbitrary linguistic or technical conventions.

2. **Undirected attachment score** disregards the directions of edges and is therefore less biased towards such conventions. For example, there is no difference whether the parser attaches prepositions to nouns or nouns to prepositions. Nevertheless, this holds for all edges, including these with undoubted directions.

3. **Neutral edge direction**[3] metric proposed by [24] is even more tolerant in assessing parsing errors than the undirected attachment score. It treats not only node's parent and child as the correct answer, but also its grandparent.

Even though the alternative scores were proposed and sometimes used, the majority of experiments were evaluated by the directed attachment scores, probably because of its simplicity and the tradition in the field and also because the other two did not prove to be substantially better.

4 Unsupervised Dependency Parsers

In this Section, we summarize and describe the most important works in the field of unsupervised dependency

---

[2]We do not want to use the abbreviation UAS for the *unlabeled attachment score* here, since it could be mistaken for *undirected attachment score*.

[3]http://www.cs.huji.ac.il/ roys02/softwae/ned.html

parsing through the last 12 years. Even though there were a couple of works before, the first paper with results better than a chain baseline [4] was the Dependency Model with Valence by Klein and Manning [13].

We first describe the methods using supervised POS tags without any other knowledge (Section 2.2) in Sections 4.1 and 4.2, then we switch to other settings. A detailed table with results over different methods and different problem settings is shown in Section 5.

4.1 Dependency Model with Valence

We start with Dependency Model with Valence (DMV), which was introduced by Klein and Manning [13]. It is the most popular approach, which was followed by many other researchers and improved in many ways. It is a generative model that generates dependency trees using two submodels:

- Stop model $p_{stop}(\cdot|t_g, dir)$ represents probability of not generating another dependent in direction dir to a node with POS tag t_g. The direction dir can be left or right. If $p_{stop} = 1$, the node with the tag t_g cannot have any dependent in direction dir. If it is 1 in both directions, the node is a leaf.

- Attach model $p_{attach}(t_d|t_g, dir)$ represents probability that the dependent of the node with POS tag t_g in direction dir is labeled with POS tag t_d.

The grammar consisting of probability distributions p_{stop} and p_{attach} is learned using the Expectation Maximization inside-outside algorithm [12]. The learning is further improved by Smith et al. [26] and Cohen et al. [8]. Headden et al. [11] introduce the Extended Valence Grammar and add lexicalization and smoothing. Besides the POS tags, the parser begin to operate with word forms as well. Blunsom and Cohn [2] use tree substitution grammars, which allow learning of larger dependency fragments by employing the Pitman-Yor process. Spitkovsky [30] improves the inference using iterated learning of increasingly longer sentences. Further improvements are achieved by better dealing with punctuation [32] and new "boundary" models [33]. Spitkovsky also improves the learning itself in [31] and [34].

Mareček and Straka [16] use so called reducibility principle to predict p_{stop} probabilities for individual POS tags from raw texts, add it to the Dependency Model with Valence and use Gibbs sampling to infer the grammar. In [19], they suppose that the function words, which can be predicted by they shortness, have fixed low number of dependents and move the parsing results even a bit higher.

4.2 Other approaches using supervised POS tagset

There are also approaches not based on DMV, even though their models are not far from it. Mareček and Žabokrtský [18] use a fertility to model number of children for particular POS tags instead of the p_{stop} model.

Sogaard [27] explores a completely different view in which a dependency structure is among other things a partial order on the nodes in terms of centrality or saliency.

Cohen et al. [7] do the grammar inference multilingually on more languages. The data do not need to be parallel, they only have to share the tagset. The inference is then less prone to skew to bad solutions due to the language differences.

Bisk and Hockenmaier [1] use the Combinatory Categorial Grammars for dependency structure induction.

4.3 Approaches using some knowledge about the POS tags

The "less unsupervised" approaches utilizing an external knowledge of the POS tagset reach often better attachment scores than the previous approaches. Any additional knowledge about the tags used can be very strong and can change the inferred structures dramatically. For example, Naseem et al. [20] follow Eisner [9] and make use of manually-specified universal dependency rules such as *Verb→Noun* or *Noun→Adjective* to guide grammar induction and improve the results by a wide margin. Mareček and Žabokrtský [17] show that only the information that "the POS tags for nouns are more frequent than the POS tags for verbs" very much improves the baseline. This however fails for example in case the POS tags for nouns are subcategorized in some way. Then we would need to know which POS tags are for nouns and group them together. Rasooli and Faili [23] identify the last verb in the sentence, minimize its probability of reduction and push it to the root position, and also make a huge improvement.

Such approaches achieve better results; however, they are useless for grammar induction for languages, for which the tagger is not available.

4.4 Approaches using unsupervised POS tags

These approaches mostly do not bring any new methods. The authors only take their unsupervised parsers we presented in Section 4.1, take a word clustering tool to produce unsupervised POS tags and run their parser on them. Spitkovsky [29] took the clustering tool by Clark [6] and Brown et al. [3] and showed that the parsing with supervised POS tags can be outperformed for English, if the word classes are used instead. Mareček [15] performed similar experiments on 30 languages and showed that on some of them the use of unsupervised word classes instead of supervised POS tags improve the parsing accuracy. The average score across the languages was however significantly worse.

---

[4] In the left or right chain baseline, each word is attached to the next or previous one respectively.

Christodoulopoulos et al. [5] try to do inference of POS tags and dependency structure together. After random initialization, they alternate the prediction of the structure based on the POS tags and prediction of the POS tags based on the structure.

4.5 Approaches using raw text only

There are couple of approaches, which do not need any word categorization. We only mention the incremental parsing by Yoav Seginer [25]. His algorithm collects lists of labels for each word, based on neighboring words, and then directly uses these labels to parse.

5 Results

In Tables 1, 2, and 3, we summarize the results over the individual parsers, data, and settings. Unfortunately, different parsers were evaluated on different data. In the beginnings, the parsers were evaluated mainly on the English Penn Treebank [14] (transformed to dependencies) and some only on the short sentences of length up to 10 (ptb10), since the shorter sentences were easier to parse and the resulting scores did not look so bad. See Table 1.

After the unsupervised parsers were improved and achieved much better results than simple baselines, they started to be evaluated across languages and on sentences of all lengths (Table 2).

In 2012, there has been a shared task on unsupervised dependency parsing named "The PASCAL challenge on Grammar Induction" [10]. Seven competing parsers were evaluated on new datasets comprising ten different languages, including simpler English used by small children. See Table 3.

Unfortunately, some of the parsers were evaluated on non-standard data or with non-standard metrics and therefor their results could not be added into any of the three tables.

All the tables share the same format: each method is labelled by a link to the references and by a group label: *SP* for using supervised POS tags, *UP* for using unsupervised POS tags, and *SP+K* when an additional knowledge about the supervised tags was used.

6 Usefulness of Unsupervised parsers in linguistics and applications

We could see a lot of work done in the field of unsupervised parsing in the last 12 years. The quality of induced structures are better than before, but the supervised parsers are still better then the unsupervised ones by a wide margin. However, for low resourced languages, for which no annotated data exists, this is the way, how to obtain their syntactic structure.

A more serious problem with unsupervised parsing is that, according to our knowledge, there were so far no works incorporating any kind of unsupervised parsing into applications, even though many papers mention that in some cases, an unsupervised structures, different from manual annotations following a given schema, may be very beneficial.

Moreover, in the last two years, no new strong paper about unsupervised parsing appeared in NLP conferences. Instead, a new techniques have arrived: The recurrent neural networks, which may fulfill the previous motivations for unsupervised parsing – to find a structure of language that would help machines to understand it better. Instead of dependency trees, some structures are hidden in hidden states of the deep neural networks.

From the linguistic point of view, the structures inferred by unsupervised parsers can be compared to the manually annotated treebanks. What are the differences? How the unsupervised methods deal with phenomena that are not clear how to parse? Should prepositions depend on nouns or vice versa? And what about coordinations? Many such questions could be answered, however, neither this topic was studied so far.

7 Conclusions

We categorized the unsupervised dependency parsers into four groups according to their needs of data, so that they could be fairly compared. We make a survey over the most important papers and works that reached state-of-the-art results when they were published. We showed a comparison of the results across the methods and languages. It is apparent that there is a big variance over the attachment scores for individual languages. The good performance of a method on one language tells nothing about the performance on another language. We hope that this paper brings to readers some system in the world of unsupervised parsing.

Acknowledgments

This work has been supported by the grant 14-06548P of the Czech Science Foundation.

References

[1] Yonatan Bisk and Julia Hockenmaier. Induction of linguistic structure with combinatory categorial grammars. *The NAACL-HLT Workshop on the Induction of Linguistic Structure*, page 90, 2012.

[2] Phil Blunsom and Trevor Cohn. Unsupervised induction of tree substitution grammars for dependency parsing. In *Proceedings of the 2010 Conference on Empirical Methods in Natural Language Processing*, EMNLP '10, pages 1204–1213, Stroudsburg, PA, USA, 2010. Association for Computational Linguistics.

	left baseline	right baseline	Klein 2004	Cohen 2008	Headden 2009	Blunsom 2010	Spitkovsky 2010	Spitkovsky 2011	Spitkovsky 2011b
link	–	–	[13]	[8]	[11]	[2]	[30]	[32]	[29]
group	–	–	SP	SP	SP	SP	SP	SP	UP
PennTreebank (up to 10 words)	27.7	38.4	47.5	59.3	68.8	67.7	57.1	69.5	
PennTreebank (all sentences)	24.0	31.7		39.0		55.7	45.0	58.4	59.1

Table 1: Results comparison on Penn treebank [14] (automatically converted to dependencies by PennConverter).

	left baseline	right baseline	Spitkovsky 2011	Spitkovsky 2012	Spitkovsky 2013	Marecek 2012	Marecek 2013	Marecek 2014	Cohen 2011	Rasooli 2012	Marecek 2015	Marecek 2011
link	–	–	[32]	[33]	[34]	[18]	[16]	[19]	[7]	[23]	[15]	[17]
group	–	–	SP	SP	SP	SP	SP	SP	SP	SP+K	UP	SP+K
Arabic 2006	55.6	7.9	32.6	10.9	9.3	26.5	38.2	35.2				
Arabic 2007	59.0	6.0	35.3	44.9	26.8	27.9	35.3			52.1		24.8
Basque 2007	23.0	30.5	29.9	33.3	24.4	26.8	35.5	35.3			28.7	34.7
Bulgarian 2006	38.8	17.9	40.5	65.2	63.4	46.0	54.9	56.8	38.6	53.9	47.9	51.4
Catalan 2007	30.0	24.8	55.2	62.1	68.0	47.0	67.0	43.3			49.2	56.3
Chinese 2006	14.0	40.7	63.2	58.4								
Chinese 2007	13.4	41.3	57.0	52.5								
Czech 2006	26.9	25.2	37.8	55.1	44.0	49.5	52.4	55.6				
Czech 2007	29.6	24.2	36.2	54.2	34.3	48.0	51.9	54.3		42.4	38.0	33.3
Danish 2006	47.8	13.1	37.1	22.2	21.4	38.6	41.6	45.5	39.9	53.1	40.8	38.6
Dutch 2006	24.5	28.0	14.0	46.6	48.0	44.2	47.5	54.8	50.2	48.8	34.4	43.4
English 2007	21.0	29.4	50.3	29.6	58.2	49.2	55.4	58.5			47.9	23.8
German 2006	22.0	23.4	28.6	39.1	56.2	44.8	52.4	45.0			41.2	21.8
Greek 2007	19.7	31.4	21.2	26.9	45.4	20.2	26.3	34.5	38.9		39.7	33.4
Hungarian 2007	5.5	41.4	8.0	58.2	58.3	51.8	34.0	34.1			24.1	48.1
Italian 2007	37.4	21.6	28.8	40.7	34.9	52.3	39.4	51.0			41.4	60.6
Japanese 2006	13.8	67.2	27.5	22.7	63.0	50.8	61.2	61.9	61.7			53.5
Portuguese 2006	31.2	25.8	33.5	72.4	74.5	50.6	69.6	75.1	51.5	55.8	31.4	41.8
Slovenian 2006	26.6	24.3	31.2	35.2	50.9	18.1	35.7	47.3	36.0	22.4	18.3	34.6
Swedish 2006	27.8	25.9	46.4	50.7	49.7	48.2	54.5	55.6	39.9	34.3	54.9	26.9
Spanish 2006	29.8	24.7	32.3	28.2	61.4	51.9	61.1	61.7	40.5	31.2	60.1	54.6
Turkish 2007	1.6	65.5	40.9	34.4	37.9	15.7	56.9	57.0	38.6	27.4	55.0	32.1
average	26.4	29.8	33.2	42.9	48.6	40.0	48.7	50.0	43.3	43.0	38.9	39.4

Table 2: Results comparison on CoNLL datasets [4, 22]. Averaged numbers are sometimes not comparable since the average can be done over different set of languages.

	left baseline	right baseline	Blunsom 2010	Bisk 2012	Marecek 2012	Sogaard 2012	Sogaard 2012	Tu 2012	Klein 2004
link	–	–	[2]	[1]	[18]	[28]	[28]	[35]	[13]
group	–	–	SP	SP	SP	SP	SP+K	SP+K	SP
Arabic	9.3	64.8	61.1	47.2	64.8	47.2	54.6	66.7	45.4
Basque	34.3	24.4	56.3	50.3	30.3	33.3	22.3	58.6	43.2
Czech	28.9	34.3	50.0	48.5	57.5	45.5	51.2	59.0	31.2
Danish	18.7	49.2	46.2	49.3	51.3	56.9	60.5	60.8	50.2
Dutch	34.0	39.5	50.5	50.8	49.5	38.9	50.0	51.7	39.7
English (childes)	36.0	23.3	48.1	62.2	47.2	50.5	53.5	56.0	51.9
English (PTB)	40.4	19.9	72.1	73.7	67.4	44.8	61.0	74.7	44.7
Portuguese	28.1	37.7	54.3	76.3	59.9	47.7	71.1	55.7	37.2
Slovenian	35.9	14.7	65.8	53.9	51.4	39.7	50.3	67.7	37.2
Swedish	33.2	31.3	65.8	66.7	63.7	48.2	72.0	76.5	44.2
average	29.9	33.9	57.0	57.9	54.3	45.3	54.7	62.7	42.5

Table 3: Results comparison in the PASCAL Challenge on Grammar Induction [10].

[3] Peter F. Brown, Peter V. deSouza, Robert L. Mercer, Vincent J. Della Pietra, and Jenifer C. Lai. Class-based n-gram models of natural language. *Computational Linguistics*, 18(4):467–479, December 1992.

[4] Sabine Buchholz and Erwin Marsi. CoNLL-X shared task on multilingual dependency parsing. In *Proceedings of the Tenth Conference on Computational Natural Language Learning*, CoNLL-X '06, pages 149–164, Stroudsburg, PA, USA, 2006. Association for Computational Linguistics.

[5] Christos Christodoulopoulos, Sharon Goldwater, and Mark Steedman. Turning the pipeline into a loop: Iterated unsupervised dependency parsing and PoS induction. In *Proceedings of the NAACL-HLT Workshop on the Induction of Linguistic Structure*, pages 96–99, June 2012.

[6] A. Clark. Combining distributional and morphological information for part of speech induction. *Proceedings of 10th EACL*, pages 59–66, 2003.

[7] Shay B. Cohen, Dipanjan Das, and Noah A. Smith. Unsupervised structure prediction with non-parallel multilingual guidance. In *Proceedings of the Conference on Empirical Methods in Natural Language Processing*, EMNLP '11, pages 50–61, Stroudsburg, PA, USA, 2011. Association for Computational Linguistics.

[8] Shay B. Cohen, Kevin Gimpel, and Noah A. Smith. Logistic normal priors for unsupervised probabilistic grammar induction. In *Neural Information Processing Systems*, pages 321–328, 2008.

[9] Jason Eisner. Three New Probabilistic Models for Dependency Parsing: An Exploration. In *Proceedings of the 16th International Conference on Computational Linguistics (COLING-96)*, pages 340–345, Copenhagen, August 1996.

[10] Douwe Gelling, Trevor Cohn, Phil Blunsom, and Joao Graca. The PASCAL Challenge on Grammar Induction. In *Proceedings of the NAACL-HLT Workshop on the Induction of Linguistic Structure*, pages 64–80, Montréal, Canada, June 2012. Association for Computational Linguistics.

[11] William P. Headden III, Mark Johnson, and David McClosky. Improving unsupervised dependency parsing with richer contexts and smoothing. In *Proceedings of Human Language Technologies: The 2009 Annual Conference of the North American Chapter of the Association for Computational Linguistics*, NAACL '09, pages 101–109, Stroudsburg, PA, USA, 2009. Association for Computational Linguistics.

[12] Dan Klein. *The Unsupervised Learning of Natural Language Structure*. PhD thesis, Stanford University, 2005.

[13] Dan Klein and Christopher D. Manning. Corpus-based induction of syntactic structure: models of dependency and constituency. In *Proceedings of the 42nd Annual Meeting on Association for Computational Linguistics*, ACL '04, Stroudsburg, PA, USA, 2004. Association for Computational Linguistics.

[14] Mitchell P. Marcus, Beatrice Santorini, and Mary A. Marcinkiewicz. Building a Large Annotated Corpus of English: The Penn Treebank. *Computational Linguistics*, 19(2):313–330, 1994.

[15] David Mareček. Multilingual unsupervised dependency parsing with unsupervised pos tags. In Grigorii Sidorov and N. Sofía Galicia-Haro, editors, *Advances in Artificial Intelligence and Soft Computing: 14th Mexican International Conference on Artificial Intelligence, MICAI 2015, Cuernavaca, Morelos, Mexico, October 25-31, 2015, Proceedings, Part I*, pages 72–82, Cham, 2015. Springer International Publishing.

[16] David Mareček and Milan Straka. Stop-probability estimates computed on a large corpus improve Unsupervised Dependency Parsing. In *Proceedings of the 51st Annual Meeting of the Association for Computational Linguistics (Volume 1: Long Papers)*, pages 281–290, Sofia, Bulgaria, August 2013. Association for Computational Linguistics.

[17] David Mareček and Zdeněk Žabokrtský. Gibbs Sampling with Treeness constraint in Unsupervised Dependency Parsing. In *Proceedings of RANLP Workshop on Ro-*

bust Unsupervised and Semisupervised Methods in Natural Language Processing, pages 1–8, Hissar, Bulgaria, 2011.

[18] David Mareček and Zdeněk Žabokrtský. Exploiting reducibility in unsupervised dependency parsing. In *Proceedings of the 2012 Joint Conference on Empirical Methods in Natural Language Processing and Computational Natural Language Learning*, EMNLP-CoNLL '12, pages 297–307, Stroudsburg, PA, USA, 2012. Association for Computational Linguistics.

[19] David Mareček and Zdeněk Žabokrtský. Dealing with function words in unsupervised dependency parsing. In *Computational Linguistics and Intelligent Text Processing, CICLing 2014*, pages 250–261, Kathmandu, Nepal, 2014.

[20] Tahira Naseem, Harr Chen, Regina Barzilay, and Mark Johnson. Using universal linguistic knowledge to guide grammar induction. In *Proceedings of the 2010 Conference on Empirical Methods in Natural Language Processing*, EMNLP '10, pages 1234–1244, Stroudsburg, PA, USA, 2010. Association for Computational Linguistics.

[21] Joakim Nivre, Marie-Catherine de Marneffe, Filip Ginter, Yoav Goldberg, Jan Hajič, Christopher Manning, Ryan McDonald, Slav Petrov, Sampo Pyysalo, Natalia Silveira, Reut Tsarfaty, and Daniel Zeman. Universal dependencies v1: A multilingual treebank collection. In *Proceedings of the 10th International Conference on Language Resources and Evaluation (LREC 2016)*, Portorož, Slovenia, 2016. European Language Resources Association.

[22] Joakim Nivre, Johan Hall, Sandra Kübler, Ryan McDonald, Jens Nilsson, Sebastian Riedel, and Deniz Yuret. The CoNLL 2007 Shared Task on Dependency Parsing. In *Proceedings of the CoNLL Shared Task Session of EMNLP-CoNLL 2007*, pages 915–932, Prague, Czech Republic, June 2007. Association for Computational Linguistics.

[23] Mohammad Sadegh Rasooli and Heshaam Faili. Fast unsupervised dependency parsing with arc-standard transitions. In *Proceedings of the Joint Workshop on Unsupervised and Semi-Supervised Learning in NLP*, ROBUS-UNSUP 2012, pages 1–9, Stroudsburg, PA, USA, 2012. Association for Computational Linguistics.

[24] Roy Schwartz, Omri Abend, Roi Reichart, and Ari Rappoport. Neutralizing linguistically problematic annotations in unsupervised dependency parsing evaluation. In *Proceedings of the 49th Annual Meeting of the Association for Computational Linguistics: Human Language Technologies*, pages 663–672, Portland, Oregon, USA, June 2011. Association for Computational Linguistics.

[25] Yoav Seginer. Fast Unsupervised Incremental Parsing. In *Proceedings of the 45th Annual Meeting of the Association of Computational Linguistics*, pages 384–391, Prague, Czech Republic, 2007. Association for Computational Linguistics.

[26] Noah Ashton Smith. *Novel estimation methods for unsupervised discovery of latent structure in natural language text*. PhD thesis, Baltimore, MD, USA, 2007. AAI3240799.

[27] Anders Søgaard. From ranked words to dependency trees: two-stage unsupervised non-projective dependency parsing. In *Proceedings of TextGraphs-6: Graph-based Methods for Natural Language Processing*, TextGraphs-6, pages 60–68, Stroudsburg, PA, USA, 2011. Association for Com-

putational Linguistics.

[28] Anders Søgaard. Two baselines for unsupervised dependency parsing. In *Proceedings of the NAACL-HLT Workshop on the Induction of Linguistic Structure*, pages 81–83, Montréal, Canada, June 2012. Association for Computational Linguistics.

[29] Valentin I. Spitkovsky, Hiyan Alshawi, Angel X. Chang, and Daniel Jurafsky. Unsupervised dependency parsing without gold part-of-speech tags. In *Proceedings of the 2011 Conference on Empirical Methods in Natural Language Processing (EMNLP 2011)*, 2011.

[30] Valentin I. Spitkovsky, Hiyan Alshawi, and Daniel Jurafsky. From baby steps to leapfrog: how "less is more" in unsupervised dependency parsing. In *Human Language Technologies: The 2010 Annual Conference of the North American Chapter of the Association for Computational Linguistics*, HLT '10, pages 751–759, Stroudsburg, PA, USA, 2010. Association for Computational Linguistics.

[31] Valentin I. Spitkovsky, Hiyan Alshawi, and Daniel Jurafsky. Lateen EM: Unsupervised training with multiple objectives, applied to dependency grammar induction. In *Proceedings of the 2011 Conference on Empirical Methods in Natural Language Processing (EMNLP 2011)*, 2011.

[32] Valentin I. Spitkovsky, Hiyan Alshawi, and Daniel Jurafsky. Punctuation: Making a point in unsupervised dependency parsing. In *Proceedings of the Fifteenth Conference on Computational Natural Language Learning (CoNLL-2011)*, 2011.

[33] Valentin I. Spitkovsky, Hiyan Alshawi, and Daniel Jurafsky. Three Dependency-and-Boundary Models for Grammar Induction. In *Proceedings of the 2012 Conference on Empirical Methods in Natural Language Processing and Computational Natural Language Learning (EMNLP-CoNLL 2012)*, 2012.

[34] Valentin I. Spitkovsky, Hiyan Alshawi, and Daniel Jurafsky. Breaking out of local optima with count transforms and model recombination: A study in grammar induction. In *Proceedings of the 2013 Conference on Empirical Methods in Natural Language Processing*, pages 1983–1995, Seattle, Washington, USA, October 2013. Association for Computational Linguistics.

[35] Kewei Tu. Combining the sparsity and unambiguity biases for grammar induction. In *Proceedings of the NAACL-HLT Workshop on the Induction of Linguistic Structure*, pages 105–110, Montréal, Canada, June 2012. Association for Computational Linguistics.

ITAT 2016 Proceedings, pp. 63–67
ISBN 978-1537016740, © 2016 O. Plátek, P. Bělohlávek, V. Hudeček, F. Jurčíček

Recurrent Neural Networks for Dialogue State Tracking

Ondřej Plátek, Petr Bělohlávek, Vojtěch Hudeček, and Filip Jurčíček

Charles University in Prague, Faculty of Mathematics and Physics
{oplatek,jurcicek}@ufal.mff.cuni.cz,
me@petrbel.cz,
vojta.hudecek@gmail.com,
http://ufal.mff.cuni.cz/ondrej-platek

Abstract: This paper discusses models for dialogue state tracking using recurrent neural networks (RNN). We present experiments on the standard dialogue state tracking (DST) dataset, DSTC2 [7]. On the one hand, RNN models became the state of the art models in DST, on the other hand, most state-of-the-art DST models are only turn-based and require dataset-specific preprocessing (e.g. DSTC2-specific) in order to achieve such results. We implemented two architectures which can be used in an incremental setting and require almost no preprocessing. We compare their performance to the benchmarks on DSTC2 and discuss their properties. With only trivial preprocessing, the performance of our models is close to the state-of-the-art results.[1]

1 Introduction

Dialogue state tracking (DST) is a standard and important task for evaluating task-oriented conversational agents [18, 7, 8]. Such agents play the role of a domain expert in a narrow domain, and users ask for information through conversation in natural language (see the example system and user responses in Figure 1). A dialogue state tracker summarizes the dialogue history and maintains a probability distribution over the (possible) user's goals (see annotation in Figure 1). Dialogue agents as introduced in [20] decide about the next action based on the dialogue state distribution given by the tracker. User's goals are expressed in a formal language, typically represented as a dialogue act items (DAIs) (see Section 2) and the tracker updates probability for each item. The dialogue state is a latent variable [20] and one needs to label the conversations in order to train a dialogue state tracker using supervised learning. It was shown that with a better dialogue state tracker, conversation agents achieve better success rate in overall completion of the their task [11].

...
Dial. state n: food:*None*, area:*None*, pricerange:*None*
System: What part of town do you have in mind?
User: West part of town.
Dial. state n+1: food:*None*, area:*west*, pricerange:*None*
System: What kind of food would you like?
User: Indian
Dial. state n+2: food:*Indian*, area:*west*, pricerange:*None*
System: India House is a nice place in the west of town serving tasty Indian food.
...

Figure 1: Example of golden annotation of Dialogue Act Items (DAIs). The dialogue act items comprise from act type (all examples have type *inform*) and slots (*food, area, pricerange*) and their values (e.g. *Indian, west, None*).

This paper compares two different RNN architectures for dialogue state tracking (see Section 3). We describe state-of-the art word-by-word dialogue state tracker architectures and propose to use a new encoder-decoder architecture for the DST task (see Section 4.2).

We focus only on the *goal* slot predictions because the other groups are trivial to predict[2].

We also experiment with re-splitting of the DSTC2 data because there are considerable differences between the standard train and test datasets [7]. Since the training, development and test set data are distributed differently, the resulting performance difference between training and test data is rather high. Based on our experiments, we conclude that DSTC2 might suggest a too pessimistic view of the state-of-the-art methods in dialogue state tracking caused by the data distribution mismatch.

2 Dialogue state tracking on DSTC2 dataset

Dialogue state trackers maintain their believes beliefs about users' goals by updating probabilities of dialogue history representations. In the DSTC2 dataset, the history is captured by dialogue act items and their probabilities. A Dialogue act item is a triple of the following form (*actionType, slotName, slotValue*).

The DSTC2 is a standard dataset for DST, and most of the state-of-the-art systems in DST have reported their per-

---
[1]**Acknowledgment:** We thank Mirek Vodolán and Ondřej Dušek for useful comments. This research was partly funded by the Ministry of Education, Youth and Sports of the Czech Republic under the grant agreement LK11221, core research funding, grant GAUK 1915/2015, and also partially supported by SVV project number 260 333. We gratefully acknowledge the support of NVIDIA Corporation with the donation of the Tesla K40c GPU used for this research. Computational resources were provided by the CESNET LM2015042 and the CERIT Scientific Cloud LM2015085, provided under the programme "Projects of Large Research, Development, and Innovations Infrastructures".

---
[2]The slots *Requested* and *Method* have accuracies 0.95 and 0.95 on the test set according to the state-of-the-art [19].

formance on this dataset [7]. The full dataset is freely available since January 2014 and it contains 1612 dialogues in the training set, 506 dialogues in the development set and 1117 dialogues in the test set.[3] The conversations are manually annotated at the turn level where the hidden information state is expressed in form of $(actionType, slotName, slotValue)$ based on the domain ontology. The task of the domain is defined by a database of restaurants and their properties[4]. The database and the manually designed ontology that captures a restaurant domain are both distributed with the dataset.

3   Models

Our models are all based on a RNN encoder [17]. The models update their hidden states h after processing each word similarly to the RNN encoder of Žilka and Jurčíček [16]. The encoder takes as inputs the previous state h_{t-1}, representing history for first $t-1$ words, and features X_t for the current word w_t. It outputs the current state h_t representing the whole dialogue history up to current word. We use a Gated Recurrent Unit (GRU) cell [5] as the update function instead of a simple RNN cell because it does not suffer from the vanishing gradient problem [10]. The model optimizes its parameters including word embeddings [3] during training.

For each input token, our RNN encoder reads the word embedding of this token along with several binary features. The binary features for each word are:

- the speaker role, representing either user or system,

- and also indicators describing whether the word is part of a named entity representing a value from the database.

Since the DSTC2 database is a simple table with six columns, we introduce six binary features firing if the word is a substring of named entity from the given column. For example, the word *indian* will not only trigger the feature for column *food* and its value *indian* but also for column restaurant *name* and its value *indian heaven*. The features make the data dense by abstracting the meaning from the lexical level.

Our model variants differ only in the way they predict *goal* labels, i.e., *food*, *area* and *pricerange* from the RNN's last encoded state.[5] The first model predicts the output slot labels independently by employing three independent classifiers (see Section 3.1). The second model uses a decoder in order to predict values one after the other from the h_T (see Section 3.2).

The models were implemented using the TensorFlow [1] framework.

---

[3]Available online at `http://camdial.org/~mh521/dstc/`.

[4]There are six columns in the database: name, food, price_range, area, telephone, address.

[5]Accuracy measure with schedule 2 on slot *food*, *area* and *pricerange* about which users can inform the system is a featured metric for DSTC2 challenge [7].

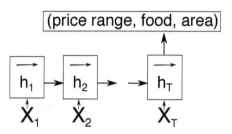

Figure 2: The joint label predictions using RNN from last hidden state h_T. The h_T represents the whole dialog history of T words. The RNN takes as input for each word i an embedding and binary features concatenated to vector X_i.

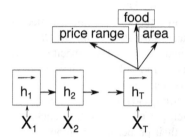

Figure 3: The RNN encodes the word history into dialogue state h_T and predicts slot values independently.

3.1   Independent classifiers for each label

The independent model (see Figure 3.1) consists of three models which predict *food*, *area* and *pricerange* based on the last hidden state h_T independently. The independent slot prediction that uses one classifier per slot is straightforward to implement, but the model introduces an unrealistic assumption of uncorrelated slot properties. In case of DSTC2 and the Cambridge restaurant domain, it is hard to believe that, e.g., the slots *area* and *pricerange* are not correlated.

We also experimented with a single classifier which predicts the labels jointly (see Figure 3) but it suffers from data sparsity of the predicted tuples, so we focused only on the independent label prediction and encoder-decoder models.

3.2   Encoder-decoder framework

We cast the slot predictions problem as a sequence-to-sequence predictions task and we use a encoder-decoder model with attention [2] to learn this representation together with slot predictions (see Figure 4). To our knowledge, we are the first who used this model for dialogue state tracking. The model is successfully used in machine translation where it is able to handle long sequences with good accuracy [2]. In DST, it captures correlation between the decoded slots easily. By introducing the encoder-decoder architecture, we aim to overcome the data sparsity problem and the incorrect independence assumptions.

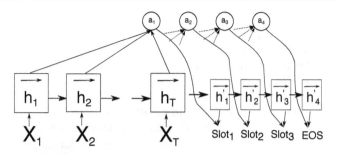

Figure 4: Encoder decoder with attention predicts goals.

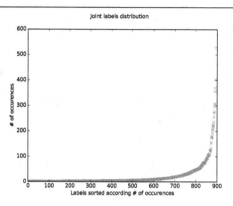

Figure 5: The number occurrences of labels in form of $(food, area, pricerange)$ triples from the least to the most frequent.

We employ the encoder RNN cell that captures the history of the dialogue which is represented as a sequence of words from the user and the system. The words are fed to the encoder as they appear in the dialogue - turn by turn - where the user and the system responses switch regularly. The encoder updates its internal state h_T after each processed word. The RNN decoder model is used when the system needs to generate its output, in our case it is at the end of the user response. The decoder generates arbitrary length sequences of words given the encoded state h_T step by step. In each step, an output word and a new hidden state h_{T+1} is generated. The generation process is finished when a special token End of Sequence (EOS) is decoded. This mechanism allows the model to terminate the output sequence. The attention part of model is used at decoding time for weighting the importance of the history.

The disadvantage of this model is its complexity. Firstly, the model is not trivial to implement[6]. Secondly, the decoding time is asymptotically quadratic in the length of the decoded sequences, but our target sequences are always four tokens long nevertheless.

4 Experiments

The results are reported on the standard DSTC2 data split where we used 516 dialogues as a validation set for early stopping [14] and the remaining 1612 dialogues for training. We use 1-best Automatic Speech Recognition (ASR) transcriptions of conversation history of the input and measure the joint slot accuracy. The models are evaluated using the recommended measure accuracy [7] with schedule 2 which skips the first turns where the believe tracker does not track any values. In addition, our models are also evaluated on a randomly split DSTC2 dataset (see Section 4.3).

For all our experiments, we train word embeddings of size 100 and use the encoder state size of size 100, together with a dropout keep probability of 0.7 for both encoder inputs and outputs. These parameters are selected by a grid search over the hyper-parameters on development data.

4.1 Training

The training procedure minimizes the cross-entropy loss function using the Adam optimizer [12] with a batch size of 10. We train predicting the goal slot values for each turn. We treat each dialogue turn as a separate training example, feeding the whole dialogue history up to the current turn into the encoder and predicting the slot labels for the current turn.

We use early stopping with patience [14], validating on the development set after each epoch and stopping if the three top models does not change for four epochs.

The predicted labels in DST task depend not only on the last turn, but on the dialogue full history as well. Since the lengths of dialogue histories vary a lot[7] and we batch our inputs, we separated the dialogues into ten buckets accordingly to their lengths in order to provide a computational speed-up. We reshuffle the data after each epoch only within each bucket.

In informal experiments, we tried to speed-up the training by optimizing the parameters only on the last turn[8] but the performance dropped relatively by more than 40%.

4.2 Comparing models

Predicting the labels jointly is quite challenging because the distribution of the labels is skewed as demonstrated in Figure 5. Some of the labels combinations are very rare, and they occur only in the development and test set so the joint model is not able to predict them. During first informal experiments the joint model performed poorly arguably due to data sparsity of slot triples. We further focus on model with independent classifiers and encoder-decoder architecture.

The model with independent label prediction is a strong baseline which was used, among others, in work of Žilka and Jurčíček [16]. The model suffers less from dataset

---

[6]We modified code from the TensorFlow 'seq2seq' module.

[7]The maximum dialogue history length is 487 words and 95% percentile is 205 words for the training set.

[8]The prediction was conditioned on the full history but we back-propagated the error only in words within the last turn.

Model	Dev set	Test set
Indep	0.892	0.727
EncDec	0.867	0.730
Vodolán et al. [15]	-	0.745
Žilka and Jurčíček [16]	0.69	0.72
Henderson et al. [6]	-	0.737
DSTC2 stacking ensemble [7]	-	0.789

Table 1: Accuracy on DSTC2 dataset. The first group contains our systems which use ASR output as input, the second group lists systems using also ASR hypothesis as input. The third group shows the results for ensemble model using ASR output nd also live language understanding annotations.

Model	Dev set	Test set
Indep	0.87	0.89
EncDec	0.94	0.91

Table 2: Accuracy of our models on the re-split DSTC2 data.

mismatch because it does not model the correlation between predicted labels. This property can explain a smaller performance drop between the test set from reshuffled data and the official test set in comparison to encoder-decoder model.

Since the encoder-decoder architecture is very general and can predict arbitrary output sequences, it also needs to learn how to predict only three slot labels in the correct order. It turned out that the architecture learned to predict quadruples with three slot values and the EOS symbol quickly, even before seeing a half of the training data in the first epoch.[9] At the end of the first epoch, the system made no more mistakes on predicting slot values in the incorrect order. The encoder-decoder system is competitive with state-of-the art architectures and the time needed for learning the output structure was surprisingly short.[10]

4.3 Data preparation experiments

The data for the DSTC2 test set were collected using a different spoken dialogue system configuration than the data for the validation and the training set.[7]. We intended to investigate the influence of the complexity of the task, hence we merged all DSTC2 data together and created splits of 80%, 10% and 10% for the training, development and test sets. The results in Table 2 show that the complexity of the task dropped significantly.

---

[9]We could have modified the decoder to always predict three symbols for our three slots, but our experiments showed that the encoder-decoder architecture does not make mistakes at predicting the order of the three slots and EOS symbol.

[10]The best model weights were found after 18 to 23 epochs for all model architectures.

5 Related work

Since there are numerous systems which reported on the DSTC2 dataset, we discuss only the systems which use RNNs. In general, the RNN systems achieved excellent results.

Our system is related to the RNN tracker of Žilka and Jurčíček [16], which reported near state-of-the art results on the DSTC2 dataset and introduced the first incremental system which was able to update the dialogue state word-by-word with such accuracy. In contrast to work of Žilka and Jurčíček [16], we use no abstraction of slot values. Instead, we add the additional features as described in Section 3. The first system which used a neural network for dialogue state tracking [6] used a feed-forward network and more than 10 manually engineered features across different levels of abstraction of the user input, including the outputs of the spoken language understanding component (SLU). In our work, we focus on simplifying the architecture, hence we used only features which were explicitly given by the dialogue history word representation and the database.

The system of Henderson et al. [9] achieves the state-of-the-art results and, similarly to our system, it predicts the dialogue state from words by employing a RNN. On the other hand, their system heavily relies on the user input abstraction. Another dialogue state tracker with LSTM was used in the reinforcement setting but the authors also used information from the SLU pipeline [13].

An interesting approach is presented in the work of Vodolán et al. [15], who combine a rule-based and a machine learning based approach. The handcrafted features are fed to an LSTM-based RNN which performs a dialog-state update. However, unlike our work, their system requires SLU output on its input.

It is worth noting that there are first attempts to train an end-to-end dialogue system even without explicitly modeling the dialogue state [4], which further simplifies the architecture of a dialogue system. However, the reported end-to-end model was evaluated only on artificial dataset and cannot be compared to DSTC2 dataset directly.

6 Conclusion

We presented and compared two dialogue state tracking models which are based on state-of-the-art architectures using recurrent neural networks. To our knowledge, we are the first to use an encoder-decoder model for the dialogue state tracking task, and we encourage others to do so because it is competitive with the standard RNN model.[11] The models are comparable to the state-of-the-art models.

We evaluate the models on DSTC2 dataset containing task-oriented dialogues in the restaurant domain. The

---

[11]The presented experiments are published at https://github.com/oplatek/e2end/ under Apache license. Informal experiments were conducted during the Statistical Dialogue Systems course at Charles University (see https://github.com/oplatek/sds-tracker).

models are trained using only ASR 1-best transcriptions and task-specific lexical features defined by the task database. We observe that dialogue state tracking on DSTC2 test set is notoriously hard and that the task becomes substantially easier if the data is reshuffled.

As future work, we plan to investigate the influence of the introduced database features on models accuracy. To our knowledge there is no dataset which can be used for evaluating incremental dialogue state trackers, so it would be beneficial to collect the word-level annotations so one can evaluate incremental DST models.

References

[1] Martın Abadi, Ashish Agarwal, Paul Barham, Eugene Brevdo, Zhifeng Chen, Craig Citro, Greg S Corrado, Andy Davis, Jeffrey Dean, Matthieu Devin, et al. TensorFlow: Large-scale machine learning on heterogeneous systems, 2015. *Software available from tensorflow. org*.

[2] Dzmitry Bahdanau, Kyunghyun Cho, and Yoshua Bengio. Neural machine translation by jointly learning to align and translate. *arXiv preprint arXiv:1409.0473*, 2014.

[3] Yoshua Bengio, Rejean Ducharme, and Pascal Vincent. A Neural probabilistic language model. *Journal of Machine Learning Research*, 3:1137–1155, 2003.

[4] Antoine Bordes and Jason Weston. Learning End-to-End Goal-Oriented Dialog. *arXiv preprint arXiv:1605.07683*, 2016.

[5] Kyunghyun Cho, Bart van Merrienboer, Çaglar Gülçehre, Fethi Bougares, Holger Schwenk, and Yoshua Bengio. Learning Phrase Representations using RNN Encoder-Decoder for Statistical Machine Translation. *CoRR*, abs/1406.1078, 2014. URL http://arxiv.org/abs/1406.1078.

[6] Matthew Henderson, Blaise Thomson, and Steve Young. Deep neural network approach for the dialog state tracking challenge. *Proceedings of the SIGDIAL 2013 Conference*, pages 467–471, 2013.

[7] Matthew Henderson, Blaise Thomson, and Jason Williams. The second dialog state tracking challenge. In *15th Annual Meeting of the Special Interest Group on Discourse and Dialogue*, volume 263, 2014.

[8] Matthew Henderson, Blaise Thomson, and Jason D Williams. The third dialog state tracking challenge. In *Spoken Language Technology Workshop (SLT), 2014 IEEE*, pages 324–329. IEEE, 2014.

[9] Matthew Henderson, Blaise Thomson, and Steve Young. Word-based dialog state tracking with recurrent neural networks. In *Proceedings of the 15th Annual Meeting of the Special Interest Group on Discourse and Dialogue (SIGDIAL)*, pages 292–299, 2014.

[10] Sepp Hochreiter, Yoshua Bengio, Paolo Frasconi, and Jürgen Schmidhuber. Gradient flow in recurrent nets: the difficulty of learning long-term dependencies, 2001.

[11] Filip Jurčíček, Blaise Thomson, and Steve Young. Reinforcement learning for parameter estimation in statistical spoken dialogue systems. *Computer Speech & Language*, 26(3):168–192, 2012.

[12] Diederik Kingma and Jimmy Ba. Adam: A method for stochastic optimization. *arXiv preprint arXiv:1412.6980*, 2014.

[13] Byung-Jun Lee and Kee-Eung Kim. Dialog History Construction with Long-Short Term Memory for Robust Generative Dialog State Tracking. *Dialogue & Discourse*, 7(3):47–64, 2016.

[14] Lutz Prechelt. Early stopping-but when? In *Neural Networks: Tricks of the trade*, pages 55–69. Springer, 1998.

[15] Miroslav Vodolán, Rudolf Kadlec, and Jan Kleindienst. Hybrid Dialog State Tracker. *CoRR*, abs/1510.03710, 2015. URL http://arxiv.org/abs/1510.03710.

[16] Lukás Žilka and Filip Jurčíček. Incremental LSTM-based dialog state tracker. *arXiv preprint arXiv:1507.03471*, 2015.

[17] Paul J Werbos. Backpropagation through time: what it does and how to do it. *Proceedings of the IEEE*, 78 (10):1550–1560, 1990.

[18] Jason Williams, Antoine Raux, Deepak Ramachandran, and Alan Black. The dialog state tracking challenge. In *Proceedings of the SIGDIAL 2013 Conference*, pages 404–413, 2013.

[19] Jason D Williams. Web-style ranking and SLU combination for dialog state tracking. In *15th Annual Meeting of the Special Interest Group on Discourse and Dialogue*, volume 282, 2014.

[20] Steve Young, Milica Gašić, Simon Keizer, François Mairesse, Jost Schatzmann, Blaise Thomson, and Kai Yu. The hidden information state model: A practical framework for POMDP-based spoken dialogue management. *Computer Speech & Language*, 24(2): 150–174, 2010.

ITAT 2016 Proceedings, pp. 68–73
ISBN 978-1537016740, © 2016 K. Přikrylová, V. Kuboň, K. Veselovská

Logical vs. Natural Language Conjunctions in Czech:
A Comparative Study

Katrin Přikrylová, Vladislav Kuboň, and Kateřina Veselovská

Charles University in Prague, Faculty of Mathematics and Physics
Czech Republic
{prikrylova,vk,veselovska}@ufal.mff.cuni.cz

Abstract: This paper studies the relationship between conjunctions in a natural language (Czech) and their logical counterparts. It shows that the process of transformation of a natural language expression into its logical representation is not straightforward. The paper concentrates on the most frequently used logical conjunctions, $\wedge$ and $\vee$, and it analyzes the natural language phenomena which influence their transformation into logical conjunction and disjunction. The phenomena discussed in the paper are temporal sequence, expressions describing mutual relationship and the consequences of using plural.

1 Introduction and motivation

The endeavor to express natural language sentences in the form of logical expressions is probably as old as logic itself. A very important role in this process is being played by natural language conjunctions and their transformation into logical connectives. The conjunctions are much more ambiguous than logical connectives and thus it is necessary to analyze their role in natural language sentences, in various contexts and types of texts. This paper presents a step towards such analysis for one particular language - Czech.

Let us recall that the fundamental task of logic is to set rules and methods for inferencing and referencing. On the other hand, natural languages serve primarily for communication. Speakers can reach and agreement or understand each other even without a strict adherence to preset rules (regardless whether they are morphological, grammatical or stylistical). A human brain can obtain substantial information also from ill-formed sentences what actually makes them to fulfill their main goal, to serve as a tool for communication. On the other hand, Noam Chomsky introduced in [1] also a famous example *Colourless green ideas sleep furiously* – a grammatically well-formed sentence which does not have any meaning and thus it cannot serve the communication task.

Sentences in any natural languge are not isolated, their meaning typically depends on the context in which they appear, on the way how they are pronounced or even on some external factors as, e.g., gestures which accompany it. Natural languages also evolve in time according to the needs of the language community and although each natural language has a set of generally applicable rules (syntactic, stylistic, morphological etc.), there are many ex-

ceptions and irregularities which do not abide the rules as strictly as it is the case in logic.

Primarily due to this difference, the transformation of natural language sentences into their logical representation constitutes a complex issue. As we are going to show in the subsequent sections, there are no simple rules which would allow automation of the process – the majority of problematic cases requires an *individual* approach.

In the following text we are going to restrict our observations to the two most frequently used conjunctions, namely *a* (and) and *nebo* (or).

2 Sentences containing the conjunction *a* (and)

The initial assumption about complex sentences containing the conjunction *a* (and) is inspired by the properties of the corresponding logical connective *and* – we suppose that the two clauses connected by the conjunction express two situations which are valid at the same time. This really holds in a number of complex sentences, as for example here:

> *Lev je kočkovitá šelma a žije v Africe.*
> (Lion is a feline and it lives in Africa.) $\qquad$ (1)

> *Jana je ve škole a Honza leží nemocný v posteli.*
> (Jana is in a school and Honza lies ill in bed.) $\qquad$ (2)

In the sentence 1 we have used the so called gnomic present[1]. The truth value of the whole sentence is TRUE only in case that both clauses are TRUE, regardless of the context or current situation.

Complex sentences with gnomic present constitute probably the simplest case. It is not necessary to investigate whether the clauses are true or what are the conditions under which they might become true – they are simply true either always or never. Such sentences can be transformed into a logical representation in a simple and straightforward manner.[2] In the logical representation of the example above we would of course use the construction $A \wedge B$ for the conjunction *a* (and).

---

[1] Present tense can be used also for the so called *extratensal* processes which are valid always, regardless of the current situation. In our example we describe properties of an animal species and its habitat.

[2] Let us point out that mathematical theorems typically contain gnomic present.

The sentence 2 describes two situations being TRUE exactly in this moment[3]. The truth value of both sentences can be determined by a *reference* from the language to a real–world, where we will find out whether both clauses describe a valid situation.[4]

None of the two clauses from the sentence 2 is absolutely true (Jana does not spend every minute of her life in the school and Honza is not ill forever). However, when we utter any of these two statements, we do not mean that Jana should stay all the time in the school. The use of the present tense implicitly carries the information that she is there just now, in this moment. If we accept that in order to determine the truth value, we have to look into the real world and also take into the account the time when the sentence was uttered, we could paraphrase the sentence into a more unambiguous variant for example like this:

> *Jana je právě teď' ve škole a Honza nyní leží*
> *nemocný v posteli.*
>
> (Jana is just now in the school and Honza is
>
> now lying ill in bed.)   (3)

– i.e. with the added information about time. Such sentence would then correspond to the logical scheme of the conjunction : $A \wedge B$.[5]

Natural languages use, of course, also other tenses – what if we would like to express the same content in the past, for example yesterday?

> *Jana byla včera ve škole a Honza včera ležel*
> *nemocný v posteli.*
>
> (Jana was in a school yesterday and Honza
>
> was lying ill in bed.)   (4)

On the first sight, there seems to be no substantial problem. The only difference seems to be in the fact that we are not referring to a current moment, but to the moment in the past (in this case, yesterday). However, what if Honza will recover till the next day, will such sentence have the same truth value also tomorrow?

Regardless to what time the expressions refer to, we are interested in them only if they are TRUE in this current moment. We should thus simplify our sentence rather in the following way:

> *Právě teď' platí, že Jana je ve škole, a současně,*
> *že Honza leží nemocný v posteli.*
>
> (Just now it is true that Jana is in the school,   (5)
>
> and, at the same time, Honza is lying ill in bed.)

---

[3]Of course, only if it is true that Jana is just now in the school and Honza lies ill in his bed.

[4]Determining the truth value of natural language expressions is studied by epistemology, a simple explanation can be found for example in [2].

[5]If we would like to consider tiniest details, we would have to consider also the issue of proper names and singular terms – our sentence does not specify which Jana and Honza we are talking about. More on this topic can be found for example in [3].

Or, we could drop the initial part which we may consider to be implicitly present:

> *Jana je ve škole, a současně Honza leží*
> *nemocný v posteli.*
>
> (Jana is in the school, and, at the same   (6)
>
> time, Honza is lying ill in bed.)

Into such template it is possible to insert also the complex sentence introduced above:

> *Jana byla včera ve škole a současně Honza*
> *včera ležel nemocný v posteli.*
>
> (Jana was in a school yesterday and, at the same   (7)
>
> time, Honza was lying ill in bed yesterday.)

All the complex sentences mentioned above can schematically be described in the form $A \wedge B$. The fact that we can express the mutual relationship of clauses by means of a logical scheme actually means that we can work with them according to logical rules. For example, logical conjunction is commutative – and we really can swap the order of clauses in our complex sentence and still retain the original truth value.

2.1 Violation of a temporal sequence

Unfortunately, the conjunction *a* (and) doesn't appear only in sentences describing actions which are happening in the same moment. All of the following sentences contain *a* (and) as its main conjunction:

> *Honza spadl a zlomil si ruku.*
> (Honza fell and broke his arm.)   (8)

> *Jana odemkla a vešla do bytu.*
> (Jana unlocked and entered the flat.)   (9)

> *Šli jsme na výstavu a potom do kina.*
> (We have visited an exhibition and   (10)
>
> then we went to a cinema.)

These sentences apparently aren't commutative. The order of clauses cannot be swapped without affecting the truth value or meaning of the whole sentence. The reason is obvious – both clauses are ordered into a temporal sequence.

The conjunction *a* (and) isn't a logical conjunction in these sentences, although it fulfills one fundamental basic condition – if the whole sentence is supposed to be true, then both clauses also have to be true.

The propositional logic nevertheless cannot cope with sentences of this kind. We might be tempted to attempt to solve this issue by means of the conditional construction *Když..., (pak) ...* (When... (then) ...):

> *Když Jana odemkla, vešla do bytu.*
> (When Jana unlocked, then she entered the flat.)   (11)

and thus to find a certain scheme corresponding to an implication. In natural languages, the modified sentence is equivalent with the original one, but this is true only because the construction *Když..., (pak)* ... (When... (then) ...) not necessarily always means an implication. In this particular case, its role is more temporal than conditional.[6] Transforming the sentence into the scheme $A \rightarrow B$ is thus incorrect. In [4], František Gahér suggests a very simple test whether a particular expression containing the conjunction *a* (and) is a logical conjunction or not. He uses the expression *a současně* (and at the same time).

The sentence:

> *Jana odemkla a současně vešla do bytu.*
> (Jana unlocked and at the same time   (12)
> entered the flat.)

does not make much sense and thus we should not directly transform it into logical conjunction. However, the author itself admits that such simple test is not 100% reliable – the construction:

> *Gödel se narodil v roce 1906 a zemřel v roce 1978.*
> (Gödel was born in 1906 and died in 1978.)
>   (13)

actually has all required properties of a conjunction: both clauses must be true if the whole sentence should be true; their order can be changed[7]. However, when we try to replace *a* (and) by the construction *a současně*, (and at the same time), we won't get a meaningful sentence:

> *Gödel se narodil v roce 1906 a současně zemřel v roce 1978.*
> (Gödel was born in 1906 and at the same   (14)
> time died in 1978.)

Let us now return to the original sentence. We have already mentioned that in predicate logic it is impossible to describe it unless we loose an important information about the order of events. What if we would use some other type of logic? The type which seems to be ideally suited for such kind of constructions is the *temporal* logic. It is in fact the propositional logic enriched by the so called *temporal operators*, by means of which we can express a temporal sequence of actions. More information about this kind of logic can be found, e.g., in [5] or [6].

2.2 Disjunction

So far, we have dealt with the conjunction *a* (and) in the cases in which it expressed conjunction. Let us now show that the same natural language conjunction may in some specific cases also serve as a logical disjunction.

Let us take the sentence:

> *Jestliže Honza neodevzdá diplomovou práci včas a nepřihlásí se ke státnicím, studia letos nedokončí.*
> (If Honza won't submit the thesis in time   (15)
> **and** doesn't subscribe for the state exams,
> he won't finish his studies in this year.)

If we would like to preserve the equivalence of *a* (and) and a logical conjunction, we could write this sentence schematically as $(\neg A \wedge \neg B) \rightarrow \neg C$. And indeed, the utterances corresponding to this scheme can be often heard from the Czech native speakers. If we look at the given sentence more closely, we will agree that in order to finish one's studies it is indeed necessary to finish the thesis in time and at the same time to subscribe also for the state exams. If **at least one** of these two conditions is not fulfilled, Honza will not finish his studies. The scheme $(\neg A \wedge \neg B) \rightarrow \neg C$, on the other hand, requires *both* conditions to be invalid in order to obtain FALSE as the truth value of the whole sentence.

It would therefore be more correct to describe the complex sentence schematically as $(\neg A \vee \neg B) \rightarrow \neg C$. The conjunction *a* (and) clearly substitutes logical disjunction in this context. Actually, even in the natural language it would be more correct to use the conjunction *nebo* (or) and to say:

> *Jestliže Honza neodevzdá diplomovou práci včas **nebo** nepřihlásí se ke státnicím, studia letos nedokončí.*
> (If Honza won't submit the thesis in time   (16)
> **or** doesn't subscribe for the state exams,
> he won't finish his studies in this year.)

The fact that this error is quite frequent in natural language communication is documented for example in the research of Vlastimil Chytrý [7] conducted among the pupils of basic and secondary schools. Only 11,5 % of them were able to correctly negate the conjunction in the antecedent of the implication, when they were asked to paraphrase it. We can only speculate why the native speakers make this error so often.[8]

2.3 Relation Expression

Let us emphasize that, e.g., a sentence:

> *Jana **a** Honza jsou studenti.*
> (Jana **and** Honza are students.)   (17)

is actually a compound sentence:

> *Jana je studentka a Honza je student.*
> (Jana is a student and Honza is a student.) (18)

---

[6]The conjunction *když* (when) is then ambiguous.

[7]Although it is more natural to use them in this order. Nevertheless, the variant with the reversed order does not violate neither linguistic rules nor the logical meaning of the sentence.

[8]More about the processes in the center of speech of a human brain can be found for example in [8].

i.e. it expresses two utterances.

In the sentence 18, the conjunction *a* (and) is equivalent to a conjunction in logic. However, let us investigate the following examples:

> *Jana a Honza jsou přátelé.*
> (Jana and Honza are friends.) (19)

> *Jana a Honza se milují.*
> (Jana and Honza love each other.) (20)

> *Barma a Myanmar je totéž.*
> (Burma and Myanmar is the same thing)[10] (21)

To rephrase the first sentence as:

> *Jana je přítelkyně a Honza je přítel.*
> (Jana is a friend and Honza is a friend.) (22)

makes no sense, since we lose the information about a relationship between Jana and Honza.

In Czech, the second sentence could be rephrased as:

> *Jana se miluje a Honza se miluje.*
> (Jana loves herself and Honza loves himself.) (23)

but it's meaning is not the same as in case of the original sentence, which is ambiguous in Czech. It contains a reflexive verb *milovat se* (to love someone), which expresses a relationship either between two subjects or of each of them to him/herself particularly. However, we usually use this verb in situations in which we want to express a relationship between two people. Anyway, this example is to illustrate that the same utterance can be formally represented using two different logical schemes. In case we would want to express the second meaning, we would write it down using the means of predicate logic as

$$love\_oneself(Jana) \land love\_oneself(Honza)$$

To catch the first meaning, we would have to use not the unary relation, but a binary one

$$Love(Jana, Honza),$$

which would be in this case symmetrical. Therefore, we would have to abandon the propositional logic to describe this type of sentences.

The last sentence from the list cannot be rephrased as:

> *Barma je totéž a Myanmar je totéž.*
> (Burma is the same thing and Myanmar (24)
> is the same thing.)

This sentence makes no sense, since the phrase *to be the same thing* again implies a relationship between the entities. These examples actually clearly document the fact that the conjunction *a* (and) used in utterances which express a relationship cannot be used as a conjunction in

logic. The following sentences represent other cases in which the conjunction *a* (and) refers to a relationship between the subjects:

> *Černé a bílé ponožky se pomíchaly.*
> (Black and white socks got mixed.) (25)

> *Jana a Honza se vzali.*
> (Jana and Honza got married.) (26)

In the above examples we have shown that if the conjunction *a* (and) is used in the utterance which expresses a relationship, it cannot be used as a conjunction in logic.

2.4 Problems with plural

The method of connecting smaller pieces of text than the whole compound sentences which we have introduced above can be called a *distributive* method in the mathematical sense of that term. However, the method is not flawless and we have already shown the examples for which it cannot be applied. We will now demonstrate the imperfections of the method that are not related only to lexicon/semantics (i.e. to particular words which do not let us use the method due to their lexical meaning), but rather to syntax.

Let us consider the following sentence:

> *Pošťák přivezl velký a těžký balík.*
> (A postman delivered a big and heavy package.) (27)

It is natural to agree with the premise that a postman delivered only one package, which was big and heavy at the same time.[11] However, if we divide the sentence into two propositions:

> *Pošťák přivezl velký balík a pošťák přivezl těžký balík.*
> (A postman delivered a big package and
> a postman delivered a heavy package) (28)

the most natural interpretation would probably be that a postman delivered two packages, one of them big and the other one heavy.

The distinction is even more obvious in the following sentence:

> *Na ulici stálo modré a zelené auto.*
> (There was a blue and green car parking (29)
> on the street.)

Although the word *car* is used here in singular, we would probably say that there were two cars parking on the street, one of them blue and the other one green. In case the author would use plural:

> *Na ulici stála modrá a zelená auta.*
> (There were blue and green cars parking (30)
> on the street.)

---

[11]That would probably be the first interpretation which would come to our mind without thinking about any further meanings.

we would probably come into conclusion that there were even more than two cars parking on the street.

These examples demonstrate that when connecting two adjectives, the interpretation of the conjunction *a* (and) is not clear. Whereas in the first example it is a description of one object having two characteristics, in the second example we describe two different objects having two different characteristics. However, we assign the same activity (same predicate) to both of these objects. The type of the structure is given by the particular adjectives. It is not common in a real word that the car would be both blue and green at the same time.[12] In the case when it would be a dirty and scratched car, it would probably be perceived as only one vehicle.

More syntactic problems are connected with a plural. While in the sentence:

> *Na ulici stálo špinavé a poškrábané auto.*
> (There was a dirty and scratched car parking   (31)
>
> on the street.)

we assign both characteristics to only one object (a car), in the sentence:

> *Na ulici stála špinavá a poškrábaná auta.*
> (There were dirty and scratched cars parking   (32)
>
> on the street.)

we do not insist on assigning both characteristics to all of the vehicles.

The second sentence thus cannot be interpreted as a conjunction, but rather as a disjunction.[13] In the case of a plural we cannot consider this feature as a specific property of particular adjectives. This phenomena is not related to a specific semantics of given lexemes, but concerns all the adjectives in their fullness.

Below we list some other sentences which should be considered:

> *Článek se zabývá aktivními a pasivními příjmy.*
> (The article discusses the active and passive   (33)
>
> incomes.)

> *Sešli se tam všichni místní slavní a bohatí lidé.*
> (All the local famous and rich people met up   (34)
>
> at the event.)

> *Jako cestovatel se dostal na mnohem zajímavější*
> *a podivuhodnější místa.*
> (As a traveler, he got to far more
>
> interesting and remarkable places.)
> (35)

3 Interpretation of the Sentences Containing the Conjunction *nebo* (or)

As we have shown in the previous section, the interpretation of the conjunction *a* (and) is not an easy task. Surprisingly, the conjunction *nebo* (or) behaves more systematically.

The conjunction *nebo* (nebo) can be interpreted in two ways:

- as a disjunction,
- as an exclusive disjunction.

Apart from English, Czech language has a rather strict rules distinguishing between these two cases.[14] If there is *nebo* (or) following the comma, it is an exclusive disjunction. In all the other cases, it is considered a common disjunction:

> *Čertovi se také říká ďábel nebo satan.*
> (The demon is also called a devil or a Satan.)   (36)
> – a disjunction

> *Honza přijede ve středu, nebo až ve čtvrtek.*
> (Honza is coming on Wednesday,   (37)
>
> or on Thursday.) – exclusive disjunction

Naturally, in the spoken language we do not have a chance to find out whether there is a comma in the sentence or not.[15] Therefore, we have a lexical distinction at our disposal: the exclusive *nebo* (or) becomes a correlative conjunction, namely *buď–nebo* (either–or):

> *Honza přijede buď ve středu, nebo až ve čtvrtek.*
> (Honza is coming either on Wednesday
>
> or on Thursday.) – exclusive disjunction
> (38)

Conjunction *nebo* (or) can also be a part of the more complex connection which can be further expressed using other logical conjunction. For illustration, see the following sentence:

> *Ať už Honza přijede, nebo ne, oslava se bude konat.*
> (Whether Honza is coming or not, we will
>
> throw the party.)
> (39)

---

[12]In this case, the car would probably rather be described as *blue-green*.

[13]However, we still need to take into account the level of which we speak. Whereas in connection with the noun (or a noun phrase) the adjective is attributed to we talk about disjunction (it is not required for both objects to have both characteristics), in context of the whole sentence the conjunction *a* (and) behaves as a conjunction again. It means that if there would be only dirty cars parking on the street, we would be wondering where are the scratched ones mentioned in the sentence as well.

[14]In English, we use a comma preceding the conjunction *or* when it connects two independent sentences, regardless the relationship between them.

[15]In Czech, we place commas based on structural rules, i.e. not in places where there is a natural break in spoken utterance.

*Ať už Honza přijede ve středu, nebo ve čtvrtek,
rozhodně navštíví také prarodiče.*

(Whether coming on Wednesday or Thursday, (40)

Honza will definitely drop by his grandparents.)

As for the sentence 39, we can write down the proposition using a special logical conjunction **Maybe and** (MA, truth depends on second proposition) described for example in [9]: *Honza is coming* MA *we will throw a party.*

The sentence 40 is however much more complex. Although it expresses the contrast of the two possibilities, one of them is not a negation of another. Therefore we cannot use the conjunction MA, since it is a binary conjunction and we need to connect three propositions.[16] The second sentence can be transformed into a logical notation in the following way:

(Honza přijede ve středu $\oplus$ Honza přijede ve čtvrtek) $\wedge$ Honza rozhodně navštíví prarodiče. ((Honza is coming on Wednesday $\oplus$ Honza is coming on Thursday) $\wedge$ Honza will drop by his grandparents.)

(41)

Therefore, we would have to use the exclusive disjunction again.[17]

4   Conclusion

In this article, we have discussed the interpretation of natural language sentences using the means of logic. We have shown that although some of the logical conjunction names are motivated by the natural language conjunctions and they quite often have similar meaning, it is not possible to translate them from natural language to logic directly. Especially for the conjunction *a* (and) we have introduced more complex problems (i.e. the issue of relations, plurals or sequence of tenses) which prevent us from identifying *a* (and) with a logical conjunction.

Also, we have brought an important analysis of the possibilities (and problems) which have to be considered when working beyond sentential level. We have shown how to transform these structures so that they could be described using the means of the propositional logic (which takes only the propositions – or, in other words, sentences).

5   Acknowledgments

This research was supported by the grant GA15-06894S of the Grant Agency of the Czech Republic and by the SVV project number 260 224. This work has been using language resources stored and/or distributed by the LINDAT-Clarin project of MŠMT (project LM2010013).

References

[1] Chomsky, N.: Syntactic Structures. Werner Hildebrandt, Berlin (2002)

[2] Dummet, M.: Origins of Analytical Philosophy. Harvard University Press, Cambrige, Massachusetts (1996)

[3] Marvan, T.: Otázka významu. Togga, Praha (2010) In Czech.

[4] Gahér, F.: Logika pre každého. Iris, Braatislava (1995) in Slovak.

[5] Øhrstrom, P., Hasle, P.F.V.: Temporal Logic: From Ancient Ideas to Artificial Intelligence. Kluwer Academic Publishers, Dorderecht, Netherlands (1995)

[6] Sag, I., Wiesler, S.: Temporal connectives and logical form. In: Proceedings of the Fifth Annual Meeting of the Berkeley Linguistics Society, Berkeley (1979) 336–349

[7] Chytrý, V.: Logika, hry a myšlení. Univerzita J. E. Purkyně, Ústí nad Labem (2015) in Czech.

[8] C.L.Baker, McCarthy, J.J.: The Logical Problem of Language Acquisition. The MIT Press, Cambridge, Massachusetts (1981)

[9] van Wijk, M.: Logical connectives in natural language. Doctoraalscriptie Algemene Taalwetenschap. Universiteit Leiden Faculteit der Letteren, Leiden (2006) Available online: https://www.era.lib.ed.ac.uk/bitstream/handle/1842/5822/VanWijk2006.pdf.

---

[16]1. Honza is coming on Wednesday. 2. Honza is coming on Thursday. 3. Honza will drop by his grandparents.

[17]Conjunction MA can be also expressed using a set of conjunctions $\{\wedge, \vee, \neg\}$. It is also interesting to consider whether the construction *Ať už (...), nebo (...)* (Whether (...) or (...)) can be captured using a common disjunction or using the exclusive one. In case we are describing an indisputable system (such as propositional logic), we already know that the situation $A \wedge \neg A$ is impossible, so both versions of the translation – with $\vee$ and with $\oplus$ – are equivalent if there is the same formula in the connection (or, more precisely, the formula and its negation). Finally, we have to mention that there were both variants (with and without a comma) found in the corpus.

ITAT 2016 Proceedings, pp. 74–79
ISBN 978-1537016740, © 2016 R. Rosa

Czechizator – Čechizátor

Rudolf Rosa

Charles University in Prague, Faculty of Mathematics and Physics,
Institute of Formal and Applied Linguistics,
Malostranské náměstí 25, 118 00 Prague, Czech Republic
rosa@ufal.mff.cuni.cz

Abstract: We present a lexicon-less rule-based machine translation system from English to Czech, based on a very limited amount of transformation rules. Its core is a novel translation module, implemented as a component of the TectoMT translation system, and depends massively on the extensive pipeline of linguistic preprocessing and postprocessing within TectoMT. Its scope is naturally limited, but for specific texts, e.g. from the scientific or marketing domain, it occasionally produces sensible results.

Prezentujeme lexikon-lesový rule-bazovaný systém machín translace od Engliše Čecha, který bazoval na verově limitované amountu rulů transformace. Jeho kor je novelový modul translace, implementovalo jako komponent systému translace tektomtu a dependuje masivně na extensivní pipelínu lingvistické preprocesování a postprocesovat v Tektomtu. Jeho skop je naturálně limitovaná, ale pro specifické texty z například scientifické nebo marketování doménu okasionálně produkuje sensibilní resulty.

1 Introduction and Motivation

In this work, we present Czechizator, a lexicon-less rule-based machine translation system from English to Czech.

Lexicon-less approach to machine translation has already been successfuly applied to closely related languages – e.g. the Czech-Slovak machine translation system Česílko [3, 4] featured a rule-based lexicon-less transformation component for handling OOV (out-of-vocabulary) words. For transliteration, which can be thought of as a low-level translation, rule-based systems are also common. However, in this work, we decided to tackle a harder problem: to use a similar approach for a full translation between a pair of only weakly related languages, namely English and Czech.

While we believe that it is impossible to achieve high-quality or even reasonable-quality general-domain translation without a large lexicon, we attempt to investigate to what degree this is possible if the domain is somewhat special. Specifically, we target the domain of scientific texts (or, more precisely, abstracts of scientific papers), which contain a large amount of terms that tend to be rather similar even across more distant languages. In this way, we operate on a pair of languages which are typologically different but lexically close. Moreover, we crucially rely on the strong linguistic abstractions provided by the TectoMT machine translation system [15], which boasts to operate on a deep layer of language representation where typological differences of languages become quite transparent, as the meaning itself, rather than the form, is captured. Abstracting away from both lexical and typological differences in this way, a smallish set of rules and heuristics should be sufficient to obtain a competitive machine translation system.

While the main focus of our work is to test the degree to which the aforementioned hypothesis is valid, our work has practical implications as well. The number of terms used in scientific texts is enormous, many of them being rare in parallel corpora or even newly created and thus bound to constitute OOV items for machine translation systems. However, as there seems to be some regularity in the way that English terms are adapted in Czech, it should be possible to use a lexicon-less system as an additional component in a standard machine translation system to handle OOVs. It may also be beneficial in scenarios where low-quality but light-weight translation system is preferred over a full-fledged but resource-heavy system.[1]

Another use-case is machine-aided translation of sientific paper abstracts, as the Czechizator output should often be a good starting point for creating the final translation by post-editing.

Before explaining the approach we used to implement the translation model, we present a set of three sample outputs of Czechizator, applied to abstracts of two scientific papers (Table 1, Table 2), and one marketing text,[2] (Table 3). Also, as an additional example, the abstract of this paper is provided both in English and in its Czechization.

2 Approach

2.1 TectoMT

TectoMT [15, 1] is a highly modular linguistically oriented machine translation system, featuring a deep-linguistic three-step processing pipeline of analysis, transfer, and

---

[1]However, TectoMT itself is rather resource-heavy even when the lexical models are omitted, so even though the component that we implemented is very light-weight, the complete system that it relies on is not – using the Czechizator model instead of the base models in TectoMT only brings a 15% speedup and 40% RAM cut, which is probably not worth the quality drop in any realistic scenario.

[2]The text was obtained from https://www.accenture.com/cz-en/strategy-index

Source	Czechization	Reference translation
Chimera is a machine translation system that combines the TectoMT deep-linguistic core with Moses phrase-based MT system. For English–Czech pair it also uses the Depfix post-correction system. All the components run on Unix/Linux platform and are open source (available from CPAN Perl repository and the LINDAT/CLARIN repository). The main website is https://ufal.mff.cuni.cz/tectomt. The development is currently supported by the QTLeap 7th FP project (http://qtleap.eu).	Chimera je systém machín translace, který kombinuje díp-lingvistické kor tektomtu z fraze-bazovaného MT systému mozesu. Pro Engliše – čechová pér také uzuje systém post-korekce Depfix. Všechny komponenty runují v Unix / platformu Linuxu a jsou openová sourc (avélabilní z CPAN Perla repositorie a LINDAT / CLARIN repositorie). Hlavní webová stránka je https://ufal.mff.cuni.cz/tectomt. Development kurentně je suport FP projektem 7th qtlípu (http://qtleap.eu).	Chimera systém strojového překladu, který kombinuje hluboce lingvistické jádro TectoMT s frázovým strojovým překladačem Moses. Pro anglicko-český překlad také používá post-editovací systém Depfix. Všechny komponenty běží na platformě Unix/Linux a jsou open-source (dostupné z Perlového repozitáře CPAN a repozitáře LINDAT/CLARIN). Hlavní webová stránka je https://ufal.mff.cuni.cz/tectomt. Vývoj je momentálně podporován projektem QTLeap ze 7th FP (http://qtleap.eu).

Table 1: Abstract of a scientific paper [7], its Czechization, and a reference translation by its author.

Source	Czechization
We propose two novel model architectures for computing continuous vector representations of words from very large data sets. The quality of these representations is measured in a word similarity task, and the results are compared to the previously best performing techniques based on different types of neural networks. We observe large improvements in accuracy at much lower computational cost, i.e. it takes less than a day to learn high quality word vectors from a 1.6 billion words data set. Furthermore, we show that these vectors provide state-of-the-art performance on our test set for measuring syntactic and semantic word similarities.	Propozujeme 2 novelová architektury modelů, že komputují kontinuální reprezentace vektorů vordů od verově largových setů dat. Kvalita těchto reprezentací je mísur ve vord similarita tasku a resulty jsou kompar s previálně nejgůdovšími, performují, techniky, kteří bazovali na diferentových typech neurálních netvorků. Observujeme largové improventy akurace v muchově lovovší komputacionální kosti, tj. takuje méně než Daie, aby se lírnovalo hajové vektory vordu kvality z dat vordů 1.6 bilionu, která setovala. Furtermorově šovujeme, že tyto vektory providují state-of-te-artovou performance na našem testu, který setoval, že mísurují syntaktické a semantické vord similarity.

Table 2: Abstract of a scientific paper [6] and its Czechization.

Source	Czechization
Accenture Operations combines technology that digitizes and automates business processes, unlocks actionable insights, and delivers everything-as-a-service with our team's deep industry, functional and technical expertise. So you can confidently chart your course to consuming your core business services on demand, accelerate innovation and speed to market. Welcome to the "as-a-service" business revolution. Accenture Strategy shapes our clients' future, combining deep business insight with the understanding of how technology will impact industry and business models. Our focus on issues related to digital disruption, redefining competitiveness, operating and business models as well as the workforce of the future helps our clients find future value and growth in a digital world. Whether focused on strategies for business, technology or operations, Accenture Strategy has the people, skills and experience to effectively shape client value. We offer highly objective points of view on C-suite themes, with an emphasis on business and technology, leveraging our deep industry experience. That's high performance, delivered.	Operacions acenturu kombinuje technologii, která digitizuje a automuje procesy businosti, unlokuje akcionabilní insajty a deliveruje everyting-as-a-servicová s funkcionální a technickou expertizou dípové industrie našeho tímu. Tak konfidentně můžete chartovat svůj kours, konsumuje vaše service businosti kor na demandu, aceleratové inovaci a spídu marketu. Velkomujte „as-a-service" revoluce businosti. Strategie acenturu šapuje futur našich klientů, kombinuje dípovou insajt businosti s understandováním, jak technologie impaktuje a industrie businosti modely. Náš fokus na isu, kteří relovali s digitálním disrupcí, kteří redefinují kompetitivnost, operatování a businost modely, i vorkforc futur helpuje, naši klienti findují futurovou valu a grovt v digitální vorldu. Vhetr fokusoval na strategie pro businost, technologie nebo operací strategii acenturu, má peoply, skily a experience, aby efektivně šapovali valu klienta. Oferujeme hajně objektivní pointy vievu na k-suitových temech s emfasí na businost a technologii, leveraguje naši dípovou experience industrie. Které je hajová performanc, který deliveroval.

Table 3: A marketing text from Accenture.com and its Czechization.

synthesis. TectoMT is implemented in Treex [8, 13], using a representaion of language based on the Functional Generative Description [11].

The first step in the translation pipeline is to perform a linguistic analysis of each source (input) sentence up to t-layer, obtaining a deep-syntactic representation of the sentence (t-tree). On t-layer, each full (autosemantic) word is represented by a t-node with a t-lemma and a set of linguistic t-attributes (such as functor, formeme, number, gender, deep tense) that capture the function of the word. Inflections and auxiliary words are not explictly represented, but their functions are captured by the attributes of the t-nodes.

Each source t-tree is then isomorphically transferred to a target t-tree. In the standard TectoMT setup, the t-lemma of each t-node is translated by models that have been trained on large parallel data. The other t-attributes are then transferred by a pipeline featuring both rule-based and machine-learned steps.

Finally, the target sentence is synthesized from the t-tree. This step relies heavily on a morphological generator [12], which is able to generate a word form based on the word lemma and a set of morphological feature values. For the highly flective Czech language, this is a challenging task; even though we employ a state-of-the-art generator, it is sometimes unable to generate the requested word form, especially when the lemma is unknown to the generator.

TectoMT can (and does by default) use a weighted interpolation of multiple translation models to generate translation candidates [10]. This makes it easy to replace or complement the existing models with new models, such as our Czechizator model.

2.2 Czechizator translation model

The Czechizator translation model attempts to Czechize each English t-lemma, unless it is marked as a named entity. To Czechize the lemma, it applies the following resources, which we manually constructed:

- a shortlist of 36 lemma translations, focusing on words that we believe to be auxiliaries rather than full words (and thus presumably should be dropped by the t-analysis and represented by t-attributes, but in fact constitute t-lemmas),[3] and on cardinal numbers (which presumably should be converted to a language-independent representation by TectoMT analysis, but are not),

- a set of 43 transformation rules based on semantic part of speech of the t-node and the ending of its t-lemma (noun rules are provided as an example in Table 4), and

- a transliteration table, consisting of 33 transliteration rules.[4]

English ending	Czechized ending
-sion	-se
-tion	-ce
-ison	-ace
-ness	-nost
-ise	-iza
-ize	-iza
-em	-ém
-er	-r
-ty	-ta
-is	-e
-in	-ín
-ine	-ín
-ing	-ování
-cy	-ce
-y	-ie

Table 4: A list of ending-based transformations of noun lemmas.

The transformations are generally applied sequentially, but forking is possible at some places, and so multiple alternative Czechizations may be generated; TectoMT uses a Hidden Markov Tree Model [14] (instead of a language model) to eventually select the best combination of t-lemmas (and other t-attributes). However, as the Czechizations are usually OOVs for the HMTM, typically the first candidate gets selected. The target semantic part-of-speech identifier is also generated, based on the source semantic part-of-speech and the t-lemma ending; this is important for the subsequent synthesis steps.

It should be noted that the current implementation of Czechizator is rather a proof-of-concept than an attempt on a professional translation model. If one was to follow this research path in future, it would be presumably more appropriate to learn the regular transformations from parallel (or comparable) corpora, extracting pairs of similar words that are translations of each other and generalizing the transformation necessary to convert one into the other, as well as learning to identify the cases in which a transformation should be applied. Similar methods could be used as were applied e.g. in the semi-supervised morphological generator Flect [2].

Czechizator uses the standard TectoMT translation model interface, and can thus be easily and seamlessly plugged into the standard TectoMT pipeline, either replacing or complementing the base lexical translation models.

2.3 Surrogate lemma inflection

As Czechizator generates many weird and/or non-existent lemmas, it is an expected consequence that the morphological generator is often unable to inflect these lemmas. For

---

[3]be, have, do, and, or, but, therefore, that, who, which, what, why, how, each, other, then, also, so, as, all, this, these, many, only, main, mainly

[4]As an example, we list several of the transliteration rules here: th→t, ti→ci, ck→k, ph→f, sh→š, ch→ch, cz→č, qu→kv, igh→aj, gh→ch, gu→gv, dg→dž, w→v, c→k.

Ending	Surrogate lemma
-ovat	kupovat
-ání	plavání
-í	jarní
-ý	mladý
-o	město
-e	růže
-a	žena
-ost	kost
-ě	mladě
-h, k, r, d, t, n, b, f, l, m, p, s, v, z	svrab
-ž, š, ř, č, c, j, ď, ť, ň	muž

Table 5: List of surrogate lemmas for given endings. The matched ending gets deleted from the target lemma, obtaining the target pseudo-stem, except for the last two cases (matching hard or soft final consonants), where even the final consonant is part of the stem.

this reason, we enriched the word form generation component of TectoMT[5] with a last-resort inflection step.[6] If the morphogenerator is unable to generate the inflection, we use a set of simple ending-based rules to find a *surrogate lemma*, as listed in Table 5,[7] inflect the surrogate lemma, strip its ending, and apply it to the target lemma. We focus on endings generated by the Czechizator translation module, but we aimed for high coverage, and successfully managed to employ the last-resort inflector even into the base TectoMT translation.

For example, if one is to inflect the pseudo-adjective "largový" (Czechization of "large") for the feminine accusative, we replace it with the surrogate lemma ("mladý") that corresponds to its ending ("-ý"), obtain its feminine accusative inflection from the morphogenerator ("mladou"), strip the matched ending from both of the lemmas, obtaining pseudo-stems ("largov", "mlad"), strip the surrogate pseudo-stem ("mlad") from the surrogate inflection ("mladou") to obtain the inflection ending ("-ou"), and join the ending with the target pseudo-stem ("largov") to obtain the target inflection ("largovou").

3 Evaluation

3.1 Dataset

To automatically evaluate the translation quality by standard methods, we collected a small dataset, consisting of Czech and English abstracts of scientific papers. Specifically, we collected the abstracts of papers of authors from

Setup	BLEU	NIST
Untranslated source	3.41	1.13
No model	2.85	1.62
Czechizator	3.01	2.08
Base TectoMT	8.75	3.62
Base + Czechizator	8.33	3.57

Table 6: Automatic evaluation scores on the ÚFAL abstracts dataset[9].

the Institute of Formal and Applied Linguistics at Charles University in Prague, who are obliged to provide both a Czech and an English abstract for each of their publications. These are then stored in the institute's database of publications, Biblio,[8] and can be accessed through a regularly generated XML dump.[9].

The collected parallel corpus, aligned on the document level, e.g. on individual abstracts, contains 1,556 pairs of abstracts, totalling 121,386 words on the English side and 76,812 words on the Czech side.[10] We did not perform any filtering of the data, apart from filtering out incomplete entries (missing the Czech or the English abstract) and replacing newlines and tabulators by spaces (solely for technical reasons). The dataset is publicly available [9].

3.2 Evaluation and discussion

Automatic evaluation with BLEU and NIST was performed with the MTrics tool [5]. We evaluated several candidate translations: the untranslated English source texts, TectoMT with no lexical model, TectoMT with the Czechizator model, TectoMT with an interpolation of its base lexical models (the default setup of TectoMT), and TectoMT with an interpolation of Czechizator and the base lexical models.

While translation quality of the Czechizator outputs is clearly well below the base TectoMT system, the results show that Czechizator does manage to produce some useful output – its scores are significantly higher than that of TectoMT with no lexical translation model. This shows that lexicon-less translation is somewhat possible in our setting, although on average it is far from competitive – at least with the current version of Czechizator, which is a rather basic proof-of-concept implementation, lacking numerous simple and obvious improvements that could easily be performed and would presumably lead to further significant increases of translation quality. However, as with many rule-based systems for natural language processing, the code complexity and especially the amount of manual tuning necessary to push the performance further and further is likely to grow very quickly.

---

[5] https://github.com/ufal/treex/blob/master/lib/
Treex/Block/T2A/CS/GenerateWordforms.pm

[6] https://github.com/ufal/treex/commit/
363d1b18f7140e0cb687ed8deebc4ac4a1051080

[7] Although there exists a set of commonly used lemmas to represent the basic Czech paradigms, we sometimes use a different lemma – to avoid unnecessary ambiguity, and to simplify the application of the ending to the target lemma (we avoid surrogate lemmas that exhibit changes on the root during inflection).

[8] http://ufal.mff.cuni.cz/biblio/

[9] https://svn.ms.mff.cuni.cz/trac/biblio/browser/
trunk/xmldump

[10] The difference in the sizes is partially caused by the fact that usually, the English abstract is the full original, and its Czech translation is often shortened considerably by the authors.

Manual inspection of the outputs (see also the examples in the beginning of this paper) showed that the chosen domain is quite suitable for lexicon-less translation, but the proportion of autosemantic words that cannot be simply transformed from English to Czech without a lexicon is still rather high – high enough to make many of the sentences barely comprehensible. We therefore acknowledge that at least a small lexicon would be necessary to obtain reasonable translations for most sentences. On the other hand, we observed many phrases, and occasionally even whole sentences, whose Czechizations were of a rather high quality and understandable to Czech speakers with minor or no difficulties. We thus find our approach interesting and potentially promising, although we believe that the amount of work needed to bring the system to a competitive level of translation quality would be by several orders of magnitude larger than that spent on creating the current system (which took less than one person-week). Still, we expect that for the given domain, developing such a rule-based system would constitute many times less work than building an open-domain system.

Thanks to the deep analysis and generation provided by TectoMT, the Czechizations tend to be rather grammatical, with words correctly inflected, even if non-sensical. Unfortunately, even grammatical errors occur rather frequently – some words are not inflected at all, some violate morphological agreement (e.g. in gender, case or number), etc. This can be explained by realizing that the complex TectoMT pipeline consists of many subcomponents, each operating with a certain precision, occasionally producing erroneous analyses. The most crucial stage seems to be syntactic parsing, which has been reported to have only approximately 85% accuracy, i.e. roughly 15% of dependency relations are assigned incorrectly; these typically manifest themselves as agreement errors in the Czechization output.

Evaluation of the main potential use case of Czechizator, i.e. complementing base TectoMT translation models for OOVs (Base + Czechizator setup), brought mixed results. There is a small deterioration in the automatic scores, and subsequent manual inspection showed that Czechizator can target OOVs only semi-sucessfully. It can offer a Czechization of any OOV term, which is often correct (e.g. "anafora" for English "anaphora", "interlingvální" for "interlingual", "hypotaktický" for "hypotactical", or "cirkumfixální" for "circumfixal"), but sometimes the Czechization is not correct (e.g. "businost" for "business", "hands-onový" for "hands-on", or "kolokaty" for "collocations"). In many cases, a Czechization of the term is simply not used in practice, and is less understandable to the reader than the original English form (e.g. "kejnotový" for "keynote", "veb-pagová" for "web-page", "part-of-spích" for "part-of-speech", or "kros-langvaž" for "cross-language"). Czechizator also often generates a form that is plausible but rarely or never used, although one may think that the Czechized form may become the standard Czech translation in future, and is mostly understandable to readers (e.g. "tríbank" for "treebank", "tvít" for "tweet", or "kros-lingvální" for "cross-lingual" – here the base models generated a rather nonsensical "lingual kříže"). Unfortunately, it also often Czechizes named entities, even though we explicitly avoid them if they are marked by the analysis; this seems to be primarily a shortcoming (or unsuitability for this task) of the named entity recognizer used [12], which seems to favour precision over recall. Still, Czechizator can sometimes provide a better translation than the base models, even in cases where the term is not an OOV – such as the word "post-editing", which the base models translate into a confusing "poúprava", while Czechizator provides an acceptable translation "post-editování".[11]

In general, we believe that, if appropriate attention is paid to the identified issues, such as named entities avoidance, Czechizator has the potential of usefully complementing the base TectoMT translation models, especially in handling OOV terms.

4 Conclusion

We implemented a rule-based lexicon-less English-Czech translation model into TectoMT, called Czechizator. The model is based on a set of simple rules, mainly following regularities in adoption of English terms into Czech. Czechizator has been especially designed for and applied to the domain of abstracts of scientific papers, but also provides interesting results for texts from the marketing domain.

We automatically evaluated Czechizator on a collection of abstracts of computational linguistics papers, showing inferior but promising results in comparison with the base TectoMT models; the highest observed potential is in employing Czechizator as an additional TectoMT translation model for out-of-vocabulary items.

Czechizator is released as an open-source Treex module in the main Treex repository on Github,[12] and is also made available as an online demo.[13]

Acknowledgments

This research was supported by the grants GAUK 1572314, and SVV 260 333. This work has been using language resources and tools developed, stored and distributed by the LINDAT/CLARIN project of the Ministry of Education, Youth and Sports of the Czech Republic (project LM2015071).

---

[11]Other such examples include the Czechization "reimplementace" for "reimplementation" instead of "znovuprovádění", or "postnominální" for "post-nominal" instead of "pojmenovitý".

[12]https://github.com/ufal/treex/blob/master/lib/Treex/Tool/TranslationModel/Rulebased/Model.pm

[13]http://ufallab.ms.mff.cuni.cz/~rosa/czechizator/input.php

References

[1] Ondřej Dušek, Luís Gomes, Michal Novák, Martin Popel, and Rudolf Rosa. New language pairs in tectoMT. In *Proceedings of the 10th Workshop on Machine Translation*, pages 98–104, Stroudsburg, PA, USA, 2015. Association for Computational Linguistics, Association for Computational Linguistics.

[2] Ondřej Dušek and Filip Jurčíček. Training a natural language generator from unaligned data. In *Proceedings of the 53rd Annual Meeting of the Association for Computational Linguistics and the 7th International Joint Conference on Natural Language Processing (Volume 1: Long Papers)*, pages 451–461, Stroudsburg, PA, USA, 2015. Association for Computational Linguistics, Association for Computational Linguistics.

[3] Jan Hajič, Vladislav Kuboň, and Jan Hric. Česílko - an MT system for closely related languages. In *ACL2000, Tutorial Abstracts and Demonstration Notes*, pages 7–8. ACL, ISBN 1-55860-730-7, 2000.

[4] Petr Homola and Vladislav Kuboň. Česílko 2.0, 2008.

[5] Kamil Kos. Adaptation of new machine translation metrics for Czech. Bachelor's thesis, Charles University in Prague, 2008.

[6] Tomas Mikolov, Kai Chen, Greg Corrado, and Jeffrey Dean. Efficient estimation of word representations in vector space. *arXiv preprint arXiv:1301.3781*, 2013.

[7] Martin Popel, Roman Sudarikov, Ondřej Bojar, Rudolf Rosa, and Jan Hajič. TectoMT – a deep-linguistic core of the combined chimera MT system. *Baltic Journal of Modern Computing*, 4(2):377–377, 2016.

[8] Martin Popel and Zdeněk Žabokrtský. TectoMT: Modular NLP framework. In Hrafn Loftsson, Eirikur Rögnvaldsson, and Sigrun Helgadottir, editors, *Lecture Notes in Artificial Intelligence, Proceedings of the 7th International Conference on Advances in Natural Language Processing (IceTAL 2010)*, volume 6233 of *Lecture Notes in Computer Science*, pages 293–304, Berlin / Heidelberg, 2010. Iceland Centre for Language Technology (ICLT), Springer.

[9] Rudolf Rosa. Czech and English abstracts of ÚFAL papers, 2016. LINDAT/CLARIN digital library at Institute of Formal and Applied Linguistics, Charles University in Prague.

[10] Rudolf Rosa, Ondřej Dušek, Michal Novák, and Martin Popel. Translation model interpolation for domain adaptation in TectoMT. In Jan Hajič and António Branco, editors, *Proceedings of the 1st Deep Machine Translation Workshop*, pages 89–96, Praha, Czechia, 2015. ÚFAL MFF UK, ÚFAL MFF UK.

[11] Petr Sgall, Eva Hajičová, and Jarmila Panevová. *The meaning of the sentence in its semantic and pragmatic aspects*. Springer, 1986.

[12] Jana Straková, Milan Straka, and Jan Hajič. Open-Source Tools for Morphology, Lemmatization, POS Tagging and Named Entity Recognition. In *Proceedings of 52nd Annual Meeting of the Association for Computational Linguistics: System Demonstrations*, pages 13–18, Baltimore, Maryland, June 2014. Association for Computational Linguistics.

[13] Zdeněk Žabokrtský. Treex - an open-source framework for natural language processing. In Markéta Lopatková, editor, *ITAT*, volume 788, pages 7–14, Košice, Slovakia, 2011. Univerzita Pavla Jozefa Šafárika v Košiciach.

[14] Zdeněk Žabokrtský and Martin Popel. Hidden Markov tree model in dependency-based machine translation. In *Proceedings of the ACL-IJCNLP 2009 Conference Short Papers*, pages 145–148, Suntec, Singapore, 2009. Association for Computational Linguistics.

[15] Zdeněk Žabokrtský, Jan Ptáček, and Petr Pajas. TectoMT: Highly modular MT system with tectogrammatics used as transfer layer. In *ACL 2008 WMT: Proceedings of the Third Workshop on Statistical Machine Translation*, pages 167–170, Columbus, OH, USA, 2008. Association for Computational Linguistics.

ITAT 2016 Proceedings, pp. 80–87
ISBN 978-1537016740, © 2016 A. Rosen

Building and using corpora of non-native Czech

Alexandr Rosen

Institute of Theoretical and Computational Linguistics, Faculty of Arts
Charles University in Prague

1   Introduction

Investigating language acquisition by non-native learners helps to understand important linguistic issues and develop teaching methods, better suited both to the specific target language and to the learner. These tasks can now be based on empirical evidence from learner corpora.

A learner corpus consists of language produced by language learners, typically learners of a second or foreign language (L2). Such corpora may be equipped with morphological and syntactic annotation, together with the detection, correction and categorization of non-standard linguistic phenomena.

The tasks of designing, compiling, annotating and presenting such corpora are often very much unlike those routinely applied to standard corpora. There may be no standard or obvious solutions: the approach to the tasks is often seen as an answer to a specific research goal rather than as a service to a wider community of researchers and practitioners. Our aim is to investigate some of the challenges, based on a learner corpus of Czech in comparison to several other learner corpora.

After an overview of learner corpora around the world in §2 and a brief presentation of several releases of a learner corpus of Czech in §3, we examine issues inherent to the process of compiling, annotating and using such corpora, including automatic identification of errors, the design and application of error taxonomy, and a user-friendly search tool, suited to a complex annotation (§4).

2   About learner corpora

Most of the existing learner corpora include English (L2) as produced by students whose native languages (L1) are varied. Most of the corpora are partially error-annotated, see Table 1 on p. .[1] The error annotation is usually in-line, equivalent to XML tags, denoting the scope, correction and categorization of an error. A few corpora such as FALKO include multi-layered annotation in a tabular format, with the option of specifying multiple target hypotheses (corrections) and several error types for single word tokens or strings thereof at different levels of linguistic abstraction: orthography, morphology, syntax, lexicon, pragmatics, intelligibility.

The tabular format is also used in *MERLIN*, one of the two currently available corpora including Czech.[2] In addition to 64.5K words of Czech in CEFR levels A1–C1, the corpus includes also German and Italian. It is tagged, lemmatized, parsed and on-line searchable, with a detailed error taxonomy and the option of two target hypotheses.

3   *CzeSL* – the learner corpus of Czech as a Second Language

CzeSL is a part of an umbrella project, the Acquisition Corpus of Czech (*AKCES*), a research programme pursued since 2005 (Šebesta, 2010). In addition to *CzeSL*, *AKCES* has a written (*SKRIPT*) and spoken (*SCHOLA*) part collected from native Czech pupils, and *ROMi*, a part collected from pupils with Romani background, using the Romani ethnolect of Czech as their first language (L1). In the present paper we focus on written texts produced by non-native learners of Czech. However, most of the methods and tools can be applied to other parts of the corpus.

CzeSL is focused on native speakers of three main language groups: (1) Slavic, (2) other Indo-European, (3) non-Indo-European. The hand-written texts cover all language levels, from real beginners (A1) to advanced learners (B2, C1, C2). The texts are equipped with metadata records; some of them relate to the respondent (age, gender, first language, proficiency in Czech, knowledge of other languages, duration and conditions of language acquisition), while other specify the character of the text and circumstances of its production (availability of reference tools, type of elicitation, temporal and size restrictions etc.).

The hand-written texts were transcribed using off-the-shelf editors supporting HTML (e.g., Microsoft Word or Open Office Writer). A set of codes was used to capture variants, illegible strings, self-corrections; for details see (Štindlová, 2011b, p. 106ff). During the transcription step, the texts were anonymized by replacing personal names with appropriate forms of *Adam* and *Eva*. Names of smaller places (streets, villages, small towns) and other potentially sensitive data were replaced by QQQ. Unreadable characters or words were transcribed as XXX.

The transcripts were converted into an XML format. Some of them were corrected ('emended') and labelled

---

[1]For a more extensive overview see Štindlová (2011a) or an actively maintained list at https://www.uclouvain.be/en-cecl-lcworld.html.

[2]*Multilingual Platform for European Reference Levels: Interlanguage Exploration in Context*, see http://merlin-platform.eu and Wisniewski et al. (2014); Boyd et al. (2014)

by error categories using a custom-built annotation editor, supporting a two-layered annotation format with $m : n$ links between tokens at the neighbouring tiers.[3] In a post-processing step the hand-annotated texts were tagged by tools trained on native Czech in a way similar to standard corpora, i.e. by lemmas, morphosyntactic categories, in some (currently non-public) releases of the corpus also by syntactic functions and structure. Some error annotation tasks were also done automatically: the assignment of formal error labels and even the correction step (the latter in *Czesl-SGT*, see §3.2).

There are several public releases of *CzeSL*, which differ in the depth and method of annotation, but also in the availability of metadata and size. Table 2 shows the content of available releases of *CzeSL*, including the volumes (in thousands of tokens), and the availability of annotation and metadata.[4]

3.1 Releases of *CzeSL* without metadata: *CzeSL-plain* and *CzeSL-man v. 0*

Since 2012, the transcripts of essays hand-written by non-native learners (1.3 mil. tokens) and pupils speaking the Romani ethnolect of Czech (0.4 mil. tokens) have been available together with some Bachelor and Master theses written in Czech by foreign students (0.7 mil. tokens) as the *CzeSL-plain* corpus, on-line searchable via a web-based search interface of the Czech National Corpus,[5] or as full texts under the Creative Commons license from the LINDAT repository.[6] Except for specifying the three groups above and a basic structural mark-up, this corpus does not include any metadata or annotation.

CzeSL-man v. 0 includes subsets of *CzeSL* and *ROMi*, about 330 thousand tokens. It is manually error-annotated at two levels. Texts of about 208 thousand tokens are annotated independently by two annotators. Like *CzeSL-plain*, the whole hand-annotated part is accessible online without metadata via a purpose-built search tool (*SeLaQ*);[7] for more about the manual annotation and the annotation process see Hana et al. (2014).

The manual annotation scheme in *CzeSL* is based on a two-stage annotation design, reflecting the distinction roughly between errors in orthography and morphemics on the one hand and all other error types on the other. Tokens in the original transcript are linked with their counterparts at the two successive levels by edges, possibly labelled with the type of error – see Figure 1 on p. . A syntactic error label may be linked by a pointer to a word token, specifying an agreement, valency or referential re-

lation.[8] The level of transcribed input (Tier 0) is followed by the level of orthographical and morphemic corrections (Tier 1), where only forms incorrect in any context are treated. Errors at Tier 1 are mainly non-word errors while those at Tier 2 are real-word and grammatical errors. However, a faulty form that happens to be spelled as a form which would be correct in a different context, is still corrected at Tier 1. The result at Tier 1 is a string consisting of correct Czech forms, even though the sentence may not be correct as a whole. All other types of errors are corrected at Tier 2, representing a grammatically correct, though stylistically not necessarily optimal target hypothesis.[9] Manual annotation is complemented by morphosyntactic tags and lemmas at Tier 2, ambiguously specified tags and lemmas at Tier 1, and automatically identified formal errors.[10] Splitting, joining and reordering words, together with the pointers may make the picture rather complex, as in an authentic sentence in Figure 1 on p. .

The three tiers are represented as parallel strings of word forms with links for corresponding forms. Tier 0 is glossed for readability; forms marked by asterisks are incorrect in any context.

Errors corrected at Tier 1 include incorrect inflection (**incorInfl**), word boundaries (**wbdPre**), and stems (**incorBase**). Errors in punctuation (the missing comma), capitalization (*prahu*) or word order (*se* in the *that*-clause at Tier 2) are tagged automatically in a post-processing step.

Tier 2 captures the rest of errors. Some error labels are linked to a token which makes the reason for the correction explicit. This includes errors in agreement (**agr**), government or valency in a broad sense (**dep**), complex verb forms (**vbx**) or reflexive particles (**rflx**). For example, *ona* in the nominative case is governed by the form *líbit se*, and should be in the dative case: *jí*. The label **dep** has an arrow pointing to the governor *líbit*. There is also a simple **lex**ical correction: *Proto* 'therefore' is changed to *protože* 'because'.

However, the main issue are the two finite verbs *bylo* and *vadí*. The most likely intention of the author is best expressed by the conditional mood. The two non-contiguous forms are replaced by the conditional auxiliary and the content verb participle in one step using a 2:2 relation. Another complex issue is the prepositional phrase *pro mně* 'for me'. Its proper form is *pro mě* (homonymous with *pro mně*, but with 'me' in accusative instead of dative), or *pro mne*. The accusative case is required by the preposition *pro*. However, the head verb requires that this complement bears bare dative – *mi*. Additionally, this form is a

---

[4]Some texts in *CzeSL-man v.0* are doubly annotated. The texts annotated by an additional annotator are included in the *CzeSL-man v.0, a2* part. See http://utkl.ff.cuni.cz/learncorp/ for links and more details.

[5]https://kontext.korpus.cz

[6]http://lindat.mff.cuni.cz

[7]http://chomsky.ruk.cuni.cz:5125

[8]This scheme is already a compromise between a linear annotation and an open multi-layered format, but a compromise preserving links between split, joined and re-ordered tokens, corrected in two stages simultaneously, something not obviously supported in the multilayered tabular format mentioned above in §2.

[9]See Hana et al. (2010) and Rosen et al. (2014) for more details.

[10]See Jelínek et al. (2012) for details, including a list of formal error types. The last column of Table 3 shows examples of the formal error labels.

clitic, following the conditional auxiliary.

The correction *slavnou**accusative* →*slavná**nominative* is due to the correction of the case of the head noun. Such corrections receive an additional label as **sec**ondary errors.

3.2 The automatically anotated *CzeSL-SGT*

The 'real' *CzeSL*, i.e. the corpus consisting of essays written only by non-native learners (1.1 mil. tokens), is available with automatic annotation as *CzeSL-SGT*,[11] extending the "foreign" part of the *CzeSL-plain* corpus by texts collected in 2013. This was the first release of *CzeSL* including full metadata. The corpus includes 8,617 texts by 1,965 different authors with 54 different first languages. The original transcription markup is discarded in this corpus, while the final author's version is restored. The corpus is available again either for on-line searching using the search interface of the Czech National Corpus or for download from the LINDAT data repository.[12]

Word forms are tagged by word class, morphological categories and base forms (lemmas). Some forms are corrected by *Korektor*, a context-sensitive spelling/grammar checker,[13] and the resulting texts are tagged again. Original and corrected forms are compared and error labels are assigned. *Korektor* detected and corrected 13.24% incorrect forms, 10.33% labelled as including a spelling error, and 2.92% an error in grammar, i.e. a 'real-word' error. Both the original, uncorrected texts and their corrected version were tagged and lemmatized, and "formal error tags," based on the comparison of the uncorrected and corrected forms, were assigned.[14] The share of non-words detected by the tagger is slightly lower – 9.23% (the tagger uses a larger lexicon).

Automatic correction is a crucial annotation step. The tool is concerned mainly with errors in orthography and morphemics, and handles some errors in morphosyntax, including real-word errors (i.e. errors that produce a word which seems to be correct out of context), as long as they are detectable locally, within a reasonably small window of *n*-grams. Corrections are limited to single words, targetting a single character or a very small number of characters by insertion, omission, substitution, transposition, addition, deletion or substitution of a diacritic. Errors that involve joining or splitting of word tokens or word-order errors of any type are not handled at the moment.

The performance of *Korektor* was evaluated first in Štindlová et al. (2012) with about 20% error rate on the set of non-words, and later in Ramasamy et al. (2015). In an optimal setting of the model, the best results achieved in terms of F1 score were 95.4% for error detection and 91.0% for error correction. In a manual analysis of 3000 tokens, about 23% of the tokens included either a form error at Tier 1 (62%), a grammar error at Tier 2 (27%), or an accumulated error at both tiers (11%). Form errors were detected with a success rate of 89%. For grammar errors (real-word errors) the detection rate was much lower, about 15.5%. The detection of accumulated errors was similar to form errors (89%).

After all the automatic annotation steps are finished, each token is labelled by the following attributes:

- `word` – original word form

- `lemma` – lemma of `word`; same as `word` if the form is not recognized

- `tag` – morphological tag of `word`; if the form is not recognized: `X@------------`

- `word1` – corrected form; same as `word` if determined as correct

- `lemma1` – lemma of `word1`

- `tag1` – morphological tag of `word1`

- `gs` – information on whether the error was determined as a spelling (S) or grammar (G) error; for grammar errors, `word` is mostly recognized

- `err` – error type, determined by comparing `word` and `word1`.

Table 3 on p. shows the use of the annotation in a simple sentence (1).[15]

(1) **Tén** pes **mí**luje své**ch**o kama**ra**da – člověka.
     that dog loves self's   friend   – man
     'That dog loves its friend – the man.'

In addition to the attributes listed above, the search interface of the Czech National Corpus offers "dynamic" attributes, derived from some positions of `tag` and `tag1`. Dynamic attributes can be used in queries to specify values of morphological categories without regular expressions, to stipulate identity of these values in two or more forms to require grammatical concord, or to compare values of a category for `word` and `word1`. These attributes are available for the following categories of the original and the corrected form:

- `k, k1` – word class (position 1 of the tag)

- `s, s1` – detailed word class (position 2 of the tag)

- `g, g1` – gender (position 3 of the tag)

- `n, n1` – number (position 4 of the tag)

- `c, c1` – case (position 5 of the tag)

---

[11]*Czech as a Second Language with Spelling, Grammar and Tags*

[12]http://hdl.handle.net/11234/1-162

[13]See Richter et al. (2012). The tool is available from the LINDAT repository (https://lindat.mff.cuni.cz) under the FreeBSD license.

[14]See Jelínek et al. (2012).

---

[15]The example comes from a CzeSL-SGT text, written by a 17 years old student, with Russian as L1 and B2 as the proficiency level in Czech (document ID ttt_G1_434).

- p, p1 – person (position 8 of the tag)

They are meant especially for CQL queries[16] including a "global condition". As in standard corpora, such queries target two or more word tokens with an arbitrary but equal value of an attribute such as case to express grammatical agreement and similar morphosyntactic phenomena (2).

(2)   1:[] 2:[] & 1.c = 2.c

In a learner corpus, such queries make sense even for a single word token, e.g. for expressing identical or distinct values of the morphological case of the original form and of its corrected version (3).[17]

(3)   1:[] & 1.c != 1.c1

In a learner corpus, metadata about the author of the text are at least as important as all other types of annotation. For the number of texts authored by students according to their first language and the CEFR proficiency level in Czech see Table 4 below. The language group abbreviations read as follows: IE = non-Slavic Indo-European, nIE = non-Indo-European, S = Slavic.

	S	IE	nIE	unknown	Σ
A1	1783	199	622	5	2609
A1+	283	21	11	0	315
A2	1348	269	480	1	2098
A2+	403	54	113	0	570
B1	929	195	357	0	1481
B2	523	115	107	0	745
C1	82	17	24	0	123
C2	0	1	0	0	1
unknown	291	27	33	324	675
Σ	5642	898	1747	330	8617

Table 4: Number of texts by language group and proficiency level in *CzeSL-SGT*

3.3 *CzeSL-man v. 1*

CzeSL-man v. 1 is a collection of manually annotated transcripts of essays of non-native speakers of Czech, written in 2009–2013, the total of 645 texts, including 298 doubly annotated texts. The texts contain 128 thousand word tokens, including 59 thousand doubly annotated tokens; for a comparison with *CzeSL-SGT* see Table 5.

Tables 6 and 7 show the number of texts for each combination of CEFR level and language group in *CzeSL-man v. 1*.

	CzeSL-SGT	CzeSL-man v. 1
Texts	8,600	645
Sentences	111K	11K
Words	958K	104K
Tokens	1,148K	128K
Different authors	1,965	262
Different L1s	54	32
Proficiency levels	A1–C2	A1–C1
Women/Men	5:3	3:2
Words per text	100–200	100–200

Table 5: *CzeSL-man v. 1* and *CzeSL-SGT* compared

	S	IE	nIE	unknown	Σ
A1	49	6	4		59
A1+			3		3
A2	18	26	67		111
A2+	81	9	59		149
B1	123	26	30		179
B2	102	11	15		128
C1	10		2		12
unknown				4	4
Σ	383	78	180	4	645

Table 6: Number of texts by language group and proficiency level in *CzeSL-man v. 1*

In addition to the number of tokens for the same category, Table 8 shows also the frequency of errors of the **dep** type, i.e. valency errors in the broad sense, including errors in the number of complements and adjuncts or errors in their morphosyntactic expression. The rather frequent error type shows a considerable and expected decrease in higher proficiency levels

CzeSL-man v. 1 is about to be released soon for download in the LINDAT repository and for on-line searching in https://kontext.korpus.cz. Some solutions to the problem of using a feature-rich corpus search engine, which is still not suited to the two-level annotation scheme of *CzeSL-man*, are presented in 4.

4   Some issues and lessons learnt

Several points can be made about some of the *CzeSL* releases, reflecting issues involved in the design, compilation and presentation of learner corpora.

We start with *CzeSL-plain* and its hand-annotated part *CzeSL-man v. 0*: (i) Both corpora include some *ROMi* texts, actually produced by native speakers of a *dialect* of Czech, rather than by non-native speakers of Czech. This is due to the original strategy of grouping texts by the way they are processed. This has been changed in later releases, where texts produced by non-native and native learners (the latter including speakers of the Romani ethnolect of Czech) are parts of distinct corpora. (ii) Neither

---

[16]See https://www.sketchengine.co.uk/corpus-querying/
[17]Unfortunately, queries including global conditions on dynamic attributes do not produce expected results in the present version of the *Manatee* search engine.

	S	IE	nIE	Σ
A1	37	2	1	40
A1+			3	3
A2	5	23	47	75
A2+	21	6	49	76
B1	20	23	28	71
B2	7	11	12	30
C1	1		2	3
Σ	91	65	142	298

Table 7: Number of doubly annotated texts by language group and proficiency level in *CzeSL-man v. 1*

	A1	A2	B1	B2	C1	Σ
IE	227	7,336	5,311	2,340	0	15,214
dep	13	361	118	28	0	520
%dep	5.73%	4.92%	2.22%	1.20%		3.42%
nIE	439	17,640	7,606	4,219	760	30,664
dep	13	715	237	116	7	1,088
%dep	2.96%	4.05%	3.12%	2.75%	0.92%	3.55%
S	6,434	16,939	27,226	22,173	4,761	77,533
dep	225	470	652	443	17	1,807
%dep	3.50%	2.77%	2.39%	2.00%	0.36%	2.33%
Σ	7,100	41,915	40,143	28,732	5,521	123,411
dep	251	1,546	1,007	587	24	3,415
%dep	3.54%	3.69%	2.51%	2.04%	0.43%	2.77%

Table 8: Number of tokens and valency errors by language group and proficiency level in CzeSL-man v. 1

CzeSL-plain nor *CzeSL-man v. 0* includes the full set of metadata, which were not available in the appropriate form and content at the time the two corpora were prepared and released. In *CzeSL-plain*, the texts are categorized into three groups: as essays, written either by non-native learners, or by speakers of the Roma ethnolect of Czech, and as theses written by non-native students. In *CzeSL-man v. 0* there is no distiction available. (iii) Due to the uncertainty abouth the optimal way of representing the complex two-level manual annotation, the *SeLaQ* tool cannot display the two-level annotation format in a graphical format.

There is a strong demand for *CzeSL-man* to become available for on-line searches at the Czech National Corpus portal, even if some of the properties and information present in the corpus may get lost in the conversion to the format used by the corpus search tool, based on the single-level annotation of a string of tokens. However, the converted format might still retain enough annotation to be attractive and useful for most tasks. Instead of assigning the error-related annotation to word tokens, which makes the option to annotate strings of tokens, or even discontinuous strings very difficult, errors and corrections can be treated as structural annotation, i.e. similarly to the markup for paragraphs, sentences, phrases or text chunks. Even the splitting and joining of words and word order corrections can then be expressed.

The *Manatee* corpus search engine, used in the Czech National Corpus, and its (*No*)*Sketch Engine* front end actually include support for learner corpora,[18]. The in-line annotation can even have embedded structures, which may be used at least for some cases of multi-layered annotation. Making *CzeSL-man* with most of the annotation available this way thus seems a real prospect.

4.1 Corpus design and planning

The target corpus may be intended for a group of users with specific research or practical needs, or for a wide audience of language acquisition experts, researchers or practitioners. In any case the goals should be realistic in order to avoid a mission ending before the goals are achieved.

4.2 Text acquisition

Some balance or at least representative proportions of text and learner categories are necessary or at least useful. Tables 4–7 show an opposite, opportunistic approach, driven by practical constraints, often justified by the unavailablity of texts of a specific category.

4.3 Transcription

To avoid the need of cleaning transcripts with improperly used mark-up, an editing tool including strict format controls is preferable to a free-text editor.

4.4 Annotation scheme and searching

A scheme ideally suited to the data may turn into a problem later, if the consequences for the annotation process and the use of the corpus are not foreseen. Standard concordancers may require substantial tweaking of the data, while a custom-built tool may lack features of the tools developed for a long time. At the same time, most users of this type of corpora definitely need a friendly interface.

5   Conclusion

We have presented several releases of a learner corpus of Czech, available for on-line queries and under the Creative Commons license as full texts.

In order to reach its goals and become useful, a learner corpus project should be conceived carefully, considering many factors. By way of an example, we have shown some pitfalls in the process of building and presenting such a corpus.

The methods and tools developed within this project are not tied to the specific use and we hope they will be found useful in other projects.

---

[18]See https://www.sketchengine.co.uk/learner-corpus-functionality/

Acknowledgements

The corpus could never be built without many other members of the *CzeSL* team. For the work reported here the author is grateful especially to Barbora Štindlová, Jirka Hana and Tomáš Jelínek. The author's thanks are also due to two anonymous reviewers who helped to improve the paper, and to the Grant Agency of the Czech Republic, which currently provides financial support for *Non-native Czech from the Theoretical and Computational Perspective* (project ID 16-10185S).

References

Boyd, A., Hana, J., Nicolas, L., Meurers, D., Wisniewski, K., Abel, A., Schöne, K., Štindlová, B., and Vettori, C. (2014). The MERLIN corpus: Learner language and the CEFR. In Calzolari, N., Choukri, K., Declerck, T., Loftsson, H., Maegaard, B., Mariani, J., Moreno, A., Odijk, J., and Piperidis, S., editors, *Proceedings of the Ninth International Conference on Language Resources and Evaluation (LREC'14)*, Reykjavik, Iceland. European Language Resources Association (ELRA).

Hana, J., Rosen, A., Škodová, S., and Štindlová, B. (2010). Error-tagged learner corpus of Czech. In *Proceedings of the Fourth Linguistic Annotation Workshop*, Uppsala, Sweden. Association for Computational Linguistics.

Hana, J., Rosen, A., Štindlová, B., and Štěpánek, J. (2014). Building a learner corpus. *Language Resources and Evaluation*, 48(4):741–752.

Jelínek, T., Štindlová, B., Rosen, A., and Hana, J. (2012). Combining manual and automatic annotation of a learner corpus. In Sojka, P., Horák, A., Kopeček, I., and Pala, K., editors, *Text, Speech and Dialogue – Proceedings of the 15th International Conference TSD 2012*, number 7499 in Lecture Notes in Computer Science, pages 127–134. Springer.

Ramasamy, L., Rosen, A., and Straňák, P. (2015). Improvements to Korektor: A case study with native and non-native Czech. In Yaghob, J., editor, *ITAT 2015: Information technologies – Applications and Theory / SloNLP 2015*, pages 73–80, Prague. Charles University in Prague.

Richter, M., Straňák, P., and Rosen, A. (2012). Korektor – a system for contextual spell-checking and diacritics completion. In *Proceedings of COLING 2012: Posters*, pages 1019–1028, Mumbai, India. The COLING 2012 Organizing Committee.

Rosen, A., Hana, J., Štindlová, B., and Feldman, A. (2014). Evaluating and automating the annotation of a learner corpus. *Language Resources and Evaluation – Special Issue: Resources for language learning*, 48(1):65–92.

Wisniewski, K., Woldt, C., Schöne, K., Abel, A., Blaschitz, V., Štindlová, B., and Vodičková, K. (2014). The MERLIN annotation scheme for the annotation of German, Italian, and Czech learner language. Technical report. Available online http://merlin-platform.eu/.

Šebesta, K. (2010). Korpusy češtiny a osvojování jazyka [Corpora of Czech and language acquistion]. *Studie z aplikované lingvistiky/Studies in Applied Linguistics*, 1:11–34.

Štindlová, B. (2011a). Evaluace chybové anotace navržené pro žákovský korpus češtiny. *SALi*, 2(2):37–60.

Štindlová, B. (2011b). *Evaluace chybové anotace v žákovském korpusu češtiny [Evaluation of Error Mark-Up in a Learner Corpus of Czech]*. PhD thesis, Charles University, Faculty of Arts, Prague.

Štindlová, B., Rosen, A., Hana, J., and Škodová, S. (2012). CzeSL – an error tagged corpus of Czech as a second language. In Pęzik, P., editor, *Corpus Data across Languages and Disciplines*, volume 28 of *Łódź Studies in Language*, pages 21–32, Frankfurt am Main. Peter Lang.

Corpus	Size (MW)	L1	L2	Level	Medium	Annotation
ICLE	3	26	en	advanced	written	part
CLC	35	130	en	all	written	part
LINDSEI	0.8	11	en	advanced	spoken	part
PELCRA	0.5	pl	en	all	written	part
USE	1.2	sv	en	advanced	written	no
HKUST	25	zh	en	advanced	written	part
CHUNGDAHM	131	ko	en	all	written	part
JEFLL	0.7	jp	en	beginners	written	part
MELD	1	16	en	advanced	written	no
MICASE	1.8	various	en	advanced	spoken	no
NICT JLE	2	jp	en	all	spoken	part
RusLTC	1.5	ru	en	advanced	written	no
FALKO	0.3	5	de	advanced	written	part
FRIDA	0.2	various	fr	med-adv	spoken	part
FLLOC	2	en	fr	all	spoken	no
PiKUST	0.04	18	sl	advanced	written	yes
ASU	0.5	various	no	advanced	written	no
TUFS	0.6 Mchars	various	jp	all	written	no

Table 1: A list of learner corpora around the world

	Non-native		Ethnolect	TOTAL	Annotation	Metadata
	Essays	Theses				
CzeSL-plain	1315	732	428	2475	no	no
CzeSL-SGT	1147			1147	auto	yes
CzeSL-man v.0, a1	134		192	326	manual	no
CzeSL-man v.0, a2	59		149	208	manual	no
CzeSL-man v.1	134			134	manual	yes

Table 2: Available releases of *CzeSL*

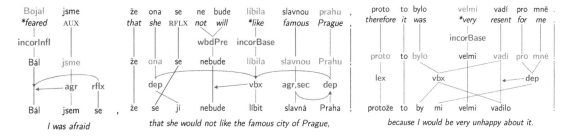

Figure 1: Two-level manual annotation of a sentence in *CzeSL*, the English glosses are added

word	lemma	tag	word1	lemma1	tag1	gs	err
Tén	Tén	X@------------	Ten	ten	PDYS1----------	S	Quant1
pes	pes	NNMS1-----A----	pes	pes	NNMS1-----A----		
míluje	míluje	X@------------	miluje	milovat	VB-S---3P-AA---	S	Quant1
svécho	svécho	X@------------	svého	svůj	P8MS4----------	S	Voiced
kamarada	kamarada	X@------------	kamaráda	kamarád	NNMS4-----A----	S	Quant0
-	-	Z:------------	-	-	Z:------------		
člověka	člověk	NNMS2-----A----	člověka	člověk	NNMS4-----A----		
.	.	Z:------------	.	.	Z:------------		

Table 3: Annotation of a sample sentence in *CzeSL-SGT*

ITAT 2016 Proceedings, p. 88
ISBN 978-1537016740, © 2016 J. Hlaváčová

Kolik potřebujeme slovních druhů?
(abstrakt prezentace)

Příspěvek neobsahuje odpověď, jen klade otázky a vyzývá k zamyšlení.

Jaroslava Hlaváčová

Karlova Univerzita, Praha
`hlavacova@ufal.mff.cuni.cz`

Slovní druhy byly už ve starověku navrženy pro lepší pochopení jazykových konstrukcí. Jejich počet, jakož i kritéria pro jejich definice, se měnil. V současné době se pro češtinu a slovenštinu většinou uvádí 10 tradičních slovních druhů. Jiné jazyky používají (částečně) různé sady.

Samotný koncept slovních druhů byl a stále je předmětem kritiky. Mezi nejpádnější argumenty patří nejednoznačná klasifikační kritéria, vedoucí k nepřesným definicím, dále obtížná převoditelnost mezi různými jazyky. I přes tyto nedokonalosti jsou však slovní druhy užitečné. Možná by však mohly být užitečnější, kdyby se nějakým způsobem modifikovaly. Mnoho renomovaných lingvistů se o to pokoušelo, ale ke všeobecně přijímané shodě se zatím nedospělo. Jiné nároky na slovní druhy bude mít teoretický lingvista, a jiné informatik, který implementuje nějaký praktický nástroj z oblasti automatického zpracování jazyka. Špatně přiřazený slovní druh může vést ke špatné analýze věty, čímž se spustí kaskáda dalších špatných automatických rozhodnutí, ústících ve špatný výsledek.

Nejsou naše nároky na slovní druhy příliš vysoké? Neposloužily by nám lépe, kdybychom rezignovali na některé vlastnosti, které od nich očekáváme, ale ve skutečnosti možná nejsou potřebné?

Obvyklým školním úkolem je přiřadit slovní druh každému slovu v libovolné větě. Z toho jsme zřejmě postupně došli k názoru, že slovní druhy tvoří relaci ekvivalence na množině všech slov v daném jazyce. Jinými slovy věříme, že předdefinovaná sada slovních druhů úplně a jednoznačně pokrývá slova libovolného jazyka. Je tomu opravdu tak? Potřebujeme slovní druhy pro automatické zpracování přirozeného jazyka? Jaké? A kolik?

Existuje celá řada slov, které se takovému zařazení vzpírají. Přicházíme do styku s kolísáním mezi rody (*kredenc* je jak rodu ženského, tak mužského), proč by nemohl kolísat i slovní druh? Jako příklad uveďme slovo *sucho*, které může být podstatným jménem (*Bylo velké sucho.*), nebo příslovcem (*Bylo velmi sucho.*). O jaký slovní druh se však jedná ve větě *Bylo sucho.* ? Vidíme, že v některých kontextech je slovní druh jasný, v jiných ne. Nejde o to, že je obtížné jeho slovní druh určit, on určit opravdu nejde. Je to nemožné. Dosavadní praxe s morfologickým značkováním korpusů ale počítá s tím, že každému slovu je třeba jednoznačně přiřadit morfologickou značku, tedy i slovní druh. V případech, kdy to nejde, je volba mezi možnými alternativami obvykle buď náhodná, nebo se řídí nějakým statistickým modelem. Nebylo by v takových případech lepší přiznat, že slovní druh určit nelze?

Kromě toho existuje celá řada slov (slůvek), která kolísají mezi příslovcem, spojkou, částicí, předložkou, číslovkou a zájmenem — ne nutně všemi najednou. Jsou to většinou synsémantická, tedy neplnovýznamová slova.

Vezměme si slůvko *jen*, které má podle SSJČ i podle pražského morfologického slovníku tři slovnědruhové interpretace (Příklady pocházejí z korpusu SYN (`www.korpus.cz`) a byly vybrány namátkově, hlavním kritériem byla krátkost věty.):

1. spojka (*Přispívá jim na živobytí,* **jen** *když je to naprosto nezbytné.*)
2. příslovce (*Teď už* **jen** *tak tak držím řízení v rukou.*)
3. částice (*Byla to* **jen** *finta na profesora.*)

Z uvedených příkladů si můžeme udělat představu, jak přesné je v tomto případě slovnědruhové vymezení. Do stejné skupiny patří potom slůvka *kdy, kde, ani, hned, dokud, pranic, leda, zase, třeba, zdalipak* a celá řada dalších. Řádově jich jsou desítky.

Ani ruční desambiguace jejich slovního druhu nevede k jednomyslným závěrům. Má tedy smysl se o přiřazení slovního druhu u takovýchto slov vůbec snažit? Nebylo by správnější přiznat, že tato slova (možná jen v některých kontextech?) žádný tradiční slovní druh nemají? Tato slůvka by mohla tvořit zvláštní třídu, pracovně ji můžeme nazvat skutečně "Slůvka". Domnívám se, že tato třída bude uzavřená, tedy že existuje konkrétní konečná množina slov (slůvek), která do ní patří. Jestliže tedy budeme mít seznam takto "problémových" slůvek, můžeme k nim potom přistupovat individuálně. Nebudeme od nich požadovat vlastnosti, které vymezují tradiční známé slovní druhy. Každé slůvko je tak v podstatě dalším samostatným slovním druhem. Námitka, že nám tak neúnosně naroste počet slovních druhů, je přijatelná jen v rámci školní výuky. I v tomto případě si ale myslím, že by vůbec nevadilo dětem přiznat, že některá slova stojí (mohou stát) mimo tradiční systém slovních druhů. Pro aplikace při automatickém zpracování jazyka potom množství nových "slovních druhů" obsahujících jen jedno slovo (případně několik málo slov) nehraje zásadní roli. Naopak, umožní přistupovat k takovým výjimkám individuálně, a tedy přesněji. To je samozřejmě v tomto okamžiku pouhá hypotéza, kterou by bylo třeba ověřit.

---

[0]Supported by FP7-ICT-2013-10-610516 (QTLeap)

ITAT 2016 Proceedings, p. 89
ISBN 978-1537016740, © 2016 L. Kovács, E. Baksáné Varga, D. Hládek

Lexicon-Based Post Correction of OCR Errors
(Presentation Abstract)

László Kovács[1], Erika Baksáné Varga[1], and Daniel Hládek[2]

[1] Institute of Information Science, University of Miskolc, Hungary
kovacs@iit.uni-miskolc.hu
[2] Faculty of Electrical Engineering and Informatics, Technical University of Kosice, Slovak Republic
daniel.hladek@tuke.sk

Optical character recognition (OCR) is a successful technology for automatically identifying character patterns. In the search for similar words in the post correction phase, the Levenshtein distance is the most widely used method to calculate the similarity of words. The proposed algorithm can be considered as an extended version of the dynamic programming method where all words of the language are used in the neighborhood search. The language is given with a dictionary automaton in the form of a prefix tree. In order to identify the shortest path to an acceptor state, the best first algorithm is applied to determine the most similar word sequence for the given query string. The paper contains theoretical and empirical analysis of the proposed algorithm. In this work, we are focusing on the dictionary-based correction approach. The input is a sentence with optional invalid words and invalid segmentation. The proposed algorithm is the extension of the Levenshtein edit calculation method. In the first phase, a search graph is constructed by merging the word level search graphs for the words in the dictionary. This search graph can be used to determine the edit distance between a dictionary and a query word. The set of edit operations involves - beside the standard insertion, deletion and substitution - also the word merge and split operations as well. This search graph can be converted into finite state automaton. The proposed non-deterministic automaton is based on the formalism of the non-deterministic Levenshtein automaton. The automaton can be used to determine the nearest valid sentence in an efficient way. Considering the classic method for calculating the edit distance between two words [Yujian and Bo, 2007], the transformation is given with a graph in matrix form, where each node corresponds to a state indexed by (i, j). Our proposed dynamic programming transformation matrix for the calculation of $d(D, w)$ is based on this idea extending it with two new components:

– adaption of the graph to the dictionary (a prefix tree instead of a chain), and

– two new operations: dictionary level split and merge.

For every word of the dictionary there is a path in the tree where the nodes of the path correspond to the characters of the word in the given sequence. The transformation graph is a triplet $G < V_G, E_G, c_v >$, where $V_G = \{v_i, j\}$: the nodes of the graph (i is the index of a node in the dictionary tree, j is an index value from 0 to $|w|$); E_G : the set of edges; $c_v : V_D \to N$: the cost assigned to each node. To get from the start node to a terminal node with minimal cost, the graph is explored with a best first traversing algorithm. The algorithm processes first the start element having zero cost value. The neighborhood nodes to be processed are mapped into buckets based on the calculated minimal cost value. The engine will always process the nodes of the bucket with lowest cost value. The proposed algorithm not only calculates the minimal transformation cost but it determines a valid sentence with minimal distance from the input string w. In the distance calculation using the dynamic programming search tree, a large number of potential neighboring nodes have to be processed to find the optimal path to a terminal node. From the viewpoint of execution cost, the finite state automaton is a good alternative mechanism, as only a smaller set of states (nodes) should be processed to get to a terminal state. On the other hand, the FSA is invented for decision problems. This mechanism is used in our context for the $NNS(D, w, m)$ problem where the automaton will determine whether the edit distance between the word w and the dictionary D is smaller than m, or not. In [Mitakin, 2005], a detailed description of the non-deterministic finite Levenshtein automaton $L_{Lev}(m, w)$ can be found. For our problem, the construction of a $NNS(D, w, m)$ automaton, the proposed dynamic optimization search tree can be converted into a non-deterministic automaton. This automaton can be used to determine whether the input sentence can be generated from the words of the dictionary within m correction operations, or not.

References

[Mitakin, 2005] Mitakin, P. (2005). *Universal Levenshtein Automata. Building and Properties. Thesis work.* Sofia University.

[Yujian and Bo, 2007] Yujian, L. and Bo, L. (2007). A normalized Levenshtein distance metric. *Pattern Analysis and Machine Intelligence, IEEE Transactions.*

Computational Intelligence and Data Mining (WCIDM 2016)

As a part of the conference ITAT 2016, the 4th international workshop "Computational Intelligence and Data Mining" has been organized. It is aimed at participants with research interests in any of these related areas, especially at PhD students and postdocs. Interested participants were invited to submit a paper in English of up to 8 double-column pages, prepared according to the instructions at the ITAT 2016 web pages.

A key factor influencing the overall quality of a workshop and of the final versions of the submitted papers is the workshop's program committee. The 4th international workshop "Computational Intelligence and Data Mining" is grateful to the 29 reviewers from 10 countries who read the submitted papers, and have provided competent, and in most cases very detailed, feedback to their authors. Most of them have a great international reputation witnessed by hundreds of WOS citations.

Martin Holeňa
Czech Academy of Sciences, Prague
Workshop organizer

Program Committee

Dirk Arnold, University of Dalhousie
Jose Luis Balcazar, Technical University of Catalonia, Barcelona
Petr Berka, University of Economics, Prague
Hans Engler, University of Georgetown
Jan Faigl, Czech Technical University, Prague
Pitoyo Hartono, University of Chukyo
Martin Holeňa, Czech Academy of Sciences, Prague
Ján Hric, Charles University, Prague
Zsolt Csaba Johanyák, University of Kecskemét
Jan Kalina, Czech Academy of Sciences, Prague
Jiří Kléma, Czech Technical University, Prague
Pavel Kordík, Czech Technical University, Prague
Tomas Krilavičius, Vytautas Magnus University, Kaunas
Jaromír Kukal, Czech Technical University, Prague
Věra Kurková, Czech Academy of Sciences, Prague

Stéphane Lallich, University of Lyon
Philippe Lenca, Telecom Bretagne, Brest
Antoni Ligęza, AGH University of Science and Technology, Krakow
Marco Lübbecke, RWTH University, Aachen
Donato Malerba, University of Bari
Mirko Navara, Czech Technical University, Prague
Engelbert Memphu Nguifo, Blaise Pascal University, Clermont-Ferrand
Ostap Okhrin, Technical University of Dresden
Tomáš Pevný, Czech Technical University, Prague
Petr Pošík, Czech Technical University, Prague
Jan Rauch, University of Economics, Prague
Heike Trautmann, University of Münster
Tingting Zhang, Mid-Sweden University, Sundsvall
Filip Železný, Czech Technical University, Prague

ITAT 2016 Proceedings, pp. 93–101
ISBN 978-1537016740, © 2016 H. Degroote, B. Bischl, L. Kotthoff, P. De Causmaecker

Reinforcement Learning for Automatic Online Algorithm Selection - an Empirical Study

Hans Degroote[1], Bernd Bischl[2], Lars Kotthoff[3], and Patrick De Causmaecker[4]

[1] KU Leuven, Department of Computer Science, CODeS & iMinds-ITEC, Belgium
hans.degroote@kuleuven.be
[2] Bernd Bischl, Department of Statistics, LMU Munich
[3] University of British Columbia, Department of Computer Science
[4] KU Leuven, Department of Computer Science, CODeS & iMinds-ITEC, Belgium

Abstract: In this paper a reinforcement learning methodology for automatic online algorithm selection is introduced and empirically tested. It is applicable to automatic algorithm selection methods that predict the performance of each available algorithm and then pick the best one. The experiments confirm the usefulness of the methodology: using online data results in better performance.

As in many online learning settings an exploration vs. exploitation trade-off, synonymously learning vs. earning trade-off, is incurred. Empirically investigating the quality of classic solution strategies for handling this trade-off in the automatic online algorithm selection setting is the secondary goal of this paper.

The automatic online algorithm selection problem can be modelled as a contextual multi-armed bandit problem. Two classic strategies for solving this problem are tested in the context of automatic online algorithm selection: ε-greedy and lower confidence bound. The experiments show that a simple purely exploitative greedy strategy outperforms strategies explicitly performing exploration.

1 Introduction

The problem considered in this paper is automatic algorithm selection. The field of algorithm selection is motivated by the observation that a unique best algorithm rarely exists for many problems. Which algorithm is best depends on the specific problem instance being solved. This can be illustrated by looking at the results of past SAT-competitions[1]. There are always problem instances that are not solved by the winning algorithm (the overall best) but that other algorithms manage to solve [25].

The complementarities between different algorithms can be leveraged through algorithm portfolios [13]. Instead of using a single algorithm to solve a set of problems, several algorithms are combined in a portfolio and a method of selecting the most appropriate algorithm for each problem instance at hand is used. This selection process is called automatic algorithm selection.

State of the art approaches for automatic offline algorithm selection use machine learning techniques to create a predictive model based on large amounts of training data.

The predictive model predicts for each instance which algorithm is likely to be best. The model is created based on characteristics of the problem under consideration. These characteristics are called problem features. The idea is that their value should be correlated with how hard a problem is for a certain algorithm.

Automatic algorithm selection methods are metaheuristics in the sense that they are general problem-independent strategies with a different implementation depending on the specific problem being considered. The difference in implementation manifests itself in the choice of features, which are distinct for every problem. For example, the ratio of the amount of clauses over the amount of variables is relevant for satisfiability problems but makes no sense for graph colouring or scheduling problems.

After the training phase the decision model remains fixed in automatic offline algorithm selection. To decide which algorithm to use to solve a new instance with, its features are calculated and input into the decision model which in turn returns an algorithm. This algorithm is then used to solve the instance with.

The observation motivating this research is that new performance data keeps being generated after the training phase every time the predictive model is used to predict the best algorithm for a new instance. This data is freely available yet not used by automatic offline algorithm selection methods. The main research question of this paper is: "Can online performance data be used to improve the predictive model underlying automatic algorithm selection?".

An interesting challenge faced in automatic online algorithm selection is finding a balance between learning a good predictive model and making good predictions. Selecting a predicted non-best algorithm might be better in the long run because the information thus obtained results in a better model and more accurate predictions for future instances, but it negatively affects the expected performance on the current instance. This challenge is an example of the exploration vs. exploitation trade-off often faced in reinforcement learning. It is also called the learning vs. earning trade-off.

The automatic online algorithm selection problem can be modelled as a multi-armed bandit problem, more specifically as a multi-armed bandit problem with covariates, also known as the contextual multi-armed bandit

---

[1]http://satcompetition.org/

problem, as for each problem instance the values of a number of problem characteristics are known. Two basic classic strategies for solving the contextual multi-armed bandit problem that incorporate explicit exploration are tested and compared to the purely exploitative approach.

The remainder of this paper is structured as follows. In section 2 the automatic online algorithm selection problem is defined. First the classic automatic offline algorithm selection problem is discussed, then the methodology for automatic online algorithm selection is presented after which the contextual multi-armed bandit problem is introduced and is shown how automatic online algorithm selection can be modelled as a contextual multi-armed bandit problem. In section 3 related work is discussed. The experimental setting and results are presented in section 4. In section 5 some remarks about the introduced methodology are made and the experimental results are discussed. Future work is also discussed in section 5. The paper concludes in section 6

2   Automatic Online Algorithm Selection

2.1   Automatic Algorithm Selection

Rice's paper "The algorithm selection problem" [23] formally introduced the algorithm selection problem. The fundamental characteristics of the problem remain unchanged up to now. In the most basic scenario identified by Rice the problem is characterised by a set of instances, a set of algorithms and a (set of) performance measure(s) and by two mappings between these sets: a selection mapping and a performance mapping. The selection mapping maps instances to algorithms and the performance mapping maps algorithm-instance pairs to their performance-measure(s). A typical formulation of the objective of automatic algorithm selection is to find the selection mapping that results in the best average performance.

It is up to the user to identify a sensible performance measure. In this paper only single-objective problems are considered. See [9] for a more formal description of what characterises an acceptable performance measure for the research in this paper. Each performance measure with totally ordered values is definitely acceptable.

Rice acknowledges the need for a set of features in practical applications and extends his model with this set. The full model is visualised in figure 1. Note that the selection mapping now maps values from the feature space instead of directly from the instance space.

To formalise the problem statement, let Q be a probability distribution on the instance set $\mathscr{I}$. Let f be the feature mapping (mapping an instance to a feature vector), s the selection mapping (mapping a feature vector to an algorithm) and p the performance mapping (mapping an instance-algorithm combination to a performance measure). The average performance of a selection mapping can now be defined as:

$$\mathbf{E}_Q[(p(s(f(i)),i)] \tag{1}$$

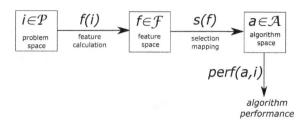

Figure 1: Rice's model for algorithm selection'

The aim is to find the feature mapping and selection mapping that optimise the average performance. The features of an instance are given, so the only leeway there is which features to consider. Limitations on the possible selection mappings can be imposed by the method used to create it.

Identifying descriptive features is a time consuming process. Luckily large amounts of features have already been proposed in literature for many interesting problems. For example in [22] an overview is given of features for the satisfiability problem and in [21] for the multi-mode resource-constrained project scheduling problem.

The automatic in automatic algorithm selection refers to the way decision models are made: automatically. Supervised learning techniques are typically used.

Two broad classes of techniques can be identified. In the first fall classification-based techniques: the decision model directly predicts which algorithm will be best for an instance based on its features. No information about the actual quality of the algorithm is communicated. Note that in general this is not a binary but a multi-class classification problem, as each instance is classified as being best-solved by one of an arbitrary amount of algorithms. In [20] for example, the k-nearest-neighbours method is used. Another example of the use of k-nearest-neighbours can be found in [6], where the more complicated problem of ranking algorithms (as opposed to only predicting the best) is considered. Another option is to use decision trees or their more powerful relative random forest, as in the latest version of Satzilla [26], an algorithm selector for the satisfiability problem.

Misclassification is cost-sensitive in automatic algorithm selection: classifying an instance incorrectly as being best solved by a horrendous algorithms is worse than classifying it as being best solved by an algorithm only marginally worse than the best one. A classification-based automatic algorithm selection technique should take this cost-sensitivity into account, as argued in [5].

The second class of automatic algorithm selection techniques consists of regression-based techniques. A regression model is created for each algorithm, predicting its performance in function of the problem features. The algorithm with the best predicted performance is selected to solve a new instance with. An overview of such techniques can be found in [14]. A recent approach is described in [10].

Note that algorithm selection itself is a cost-sensitive classification problem: the goal is to classify instances as belonging to the algorithm that best solves them. The distinction between classification and regression methods refers to how this classification problem is solved behind the scenes.

A thorough overview of algorithm selection methodology can be found in [24] and more recently in [17].

Both classes of automatic algorithm selection methods use the same kind of input to initialise their decision models: performance data of all algorithms on a set of training instances. For the classification-based techniques it is strictly necessary for the performance of all algorithms to be available for each instance. Otherwise it is not possible to say which algorithm is best for the instance. This is not the case for regression-based techniques. As long as each algorithm's model has access to datapoints it can be initialised, it is not necessary to know the performance of each algorithm on each training instance.

2.2 Solution Strategy for Automatic Online Algorithm Selection

During the online phase performance data is generated every time a new instance is solved. This performance data consists of the performance of the selected algorithm on the new instance. The performance data of the other algorithms on the new instance is not available. Since this type of data can only be processed by the regression-based methods, the proposed methodology will be limited to regression-based techniques.

The methodology for automatic online algorithm selection is the following. During the offline training phase an initial regression model is trained for each algorithm , using training data consisting of algorithm performance on instances described by feature values. During the online phase the algorithm to solve the first online instance with is selected based on the models created during the training phase. The model of the selected algorithm is retrained with the new datapoint. The performance of all other algorithms on the instance remains unknown. The algorithm to solve the second online instance with is selected based on the models created after having solved the first instance, thus one of the models has been updated to incorporate the performance information about the first online instance. Selection for the third online instance is influenced by the two previous etc. As more instances are solved, more datapoints are gathered and the models are expected to improve, which in turn is expected to result in better algorithm selection.

2.3 Automatic Online Algorithm Selection Problem Statement

As discussed in section 2.1, the goal of automatic algorithm selection is to find the feature mapping and selection mapping that optimise the average performance as defined in equation 1.

In the setting of this paper the instance set is defined by a fixed set of benchmark instances and the distribution is uniform. The feature mapping is defined by considering all features available for the benchmark instances. The problem of selecting the most informative features is not considered: the feature mapping is fixed. A selection mapping is defined by considering a regression model for each algorithm and selecting an algorithm in function of these predicted values. The most straightforward selection mapping is to select the algorithm with the predicted best performance. This and other options are discussed in section 2.4. The performance mapping used is discussed in section 4.1.

In the offline setting the selection mapping remains fixed. However, in the online setting it changes over time as more instances are solved. The selection at each point in time depends explicitly on earlier selections. For this reason equation 1 cannot be used directly to formally define a general problem statement for automatic online algorithm selection.

In the empirical setting of this paper the quality of a solution to the automatic online algorithm selection problem is measured as its average performance on a time-ordered set of instances, as presented during the online phase. The empirical performance measurement process is explained in more detail in section 4 where the experimental setting and results are described.

2.4 Contextual Multi-armed Bandits

In the standard multi-armed bandit a gambler has access to a set of slot machines (bandits) and must decide on a strategy in which order to pull their arms. His goal is to realise as much profit as possible. Each time an arm is pulled the gambler receives a random reward sampled from a distribution belonging to the selected arm. Initially all distributions are unknown, but as the gambler gambles on he obtains more information about the distributions of the available arms and can make more informed choices.

The central dilemma faced by the gambler is whether to keep pulling the arm proven to be best so far or to try another arm about which little is known and that might be better. If the other arm turns out to be more profitable never having explored its potential further would have lost the gambler a lot of money.

See [1] for a formal definition of the multi-armed bandit problem. In this paper a number of policies for pulling arms are analysed in terms of how fast the total profit diverges from the maximal profit in function of the total amount of pulls.

The contextual multi-armed bandit problem generalises the multi-armed bandit problem. To stay within the metaphor: before pulling an arm the gambler sees a context vector. This context vector contains values for predefined properties that describe the current situation. In the contextual multi-armed bandit problem the reward of each arm depends on the context. As in the classic multi-armed bandit problem the gambler's goal is to maximize his profit, but in order to do so he has to learn how the context vector relates to the rewards.

The automatic online algorithm selection problem is a contextual multi-armed bandit problem. Each algorithm is an arm and pulling an arm is the equivalent of selecting an algorithm. When selecting an algorithm for an instance its feature values are known, which is the equivalent of having shown a context vector. Maximizing profit in this context boils down to minimizing the performance difference between the selected algorithm and the actual best algorithm.

A number of solution strategies for the contextual bandit have been introduced and analysed in literature, such as LinUCB [7] where the reward is assumed to linearly depend on the feature vector. However, for the preliminary research presented in this paper three straightforward and simple strategies have been implemented.

The first strategy that is considered is the greedy strategy. The greedy strategy does not perform any explicit exploration: it always selects the algorithm that is predicted to be best.

The second strategy that is considered is the ε-greedy strategy, which is parametrised by a value ε between 0 and 1. The strategy is equivalent with the simple greedy strategy with probability $(1 - \varepsilon)$ and selects a random algorithm with probability ε.

The third strategy is the is the UCB strategy, short for upper confidence bound. It is parametrised by parameter λ (with $\lambda \geq 0$). The UCB strategy consists of calculating for each algorithm its predicted performance p and the standard error on this prediction e. The algorithm with highest value for $p + e * \lambda$ is selected. Since algorithms for which few datapoints exist typically have high variance on their predictions, an algorithm with predicted poor performance might be preferred over an algorithm with decent performance, depending on the performance difference, variance sizes and the value of λ. A higher λ-value results in more exploration.

The equivalent of the UCB strategy for minimisation problems is the LCB strategy, short for lower confidence bound. Its selection rule is: $p - e * \lambda$.

Unlike the two previous strategies, which only rely on a predicted value, the LCB strategy also relies on a notion of variance. Hence it can be applied only to regression methods for which the variance on a prediction is calculable.

3 Related work

Reinforcement learning and multi-armed bandit methodology have been applied to some related topics in automatic algorithm selection literature. However, the authors believe the setting considered in this paper, applying reinforcement learning to the standard automatic algorithm selection problem where one has to select one algorithm from a limited pre-defined set of algorithms to solve an instance with, has not yet been investigated. In the remainder of this section some related research is discussed and is mentioned how it differs from this work.

In [11] multi-armed bandit methodology is applied to the online learning of dynamic algorithm portfolios. Their goal differs from this paper's. They want to learn for each instance a separate algorithm portfolio while the goal here is to predict one algorithm to solve the instance with. In an algorithm portfolio a bunch of algorithms are run simultaneously. The dynamic goal is to learn the optimal assignment of time slices to algorithms while the portfolio is in use. This paper's setting is not dynamic in this sense. Once an algorithm has been selected to solve an instance with this decision will not be come back on, even if the algorithm appears to perform poorly on the instance.

In [8] a new multi-armed bandit model is proposed and applied to search heuristic selection, a kind of algorithm selection. However, their objective differs from this paper's. In terms of algorithm selection they have access to a number of stochastic algorithms and a budget of N trials. The goal is to find an as good as possible solution for one instance within the budget of N trials, whereas this paper's goal is to find an as good as possible solution on average over many instances, each with a budget of one trial. Their stochasticity is caused by the algorithms but the instance remains fixed. In this paper stochasticity is also caused by the instances as at each point in time a new random instance is solved.

In [12] a notion of online algorithm selection is introduced for decision problems. They focus on the problem of deciding how to distribute time shares over the set of available algorithms and make this decision on an instance per instance basis. They model the problem on two levels. On the upper level they use bandit methodology to decide which time allocator to use (choosing from a uniform allocator and various dynamic allocators) and on the lower level the algorithms are run in parallel (or simulated to run in parallel) according to the time shares predicted by the allocator selected on the higher level. Thus the arms of their bandit problem are 'time allocators' and not algorithms.

4 Experiments

4.1 Experimental Setting

A standard database with automatic algorithm selection data, called ASLIB [3], is used. This database consists of 17 problems, each with a number of algorithms (2-30) and instances (500-2500). The value of one or more performance measures is available for each algorithm-instance pair. Using this database it is possible to simulate different algorithm selection strategies without having to waste time on calculating the performance of algorithms and instances.

Information about the feature values for each instance is stored as well. The amount of features ranges from 22 to 155.

In all experiments performed performance is measured as how fast an algorithm solves an instance. To differentiate between solving an instance just within the time-limit and failing to solve an instance, time-outs are penalised by multiplying them with a fixed factor. A penalty factor commonly used in literature is 10. resulting in the PAR10 criterion (with PAR an abbreviation for penalised average runtime). Suppose the time-out limit is 1 hour. An unsolved instance will have a PAR score of 10 hours. In terms of the problem definition of automatic algorithm selection (equation 1): all results in this paper are presented with as performance mapping applying the PAR10 criterion to the stored runtime.

Since for all problems being considered performance is measured as time taken until a solution is found, they are all minimisation problems. This implies specifically that the lower confidence bound method (LCB) will be used instead of the upper confidence bound method (UCB).

As content management system for the experiments and as interface to the remote cluster the R-package BatchExperiments was used [4].

As described in section 2.2 a regression model is trained for each algorithm during a training phase and these models are subsequently updated during an online phase. To evaluate how well each strategy has managed to learn models, the final model quality at the end of the online phase is evaluated during a verification phase. During the verification phase each strategy's resulting model quality is evaluated by using the models to make predictions. Note that during this verification phase models are no longer updated and no explicit exploration is performed. For each strategy the basic greedy selection criterion is used.

The set of available instances is split into three subsets to represent three experimental phases: a set of training instances, a set of online instances and a set of verification instances.

As regression model 'regression forest' is used. The implementation from R-package randomForest [19] with the standard parameter values is used. The randomForest method is interfaced through the R-package MLR [2]. Note that the prediction variance reported by random forest is calculated using a bootstrap methodology. See [19] for a description of this method.

Even though a database of performance data is used, running the experiments still proved too time-consuming for most ASLIB-scenarios. Most time is spent on retraining models. Therefore an optimisation was introduced: retraining the model of an algorithm is postponed until a minimal amount of new datapoints is available.

All results have been normalised on an per-instance basis before the average PAR10 performances (averaged over all repeats of the experiment) are calculated. A value of 0 is the best possible (recall that minimisation problems are considered, so a lower value is a better value). This score

is achieved by the so-called virtual best solver. The virtual best solver selects for each instance the best possible algorithm. It is defined only for instances for which performance data is available for all algorithms. Note that the PAR-score of the virtual best solver itself is not 0, it is simply normalised to 0.

The virtual best solver is artificial because it requires calculating the performance of each algorithm before selecting one, hence it cannot be used in practice. However, it is easy to define for an ASLIB scenario and is commonly used to evaluate the quality of an algorithm selection approach, for example in [25] and [15]. A score of 1 equals the score of the single best solver. The single best solver corresponds to the classical notion of 'best algorithm': it is the best solver on average over the entire dataset. Any algorithm selection strategy should improve on the single best solver to be considered useful, but the score of 1 does not provide a strict upper bound and it is possible to obtain scores higher than 1. An algorithm selection method with a score higher than 1 performs worse than the single best solver.

To enable comparison with the current state of the art in automatic offline algorithm selection, the performance of regression random forest as reported on the ASLIB website[2] is shown as a horizontal red line on each plot. LLAMA is an R-package for algorithm selection interfacing a number of machine learning algorithms [16]. On the website the performance of some popular machine learning algorithms applied to ASLIB algorithm selection scenarios is reported. Since regression random forest is also used in this paper's experiments this allows comparison with a current state of the art automatic offline algorithm selection method.

The results are presented using box plots. The hinges correspond to the first and third quartiles. The whiskers extend to the highest value within a 1.5 inter-quartile range from the hinges. The remaining points are outliers.

Several parameters must be defined to run the experiments. They are kept at a fixed value for all experiments reported in this paper.

- LCB λ: 1
- ε-greedy ε: 0.05
- Proportion of training instances: 0.1
- Proportion of online instances: 0.8
- Proportion of verification instances: 0.1
- Minimal amount of instances before retraining: 16
- Amount of repitions per experiment: 10

For the exploration methods standard parameters were chosen. The proportions of training and online instances were chosen ad hoc. The proportion of 0.1 for verification instances was chosen more consciously because it is standard practice to evaluate models on 10% of the data. The other parameters were also chosen ad hoc. For follow-up studies a parameter study can be useful.

---

[2]http://coseal.github.io/aslib-r/scenario-pages/QBF-2011/llama.html

Only results for the QBF-2011 scenario are reported in this paper. Results for other scenarios are qualitatively similar with regards to the two research questions considered[3]. The QBF-2011 scenario contains performance data obtained from the quantified Boolean formula competition of 2011. The QBF-2011 scenario contains 5 algorithms, 46 features and 1368 instances, of which 1054 were solved by at least one algorithm. There are 136 training instances, 1094 online instances and 136 verification instances.

The PAR10 score of the virtual best solver fluctuates around 8400 and that of the single best solver around 15300, depending on the specific split in training, online and verification instance set. Recall that the virtual best solver's score is normalised to 0 and the single best's to 1.

4.2   Is Automatic Online Algorithm Selection Useful for the Greedy Approach?

Adding additional data to the regression models is expected to result in better performance. To validate this hypothesis the performance of the most basic learning strategy (greedy) is compared with that of a strategy that does not learn.

The greedy strategy picks the algorithm predicted to be best.

The strategy that does not learn is called the greedy-no-learning strategy and is abbreviated as greedyNL in the plots. It is equivalent to the simply greedy strategy but it does not do any learning: it keeps using the models it learned during the training phase, never adding new datapoints. This strategy is the strategy used by offline algorithm selection approaches.

The greedy-no-learning strategy uses its models to predict the best algorithm for all online instances and its PAR10-score is calculated on these online instances. The learning strategy does the same, but updates its models with the data it gathers during the online phase.

A third strategy is considered as well: the greedy-full-information strategy, abbreviated as greedyFI. Greedy-full-information is an artificial strategy that has access to the online information of each algorithm on all handled instances. Thus not only the result of the selected algorithm is used to update the models, but also the results of all other algorithms, hence the full-information. It does not have to explore as it has access to all information regardless, hence its greedy selection criterion.

The Greedy-full-information strategy is introduced to serve as a sort of upper bound on the performance of any selection strategy. It always makes the best decision given the current information (pure exploitation) and it has access to the maximal amount of information (performance of all algorithms on all handled instances). Each actual selection strategy will have access to only a part of the information and might at times make suboptimal decisions if it explores.

---

[3]Plots for all performed experiments are available on http://www.kuleuven-kulak.be/~u0075355/Plots_ITAT_2016

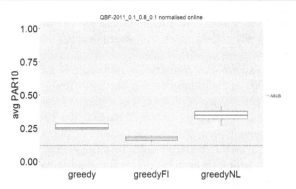

Figure 2: Boxplot summarising the answer to the question 'Is active learning useful?'. The presented data is collected during the online phase

Note that the Greedy-full-information strategy does not provide a real upper bound: it is possible to perform better than this strategy as more information is not guaranteed to always result in better predictions.

The plot with the results of the online phase is presented in figure 2. Online learning appears to be useful as the greedy strategy outperforms the greedy-no-learning strategy. The good performance of the greedy-full-information strategy shows the value of having access to more information.

The performance reported in figure 2 is the average performance over all online instances. For the first online instance the performance of the greedy-no-learning strategy is equal to that of the greedy strategy that does learn, but for the last online instance the performance of the greedy strategy that does learn is expected to be better because it has access to more data. The performance reported in figure 2 is the average of these (most likely) increasing performances.

To quantify how much the greedy strategy has learned during the online phase, the quality of its predictions is tested on a set of verification instances. During the verification phase the models are no longer updated. The difference in PAR10-score between the greedy strategy and the greedy-no-learning strategy is a measure for how much using the online data improves the quality of the selection.

The plot with the results of the verification phase is presented in figure 3. Note that the performance of the greedy-full-information strategy is similar to the performance of llama. This is expected because the benchmark performance was calculated using a 10-fold cross-validation where performance of models trained on 90% of the data is measured on the remaining 10%. The models of the greedy-full-information strategy have also been trained on 90% of the data: 10% training data and 80% online data.

To answer the question titling this section: automatic online algorithm selection appears to be useful for the greedy approach.

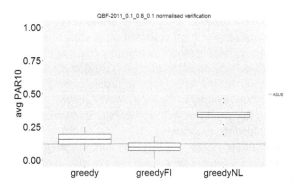

Figure 3: Boxplot summarising the answer to the question 'Is active learning useful?'. The presented data is collected during the verification phase

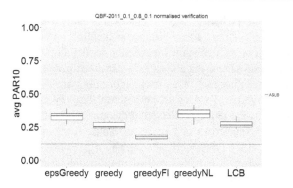

Figure 4: Boxplot summarising the answer to the question 'is explicit exploration useful?'. The presented data is collected during the online phase

4.3 Handling the Exploration vs. Exploitation Trade-off

When performing reinforcement learning one is typically faced with an exploration vs. exploitation trade-off. When no online learning is performed the predicted best algorithm is always selected because the only reason for selecting an algorithm is solving the next instance as well as possible. In an online learning setting a second reason for selecting an algorithm surfaces: additional information will be obtained and this information will increase the quality of future decisions.

Two exploration-incorporating strategies are compared to the simple greedy approach: ε-greedy (epsGreedy on the plots) and lower confidence bound (LCB on the plots). See section 2.4 for a description of these two strategies.

A first test is to compare each strategy's performance during the online phase. This measures their ability to solve the exploration vs. exploitation trade-off: do they manage to benefit from exploring more by obtaining a better average performance?

The plot with the results of the online phase is presented in figure 4. The answer appears to be negative: explicit exploration does not result in a better average performance than greedy and the ε-greedy strategy even drops down to the level of the greedy-no-learning strategy.

A second test is to check whether the exploration strategies managed to learn better models than the greedy strategy by comparing their performance on the verification data. If the exploration strategies managed to learn better models they have merit as they traded off some exploitation in favour of useful exploration. If this is not the case the exploration was not useful and simply resulted in picking inferior algorithms without any noticeable gain.

The plot with the results of the verification phase is presented in figure 5. Exploration does not appear to have been useful as the models learned by the ε-greedy and lower confidence bound strategy do not outperform the model learned by the greedy strategy. Note however that the additional information obtained during the online phase does result in better models than the greedy-

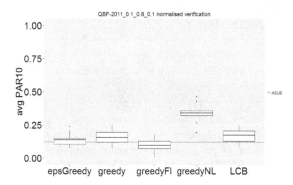

Figure 5: Boxplot summarising the answer to the question 'is explicit exploration useful?'. The presented data is collected during the verification phase

no-learning strategy for all learning strategies.

5 Discussion and future work

The automatic online algorithm selection method presented in section 2.2 is inefficient. Every time a new datapoint is collected for an algorithm, the corresponding regression model is retrained from scratch using all previous data and the newly obtained datapoint. If the fitting of a model takes a long time this approach can become prohibitively expensive, especially if its complexity is influenced heavily by the amount of instances, as for each online instance a new model is trained and the models are trained based on an ever increasing amount of instances. Identifying and implementing more efficient updating strategies is future work. Mondrian forests [18] for example are an online version of random forests that could be useful in this context.

There might be a theoretical problem with the proposed automatic online algorithm selection method. During the online phase an algorithm's regression model is extended only with datapoints for which the algorithm was predicted to be best. Hence the new datapoints are all clustered in the same region(s) of the problem domain. Note also that the region(s) where an algorithm is best is likely to change slightly every time a new instance is handled, as with the changing of an algorithm's regression model all points in the domain where the algorithm's predicted performance was better than that of another algorithm's are likely to move slightly. Then again, in a sense the property that datapoints are mostly collected in the area where an algorithm is expected to be best is desirable. Knowing with high accuracy how poorly an algorithm performs on instances where it is bad is useless in this context whereas accurate predictions on instances for which the algorithm is likely to be one of the best are very relevant. However, note that predicting performance accurately is not the goal itself. What is important is that the actual best algorithm is the algorithm with predicted best score. The selection mapping does not change if a fixed value is added to each performance prediction.

At the start of this project it was thought that the explicit exploration would be useful. Current and future work is investigating why this does not appear to be the case. There are two main hypotheses.

The first hypothesis is that the amount of exploration data collected during the online phase is negligible compared to the data gathered during the training phase, thus the influence of the exploration cannot be observed. A training set of 100 instances for 5 algorithms can be seen as a combination of 100 greedy choices and 400 explorative choices. The epsilon greedy strategy will explore 5% of the time, resulting in on average 50 new explorative datapoints during an online phase of 1000 instances. This hypothesis is currently being investigated

The second hypothesis is that exploration is already implicitly performed by the greedy strategy, rendering additional explicit exploration unnecessary. The greedy method is greedy in the sense that it always selects the best algorithm, but which the best algorithm is depends from instance to instance, thus over time performance datapoints for all algorithms are collected. In this way the greedy strategy implicitly explores. Investigating this hypothesis is future work.

In order to better quantify the improvements realised during the online phase, future work is to investigate the way in which the selection model improves in detail, by not only evaluating the overall models before and after the online phase, but also at several points during the online phase and by also dropping down a level and investigating how the individual regression models (one for each algorithm) evolve over time.

In future work the overhead of retraining the models should be explicitly considered and quantified in order to be able to quantify the net improvement of using the online data. In the experiments here reported this overhead is ignored.

An interesting path for future work is te develop an algorithm that learns how to perform automatic online algorithm selection form scratch, without any training data whatsoever. A straightforward initial methodology would be to perform random or round-robin selection until sufficient samples have been collected for each algorithm to construct a regression model. Interesting challenges would be to include the option to add new algorithms at runtime and even identifying which kind of instances are hard for all algorithms, thereby inspiring the development of a new algorithm that performs well on these instances which can then be added to the system.

Other future work consists of implementing solution strategies specifically designed for the contextual multi-armed bandit problem which are more theoretically founded, for example LinUCB [7].

6 Conclusions

A reinforcement learning methodology for automatic online algorithm selection has been introduced. It is limited to automatic algorithm selection methods based on performance predictions for each individual algorithm. It has been shown experimentally that the method is capable of learning from online data and thereby improves on automatic offline algorithm selection methods.

It has been shown that automatic online algorithm selection can be modelled as a contextual multi-armed bandit problem.

A total of three solution strategies have been implemented and empirically tested: an approach that always greedily selects the best algorithm and two approaches that perform exploration: ε-greedy and lower confidence bound. The experiments suggest that the greedy strategy outperforms the explorative strategies.

Acknowledgements

Work supported by the Belgian Science Policy Office (BELSPO) in the Interuniversity Attraction Pole COMEX. (http://comex.ulb.ac.be).

The computational resources and services used in this work were provided by the VSC (Flemish Supercomputer Center), funded by the Research Foundation - Flanders (FWO) and the Flemish Government – department EWI

References

[1] P. Auer, N. Cesa-Bianchi, and P. Fischer. Finite-time analysis of the multiarmed bandit problem. *Machine learning*, 47(2-3):235–256, 2002.

[2] B. Bernd. mlr: A new package to conduct machine learning experiments in r.

[3] B. Bischl, P. Kerschke, L. Kotthoff, M. Lindauer, Y. Malitsky, A. Fréchette, H. Hoos, F. Hutter, K. Leyton-Brown, K. Tierney, et al. Aslib: A benchmark library for algorithm selection. *arXiv preprint arXiv:1506.02465*, 2015.

[4] B. Bischl, M. Lang, O. Mersmann, J. Rahnenführer, and C. Weihs. BatchJobs and BatchExperiments: Abstraction mechanisms for using R in batch environments. *Journal of Statistical Software*, 64(11):1–25, 2015.

[5] B. Bischl, O. Mersmann, H. Trautmann, and M. Preuss. Algorithm selection based on exploratory landscape analysis and cost-sensitive learning. In *Genetic and Evolutionary Computation Conference (GECCO)*, 2012.

[6] P. B. Brazdil, C. Soares, and J. P. Da Costa. Ranking learning algorithms: Using ibl and meta-learning on accuracy and time results. *Machine Learning*, 50(3):251–277, 2003.

[7] W. Chu, L. Li, L. Reyzin, and R. E. Schapire. Contextual bandits with linear payoff functions. In *International Conference on Artificial Intelligence and Statistics*, pages 208–214, 2011.

[8] V. A. Cicirello and S. F. Smith. The max k-armed bandit: A new model of exploration applied to search heuristic selection. In *AAAI*, pages 1355–1361, 2005.

[9] H. Degroote and P. De Causmaecker. Towards a knowledge base for performance data: A formal model for performance comparison. In *Proceedings of the Companion Publication of the 2015 on Genetic and Evolutionary Computation Conference*, pages 1189–1192. ACM, 2015.

[10] T. Doan and J. Kalita. Selecting machine learning algorithms using regression models. In *2015 IEEE International Conference on Data Mining Workshop (ICDMW)*, pages 1498–1505. IEEE, 2015.

[11] M. Gagliolo and J. Schmidhuber. Learning dynamic algorithm portfolios. *Annals of Mathematics and Artificial Intelligence*, 47(3-4):295–328, 2006.

[12] M. Gagliolo and J. Schmidhuber. Algorithm selection as a bandit problem with unbounded losses. In *International Conference on Learning and Intelligent Optimization*, pages 82–96. Springer, 2010.

[13] B. A. Huberman, R. M. Lukose, and T. Hogg. An Economics Approach to Hard Computational Problems. *Science*, 275(5296):51–54, 1997.

[14] F. Hutter, L. Xu, H. H. Hoos, and K. Leyton-Brown. Algorithm runtime prediction: Methods & evaluation. *Artificial Intelligence*, 206:79–111, 2014.

[15] S. Kadioglu, Y. Malitsky, A. Sabharwal, H. Samulowitz, and M. Sellmann. Algorithm selection and scheduling. In *Principles and Practice of Constraint Programming–CP 2011*, pages 454–469. Springer, 2011.

[16] L. Kotthoff. Llama: leveraging learning to automatically manage algorithms. *arXiv preprint arXiv:1306.1031*, 2013.

[17] L. Kotthoff. Algorithm Selection for Combinatorial Search Problems: A Survey. *AI Magazine*, 35(3):48–60, 2014.

[18] B. Lakshminarayanan, D. M. Roy, and Y. W. Teh. Mondrian forests: Efficient online random forests. In *Advances in Neural Information Processing Systems*, pages 3140–3148, 2014.

[19] A. Liaw and M. Wiener. Classification and regression by randomforest. *R news*, 2(3):18–22, 2002.

[20] Y. Malitsky, A. Sabharwal, H. Samulowitz, and M. Sellmann. Non-model-based algorithm portfolios for sat. In *Theory and Applications of Satisfiability Testing-SAT 2011*, pages 369–370. Springer, 2011.

[21] T. Messelis and P. De Causmaecker. An automatic algorithm selection approach for the multi-mode resource-constrained project scheduling problem. *European Journal of Operational Research*, 233(3):511–528, 2014.

[22] E. Nudelman, K. Leyton-Brown, H. H. Hoos, A. Devkar, and Y. Shoham. Understanding random sat: Beyond the clauses-to-variables ratio. In *Principles and Practice of Constraint Programming–CP 2004*, pages 438–452. Springer, 2004.

[23] J. R. Rice. The algorithm selection problem. *Advances in Computers*, 15:65–118, 1976.

[24] K. A. Smith-Miles. Cross-disciplinary perspectives on meta-learning for algorithm selection. *ACM Computing Surveys (CSUR)*, 41(1):6, 2009.

[25] L. Xu, F. Hutter, H. Hoos, and K. Leyton-Brown. Evaluating component solver contributions to portfolio-based algorithm selectors. In *Theory and Applications of Satisfiability Testing–SAT 2012*, pages 228–241. Springer, 2012.

[26] L. Xu, F. Hutter, J. Shen, H. H. Hoos, and K. Leyton-Brown. Satzilla2012: Improved algorithm selection based on cost-sensitive classification models. *Proceedings of SAT Challenge*, pages 57–58, 2012.

ITAT 2016 Proceedings, pp. 102–109
ISBN 978-1537016740, © 2016 N. Jajcay, M. Paluš

Statistical modelling in climate science

Nikola Jajcay[1,2] and Milan Paluš[1]

[1] Dept. of Nonlinear Dynamics and Complex Systems, Institute of Computer Science, Academy of Sciences of the Czech Republic
[2] Dept. of Atmospheric Physics, Faculty of Mathematics and Physics, Charles University in Prague

Abstract: When it comes to modelling in atmospheric and climate science, the two main types of models are taken into account – dynamical and statistical models. The former ones have a physical basis: they utilize discretized differential equations with a set of conditions (boundary conditions + present state as an initial condition) and model the system's state by integrating the equations forward in time. Models of this type are currently used e.g. as a numerical weather prediction models. The statistical models are considerably different: they are not based on physical mechanisms underlying the dynamics of the modelled system, but rather derived from the analysis of past weather patterns. An example of such a statistical model based on the idea of linear inverse modelling, is examined for modelling the El Niño – Southern Oscillation phenomenon with a focus on modelling cross-scale interactions in the temporal sense. Various noise parameterizations and the possibility of using a multi-variable model is discussed among other characteristics of the statistical model. The prospect of using statistical models with low complexity as a surrogate model for statistical testing of null hypotheses is also discussed.

1 Modelling in climate science

Climate models, which rely on the use of quantitative methods to simulate interactions in the climate system, are one of the most important tools to predict and asses future climate projections or to study the climate of the past. In general, two types of models are mainly used: dynamical models and statistical models. The base for a dynamical model is a set of discretized differential equations which are integrated forward in time from the present state, posing as an initial condition. The most prominent example of the usage of dynamical models is without doubt a general circulation model (GCM hereafter). It employs a mathematical model of circulation of the planetary atmosphere and oceans, therefore it uses the Navier-Stokes equations on a rotating sphere (describing a motion of viscous fluid) with thermodynamic terms for energy sources and sinks. The above described model is used in numerical weather prediction, to infer the reanalysis datasets of the past climate and for future climate projections in climate model intercomparison projects CMIP3 [1] and CMIP5 [2].

The uncertainties of the forecast arisen from the GCM models are usually classified into two types: the first one is related to the initial errors (errors in determining the "true" present state of the climate), while the second one is due to

the model errors [3] and these are intrinsic. The problem with initial errors is usually tackled by considering an ensemble of model forecasts (instead of just one realization - integration from single initial state), starting with slightly different initial conditions. The model errors are intrinsically connected with the exponential error growth emerging from the chaotic behaviour related to nonlinearities in discretized equations [4]. This limits the predictability of such GCMs to 6-10 days maximum (e.g. [5]).

1.1 Statistical models

The second kind of models used in climate science are statistical models. In their design, they are considerably different than the dynamical models in the sense that they are not based on physical mechanism underlying the dynamics of the modelled system, but rather derived from the analysis of past weather patterns. Probably the most used concept is that of inverse stochastic model [6], where the model is designed, then estimated using past data and, finally, stochastically integrated forward in time to obtain the prediction. The disadvantages connected to this type of models consist of the selection of variables that capture the system we are trying to model. Other possible issue could be the non-stationarity of the modelled system - since the statistical model does not involve the underlying physical mechanisms, just the interaction between subsystems (ignoring hidden variables), the model estimated on some subset of the past data may not correctly capture all possible states of the system. In other words, the training period of the past data used to estimate the statistical model may not capture the full phase space of the modelled system.

The motivation for building a statistical model for particular phenomenon, apart from its forecasting, would be to scale down the complexity of the problem. When we find some e.g. nonlinear interactions in the observed data, and we are interested in uncovering the mechanisms, constructing a models of different complexity and seeking such interactions in them would help to expose the mechanisms and shed some light on the problem.

In the following sections, the inverse stochastic model for forecasting the El Niño - Southern Oscillation (ENSO hereafter) phenomenon is built following [7], with the focus on various noise parametrizations and possible use of multiple variables.

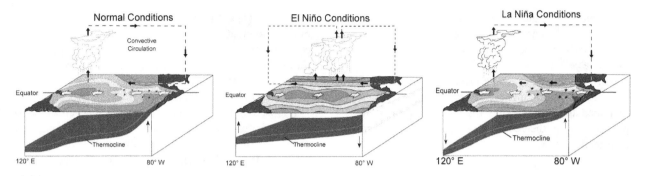

Figure 1: ENSO phenomenon, its phases and mechanisms: (left) neutral, (center) positive and (right) negative. Figures taken from [10].

2 Data-based ENSO model

The ENSO phenomenon exhibits strong interannual climate signal and has a great economic and societal impact. It originates from the coupled ocean-atmosphere dynamics of the tropical Pacific [8], but has a strong influence on circulation and air-sea interaction also outside the tropical belt through teleconnections associated with it [9].

The ENSO phenomenon expresses itself as a sea surface temperature (SST hereafter) anomaly and exists in three distinct phases - the neutral, positive (El Niño) and negative (La Niña). The basic physical mechanisms for each of the phases are depicted in Fig. 1. The normal state of the equatorial Pacific (Fig. 1 left) is warm SST in the western basin, near Australia and cold SST in the eastern basin, near the coast of Peru. Above the warm water in the west, the deep convection takes place, where warm and moist air is ascending to the border of troposphere, creating an area of low atmospheric pressure and area of persistent precipitation. From the upper part of the troposphere, the air is moving eastward and then it descends already as cold and dry, creating an area of high atmospheric pressure above the eastern equatorial Pacific. From this basin, the air is blowing westward on the surface, in agreement with the trade winds, finishing the circulation loop known as the Walker circulation. The easterly surface air flow triggers the oceanic surface current to flow poleward, effectively removing water from the surface, thus the water needs to be replaced and this is due to the upwelling, where in the equatorial area, the water is upwelled from roughly 50 meters depth to the surface. Since the thermocline (a border between cold deep ocean and warm surface ocean) is located below 50 meters in the west, the upwelled water is warm, but in the eastern Pacific the thermocline level is above the 50 meters, thus the upwelled water is cold, creating the cold SST in the east and warm SST in the west.

The warm phase of ENSO (Fig. 1 center) creates a warm SST anomaly in the eastern Pacific, acting to weaken the Walker circulation, to move the area of persistent precipitation eastward, to diminish the difference between eastern and western Pacific surface pressures and to level off the thermocline. Reversely, the negative phase of ENSO (Fig. 1 right) is acting to strengthen the Walker circulation, to move the area of persistent precipitation even more westward, the differences in surface pressure is now larger and the thermocline is even more tilted. The ENSO tends to naturally oscillate between these three phases without a distinct period (there is no distinct peak in ENSO signal's spectrum) and the reasons why are still largely unknown.

The important aspect of ENSO is that its positive phase - El Niño is generally characterized by a larger magnitude than its negative phase - La Niña. This statistical skewness is one of the indicators that, at least to some extent, the dynamics of ENSO involves nonlinear processes [11]. At the same time, the most detailed numerical dynamical models seem to severely underestimate this nonlinearity [12], hence the quality of the forecast is not satisfactory.

From the reviews of statistical models for ENSO forecasting before 2000 [13] it was clear, that majority of models were still linear, but lately the nonlinear models are getting more attention (e.g. [14]). In the following, we describe easy-to-interpret nonlinear model for ENSO forecasting.

2.1 Inverse models

The concept of inverse stochastic models are used as the starting point in developing the ENSO model. Let $\mathbf{x}(t)$ be the state vector of anomalies, so $\mathbf{x}(t) = \mathbf{X}(t) - \overline{\mathbf{X}}$, where $\mathbf{X}(t)$ is the climate state vector (could be multi- or univariate climate observations e.g. temperature, pressure etc. or a PCA time series from eigen-decomposition of some climate field) and $\overline{\mathbf{X}}$ is its time-mean. The evolution of anomalies could be expressed as

$$\dot{\mathbf{x}} = \mathbf{L}\mathbf{x} + \mathbf{N}(\mathbf{x}) \qquad (1)$$

where $\mathbf{L}$ is a linear operator, $\mathbf{N}$ represents the nonlinear terms and dot denotes time derivative.

The simplest type of inverse models is linear inverse models (LIM, [6]). By assuming, in eq. (1), that $\mathbf{N}(\mathbf{x})\mathrm{d}x \approx \mathbf{T}\mathbf{x}\mathrm{d}t + \mathrm{d}\mathbf{r}^{(0)}$, where $\mathbf{T}$ is the matrix describing linear feedbacks of unresolved (hidden) processes on $\mathbf{x}$ and $\mathrm{d}\mathbf{r}^{(0)}$ is a white-noise process, eq. (1) could be written as

$$\mathrm{d}\mathbf{x} = \mathbf{B}^{(0)}\mathbf{x}\mathrm{d}t + \mathrm{d}\mathbf{r}^{(0)}, \quad \mathbf{B}^{(0)} = \mathbf{L} + \mathbf{T}. \qquad (2)$$

The matrix $\mathbf{B}^{(0)}$ and the covariance matrix of the noise $\mathbf{Q} \equiv \langle \mathbf{r}^{(0)} \mathbf{r}^{(0)T} \rangle$ can be directly estimated from the observed statistics of $\mathbf{x}$ by multiple linear regression [15]. The state vector $\mathbf{x}$, or predictor-variable vector, consists of amplitudes of corresponding principal components (PCA analysis [16] yields spatial patterns - empirical orthogonal functions and its respective time series - principal components), while the vector of response variables contains their tendencies $\dot{\mathbf{x}}$.

2.2 Nonlinear multilevel model

The assumptions of linear, stable dynamics and of additive white-noise used to construct LIMs are only valid to certain degree of approximation. In particular, the stochastic forcing $\mathrm{d}\mathbf{r}^{(0)}$ typically involves serial correlations, and, in addition, the matrices $\mathbf{B}^{(0)}$ and $\mathbf{Q}$ obtained from the data exhibit substantial dependence on the lag, that was used to fit them [17]. The two modifications of the basic inverse model, that address both nonlinearity and serial correlations are taken into account, as in [18].

The first modification is obtained by assuming polynomial, rather than linear form of $\mathbf{N}(\mathbf{x})$ in eq. (1), in particular, a quadratic dependence. The ith component $N_i(\mathbf{x})$ could be written as

$$N_i(\mathbf{x}) \approx \left(\mathbf{x}^T \mathbf{A}_i \mathbf{x} + \mathbf{t}_i \mathbf{x} + c_i^{(0)} \right) \mathrm{d}t + \mathrm{d}r_i^{(0)} \qquad (3)$$

The matrices $\mathbf{A}_i$ represent the blocks of a third-order tensors, while the vectors $\mathbf{b}_i^{(0)} = \mathbf{l}_i + \mathbf{t}_i$ are the rows of the matrix $\mathbf{B}^{(0)} = \mathbf{L} + \mathbf{T}$ (as in eq. (2)). These objects, as well as components of the vector $\mathbf{c}^{(0)}$, are estimated by multiple polynomial regression [19].

The second modification, considering the serial correlations in residual forcing, is due to the multilevel structure of our model. In particular, consider the ith component of the first, main level of the inverse stochastic model

$$\mathrm{d}x_i = \left(\mathbf{x}^T \mathbf{A}_i \mathbf{x} + \mathbf{b}_i^{(0)} + c_i^{(0)} \right) \mathrm{d}t + \mathrm{d}r_i^{(0)}, \qquad (4)$$

where $\mathbf{x} = \{x_i\}$ is the state vector and matrices $\mathbf{A}_i$, vectors $\mathbf{b}_i^{(0)}$ and the components $c_i^{(0)}$ of the vector $\mathbf{c}^{(0)}$ as well as the components $r_i^{(0)}$ of the residual forcing vector $\mathbf{r}^{(0)}$ are determined by the least squares. The additional model level is added to express the known increments $\mathrm{d}\mathbf{r}^{(0)}$ as a linear function of an extended state vector $[\mathbf{x}, \mathbf{r}^{(0)}]$. We estimate this level's residual forcing again by the least squares. More levels are added the same way, until the Lth level's residual, $\mathbf{r}^{(L+1)}$, becomes white in time, and its lag-0 correlation matrix converges to constant, hence

$$\begin{aligned}
\mathrm{d}r_i^{(0)} &= \mathbf{b}_i^{(1)}[\mathbf{x}, \mathbf{r}^{(0)}]\mathrm{d}t + r_i^{(1)}\mathrm{d}t, \\
\mathrm{d}r_i^{(1)} &= \mathbf{b}_i^{(2)}[\mathbf{x}, \mathbf{r}^{(0)}, \mathbf{r}^{(1)}]\mathrm{d}t + r_i^{(2)}\mathrm{d}t, \\
&\cdots \\
\mathrm{d}r_i^{(L)} &= \mathbf{b}_i^{(L+1)}[\mathbf{x}, \mathbf{r}^{(0)}, \ldots, \mathbf{r}^{(L)}]\mathrm{d}t + r_i^{(L+1)}\mathrm{d}t \quad (5)
\end{aligned}$$

The eqs. (4) and (5) describe a wide variety of processes in a fashion that explicitly accounts for the modeled process $\mathbf{x}$ feeding back on the noise statistics. The linear multilevel model is obtained by assuming $\mathbf{A}_i \equiv 0$ and $\mathbf{c}^{(0)} \equiv 0$ in eq. (4). Details of the methodology and further discussion could be found in [7].

It is well known, that the extreme ENSO events tend to occur in boreal winter. From several ways to include this phase locking to the annual cycle, the alternative approach used here is to include seasonal dependence in the dynamical part of the first level. Namely, we assume the matrix $\mathbf{B}^{(0)}$ and vector $\mathbf{c}^{(0)}$ to be periodic, with period $T = 12$ months:

$$\begin{aligned}
\mathbf{B}^{(0)} &= \mathbf{B}_0 + \mathbf{B}_s \sin(2\pi t/T) + \mathbf{B}_c \cos(2\pi t/T), \\
\mathbf{c}^{(0)} &= \mathbf{c}_0 + \mathbf{c}_s \sin(2\pi t/T) + \mathbf{c}_c \cos(2\pi t/T) \quad (6)
\end{aligned}$$

In this case, the whole record is used to estimate four seasonal-dependent coefficients. The model is trained in the leading EOF (empirical orthogonal function) space [16] of tropical Pacific SST anomalies. The optimal number of state-vector components and the degree of nonlinearity has to be assessed by cross-validation. The parameters in this paper were used as in [7].

3 Results

In this section, the brief results are presented of how the statistical model is able to simulate the ENSO signal. The skill of the model is determined in the sense of basic linear ENSO metrics such as the amplitude of the ENSO signal, the seasonality (since the seasonality is important aspect of ENSO dynamics) and finally, the power spectrum of ENSO signal. The model is employed as described in the previous section, the matrices and vectors are estimated from the previous data and then the model is integrated to obtain the time series of same length as the training data. Since the model is stochastic (forced by a white noise), we employed an ensemble of 20 members. Each member is integrated with slightly different initial conditions and these members are referred to as realizations.

The basic ENSO metric is its amplitude, which could be characterized by the standard deviation of SST anomalies averaged over Nino3.4 box (bounded by 5°S - 5°N and 120°W - 170°W). In Fig. 2 we can see the ENSO amplitude as derived from the Nino3.4 index [20] (thick black line), along with 20 realizations from the data-based ENSO model, both linear and quadratic (gold for linear, red for quadratic).

As can be seen, the linear model slightly overestimates the ENSO amplitude, while the quadratic model slightly underestimate the ENSO amplitude. From the spread of the ensemble members we could infer that the model is sensitive to initial conditions and the forcing. Still, the ensemble averages for both models are within reasonable distance from the data borderline, therefore in this aspect the model performs adequately.

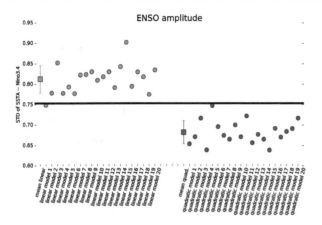

Figure 2: ENSO amplitude as standard deviation of SST anomalies in data (black line) and in 20 realizations of linear (gold) and quadratic (red) model.

Other metric connected with ENSO amplitude is its seasonality. As written above, the ENSO phenomenon exhibits seasonal changes in variance, with elevated variance in winter months and lower variance in spring and summer months. This can be also seen in Fig. 3, where the monthly variance is plotted for the data and for both models. Both models are capable of modelling higher variance in winter months and drop in variance through spring and summer, although the difference in variance is higher in data than in both models. Still, the ensemble averages are reasonably close to the data.

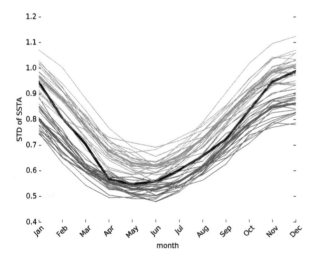

Figure 3: ENSO seasonality as standard deviation per month in data (black curve) and in 20 realizations of linear (gold) and quadratic (red) model. Thicker lines represent the mean over 20 realizations in the respective model.

The last metric taken into account was the power spectrum of Nino3.4 time series. The spectrum for the Nino3.4 data and both linear and quadratic model realizations can be seen in Fig. 4. The main peak in data occurs at roughly 5 year period, but still the ensemble averages for respec-

tive models are more flat in this area of frequencies. In the higher frequencies (around annual frequency and less) the power spectra are in agreement. In general, the spectra of modelled time series could be said to copy the actual Nino3.4 time series. The power spectra were computed using the Welch method [21].

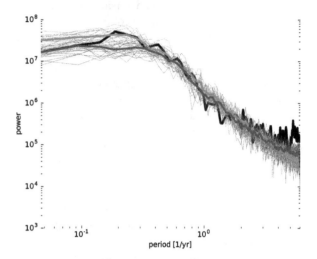

Figure 4: ENSO power spectra estimated using the Welch method in data (black curve) and in 20 realizations of linear (gold) and quadratic (red) model. Thicker lines represent the mean over 20 realizations in the respective model.

4 Noise parametrization in the model

The statistical model, once estimated, is integrated forward in time and forced by a noise - usually a realization of spatially correlated random process. In the most intuitive and basic case, the last level residuals' covariance matrix is estimated and decomposed using Cholesky factorization yielding a lower triangular matrix $\mathbf{R}$. When the model is integrated, the random realization of white noise is multiplied by the matrix $\mathbf{R}$, yielding spatially correlated white noise which is used as a random forcing in the model. The results for quadratic and linear ENSO models from the previous section were obtained using this simple noise parametrization, and the question is whether looking deeper into the residuals' structure could aid the model's performance.

4.1 Dependence on the system's state

First refinement for the noise parametrization arises from the concept of modelling climate processes which exhibit low-frequency variability (LFV). In this method, we find and select noise samples, snippets, from the past noise (residuals) which have forced the system during short time intervals that resemble the LFV phase just preceding the currently observed state, and then use these snippets (or information contained in them) to drive the current state into the future. For full methodology and discussion, see [22].

The found past noise snippets can be used in two different ways. The first one (as used in [22]) seeks various snippets from the past observations and then directly uses them to force the model as an ensemble. When e.g. we find 4 intervals which resemble the LFV phase, we integrate the model 4 times using all 4 noise snippets directly and than average over them. The second version (as used in our study) is to find, say, 100 samples of the past noise closest to the current state of the system, cluster them together and create covariance matrix from them. Afterwards, the Cholesky decomposition is used to obtain the matrix $\mathbf{R}$ and finally, the random white noise realization is multiplied by the matrix $\mathbf{R}$. Using this matrix, the spatial covariance of the forcing is dependent on the current state of the system. In both noise parametrizations, the current system state could be estimated in multiple ways: either using correlation of the SSA time series, or using the Euclidean distance in the subspace spanned by first few EOFs.

As can be seen in Fig. 5, although the amplitude statistics are not substantially shifted, the transient from high-variance winter period to low-variance spring and summer are better captured by the later model, with noise forcing conditioned on system's state. The power spectra for both models are practically the same (not shown).

4.2 Seasonal dependence of the forcing

Although the seasonal dependence of the model is captured in model's dynamics by fitting the seasonally dependent matrices $\mathbf{B}^{(0)}$ and $\mathbf{c}^{(0)}$ (recall eq. (6)), our analysis showed, that the last level's residuals still exhibit seasonally dependent amplitude. To address this issue, we computed the standard deviations for each month from the last level's residuals, then fitted the 5 harmonics of the annual cycle to capture the seasonal dependence, removed this dependence from the residuals, then estimated covariance matrix and subsequently the matrix $\mathbf{R}$ and finally generated spatially correlated white noise realization which was multiplied back by the requisite seasonal amplitude to account for the seasonally dependent amplitude of the forcing. The fitted harmonics of the annual cycle were selected as

$$P_i = \cos(2\pi i t/T) + \sin(2\pi i t/T), \; i = 1, \ldots, 5 \quad (7)$$

and then regressed on the seasonally varying standard deviation of the last level's residuals.

4.3 Using extended covariance matrix

The last modification to the noise is to use the extended covariance matrix instead of lag-0 covariance matrix. When evaluating system's state we do not take just the state closest to the current state of the model, but, say 5 consecutive months and construct the extended matrix out of this snippet. Then the matrix is decomposed using Cholesky factorization and used as a spatial correlation matrix $\mathbf{R}$ is random forcing generation.

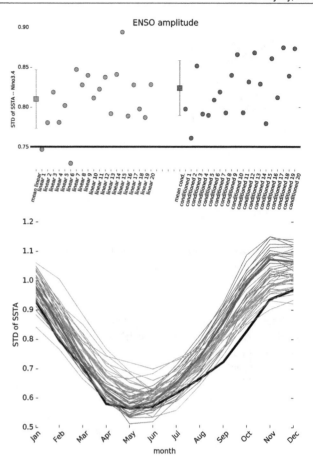

Figure 5: ENSO amplitude (upper) and seasonality (bottom) in data (black curve) and in 20 realizations of linear (gold) and linear with conditioned noise on the system's state (red) model. Thicker lines represent the mean over 20 realizations in the respective model.

The two latter modifications bring just a slight improvements into ENSO metrics (not shown), but could have more substantial advancements in modelling different atmospheric phenomena.

5 Synchronization and causality in the observed and modelled data

Better understanding of the complex dynamics of the atmosphere and climate is one of the challenges for contemporary science. Considering the climate system as a complex network of interacting subsystems [23] is a new paradigm bringing new data analysis methods helping to detect, describe and predict atmospheric phenomena [24]. A crucial step in constructing climate networks is inference of network links between climate subsystem [25]. Directed links determine which subsystems influence other subsystems, i.e. uncover the drivers of atmospheric phenomena. Inference of causal relationships from climate data is an intensively developing research field, e.g. [26, 27]. Typically, a causal relation is sought between different variables or modes of atmospheric variability.

Paluš [28] has open another view at the complexity of atmospheric dynamics by uncovering causal relations or information flow between dynamics on different time scales in the same variable. Recently, phase-phase and also phase-amplitude interactions between dynamics on different temporal scales were observed in the ENSO dynamics (captured by the Nino3.4 index) using the approach as in [28]. Shortly, we use the continuous wavelet transform to the time series for particular time scales to obtain the instantaneous phase and amplitude of the oscillatory mode as

$$\psi(t) = s(t) + i\hat{s}(t) = A(t)e^{(i\phi(t))}, \quad (8)$$

$$\phi(t) = \arctan\frac{\hat{s}(t)}{s(t)}, \quad (9)$$

$$A(t) = \sqrt{s^2(t) + \hat{s}^2(t)}. \quad (10)$$

Then the time series of phase and / or amplitude are used to study the interactions. We adopt measures from information theory, namely mutual information and conditional mutual information, where the mutual information could be expressed as

$$I(X;Y) = \sum_{x \in X}\sum_{y \in Y} p(x,y)\log\frac{p(x,y)}{p(x)p(y)}, \quad (11)$$

where $p(\cdot)$ is the probability distribution or joint probability distribution and X and Y are our time series of either phase or amplitude derived from the ENSO SST data. Finally, the measures we are interested in could be written as:

- phase synchronization – $I(\phi_1(t); \phi_2(t))$,

- phase-phase causality – $I(\phi_1(t); \phi_2(t + \tau) - \phi_2(t)|\phi_2(t))$,

- phase-amplitude causality – $I(\phi_1(t); A_2(t + \tau)|A_2(t), A_2(t - \eta), A_2(t - 2\eta))$,

5.1 Interactions in the data

As can be seen from Fig. 6, in ENSO dynamics captured by the Nino3.4 index, the synchronization of annual cycle with quasi-biennal and combination frequencies (frequencies that arise from the interactions between annual and the most prominent ENSO period) is observed. Also, the 4-6 year cycle of phase in ENSO dynamics influence the quasi-biennal range of the amplitude time series.

5.2 Interactions in the model

Our goal was to simulate the nonlinear cross-scale interactions in the model. This is important since it might help

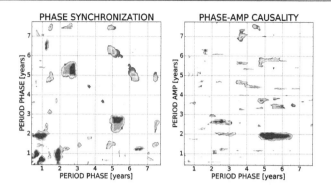

Figure 6: Phase synchronization (left) and phase-amplitude causality (right) in Nino3.4 time series. Shown is the significance (over 95th percentile against 500 Fourier transform surrogates) of k-nearest neighbours estimate of mutual information and conditional mutual information.

to uncover the mechanisms of these interactions and shed more light onto the dynamics of ENSO in general. We constructed the ENSO model and repeated the above analysis to modeled ensemble of the Nino3.4 time series.

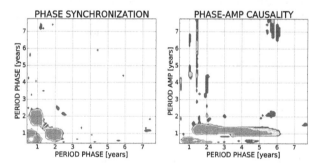

Figure 7: Phase synchronization (left) and phase-amplitude causality (right) in modeled Nino3.4 time series by the data-based model. Shown is the aggregate of 5 realizations of k-nearest neighbours estimate of mutual information and conditional mutual information. Significance against 500 Fourier transform surrogate data.

As seen from the analysis of modelled data (Fig. 7), the main phase synchronization bands (annual cycle with quasi-biennal cycle and combination frequencies) are also captured by the modelled data, while the phase - amplitude interactions are not very well captured. This might arise from the low complexity of the model, or the absence of some nonlinear interactions in the model design (apart from quadratic).

6 Modelling surrogate data with statistical model

Surrogate data (or analogous data) is a method to generate synthetic data set (time series) that preserve some of the statistical properties, while omitting the others. One way of using them, is to test statistical significance by contradiction. This involves posing a null hypothesis describing some kind of a process and then generating an ensemble of surrogate data according to null hypothesis using Monte Carlo methods. One of the most used technique for generating surrogate data is the Fourier transform surrogate [29] (FT surrogates), which preserve the linear correlations in the data (periodogram or spectrogram, including autocorrelation) of the time series, but omits any other interactions in them.

As an example, consider two intertwined Lorenz systems, where one of them drives the other. Now, using the time series in one dimension, say the x dimension from both Lorenz systems, we can use some method for detecting causality, e.g. conditional mutual information between the two time series of two Lorenz systems. We get the value of conditional mutual information, but this is still not enough to interpret it in the means of whether there is a causal relationship between them or the result arose by chance. For this purpose, we construct an ensemble of Fourier transform surrogate data (which qualitatively preserves properties of the time series, but allows no causal relationship between them) and repeat the analysis using the very same method on this ensemble and finally compare the value for actual data with the histogram of values obtained from the ensemble of surrogate data. When the value from the data exceeds some percentile (e.g. 95th) of the surrogate data distribution, we say that the causal relationship is significant in comparison with e.g. 500 FT surrogates.

When studying nonlinear cross-scale interactions in time series using the above method, the statistical test involves creating an ensemble of surrogate, synthetic time series and repeat the analysis for the whole ensemble. Then we computed the percentile, where the observed interactions could not arose by random chance. Of course, one could use Fourier transform method to generate the surrogate time series, effectively posing a null hypothesis of a linear process which has the same spectrum to that of an observed data. On the other hand, one can create a more sophisticated null hypothesis by exploiting the options of a data-based model: when one consider just a linear model, omit the dynamical seasonal dependence in $\mathbf{B}^{(0)}$ and $\mathbf{c}^{(0)}$ terms (as in eq. (6)) and use the simplest noise parametrisation (just consider the spatial covariance structure), the model will omit the nonlinear interactions and could pose as a surrogate data model copying the basic statistical properties of a modelled time series. This way, the analysis would show whether the cross-scale interactions are arising from the seasonal dependent dynamics, or from nonlinear (e.g. quadratic) interactions between subsystems and so on.

When comparing Fig. 6 (testing against 500 Fourier transform surrogates) and Fig. 8 (testing against 500 data-based model surrogates), the significant interactions are virtually the same, expect in the latter, the "fluctuations" (or they might be false positives as well) are attenuated to

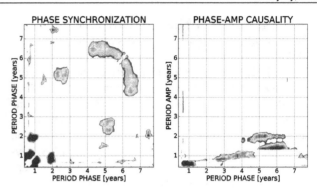

Figure 8: Phase synchronization (left) and phase-amplitude causality (right) in modelled Nino3.4 time series by the data-based model. Shown is the aggregate of 5 realizations of k-nearest neighbours estimate of mutual information and conditional mutual information. Significance against 500 surrogate time series created with data-based model.

minimum. This way, we can get better idea of the statistical significance of the interactions between subsystems, in particular the nonlinear ones, since we are testing against the model with just linear interactions.

7   Conclusions

Statistical modelling in climate science is continuously getting more attention, since their usage is not limited to forecast some of the phenomena of interest (like ENSO), but could also be used to infer some of the statistical properties and relationships among different subsystems. Since the statistical models live in phase space of particularly reduced dimensionality, when we could observe the interactions of interest, the identification of their sources will become more feasible.

We showed that the statistical model with the right settings, which were selected based on careful inspection of the modelled system, could generate synthetic time series of interest, copying the desired properties of the system - both linear and nonlinear statistics. Since the stochasticity is the important aspect of the data-based model, various parametrization techniques exist to correctly model the system's external forcing. Finally, the possibility of usage of the low complexity model as surrogate data was discussed, showing advantages of usage of such technique to infer statistical significance.

The outlook for future work combines various different paths which appeared. One direction would be focusing on statistical modelling itself, experimenting with various variable model, with input time series and their preprocessing and so on and so forth. Other direction would be connecting the statistical models with dynamical ones, in the sense, that statistical models could be used for parametrization of e.g. sub-grid phenomena (microphysics of clouds, local convection etc.) in large coupled atmospheric-oceanic models.

References

[1] Meehl, G. A., C. Covey, T. Delworth, M. Latif, B. McAvaney, J. F. B. Mitchell, R. J. Stouffer, and K. E. Taylor: The WCRP CMIP3 multi-model dataset: A new era in climate change research. *A Bull. Amer. Meteor. Soc.* **88** (2007) 1383–1394

[2] Taylor, K.E., R.J. Stouffer and G.A. Meehl: An Overview of CMIP5 and the experiment design. *A Bull. Amer. Meteor. Soc.* **93** (2012) 485–498

[3] Bjerknes, V.: Dynamic meteorology and hydrology, Part II. Kinematics. *Gibson Bros.*, Carnegie Institute, New York. (1911)

[4] Lorenz, E. N.: Deterministic nonperiodic flow. *J. Atmos. Sci.* **20** (1963) 130–141

[5] Van den Dool, H. M.: Long-range weather forecasts through numerical and empirical methods. *Dyn. Atmos. Oceans* **20** (1994) 247–270

[6] Penland, C.: Random forcing and forecasting using principal oscillation pattern analysis. *Mon. Weat. Rev.* **117** (1989) 2165–2185

[7] Kravtsov, S., D. Kondrashov, and M. Ghil: Multilevel regression modeling of nonlinear processes: Derivation and applications to climate variability. *J. Climate* **18** (2005) 4404—4424

[8] Philander, S. G. H.: El Niño, La Niña, and the Southern Oscillation. *Academic Press* (1990)

[9] Alexander, M. A., I. Bladé, M. Newman, J. R. Lanzante, N.-C. Lau, and J. D. Scott: The atmospheric bridge: The influence of ENSO teleconnections on air–sea interaction over the global oceans. *J. Climate* **15** (2002) 2205–2231

[10] WIKIPEDIA.ORG: El Niño–Southern Oscillation `https://en.wikipedia.org/wiki/El_Ni%C3%B1o% E2%80%93Southern_Oscillation`, downloaded June 27, 2016.

[11] Ghil, M. and A. W. Robertson: Solving problems with GCMs: General circulation models and their role in the climate modeling hierarchy. *Academic Press*, (2000) 285–325

[12] Hannachi, A., D. B. Stephenson, and K. R. Sperber: Probability-based methods for quanfifying nonlinearity in the ENSO. *Clim. Dyn.* **20** (2003) 241–256

[13] Ghil, M. and N. Jiang: Recent forecast skill for the El Niño / Southern Oscillation. *Geophys. Res. Lett.* **25** (1998) 171–174

[14] Timmermann, A., H. U. Voss, and R. Pasmanter: Empirical dynamical system modeling of ENSO using nonlinear inverse techniques. *J. Phys. Oceanogr.* **31** (2001) 1579–1598

[15] Wetherill, G. B.: Regression Analysis with Applications. *Chapman and Hall* (1986)

[16] Hannachi, A., I. T. Jolliffe and D. B. Stephenson: Empirical orthogonal functions and related techniques in atmospheric science: A review. *Int. J. Climatol.* **27** (2007) 1119–1152

[17] Penland, C. and M. Ghil: Forecasting Northern Hemisphere 700-mb geopotential height anomalies using empirical normal modes. *Mon. Wea. Rev.* **121** (1993) 2355—2372

[18] Kondrashov, D., S. Kravtsov, A. W. Robertson and M. Ghil: A Hierarchy of Data-Based ENSO Models. *J. Climate* **18** (2005) 4425–4444

[19] McCullagh, P., and J. A. Nelder: Generalized Linear Models. *Chapman and Hall* (1989)

[20] Rayner N. A., D. E. Parker, E. B. Horton, C. K. Folland, L. V. Alexander, D. P. Rowell, E. C. Kent and A. Kaplan: Global analyses of sea surface temperature, sea ice, and night marine air temperature since the late nineteenth century. *J. Geophys. Res.* **108** (2003) 4407

[21] Welch, P. D.: The use of Fast Fourier Transform for the estimation of power spectra: A method based on time averaging over short, modified periodograms. *IEEE Trans. Audio* **AU-15** (1967) 70–73

[22] Chekroun, M. D., D. Kondrashov and M. Ghil: Predicting stochastic systems by noise sampling, and application to the El Niño-Southern Oscillation. *P. Natl. Acad. Sci. USA* **108** (2011) 11766–11771

[23] A. A. Tsonis and P. J. Roebber: The architecture of the climate network. *Physica A: Statistical Mechanics and its Applications*, **333** (2004) 497–504

[24] S. Havlin, D. Y. Kenett, E. Ben-Jacob, A. Bunde, R. Cohen, H. Hermann, J. Kantelhardt, J. Kertész, S. Kirkpatrick, J. Kurths, et al.: Challenges in network science: Applications to infrastructures, climate, social systems and economics. *The European Physical Journal Special Topics*, **214** (2012) 273–293

[25] M. Paluš, D. Hartman, J. Hlinka, and M. Vejmelka: Discerning connectivity from dynamics in climate networks. *Nonlinear Processes in Geophysics* **18** (2011) 751–763

[26] Ebert-Uphoff and Y. Deng: Causal discovery for climate research using graphical models. *Journal of Climate* **25** (2012) 5648–5665

[27] Y. Deng and I. Ebert-Uphoff: Weakening of atmospheric information flow in a warming climate in the community climate system model. *Geophysical Research Letters* **41** (2014) 193–200

[28] Paluš, M.: Multiscale atmospheric dynamics: Cross-frequency phase-amplitude coupling in the air temperature. *Phys. Rev. Lett.* **112** (2014) 1–5

[29] Theiler, J., S. Eubank, A. Longtin, B. Galdrikian, and J. Doyne Farmer: Testing for nonlinearity in time series: The method of surrogate data. *Physica D* **58** (1992) 77–94

ITAT 2016 Proceedings, pp. 110–117
ISBN 978-1537016740, © 2016 M. Kopp, M. Pištora, M. Holeňa

How to Mimic Humans, Guide for Computers

Martin Kopp[1,2], Matouš Pištora[1], and Martin Holeňa[1,3]

[1] Faculty of Information Technology, Czech Technical University in Prague
Thákurova 9, 160 00 Prague
[2] Cisco Systems, Cognitive Research Team in Prague
[3] Institute of Computer Science, Academy of Sciences of the Czech Republic
Pod Vodárenskou věží 2, 182 07 Prague

Abstract: This paper studies reverse Turing tests to tell humans and computers apart. Contrary to classical Turing tests, the judge is not a human but a computer. These tests are often called Completely Automated Public Turing tests to tell Computers and Humans Apart (CAPTCHA). The main purpose of such test is avoiding automated usage of various services, preventing bots from spamming on forums, securing user logins against dictionary or brute force password guessing and many others.

During years, a diversity of tests appeared. In this paper, we focused on the two most classical and widespread schemes, which are text-based and audio-based CAPTCHA, and on their use in the Czech internet environment. The goal of this paper is to point out flaws and weak spots of often used solutions and consequent security risks. To this end, we pipelined several relatively easy algorithms like flood fill algorithm and k-nearest neighbours, to overcome CAPTCHA challenges at several web pages, including state administration.

Keywords: CAPTCHA, machine learning, network security, optical character recognition, speech recognition

1 Introduction

In the past few decades, the rise of the internet has revolutionised our lives. We use it for work, study, socialising, shopping and many other activities on a daily basis. With the increasing popularity of the web, many public services have became a target of a malicious activity of some kind. There were attempts to, e.g., exploit mail servers for sending massive amounts of spam messages, create numerous fake profiles on social networks or make fraudulent offers on online marketplaces. In order to block the access of automated scripts and bots, the web sites had started to use various captchas[1] based security protocols in hopes of ensuring their safety. Over the years, such schemes have evolved in one of the standard security measures.

The acronym CAPTCHA stands for Completely Automated Public Turing test to Tell Computers and Humans Apart, and was coined in 2003 by von Ahn et al [19]. The fundamental idea of its authors is to use a yet unsolved hard AI problem which is easy for humans to solve. In theoretical informatics, the Standard Turing test [18] is defined as a test in which a human judge is supposed to con-

sistently distinguish whether he/she is communicating via text with a human counterpart or a computer pretending to be a human. However, for the automatic and effective testing, the judge must also be a computer. This is where captcha, often called a reverse Turing test, comes into play.

Nowadays, a captcha is a program that generates a test which the majority of humans are able to solve, but current computer programs are not. Its mainly used on websites to distinguish whether the user is a human or a robot. The need for this type of challenge arose with the increasing amount of internet bots and automated scripts attempting to exploit public web services. Nowadays, it is an established security mechanism to prevent mailing spam messages, mass posting on internet forums, mass voting in online polls and downloading files in large amounts.

An interesting work has been done by the Microsoft researcher Chellapilla [11] who calls these tests Human interaction proofs. His work focuses on distinguishing effective distortion features and specifying best practices for designing captchas which are resistant to computers while remaining relatively easy for humans to solve. He also states that, depending on the cost of the attack, automated scripts should not be more successful than 1 in 10 000 attempts, while human success rate should approach 90%. It is generally considered a too ambitious goal, as random guesses can be successful [10], and consequently, a captcha is considered compromised when the attacker success rate surpasses 1%.

This is a work in progress, and we started it with websites that are most familiar to our everyday life, which are websites in Czech. More precisely, we focused on webpages of the state administration and similar to show them the vulnerability of sometimes critical systems of the national infrastructure. The main purpose of this paper is to show that the captcha schemes used on such webpages are easy to solve and therefore unsafe and to alarm the responsible offices. This is especially alarming on the webpages like State Office for Nuclear Safety or the Czech State Administration of Land Surveying and Cadastre.

The rest of this paper is organised as follows. The related work is briefly reviewed in the next section. Section 3 surveys the current captcha solutions. Section 4 presents our approach to breaking text-based and audio-based captcha challenges. The experimental evaluation is summarised in Section 5 and the paper closes with a conclusion.

---

[1] We will write captcha in lowercase for typographical reasons.

2   Related work

Most papers about breaking captcha heavily focus on some particular scheme. As an example may serve [12] with scheme reCapthca 2011. To our knowledge, the most general approach is presented in [6]. This approach is based on effective selection of the best segmentation cuts. It was tested on many up-to-date text-based schemes with better results than most of specialised solutions. But even that work was focused solely on the text-based schemes. We focused our efforts in a different way and instead of targeting one particular scheme, we tried to break captchas of different types, but all in the Czech internet environment. Unfortunately, we found only text-based and audio based captcha. Therefore, we tried to break both of them on several web sites including the Czech State Administration of Land Surveying and Cadastre[1] or the State Office for Nuclear Safety[4].

The most recent approaches use neural networks like [16]. The results are still not that impressive compared to the previous approaches, but the neural-net-based approaches improve very quickly. We intend to use convolution neural networks in our future work as well. But in this paper we tried to use as simple techniques as possible and show that even with them, we were able to compromise all captcha schemes presented in this study.

Not all captcha schemes support the audio as an alternative. Consequently, there was not that much effort spent in this topic. One of the first really successful attacks is well described in [17], followed by even greater success in [8]. More recent results of the same team are presented in [7]. The reason for our investment into audio captcha is to decide if it is generally easier to break text-based or audio-based captcha when both are available. Again, we used only the most simple techniques to point out the vulnerability of audio-based captchas.

An excellent assessment of humans success rate in completing captcha challenges can be found in [9]. As our paper is work in progress, we have human results only for the audio-based schemes.

3   Captcha schemes survey

This section surveys the currently available captcha schemes and challenges they present.

3.1   Text-based

The first ever use of captcha was in 1997 by the software company Alta-Vista, which sought a way to prevent automated submissions to their search-engine. It was a simple text-based test which was sufficient for that time, but it was eventually proven ineffective. At that time, the computer recognition rates of single characters were already on par with those of humans, and thus the development of captchas shifted to the prevention of segmenta-

tion like noise addition, cluttering and other various anti-segmentation techniques. With the effort to prevent breaking of captchas with increasing the amount of distortion and cluttering, the challenges faced the risk of becoming almost illegible. The design of human friendly, yet secure captchas becomes a serious challenge. The most commonly used techniques to prevent automatic recognition can be divided into two groups called anti-recognition features and anti-segmentation features.

The anti-recognition features such as the use of different size of characters in multiple fonts was a straightforward first step to the text-based captcha schemes. Those and other anti-recognition features, like character rotation, are typically no problem for humans because we see it on everyday basis. The only exception is distortion. Distortion is a technique in which ripples and warp are added to the image. It is one of the easiest and most effective ways of reducing the classifier accuracy. But excessive distortion can make it very difficult even for humans and thus usage of this feature slowly vanishes. Due to advances in pattern recognition and optical character recognition, all those features became obsolete and were to some extend replaced by anti-segmentation features.

The anti-segmentation features are not designed to complicate a single character recognition but instead they try to make the segmentation of the captcha image unmanageable, preserving the readability by humans. The first two features used for this purpose were added noise and confusing background. But it showed up that both of them are bigger obstacle for humans than for computers. After that the occlusion lines appeared in the wild. A good implementation of occluding lines is one of the most effective and human-friendly ways of preventing segmentation, an example can be seen at Figure 1. The most recent feature is called negative kerning. It means that the neighbouring letters are moved so close to each other that they can eventually overlap. It showed up that humans are still able to read the overlapping text with only a small error rate, but for computers it is almost impossible to found the right segmentation.

Figure 1: Older Google reCaptcha with the occlusion line.

3.2   Audio-based

From the beginning, the adoption of captcha schemes was not the ideal state. Users were annoyed with captchas that were hard to solve and had to try multiple times in order to solve them. The people affected the most were those with visual impairments or various reading disorders such as dyslexia. Soon, an alternative emerged in the form of audio captchas. Instead of looking at the image and transcribing the displayed characters, the user was given the option, usually alongside with a traditional text-based captcha, to play a sound puzzle and write the characters that he/she heard. In order to remain effective and secure, the captcha has to be resistant to automated sound analysis. For this purpose various background noise and sound distortion are added. Still a human visitor should have no problem in hearing and recognising the code. Generally, this scheme is now a standard option on major websites that implement captcha.

The major anti-automation tools are changing speakers, involving both males and females of ages ranging from children to retired. Most of the current solutions rely on the added noise. The level of sophistication is very diverse, ranging from buzz, singing birds to human speakers played backwards.

3.3 Image-based

With the advancement of captchas, criticism soon began to appear. The obstacle of solving a puzzle every time someone wants to enter a site is at least annoying and discouraging for the common user. It is in the everyones best interest to keep the customer satisfied all the time and make their user experience the most pleasant. In order to preserve security against spam-bots, new captcha designs were developed. The most prominent design was image-based captcha. The user is presented with a series of images showing various objects and the task lies usually in detecting which of them have a common topic and selecting them. For example a user is shown a series of images of various landscapes and is asked to select those with trees, like in Figure 2. This type of captcha has gained huge popularity on touchscreen devices like tablets and smart phones, where simply tapping the screen is the preferable option over typing the code.

3.4 Other types

In parallel with the image-based captcha developed by google and other big players, many alternative schemes appeared. They are different variations of text-based schemes hidden in video instead of distorted image, some simple logical games or puzzles. As an example of an easy to solve logical game we selected the naughts and crosses, Figure 5. As a special type of of text-based scheme can be considered the metal captcha. This scheme shows to the user not the automatically distorted characters but a logos of metal bands which are typically unreadable, see Figure 3. All of those got recently dominated by Google's no-Captcha button, Figure 4. They say that this single button can distinguish between humans and computers. It uses browser cookies and somehow track user behaviour on the webpage, but implementation detail were not disclosed.

Figure 2: Current Google reCaptcha with image recognition challenge.

Figure 3: An example of the HeavyGifts group Metal Captcha.

4 Recognition pipeline

In this section, the algorithm pipelines for both text-based and audio-based captcha schemes are described. We are aware that there are some very advanced approaches e.g. [6, 16] but we intentionally used simple algorithms in the basic pre-process, segment and recognize pipeline. Our motivation is to show that even using simple approaches, most currently used captchas in the Czech internet environment can be compromised.

4.1 Text-based

The text-based captchas are still the most widely used ones. Their goal is to present an image with distorted characters using anti-recognition and anti-segmentation features combined in such a way that humans can easily read it but computers do not. Our goal, on the contrary, is to successfully recognize all those characters automatically.

The first step in the intended pipeline is conversion of an image to the grayscale. The image is converted from

Figure 4: Current Google noCaptcha button.

Figure 5: A naughts and crosses game used as a captcha.

the RGB colorspace to the greyscale space according to the following equation:

$$Y = 0.299 \cdot R + 0.587 \cdot G + 0.114 \cdot B. \tag{1}$$

This equation was adopted in the Rec. BT 601 standard by the International Telecommunication Union [14].

The image is then transformed to a binary image by a thresholding method. Pixels with an intensity higher than the threshold are converted to the white colour and those with a lower intensity are converted to black. For a given threshold T the equations is:

$$Y(x) = \begin{cases} 0 & \text{if } x < T \\ 1 & \text{otherwise} \end{cases} \tag{2}$$

The threshold is computed by iterating through all possible thresholds and selecting the one which minimises the within-class variance. This method was proposed by Otsu in [13]. The class probabilities and the class variances are computed from the image brightness histogram:

$$\sigma_\omega^2(t) = \omega_0(t)\sigma_0^2(t) + \omega_1(t)\sigma_1^2(t) \tag{3}$$

$$\omega_0(t) = \sum_{i=0}^{t-1} p(i) \tag{4}$$

$$\omega_1(t) = \sum_{i=t}^{L-1} p(i) \tag{5}$$

where p is a greyscale level probability and L is the number of the greyscale levels.

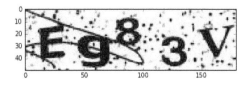

Figure 6: An example of a greyscale cuzk captcha with characters $Eg83V$

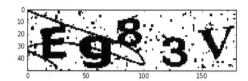

Figure 7: The thresholded captcha example

Next part is a noise removal. For this we used morphological operations followed by the flood fill algorithm. Morphological operations are a simple yet powerful approach to remove speckles and occluding lines. With the closing operation, we can fill small holes and gaps in the image, and with the opening operation loosely connected segments are disjointed and small points and lines are removed. The four basic binary morphological operations: dilation $\oplus$, erosion $\ominus$, opening $\circ$ and closing $\bullet$ are defined as follows:

$$X \oplus H = \{(x,y) : H_{(x,y)} \cap X \neq \emptyset\} \tag{6}$$

$$X \ominus H = \{(x,y) : H_{(x,y)} \subseteq X\} \tag{7}$$

$$X \circ H = (X \ominus H) \oplus H \tag{8}$$

$$X \bullet H = (X \oplus H) \ominus H \tag{9}$$

where X is the original image, H the structuring element and $H(x,y)$ the translation of H by the vector (x,y). The effect of the closing operation can be described as erasing the object border and then regrowing it back. If in the first step an object is small enough to be considered a border as a whole, there is subsequently nothing to regrow and thus it is deleted.

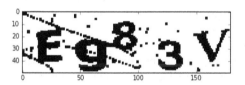

Figure 8: The effect of one iteration of closing

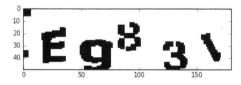

Figure 9: Deterioration of character details after three iterations of *closing*

The next approach is to count areas of all connected components (in terms of pixels it contains) and delete the ones with the area below a certain threshold. The idea is to iterate on each pixel of the image and when a white pixel is found a flood fill algorithm is used to count the number of pixels in the area. Individual characters are large objects and such can be easily distinguished from noise by empirically setting a certain threshold. The objects with area count below the threshold are then deleted, which results in an almost noiseless image.

Even with our simplistic approach, only the individual characters and a few lines remain. At first we isolate all the objects left in the image, which is done by iterating through every pixel. When an unlabelled pixel with a foreground colour is found, the flood fill algorithm is used to paint it with a new unique colour. Due to the nature of occluding lines, their position is generally horizontal. That is unlike any of the characters the captchas contain and as such the isolated lines can be easily eliminated by deleting all objects with their height under an empirically set threshold.

If the number of isolated objects is the desired number of characters, a captcha is considered successfully segmented. In the other case, we have two possibilities. If the number of objects is greater than number of characters, it implies that there are some speckles or line segments left. They are eliminated by deleting objects with the lowest pixel count. This usually provides good results. If there are fewer objects than the number of characters it indicates a connection of multiple characters either by a remaining line or by collapsing. This situation is resolved by the X-axis projection algorithm.

Its main idea for two or more joined characters is that the pixel count between them is generally lower than in the centre of the character. First, we construct the X-axis projection by summing pixels of each column. Next, all local minima are found which will be later considered for cutting points. The next step is to remove all local minima which have their pixel count under the empirically set threshold to eliminate most cutting points positioned in the middle of a character. All possible segmentations into two parts left are then considered for the subsequent classification. Finally the cutting point which maximises the classification performance is selected. Fortunately, this is a really rare event.

When the segmentation step is done, each segment is resized to 20x20 pixels, resulting in a vector of 400 binary values. These vectors are then used as features for the k-nn classifier. Parameters of the k-nn classifier are discussed in Section 5.

4.2   Audio captcha

For the audio-based captchas the pipeline is even simpler. The most advanced audio captcha looks like the one at Figure 10. A human speaker with a lot of noise making it very hard to do a good segmentation. Contrary, the ones we found on the Czech internet looks more like Figure 11. A synthetic voice was used and the level of added noise is almost negligible. Therefore, we can simply skip the

noise cancelation step. Furthermore, the segmentation is much simpler than in the text-based case. The audio data are normalised to zero mean and unit variance. The segmentation is done based on amplitude thresholding with an empirically set threshold.

According to [15], speech signals are time-varying signals, which are stationary for a short time periods (5-100 ms). The change of the signal then reflects different phonemes. The information in a speech signal is actually represented by a short term amplitude spectrum of the speech wave form. Therefore, we split the character wave form into 10 bins, extracted means and variances of amplitudes from each bin and used them as features. The last feature is the length of sound wave in seconds.

Those feature vectors, containing 21 scalar values, are then presented to a k-nn classifier.

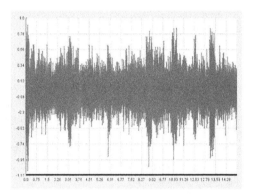

Figure 10: The visualisation of audio captcha from Securimage containing phonemes "h86gpd". The added noise effectively covers gaps between characters.

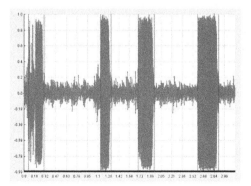

Figure 11: The visualisation of audio captcha from uloz.to. Added noise is weak and the phonemes can be simple separated by thresholding the amplitude.

5   Experimental evaluation

This section describes all the experiments we have done so far, setting of k-nn parameters for both audio and text-based captchas and evaluating of the successful recognition rate for each analysed scheme. Because this is work in progress, there are still some missing values and not all experiments were finished yet.

We have tested text-based captchas recognition at the following web sites: cuzk.cz[1], mojedatovaschranka.cz[3], sujb.cz[4], uloz.to[5], centralniregistrdluzniku.cz[2] and the audio-based captchas recognition at: sujb.cz[4] and again uloz.to[5].

5.1 Parameters setting

For the parameters setting, we used together 510 text-based and audio-based captchas, which were manually labelled. We used a 3-fold cross-validation, entailing 340 samples for training and remaining 170 for testing.

Our experimental results on the uloz.to dataset suggests that the best option for the text-based captchas are manhattan distance and $k = 6$, see Figure 12. For the audio-based captchas the graph looked pretty similar, but we used euclidean instead of manhattan distance. It showed up that the euclidean metric is the best and together with $k = 9$ it achieved recognition rate 86,5%, followed by the cosine metric with 84.1%.

The uloz.to was chosen as the primary testing dataset for multiple reasons. It has the most advanced captcha we found on the Czech internet in both text-based and audio-based cases. We didn't found any design or implementation flaws like for e.g. for the cuzk.cz web site. Therefore, we expected the parameters set on the uloz.to dataset will be robust enough even for the other schemes and according to Figure 13, this is more or less true.

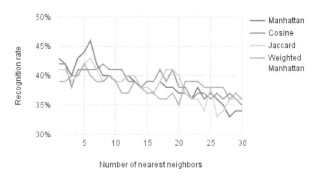

Figure 12: Comparison of different metrics and the influence of increasing k for text-based captcha.

5.2 Results

uloz.to The uloz.to is a file sharing service which uses captchas to prevent automated file downloading. They support both text-based and audio-based schemes. Their text-based scheme is very good compared to others we analysed. They use distortion, rotation a lot of noise and occluding lines. Their audio captcha use one synthetic voice with addition of a weak noise signal.

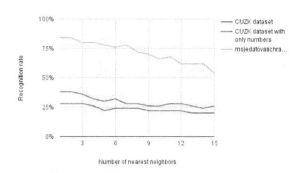

Figure 13: Checking the robustness of parameters setting estimated on uloz.to on other schemes.

Figure 14: Example of text-based captcha from uloz.to.

We have analysed 510 samples of audio and text-based challenges. Our average recognition rate for whole captchas estimated by 10-fold cross-validation was 14% for text-based and 86% for audio-based captchas. The 14% recognition rate does not seem much, but lets recall that there is the 1% threshold to consider a captcha scheme compromised. Furthermore, we have tested up to ten humans to solve the random audio captchas and their success rate ranged from 54% to 76%. This in fact means that the computers are better than humans in test which should tell them apart.

sujb.cz The State Office for Nuclear Safety uses a captcha to secure their public forum. Both text-based and audio-based schemes are available and easy to solve. Both schemes lack noise and anti-recognition features. The text-based scheme has occluding lines, but they have a different colour than characters so it is easy to filter them out.

The overall recognition rate was 98% for audio-based and 86% for text-based captchas. But we have to admin that we used only 50 images and audio files to obtain those results.

cuzk.cz The Czech State Administration of Land Surveying and Cadastre uses only the text-based captcha to disable automatic queries to their database. The images generated by their scheme look well on the first sight but there is a serious design bug. The captcha shown on an im-

Figure 15: Example of text-based captcha from sujb.cz.

Figure 16: Example of text-based captcha from cuzk.cz.

Figure 17: Example of text-based captcha from mojedato-vaschranka.cz.

age is not a standard GIF or JPEG format but rather a *.axd* file, which is the HTTP Handler used by ASP.NET applications. Therefore, the image is generated on runtime. Simply refreshing the image (not the whole page) then generates a new captcha challenge containing the same characters.

Thanks to the bug, we were able to obtain and label 2100 different images. This flaw can be easily exploited to achieve a nearly 100% precision, by downloading more and more images until we are sure about correct recognition. To be fair we did not used this bug in our evaluation and still were able to obtain 46% captcha recognition rate.

mojedatovaschranka.cz This scheme is pretty weak, lacking any anti-segmentation features, with a differently coloured noise and using only digits. Our result is a 82% success recognition rate over the testing set of 50 samples.

centralniregistrdluzniku.cz This page serves as the central registry of debtors and captcha must be solve before you can upload your customer experience with some company. Adopted scheme is again easy to solve, the distortion is weak and occluding lines have a different colour than the characters. Our result is a 61% success recognition rate over a testing set of 50 samples.

5.3 Summary

The final results are summarised in Table 1. The reported numbers are captcha recognition rates, estimated by a 10-fold cross-validation. Some values are missing, because the audio-based captcha alternative is available only for uloz.to and sujb.cz.

Finally, the overall misclassification overview is given for the text-based captcha in Figure 19, and for the audio-based in Table 2.

Figure 18: Example of text-based captcha from central-niregistrdluzniku.cz.

webpage	audio	text
uloz.to	0.86	0.14
sujb.cz	0.98	0.86
cuzk.cz	-	0.46
mojedatovaschranka.cz	-	0.82
centralniregistrdluzniku.cz	-	0.61

Table 1: The summary off successful recognition rates on all tested captcha challenges.

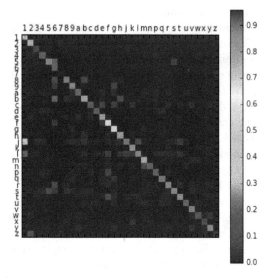

Figure 19: Confusion matrix for all text-based schemes.

6 Conclusion

This research was driven by curiosity of security enthusiasts and will be used for academic purposes only. None of us have any malevolent or business intentions.

We have tested the security of several captcha solutions across Czech internet environment. We intentionally used the out of the shelf algorithms to simulate simple attacks. The final result is that the current state is alarming. All tested solution have been compromised with recognition rate highly over 1%. The most secure solution was the text-based scheme at uloz.to, where we achieved only 14% recognition rate. On the other hand we were about 10% more accurate than humans in terms of average recognition rate on their audio-based captchas.

The second most secure were challenges generated at the web site of the Czech State Administration of Land Surveying and Cadastre. The captcha is used to block automated queries to the database and it should prevent massive downloads of private informations about the ownership of real estates. Our recognition rate was almost one half, more precisely 46%. But due to the design flaw of this captcha, described in Section 5, it can be easily boosted to almost 100% precision.

The key messages of this paper should be: do not rely on any captcha as the only defence agains automation and

phoneme	success rate	misclassified as phoneme	rate
a	97.2	r	2.8
b	96.8	t	3.2
c	82.1	s	10.7
d	92.1	r	5.3
e	92.3	a	3.8
f	96.3	x	3.7
g	96.3	n	3.7
h	97.4	k	2.6
i	100	-	-
j	93.1	a	3.4
k	100	-	-
l	80	r	20
m	96.8	b	3.2
n	100	-	-
o	100	-	-
p	93.3	o	6.7
q	96.4	r	3.6
r	100	-	-
s	87.5	x	3.1
t	87.9	k	6.1
u	89.3	o	3.6
v	95.7	g	4.3
x	92.3	s	2.6
z	95.1	g	2.4

Table 2: The misclassification rate for the audio captchas.

never use captcha as the only security solution and for the attacker it is: if you can choose, try audio captchas, they are typically easier to break.

As to our future work, we are still preparing a more complete survey of captcha solutions used on the Czech internet. We are especially searching for more state administration pages, that use completely insufficient solutions or design flaws. Currently we are devoting our research efforts to the application of convolution neural networks in this context as we believe that they can replace our whole text-based pipeline. We are also starting to pay attention to image-based captchas like the one in Figure 2

Acknowledgement

The research reported in this paper has been supported by the Student Grant SGS16/119/OHK3/1T/18.

References

[1] Nahlížení do katastru nemovitostí [online], 2004-2016. [Cited 2016-06-01].

[2] Centrální registr dlužníků [online], 2016. [Cited 2016-06-01].

[3] Datové schránky [online], 2016. [Cited 2016-06-01].

[4] Státní úřad pro jadernou bezpečnost [online], 2016. [Cited 2016-06-01].

[5] Ulož.to [online], 2016. [Cited 2016-06-01].

[6] Elie Bursztein, Jonathan Aigrain, Angelika Moscicki, and John C Mitchell. The end is nigh: Generic solving of text-based captchas. In *8th USENIX Workshop on Offensive Technologies (WOOT 14)*, 2014.

[7] Elie Bursztein, Romain Beauxis, Hristo Paskov, Daniele Perito, Celine Fabry, and John Mitchell. The failure of noise-based non-continuous audio captchas. In *Security and Privacy (SP), 2011 IEEE Symposium on*, pages 19–31. IEEE, 2011.

[8] Elie Bursztein and Steven Bethard. Decaptcha: breaking 75% of ebay audio captchas. In *Proceedings of the 3rd USENIX conference on Offensive technologies*, page 8. USENIX Association, 2009.

[9] Elie Bursztein, Steven Bethard, Celine Fabry, John C Mitchell, and Dan Jurafsky. How good are humans at solving captchas? a large scale evaluation. In *2010 IEEE Symposium on Security and Privacy*, pages 399–413. IEEE, 2010.

[10] Elie Bursztein, Matthieu Martin, and John Mitchell. Text-based captcha strengths and weaknesses. In *Proceedings of the 18th ACM conference on Computer and communications security*, pages 125–138. ACM, 2011.

[11] Kumar Chellapilla, Kevin Larson, Patrice Simard, and Mary Czerwinski. Designing human friendly human interaction proofs (hips). In *Proceedings of the SIGCHI conference on Human factors in computing systems*, pages 711–720. ACM, 2005.

[12] Claudia Cruz-Perez, Oleg Starostenko, Fernando Uceda-Ponga, Vicente Alarcon-Aquino, and Leobardo Reyes-Cabrera. Breaking recaptchas with unpredictable collapse: heuristic character segmentation and recognition. In *Pattern Recognition*, pages 155–165. Springer, 2012.

[13] Nobuyuki Otsu. A threshold selection method from gray-level histograms. *Automatica*, 11(285-296):23–27, 1975.

[14] ITUR Rec. Bt 601: Studio encoding parameters of digital television for standard 4: 3 and wide-screen 16: 9 aspect ratios. *ITU-R Rec. BT*, 656, 1995.

[15] Urmila Shrawankar and Vilas M Thakare. Techniques for feature extraction in speech recognition system: A comparative study. *arXiv preprint arXiv:1305.1145*, 2013.

[16] F. Stark, C. Hazırbaş, R. Triebel, and D. Cremers. Captcha recognition with active deep learning. In *GCPR Workshop on New Challenges in Neural Computation*, 2015.

[17] Jennifer Tam, Jiri Simsa, Sean Hyde, and Luis V Ahn. Breaking audio captchas. In *Advances in Neural Information Processing Systems*, pages 1625–1632, 2008.

[18] Alan M Turing. Computing machinery and intelligence. *Mind*, 59(236):433–460, 1950.

[19] Luis Von Ahn, Manuel Blum, Nicholas J Hopper, and John Langford. Captcha: Using hard ai problems for security. In *Advances in Cryptology—EUROCRYPT 2003*, pages 294–311. Springer, 2003.

ITAT 2016 Proceedings, pp. 118–122
ISBN 978-1537016740, © 2016 V. Kůrková

Multivariable Approximation by Convolutional Kernel Networks

Věra Kůrková

Institute of Computer Science, Academy of Sciences of the Czech,
vera@cs.cas.cz,
WWW home page: http://www.cs.cas.cz/~vera

Abstract: Computational units induced by convolutional kernels together with biologically inspired perceptrons belong to the most widespread types of units used in neurocomputing. Radial convolutional kernels with varying widths form RBF (radial-basis-function) networks and these kernels with fixed widths are used in the SVM (support vector machine) algorithm. We investigate suitability of various convolutional kernel units for function approximation. We show that properties of Fourier transforms of convolutional kernels determine whether sets of input-output functions of networks with kernel units are large enough to be universal approximators. We compare these properties with conditions guaranteeing positive semidefinitness of convolutional kernels.

1 Introduction

Computational units induced by radial and convolutional kernels together with perceptrons belong to the most widespread types of units used in neurocomputing. In contrast to biologically inspired perceptrons [15], localized radial units [1] were introduced merely due to their good mathematical properties. Radial-basis-function units (RBF) computing spherical waves were followed by kernel units [7]. Kernel units in the most general form include all types of computational units, which are functions of two vector variables: an input vector and a parameter vector. However, often the term kernel unit is reserved merely for units computing symmetric positive semidefinite functions of two variables. Networks with these units have been widely used for classification with maximal margin by the support vector machine algorithm (SVM) [2] as well as for regression [21].

Other important kernel units are units induced by convolutional kernels in the form of translations of functions of one vector variable. Isotropic RBF units can be viewed as non symmetric kernel units obtained from convolutional radial kernels by adding a width parameter. Variability of widths is a strong property. It allows to apply arguments based on classical results on approximation of functions by sequences of their convolutions with scaled bump functions to prove universal approximation capabilities of many types of RBF networks [16, 17]. Moreover, some estimates of rates of approximation by RBF networks exploit variability of widths [9, 10, 13].

On the other hand, symmetric positive semidefinite kernels (which include some classes of RBFs with fixed widths parameters) benefit from geometrical properties of reproducing kernel Hilbert spaces (RKHS) generated by these kernels. These properties allow an extension of the maximal margin classification from finite dimensional spaces also to sets of data which are not linearly separable by embedding them into infinite dimensional spaces [2]. Moreover, symmetric positive semidefinite kernels generate stabilizers in the form of norms on RKHSs suitable for modeling generalization in terms of regularization [6] and enable characterizations of theoretically optimal solutions of learning tasks [3, 19, 11].

Arguments proving the universal approximation property of RBF networks using sequences of scaled kernels might suggest that variability of widths is necessary for the universal approximation. However, for the special case of the Gaussian kernel, the universal approximation property holds even when the width is fixed and merely centers are varying [14, 12].

On the other hand, it is easy to find some examples of positive semidefinite kernels such that sets of input-output functions of shallow networks with units generated by these kernels are too small to be universal approximators. For example, networks with product kernel units of the form $K(x,y) = k(x)k(y)$ generate as input-output functions only scalar multiples $ck(x)$ of the function k.

In this paper, we investigate capabilities of networks with one hidden layer of convolutional kernel units to approximate multivariable functions. We show that a crucial property influencing whether sets of input-output functions of convolutional kernel networks are large enough to be universal approximators is behavior of the Fourier transform of the one variable function generating the convolutional kernel. We give a necessary and sufficient condition for universal approximation of kernel networks in terms of the Fourier transforms of kernels. We compare this condition with properties of kernels guaranteeing their positive definitness. We illustrate our results by examples of some common kernels such as Gaussian, Laplace, parabolic, rectangle, and triangle.

The paper is organized as follows. In section 2, notations and basic concepts on one-hidden-layer networks and kernel units are introduced. In section 3, a necessary and sufficient condition on a convolutional kernel that guarantees that networks with units induced by the kernel have the universal approximation property. In section 4 this condition is compared with a condition guaranteeing that a kernel is positive semidefinite and some examples of kernels satisfying both or one of these conditions are given. Section 5 is a brief discussion.

2 Preliminaries

Radial-basis-function networks as well as kernel models belong to the class of one-hidden-layer networks with one linear output unit. Such networks compute input-output functions from sets of the form

$$\operatorname{span} G = \left\{ \sum_{i=1}^{n} w_i g_i \,|\, w_i \in \mathbb{R}, g_i \in G, n \in \mathbb{N}_+ \right\},$$

where the set G is called a *dictionary* [8], and $\mathbb{R}$, $\mathbb{N}_+$ denote the sets of real numbers and positive integers, resp. Typically, dictionaries are parameterized families of functions modeling computational units, i.e., they are of the form

$$G_K(X,Y) = \{K(.,y) : X \to \mathbb{R} \,|\, y \in Y\}$$

where $K : X \times Y \to \mathbb{R}$ is a function of two variables, an input vector $x \in X \subseteq \mathbb{R}^d$ and a parameter $y \in Y \subseteq \mathbb{R}^s$. Such functions of two variables are called *kernels*. This term, derived from the German term "kern", has been used since 1904 in theory of integral operators [18, p.291].

An important class of kernels are *convolutional kernels* which are obtained by translations of one-variable functions $k : \mathbb{R}^d \to \mathbb{R}^d$ as

$$K(x,y) = k(x-y).$$

Radial convolutional kernels are convolutional kernels obtained as translations of radial functions, i.e., functions of the form

$$k(x) = k_1(\|x\|),$$

where $k_1 : \mathbb{R}_+ \to \mathbb{R}$.

The *convolution* is an operation defined as

$$f * g(x) = \int_{\mathbb{R}^d} f(y-x)g(y)dy = \int_{\mathbb{R}^d} f(y)g(x-y)dy$$

[20, p.170].

Recall, that a kernel $K : X \times X \to \mathbb{R}$ is called *positive semidefinite* if for any positive integer m, any $x_1, \ldots, x_m \in X$ and any $a_1, \ldots, a_m \in \mathbb{R}$,

$$\sum_{i=1}^{m} \sum_{j=1}^{m} a_i a_j K(x_i, x_j) \geq 0.$$

Similarly, a function of one variable $k : \mathbb{R}^d \to \mathbb{R}$ is called positive semidefinite if for any positive integer m, any $x_1, \ldots, x_m \in X$ and any $a_1, \ldots, a_m \in \mathbb{R}$,

$$\sum_{i=1}^{m} \sum_{j=1}^{m} a_i a_j k(x_i - x_j) \geq 0.$$

For symmetric positive semidefinite kernels K, the sets $\operatorname{span} G_K(X)$ of input-output functions of networks with

units induced by the kernel K are contained in Hilbert spaces defined by these kernels. These spaces are called *reproducing kernel Hilbert spaces (RKHS)* and denoted $\mathscr{H}_K(X)$. They are formed by functions from

$$\operatorname{span} G_K(X) = \operatorname{span}\{K_x \,|\, x \in X\},$$

where

$$K_x(.) = K(x,.),$$

together with limits of their Cauchy sequences in the norm $\|.\|_K$. The norm $\|.\|_K$ is induced by the inner product $\langle ., . \rangle_K$, which is defined on

$$G_K(X) = \{K_x \,|\, x \in X\}$$

as

$$\langle K_x, K_y \rangle_K = K(x,y).$$

So $\operatorname{span} G_K(X) \subset \mathscr{H}_K(X)$.

3 Universal approximation capability of convolutional kernel networks

In this section, we investigate conditions guaranteeing that sets of input-output functions of convolutional kernel networks are large enough to be universal approximators.

The universal approximation property is formally defined as density in a normed linear space. A class of one-hidden-layer networks with units from a dictionary G is said to have the *universal approximation property in a normed linear space* $(\mathscr{X}, \|.\|_{\mathscr{X}})$ if it is *dense* in this space, i.e., $\operatorname{cl}_{\mathscr{X}} \operatorname{span} G = \mathscr{X}$, where $\operatorname{span} G$ denotes the *linear span* of G and $\operatorname{cl}_{\mathscr{X}}$ denotes the closure with respect to the topology induced by the norm $\|.\|_{\mathscr{X}}$. More precisely, for every $f \in X$ and every $\varepsilon > 0$ there exist a positive integer $n, g_1, \ldots, g_n \in G$, and $w_1, \ldots, w_n \in \mathbb{R}$ such that

$$\|f - \sum_{i=1}^{n} w_i g_i\|_{\mathscr{X}} < \varepsilon.$$

Function spaces where the universal approximation property has been of interest are spaces $(\mathbb{C}(X), \|.\|_{\sup})$ of continuous functions on subsets X of $\mathbb{R}^d$ (typically compact) with the supremum norm

$$\|f\|_{\sup} = \sup_{x \in X} |f(x)|$$

and spaces $(\mathscr{L}^p(\mathbb{R}^d), \|.\|_{\mathscr{L}^p})$ of functions on $\mathbb{R}^d$ with finite $\int_{\mathbb{R}^d} |f(y)|^p dy$ and the norm

$$\|f\|_{\mathscr{L}^p} = \left(\int_{\mathbb{R}^d} |f(y)|^p dy \right)^{1/p}.$$

Recall that the *d-dimensional Fourier transform* is an isometry on $\mathscr{L}^2(\mathbb{R}^d)$ defined on $\mathscr{L}^2(\mathbb{R}^d) \cap \mathscr{L}^1(\mathbb{R}^d)$ as

$$\hat{f}(s) = \frac{1}{(2\pi)^{d/2}} \int_{\mathbb{R}^d} e^{-ix \cdot s} f(x) dx$$

and extended to $\mathscr{L}^2(\mathbb{R}^d)$ [20, p.183].

Note that the Fourier transform of an even function is real and the Fourier transform of a radial function is radial. If $k \in cL^1(\mathbb{R}^d)$, then $\hat{k}$ is uniformly continuous and with increasing frequencies converges to zero, i.e.,

$$\lim_{\|s\|\to\infty} \hat{k}(s) = 0.$$

The following theorem gives a necessary and sufficient condition on a convolutional kernel that guarantees that the class of input-output functions computable by networks with units induced by the kernel can approximate arbitrarily well all functions in $\mathscr{L}^2(\mathbb{R}^d)$. The condition is formulated in terms of the size of the set of frequencies for which the Fourier transform is equal to zero. By λ is denoted the Lebesgue measure.

Theorem 1. *Let d be a positive integer, $k \in \mathscr{L}^1(\mathbb{R}^d) \cap \mathscr{L}^2(\mathbb{R}^d)$ be even, $K : \mathbb{R}^d \times \mathbb{R}^d \to \mathbb{R}$ be defined as $K(x,y) = k(x-y)$, and $X \subseteq \mathbb{R}^d$ be Lebesgue measurable. Then $\operatorname{span} G_K(X)$ is dense in $(\mathscr{L}^2(X), \|.\|_{\mathscr{L}^2})$ if and only if $\lambda(\{s \in \mathbb{R}^d \,|\, \hat{k}(s) = 0\}) = 0$.*

Proof. First, we prove the necessity. To prove it by contradiction, assume that $\lambda(S) \neq 0$. Take any function $f \in \mathscr{L}^2(\mathbb{R}^d) \cap \mathscr{L}^1(\mathbb{R}^d)$ with a positive Fourier transform (for example, f can be the Gaussian). Let $\varepsilon > 0$ be such that

$$\varepsilon < \int_{\mathbb{R}^d} \hat{f}(s)^2 ds.$$

Assume that there exists n, $w_i \in \mathbb{R}$, and $y_i \in \mathbb{R}^d$ such that

$$\left\| f - \sum_{j=1}^n w_i k(. - y_i) \right\|_{\mathscr{L}_2} < \varepsilon.$$

Then by the Plancherel Theorem [20, p.188],

$$\left\| \hat{f} - \sum_{j=1}^n w_i \widehat{k(. - y_i)} \right\|_{\mathscr{L}_2}^2 = \left\| \hat{f} - \sum_{j=1}^n \bar{w}_i \hat{k} \right\|_{\mathscr{L}_2}^2,$$

where $\bar{w}_i = w_i e^{iy_i}$. Hence

$$\left\| \hat{f} - \sum_{j=1}^n \bar{w}_i \hat{k} \right\|_{\mathscr{L}_2}^2 =$$

$$\int_{\mathbb{R}^d \setminus S} \left(\hat{f}(s) - \sum_{j=1}^n \bar{w}_i \hat{k}(s) \right)^2 ds + \int_S \hat{f}(s)^2 ds > \varepsilon,$$

which is a contradiction.

To prove the sufficiency, we first assume that $X = \mathbb{R}^d$. We prove it by contradiction, so we suppose that

$$\operatorname{cl}_{\mathscr{L}^2} \operatorname{span} G_K(\mathbb{R}^d) = \operatorname{cl}_{\mathscr{L}^2} \operatorname{span} \{K(.,y) \,|\, y \in \mathbb{R}^d\} \neq \mathscr{L}^2(\mathbb{R}^d).$$

Then by the Hahn-Banach Theorem [20, p. 60] there exists a bounded linear functional l on $\mathscr{L}^2(\mathbb{R}^d)$ such that for all $f \in \operatorname{cl}_{\mathscr{L}^2} \operatorname{span} G_K(\mathbb{R}^d)$, $l(f) = 0$ and for some $f_0 \in$

$\mathscr{L}^2(\mathbb{R}^d) \setminus \operatorname{cl}_{\mathscr{L}^2} \operatorname{span} G_K(\mathbb{R}^d)$, $l(f_0) = 1$. By the Riesz Representation Theorem [5, p.206], l can be expressed as an inner product with some $h \in \mathscr{L}^2(\mathbb{R}^d)$.

As k is even, for all $y \in \mathbb{R}^d$,

$$\langle h, K(.,y) \rangle = \int_{\mathbb{R}^d} h(x)k(x-y)dx =$$

$$\int_{\mathbb{R}^d} h(x)k_1(y-x)dx = h * k_1(x) = 0.$$

By the Young Inequality for convolutions $h * k \in \mathscr{L}^2(\mathbb{R}^d)$ and so by the Plancherel Theorem [20, p.188],

$$\|\widehat{h * k_1}\|_{\mathscr{L}^2} = 0.$$

As

$$\widehat{h * k_1} = \frac{1}{(2\pi)^{d/2}} \hat{h}\hat{k}$$

[20, p.183], we have $\|\hat{h}\hat{k}\|_{\mathscr{L}^2} = 0$ and so

$$\int_{\mathbb{R}^d} (\hat{h}(s)\hat{k}(s))^2 ds = 0.$$

As the set

$$S = \{s \in \mathbb{R}^d \,|\, \hat{k}(s) = 0\}$$

has Lebesgue measure zero we have

$$\int_{\mathbb{R}^d} \hat{h}(s)^2 \hat{k}(s)^2 ds = \int_{\mathbb{R}^d \setminus S} \hat{h}(s)^2 \hat{k}(s)^2 ds = 0.$$

As for all $s \in \mathbb{R}^d \setminus S$, $\hat{k}(s)^2 > 0$, we have $\|\hat{h}\|_{\mathscr{L}^2}^2 ds = 0$. So $\|h\|_{\mathscr{L}^2} = 0$ and hence by the Cauchy-Schwartz Inequality we get

$$1 = l(f_0) = \int_{\mathbb{R}^d} f_0(y)h(y)dy \leq \|f_0\|_{\mathscr{L}^2} \|h\|_{\mathscr{L}^2} = 0,$$

which is a contradiction.

Extending a function f from $\mathscr{L}^2(X)$ to $\bar{f}$ from $\mathscr{L}^2(\mathbb{R}^d)$ by setting its values equal to zero outside of X and restricting approximations of $\bar{f}$ by functions from $\operatorname{span} G_K(\mathbb{R}^d)$ to X, we get the statement for any Lebesgue measurable subset X of $\mathbb{R}^d$. $\square$

Theorem 1 shows that sets of input-output functions of convolutional kernel networks are large enough to approximate arbitrarily well all $\mathscr{L}^2$-functions if and only if the Fourier transform of the function k is almost everywhere non-zero.

Theorem 1 implies that when $\hat{k}(s)$ is equal to zero for all s such that $\|s\| \geq r$ for some $r > 0$ (the Fourier transform is band-limited), then the set $\operatorname{span} G_K(\mathbb{R}^d)$ is too small to have the universal approximation capability. In the next section we show, that some of such kernels are positive semidefinite. So they can be used for classification by the SVM algorithm but they are not suitable for function approximation.

4 Positive semidefinitness and universal approximation property

In this section, we compare a condition on positive semidefinitness of a convolutional kernel with the condition on the universal approximation property derived in the previous section.

As the inverse Fourier transform of a convolutional kernel can be expressed as

$$K(x,y) = k(x-y) = \frac{1}{(2\pi)^{d/2}} \int_{\mathbb{R}^d} \hat{k}(s) e^{i(x-y)\cdot s} ds$$

it is easy to verify that when $\hat{k}$ is positive or non negative than K defined as $K(x,y) = k(x-y)$ is positive definite, semidefinite, resp.

Indeed, to verify that $\sum_{j,l=1}^n a_j a_l K(x_j,x_l) \geq 0$ we express K in terms of the inverse Fourier transform. Thus we get

$$\sum_{j,l=1}^n a_j a_l K(x_j,x_l) = \sum_{j,l=1}^n a_j a_l \frac{1}{(2\pi)^{d/2}} \int_{\mathbb{R}^d} \hat{k}(s) e^{i(x_j-x_l)\cdot s} ds =$$

$$\frac{1}{(2\pi)d/2} \int_{\mathbb{R}^d} \left(\sum_j^n a_j e^{i(x_j)\cdot s} \right) \left(\sum_l^n a_k e^{-i(x_l)\cdot s} \right) \hat{k}(s) ds =$$

$$\frac{1}{(2\pi)d/2} \int_{\mathbb{R}^d} \left| \sum_j^n a_j e^{i(x_j)\cdot s} \right|^2 \hat{k}(s) ds \geq 0.$$

The following proposition is well-known (see, e.g., [4]).

Proposition 2. Let $k \in \mathscr{L}^1(\mathbb{R}^d) \cap \mathscr{L}^2(\mathbb{R}^d)$ be an even function such that $\hat{k}(s) \geq 0$ for all $s \in \mathbb{R}^d$. Then $K(x,y) = k(x-y)$ is positive semidefinite.

A complete characterization of positive semidefinite bounded continuous kernels follows from the Bochner Theorem.

Theorem 3 (Bochner). *A bounded continuous function $k : \mathbb{R}^d \to \mathbb{C}$ is positive semidefinite iff k is the Fourier transform of a nonnegative finite Borel measure μ, i.e.,*

$$k(x) = \frac{1}{(2\pi)^{d/2}} \int_{\mathbb{R}^d} e^{-x \cdot s} \mu(ds).$$

The Bochner Theorem implies that when the Borel measure μ has a distribution function then the condition in Proposition 2 is both sufficient and necessary.

Comparison of the characterization of kernels for which by Theorem 1 one-hidden-layer kernel networks are universal approximators with the condition on positive semidefinitness from Proposition 2 shows that there are positive semidefinite kernels which do not generate networks possessing the universal approximation capability

and there also are kernels which are not positive definite but induce networks with the universal approximation property. The first ones are suitable for SVM but not for regression, while the second ones can be used for regression but are not suitable for SVM. In the sequel, we give some examples of such kernels.

A paradigmatic example of a convolutional kernel is the *Gaussian kernel* $g_a : \mathbb{R}^d \to \mathbb{R}$ defined for a width $a > 0$ as

$$g_a = e^{-a^2 \|.\|^2}.$$

For any fixed width a and any dimension d,

$$\hat{g_a} = (\sqrt{2}a)^{-d} e^{-1/a^2 \|.\|^2}.$$

So the Gaussian kernel is positive definite and the class of Gaussian kernel networks have the universal approximation property.

The *rectangle kernel* is defined as

$$\text{rect}(x) = 1 \text{ for } x \in (-1/2, 1/2),$$
$$\text{otherwise rect}(x) = 0.$$

Its Fourier transform is the sinc function

$$\widehat{\text{rect}}(s) = \text{sinc}(s) = \frac{\sin(\pi s)}{\pi s}.$$

So the Fourier transform of rect is not non negative but its zeros form a discrete set of the Lebesgue measure zero. Thus the rectangle kernel is not positive semidefinite but induces class of networks with the universal approximation property. On the other hand, the Fourier transform of sinc is the rectangle kernel and thus it is positive semidefinite, but does not induce networks with the universal approximation property.

The *Laplace kernel* is defined for any $a > 0$ as

$$l(x) = e^{-a|x|}.$$

Its Fourier transforms is positive as

$$\hat{l}(s) = \frac{2a}{a^2 + (2\pi s)^2}.$$

The *triangle kernel* is defined as

$$\text{tri}(x) = 2x - 1/2 \text{ for } x \in (-1/2, 0),$$
$$\text{tri}(x) = -2(x+1/2) \text{ for } x \in (0, 1/2),$$
$$\text{otherwise tri}(x) = 0.$$

Its Fourier transforms is positive as

$$\widehat{\text{tri}}(s) = \text{sinc}(s)^2 = \left(\frac{\sin(\pi s)}{\pi s} \right)^2.$$

Thus both the Laplace and the triangle kernel are positive definite and induce networks having the universal approximation property.

The *parabolic (Epinechnikov) kernel* is defined

$$\text{epi}(x) = \tfrac{3}{4}(1-x^2) \text{ for } x \in (-1,1),$$
$$\text{otherwise epi}(x) = 0.$$

Its Fourier transforms is

$$\widehat{\text{epi}}(s) = \frac{3}{s^3}\left(\sin(s) - \frac{1}{2}s\cos(s)\right) \text{ for } s \neq 0,$$
$$\widehat{\text{epi}}(s) = 1 \text{ for } s = 0.$$

So the parabolic kernel is not positive semidefinite but induces networks with the universal approximation property.

5 Discussion

We investigated effect of properties of the Fourier transform of a kernel function on suitability of the convolutional kernel for function approximation (universal approximation property) and for maximal margin classification algorithm (positive semidefinitness). We showed that these properties depend on the way how the Fourier transform converges with increasing frequencies to infinity. For the universal approximation property, the Fourier transform can be negative but cannot be zero on any set of frequencies of non-zero Lebesgue measure. On the other hand, functions with non-negative Fourier transforms are positive semidefinite even if they are compactly supported. We illustrated our results by the paradigmatic example of the multivariable Gaussian kernel and by some one-dimensional examples. Multivariable Gaussian is a product of one variable functions and thus its multivariable Fourier transform can be computed using transforms of one-variable Gaussians. Fourier transforms of other radial multivariable kernels are more complicated, their expressions include Bessel functions and the Hankel transform. Investigation of properties of Fourier transforms of multivariable radial convolutional kernels is subject of our future work.

Acknowledgments. This work was partially supported by the grant GAČR 15-181085 and institutional support of the Institute of Computer Science RVO 67985807.

References

[1] D. S. Broomhead and D. Lowe. Error bounds for approximation with neural networks. *Complex Systems*, 2:321–355, 1988.

[2] C. Cortes and V. N. Vapnik. Support vector networks. *Machine Learning*, 20:273–297, 1995.

[3] F. Cucker and S. Smale. On the mathematical foundations of learning. *Bulletin of AMS*, 39:1–49, 2002.

[4] F. Cucker and D. X. Zhou. *Learning Theory: An Approximation Theory Viewpoint*. Cambridge University Press, Cambridge, 2007.

[5] A. Friedman. *Modern Analysis*. Dover, New York, 1982.

[6] F. Girosi. An equivalence between sparse approximation and support vector machines. *Neural Computation*, 10:1455–1480 (AI memo 1606), 1998.

[7] F. Girosi and T. Poggio. Regularization algorithms for learning that are equivalent to multilayer networks. *Science*, 247(4945):978–982, 1990.

[8] R. Gribonval and P. Vandergheynst. On the exponential convergence of matching pursuits in quasi-incoherent dictionaries. *IEEE Trans. on Information Theory*, 52:255–261, 2006.

[9] P. C. Kainen, V. Kůrková, and M. Sanguineti. Complexity of Gaussian radial basis networks approximating smooth functions. *J. of Complexity*, 25:63–74, 2009.

[10] P. C. Kainen, V. Kůrková, and M. Sanguineti. Dependence of computational models on input dimension: Tractability of approximation and optimization tasks. *IEEE Transactions on Information Theory*, 58:1203–1214, 2012.

[11] V. Kůrková. Neural network learning as an inverse problem. *Logic Journal of IGPL*, 13:551–559, 2005.

[12] V. Kůrková and P. C. Kainen. Comparing fixed and variable-width gaussian networks. *Neural Networks*, 57:23–28, 2014.

[13] V. Kůrková and M. Sanguineti. Model complexities of shallow networks representing highly varying functions. *Neurocomputing*, 171:598–604, 2016.

[14] H. N. Mhaskar. Versatile Gaussian networks. In *Proceedings of IEEE Workshop of Nonlinear Image Processing*, pages 70–73, 1995.

[15] M. Minsky and S. Papert. *Perceptrons*. MIT Press, 1969.

[16] J. Park and I. Sandberg. Universal approximation using radial–basis–function networks. *Neural Computation*, 3:246–257, 1991.

[17] J. Park and I. Sandberg. Approximation and radial basis function networks. *Neural Computation*, 5:305–316, 1993.

[18] A. Pietsch. *Eigenvalues and s-Numbers*. Cambridge University Press, Cambridge, 1987.

[19] T. Poggio and S. Smale. The mathematics of learning: dealing with data. *Notices of AMS*, 50:537–544, 2003.

[20] W. Rudin. *Functional Analysis*. Mc Graw-Hill, 1991.

[21] B. Schölkopf and A. J. Smola. *Learning with Kernels – Support Vector Machines, Regularization, Optimization and Beyond*. MIT Press, Cambridge, 2002.

ITAT 2016 Proceedings, pp. 123–130
ISBN 978-1537016740, © 2016 T. Kuzin, T. Borovička

Early Failure Detection for Predictive Maintenance of Sensor Parts

Tomáš Kuzin, Tomáš Borovička

Faculty of Information Technology,
Czech Technical University in Prague,
Prague, The Czech Repubic
kuzintom@fit.cvut.cz,
tomas.borovicka@fit.cvut.cz

Abstract: Maintenance of a sensor part typically means renewal of the sensor in regular intervals or replacing the malfunctioning sensor. However optimal timing of the replacement can reduce maintenance costs. The aim of this article is to suggest a predictive maintenance strategy for sensors using condition monitoring and early failure detection based on their own collected measurements.

Three different approaches that deal with early failure detection of sensor parts are introduced 1) approach based on feature extraction and status classification, 2) approach based on time series modeling and 3) approach based on anomaly detection using autoencoders. All methods were illustrated on real-world data and were proven to be applicable for condition monitoring.

1 Introduction

In the last decade the amount of used sensors across all sectors has significantly raised. This is important and a still continuing trend.

In the classical concept, predictive maintenance takes place when the maintained asset is expensive or important for key business processes. In other words when proper utilization of the machinery has important economic or safety consequences. This is not the characteristic case of sensor parts which are usually cheap and play a minor role. For such assets maintenance typically means simple replacement and reactive maintenance strategy would be the most common choice. However, machines become more and more dependent on sensor parts and that brings new challenges in their maintenance. Proper timing of replacement has direct influence on maintenance expenses. Especially in cases where other processes depend on the sensor readings and the sensor failure or malfunction may stop the operation or cause collateral loses of a machinery.

In case of sensors "classical" condition monitoring scheme utilizing properly chosen set of external sensors makes no sense. On the other hand sensors themselves provide on-line measurements during their whole operational service. These data may be exploited to estimate the current state of the measuring device. Therefore applying smarter maintenance strategy for sensor parts makes perfect sense and may introduce significant savings.

This article deals with the possibilities of smarter maintenance strategies for sensor parts. The main idea is to apply machine learning techniques in order to monitor the current condition or predict failure of sensors based on their own measurements and propose an optimal time for their replacement in order to avoid failures.

2 Related Work

Several articles and works on "classical" predictive maintenance and condition monitoring [1, 2] were published in the literature. Predictive maintenance strategy is usually a rule-based maintenance grounded on on-line condition monitoring, which relies on an appropriately chosen set of external sensors. The proper sensor set plays the key role [2]. Unfortunately none of these techniques are useful if it is needed to monitor the state of sensors themselves. Moreover, many published works base their approaches on sensor networks, where malfunction of one sensor can be identified utilizing measurements of other sensors in the network. However, this paper focuses on "standalone" sensors where no more devices sensing the same or correlated phenomena are available. Thus these approaches use only measurements of the sensor itself. Since there are not many available publications for this case, further review is focused on categorization of faults and fault detection techniques of both the sensors and sensor networks.

Sensors provide a huge amount of information about observed phenomena. However, to make meaningful conclusions, the quality of the data has to be ensured. Sensors alone can malfunction and that can distort an image of the phenomena. Most of the methods follow a common framework, characterize the normal behavior of sensor readings, identify significant deviations and mark them as faults.

In case of sensor networks the most frequent types of faults have been described and categorized by Ni, K. et al[3]. They describe two distinct approaches to deal with faults. The first is a data-centric view which examines the data collected by a given sensor and describes fault models based on data features. In contrary there is a system-centric view which examines physical malfunctions of a sensor and how those may manifest themselves in the resulting data. According to Ni et. al. these two views are related to one another and every fault can be mapped between these two. The important fault categories discussed in [3] are summarized in Table 1. In this article the focus is on the data centric point of view.

Sharma, A.B. et al.[4] loosely follow on the work of Ni et al. and propose specific algorithms for fault detection.

They focus only on a subset of fault types examined in [3] and summarized in Table 1.

Table 1: Taxonomy of Faults described by Ni et al.[3].

Data-centric point of view

Fault	Definition
Outlier	Isolated data point or sensor unexpectedly distant from models.
Spike	Multiple data points with a much greater than expected rate of change.
"Stuck-at"	Sensor values experience zero variation for an unexpected length of time.
High Noise or Variance	Sensor values experience unexpectedly high variation or noise.

Four different classes of approaches for detecting above mentioned faults are discussed.

Rule-based Methods use domain knowledge to develop heuristic constraints that the sensor readings must satisfy. Violations of those constraints imply faults. For above mentioned fault types following simple rules are typically used [4]:

The variance (or the standard deviation) of the sample readings within a window of size w_{size} is computed. If it is above a certain threshold, the samples are corrupted by the noise fault. If the variance is zero the samples are corrupted by the constant fault. In order to detect short noise faults, the data had to be appropriately preprocessed. If the rate of change is above a threshold, it can be assumed that the data were affected by short faults.

The performance of this method strongly depends on parameters w_{size} and the threshold. Parameter setting is not trivial and usually requires domain knowledge of the examined problem.

Estimation-based Methods can be used when a physical phenomena is sensed concurrently by multiple sensors and dependence between sensor measurements can be exploited to generate estimates for the individual sensor measurements. The dependence can be expressed by spatial correlation. Regardless of the cause of the correlation, it can be used to model the normal behavior. The estimation can be done for example by Linear Least-Squares Estimation. This method is most suitable for cases when the phenomena is sensed by almost identical sensors. As an example one can imagine multiple barometric altimeters on a single aircraft. In this case there is a strong presumption that the values are strongly correlated.

Time-series-based Methods utilize the fact, that measurements of a sensor are not random and therefore contain some kind of regular patterns. This patterns can be described through autocorrelations in measurements collected by a single sensor. These can be used to create a regressive model of sensed phenomena. A sensor measurement can be than compared against its predicted value to determine if it is faulty.

Advantage is that this approach is more general than classification and can be used even if there are no labeled data available nor multiple strongly correlated sensors.

Learning-based Methods use training data to infer model of "normal" sensor behavior. If the "normal" sensor behavior and the effects of sensor faults are well understood, learning-based methods may be suitable to detect and classify sensor faults. In [4] authors successfully use Hidden Markov Models to construct a model of sensor measurements. The main advantage of learning based methods is that they can simultaneously detect and classify faults.

3 Preliminaries

3.1 Classification

In the terminology of machine learning, classification is considered an instance of supervised learning, i.e. machine learning technique where a training set of correctly identified observations is available [5]. The main goal of classification is assigning a new observation X to one from a finite set of categories with the use of the training data set containing instances whose category membership is known.

Every instance of the input dataset is a vector $X = (x_1, x_2, \ldots, x_d)$ typically called feature vector, where d is the number of features ($0 < i <= d$) and x_i is the value of the $i^t h$ feature. Every instance belongs to one of the k classes $C = c_1, c_2, \ldots, c_k$.

The classification process consists of two phases. In the first phase, called learning phase, the training data set with labels is used to build a model. It means that the knowledge from reference data is being extracted and stored in form of a model. In the second phase, the model is used to classify unlabeled data. This phase is often called recall. An algorithm that implements classification is called classifier.

Naive Bayes In machine learning naive Bayes classifiers are a family of probabilistic classifiers based on Bayes theorem. It assumes that a value of a particular feature is independent of a value of any other feature, given the class variable [6]. This assumption is often violated in practice but even though Naive Bayes classifier is still powerful classification techniques.

Learning naive Bayes model proceeds with calculation of probabilities from the training data set. The probability to be estimated is a conditional probability $P(c_j|x_1, \ldots, x_d)$

for each class c_j when object $X = (x_1, x_2, \ldots, x_d)$ is given [7].

Using the Bayes rule

$$P(A \mid B) = \frac{P(A)P(B \mid A)}{P(B)} \quad (1)$$

the posterior probability can be expressed by Equation

$$P(c_j \mid X_1, \ldots, X_d) = \frac{P(c_j)P(x_1, \ldots, x_d \mid c_j)}{P(x_1, \ldots, x_d)}, \quad (2)$$

where

- $P(c_j \mid x_1, \ldots, x_d)$ is the posterior probability of class c_j when object $X = (x_1, x_2, \ldots, x_d)$ is given.

- $P(c_j)$ is the prior probability of class c_j.

- $P(x_1, \ldots, x_d \mid c_j)$ is the posterior probability of an object $X = (x_1, \ldots, x_d)$ when class c_j is given. We call this probability likelihood.

- $P(x_1, \ldots, x_d)$ is the prior probability of an object $X = (x_1, x_2, \ldots, x_d)$.

The resulting model is represented by prior probabilities of each class and likelihood probabilities for each combination of class and feature. The likelihoods are usually represented by a mean and variance of normal distribution estimated from the training set.

The recall of naive Bayes algorithm is done by looking up the prior and likelihood probabilities which belong to input data and calculating posterior probabilities for each class. Thanks to the assumption of strong conditional independence between all features conditioned by the class, the likelihood can be calculated as follows.

$$P(x_1, \ldots, x_d \mid c_j) = \prod_{i=1}^{n} P(x_i \mid c_j) \quad (3)$$

The resulting class is determined by the highest posterior probability.

3.2 Time Series Modeling

Time series is a series of observations of a process or an event in equal time intervals. It is called time series, because the observations are usually taken with respect to time. This is however not necessity, because the observations may be taken with respect to space as well [8].

Modeling techniques try to find a model which describes the series, i.e. a model capable to generate identical series. The model may help to better understand the underlying phenomena or serve as forecasting tool to predict future values of the series.

Stochastic models like ARIMA assume that the time series consist of regular pattern manifesting the underlying phenomena and a random noise.

The ARIMA Model ARIMA (autoregressive integrated moving average model) is a general time series model. It combines two independent models, autoregressive (AR) and moving-average (MA). They are combined in a single equation (Equation 4). By convention the AR terms are added and the MA terms are subtracted.

$$x_t = C + \varphi_1 \cdot x_{t-1} + \cdots + \varphi_p \cdot x_{t-p} - \theta_1 \cdot \varepsilon_{t-1} - \cdots - \theta_q \cdot \varepsilon_{t-q} \quad (4)$$

where

- x_i is i-th element of the series,

- C is a constant,

- φ_1, φ_2 are parameters of the autoregressive model,

- ε_i is random error component of i-th member of the series.

- θ_1, θ_2 are parameters of the moving average model.

ARIMA models are extensively examined in literature. For more information the reader is reffered to [9] or [10].

3.3 Artificial Neural Networks

Artificial neural network is an information processing paradigm inspired by biological nervous systems. It is composed of a large number of highly interconnected processing units (neurons) working in unity to solve a specific problems.

A neuron is a simplistic model of a biological neural cell. Each neuron has one or more inputs and produces single output. The inputs simulate the stimuli signals that the neuron gets from other neurons, while the output simulates the response signal which the neuron generates.

The biological neuron fires (i.e generates the response signal) only if the gathered stimuli signals exceed a certain threshold. In other word the neuron fires only if the $stimuli - treshold > 0$. In the context of ANNs the term bias b is used instead of "threshold"[1].

The artificial equivalent to gathered stimuli signals is called inner potential (ξ) and typically is defined as a weighted sum of the input signals plus the bias. Each input (x_j) is multiplied by a specific real number w_j called the weight. These weights are parameters of each neuron. The calculation of inner potential is summarized in Equation 5.

$$\xi = \sum_{all\, j} w_j * x_j + b = W \cdot X + b \quad (5)$$

The actual output is obtained by applying activation function $\varphi(\cdot)$ on the gathered inner potential. There can be used variety of activation functions. Very popular for

---

[1]Due the conventions $bias = (-1 \cdot threshold)$.

its properties is sigmoid function, where the output of the neuron y is given by formula in Equation 6.

$$y = \varphi(\xi) = \frac{1}{1 + e^{-\xi}} \qquad (6)$$

For more complex tasks like anomaly detection a single neuron is not powerful enough and therefore more complex structures are introduced. A neural network is a group of neurons connected together. Connecting neurons to form a ANN can be done in various ways.

Networks where the neurons are arranged in separate layers and the output from one layer is used as an input to the next layer are called feed-forward networks. This means there are no loops in the network and information is always fed forward, never fed back.

ANNs, like their biological artworks, learn by example. Therefore in order to train a neural network a set of input examples with known expected responses is necessary. Classical method of training ANNs is called "backpropagation" which is an abbreviation for "backward propagation of errors".

Typical goal in a training of neural networks is to find weights $W = (w_1, \ldots, w_k)$ and biases $B = (b_1, \ldots, b_l)$ which minimize the error or cost function $C(W, B)$ over all instances in the training set.

More specific information about different ANN types can be found in literature [11, 12].

Autoencoder is a specific type of feed-forward neural network, with an input layer, an output layer and one or more hidden layers. The main properties of an autoencoder are, that the output layer has the same number of neurones as the input layer and instead of being trained to predict some target value Y given inputs X, autoencoders are trained to reconstruct their own inputs X'.

Especially interesting are autoencoders, where hidden layers have less nodes than input/output layer. Such a network is forced to comprehend nonlinear, reduced representation of the original data.

Such a autoencoder network can have a variety of uses. They can serve for non linear dimensionality reduction, data compression or to learn generative model of the data[13].

4 Approach

Influenced by related work reviewed in the Section 2, three different approaches to deal with condition monitoring of sensor parts are introduced. Each approach is based on a different principle; the first approach is based on feature extraction and status classification, the second approach is based on time series modeling and the third approach is based on anomaly detection using autoencoders. Approaches are illustrated on data set with measurements from 2000 accelerometers (hereafter referred as sensors). For each sensor the data set contains one time series with minimum of 14 days measurements before the sensor failed. The aim is to label the sensor faulty within two days before the failure. More than two days before the failure the sensor can be considered faultless. All three approaches are described in detail in the following subsections.

4.1 Classification-based approach

The first suggested approach is based on supervised learning, namely classification. Supervised learning techniques require examples with labels to learn from. This approach, therefore, requires information about failures to prepare the labels. If no information about the failures is available and the labels can not be supplied this approach can not be applied.

The sensor readings are in a form of a time-series. Sliding window of N measurements is used to calculate the feature vector for classification. The raw measurements itself can be used directly as a feature vector, however, the dimensionality is then equal to the size of the sliding window multiplied by the number of measured phenomenons. Typically, simple features (such as variance, average, median or slope) or more complex features (e.g. Fourier or wavelet coefficients) are extracted from the sliding window [14, 15, 16]. For on-line condition monitoring the feature vector is extracted from a window aligned with the most current readings. The instance is then classified by pre-trained classifier. If the instance is classified as "failed" the current condition of the sensor is evaluated as faulty.

In order to train a model the labels have to be prepared. To prepare the training dataset historical readings and a set of times related to the failures or generally the events to be detected are used. To obtain faulty instance sliding window is placed over the readings of a failed sensor and aligned with the time of failure. A feature vector is extracted from such a window and marked with label "failed" (i.e. class y=1). For each failure one instance with a label "failed" is obtained. Non-faulty instances can be extracted by sliding the window over the time series of non-failed sensor[2].

However, by using every possible shift unnecessarily large number of instances is obtained. Therefore, non-faulty instances are extracted by placing the window randomly over readings. Extracted feature vectors are marked with label 'ok' (i.e. class y=0). In this case the ratio between classes can be easily controlled. The whole process demonstrates Figure 1.

The number of features is reduced with iterative forward feature selection method. Initially a model is trained with only one feature, in each iteration one feature as added and model is retrained. If the new model performs significantly better than the previous, the feature is kept in the feature vector, otherwise the feature is discarded.

---

[2]Non-failed sensor is a sensor for which do not exist any record of failure.

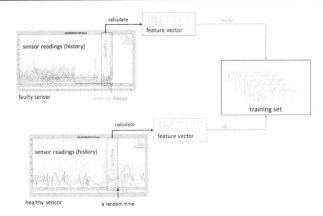

Figure 1: Working scheme of creating the training set.

Classification model is trained with extracted feature vectors to recognize faulty and non-faulty instances. Arbitrary classifier can be used. The aim of this article is to prove the concept that classification can be used for condition monitoring and thus maintenance strategy for sensor parts. Therefore for simplicity and interpretability the Naive Bayes classifier is applied.

In Naive Bayes the instance is typically classified to a class with higher posterior probability. To increase confidence of positive classification the minimal threshold value of posterior probability can be set on the class with failed instances. With this threshold of minimal probability for positive class can be controlled trade-off between sensitivity and specificity of the naive Bayes classifier. With a higher threshold the classifier will be more certain about the prediction, however, it may mark more failures as non-faulty and vice versa.

4.2 Time-series Modeling-based approach

The second approach basically follows the method suggested in [4]. It assumes that malfunction of a sensor is preceded by an abnormal behavior. The working principle basically follows the common framework for anomaly detection. It uses time-series modelling in order to model "normal" sensor behavior.

A regressive model is trained on the historical measurements of a specific sensor and used to generate predictions. The ARIMA model[9, 10] is general regressive model popular in time-series modeling. Especially in cases, when the time-series contains significant regular patterns, which is more or less the case of sensor readings [4]. For that reason the general ARIMA model is used to obtain the predictions.

Predicted values are compared with the actual readings and if the difference is higher than a certain threshold, measurements are marked as faulty.

The working scheme is depicted in Figure 2.

The ARIMA model prescription contains random members, therefore it is a stochastic process. In order to re-

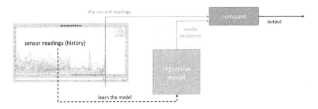

Figure 2: Working scheme of regression-model-based approach

duce random component and get the most precise predictions Monte Carlo principle is typically engaged to generate multiple predictions. The final prediction is obtained as a mean value of k predicted values.

Knowing how the prediction is obtained allows us to create hypothesis about the expected value and construct a confidence interval for the predicted value as shown in Figure 3.

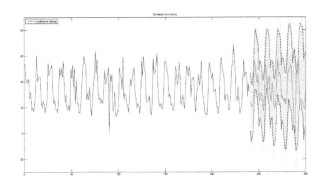

Figure 3: ARIMA model predictions with the confidential interval.

If the actual reading of a sensor is out of the confidence interval of the corresponding predicted value the sensor is marked as 'faulty'.

4.3 Autoencoder-based approach

The last suggested approach is, similarly to the previous approach, based on an assumption that the failure of a sensor is preceded by its anomalous behavior. In this particular case auto-encoders are utilized to detect anomalies.

Inputs to the autoencoder network are the raw values from a sliding window drawn over historical measurements of the sensor. However, it is also possible to extract different features and use them as inputs of the autoencoder. As a result, this method requires a certain amount of historical data, in order to train an autoencoder network.

The whole working scheme is shown in Figure 4.

The structure of an autoencoder is defined by following parameters: size of the input and output layer, number of hidden layers and number of nodes in the hidden layers.

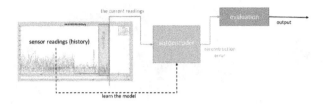

Figure 4: Working scheme of anomaly-detection-based approach.

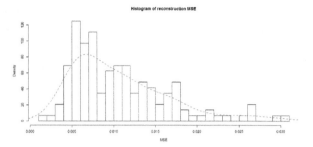

Figure 5: Histogram of reconstruction errors.

Since the raw data from the sensor are used as inputs to the autoencoder network, the number of nodes in the input and also the output layer is determined by size of the sliding window. Influenced by [13] the autoencoder has three hidden layers. The number of neurons is related to the number of neurons in the input / output layer. Let n be the number of input respectively output neurons than the hidden layers have $0.75n, 0.5n, 0.75n$ neurons.

The output of an autoencoder itself is not especially interesting. Rather a reconstruction error, defined as mean squared error between the real measurements and output of the autoencoder, is calculated. Let $X = (x_1 \ldots x_n)$ be the input vector of an autoencoder network and $X' = (x'_1 \ldots x'_n)$ is the corresponding output, the reconstruction error is

$$RE(X) = \frac{1}{n} \sum_1^n (x_i - x'_i)^2$$

If the reconstruction error is higher than a certain threshold τ the current condition of a sensor is marked as "faulty".

The threshold is estimated with a heuristic method. The main idea is to consider the reconstruction error being a random variable. Then the underlying distribution of the random variable can be easily estimated. Having a distribution of the reconstruction error, if the value of the error does not lie in a right-sided (upper) confidence interval with confidence level α it is marked "faulty".

$$P(RE(X) < \tau) = 1 - \alpha$$

Figure 5 demonstrated the histogram which is used in order to estimate the underlying distribution function of the reconstruction error.

5 Experimental Results

5.1 Classification-based Approach

Having labeled data, performance of a classifier can be easily measured. TPR (true positive rate) is defined as number of detected failures to the number of all failures in a given dataset. FPR (false positive rate) is defined as the number of positively identified to the number of all negative samples in a dataset. The acquired results are presented by the ROC curve showed in Figure 6. In a ROC

curve the TPR (i.e. True Positive Rate or Sensitivity) is plotted in function of the FPR (False Positive Rate or (1-Specificity)) for different setting of model's parameters.

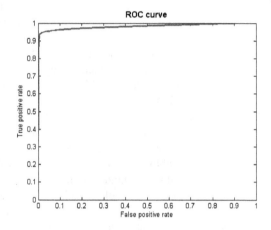

Figure 6: Classification-based approach - ROC curve.

5.2 Time-series Modeling-based Approach

In order to evaluate this approach on predicting failures the method is evaluated as a binary classifier.

A window of a size M is placed before the time of a failure and if an anomaly is within the window, the failure is considered as detected. If an anomaly is detected outside of this window it is considered as false positive detection.

As presented in the section 4.2 this method marks as anomalies all the moments, where the actual reading is not within the confidence interval.

The level of significance α can be set explicitly, and its effect can be examined. In Figure 7 are shown detected anomalies for $\alpha = 0.0015$. The red segments mark the times of failures.

The experiment is repeated multiple times for different α. The results are presented by the ROC curve showed in Figure 8. Each point on the ROC curve represents a TPR/FPR pair corresponding to a particular value of α. It demonstrates how the sensitivity versus specificity can be controlled by choosing the α.

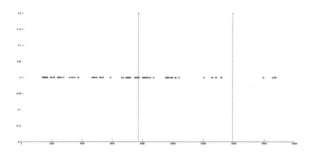

Figure 7: Time-series modeling based approach - detected failures.

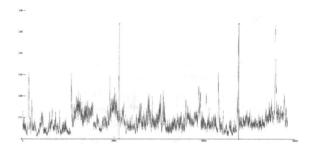

Figure 9: Anomaly-detection-based approach - detected failures.

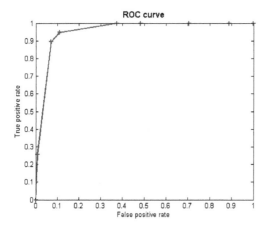

Figure 8: TS-modeling-detection-based approach - ROC curve.

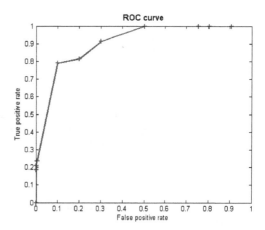

Figure 10: Anomaly-detection-based approach - ROC curve.

5.3 Autoencoder-based Approach

In order to evaluate the autoencoder-based method, the same procedure as in the case of time-series modeling based approach, is used. In Figure 9 is shown the resulting series of the reconstruction errors. The red-marked points are the moments of failure(i.e. the event one intend to predict). It is visible that the time of failure is preceded by significant raise of reconstruction error. However, there are also other anomalous moments(peaks in the series of reconstruction errors), that are not related to the incoming failure of the sensor. Having the domain knowledge of the sensor operation, those can be easily explained, since they are related to the observed phenomena.

The ROC curve in Figure 10 presents the results of this approach. Sensitivity and specificity trade-off is controlled by the *level of significance* described in the the Section 4.3.

6 Conclusion

Three different approaches to deal with the condition monitoring and predictive maintenance of sensors have been described and illustrated on real-world data. All those approaches are chosen with a regard to be general and thus applicable with various sensor devices. All three methods exploit different principles and hence have different assumptions and requirements.

Classification based approach utilizes labels if available. If not this approach is not applicable. The other two approaches are more general since they do not require any meta-data and work just with the sensor measurements. However, both assume that the failure is preceded by anomalous behavior. The time series modeling approach exploits the fact that sensors measurements are in a form of time-series and often contain regular patterns, which manifest themselves in a form of autocorrelations. Therefore they it can be described by a model. The autoencoder-based approach contrary to the time-series modeling does not model the "normal" behavior.

All methods were able to detect failures before they occurred and thus proved to be applicable for condition monitoring and utilized for predictive maintenance of sensor parts. Further more, all the approaches can be parametrize to find an ideal trade-off between sensitivity and specificity of the prediction. The best results has the approach based on classification. This can be expected considering the fact that, unlike the other two approaches, it uses additional meta-data (labels) about the sensor failures.

References

[1] Inc., M. A. Common maintenance strategies. 2015, [Online; accessed 17-January-2016]. Available from: `https://www.maintenanceassistant.com/`

[2] Kennedy, S. New tools for PdM. 2006, [Online; accessed 17-February-2016]. Available from: `http://www.plantservices.com/articles/2006/072/`

[3] Ni, K.; Ramantahan, N.; Nabil, M.; et al. Sensor Network Data Fault Types. *ACM Transactions on Sensor Networks*, volume 5, no. 3, May 2009.

[4] Sharma, A. B.; Golubchi, L.; Govindan, R. Sensor Faults: Detection Methods and Prevalence in Real-World Datasets. *ACM Transactions on Sensor Networks*, volume 6, no. 3, June 2010.

[5] Alpaydin, E. *Introduction to machine learning*. MIT Press, second edition, 2010, ISBN 978-0-262-01243-0.

[6] Russell, S.; Norvig, P. *Artificial Intelligence: A Modern Approach*. Prentice Hall, second edition, 2003, ISBN 978-0137903955.

[7] StatSoft. Naive Bayes Classifier. 2016, [Online; accessed 19-February-2016]. Available from: `http://www.statsoft.com/textbook/naive-bayes-classifier`

[8] Vu, K. M. *Optimal Discrete Control Theory: The Rational Function Structure Model*. Ottawa: AuLac Technologies, 2007, ISBN 978-0-9783996-0-3, 51–99 pp.

[9] Nau, R. Lecture notes on forecasting. 2014, [Online; accessed 19-February-2016]. Available from: `http://people.duke.edu/~rnau/Slides_on_ARIMA_models--Robert_Nau.pdf`

[10] Lu, Y.; Simaan, M. A. Automated Box–Jenkins forecasting modelling. *Elsevier Automation in Construction 18*, November 2008: pp. 547–558.

[11] Nielsen, M. *Neural Networks and Deep Learning*. Determination Press, 2015. Available from: `http://neuralnetworksanddeeplearning.com/index.htm`

[12] Goodfellow, I.; Bengio, Y.; Courville, A. Deep Learning, 2016, book in preparation for MIT Press. Available from: `http://www.deeplearningbook.org`

[13] Candel, A.; Lanford, J.; LeDell, E.; et al. Deep Learning with H2O. 2015, third Edition. Available from: `https://h2o.gitbooks.io/deep-learning/`

[14] Fu, T.-c. A review on time series data mining. *Engineering Applications of Artificial Intelligence*, volume 24, no. 1, 2011: pp. 164–181.

[15] Chen, Y.; Nascimento, M. A.; Ooi, B. C.; et al. Spade: On shape-based pattern detection in streaming time series. In *Data Engineering, 2007. ICDE 2007. IEEE 23rd International Conference on*, IEEE, 2007, pp. 786–795.

[16] Xing, Z.; Pei, J.; Philip, S. Y.; et al. Extracting Interpretable Features for Early Classification on Time Series. In *SDM*, volume 11, SIAM, 2011, pp. 247–258.

ITAT 2016 Proceedings, pp. 131–137
ISBN 978-1537016740, © 2016 P. Milička, P. Čížek, J. Faigl

On Chaotic Oscillator-based Central Pattern Generator for Motion Control of Hexapod Walking Robot

Pavel Milička, Petr Čížek, and Jan Faigl

Czech Technical University in Prague, Technická 2, 166 27 Prague, Czech Republic
`milicpav|cizekpe6|faiglj@fel.cvut.cz`

Abstract: In this paper, we address a problem of motion control of a real hexapod walking robot along a trajectory of the prescribed curvature and desired motion gait. The proposed approach is based on a chaotic neural oscillator that is employed as the central pattern generator (CPG). The CPG allows to generate various motion gaits according to the specified period of the chaotic oscillator. The output signal of the oscillator is processed by the proposed trajectory generator that allows to specify a curvature of the trajectory the robot is requested to traverse. Such a signal is then considered as an input for the inverse kinematic task which provides particular trajectories of individual legs that are directly send to the robot actuators. Thus, the main benefit of the proposed approach is that only two natural parameters are necessary to control the gait type and the robot motion. The proposed approach has been verified in real experiments. The experimental results support feasibility of the proposed concept and the robot is able to crawl desired trajectories with the tripod, ripple, low gear, and wave motion gaits.

1 Introduction

Hexapod crawlers have a great potential in many applications such as rescue missions or exploration of unknown environments that are hostile or unreachable to human beings and where motion capabilities of legged robots can be utilized to walk over rough terrains. Regarding a particular mission, it is desirable a robot can deal with various locomotor skills to adapt and react to its environment. On the other hand, a solution of such a task has already been found in nature by the process of evolution. Hence, it is a source of motivation for the presented approach based on biologically inspired locomotion controller for the hexapod walking robot showed in Figure 1.

The considered approach builds on the idea that the insect locomotion is generated by the so called Central Pattern Generators (CPGs) located in central nervous system [1, 2, 3], which generates the rhythmic motor patterns carried out by muscles without the sensory feedback. The feedback is; however, essential in structuring the motor patterns when walking on uneven terrains [4]. In addition, the locomotion is also enhanced by muscle dynamics reacting immediately to terrain irregularities and thus creating reactions (preflexes) faster than any neural feedback [5].

Figure 1: Hexapod robot used for experimental evaluation of the proposed chaotic oscillator-based motion control.

According to [6], individual limbs can produce motor patterns, which can be viewed as an evidence that each leg, or even each joint has its own pattern generator. The coordination of multiple legs is done by coupling the individual CPGs by mutual connections and the overall locomotion is composed of a synchronized motion of individual legs. Two phases can be recognized in a single motion step of each leg: the support phase and the swing phase. In the support phase, a leg is firmly touching the ground and moving backward relatively to the body, which results in the body moving forward relatively to the ground. On the other hand, in the swing phase, a leg swings forward in the air relative to the body to reach a position enabling another support phase.

Findings from biological observations of walking insects have been summarized by Wilson [7], who created a simple locomotion model consisting of five rules that are essential to the construction of motion patterns:

1. Swing phases go from rear to front and no leg swings until the one behind is in the support phase;
2. Contralateral legs of the same segment alternate in phase, i.e., they cannot both be in the swing phase simultaneously;
3. The swing phase duration is constant;
4. The support phase duration varies with the frequency of CPG oscillations, i.e., a lower frequency, which generates a slower gait, results in a longer support phase;
5. Intervals between steps of the hind leg and the middle leg and between the middle leg and the front leg are

constant, while the interval between the foreleg and the hind leg steps varies with the CPG frequency.

Based on these rules following locomotion patterns (gaits) can be identified. The most safe gait is called *wave* in which each leg swings separately. Another example is the *low gear* gait where an insect alternates between swinging two legs and one. Another types are *tetrapod* and *ripple* gaits which differ in phase lag between the left and right legs. Legs in the tetrapod gait are synchronized, whereas the ripple gait seems to be more fluent. Finally the fastest motion pattern is called the *tripod* gait. It is also worth mentioning that there are further variants of the tetrapod, ripple and low gear gaits depending on the phase lags between the left and right legs [8].

The main motivation of this work is to design and experimentally verify a biologically inspired locomotion controller for a hexapod walking robot to develop a suitable framework for further processing various sensory inputs and produce adequate control actions. Therefore, the design of the proposed controller is based on chaotic oscillator [9] for which we propose to post-process the oscillator output with a trajectory generator to generate the position of each leg's foot-tip and inverse kinematics module, which transforms the signal to the actual joints' positions. The proposed controller is comprehensible and it allows to control the hexapod locomotion with only two natural parameters: the turning rate *turn* of the robot and the period p influencing the gait type according to the aforementioned locomotion patterns.

The rest of the paper is organized as follows. Section 2 overviews the related work to give an insight in possible approaches and CPG implementation methods. Section 3 describes the design of the proposed locomotion controller and methods used for its development. Results of the performed experimental evaluation with the real robot are presented in Section 4. Concluding remarks and suggestions for further work are dedicated to Section 5.

2 Related Work

Biologically inspired strategies based on the CPGs have already been utilized in the control of legged locomotion. The existing methods mainly differs in the way how the CPG is implemented and how its output signal is processed. In strictly biological approaches, the signal is processed by neural networks with the motoneurons as the output layer. Alternatively, the signal can be postprocessed and utilized in a trajectory generator to compute the desired foot-tips locations that are further transformed to the individual joints' positions using the inverse kinematics.

Regarding the CPG itself, there are many ways of achieving a patterned output [6, 10] that can be characterized as one of the three main types of implementation. First, the CPG can be implemented using neuron models mutually connected together, which produces (with a

correct set of design parameters) a dynamical system capable of oscillations [11, 12]. The second type are CPG implementations based on the coupled non-linear oscillators (NLO), which are not strictly biologically based, but share many common characteristics with biophysical models. One of the most used models is Matsuoka oscillator [13] implementing the half centre principle: extensor and flexor neurons inhibiting each other with an adaptation mechanism. The Matsuoka NLO model was successfully simulated and implemented in hexapod [14, 15] and biped walking [16]. Finally, connectionist models are CPG implementations which tend to use simplified neuron models while focusing on the effect of inter-neuron connections. An example of this approach is a cellular neural network used in [17], where the network consists of identical cells arranged in a rectangular grid. Each cell is usually a first order dynamical system affected only by itself and its neighbours in the specified radius. Another example are spiking neurons used for hexapod locomotion in [18].

In this paper, we consider NLO-based approach for which we utilized chaotic neural oscillator proposed in [9] to produce rhythmic patterns of the desired CPG. The proposed solution is presented in the following section.

3 Proposed Solution

The proposed solution builds on the chaotic CPG [9] and the ideas of the adaptive locomotion controller for hexapod robots [14], where non-neural post-processing is suggested. However, this paper provides different method of the post-processing resulting in more emphasis put on the insect's locomotion rules. Moreover, the proposed approach utilizes the trajectory generator in the way that the hexapod is able to follow any given trajectory consisting of circular arcs.

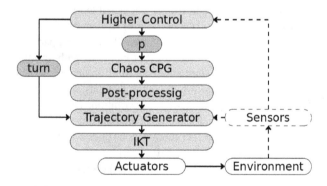

Figure 2: Structure of the proposed control system

The overall block scheme of the proposed modular controller is depicted in Figure 2. Note, the dashed lines denote the sensory feedback part of the system which has not yet been implemented but is considered future work. In general, the proposed controller works as follows. First of all, data from sensors are processed by the Higher Control module which sets the locomotion control parameters, namely the turning radius *turn* and the period p.[1] The period p is used to adjust the CPG output which is then shaped and delayed by the post-processing module to generate a signal for each leg. Afterwards, this signal is fed into the trajectory generator which generates foot-tip positions using the second control parameter *turn*. Finally, the foot-tips' positions are transformed by the inverse kinematics module into the joint angles that are directly applied to the servo drives. The particular controller blocks are detailed in the following subsections.

3.1 Chaos CPG

The proposed CPG implementation is based on the chaotic neural oscillator [9]. The main feature of this oscillator is its ability to stabilize different periodic orbits by changing only a single parameter, the period p. A diagram of the used neural oscillator is shown in Figure 3.

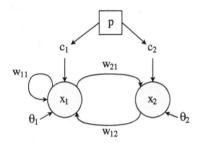

Figure 3: Chaotic neural oscillator

The oscillator is considered with the particular parameters $w_{11} = -22.0$, $w_{12} = 5.9$, $w_{21} = -6.6$, $w_{22} = 0$, $\theta_1 = -3.4$, $\theta_2 = 3.8$ for the network output computed as

$$x_i(t+1) = \sigma\left(\theta_i + \sum_{j=1}^{2} w_{ij}x_j(t) + c_i(t)\right),\qquad (1)$$

where w_{ij} is the synaptic weight from the neuron j to the neuron i, θ_i is the neuron bias and c_i is the control signal utilized for stabilizing periodic orbits. It is applied every $p+1$ step, otherwise it is set to zero. The signal is determined from

$$c_i(t) = \mu(t)\sum_{j=1}^{2} w_{ij}\Delta_j(t),\qquad (2)$$

where Δ_j is the signal difference of the j-th neuron state separated by one period

$$\Delta_j(t) = x_j(t) - x_j(t-p),\qquad (3)$$

and $\mu(t)$ is the adaptive control strength given as

$$\mu(t+1) = \mu(t) + \frac{\lambda}{p}\left(\Delta_1(t)^2 + \Delta_2(t)^2\right).\qquad (4)$$

The period which is set to be stabilized is denoted as p. The adaptation speed λ has to be set carefully as too high

---

values can prevent the stabilization of the given periodic orbit or the stabilization could take a long time. Besides, an usable learning rate gets lower with increasing period; so, we scale it by $1/p$. The adaptation speed λ has been empirically set to 0.05 in our implementation. The control strength μ is reset to -1 whenever the period p is changed.

Based on the real insect locomotion, periods p from the set $\{2, 3, 4, 6\}$ would be ideal for further processing. Unfortunately, not all periodic orbits can be stabilized or even exist in the proposed chaotic oscillator, such as the period $p = 3$. Therefore, p is selected from a set $\{4, 6, 8, 12\}$ which is then further utilized for the gait generation, where the swing phase is always constant.

Another drawback is that due to sensitivity of the oscillator to the initial conditions together with the control method used, the final stabilized period can differ from the desired one. For example, the control method cannot recognize that it actually stabilized period–2 orbit when period–6 orbit was set. This can be addressed by resetting the network states to zero every time the period is changed; so, the initial condition of the oscillator will not spoil the stabilization.

3.2 CPG Post-processing

The output produced by the chaos CPG has to be shaped and processed to get information about the current phase of each leg and to obtain an input for the trajectory generator, which can be used to position the legs' foot-tips. For this purpose, partially neural-based signal post-processing is proposed, which scheme is depicted in Figure 4.

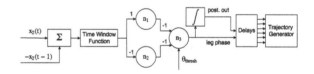

Figure 4: Post-processing module. n_1, n_2 and n_3 are neurons used for processing the output of the CPG.

The difference of the oscillator neuron output and its delay is used to obtain the signal for the phase generation

$$\Delta x_2(t) = x_2(t) - x_2(t-1).\qquad (5)$$

This signal goes through a time window function, which passes the signal every Δt step to the neural post-processing network. A suitable value Δt has been found experimentally as $\Delta t = 13$. The neural network compares the absolute difference of the signal with the threshold θ_{thresh} that is selected according to the actual period p and is listed in Table 1.

The output of the neural network corresponds to the current leg phase. If it is equal to -1, the leg is in the swing phase; otherwise it is in the support phase. Outputs of the

Table 1: Post-processing constants

p	Gait	θ_{thresh}	τ_L
4	Tripod	0.20	26
6	Ripple	0.20	39
8	Low gear	0.50	26
12	Wave	0.78	78

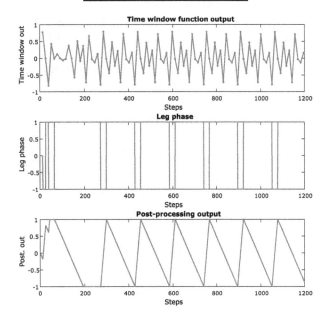

Figure 5: Post-processed signals, $p = 6$

individual neurons n_1, n_2, n_3 are computed as

$$n_1(t) = \max(0, \Delta x_2(t)), \quad (6)$$
$$n_2(t) = \max(0, -\Delta x_2(t)), \quad (7)$$
$$n_3(t) = f(-n_1(t) - n_2(t) + \theta_{thresh}), \quad (8)$$

where

$$f(x) = \begin{cases} -1 & \text{if } x \in (-\infty, 0), \\ 1 & \text{if } x \in [0, \infty). \end{cases} \quad (9)$$

Note, the neurons here serve only as processing units with no ability to learn or adapt.

According to the leg phase, a constant value is added to the previously post-processed output to achieve a suitable input for the trajectory generator *post*. This signal alternates from -1 to 1 in triangle waves after the period stabilization, where the up slope (swing phase) is a constant and the down slope (support phase) depends on the period p. Figure 5 shows the results of post processing of a CPG signal with the period $p = 6$.

The last part of the post-processing module is signal delaying. This is rather a simplification compared to biological systems as only a single oscillator is used to control all legs. By adjusting the delay τ_L (Table 1) and thus changing the phase lag between the right rear and the left rear leg,

different walking patterns (i.e., *tripod*, *ripple*, *low gear*, and *wave* gaits) observed in nature can be achieved.

3.3 Trajectory Generator

The trajectory generator module decides the foot-tip coordinates $\hat{x}_i(t), \hat{y}_i(t), \hat{z}_i(t)$ of each leg i based on the post-processed output of the CPG – $post(t)$ at the time t, and a particular parameter determining the rate of the robot turning – *turn*. Foot-tips positions generation is generalized by considering the robot is always turning. Nevertheless, a turning radius set to a very high value results in a seemingly straight walking.

The $\hat{z}_i(t)$ coordinate of the foot tip is computed using

$$\hat{z}_i(t) = \begin{cases} \sin((post(t)+1)\frac{\pi}{2}) \cdot z_{max}, & \text{if swing} \wedge post(t) \leq 0, \\ \sin((-post(t)+1)\frac{\pi}{2}) \cdot z_{max}, & \text{if swing} \wedge post(t) > 0, \\ 0 & \text{if support,} \end{cases} \quad (10)$$

where z_{max} is the maximum step height. Unlike $\hat{z}_i(t)$, the coordinates $\hat{x}_i(t)$ and $\hat{y}_i(t)$ are influenced by the turning radius *turn*. In order to turn the hexapod, each leg has to move along an arc of a circle going through the foot default position and having center at the turn point, which is located on a line given by the default foot-tips positions of the middle legs. Therefore, only a single parameter, the turning radius *turn*, is sufficient to parametrize the robots' trajectory. Figure 6 shows how the *turn* parameter influences the foot-tip trajectories of the middle legs.

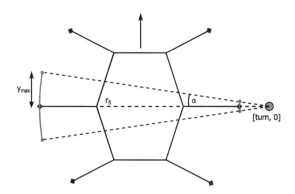

Figure 6: Trajectory generation – the turning point denoted as red circle is given and α is computed with the distance of the turning point to the furthest middle leg and with defined step length. α is then used to specify the trajectory of each foot-tip.

The next step of the trajectory generation is to find an angle determining the arc used for the foot-tips locations, because the step length is limited by the robot and leg construction. y_{max} is experimentally set to 35 mm, which means a leg can move about this distance in both forward and backward directions, i.e., the step length is at most 70 mm. When turning, each leg has a different step length and the longest step is always performed by the furthest leg j from the turning center

$$j = \text{argmax}_{j=\{2,5\}}(|P_{x_j} - turn|), \quad (11)$$

where P_{x_j} is the x-coordinate of the default foot-tip with respect to the robots' center. The angle α is then given as

$$\alpha = \text{asin}\left(\frac{y_{max}}{(P_{x_j} - turn)}\right). \tag{12}$$

Now, the arc radius r_i is computed for each leg foot-tip $i \in \{1, 2, \ldots, 6\}$ and the angle offset θ_{rad} given by the default leg position as

$$\theta_{rad_i} = \text{atan2}\left(P_{y_i}, P_{x_i} - turn\right), \tag{13}$$

$$r_i = \sqrt{(P_{x_i} - turn)^2 + (P_{y_i})^2}. \tag{14}$$

Then, the foot-tip location is computed

$$\hat{x}_i(t) = r_i \cos(\theta_{rad_i} + \alpha post(t)), \tag{15}$$
$$\hat{y}_i(t) = r_i \sin(\theta_{rad_i} + \alpha post(t)). \tag{16}$$

3.4 Inverse Kinematics

The last step of the trajectory generation is to transform the generated foot-tip positions into the joint angles which can be directly send to the actuators. The input of our inverse kinematic task (IKT) module are foot coordinates in the leg reference system. For brevity, the inputs $x^{leg_i}_{foot_i}$, $y^{leg_i}_{foot_i}$, $z^{leg_i}_{foot_i}$ are written as x_i, y_i, z_i in this section, where i stands for leg index. The coxa joint angles can be computed as

$$\theta_{1_i} = \text{atan2}(y_i, x_i) - \theta^{off}_{1_i}. \tag{17}$$

The other two joint angles are calculated using the following formulas. Note, the provided formulas do not hold in the whole operational space of the legs; however, they are correct for the foot-tip positions generated by our locomotion controller within the restricted operational space. The joint angles are determined as follows.

$$\theta_{2_i} = k_i(\beta + \omega_i) - \theta^{off}_{2_i}, \tag{18}$$
$$\theta_{3_i} = k_i(\gamma - \pi) - \theta^{off}_{3_i}, \tag{19}$$

where

$$\beta = \text{acos}\left(\frac{-l_3^2 + l_2^2 + d^2}{2l_2 d}\right), \tag{20}$$

$$\gamma = \text{acos}\left(\frac{-d^2 + l_2^2 + l_3^2}{2l_2 l_3}\right), \tag{21}$$

$$\omega_i = \text{atan2}\left(z_i, \sqrt{(B_{x_i} - x_i)^2 + (B_{y_i}) - y_i)^2}\right). \tag{22}$$

In which

$$d = \sqrt{(B_{x_i} - x_i)^2 + (B_{y_i} - y_i)^2 + (B_{z_i} - z_i)^2} \tag{23}$$

and B_i is the location of the i-th leg femur joint in the leg coordinates that can be computed as the first three values

Table 2: IKT Constants

Leg	k_i	$\theta^{off}_{1_i}$	$\theta^{off}_{2_i}$	$\theta^{off}_{3_i}$
1 (RR)	1	$-\pi/4$	θ^{off}_2	θ^{off}_3
2 (RM)	1	0	θ^{off}_2	θ^{off}_3
3 (RF)	1	$\pi/4$	θ^{off}_2	θ^{off}_3
4 (LR)	-1	$-3\pi/4$	$-\theta^{off}_2$	$-\theta^{off}_3$
5 (LM)	-1	π	$-\theta^{off}_2$	$-\theta^{off}_3$
6 (LF)	-1	$3\pi/4$	$-\theta^{off}_2$	$-\theta^{off}_3$

of

$$B_i = R_z(\theta_{1_i} + \theta^{off}_{1_i})T_x(l_1)\begin{bmatrix} 0 \\ 0 \\ 0 \\ 1 \end{bmatrix} = \begin{bmatrix} l_1 \cos\left(\theta_{1_i} + \theta^{off}_{1_i}\right) \\ l_1 \sin\left(\theta_{1_i} + \theta^{off}_{1_i}\right) \\ 0 \\ 1 \end{bmatrix}, \tag{24}$$

where $R_z(\cdot)$, $T_x(\cdot)$ stands for the rotation around z-axis and translation along x-axis, respectively. Joint offsets caused by the mechanical construction are listed in Table 2 among with k_i. The signs are influenced by the "asymmetric" behaviour of the left and right legs along with the fact that the x-axis of the leg coordinate system is heading right no matter whether it is on the hexapod right or left side. Values of θ^{off}_2 and θ^{off}_3 are obtained from the leg dimensions.

4 Experimental Evaluation

The conducted experiments focus on the evaluation of the controller performance to follow trajectories consisting of straight line segments and arcs of circles with various radii and different gait types.

4.1 Walking Platform

The proposed locomotion controller is considered with an off-the-shelf hexapod walking robot *PhantomX Hexapod Mark II* (depicted in Figure 1). The robot consists of six legs each granting three Degrees-Of-Freedom (DOF), summing up to 18 controllable DOF for the whole robot. That gives us great maneuverability and agility that is useful for obstacle traversing and rough terrain walking. Each leg has three revolute joints motorized by the Dynamixel AX series intelligent servo motors. The servos are connected in daisy chain and communicate using a serial interface.

4.2 Results

The robot real trajectory is captured by a vision-based external localization system [19], which grants us an ability to measure the robot forward velocity for different gaits

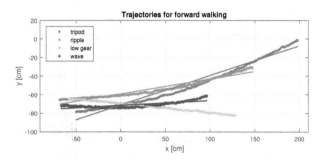

Figure 7: Trajectories of the forward motion

and quantify the relative radius error (RRE) given a particular value of the *turn* parameter. Thus, the herein presented empirical evaluation of the proposed stochastic-based CPG motion controller is focused on two control parameters: the period p and the turning radius *turn*.

The tracked body position is denoted as $X^{glob}(t) = [O_x^{glob}(t), O_y^{glob}(t)]$ with $t = 0, 1, \ldots N$, where N is the number of frames taken by the localization system during the experiment. Having the robot position in time, we can estimate the forward velocity for individual gaits defined by the parameter p as

$$v = \frac{\|X^{glob}(1) - X^{glob}(N)\|}{t_r} \quad [m \cdot s^{-1}], \quad (25)$$

where t_r is the experiment runtime. The straight forward motion is achieved by setting the parameter *turn* to very high value, e.g., 10^9; however, too high values may cause numerical instability. The robot does not perfectly follow a straight line path, see Figure 7, due to the gaits and mechanical imprecision. Therefore, the forward velocity is established from a line fitted to the captured data. The established forward velocities for each individual gait are reported in Table 3.

Table 3: Forward Velocity

| p | 4 | 6 | 8 | 12 |
Gait	Tripod	Ripple	Low gear	Wave
Speed $[m \cdot s^{-1}]$	0.172	0.097	0.062	0.036

The value of the *turn* parameter equals to the radius of the circle the hexapod body should follow and it is denoted as r_{ref}. Different values of *turn* allows to achieve various circular motion as rotation on the spot or crawling an arc trajectory of specified radius. Therefore, the robot has been requested to crawl circular trajectories with the radius 0.01 cm, i.e., rotating on the spot, and radii $r_{ref} \in \{20, 40, 60, 80, 100\}$ cm. A circle fitting method proposed by Pratt [20] is utilized to estimate the real circular trajectory with the radius r_{fit} and center $S = [S_x^{glob}, S_y^{glob}]$ in the global coordinate system of the localization system. The relative radius error (RRE) η_{turn} is used to quantify the robot performance in crawling circular trajectories as

$$\eta_{turn} = \frac{|r_{fit} - r_{ref}|}{r_{ref}} \cdot 100 \quad [\%]. \quad (26)$$

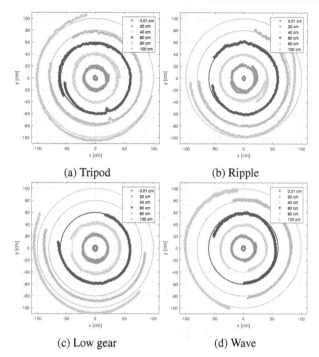

(a) Tripod   (b) Ripple

(c) Low gear   (d) Wave

Figure 8: Trajectories for circular motion and different gaits. Crosses show the tracked hexapod body positions and the circles the reference trajectory. Trajectories and centres are aligned to have their center in the plot origin.

Particular trajectories for each gait type are depicted in Figure 8, where the detected hexapod positions are marked with crosses and reference orbits are drawn with the solid line. The resulting trajectories are collocated to share the same orbit point. The established η_{turn} are listed in Table 4 for $r_{ref} \geq 20$ cm, since for rotating on the spot η_{turn} would give too large number without carrying any information because of the division with small r_{ref}.

Table 4: Relative radius error η_{turn} for circular motion

turn [cm]/p	4	6	8	12
20	0.83 %	9.89 %	11.63 %	1.34 %
40	0.92 %	0.41 %	7.54 %	1.42 %
60	0.40 %	0.97 %	0.32 %	4.60 %
80	2.78 %	1.78 %	10.00 %	2.32 %
100	3.15 %	5.37 %	7.23 %	0.54 %

Discussion

The presented results indicate that the circular locomotion can be controlled with the proposed method, i.e., the robot is able to follow the orbit defined by the *turn* parameter with the error not exceeding more than 2.5 % for the majority of combinations of gait types and turn ratios. The outliers, e.g., for $p = 6$ and *turn* = 20 cm, are caused by a leg slippage on the floor and other factors like the experiment imperfections. The results obtained for wave gait tend to have greater relative errors which can indicate that the "period stabilization" might have spoiled the resulting trajectory. The stabilization is a process in which the robot does not exactly have to be walking as desired and its legs move in a way not resulting in locomotion specified by the control parameters. It even may turn during forward locomotion as it can drag wrong legs while they should be swinging. The uncertain or even wrong foot coordination during the stabilization is caused by the time it takes the chaotic oscillator producing the patterned outputs to achieve oscillations with the specified period. This phenomenon is hardly noticeable for gaits other than wave as it takes less than a second, but in the case of the wave gait, it takes up to 4 seconds to achieve the desired motion, which is caused by the period stabilization.

5 Conclusion

In this paper, we have proposed a locomotion controller for a hexapod walking robot based on combination of the biologically inspired approach with a trajectory generator and inverse kinematics. The proposed controller is capable of controlling the hexapod locomotion by tuning only two parameters: the period p which modulates the chaotic CPG in order to stabilize different periodic orbits, hence different motion gaits, and the turning radius *turn* which allows the robot to perform different movements from turning on the spot to straight-forward walking. The designed control method has been evaluated using the real hexapod walking robot. The presented results of the experimental evaluation show that the proposed controller is plausible and can be used for walking on flat surfaces. The key concept in development has been to keep the controller modular to be easily usable with additional sensors. Therefore, our future work is to consider sensor feedback in the trajectory generator to allow the robot to negotiate rough terrains and autonomously set-up the control parameters. Also, chaotic state of the oscillator could be exploited for leg untrapping.

Acknowledgments – This work was supported by the Czech Science Foundation (GAČR) under research project No. 15-09600Y. The support of the Grant Agency of the CTU in Prague under grant No. SGS16/235/OHK3/3T/13 to Petr Čížek is also gratefully acknowledged.

References

[1] A. J. Ijspeert, "Central pattern generators for locomotion control in animals and robots: a review," *Neural Networks*, vol. 21, no. 4, pp. 642–653, 2008.

[2] T. G. Brown, "On the nature of the fundamental activity of the nervous centres; together with an analysis of the conditioning of rhythmic activity in progression, and a theory of the evolution of function in the nervous system," *The Journal of Physiology*, vol. 48, no. 1, pp. 18–46, 1914.

[3] D. M. Wilson, "The central nervous control of flight in a locust," *J. exp. Biol*, vol. 38, no. 47, pp. 1–490, 1961.

[4] M. H. Dickinson, C. T. Farley, R. J. Full, M. Koehl, R. Kram, and S. Lehman, "How animals move: an integrative view," *Science*, vol. 288, no. 5463, pp. 100–106, 2000.

[5] J. Proctor and P. Holmes, "Reflexes and preflexes: on the role of sensory feedback on rhythmic patterns in insect locomotion," *Biological cybernetics*, vol. 102, no. 6, pp. 513–531, 2010.

[6] E. Marder and D. Bucher, "Central pattern generators and the control of rhythmic movements," *Current biology*, vol. 11, no. 23, pp. R986–R996, 2001.

[7] D. M. Wilson, "Insect walking," *Annual review of entomology*, vol. 11, no. 1, pp. 103–122, 1966.

[8] N. Porcino, "Hexapod gait control by a neural network," in *International Joint Conference on Neural Networks (IJCNN)*. IEEE, 1990, pp. 189–194.

[9] S. Steingrube, M. Timme, F. Wörgötter, and P. Manoonpong, "Self-organized adaptation of a simple neural circuit enables complex robot behaviour," *Nature physics*, vol. 6, no. 3, pp. 224–230, 2010.

[10] J. Yu, M. Tan, J. Chen, and J. Zhang, "A survey on cpg-inspired control models and system implementation," *IEEE Transactions on Neural Networks and Learning Systems*, vol. 25, no. 3, pp. 441–456, 2014.

[11] R. Haschke, "Bifurcations in discrete-time neural networks: controlling complex network behaviour with inputs," Ph.D. dissertation, Bielefield University, 2003.

[12] F. Pasemann, "Complex dynamics and the structure of small neural networks," *Network: Computation in neural systems*, vol. 13, no. 2, pp. 195–216, 2002.

[13] K. Matsuoka, "Sustained oscillations generated by mutually inhibiting neurons with adaptation," *Biological cybernetics*, vol. 52, no. 6, pp. 367–376, 1985.

[14] W. Chen, G. Ren, J. Wang, and D. Liu, "An adaptive locomotion controller for a hexapod robot: CPG, kinematics and force feedback," *Science China Information Sciences*, vol. 57, no. 11, pp. 1–18, 2014.

[15] L. Xu, W. Liu, Z. Wang, and W. Xu, "Gait planning method of a hexapod robot based on the central pattern generators: Simulation and experiment," in *ROBIO*, 2013, pp. 698–703.

[16] G. L. Liu, M. K. Habib, K. Watanabe, and K. Izumi, "Central pattern generators based on matsuoka oscillators for the locomotion of biped robots," *Artificial Life and Robotics*, vol. 12, no. 1-2, pp. 264–269, 2008.

[17] M. Frasca, P. Arena, and L. Fortuna, *Bio-inspired emergent control of locomotion systems*, ser. Nonlinear Science A. World Scientific, 2004, vol. 48.

[18] H. Rostro-Gonzalez, P. Cerna-Garcia, G. Trejo-Caballero, C. Garcia-Capulin, M. Ibarra-Manzano, J. Avina-Cervantes, and C. Torres-Huitzil, "A CPG system based on spiking neurons for hexapod robot locomotion," *Neurocomputing*, vol. 170, pp. 47–54, 2015.

[19] T. Krajník, M. Nitsche, J. Faigl, P. Vaněk, M. Saska, L. Přeučil, T. Duckett, and M. Mejail, "A practical multi-robot localization system," *Journal of Intelligent & Robotic Systems*, vol. 76, no. 3-4, pp. 539–562, 2014.

[20] V. Pratt, "Direct least-squares fitting of algebraic surfaces," *ACM SIGGRAPH computer graphics*, vol. 21, no. 4, pp. 145–152, 1987.

ITAT 2016 Proceedings, pp. 138–146
ISBN 978-1537016740, © 2016 N. Orekhov, L. Bajer, M. Holeňa

Testing Gaussian Process Surrogates on CEC'2013 multi-modal benchmark

Nikita Orekhov[1], Lukáš Bajer[2], and Martin Holeňa[3]

[1] Faculty of Information Technology, Czech Technical University, Prague, orekhnik@fit.cvut.cz
[2] Faculty of Mathematics and Physics, Charles University, Prague, bajeluk@matfyz.cz
[3] Czech Academy of Sciences, Prague, martin@cs.cas.cz

Abstract: This paper compares several Gaussian-process-based surrogate modeling methods applied to black-box optimization by means of the Covariance Matrix Adaptation Evolution Strategy (CMA-ES), which is considered state-of-the-art in the area of continuous black-box optimization. Among the compared methods are the Model-assisted CMA-ES, the Robust Kriging Metamodel CMA-ES, and the Surrogate CMA-ES. In addition, a very successful surrogate-assisted self-adaptive CMA-ES, which is not based on Gaussian processes, but on ordinary regression by means of support vector machines has been included into the comparison. Those methods have been benchmarked using CEC'2013 testing functions. We show that the surrogate CMA-ES achieves best results at the beginning and later phases of optimization process, conceding in the middle to surrogate-assisted CMA-ES.

the original objective function [2]. The aim of this paper is to compare several GP-based surrogate-modeling techniques against another successful surrogate modeling method used in connection with CMA-ES. In particular, we examine the POI-based approach [13], the robust kriging metamodel [9] and the surrogate CMA-ES (S-CMA-ES) [2] and compare them against the support vector machines-based method called ^{s*}ACM-ES [11] and the basic CMA-ES without a surrogate model. The comparison has been performed on the multi-modal benchmark from CEC'2013.

The remainder of the paper is organized as follows. Section 2 introduces the necessary background of the Covariance Matrix Adaptation ES and Gaussian processes in the context of black-box optimization. Section 3 briefly recalls tested surrogate models, while section 4 describes the performed experiments and comments on obtained results.

1 Introduction

Evolutionary computation has been successfully applied to a wide spectrum of engineering problems. The randomized exploration guided by a set of candidate solutions (population) may be resistant against most optimization obstacles such as noise or multi-modality. It makes evolutionary algorithms (EAs) suitable for black-box optimization where an analytic form of the objective function is not known. In such cases, values of the objective function evaluations are the only available information to optimize the function.

The evaluation of the objective function can often be costly, i.e., it takes a significant amount of time and/or money. Typically, a black-box objective function is evaluated empirically during some experiment such as gas turbine profiles optimization [3] or protein folding stability optimization [4].

Today, a state-of-the-art among evolutionary black-box optimizers is the Covariance Matrix Adaptation evolution strategy (CMA-ES), which was initially introduced in [7]. However, as any other evolutionary optimization methods, CMA-ES may suffer from insufficient convergence speed w.r.t. the budget of expensive function evaluations. This can be avoided by the introduction of so-called surrogate models (aka metamodels), which provide regression-based predictions of the expensive objective function values.

Past works on surrogate-assisted optimization showed that models based on Gaussian Processes (GP) can lead to a significant reduction as to the number of evaluations of

2 Background

2.1 Surrogate modeling in black-box optimization

In the context of black-box optimization by CMA-ES, a surrogate model is built using some points sampled by the CMA-ES and their objective values. Then, the model is used to predict the quality of the sampled points in order to reduce number of function evaluations. However, the points should be carefully selected. Generally, there are two main ways to select them. The first approach proposed in [3] means that in each iteration of the overall optimization algorithm, one replaces the original objective function by its surrogate model, *estimates the model's global optimum* and evaluates it with the original objective function.

The other way consists in selecting a *controlled fraction* of individuals that should be evaluated on the original objective function. Such approach is thus called *evolution control* (EC) [8]. More specifically, costly evaluating the original objective for the entire population only at certain generations is called *generation-based* EC, while evaluating it only for a part of the population at each generation is called *individual-based* EC.

Using a surrogate model to find the global optimum, one *exploits* model's knowledge regarding the unknown objective function. However, this can potentially prevent the optimization algorithm from convergence to an optimal solution due to unexplored regions that were incorrectly modeled. To protect the model from making such predictions there is a need for some mechanism which cares about the *exploration* of new regions in the solution space. The *merit functions* were introduced precisely for this reason: they incorporate both exploration and exploitation patterns into the decisions performed during the surrogate modeling.

The variance σ^2 of the model predictions may be used as a merit function. Thus, the larger the variance, the higher the uncertainty of the predicted objective function value. The merit function is expressed as:

$$f_{\text{var}}(\boldsymbol{x}) = \sigma^2(\boldsymbol{x}),$$

where $\sigma^2(\boldsymbol{x})$ is the variance of the model's prediction at $\boldsymbol{x}$.

Lower confidence bound (LCB) is another merit function, which has the following form:

$$f_\alpha(\boldsymbol{x}) = \hat{f}(\boldsymbol{x}) - \alpha\sigma^2(\boldsymbol{x}),$$

where $\alpha \geq 0$ balances between the exploration and exploitation and $\hat{f}(\boldsymbol{x})$ is the model's prediction of the objective function value at $\boldsymbol{x}$.

The next merit function is a probability of improvement (POI). For any given solution vector $\boldsymbol{x}$, the model predictions about the function value at $\boldsymbol{x}$ is a realization of the random variable $Y(\boldsymbol{x})$. Having f_{min} as the current best obtained value of the original objective function, we define for any $T \leq f_{\text{min}}$ the probability of improvement as:

$$f_{\text{T}}(\boldsymbol{x}) = p(Y(\boldsymbol{x}) \leq T). \tag{1}$$

2.2 Gaussian processes

Gaussian process is a random process indexed by $\mathbb{R}^n$ such that its marginal indexed by a finite set of points $\boldsymbol{X}_N = \{\boldsymbol{x}_1, \ldots, \boldsymbol{x}_N\} \subset \mathbb{R}^n$ has an N-dimensional Gaussian distribution. Evaluating the objective function at those points results in a vector of function values $\boldsymbol{t}_N \in \mathbb{R}^N$. If that vector is viewed as a particular realization of the respective Gaussian distribution, the GP provides a prediction of the distribution of the function value t_{N+1} at some point $\boldsymbol{x}_{N+1}$.

Gaussian process models are determined by their mean and covariance matrix. This matrix is constructed by applying a covariance function $k : \mathbb{R}^n \times \mathbb{R}^n \mapsto \mathbb{R}$ to each pair of points in $\boldsymbol{X}_N$. The covariance functions have a certain set of parameters, usually called hyper-parameters due to the fact that the covariance function itself is a parameter of the Gaussian process. Typically, the hyper-parameters are obtained through the maximum likelihood estimation.

We recall the covariance functions employed in the observed methods. Note that the hyper-parameters below are marked as θ. The first one is *exponential* covariance function. It is used in [9] and has the following form:

$$k_{\text{E}}(\boldsymbol{x}_p, \boldsymbol{x}_q) = \exp\left(-\frac{r}{\theta}\right),$$

where $r = \|\boldsymbol{x}_p - \boldsymbol{x}_q\|$ is the distance between points.

The next covariance function is called *squared exponential*. This is used in [13] and its basic variant can be expressed as:

$$k_{\text{SE}}(\boldsymbol{x}_p, \boldsymbol{x}_q) = \exp\left(-\frac{r^2}{\theta}\right).$$

In [2], the isotropic *Matérn* covariance function $k_{\text{Matérn}}^{5/2}$ is used in its form:

$$k_{\text{Matérn}}^{5/2}(\boldsymbol{x}_p, \boldsymbol{x}_q) = \theta_1\left(1 + \frac{\sqrt{5}r}{\theta_2} + \frac{5r^2}{3\theta_2^2}\right)\exp\left(-\frac{\sqrt{5}r}{\theta_2}\right).$$

Having defined the covariance matrix for N points, an extension of $\boldsymbol{C}$ after including an $(N+1)$th point reads:

$$\boldsymbol{C}_{N+1} = \left(\begin{array}{cc} \boldsymbol{C}_N & \boldsymbol{k} \\ \boldsymbol{k}^{\text{T}} & \kappa \end{array} \right),$$

where $\boldsymbol{k} = k(\boldsymbol{x}_{N+1}, \boldsymbol{X}_N)$ is an N-dimensional real vector of covariances between the new point and points from training set, while $\kappa = k(\boldsymbol{x}_{N+1}, \boldsymbol{x}_{N+1})$ is a variance of the new point [3]. Consequently,

$$t_{N+1} \sim \mathcal{N}(\mu_{N+1}, \sigma_{N+1}^2), \tag{2}$$

where $\mu_{N+1} = \boldsymbol{k}^{\text{T}}\boldsymbol{C}_N^{-1}\boldsymbol{t}_N$ is the predictive mean and $\sigma_{N+1}^2 = \kappa - \boldsymbol{k}^{\text{T}}\boldsymbol{C}_N^{-1}\boldsymbol{k}$ is the predictive variance.

In the context of Gaussian processes, we have $f_{\text{min}} = \min(t_1, \ldots, t_N)$. Then, considering distribution from (2), the POI criterion can be rewritten from (1) as follows:

$$f_{\text{T}}(\boldsymbol{x}) = \Phi\left(\frac{T - \hat{t}(\boldsymbol{x})}{\sigma(\boldsymbol{x})}\right),$$

where Φ is the cumulative distribution function of the normal distribution $\mathcal{N}(0, 1)$.

Areas with high POI value have a high probability to sample point with objective value better than f_{min}. Regions with model prediction $\hat{t}(\boldsymbol{x}) \gg f_{\text{min}}$ will have POI value close to zero, which encourages the model to search somewhere else. The POI value becomes large when the variance (i.e. σ^2) is large, which is typical for unexplored areas. Therefore, the use of POI may be useful for dealing with multi-modal functions.

2.3 CMA-ES

The CMA-ES employs the concept of the adaptation of internal variables from the data. Particularly, it adapts several components such as mutation step size, distribution mean and the covariance matrix, which represents a local approximation of the function landscape.

In the CMA-ES, a generation of candidate solutions is usually obtained by sampling a *normally-distributed* random variable:

$$\boldsymbol{x}_k^{(g+1)} \sim \boldsymbol{m}^{(g)} + \sigma^{(g)}\mathcal{N}\left(\boldsymbol{0}, \boldsymbol{C}^{(g)}\right) \text{ for } k = 1, \ldots, \lambda,$$

where $\lambda \geq 2$ is a population size, $\boldsymbol{x}_k^{(g+1)} \in \mathbb{R}^n$ is the k-th offspring in $g+1$-th generation, $\boldsymbol{m}^{(g)} \in \mathbb{R}^n$ is the mean of the sampling distribution, $\sigma^{(g)} \in \mathbb{R}_+$ is a step-size, $\boldsymbol{C}^{(g)} \in \mathbb{R}_{n \times n}$ is a covariance matrix. Below we list basic equations for the adaptation of the mean, step-size and covariance matrix used in CMA-ES. For details we refer to [5].

The mean of the sampling distribution is a weighted average of μ best-ranked points from $\boldsymbol{x}_1^{(g+1)}, \dots, \boldsymbol{x}_\lambda^{(g+1)}$:

$$\boldsymbol{m}^{(g+1)} \quad = \quad \sum_{i=1}^{\mu} w_i \, \boldsymbol{x}_{i:\lambda}^{(g+1)},$$

where $\sum_{i=1}^{\mu} w_i = 1$, $w_1 \geq w_2 \geq \cdots \geq w_\mu > 0$ are weight coefficients and $i : \lambda$ notation means i-th best individual out of $\boldsymbol{x}_1^{(g+1)}, \dots, \boldsymbol{x}_\lambda^{(g+1)}$.

The covariance matrix $\boldsymbol{C}$, being initially set to identity matrix, is updated by *rank-one-update* and *rank-μ-update* during each iteration. A *cumulation* strategy [5] is applied to combine consecutive steps in the search space.

$$\boldsymbol{C}^{(g+1)} = (1 - c_1 - c_\mu) \, \boldsymbol{C}^{(g)}$$
$$+ \; c_1 \underbrace{\boldsymbol{p}_c^{(g+1)} \boldsymbol{p}_c^{(g+1)\top}}_{\text{rank-one update}} + c_\mu \underbrace{\sum_{i=1}^{\mu} w_i \, \boldsymbol{y}_{i:\lambda}^{(g+1)} \boldsymbol{y}_{i:\lambda}^{(g+1)\top}}_{\text{rank-}\mu \text{ update}},$$

where c_1 and c_μ are learning rates for rank-one-update and rank-μ-update, $\boldsymbol{p}_c^{(g+1)}$ is an evolution path and $\boldsymbol{y}_{i:\lambda}^{(g+1)} = \left(\boldsymbol{x}_{i:\lambda}^{(g+1)} - \boldsymbol{m}^{(g)} \right) / \sigma^{(g)}$.

The step length update reads:

$$\sigma^{(g+1)} = \sigma^{(g)} \exp\left(\frac{c_\sigma}{d_\sigma} \left(\frac{\|\boldsymbol{p}_\sigma^{(g+1)}\|}{\mathbb{E}\|\mathcal{N}(\boldsymbol{0}, \boldsymbol{I})\|} - 1 \right) \right),$$

where c_σ is a learning rate and $\boldsymbol{p}_\sigma^{(g+1)}$ is an evolution path.

The CMA-ES is considered as a *local* optimizer. So in case of multi-modal functions, it tends to end up in a local optima. Hence, to reduce the influence of such behavior, several restart strategies were introduced. The perhaps best known one is the IPOP-CMA-ES [1]. In this modification, an optimization process is being interrupted several times and independently restarted with the population size increased by a certain factor (typically 2). IPOP version is set default for all of the CMA-ES algorithms throughout the article.

3 Tested methods

3.1 POI MAES

Ulmer et al. refer to this algorithm as Probability of Improvement Model-assisted Evolution Strategy (POI MAES) [13]. The method uses a modification of the covariance function SE, which has $n + 2$ hyper-parameters,

obtained by likelihood maximization:

$$k(\boldsymbol{x}_p, \boldsymbol{x}_q, \boldsymbol{\theta}) = \theta_1 \exp\left(-\frac{1}{2} \sum_{i=1}^{n} \frac{(x_{p_i} - x_{q_i})^2}{r_i^2} \right) + \delta_{pq} \theta_2,$$

where r_i^2 are length-scales for the individual dimensions and $\delta_{pq} = \begin{cases} 0, & \text{if } p \neq q \\ 1, & \text{if } p = q \end{cases}$ is the Kronecker delta.

The model is incorporated into the CMA-ES via individual-based EC, which the authors call *pre-selection*. In every iteration, $\lambda_{\text{pre}} > \lambda$ new individuals are sampled from μ parents and evaluated on the surrogate model using the POI merit function. Then, the λ offsprings with the highest POI are selected and evaluated on the objective function. In the end, the surrogate model is updated.

3.2 Robust CMA-ES

The approach below was designed to provide robustness approximations of the objective function values. It is also combined with a special method to select promising solutions [9].

One can imagine robustness approximation as an attempt to predict function values within noisy or imprecise environment. Considering expensive optimization, it becomes extremely important to make precise predictions for noisy problems as it requires a certain trade-off between limiting the noise and reducing the number of evaluations.

The robustness approximation is achieved in a way that the local model is trained around every point $\boldsymbol{x}_k$ to be estimated. To achieve this, the algorithm chooses n_{krig} pairs $(\boldsymbol{x}, t)$ in a specific way described below from a given archive $\mathscr{A}$ and stores them in a local training set $\mathscr{D}$. If the amount of points does not suffice, the algorithm returns also a set $\boldsymbol{X}_{\text{cand}} = \{\boldsymbol{x}_1, \dots, \boldsymbol{x}_l\}$ of length $l = n_{\text{krig}} - |\mathscr{D}|$. Points from $\boldsymbol{X}_{\text{cand}}$ are then evaluated with the original objective function and added to both $\mathscr{A}$ and $\mathscr{D}$.

The procedure to select the pairs $(\boldsymbol{x}, t)$ from the archive $\mathscr{A}$ is as follows. First, the n_{krig} points are generated via the Latin hypercube sampling method and are stored in a reference set $\mathscr{R}$. Then, for every point $\boldsymbol{x} \in \mathscr{R}$ (subsequently called reference point), the closest $\boldsymbol{x}$ from $\mathscr{A}$ is assigned. An important note here is that the reference point from $\mathscr{R}$ must be closest to the archive point $\boldsymbol{x}$ as well. If this is the case, the archive point with its corresponding objective function value are added to the training set. Otherwise, the reference point is considered a suitable candidate for sampling and added to $\boldsymbol{X}_{\text{cand}}$. When all points from $\mathscr{R}$ are assigned, the reference point from the assigned pair (archive point, reference point), for which the distance between both points is the largest among all assigned pairs, is selected and evaluated.

Using the procedure above a separate training set is selected for every point $\boldsymbol{x}^{(g)}$ to be estimated at generation g and the model is trained. Then, the fitness value at $\boldsymbol{x}^{(g)}$ is estimated according to so-called *multi evaluation method*

(MEM). In this method the approximation is obtained as a mean value of several approximations at points with random perturbation in the input space, i.e.:

$$\hat{f}_{MEM}(\boldsymbol{x}) = \frac{1}{m} \sum_{i=1}^{m} \hat{f}(\boldsymbol{x} + \boldsymbol{\delta}_i),$$

where m is the predefined amount of points to perform approximation and $\boldsymbol{\delta}_i$ denotes a random variation.

3.3 S-CMA-ES

Another surrogate-assisted approach is called *Surrogate CMA-ES* (S-CMA-ES). It was initially proposed in [2] and later extended to the *Doubly Trained* S-CMA-ES (DTS-CMA-ES) in [12]. The S-CMA-ES employs the Matérn covariance function mentioned in 2.2 with hyper-parameters $\boldsymbol{\theta} = \{\sigma_f^2, l, \sigma_n^2\}$ optimized by the maximum-likelihood approach.

The S-CMA-ES algorithm uses generation-based evolution control which means that an *original*-evaluated generation and *model*-evaluated generations interleave. During the *original* generations, all the points are evaluated by the expensive objective function. In every *model* generation, at least n_{MIN} archive points have to be selected to train the surrogate model. The selection process is restricted to points that do not have the Mahalanobis distance from the CMA-ES' mean value $\boldsymbol{m}$ larger than some prescribed limit r:

$$\mathscr{D} \leftarrow \{(\boldsymbol{x},t) \in \mathscr{A} \,|\, \sqrt{(\boldsymbol{m}-\boldsymbol{x})^\top (\sigma^2 \boldsymbol{C})^{-1}(\boldsymbol{m}-\boldsymbol{x})} \leq r\},$$

where $\boldsymbol{C}$ is the CMA-ES covariance matrix and σ is the step-size at the considered generation.

If there are not enough points, building the model is postponed and all fitness evaluations are performed on the original objective function. When there are enough points, at most n_{MAX} points are selected via k-NN clustering to train a GP model.

The extension DTS-CMA-ES selects $n_{orig} < \lambda$ most uncertain points w.r.t. the employed merit function and evaluates them on the original objective function. Then, the surrogate model is being retrained on the archive extended with the newly evaluated n_{orig} points. Finally, the $\lambda - n_{orig}$ remaining points function values are predicted by the model and returned to the CMA-ES.

3.4 s*ACM-ES

This subsection describes a method called Self-adaptive Surrogate-assisted CMA-ES (^{s*}ACM-ES) [11], which is not GP-based, but is used for comparison.

This method employs the ordinal regression based on Ranking support vector machines. Evaluations made by such model provide only rankings of the points in order to achieve the invariance to the rank-preserving transformations of f. The method adapts the model hyper-parameters

in an on-line manner. In addition, it also depends on much larger population size while operating on surrogate and preserving original population size for the original objective function evaluations.

A generation-based EC is used, the number $\hat{n}$ of model-evaluated generations is adjusted according to the model error, assessed in the interleaving generation in which the original objective function is evaluated.

The algorithm adjusts $\hat{n}$ by a linear function inversely proportional to a *global* model error $\mathrm{Err}(\boldsymbol{\theta})$. The global error is updated with some relaxation from a *local* error on λ most recent evaluated points. Denoting Λ to be the set of those λ points, the local error is estimated as follows:

$$\mathrm{Err}(\boldsymbol{\theta}) = \frac{2}{|\Lambda|(|\Lambda|-1)} \sum_{i=1}^{|\Lambda|} \sum_{j=i+1}^{|\Lambda|} w_{i,j} \cdot 1_{\hat{f}_{\boldsymbol{\theta},i,j}},$$

where $1_{\hat{f}_{\boldsymbol{\theta},i,j}}$ is true if $\hat{f}$ violates the ordering of pair (i,j) given by the real objective function f and $w_{i,j}$ defines the weights of such violations.

The procedure of the surrogate error optimization is done in the end of every ES generation, where the model hyper-parameters are optimized by one iteration of an additional CMA-ES (referred to as CMA-ES #2 in [11]). Here, the algorithm samples λ_{hyp} different points in a space of hyper-parameters and builds λ_{hyp} surrogate models. Then, those models are evaluated using the $\mathrm{Err}(\boldsymbol{\theta})$ metric and $\mu_{hyp} = \lfloor \lambda_{hyp}/2 \rfloor$ best performing are used to update internal variables of the CMA-ES #2. The resulting mean of the hyper-parameter distribution is used to obtain $\boldsymbol{\theta}$ for the next generation of ^{s*}ACM-ES.

Finally, the standard CMA-ES configurations differ if it optimizes the surrogate model $\hat{f}$. In such cases, it uses larger population sizes $\lambda = k_\lambda \lambda_{default}$ and $\mu = k_\mu \mu_{default}$, where $k_\lambda, k_\mu \geq 1$. In order to prevent degradation when the model is inaccurate, k_λ is also adjusted w.r.t. the $\mathrm{Err}(\boldsymbol{\theta})$.

4 Experiments

4.1 Benchmark functions

The experiments has been conducted on a recently proposed benchmark, introduced on the special session for multi-modal function optimization during the Congress of Evolutionary Computation (CEC) in 2013 [10]. The benchmark contains 12 noiseless multi-modal functions being defined for dimensions $1 - 20D$. Note that this test set differs from the one used in [9], where the noise was introduced by oscillations in the input space. In addition, the experiments has been conducted within the BBOB framework [6] via introducing 9 new benchmark functions. Since the CMA-ES is not able to run in 1D, we excluded 1D functions from our experiments. Altogether, the following set of functions was employed (dimensionality is shown in brackets): Himmelblau (2D), Six-Hump Camel Back (2D), Shubert (2D, 3D), Vincent (2D, 3D), Modified Rastrigin (2D), Composition Function

1 (2D), Composition Function 2 (2D), Composition Function 3 (2D, 3D, 5D, 10D), Composition Function 4 (3D, 5D, 10D, 20D).

4.2 Experimental setup

The experimental testing has been prepared according to the BBOB framework specifications [6]. First, for every benchmark function, the global minimum is denoted as f_{opt}. The target function value f_{target} was set to $f_{\text{opt}} + 10^{-8}$. This value is considered as a stopping criterion for tested algorithms. The performance of the tested methods is measured as a difference of the best objective value found so far t_{best} and global minimum of the function: $\Delta_f = t_{\text{best}} - f_{\text{opt}}$ for respective numbers of original fitness evaluations. The resulting Δ_f values are calculated for Ntrials = 15 algorithm runs for every benchmark function and every dimension.

The tested algorithms had the following settings:

- *CMA-ES*: the Matlab code version 3.62 of the IPOP-CMA-ES has been used, with the number of restarts = 4, *IncPopSize* = 2, $\sigma_{\text{start}} = \frac{8}{3}$, $\lambda = 4 + \lfloor 3 \log n \rfloor$ and setting the remaining parameters to its defaults [6]. Note that since the tested surrogate methods perform within the CMA-ES environment, they also had those settings.

- *POI MAES*: the only algorithm, which does not use the original author's implementation. We implemented it in Matlab according to its description in [13]. The λ_{pre} was set to 3λ and the number of points to train the model to 2λ. Here we weren't able to confirm or deny if the algorithm replicates the results from the original paper.

- *Robust CMA*: the n_{krig} is set to $2n$, the m parameter is 10.

- *S-CMA-ES*: the DTS-CMA-ES extension was used, the Mahalanobis distance limit r was set to 8, the covariance function $k_{\text{Matérn}}^{5/2}$ was used with the starting values $(\sigma_n^2, l, \sigma_f^2) = \log(0.01, 2, 0.5)$, n_{orig} was set to $\lceil 0.1\lambda \rceil$ and f_{var} was used as the merit function, see [12] for details.

- *ᔆ*ACM-ES*: uses settings from [11].

4.3 Results and their assessment

The results of testing are now analyzed in two-stages. During the first stage, the algorithm's performance is analyzed for every benchmark function and every dimension separately. The second stage concentrates on the analysis of results aggregated over individual functions and dimensions, and finally over the entire benchmark set.

The results of testing over individual CEC functions are shown in Figure 1. The performance of every method has been calculated for Ntrials runs and is represented by the empirical median Δ_f^{med} (straight lines) and quartiles (translucent area) of the Δ_f.

It can be seen that the S-CMA-ES and ᔆ*ACM-ES methods have the best performance on the majority of benchmark functions. However, for the Shubert function in 2D and 3D and for the Composition Function 4 in 5D both methods seem to miss the global optimum and do not noticeably speed up the original CMA-ES. An example visualization of the experiment on 2D Shubert function is shown in Figure 2. In addition, the ᔆ*ACM-ES fails to find the global optimum for the Vincent function in 3D.

The other methods lead to a deceleration of the CMA-ES convergence speed in most cases. The global optimum remains undiscovered except for the Vincent, Himmelblau and Six-Hump Camel Back functions by POI MAES. POI MAES was the best method on the Shubert function. Also, this method outperformed the original CMA-ES on 20 dimensional Composite Function 4, which may indicate its ability to speed up the CMA-ES for higher dimensions.

The Robust CMA method achieved the worst results in our experiments; comparable performance was shown only for Shubert function. However, this can be due to the fact that the considered benchmark functions were noiseless whereas this method has been developed primarily for noisy objective functions.

Next, Figure 3 depicts results aggregated over different functions, while Figure 4 shows results aggregated over the entire benchmark set. To enable aggregation, we use scaled logarithms of medians. First of all, the evaluation budgets are normalized by the dimensionality. For benchmarking, the budgets were limited to 250 function evaluations per dimension (FE/D). Then, the scaled logarithm Δ_f^{log} of the median Δ_f^{med} is calculated as follows:

$$\Delta_f^{\text{log}} = \frac{\log \Delta_f^{\text{med}} - \Delta_f^{\text{MIN}}}{\Delta_f^{\text{MAX}} - \Delta_f^{\text{MIN}}} \log_{10}(1/10^{-8}) + \log_{10} 10^{-8},$$

where Δ_f^{MIN} and Δ_f^{MAX} are the lowest and the highest $\log \Delta_f^{\text{med}}$ values obtained by any of the compared algorithms for the particular benchmark function f and dimension D within the evaluation budget 250 FE/D.

Figures 3 and 4 show that S-CMA-ES and ᔆ*ACM-ES have the fastest convergence rates. S-CMA-ES converges fastest at the beginning of the optimization (till approx. 75 FE/D) as well as at the later phases ($125 - 250$ FE/D). However, it slows down from 75 till 125 FE/D, being outperformed by ᔆ*ACM-ES, especially due to the results on Shubert, CF3 (in 5D and 10D) and CF4 (in 5D and 20D).

It can be seen that POI MAES finally converges (at 250 FE/D) close to the other algorithms (outperforming CMA-ES and ᔆ*ACM-ES for 3D) for low-dimensional problems. An interesting case, however, is that POI MAES outperforms CMA-ES on 20-dimensional f_{12}. Such behavior may be associated with the fact that POI-based approach tends to explore areas with high model uncertainties which is useful for multi-modal problems [13], especially in case of high dimensionality, where the classic CMA-ES is not capable to learn the landscape sufficiently. Also, slower convergence rates of POI MAES may be explained by the fact that the model requires more time to move from exploration phase to exploitation. However, one can consider the method to be not flexible enough. The reason is that the model selects 2λ most recently evaluated points for training which is not the best decision if the algorithm moves far from the global optimum. Hence, a more sophisticated selection strategy may be required to obtain better results.

5 Conclusion

Experimental testing has shown that the best performing among all compared methods for smaller evaluation budgets (up to approx. 75FE/D) appears to be S-CMA-ES. However, it is being outperformed by the ^{s*}ACM-ES for the budgets $75-125$FE/D. For even larger evaluation budgets the former method performed the best again. The POI MAES has shown a slightly worse performance compared to CMA-ES with rare improvements. However, we believe that the method can be further enhanced by introducing a new selection strategy. The method from [9] has shown inadequate performance in our experiments. However, that method was designed to perform in noisy environment, which was not the case of the employed CEC benchmark.

Today many experiments in the field of black-box optimization are conducted on the functions from the BBOB framework [2] [11]. Thereby, this paper is considered as an extension to the BBOB benchmark. The paper concentrates only on the relatively small set of test functions, which prevents from making clear conclusions. However, we believe that the performance of the methods may be clarified by the combination of this paper's results with other comparisons.

6 Acknowledgments

Access to computing and storage facilities owned by parties and projects contributing to the National Grid Infrastructure MetaCentrum, provided under the programme "Projects of Large Research, Development, and Innovations Infrastructures" (CESNET LM2015042), is greatly appreciated.

References

[1] Anne Auger and Nikolaus Hansen. A restart CMA evolution strategy with increasing population size. In *Evolutionary Computation, 2005. The 2005 IEEE Congress on*, volume 2, pages 1769–1776. IEEE, 2005.

[2] Lukáš Bajer, Zbyněk Pitra, and Martin Holeňa. Benchmarking Gaussian processes and random forests surrogate models on the BBOB noiseless testbed. In *Proceedings of the Companion Publication of the 2015 Annual Conference on Genetic and Evolutionary Computation*, pages 1143–1150. ACM, 2015.

[3] Dirk Büche, Nicol N Schraudolph, and Petros Koumoutsakos. Accelerating evolutionary algorithms with Gaussian process fitness function models. *IEEE Transactions on Systems, Man, and Cybernetics, Part C: Applications and Reviews*, 35(2):183–194, 2005.

[4] John C Chaput and Jack W Szostak. Evolutionary optimization of a nonbiological ATP binding protein for improved folding stability. *Chemistry & biology*, 11(6):865–874, 2004.

[5] Nikolaus Hansen. The CMA evolution strategy: a comparing review. In *Towards a new evolutionary computation*, pages 75–102. Springer, 2006.

[6] Nikolaus Hansen, Anne Auger, Steffen Finck, and Raymond Ros. Real-parameter black-box optimization benchmarking 2010: Experimental setup. *INRIA*, 2010. <inria-00462481>.

[7] Nikolaus Hansen and Andreas Ostermeier. Adapting arbitrary normal mutation distributions in evolution strategies: The covariance matrix adaptation. In *Evolutionary Computation, 1996., Proceedings of IEEE International Conference on*, pages 312–317. IEEE, 1996.

[8] Yaochu Jin. A comprehensive survey of fitness approximation in evolutionary computation. *Soft computing*, 9(1):3–12, 2005.

[9] Johannes W Kruisselbrink, Michael Emmerich, André H Deutz, and Thomas Bäck. A robust optimization approach using kriging metamodels for robustness approximation in the CMA-ES. In *Evolutionary Computation (CEC), 2010 IEEE Congress on*, pages 1–8. IEEE, 2010.

[10] Xiaodong Li, Andries Engelbrecht, and Michael G Epitropakis. Benchmark functions for CEC'2013 special session and competition on niching methods for multimodal function optimization.

[11] Ilya Loshchilov, Marc Schoenauer, and Michèle Sebag. Intensive surrogate model exploitation in self-adaptive surrogate-assisted CMA-ES (saACM-ES). In *Proceedings of the 15th annual conference on Genetic and evolutionary computation*, pages 439–446. ACM, 2013.

[12] Zbyněk Pitra, Lukáš Bajer, and Martin Holeňa. Doubly trained evolution control for the surrogate CMA-ES. Accepted for publication at PPSN 2016.

[13] Holger Ulmer, Felix Streichert, and Andreas Zell. Evolution strategies assisted by Gaussian processes with improved preselection criterion. In *Evolutionary Computation, 2003. CEC'03. The 2003 Congress on*, volume 1, pages 692–699. IEEE, 2003.

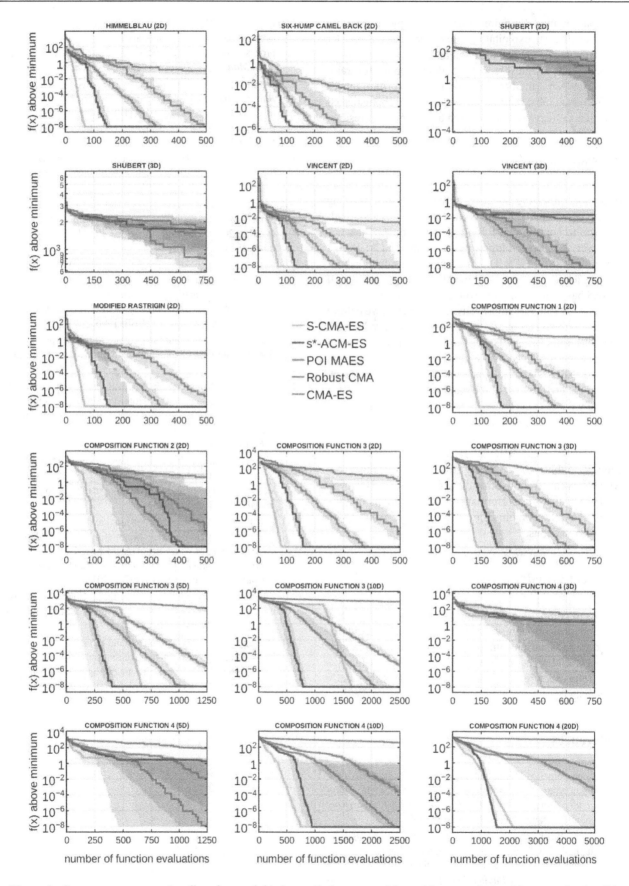

Figure 1: Convergence curves (median, first and third quartiles) computed from 15 repeated algorithm runs for feasible combinations of CEC functions and dimensions $n \in \{2, 3, 5, 10, 20\}$.

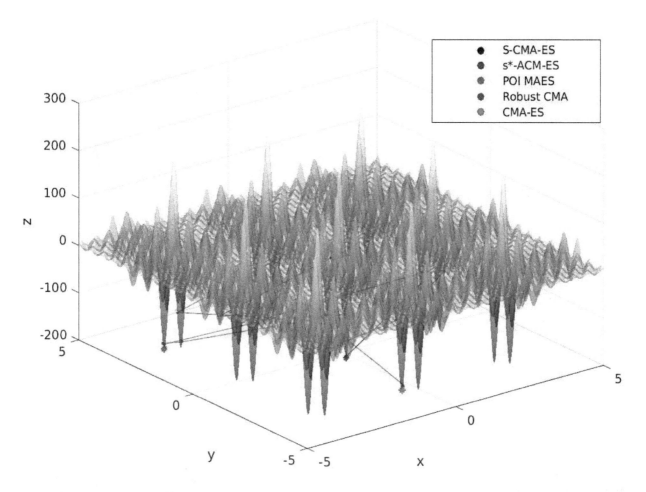

Figure 2: Best solutions found by algorithms mapped on 2D Shubert function landscape. Points represent transitional solutions found at some number of function evaluations during the optimization process. The solutions are sorted according to that number, the lines represent ordering of points. The resulting solutions found in the end of optimization are denoted by asterisks.

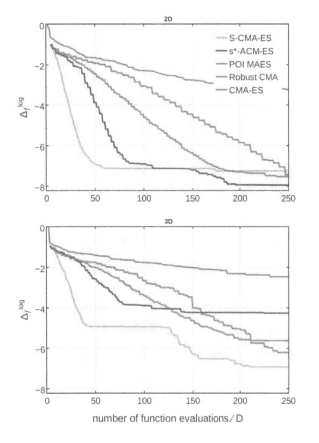

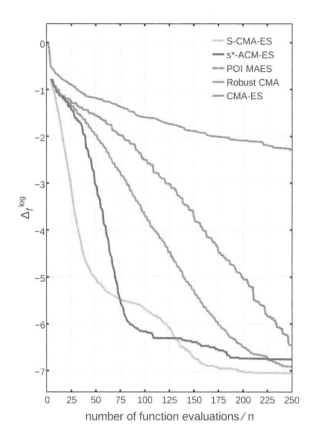

Figure 3: Scaled logarithms of the empirical medians (Δ_f^{med}) depending on FE/D. The graphs show the benchmark results achieved by averaging all functions defined in 2D and 3D.

Figure 4: Scaled logarithms of the empirical medians (Δ_f^{med}) depending on FE/D. The results are aggregated over all benchmark functions.

ITAT 2016 Proceedings, pp. 147–154
ISBN 978-1537016740, © 2016 J. Outrata, M. Trnecka

Evaluating Association Rules in Boolean Matrix Factorization

Jan Outrata and Martin Trnecka*

Department of Computer Science
Palacký University Olomouc, Czech Republic
jan.outrata@upol.cz, martin.trnecka@gmail.com

Abstract: Association rules, or association rule mining, is a well-established and popular method of data mining and machine learning successfully applied in many different areas since mid-nineties. Association rules form a ground of the Asso algorithm for discovery of the first (presumably most important) factors in Boolean matrix factorization. In Asso, the confidence parameter of association rules heavily influences the quality of factorization. However, association rules, in a more general form, appear already in GUHA, a knowledge discovery method developed since mid-sixties. In the paper, we evaluate the use of various (other) types of association rules from GUHA in Asso and, from the other side, a possible utilization of (particular) association rules in other Boolean matrix factorization algorithms not based on the rules. We compare the quality of factorization produced by the modified algorithms with those produced by the original algorithms.

1 Introduction

1.1 The problem and algorithms

Boolean matrix factorization (BMF), called also Boolean matrix decomposition, aims to find for a given $n \times m$ object-attribute incidence Boolean matrix I a $n \times k$ object-factor Boolean matrix A and a $k \times m$ factor-attribute Boolean matrix B such that the Boolean matrix product (see below) of A and B (approximately) equals I. A decomposition of I into A and B may be interpreted as a discovery of k factors exactly or approximately explaining the data. Interpreting the matrices I, A and B as the object-attribute, object-factor and factor-attribute incidence matrices, respectively, A and B explain I as follows: the object i has the attribute j (the entry I_{ij} corresponding to the row i and the column j is 1) if and only if there exists factor l such that l applies to i and j is one of the particular manifestations of l. The optimization version of this basic BMF problem demands k to be as small as possible. The least k for which an exact decomposition of I exists is called the *Boolean rank* (or Schein rank) of I.

In the literature, two common variants of the optimization problem are defined and dealt with: the approximate factorization problem (AFP) [3], where the number k of factors is sought to be minimal for a prescribed maximal

difference (error) of the Boolean product of A and B from I (usualy zero), and the discrete basic problem (DBP) [11], where the error is sought to be minimal for a prescribed (fixed) k. The formal definitions of the problems are given below. For the former problem, greedy approach algorithms seem popular. One of the most efficient ones, GRECOND, is proposed in [3] (where it is called Algorithm 2). Another one, GREESS [4], refines GRECOND based on a deeper insight into the problem. For the latter problem, probably the most known (and a basic one) algorithm is ASSO, proposed in [11], together with a few of its variants. Other BMF algorithms proposed in the recent data mining literature that can be tailored for either of the two problems are e.g. HYPER [16] or PANDA [10].

GRECOND (and GREESS and their variants) finds factors as *maximal rectangles*, Boolean matrices whose entries with 1 form a maximal rectangular area (full of 1s), upon a suitable permutation of rows and columns. This concept comes from the geometric view on BMF and *formal concept analysis* (FCA). The view tells us that finding a decomposition of I means finding a *coverage* of 1s in I by rectangles full of 1s [3, 4] and in FCA maximal rectangles full of 1s correspond to so-called formal concepts [5]. We will use maximal rectangles as factors to describe the algorithms now. The GRECOND algorithm, in its seek for a factor, starts with the empty set of attributes to which a selected attribute with possibly other attributes are repeatedly added. The constructed set of attributes together with the set of all objects having all the attributes determine a maximal rectangle (form a formal concept). The selected attribute is such that the rectangle with the attributes added *covers* as many still *uncovered* 1 in I as possible. The attributes are added repeatedly as long as the number of still uncovered 1s in I covered by the rectangle grows (note the greedy approach here). Further factors are sought the same way and the algorithm stops when the prescribed number of 1s in I is covered by the maximal rectangles corresponding to factors (i.e. the algorithm is designed for the AFP). Characteristic vectors of object sets determining found maximal rectangles then constitute columns of matrix A and characteristic vectors of attribute sets of the maximal rectangles constitute rows of matrix B.

ASSO, on the other hand, starts in its seek for each of (at most) the prescribed number k of factors with a selected set of attributes and searches for a set of objects such that the Boolean product of the characteristic vectors of the two sets, as a rectangle (not necessarily maximal) correspond-

---
*Support by grant No. GA15-17899S of the Czech Science Foundation is acknowledged. M. Trnecka also acknowledges partial support by grant No. PrF_2016_027 of IGA of Palacký University Olomouc.

ing to the factor, covers as many 1s in I as possible. At the same time, however, the rectangle must also *overcover* as few 0 in I by 1 as possible (i.e. the algorithm is designed for the DBP). Note here that ASSO is admitted to overcover 0 in I in its aim to cover 1s, while GRECOND does not do that (thereby it is said it performs a from-bellow decomposition of I). Characteristic vectors of the selected sets of attributes constitute rows of matrix B while characteristic vectors of the corresponding found sets of objects constitute columns of matrix A. The sets of attributes are selected, under the same conditions as for the search of objects, among candidate sets represented by rows of the attribute-attribute matrix called association matrix. This $m \times m$ Boolean matrix, created in the first step of the algorithm, contains 1 in the row corresponding to an attribute i and the column corresponding to an attribute j if the association rule $i \Rightarrow j$ has the (so-called) confidence – the ratio of the number of objects having both i and j to the number of objects having i – greater than a user-defined parameter τ; otherwise it contains 0 in the row and the column.

1.2 Associations in BMF

The association rules in ASSO, also known from association rule mining [1], are of one type of relationship between two (Boolean) attributes in (Boolean) object-attribute data. There are other types, in general between two logical formulas above attributes instead of between just two single attributes, introduced in the literature. After all, general association rules whose validity in data is defined through a function of the numbers of objects having and not having both or one of the attributes (or, in general, satisfying and not satisfying the formulas above attributes) are introduced and operated with in GUHA [7, 8, 9, 13], one of the oldest, less known but most sophisticated, method of knowledge discovery. In GUHA, several logical and statistical functions, called quantifiers, used to interpret several different types of association rules are introduced. Actually, one of the quantifiers (the basic one), founded implication, interprets the association rule used in ASSO (and association rule mining, see below).

The topic of this paper is twofold. First, we pick up several (other) types of association rules, interpreted by selected GUHA quantifiers, and use them in place of the ASSO's association rule in the ASSO algorithm. Second, vice versa, we take the concept of association matrix from ASSO and utilize it in greedy-approach algorithms. Namely, we take a particular association matrix and use the rows of the matrix as characteristic vectors of candidates to initial sets of attributes to which further attributes are added in GRECOND instead of the empty set. Both modifications of the algorithms are novel ideas not previously discussed in the literature. The main purpose of the paper is to evaluate the use of various types of association rules in ASSO algorithm and the use of association matrix in GRECOND algorithm. The evaluation is done by experimental comparison of quality of decompositions

obtained from the modified algorithms with those obtained from their respective original versions.

The rest of the paper is organized as follows. In the following section 2 we briefly precise the BMF problems introduced above and recall GUHA, namely the quantifiers and general association rules. Then, in section 3 the modification of ASSO with GUHA association rules and the modification of GRECOND with rows of particular association matrix as initial attributes sets are presented. The modified algorithms are experimentally evaluated in section 4 and section 5 draws a conclusion and future research directions.

2 Basic notions of BMF and GUHA

2.1 Boolean Matrix Factorization

We precise the basic BMF notions and problems recalled in the beginning of the previous section. Denote by $\{0,1\}^{n \times m}$ the set of all $n \times m$ Boolean matrices (i.e. with entries either 1 or 0). The basic problem in BMF is to find for a given $I \in \{0,1\}^{n \times m}$ matrices $A \in \{0,1\}^{n \times k}$ and $B \in \{0,1\}^{k \times m}$ for which

$$I \text{ (approximately) equals } A \circ B, \tag{1}$$

where $\circ$ is the Boolean matrix product, i.e.

$$(A \circ B)_{ij} = \max_{l=1}^{k} \min(A_{il}, B_{lj}).$$

The approximate equality in (1) is assessed by means of the well-known L_1-norm $\|I\| = \sum_{i,j=1}^{m,n} |I_{ij}|$ and the corresponding distance (error) function $E(I, A \circ B)$ defined by

$$E(I, A \circ B) = \|I - A \circ B\| = \sum_{i,j=1}^{m,n} |I_{ij} - (A \circ B)_{ij}|.$$

In BMF, one is usually interested in two parts of the error function E, E_u corresponding to 1s in I that are 0s (and hence *uncovered*) in $A \circ B$ and E_o corresponding to 0s in I that are 1s (and hence *overcovered*) in $A \circ B$:

$$E(I, A \circ B) = E_u(I, A \circ B) + E_o(I, A \circ B), \text{ where}$$
$$E_u(I, A \circ B) = |\{\langle i, j \rangle ; I_{ij} = 1, (A \circ B)_{ij} = 0\}|,$$
$$E_o(I, A \circ B) = |\{\langle i, j \rangle ; I_{ij} = 0, (A \circ B)_{ij} = 1\}|,$$

or, more often, in the relative errors

$$e_u(l) = E_u(I, A \circ B)/\|I\|, \quad e_o(l) = E_o(I, A \circ B)/\|I\|. \tag{2}$$

e_u and e_o are functions of the first l factors delivered by the particular algorithm and measure how well the data is explained by the l factors. The value of $1 - e_u$ represents the (pure) coverage of data by the observed factors. We will use $1 - e_u$ and e_o in the experiments section 4 below. Note that the value of $c = 1 - e_u - e_o$ represents the overall coverage of data by the factors and is commonly used to assess quality of decompositions delivered by BMF algorithms [3, 4, 6, 11].

The two optimization BMF problems are defined as follows:

Definition 1 (Approximate Factorization Problem, AFP [3]). *Given $I \in \{0,1\}^{n \times m}$ and prescribed error $\varepsilon \geq 0$, find $A \in \{0,1\}^{n \times k}$ and $B \in \{0,1\}^{k \times m}$ with k as small as possible such that $\|I - A \circ B\| \leq \varepsilon$.*

AFP emphasizes the need to account for (and thus to explain) a prescribed (presumably reasonably large) portion of data, which is specified by ε.

Definition 2 (Discrete Basis Problem, DBP [11]). *Given $I \in \{0,1\}^{n \times m}$ and a positive integer k, find $A \in \{0,1\}^{n \times k}$ and $B \in \{0,1\}^{k \times m}$ that minimize $\|I - A \circ B\|$.*

DBP emphasizes the importance of the first k (presumably most important) factors. A throughout study of Boolean matrix factorization from the point of views of the two problems is provided in [4].

2.2 GUHA

We will only recall the necessary notions from the GUHA (General Unary Hypotheses Automaton) method [7, 8] which are required to describe the various types of association rules used in the modified ASSO algorithm. For throughout treatise of the foundations of the method (of mechanized formation of hypotheses, in particular its observational predicate calculi), see books [9] or [13].

GUHA, more precisely its ASSOC procedure [9] (do not confuse with the ASSO algorithm!) or more enhanced 4FT-MINER procedure [14] for Boolean data, inputs (Boolean) object-attribute incidence data with Boolean attributes which we represent by a $n \times m$ Boolean matrix I. (General) association rule (over a given set of attributes) is an expression

$$i \approx j$$

where i and j are attributes. (Note that in its full form, GUHA general association rule is an expression $\varphi \approx \psi$ where φ and ψ are arbitrary complex logical formulas above the attributes. We consider the simplified case with just single attributes for the formulas, as in the association rules used in ASSO and association rule mining.) $i \approx j$ is true in I if there is an association between i and j interpreted by a function q assigning to the four-fold table 4ft(i, j, I) corresponding to $i \approx j$ and I the value 1 (logical true). 4ft(i, j, I) is the quadruple

$$\langle a, b, c, d \rangle =$$
$$\langle fr(i \wedge j), fr(i \wedge \neg j), fr(\neg i \wedge j), fr(\neg i \wedge \neg j) \rangle$$

where $fr(i \wedge j)$ is the number of objects having both i and j in I (rows in I in which there is 1 in both columns corresponding to i and j) and $\neg i$ is an attribute corresponding to the negation of attribute i (i.e. the column in I corresponding to i in which 1s are replaced by 0s and vice versa).

4ft(i, j, I) is usually depicted as

I	j	$\neg j$
i	$a = fr(i \wedge j)$	$b = fr(i \wedge \neg j)$
$\neg i$	$c = fr(\neg i \wedge j)$	$d = fr(\neg i \wedge \neg j)$.

Function q which assigns to any four-fold table 4ft(i, j, I) a logical value 0 or 1 defines a so-called (generalized, GUHA) quantifier. There are several different quantifiers, summarized e.g. in [13], logical and statistical, which interpret different types of association rules (with different meaning of the association $\approx$ between attributes):

- *founded (p-)implication, $\Rightarrow_p$ (for $\approx$)*

$$q(a,b,c,d) = \begin{cases} 1 \text{ if } \frac{a}{a+b} \geq p, \\ 0 \text{ otherwise.} \end{cases}$$

Parameter $0 < p \leq 1$ has a meaning of threshold for the confidence of the association rule $i \Rightarrow_p j$, i.e. the ratio of the number of objects having in I both attributes i and j to the number of objects having i. Founded implication interprets the association rule used in the original ASSO algorithm (with p denoted as τ instead) and association rule mining, which is thus a particular case of GUHA general association rules.

- *double founded implication, $\Leftrightarrow_p$*

$$q(a,b,c,d) = \begin{cases} 1 \text{ if } \frac{a}{a+b+c} \geq p, \\ 0 \text{ otherwise.} \end{cases}$$

Compared to founded implication, double founded implication, to evaluate to 1, requires that the number of objects having in I both i and j is at least $100 \cdot p\%$ of the number of objects having i or j.

- *founded equivalence, $\equiv_p$*

$$q(a,b,c,d) = \begin{cases} 1 \text{ if } \frac{a+d}{a+b+c+d} \geq p, \\ 0 \text{ otherwise.} \end{cases}$$

Meaning: At least $100 \cdot p\%$ among all objects in I have the same attributes.

- *E-equivalence, $\sim_\delta^E$*

$$q(a,b,c,d) = \begin{cases} 1 \text{ if } \max\left(\frac{b}{a+b}, \frac{c}{c+d}\right) < \delta, \\ 0 \text{ otherwise.} \end{cases}$$

Meaning: Less than $100 \cdot \delta\%$ ($0 < \delta \leq 0.5$) of objects among the objects having i do not have j and among the objects not having i have j.

- *negative Jaccard distance*

$$q(a,b,c,d) = \begin{cases} 1 \text{ if } \frac{b+c}{b+c+d} \geq p, \\ 0 \text{ otherwise.} \end{cases}$$

This is our new quantifier resembling Jaccard distance dissimilarity measure used in data mining (which is one minus Jaccard similarity coefficient [15] which in turn is equal to double founded implication above). Compared to double founded implication, this quantifier, to evaluate to 1, requires that at least $100 \cdot p\%$ objects have i or j among the objects *not* having i or j.

In fact, the above presented quantifiers, except for the last one, are simplified versions of quantifiers defined in [9] where additional parameter $s > 0$ is included:

- *founded implication,* $\Rightarrow_{p,s}$

$$q(a,b,c,d) = \begin{cases} 1 \text{ if } \frac{a}{a+b} \geq p \text{ and } a \geq s, \\ 0 \text{ otherwise.} \end{cases}$$

and similarly for the other quantifiers. For association rule $i \approx j$, s has a meaning of threshold for the so-called support of the rule – the number of objects having in I both attributes i and j (or, if normalized as in association rule mining, the ratio of the number to the number of all objects in I).

3 The modified algorithms

3.1 Asso with GUHA association rules

The modified Asso algorithm involving GUHA (general) association rule interpreted by a GUHA quantifier is depicted in Algorithm 1.

Algorithm 1: Modified Asso algorithm

Input: A Boolean matrix $I \in \{0,1\}^{n \times m}$, a positive integer k, a threshold value $\tau \in (0,1]$, real-valued weights w^+, w^- and a quantifier q_τ (with parameter τ) interpreting $i \approx j$

Output: Boolean matrices $A \in \{0,1\}^{n \times k}$ and $B \in \{0,1\}^{k \times m}$

1 **for** $i = 1, \ldots, m$ **do**
2 | **for** $j = 1, \ldots, m$ **do**
3 | | $Q_{ij} = q_\tau(a,b,c,d)$
4 | **end**
5 **end**
6 $A \leftarrow$ empty $n \times k$ Boolean matrix
7 $B \leftarrow$ empty $k \times m$ Boolean matrix
8 **for** $l = 1, \ldots, k$ **do**
9 | $(Q_{i\_}, e) \leftarrow \arg\max_{Q_{i\_}, \, e \in \{0,1\}^{n \times 1}}$
   | $\quad cover\left(\begin{bmatrix} B \\ Q_{i\_} \end{bmatrix}, [A \, e], I, w^+, w^-\right)$
10 | $A \leftarrow [A \, e], B \leftarrow \begin{bmatrix} B \\ Q_{i\_} \end{bmatrix}$
11 **end**
12 **return** A and B

$Q_{i\_}$ denotes the ith row vector of the (Boolean) association matrix Q and the function $cover(B,A,I,w^+,w^-)$ is defined as

$$w^+ |\{\langle i,j \rangle ; I_{ij} = 1, (A \circ B)_{ij} = 1\}| \\ -w^- |\{\langle i,j \rangle ; I_{ij} = 0, (A \circ B)_{ij} = 1\}|.$$

The original algorithm was described in the introduction section 1. The only modification in Algorithm 1 to the

(generic) version of the original algorithm in [11] is computing the association matrix Q (lines 1–5) using the given quantifier $q_\tau(a,b,c,d)$ interpreting a (general) association rule $i \approx j$ instead of using the confidence of the association rule $i \Rightarrow_\tau j$.

3.2 GreCond using association matrix

Due to the particular way of finding factors in the Gre-Cond algorithm, namely as maximal rectangles, we need to use a particular association matrix of which the rows are used as characteristic vectors of candidates to initial attribute sets in the algorithm. The matrix used is computed using the GUHA quantifier founded implication with parameter p set to 1; hence the confidence of the interpreted association rule $i \Rightarrow_p j$ must be 1 for the rule to be true (which precisely coincides with the notion of attribute implication between attributes i and j in formal concept analysis, see [5]). This, at the same time, means that the association matrix is the special case of the association matrix of the Asso algorithm with $\tau = 1$.

The modified GreCond algorithm using the association matrix is depicted in Algorithm 2.

Algorithm 2: Modified GreCond algorithm

Input: A Boolean matrix $I \in \{0,1\}^{n \times m}$ and a prescribed error $\varepsilon \geq 0$

Output: Boolean matrices $A \in \{0,1\}^{n \times k}$ and $B \in \{0,1\}^{k \times m}$

1 $Q \leftarrow$ empty $m \times m$ Boolean matrix
2 **for** $i = 1, \ldots, m$ **do**
3 | **for** $j = 1, \ldots, m$ **do**
4 | | **if** $i \Rightarrow_1 j$ is *true* in I **then**
5 | | | $Q_{ij} = 1$
6 | | **end**
7 | **end**
8 **end**
9 $A \leftarrow$ empty $n \times k$ Boolean matrix
10 $B \leftarrow$ empty $k \times m$ Boolean matrix
11 **while** $\|I - A \circ B\| > \varepsilon$ **do**
12 | $D \leftarrow \arg\max_{Q_{i\_}} cover(Q_{i\_}, I, A, B)$
13 | $V \leftarrow cover(D, I, A, B)$
14 | **while** there is j such that $D_j = 0$ and
   | $\quad cover(D + [j], I, A, B) > V$ **do**
15 | | $j \leftarrow \arg\max_{j, D_j = 0} cover(D + [j], I, A, B)$
16 | | $D \leftarrow (D + [j])^{\downarrow \uparrow}$
17 | | $V \leftarrow cover(D, I, A, B)$
18 | **end**
19 | $A \leftarrow [A \, D^{\downarrow}], B \leftarrow \begin{bmatrix} B \\ D \end{bmatrix}$
20 **end**
21 **return** A and B

D_j denotes the jth item of (row Boolean) vector $D \in \{0,1\}^{1 \times m}$, $[j] \in \{0,1\}^{1 \times m}$ denotes the (row Boolean) vec-

Dataset	k	dens A	dens B	dens I
Set C1	40	0.07	0.04	0.10
Set C2	40	0.07	0.06	0.15
Set C3	40	0.11	0.05	0.20

Table 1: Synthetic data

Dataset	Size	$\|I\|$
DNA	4590×392	26527
Mushroom	8124×119	186852
Zoo	101×28	862

Table 2: Real data

tor with jth item equal to 1 and all other items equal to 0, the function $cover(D, I, A, B)$ is defined as

$$\|(D^\downarrow \times D^{\downarrow\uparrow}) \cdot (I - A \circ B)\|$$

and the (formal concept-forming [5]) operators $C^\uparrow$ and $D^\downarrow$ for (column Boolean) vector $C \in \{0,1\}^{n\times 1}$ and vector D, respectively, are defined as

$$C^\uparrow = +[j] \in \{0,1\}^{1\times m}; \text{ for each } i, C_i = 1 : I_{ij} = 1,$$
$$D^\downarrow = +[i] \in \{0,1\}^{n\times 1}; \text{ for each } j, D_j = 1 : I_{ij} = 1.$$

Again, the original algorithm was described in the introduction section 1. The only modifications in Algorithm 2 to the (generic) version of the original algorithm in [3] are computing the particular association matrix Q (lines 1–8) using the quantifier founded implication with $p = 1$ interpreting the association rule $i \Rightarrow_1 j$ and using the rows of the matrix as characteristic vectors of candidates to initial attribute sets (line 12) in the factor construction (lines 12–19).

4 Experimental evaluation

In this section, we provide an experimental evaluation of the modified algorithms and their comparison to the original versions, the ASSO algorithm and the GRECOND algorithm. Due to the lack of space we do not present a comparison with other algorithms and approaches to the general BMF. A comparison that includes both the algorithms can be found for example in [4].

As in the typical experiment scenario—which occurs in various BMF papers—we use both synthetic and real datasets. Experiments on synthetic datasets enable us to analyze performance of the algorithms on data with the same and known characteristics—we can analyze results in average case. On real data, we can study meaning of obtained results. Let us also note, that synthetic data are artificial while real data are influenced by real factors.

Synthetic data. We created 1000 of randomly generated datasets. Every dataset X_i has 500 rows and 250 columns and was obtained as a Boolean product $X_i = A_i \circ B_i$ of matrices A_i and B_i that were generated randomly with parameters shown in Table 1. The inner dimmension k was for all X_i set to 40, i.e. the expected number of factors is 40.

Real data. We used datasets DNA [12], Mushroom [2], and Zoo [2], the characteristics of which are shown in Table2. All of them are well known and widely used in the literature on BMF.

4.1 ASSO with GUHA association rules

We observe the values of $1 - e_u(l)$ (2) for $l = 0, \ldots, k$ where k is the number of factors delivered by a particular algorithm. Clearly, for $l = 0$ (no factors, A and B are "empty") we have $1 - e_u(l) = 0$. In accordance with general requirements on BMF, for a good factorization algorithm $1 - e_u(l)$ should be increasing in l, should have relatively large values for small l, and it is desirable that for $l = k$ we have $I = A \circ B$, i.e. the data is fully explained by all k factors computed (in which case $1 - e_u(l) = 1$). For synthetic datasets C_1, C_2 and C_3, values of $1 - e_u(l)$ are shown in Figures 1, 2 and 3, respectively.

As we mentioned above the ASSO algorithm admits overcovering of 0s of input data matrix. The number of overcovered 0s is a very important value and the values of $e_o(l)$ (2) for synthetic datasets C_1, C_2 and C_3 are shown in Figures 4, 5 and 6. Let us note that the results marked as "founded implication" are in fact results for the original ASSO algorithm. Note also that all variants of ASSO require us to set τ and (one of) $w+$ and $w-$, see Algorithm 1. Based on some previous experimental results (see [4]) we fixed $w+ = w- = 1$ and used the value of τ for which the particular algorithm produces the best results. In most cases, the best choice was $0.8 < \tau < 1$. This observation corresponds with results in [4].

We can see that the original algorithm is outperformed in terms of both coverage $(1 - e_u)$ and overcoverage (e_o) by the modification utilizing double founded implication. This modification produces large values of coverage and compared to the original ASSO algorithm commits smaller overcoverage error. This is true for both synthetic and real datasets. Very promising is also the modification utilizing the negative Jaccard distance quantifier.

Modifications utilizing founded equivalence and E-equivalence, however, do not perform well, for synthetic datasets. In case of dataset C_1—the most sparse one—both modifications commit extremely large overcover error, the values are beyond the scale of Figure 4. In cases of C_2 and C_3, Figures 2 and 3, they produce poor coverage while the overcoverage error is not much different from the modifications utilizing other quantifiers, for higher number of factors. On the other side, for real datasets the results are comparable with the other modifications (Figures 7, 8), with significantly smaller overcoverage errors (Figures 10, 11). The only exception is the Mushroom dataset where founded equivalence is again beyond the scale of Figure 10. Due to the limited space we do not include results for the DNA dataset which are very close to the results obtained for the Zoo dataset.

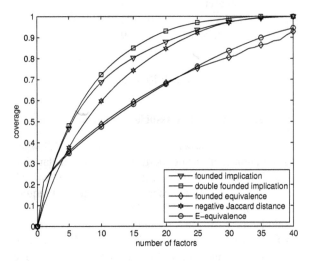

Figure 1: Coverage for synthetic dataset C_1

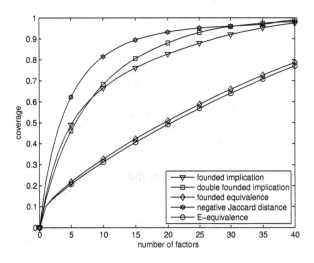

Figure 2: Coverage for synthetic dataset C_2

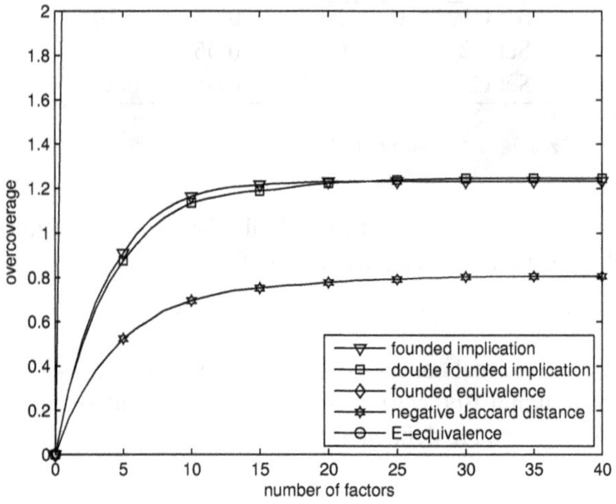

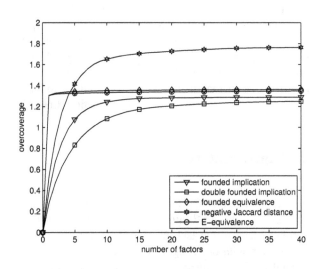

Figure 4: Overcoverage for synthetic dataset C_1

Figure 5: Overcoverage for synthetic dataset C_2

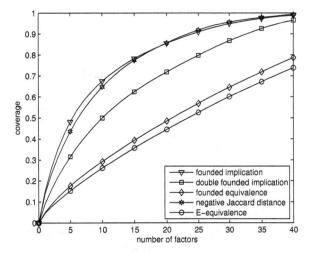

Figure 3: Coverage for synthetic dataset C_3

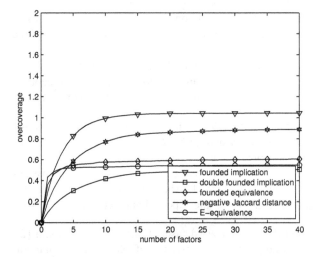

Figure 6: Overcoverage for synthetic dataset C_3

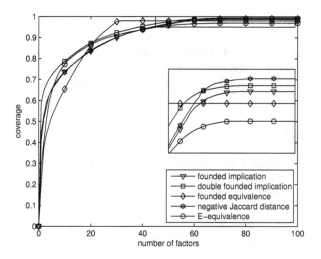

Figure 7: Coverage for Mushroom dataset

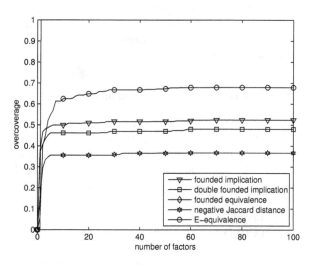

Figure 10: Overcoverage for Mushroom dataset

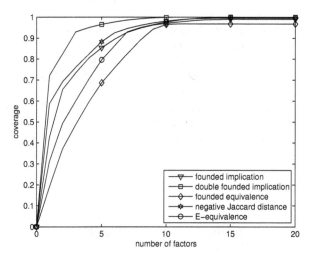

Figure 8: Coverage for Zoo dataset

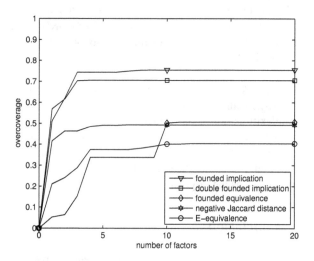

Figure 11: Overcoverage for Zoo dataset

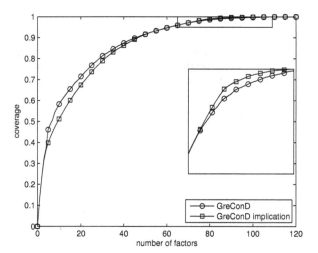

Figure 9: Original and modified GRECOND on Mushroom dataset

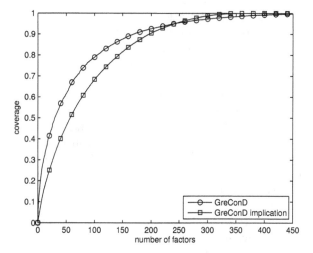

Figure 12: Original and modified GRECOND on DNA dataset

Presented results are representative. We performed the same evaluations for several other datasets which we have not included in the paper and observed the same type of results described above.

4.2   GRECOND using association matrix

Do to the limited space we do not present a comparison of the original GRECOND algorithm and the modification utilizing the association matrix (Algorithm 2) on the synthetic datasets. On each X_i the modified GRECOND slightly outperforms the original algorithm from the standpoint of coverage. Moreover, the modified algorithm also tends to produce less factors, i.e. outperforms the original GRECOND from both the AFP and DBP views (see Section 2).

Values of $1 - e_u$ for the Mushroom and DNA datasets are shown in Figures 9 and 12, respectively. We can see that the modified algorithm first looses for small numbers of factors but in the end, it outperforms the original GRECOND algorithm—i.e. it outperforms GRECOND from the AFP view. We observed similar behavior also for the other real datasets.

Time complexity. We implemented all used algorithms in MATLAB with critical parts written in C. Theoretical time complexity is not of our primary concern. Practically, it follows from our observations that the modification of the GRECOND algorithm is slightly faster than the original algorithm and all modifications of the ASSO algorithm are equally fast as the original.

5   Conclusion

We evaluated the use of various types of (general) association rules from the GUHA knowledge discovery method in the Boolean matrix factorization (BMF) algorithm ASSO and an utilization of (particular) association rules in the greedy-approach BMF algorithm GRECOND which is not based on association rules. The comparison of the quality of factorization produced by the modified algorithms with those produced by the original algorithms on both synthetic and selected real data showed that our modified algorithms outperform, for some types of rules, the original ones. Namely the double founded implication and (our new) negative Jaccard distance quantifiers interpreting the association rules in ASSO perform better than the founded implication quantifier used in the original ASSO. Also the utilization of association matrix in the factor search initialization stage of the GRECOND algorithm improves factorization results produced by the algorithm.

The observed results encourage us to the following future research directions. First, as the role of association matrix is crucial for the ASSO algorithm (and, as we have seen, the algorithm can be improved by using other types of association rules), we have an idea about algorithm which computes, or updates, the matrix in the process of searching for factors instead of computing it once before the search. Second, we will look for a way how to use in the utilization of association matrix the so-called *essential elements* of the input data matrix, which are crucial for the GREESS algorithm [4] (which improves the GRECOND algorithm).

References

[1] Agrawal R., Imieliński T., Swami A.: Mining association rules between sets of items in large databases, Proc. ACM SIGMOD 1993, 207–216.

[2] Bache K., Lichman M., UCI Machine Learning Repository [http://archive.ics.uci.edu/ml], Irvine, CA: University of California, School of Information and Computer Science, 2013.

[3] Belohlavek R., Vychodil V., Discovery of optimal factors in binary data via a novel method of matrix decomposition, J. Comput. Syst. Sci. 76(1)(2010), 3–20 (preliminary version in Proc. SCIS & ISCIS 2006).

[4] Belohlavek R., Trnecka M., From-below approximations in Boolean matrix factorization: Geometry and new algorithm, J. Comput. Syst. Sci. 81(8)(2015), 1678–1697.

[5] Ganter B., Wille R., Formal Concept Analysis: Mathematical Foundations, Springer, Berlin, 1999.

[6] Geerts F., Goethals B., Mielikäinen T., Tiling databases, Proc. Discovery Science 2004, 278–289.

[7] Hájek P., Holeňa M., Rauch J.: The GUHA method and its meaning for data mining. Journal of Computer and System Science 76(1)(2010), 34-–48.

[8] Hájek P., Havel I., Chytil M.: The GUHA method of automatic hypotheses determination. Computing 1(1966), 293-–308.

[9] Hájek P., Havránek T.: Mechanizing Hypothesis Formation (Mathematical Foundations for a General Theory), Springer-Verlag 1978, 396 pp. New edition available online at http://www.cs.cas.cz/~hajek/guhabook/.

[10] Lucchese C., Orlando S., Perego R., Mining top-K patterns from binary datasets in presence of noise, SIAM DM 2010, 165–176.

[11] Miettinen P., Mielikäinen T., Gionis A., Das G., Mannila H., The discrete basis problem, IEEE Trans. Knowledge and Data Eng. 20(10)(2008), 1348–1362 (preliminary version in Proc. PKDD 2006).

[12] Myllykangas S. et al, 2006, DNA copy number amplification profiling of human neoplasms, Oncogene 25(55)(2006), 7324–7332.

[13] Rauch J.: Observational Calculi and Association Rules. Springer-Verlag, 2013.

[14] Rauch J., Šimůnek M.: Mining for 4ft rules, in: Proceedings of Discovery Science, Springer-Verlag, 2000.

[15] Tan P.-N., Steinbach M., Kumar V.: Introduction to Data Mining. Addison Wesley, Boston, MA, 2006.

[16] Xiang Y., Jin R., Fuhry D., Dragan F. F., Summarizing transactional databases with overlapped hyperrectangles, Data Mining and Knowledge Discovery 23(2011), 215–251 (preliminary version in Proc. ACM KDD 2008).

ITAT 2016 Proceedings, pp. 155–162
ISBN 978-1537016740, © 2016 P. Pulc, E. Rosenzveig, M. Holeňa

Image Processing in Collaborative Open Narrative Systems

Petr Pulc[1], Eric Rosenzveig[2], Martin Holeňa[3]

[1] Faculty of information technology, Czech Technical University in Prague
Thákurova 9, 160 00 Prague
petr.pulc@fit.cvut.cz

[2] Film and TV School, Academy of Performing Arts in Prague
Smetanovo nábřeží 2, 116 65 Prague
eric.rosenzveig@famu.cz

[3] Institute of Computer Science, Academy of Sciences of the Czech Republic
Pod Vodárenskou věží 2, 182 07 Prague
martin@cs.cas.cz

Abstract: Open narrative approach enables the creators of multimedia content to create multi-stranded, navigable narrative environments. The viewer is able to navigate such space depending on author's predetermined constraints, or even browse the open narrative structure arbitrarily based on their interests. This philosophy is used with great advantage in the collaborative open narrative system NARRA. The platform creates a possibility for documentary makers, journalists, activists or other artists to link their own audiovisual material to clips of other authors and finally create a navigable space of individual multimedia pieces.

To help authors focus on building the narratives themselves, a set of automated tools have been proposed. Most obvious ones, as speech-to-text, are already incorporated in the system. However other, more complicated authoring tools, primarily focused on creating metadata for the media objects, are yet to be developed. Most complex of them involve an object description in media (with unrestricted motion, action or other features) and detection of near-duplicates of video content, which is the focus of our current interest.

In our approach, we are trying to use motion-based features and register them across the whole clip. Using Grid Cut algorithm to segment the image, we then try to select only parts of the motion picture, that are of our interest for further processing. For the selection of suitable description methods, we are developing a meta-learning approach. This will supposedly enable automatic annotation based not only on clip similarity per se, but rather on detected objects present in the shot.

1 Introduction

Amounts of multimedia content in archives of documentarists and other multimedia content creators were always large, even in the era of analogue film. With higher availability and much lower price of capturing devices suitable for cinema- or television-grade multimedia production, much more content is stored archivally and only a fraction is later published as a typical "closed narrative" ie. a traditional media work of say 30, 60 or feature length 90 minutes.

With a wider access to broadband internet connections and higher participation of individual users in the creation of internet content, the publication of such archives is now theoretically possible, yet they are usually difficult to navigate by users unfamiliar with the structure proposed by the author. Even the authors themselves tend to lose track of the entirety of their own content. And many time constrained projects or longer term project's media archives lack any structure at all.

To enable a creation of structure maintainable by a group of authors, the open narrative principle can be used. Although the original meaning refers rather to soap operas or other pieces of art with no foreseeable end, the main idea of multi-stranded narrative is easily transferable to other environments, such as documentaries.

In our example system, NARRA, that will be described in section 2, multiple strands of narrative created by multiple authors are combined and structured using data visualizations into coherent multiple narratives and can be mapped to a single graph, therefore extending the viewpoint of one author as opposed to more traditional narratives. However, such approach to multimedia clip connection discovery may be insufficient in certain cases.

One of them involves a discovery of near-identical video clips, that are created by editing the original (raw) footage. Authors tend to lose track through multiple iterated versions (including cropping, colour corrections, visual effects, retouching, soundtrack alterations or "sweetening", etc.) before arriving at a sequence used in the final edit. This brings a need for automated moving picture processing, that will be discussed in section 3.

To be able to work efficiently with only a relatively small set of interest points, instead of the whole image, common image feature extraction algorithms will be briefly presented in subsection 3.3. These algorithms will be than compared in a task of basic motion detection.

In subsection 3.4, we will present on idea of motion-based image segmentation. The basic notion is based on a similar approach used in object recognition from static images, however instead of using just the image itself for segmentation, hints from object movement will be used for object determination.

As most of the topics are still open, further research in these areas will be briefly discussed in section 4. Based on that direction of research, not only the recognition of objects, but also a recognition of the properties of the objects will be supposedly possible. In this area, we would like to use a meta-learning approach. This approach will be outlined in subsection 4.1.

2   NARRA

Open narrative systems were usually created as one-of-a-kind tools that enabled the user to browse authored content in a somewhat open manner. First approaches similar to open narrative platforms stemmed from multimedia archives at the end of 20th century, with annotations and connections curated by hand. David Blair's Waxweb, besides being the first streaming video on the web, is often cited as the first online video based navigable narrative [9].

One of the major projects of the second author, Eric Rosenzveig, on which we are building, is playListNetWork. A system developed from 2001 to 2003 in collaboration with Willy LeMaitre and other media artists and programmers. This software enabled multiple users in different locations to simultaneously work with an underlying audiovisual database, annotating the media clips and joining them into branching playlists. The publicly accessible part of the software, disPlayList, enabled a 3D visualization of the playlist structure created by playListNetWork and a subsequent unique "run" or cinematic experience through the material.

NARRA is an evolution of playListNetWork concepts, brought to a new world of hyper-linked media and direct audiovisual playback, as opposed to the more complicated multimedia streaming approaches of the past. With the increasing processing power of computers, it has been proposed that some parts of media annotation or linking can be handed over to automated processing tools.

The main task of NARRA is to create a platform for collaboration of multiple artists, and therefore the system is being built modularly, with an extensible API. During the use of NARRA on multiple projects, we discovered diverse ideas about multimedia collaboration and that different kinds of annotations are needed. To this end, NARRA uses a NoSQL database to avoid any possible limitations in the future.

Modules themselves are of three distinct types:

Connectors are used to ingest the multimedia data, yet because NARRA is not a multimedia archive, only a preview and proxy is stored alongside basic metadata.

Generators are automated tools, that process the multimedia and create a set of new metadata. An example of such a module uses an AT&T speech recognition API for automated transcription of human speech.

Synthesizers find any structure in the (meta-) data already present in storage to link the items together. For example, the synthesizer looks for a keyword similarity between two items, or is used to create and enhance links between clips used in stored video sequences.

NARRA can be then used for presentation of generated multimedia sequences, allowing for media discovery due to navigation during sequence playback or to show any user interface or visualization created in Processing.js or P5.js scripts.

This article will propose a generator creating annotations based on motion vectors in the video. Further research is intended to create a synthesizer that will enable a final linking of similar audiovisual clips automatically.

Detection and description of objects is proposed as another metadata generator. Currently, motion vectors can be used for detection of individual objects in unconstrained motion picture. Evolving rules connecting the detected objects with salient features contained in their description is a goal for our further research.

3   Moving Picture Processing

Computer vision, moving picture processing and still image processing are interconnected areas that use a very similar set of processing techniques. Using edge detection to create outlines of objects in the scene, detecting occurrences of previously defined shapes, detection of interest points and registering them among multiple pictures, etc.

Opposed to static image, moving picture brings a possibility of motion detection, yet on the other hand a problem of high data amounts that we need to deal with.

3.1   State of the Art

Many of the traditional approaches analyse individual multimedia frames, and such extracted data is taken as a discrete time sequence. Or even only statistical properties of such sequence are used for further processing.

Examples of single-frame processing methods include the classification of textures [14], bag-of-features classification [12], text recognition [11], object recognition [2] or face recognition [16].

The method created by Lukáš Neumann and Jiří Matas [11] has been also further extended into text transcription from live video. But opposed to a later mentioned approach of Fragoso et al. [3], frames were still processed one-by-one.

Other systems process pairs of frames, but have to introduce certain limitations to the acquisition process – such as limiting the motion of either the camera or the object. The camera motion limitation is for example acceptable in security camera applications, the second one in static object or environment scanning.

Especially the static camera is widely used, as it allows us a very simple motion detection concept: If many pixels change significantly in-between frames, it can be assumed that motion had happened. The location of the changed pixels tells us the position of such a motion and the difference between positions in individual frames can be deduced as a motion vector.

If we have enough information about the background or gather it during the processing, it can be subtracted from all frames to enable not only the detection of movement, but detection of whole objects. Yet still, the camera has to be static and the gathered background has to be as invariant as possible, which is not always achievable.

To enhance the information from image segmentation, other specialised sensors or camera arrays can be used to gather a depth information, however distance sensors do not usually have high-enough resolution and scene reconstruction from multiple sources is costly. There is a new method developed by Disney Research Zurich [5] to eliminate such problems, yet they are still based on processing of individual pixels into 3D point clouds.

Another problem that is currently based mostly on still image comparison, is measuring similarity between individual clips. Existing approaches try to gather similar patches from two sets of frames and compare them with invariance to very little or no editing operations [15].

3.2 Interest Point Based Image Processing

A very different approach to image processing can be based on detection and registration of interest points among a set of individual multimedia frames. This brings an advantage of much smaller data processing requirements with only a slight compromise in quality and precision. Technically, the worst type of error is a detection of similar, yet not related, points of interest. But these outliers can be filtered out later on.

To contrast with previously mentioned methods, we try to use primarily the information about interest points, especially their motion. An example of such use of motion tracking can be seen in the already mentioned translation application [3]. Image is sent to the recognition service only once, and the returned result is kept in track with the moving picture thanks to extracted motion vectors.

Image segmentation, as another example of widely used image processing technique, have to be still based on the image information itself, yet the motion information can be used to discover and track position of the detected object.

In our use case, the motion vectors extracted from all frames can be divided into two basic groups – motion of the camera itself and motion of the objects in the scene. For both groups, we can make some basic assumptions that will help us to distinguish them. In case of object motion, we can safely assume that the singular motion vectors exceeding some interframe distance are false detections and can be avoided. Also, we can assume that the motion of the

object is at least to some extent smooth. Therefore, rapid movement of an object is impossible without a jump-cut in the post-production. And higher frame rate footage will be supposedly able to rely on this property even more.

The camera motion can be proposed as a smallest deviation to a global motion model. However, several problems arise as the camera can not only translate and rotate, but also change focus and in case of some lenses also zoom. The detection model therefore needs to incorporate all possible deformations of the field.

Currently, we will incorporate such moving picture description into NARRA, as a more robust computation of item similarity. By combining this approach with meta-learned rules concerning item description, we should be then able to correctly describe both the environment where the action takes place and the objects themselves. However, to validate the applicability of such a complex description, more experimentation with extracted image features and segmentation needs to be performed.

3.3 Experiments with Image Descriptor Matching

Because of distinct properties of currently used image feature descriptors and specificity of our use-case, we used the following image descriptors with two distinct matching algorithms. Brute-force (BF) searches for the closest descriptors directly, in linear time, and ends. More elaborate Fast Library for Approximate Nearest Neighbours (FLANN) [10] first creates a set of binary trees and indexes all descriptors. During search, the trees are recursively traversed many times to increase match precision – currently 50 times, which is possibly excessive. In both cases we perform a ratio check proposed by Lowe [7].

Scale-invariant feature transform (SIFT) is an algorithm for detection and description of local features in images, published by David Lowe in 1999 [7]. This algorithm takes the input image, and returns a description of the individual interest points as 8-binned gradient direction histogram of 16×16 surrounding blocks, collected on 4×4 sub-blocks. Therefore, SIFT creates a vector of 128 numbers for each interest point.

Speeded up Robust Features (SURF) is merely an enhancement of the SIFT descriptor. The Laplacian of Gaussian used in SIFT is approximated with a Box filter, and both orientation assignment and feature description are gathered from wavelet responses. Around the interest points, 4×4 sub-regions are considered, each being described by four properties of the wavelet responses. SURF descriptor therefore creates by default a vector of 64 values for each interest point.

ORB is a fairly new image feature descriptor presented by Rublee in 2011 [13] which uses Binary Robust Independent Elementary Features descriptor of detected points of interest.

Due to the binary nature of ORB, the search of matching points of interest is much faster in case of either algorithm, as can be seen in Table 2. Yet the resulting set of matches

Table 1: Number of detected motion vectors in a 50 frames long clip, frame 29 is shown in Figure 1

Resolution	ORB BF	ORB FLANN	SIFT BF	SIFT FLANN	SURF BF	SURF FLANN
480 × 270	16 232	18 200	23 830	23 554	35 628	34 312
960 × 540	15 290	16 255	49 937	49 249	120 790	116 561
1920 × 1080	14 321	14 102	165 376	161 337	387 938	363 926
3840 × 2160	13 740	12 926	1 590 839	1 496 823	1 007 805	835 092

Table 2: Computation time [s] needed for motion vector detection in a 50 frames long clip, frame 29 is shown in Figure 1

Resolution	ORB BF	ORB FLANN	SIFT BF	SIFT FLANN	SURF BF	SURF FLANN
480 × 270	7.600	7.872	27.576	30.268	51.411	51.608
960 × 540	14.200	13.796	84.212	97.040	243.257	284.860
1920 × 1080	39.280	39.248	476.160	702.644	1 601.080	2 094.176
3840 × 2160	127.700	128.960	26 868.699	57 399.776	8 997.271	12 667.774

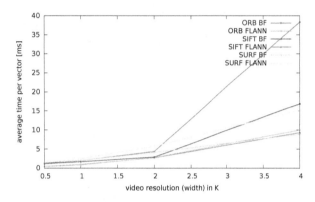

Figure 2: Comparison of time requirements for computation of one motion vector.

consist of much fewer points. The number of resulting vectors is shown in Table 1

Visual comparison of detected motion by all three algorithms is shown in Figure 1. It indicates that ORB would be useful for direct classification of actions in the image and possibly also the multimedia clip comparison. Whereas SURF, as a most time-consuming method with results exceeding the ones of SIFT by much more detected motion vectors, would be beneficial for the detailed image segmentation. However, as we are working on a proof of concept only, the much faster ORB descriptors will be in focus of our further interest.

The graph in Figure 2 also shows that SIFT does not scale well and that simple brute force based matching has a better time performance. Yet the visual comparison of outputs in Figure 1 shows that vectors matched by the FLANN algorithm are more precise. Meaning that not as many false motion vectors (long green lines) are detected. Also, the FLANN algorithm can be tuned a lot, for example by reducing the number of checks. Therefore, image segmentation will be tested on vectors obtained from ORB descriptors matched with FLANN.

It is needed to say that the current time performance of any of these algorithms is insufficient for any real-time or

large archive application. Yet these results were obtained on a weak CPU (Intel 997 mobile) with no GPU acceleration, using a Python binding to OpenCV 2.4.12.2 and without any code optimization.

3.4 Image Segmentation

Image segmentation itself is a very important discipline in computer vision, as it enables to bring our focus to narrow details of a particular part of the image, as opposed to a complicated description of the whole scene.

The basic image segmentation may be derived from a detection of connected components in the image and provide a set of areas, ideally affine to the local texture of the image. Such approaches, partially discussed in [8], bring a possibility to categorize such areas and therefore describe the whole image.

A bit more sophisticated image segmentation algorithm uses a principle of minimal energy cuts in the space of the image, where the inlets and outlets to the graph are assigned by rather imprecise scribbles. More precisely, we will be using a speeded-up version of Boykov-Kolmogorov algorithm – Grid Cut [4].

For better segmentation, the image is converted into an edge-representation. To this end, a convolution with the Laplacian of Gaussian kernel is performed. The inlets are then generated from the clustered motion vectors.

Such clustering is crucial as we need to assign inlets corresponding to whole objects, not individual motion vectors. To this end, all vectors of motion are represented as 6-dimensional data points, storing frame number, location and motion vector as angle sine, cosine and length.

For clustering, we have used a partially normalised data representation, where the position of the starting pixel in the image was divided by the image resolution and frame number has been made relative to the the length of the processed clip. This had a consequence that the role of those features in the performed hierarchical clustering decreased, in favour of the motion vector length and direction. Ward's linkage [17] yielded a dendrogram shown in Figure 3.

(a) ORB, exact match

(b) ORB FLANN table

(c) SIFT 2-NN selection

(d) SIFT FLANN 2-NN

(e) SURF 2-NN selection

(f) SURF FLANN 2NN

Figure 1: Visual comparison of motion vectors detected on image of resolution 960×540 pixels with different local image descriptors and matching algorithms. Red dots represent a vector of no motion, green lines represent a detected motion vector to next frame.

In-between shown and next frame, camera rolls slightly (at most 1 pixel distance) counter clockwise and the two people in foreground move to the right side of the image. The man on left with an average speed of 2 pixels, the woman on right with an average speed of 4 pixels per frame.

As the motion of objects and background between individual frames is minuscule, correctly detected motion vectors appear from this scale as green dots. Longer green lines are actually false matches of interest points.

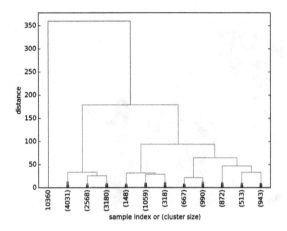

Figure 3: Dendrogram generated from hierarchical clustering of motion vectors acquired by ORB FLANN detection, see Figure 1b.

Figure 4: Resulting clustering of motion vectors.

Figure 5: Resulting segmentation of the image using a Grid Cut algorithm.

Based on this dendrogram, a division of motion vectors into 5 clusters has been performed and the resulting clusters are shown in Figure 4. Cyan and red points represent correctly the background and the yellow and green points mostly represent the moving objects. Sadly, both of the objects have similar vectors of motion and normalization of point positions reduced the possibility to discriminate them.

Any detected cluster in this space is then assigned a unique descriptor that is used as a scribble index. Scribble pixels (min-cut inlets) are assigned from neighbourhood of the clustered motion vector start points.

Although we have used the approach resulting in the minimal amount of detected motion vectors, the preliminary result of segmentation in Figure 5 shows that this approach is valid and can be used at least for motion description of both the background and foreground objects. Investigating other clustering and segmentation algorithms is a part of our further research interests.

4 Further Research

The main problem with ORB descriptor is that it creates a small set of interest point matches and therefore, in Figure 5, only the upper torso containing at least some motion vectors has been correctly segmented.

Also, the process of minimal cut detection is still somewhat costly. A possible extension, that would speed-up the process significantly, is an introduction of "supernodes", i.e., whole areas of the convoluted image will be treated as one large pixel with many connections. Although the first author had already developed such solution, its incorporation into the NARRA project will be carried out only later.

4.1 Meta-learning in Object Detection

So far, the information gathered can be used for a simple indexing tasks. For example gathering a number of objects present in the scene, their shape, colour histograms, present textures and points of interest. Motion vectors can be also indexed for later comparison of multimedia clips. Such index will be invariant to scale, crop, colour edits and other, more complex modifications of the multimedia, as the final descriptor would be deduced only from motion vectors and their relative displacement.

The final goal of our research is, however, to enable an automatic description of objects and environments in an unconstrained multimedia item. For such description, we may propose a custom baseline classifier, that would use the information about the segment contour, relative colour histogram and / or texture. However, we aim for utilisation of some already existing and previously mentioned single-frame processing methods. As the content of each multimedia segment should be now composed only of a single object in ideal case, only the classification part of such methods may be used.

Yet, we have no prior information about the type of the recognized object. The custom classifier would be difficult to train. If we would run all of the already existing classifiers and combine their outputs to deduce the final class of the object, high amount of noise and possibly contradictory information would be introduced. Also there is no sense to run the recognition algorithms on all media frames, as the ones with blurred or highly occluded objects will just confuse the classifiers.

Therefore, we are currently studying a meta-learning approaches that will select only several best-performing classification algorithms, based on the meta-features describing the considered video – such as coarsely binned colour histogram and edge information. Although meta-learning itself has been used on text corpora [1] for several decades, its application to the classification of multimedia content is rather novel.

We are currently investigating two levels, on which we can apply meta-learning to multimedia. The first, and higher-level, introduces a processing method recommendation – a classifier on the meta level that chooses the most appropriate from a set of available processing methods, based on easily extractable meta-features. In our current case, the computed boundary of segmented object, its histogram and other meta-features will be used to select more complex and thorough extraction and classification methods, such as face description or texture processing. A set of methods is used, to enable an evolution of meta-learner. To accomplish that, the best-performing method is associated with input meta-features for next rounds of the meta-learning.

This approach can be even stacked to multiple layers. An example of such situation is a more precise recognition of people, where the meta-learning classifier recognizes the shape as a human, and subsequent classification, possibly also obtained through meta-learning, brings information about recognized face, clothes, eye-wear, carried objects, types of movement and other features.

However, using more methods will also introduce much higher time complexity. To eliminate such problem, a meta-learning with multiobjective optimization can be introduced. Such meta-learning will then try to select methods both from the point of view of predictive accuracy and from the point of view of computational demands.

The second level will aim on optimization of the individual media processing units on their own. As some of the data description methods incorporate trainable and tunable methods (such as regression or classification), we can either trust their recommended settings during training, or consider multiple methods and/or their set-ups. This way, we would like to increase the precision and also possibly discover a wider variety of classes reflecting any drift in the input data.

Acknowledgements

The research reported in this paper has been carried out on Academy of Performing Arts, within project "NARRA" supported by the Institutional Support for Long-term Conceptual Development of Research Organization programme, provided by Ministry of Education, Youth and Sports, Czech Republic.

References

[1] Brazdil, P.; Giraud-Carrier, C.; Soares, C.; et al. *Metalearning*. Cognitive Technologies, Berlin, Heidelberg: Springer Berlin Heidelberg, 2009, ISBN 978-3-540-73262-4. Available from: http://link.springer.com/10.1007/978-3-540-73263-1

[2] Duygulu, P.; Barnard, K.; Freitas, J. F. G.; et al. *Computer Vision — ECCV 2002: 7th European Conference on Computer Vision Copenhagen, Denmark, May 28–31, 2002 Proceedings, Part IV*, chapter Object Recognition as Machine Translation: Learning a Lexicon for a Fixed Image Vocabulary. Berlin, Heidelberg: Springer Berlin Heidelberg, 2002, ISBN 978-3-540-47979-6, pp. 97–112. Available from: http://dx.doi.org/10.1007/3-540-47979-1_7

[3] Fragoso, V.; Gauglitz, S.; Zamora, S.; et al. Translatar: A mobile augmented reality translator. In *Applications of Computer Vision (WACV), 2011 IEEE Workshop on*, IEEE, 2011, pp. 497–502.

[4] Jamriška, O.; Sýkora, D.; Hornung, A. Cache-efficient graph cuts on structured grids. In *IEEE Conference on Computer Vision and Pattern Recognition (CVPR), 2012*, June 2012, ISSN 1063-6919, pp. 3673–3680.

[5] Klose, F.; Wang, O.; Bazin, J.-C.; et al. Sampling based scene-space video processing. *ACM Transactions on Graphics (TOG)*, volume 34, no. 4, 2015: p. 67.

[6] Kuncheva, L. I. *Combining Pattern Classifiers*. John Wiley & Sons, Inc., 2004, ISBN 0471210781.

[7] Lowe, D. G. Object recognition from local scale-invariant features. In *Computer vision, 1999. The proceedings of the seventh IEEE international conference on*, volume 2, Ieee, 1999, pp. 1150–1157.

[8] Lu, W.; Li, L.; Li, J.; et al. A multimedia information fusion framework for web image categorization. *Multimedia Tools and Applications*, volume 70, no. 3, jun 2014: pp. 1453–1486, ISSN 1380-7501. Available from: http://link.springer.com/10.1007/s11042-012-1165-2

[9] Meyer, T.; Blair, D.; Hader, S. WAXweb: a MOO-based collaborative hypermedia system for WWW. *Computer Networks and ISDN Systems*, volume 28, no. 1, 1995: pp. 77–84.

[10] Muja, M.; Lowe, D. G. Fast Approximate Nearest Neighbors with Automatic Algorithm Configuration. *VISAPP (1)*, volume 2, 2009: pp. 331–340.

[11] Neumann, L.; Matas, J. *Computer Vision – ACCV 2010: 10th Asian Conference on Computer Vision, Queenstown, New Zealand, November 8-12, 2010, Revised Selected Papers, Part III*, chapter A Method for Text Localization and Recognition in Real-World Images. Berlin, Heidelberg:

Springer Berlin Heidelberg, 2011, ISBN 978-3-642-19318-7, pp. 770–783. Available from: `http://dx.doi.org/10.1007/978-3-642-19318-7_60`

[12] Nowak, E.; Jurie, F.; Triggs, B. Sampling strategies for bag-of-features image classification. In *Computer Vision–ECCV 2006*, Springer, 2006, pp. 490–503.

[13] Rublee, E.; Rabaud, V.; Konolige, K.; et al. ORB: an efficient alternative to SIFT or SURF. In *Computer Vision (ICCV), 2011 IEEE International Conference on*, IEEE, 2011, pp. 2564–2571.

[14] Selvan, S.; Ramakrishnan, S. SVD-based modeling for image texture classification using wavelet transformation. *Image Processing, IEEE Transactions on*, volume 16, no. 11, 2007: pp. 2688–2696.

[15] Shang, L.; Yang, L.; Wang, F.; et al. Real-time Large Scale Near-duplicate Web Video Retrieval. In *Proceedings of the 18th ACM International Conference on Multimedia*, MM '10, New York, NY, USA: ACM, 2010, ISBN 978-1-60558-933-6, pp. 531–540. Available from: `http://doi.acm.org/10.1145/1873951.1874021`

[16] Turk, M.; Pentland, A. Face recognition using eigenfaces. In *Computer Vision and Pattern Recognition, 1991. Proceedings CVPR '91., IEEE Computer Society Conference on*, Jun 1991, ISSN 1063-6919, pp. 586–591.

[17] Ward Jr, J. H. Hierarchical grouping to optimize an objective function. *Journal of the American statistical association*, volume 58, no. 301, 1963: pp. 236–244.

ITAT 2016 Proceedings, pp. 163–171
ISBN 978-1537016740, © 2016 J. Repický, L. Bajer, M. Holeňa

Traditional Gaussian Process Surrogates in the BBOB Framework

Jakub Repický[1], Lukáš Bajer[1], and Martin Holeňa[2]

[1] Faculty of Mathematics and Physics
Charles University in Prague
Malostranské nám. 25
Prague, Czech Republic
{j.repicky,bajeluk}@gmail.com
[2] Institute of Computer Science,
Czech Academy of Sciences
Pod Vodárenskou věží 2
Prague, Czech Republic
martin@cs.cas.cz

Abstract: Objective function evaluation in continuous optimization tasks is often the operation that dominates the algorithm's cost. In particular in the case of black-box functions, i.e. when no analytical description is available, and the function is evaluated empirically. In such a situation, utilizing information from a surrogate model of the objective function is a well known technique to accelerate the search. In this paper, we review two traditional approaches to surrogate modelling based on Gaussian processes that we have newly reimplemented in MATLAB: Metamodel Assisted Evolution Strategy using probability of improvement and Gaussian Process Optimization Procedure. In the research reported in this paper, both approaches have been for the first time evaluated on Black-Box Optimization Benchmarking framework (BBOB), a comprehensive benchmark for continuous optimizers.

1 Introduction

An analytical definition of the objective function in real-world optimization tasks is sometimes hard to obtain. Therefore, neither information about the function's smoothness nor its derivatives are available. Moreover, evaluation of the function is usually expensive as it can only be done empirically, e.g. by measurement, testing, or running a computer simulation. Such functions are called black-box.

One class of optimization algorithms that are successfully applied to black-box optimization are evolution strategies. An evolution strategy is an optimization method that works on a population of candidate solutions using evolutionary operators of selection, mutation and recombination [10] [11]. In particular, the Covariance Matrix Adaptation Evolution Strategy (CMA-ES) [4] is considered to be the state-of-the-art continuous black-box optimizer. It samples each population according to a multivariate normal distribution determined by a covariance matrix. A notable property of the algorithm is the adaptation of the covariance matrix along the path of past successful search steps.

Still the whole population must be evaluated which might make running the algorithm for a sufficient number of generations infeasible due to expensive evaluation. To address this issue, techniques that involve a surrogate regression model of the fitness have been proposed.

Two major requirements of incorporating a surrogate model (also called metamodel in the literature) into evolutionary strategies are model management and model selection.

Model management is the task to control the surrogate model's impact on algorithm's convergence by using the original fitness alongside its surrogate model in the course of the search.

In *evolution control*, a certain fraction of individuals or generations is controlled, i.e. evaluated with the fitness function, while the remainder is evaluated with the surrogate model [8].

For example, *Metamodel-Assisted Evolution Strategy* (MAES) uses a surrogate model to pre-select the most promising individuals before they enter a selection procedure of a standard ES [3].

In contrast to evolution control, *surrogate approach* [2] directly optimizes the model output in an iterative procedure, thus avoiding the issue of determining the correct fraction of controlled individuals. In each iteration, a fixed number of candidate solutions are found by minimizing the model with an evolution strategy. These solutions are thereafter evaluated on the real fitness and the model is updated.

Regarding the model selection, Gaussian processes (GPs) are a non-parameterized regression model that is appealing for the task as it gives its prediction in terms of a Gaussian distribution. The variance of this prediction can be utilized as a confidence measure that promotes exploration of insufficiently modelled areas.

This paper reviews two traditional algorithms interconnecting Gaussian process-based surrogate models with the CMA-ES: Metamodel-Assisted Evolution strategy with improved pre-selection criterion by Ulmer, Strechert and Zell [13] and Gaussian Process Optimization Procedure (GPOP) by Büche, Schraudolph and Koumoutsakos [2].

The former is a GP-based MAES with probability of improvement (POI) as a pre-selection criterion.

The latter represents the surrogate approach – in each iteration, a local GP model is built and four functions designed to balance predicted value and variance are optimized.

While both algorithms are GP-based, they differ both in the model-management approach as well as in utilizing GP's confidence.

The framework COCO/BBOB (Comparing Continuous Optimizers / Black-Box Optimization Benchmarking) [7] provides an experimental setup for benchmarking blackbox optimizers. In particular, its noiseless testbed [6] comprises of 24 functions with properties that are to different extents challenging for continuous optimizers.

Both tested methods had been proposed before the BBOB framework originated. In the research reported in this paper, we evaluated both methods on the noiseless part of the BBOB framework. For that purpose a new implementation[1] was required as the original source codes were not available to us.

In the following, we first briefly introduce Gaussian processes as a suitable surrogate fitness model in Section 2. An exposition of the tested methods is given in Section 3 and experimental setup in Section 4. Section 5 presents experimental results and finally Section 6 concludes the paper.

2   Gaussian processes

Both algorithms under review feature the choice of Gaussian processes as a surrogate fitness function model.

GPs are a probabilistic model with several properties that make it well suited for fitness function modelling: its hyperparameters are comprehensible and limited in number and it provides a confidence measure given by standard deviation of predicted value at new data points.

In the following, we define a GP using notation and equations from Büche [2].

Consider $f \colon \mathbb{R}^D \to \mathbb{R}$ an unknown real-parameter function to be approximated. GP model is specified by a set $\mathbf{X}_N = \left\{ x_i \,|\, x_i \in \mathbb{R}^D \right\}_{i=1}^N$ of N training data points with known function values $\mathbf{t}_N = \{ t_i \,|\, f(\mathbf{x}_i) = t_i \}_{i=1}^N$. The data are assumed to be a sample of zero-mean multivariate Gaussian distribution with joint probability density

$$p(\mathbf{t}_N \,|\, \mathbf{X}_N) = \frac{\exp(-\frac{1}{2}\mathbf{t}_N^T \mathbf{C}_N^{-1} \mathbf{t}_N)}{\sqrt{(2\pi)^N \det(\mathbf{C}_N)}} \qquad (1)$$

where the covariance matrix $\mathbf{C}_N$ is defined by means of a covariance function $C(\mathbf{x}_i, \mathbf{x}_j, \Theta)$ $i, j \in \{1, \ldots, N\}$ with a fixed set of hyperparameters Θ.

For a set $\mathbf{t}_{N+1}$ that includes a new observation $t_{N+1} = f(\mathbf{x}_{N+1})$, we obtain

$$p(\mathbf{t}_{N+1} \,|\, \mathbf{X}_{N+1}) = \frac{\exp(-\frac{1}{2}\mathbf{t}_{N+1}^T \mathbf{C}_{N+1}^{-1} \mathbf{t}_{N+1})}{\sqrt{(2\pi)^{N+1} \det(\mathbf{C}_{N+1})}}. \qquad (2)$$

Using Bayesian rule for conditional probabilities, the prediction at a new data point has the density function

$$p(t_{N+1} \,|\, \mathbf{X}_{N+1}, \mathbf{t}_N) = \frac{p(\mathbf{t}_{N+1} \,|\, \mathbf{X}_{N+1})}{p(\mathbf{t}_N \,|\, \mathbf{X}_N)}. \qquad (3)$$

The covariance matrix $\mathbf{C}_{N+1}$ can be written with the use of the covariance matrix $\mathbf{C}_N$ as

$$\mathbf{C}_{N+1} = \begin{pmatrix} \mathbf{C}_N & \mathbf{k} \\ \mathbf{k}^T & \kappa \end{pmatrix} \qquad (4)$$

where $\mathbf{k} = (C(\mathbf{x}_i, \mathbf{x}_{N+1}))_1^N$ is a vector of covariances between the new point and $\mathbf{X}_N$ and $\kappa = C(\mathbf{x}_{N+1}, \mathbf{x}_{N+1})$ is the new point's variance.

Using (1) and (2) together with the fact that the inverse $\mathbf{C}_{N+1}^{-1}$ can also be expressed by the means of $\mathbf{C}_N^{-1}$, (3) can be simplified to a univariate Gaussian [2]

$$p(t_{N+1} \,|\, \mathbf{X}_{N+1}, \mathbf{t}_N) \propto \exp\left(-\frac{1}{2} \frac{(t_{N+1} - \hat{t}_{N+1})^2}{\sigma_{t_{N+1}}^2} \right) \qquad (5)$$

with mean and variance given by

$$\hat{t}_{N+1} = \mathbf{k}^T \mathbf{C}_N^{-1} \mathbf{t}_N,$$
$$\sigma_{t_{N+1}}^2 = \kappa - \mathbf{k}^T \mathbf{C}_N^{-1} \mathbf{k}.$$

A comprehensive exposition of Gaussian processes can be found in [9].

The covariance function plays an important role as it expresses prior assumptions about the shape of the modelled function. The vector Θ of model's hyperparameters is usually fitted with the maximum likelihood method.

One of the most commonly used covariance functions is squared exponential covariance function:

$$C(\mathbf{x}_p, \mathbf{x}_q) = \theta \exp\left(-\frac{1}{2} \frac{(\mathbf{x}_p - \mathbf{x}_q)^T (\mathbf{x}_p - \mathbf{x}_q)}{r^2} \right) \qquad (6)$$

where the parameter θ scales the covariance between two points and radius r is the characteristic length scale of the process.

When two points are close to each other compared to the characteristic length scale r, the covariance is close to one while it exponentially decays to zero with their distance growing.

The squared exponential covariance function can be improved with automatic relevance determination (ARD):

$$C(\mathbf{x}_p, \mathbf{x}_q) = \theta \exp\left(-\frac{1}{2} \sum_{i=1}^D \frac{(x_{p,i} - x_{q,i})^2}{r_i^2} \right) \qquad (7)$$

---

[1]The sources are available at `https://github.com/repjak/surrogate-cmaes/`

where the radii r_i scale the impact of two points distance on their correlation separately in each dimension.

To address the need to balance the exploitation of a fitted model prediction and the exploration of regions where model's confidence is low, the standard deviation of GP's prediction can be utilized.

One possibility are *merit functions* proposed in [12] for the purpose of balancing exploration and exploitation in engineering design optimization. Consider M to be a trained Gaussian process model. A merit function combines the goals of finding a minimum predicted by the model M and improving the accuracy of M into a single objective function:

$$f_{M,\alpha}(\mathbf{x}) = \hat{t}(\mathbf{x}) - \alpha\sigma(\mathbf{x}) \qquad (8)$$

where $\hat{t}(\mathbf{x})$ is the mean of the prediction of the function value in $\mathbf{x}$, $\sigma(\mathbf{x})$ is the prediction standard deviation and $\alpha \geq 0$ is a balancing parameter.

Another option is the probability of improvement (POI). Let us assume Gaussian process prediction to be a random variable $Y(\mathbf{x})$ with mean $\hat{t}(\mathbf{x})$ and standard deviation $\sigma(\mathbf{x})$. For a chosen threshold T less than or equal to the so-far best obtained fitness value $f_{\min}$, the probability of improvement in point $\mathbf{x}$ is defined as:

$$POI_T(\mathbf{x}) = p(Y(\mathbf{x}) \leq T) = \Phi\left(\frac{T - \hat{t}(\mathbf{x})}{\sigma(\mathbf{x})}\right) \qquad (9)$$

where Φ is the cumulative distribution function of the distribution $\mathcal{N}(0,1)$.

3 Tested Methods

3.1 GP Model Assisted Evolution Control

A standard ES operates on λ offsprings generated from μ parents by evolutionary operators of recombination and mutation. After the fitness of the offsprings is evaluated, a population of μ best individuals is selected to reproduce to a new offspring in the next iteration. In (μ,λ) ES, μ best individuals are selected from the λ offsprings, whereas in $(\mu+\lambda)$ ES, μ best individuals are selected from the union of the offprings and their parents.

MAES [3] modifies the standard evolution strategy with producing $\lambda_{\text{Pre}} > \lambda$ instead of λ individuals from μ parents by the same operators of recombination and mutation (steps 4 and 5 in the Algorithm 1). Given a fitted Gaussian process M, individuals $\mathbf{x}_i$, $i = 1,\ldots,\lambda_{\text{Pre}}$ are then preselected according to a criterion χ_M defined for the model M to create λ offsprings (step 6).

The GP model is trained in every generation on a set of N_{tr} most recently evaluated individuals (step 8).

In this paper we consider two pre-selection criteria in accordance with [13]: mean model prediction (MMP) (5) which selects λ_{Pre} points with the best mean predicted fitness $\hat{t}(\mathbf{x})$ and POI (9). The authors of [13] prefer POI to merit functions (8), as it does not depend on finding the appropriate value of the scale parameter α.

Algorithm 1 GP Model-Assisted Evolution Strategy

Input: f – fitness function
    μ – number of parents
    λ – population size
    λ_{Pre} – size of pre-selected population
    N_{tr} – size of training dataset
    χ_M – the preselection criterion that depends on a GP model M, e.g. mean model prediction or POI
1: Pop ← generate and evaluate λ initial samples
2: M ← a GP model trained on points from Pop
3: **while** termination criteria not reached **do**
4:     Offspring ← reproduce Pop into λ_{Pre} new points
5:     Offspring ← mutate Offspring
6:     Offspring ← select best λ points according to the pre-selection criterion χ_M
7:     evaluate Offspring with f
8:     M ← update model M on N_{tr} points most recently evaluated with f
9:     Pop ← select μ points best according to f
10: **end while**

3.2 Gaussian Process Optimization Procedure

Gaussian Process Optimization Procedure is due to Büche, Schraudolph and P. Koumoutsakos [2]. A Gaussian process is trained on a subset of already evaluated data and optimized by an ES instead of the original fitness. As optimization of the surrogate is cheaper than optimization of the original fitness, this can be repeated until reaching some termination criteria.

CMA-ES is used as the evolution strategy, with the number of parents μ set to 2 and the population size λ set to 10.

The pseudocode is given in Figure 2. After generating an initial population, a local GP model is built and utilized in an iterative procedure. Considering possibly low accuracy and computational infeasibility of global models, the training dataset is restricted to N_C points closest to the current best known solution $\mathbf{x}^{\text{best}}$ (step 6) and N_R most recently evaluated points (step 7).

If the GP model M has been successfully trained then the CMA-ES optimizes four merit functions $f_{M,\alpha}$ (8) for each $\alpha \in \{0,1,2,4\}$. Areas that might be approximated inaccurately are avoided by bounding the ES to the hypercube spanning the set of N_C points selected from $\mathbf{x}^{\text{best}}$'s neighborhood (steps 10 and 12). The points that are optima of the considered merit functions are evaluated by the original fitness and added to the dataset of known points.

In the case that no new solution is found, a random perturbation (step 23) is evaluated and added to the dataset. Unfortunately, authors don't specify the parameter m that occurs in 23. We set it to the value $m = 1$.

The authors used the following covariance function in their GP model:

$$C(\mathbf{x}_p, \mathbf{x}_q) = \theta_1 \exp\left(-\frac{1}{2}\sum_{i=1}^{n} \frac{(x_{p,i} - x_{q,i})^2}{r_i^2}\right) \tag{10}$$
$$+ \theta_2 + \delta_{pq}\theta_3$$

where $r_i, \theta_1, \theta_2, \theta_3 > 0$ and δ_{pq} is the Kronecker delta. The function is the sum of the squared exponential covariance function with ARD (7), constant shift θ_2 and a white noise scaled with θ_3.

Algorithm 2 Gaussian Process Optimization Procedure

Input: N_C – number of training points selected according to their distance to $\mathbf{x}^{\text{best}}$

N_R – number of training points selected according to most recent time of evaluation

f – fitness function

μ – the number of parents for CMA-ES

λ – population size for CMA-ES

1: $\{\mathbf{x}_1, \ldots, \mathbf{x}_{N_C/2}\} \leftarrow$ a set of $N_C/2$ points generated by CMA-ES
2: $y_i \leftarrow f(\mathbf{x}_i) \quad i \in \{1, \ldots, N_C/2\}$
3: $A \leftarrow \{(\mathbf{x}_i, y_i) \mid i \in \{1, \ldots, N_C/2\}\}$
4: $\mathbf{x}^{\text{best}} \leftarrow \arg\min_{\mathbf{x} \in \{\mathbf{x}_i \mid i \in \{1, \ldots, N_C/2\}\}}(f(\mathbf{x}))$
5: **while** stopping criteria not reached **do**
6:     $T_C \leftarrow N_C$ points from $\{\mathbf{u} \mid \exists z(\mathbf{u}, z) \in A\}$ closest to $\mathbf{x}^{\text{best}}$
7:     $T_R \leftarrow N_R$ points most recently evaluated
8:     $M \leftarrow$ a GP model trained on $T_C \cup T_R$
9:     $S \leftarrow \emptyset$
10:     $\mathbf{d} \leftarrow (d_i)_{i=1}^{D}, d_i = \max_{\mathbf{x} \in T_C}(x_i) - \min_{\mathbf{x} \in T_C}(x_i)$
11:     **for all** $\alpha \in \{0, 1, 2, 4\}$ **do**
12:         $B \leftarrow \{\mathbf{x} \mid \mathbf{x}^{\text{best}} - \frac{\mathbf{d}}{2} \leq \mathbf{x} \leq \mathbf{x}^{\text{best}} + \frac{\mathbf{d}}{2}\}$
13:         $\mathbf{x} \leftarrow$ optimize $f_{M,\alpha}$ within B by (μ, λ)-CMA-ES
14:         **if** $\nexists z(\mathbf{x}, z) \in A$ **then**
15:             $y \leftarrow f(\mathbf{x})$
16:             $S \leftarrow S \cup \{\mathbf{x}, y\}$
17:         **end if**
18:     **end for**
19:     **if** $S \neq \emptyset$ **then**
20:         $A \leftarrow A \cup S$
21:         $\mathbf{x}^{\text{best}} \leftarrow \arg\min_{\mathbf{x} \in \{\mathbf{u} \mid \exists z(\mathbf{u}, z) \in A\}}(f(\mathbf{x}))$
22:     **else**
23:         $\mathbf{x}^R \leftarrow \left(x_i^{\text{best}} + \frac{z_i d_i}{100}m\right)_{i=1}^{D} \quad z_i \sim \mathcal{N}(0, 1)$
24:         $y^R \leftarrow f(\mathbf{x})$
25:         $A \leftarrow A \cup \{(\mathbf{x}^R, y^R)\}$
26:     **end if**
27: **end while**
28: **return** $\mathbf{x}^{\text{best}}$

4　Experimental Setup

The framework COCO/BBOB (Comparing Continuous Optimizers / Black-Box Optimization Benchmarking) [6] [7] is intended for systematic experimentation with black-box optimizers. We use the noiseless testbed of the BBOB framework, which is comprised of 24 real-parameter benchmark functions with different characteristics such as non-separability, multi-modality, ill-conditioning etc.

Each function is defined on $[-5, 5]^D$ for all $D \geq 2$. For every function and every dimensionality, 15 trials of the optimizer are run. A different instance of the original function is used for each trial. We used dimensionalities $2, 3, 5, 10$, thus 1440 trials in total were run for each set of parameters and each method.

Since source codes were available for neither of the tested methods, we implemented them in MATLAB.

For Gaussian processes, we chose MATLAB's default implementation, `fitrgp`, a part of Statistics and Machine Learning Toolbox. The GP hyperparameters fitting was done with a quasi-newton optimizer, which is the default in `fitrgp`.

Parameters of the benchmarked algorithms were set as follows:

CMA-ES. A multi-start version with the population size doubled after each restart was used in the tests (MATLAB code v. 3.62.beta). Number of restarts was set to 4, while other parameters settings were left default: $\lambda = 4 + \lfloor 3\log_{10}D \rfloor$, $\sigma_{\text{start}} = \frac{8}{3}$, IncPopSize = $\lfloor \lambda/2 \rfloor$.

MAES. We implemented GP Model Assisted Evolution Strategy on top of a framework developed for S-CMA-ES algorithm, which employs a GP model in conjunction with a generation evolution control [1]. The S-CMA-ES implementation allows to conveniently replace the population sampling step of the CMA-ES with a custom procedure. In this case, a population intended for pre-selection is sampled and processed as described in Subsection 3.1. The control is then handed over back to the CMA-ES.

The number of parents and population size were set to correspond with the CMA-ES settings.

Two pre-selection criteria were tested: MMP and the POI with threshold equal to the so-far best sampled fitness value $f_{\min}$. In both cases λ_{Pre} was set to 3λ. The training set was comprised from 2λ most recently evaluated points.

We used the same covariance function as in the GPOP case, i.e. (10).

GPOP. We adhered to [2] in usage of the proposed covariance function (10).

The termination criteria were chosen as follows:

- number of consecutive iterations with no new solution found is larger than 2 while the tolerance on the two points euclidean distance for them to be considered equal is 10^{-8}

- the overall change of fitness values during the last 10 iterations is lower than 10^{-9}

- the target fitness value is reached

Training set size parameters N_C and N_R were chosen in accordance with empirical results reported in [2], particularly $N_C = N_R = 5 * D$.

Although the performance is measured in terms of the number of fitness evaluations, other operations such as optimizing a surrogate model may also be costly in benchmarking scenarios. If we consider functions in 10 D, a run of GPOP on one core of a computational grid took approximately 27.8 real hours per function on average. For those reasons, we limited the maximum number of fitness evaluations to $100 * D$ for all tested methods.

5   Experimental Results

Results from experiments on all the 24 noiseless BBOB benchmark functions are presented in Figures 1–3.

The expected running time (ERT) depicted in Figure 1 depends on a given target value, $f_t = f_{opt} + \Delta f$, i.e. the true optimum f_{opt} of the respective benchmark function raised by a small value Δf. The ERT is computed over all relevant trials as the number of the original function evaluations (FE) executed during each trial until the target function value f_t reached, summed over all trials and divided by the number of successful trials, i.e. trials that actually reached f_t: [7]

$$\text{ERT}(f_t) = \frac{\#\text{FE}(f_{best} \geq f_t)}{\#\text{succ}} \quad (11)$$

In the graphs for functions 1, 2, 5, 8, 9, 12, 14, GPOP achieved significantly better results compared to all other algorithms for some dimensions. In contrast, the differences between MAES and CMA-ES are rather small, regardless of the pre-selection criterion.

The graphs in Figure 2 summarize the performance over subgroups of the benchmark functions for the highest tested dimension 10. The graphs show the proportion of algorithm runs that reached a target value $f_t \in 10^{[-1..2]}$ (see the figure caption for further details).

The GPOP speedup is most eminent on the group of separable functions (functions 1–5), that is functions, optimization of which can be reduced to D one-dimensional problems [6]. On the other hand, GPOP has the worst results of all methods on multi-modal functions (functions 15–19).

Similar results may be observed on Figure 3 that for each function shows the dependence of the relative best fitness value on the number of evaluations in 10 D. As can be seen on the graphs for functions 13 and 24, GPOP in some cases outperforms all other algorithms in early stages, but then gets trapped in a local minimum.

On the graph for functions 21 on Figure 3, MAES with MMP as the pre-selection criterion visibly outperforms all other algorithms.

6   Conclusion

In this paper, we compared the CMA-ES and our implementation of two traditional methods which improve upon the CMA-ES with Gaussian process-based surrogate models: MAES, which extends the CMA-ES with a pre-selection step, and GPOP, which iteratively optimizes the GP model.

The benchmarks on the BBOB framework did not show any significant speedup of MAES compared to the CMA-ES. On the other hand, GPOP in many cases outperforms all the other methods, especially in early optimization stages. On some functions, though, it tends to get trapped in local minima. This might be explained with the fact that GPOP requires considerably fewer function evaluations per iteration than other methods. However, the model is built locally and might not be sufficient for exploration of the search space in later phases.

Our MAES implementation relies on a modification of the sampling step in CMA-ES, thereby changing the distribution of the sampled population. This might mislead CMA-ES a bit and requires further research, in particular considering the proposal in [5].

Another area for further research is the exploration of various confidence measures across tested methods, especially in connection with GPOP.

7   Acknowledgments

Access to computing and storage facilities owned by parties and projects contributing to the National Grid Infrastructure MetaCentrum, provided under the programme "Projects of Large Research, Development, and Innovations Infrastructures" (CESNET LM2015042), is greatly appreciated.

The research performed by Lukáš Bajer has been supported by the Czech Health Research Council project NV15-33250A.

The research performed by Jakub Repický was supported by SVV project number 260 224.

References

[1] L. Bajer, Z. Pitra, and M. Holeňa. Benchmarking Gaussian processes and random forests surrogate models on the BBOB noiseless testbed. In *Proceedings of the Companion Publication of the 2015 Annual Conference on Genetic and Evolutionary Computation*, GECCO Companion '15, 2015.

[2] D. Büche, N. N. Schraudolph, and P. Koumoutsakos. Accelerating evolutionary algorithms with Gaussian process fitness function models. *IEEE Transactions on Systems, Man and Cybernetics*, 35(2):183–194, 2005.

[3] M. Emmerich, A. Giotis, M. Özdemir, T. Bäck, and K. Giannakoglou. Metamodel-assisted evolution strategies. In *In Parallel Problem Solving from Nature VII*, pages 361–370. Springer, 2002.

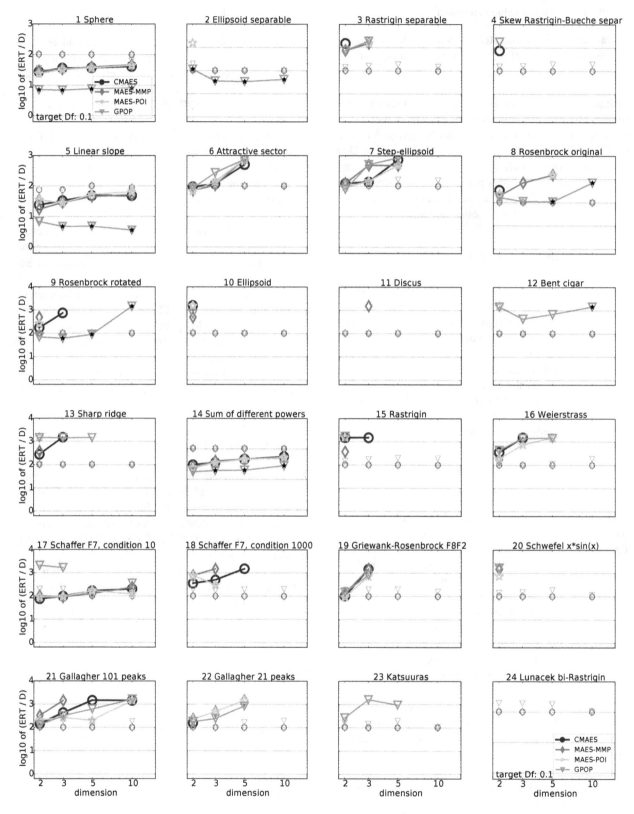

Figure 1: Expected running time (ERT as $\log_{10}$ of the number of f-evaluations) for target function value 0.1 divided by dimension, versus dimension. Different symbols correspond to different algorithms given in the legend of f_1 and f_{24}. Values are plotted up to the highest dimensionality with at least one successful trial. Light symbols give the maximum number of function evaluations from the longest trial divided by dimension. Black stars indicate a statistically better result compared to all other algorithms with $p < 0.05$ using Hommel correction.

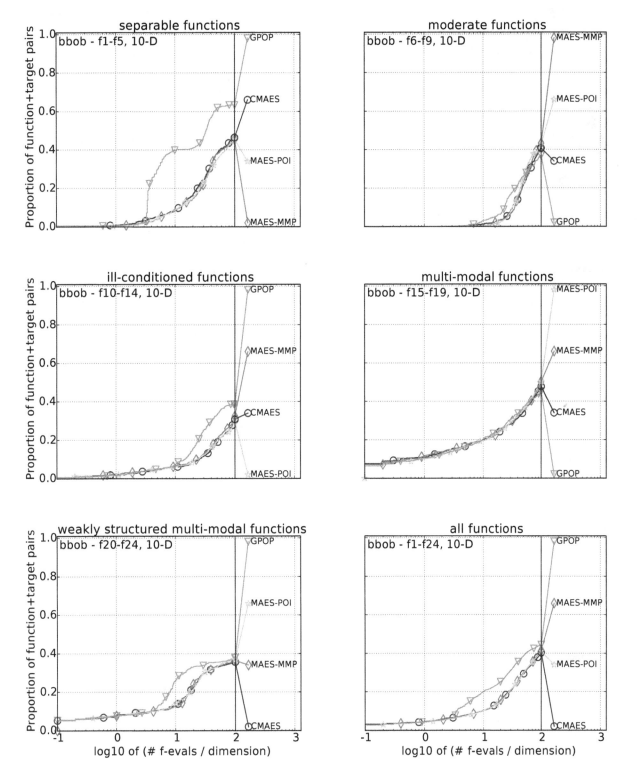

Figure 2: Bootstrapped empirical cumulative distribution of the number of objective function evaluations divided by dimension (FE/D) for 61 targets with target precision in $10^{[-1..2]}$ for different subgroups of BBOB benchmark functions in 10 D.

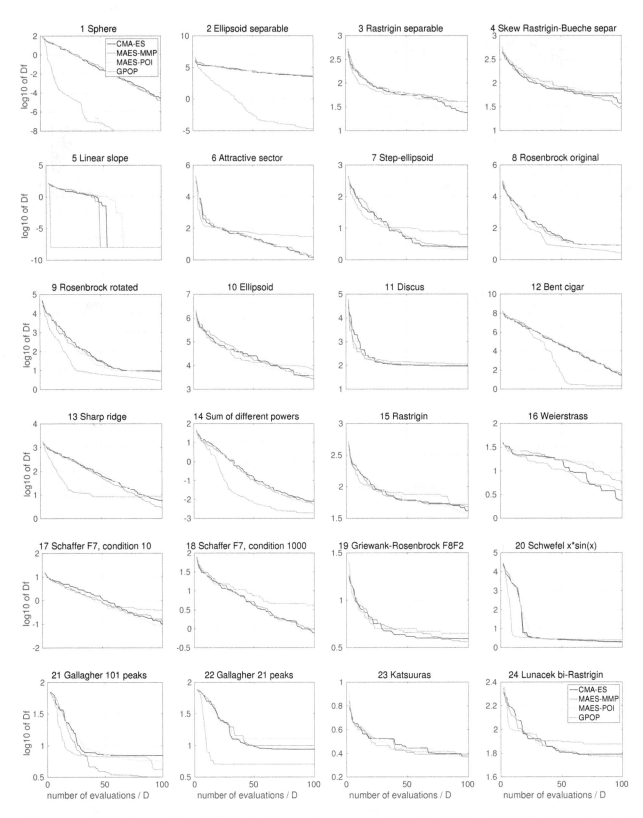

Figure 3: Relative fitness of best individual as $\log_{10}$ value versus number of evaluations divided by dimension for all functions in 10 D. Best fitness value at each number of evaluations is computed as the median of all trials.

[4] N. Hansen. The CMA evolution strategy: a comparing review. In I. Inza J. A. Lozano, P. Larrañaga and E. Bengoetxea, editors, *Towards a new evolutionary computation. Advances on estimation of distribution algorithms*, pages 75–102. Springer, 2006.

[5] N. Hansen. Injecting external solutions into CMA-ES. *CoRR*, abs/1110.4181, 2011.

[6] N. Hansen, S. Finck, R. Ros, and A. Auger. Real-parameter black-box optimization benchmarking 2009: Noiseless functions definitions. technical report rr-6829. Technical report, INRIA, 2009. Updated February 2010.

[7] N. Hansen, S. Finck, R. Ros, and A. Auger. Real-parameter black-box optimization benchmarking 2012: Experimental setup. technical report. Technical report, INRIA, 2012.

[8] Y. Jin and B. Sendhoff. Fitness approximation in evolutionary computation-a survey. In *GECCO 2002 Proceedings of Genetic and Evolutionary Computation Conference*, pages 1105–1111, 2002.

[9] C. E. Rassmusen and C. K. I. Williams. *Gaussian Processes for Machine Learning*. Adaptive computation and machine learning series. MIT Press, 2006.

[10] I. Rechenberg. *Evolutionsstrategie – Optimierung technischer Systeme nach Prinzipien der biologischen Evolution.* Frommann-Holzboog, Stuttgart, 1973.

[11] H.-P. Schwefel. *Numerische Optimierung von Computer-Modellen.* Birkhäuser, Basel, 1977.

[12] V. Torczon and M. W. Trosset. Using approximations to accelerate engineering design optimization. In *Proceedings of the 7th AIAA/USAF/NASA/ISSMO Multidisciplinary Analysis & Optimization Symposium (Held at Saint Louis, Missouri), paper 98-4800*, pages 507–512, 1998.

[13] H. Ulmer, F. Streichert, and A. Zell. Evolution strategies assisted by Gaussian processes with improved pre-selection criterion. *IEEE Congress on Evolutionary Computation*, pages 692–699, 2003.

ITAT 2016 Proceedings, pp. 172–178
ISBN 978-1537016740, © 2016 T. Šabata, T. Borovička, M. Holeňa

Modeling and Clustering the Behavior of Animals Using Hidden Markov Models

Tomáš Šabata[1], Tomáš Borovička[1], and Martin Holeňa[2]

[1] Faculty of Information Technology,
Czech Technical University in Prague,
Prague, The Czech Republic
[2] Institute of Computer Science,
Czech Academy of Sciences,
Prague, The Czech Republic

Abstract: The objectives of this article are to model behavior of individual animals and to cluster the resulting models in order to group animals with similar behavior patterns. Hidden Markov models are considered suitable for clustering purposes. Their clustering is well studied, however, only if the observable variables can be assumed to be Gaussian mixtures, which is not valid in our case. Therefore, we use the Kullback-Leibler divergence to cluster hidden Markov models with observable variables that have an arbitrary distribution. Hierarchical and spectral clustering is applied. To evaluate the modeling approach, an experiment was performed and an accuracy of 83.86% was reached in predicting behavioral sequences of individual animals. Results of clustering were evaluated by means of statistical descriptors of the animals and by a domain expert, both methods confirm that the results of clustering are meaningful.

1 Introduction

A mathematical model that describes behavior is called behavioral model. In particular, we assume that patterns of animals' behavior are reflected in their behavioral models and the differences can be identified and analyzed on the individual level.

For each animal, a model that represents its behavior in a certain time period is created. A comparison of models of one animal from different periods of time can show changes in its behavior over time. Rapid changes in the behavior can indicate an important event or disorder.

Moreover, different animals can be compared based on their behavioral models. The behavioral model as a descriptor of the behavioral patterns can be used to group and classify the animals. Furthermore, characteristics of each group can be extracted and changes of behavioral patterns can be tracked.

2 Related work

The field of the behavioral analysis is very wide [2]. However, the paper focuses on a specific kind of behavioral analysis, behavioral analysis of animals as a sequence of states.

To create a sufficiently accurate behavioral model, an abstraction and simplification of the behavior is used. The most common abstraction of an animals' behavior is the abstraction as a sequence of states

The description of behavior as a sequence of states is a commonly used abstraction and simplification in modeling behavior [6, 13, 14]. This allows to create generalised and sufficiently accurate behavioral model. Each state of the sequence corresponds to an action. Actions are organized in a finite sequence [6, 13, 14, 17, 20]. The model is expected to be more accurate if actions are easily separable. Thus, these actions should be mutually disjoint and cover all activities that an animal can do. It means that the animal is doing exactly one action at a time.

An abstraction of an animal living in a closed environment is much simpler than for example an abstraction of the behavior of a human. Such animals can do only a limited number of actions. These actions are reactions to the internal state of the animal (hunger, thirst, ...), reactions to other animals' behavior or to the environment.

The most commonly used methods to model sequences are Hidden Markov Models [14], Dynamic Bayesian networks [16], Conditional Random Fields [12], Neural Networks [15], Linear regression model [4] or Structured Support Vector machines [22]. All these methods belong to methods of supervised learning. Even though, Hidden markov models can be also estimated in a semisupervised way [23]. There are also approaches that utilize unsupervised learning methods to deal with modeling of behavior. The Fuzzy Q-state Learning is an example of unsupervised method that was used to model humans' behavior. In this approach labels are created by the Iterative Bayesian Fuzzy Clustering algorithm [13].

3 Preliminaries

3.1 Hidden Markov Models

Influenced by [6, 14, 20], we have decided to use hidden Markov models for behavioral modeling. In this subsection, the principles of a hidden Markov model (HMM) will be recalled.

With each HMM, a random process indexed by time is connected, which is assumed to be in exactly one of a set of

N distinct states at any time. At regularly spaced discrete times, the system changes its state according to probabilities of transitions between states. Time steps associated with time changes are denoted $t = 1, 2, 3, \ldots$. The actual state at a time step t is denoted q_t.

The process itself is assumed to be a Markov chain, usually a first-order Markov chain, although a Markov chain of any order can be used. It is usually assumed that the Markov chain is homogeneous. This assumption allows the Markov chain to be described as a matrix of transition probabilities $A = \{a_{ij}\}$, which is formally defined in the Equation (1).

$$a_{ij} = P(q_t = y_j | q_{t-1} = y_i), \quad 1 \leq i, j \leq N \quad (1)$$

The simple observable Markov chain is too restrictive to describe the reality, however it can be extended. Denoting Y the variable recording the states of the Markov chain, a HMM is obtained through completing Y with a multivariate random variable X. In the context of that HMM, X is called 'observation variable' or 'output variable', whereas Y is called 'hidden variable'. The the hidden variable takes values in the set $\{y_1, y_2, \ldots, y_N\}$ and observable variable X takes values in the set $\{x_1, x_2, \ldots, x_M\}$.

We assume to have an observation sequence $O = o_1 o_2 \ldots o_T$ and a state sequence $Q = q_1 q_2 \ldots q_T$ which corresponds to the observation sequence. HMM can be characterized using three probability distributions:

1. A state transition probability distribution $A = \{a_{ij}\}$ which is formally defined by the Equation (1).

2. An probability distribution of observation variables, $B = \{b_{i,j}\}$, where $b_{i,j}$ is a probability of observation variables in state y_i and it is formally defined as (2).

$$b_{i,j} = P(o_t = x_j | q_t = y_i) \quad (2)$$

The matrix B of the discrete variable can be described using $N \times M$ stochastic matrix, where M denotes number of possible values of X.

3. An initial state distribution $\pi = \{\pi_i\}$ is defined by

$$\pi_i = P(q_1 = y_i) \quad (3)$$

When the initial state distribution is assumed to be stationary, then a initial state distribution is usually computed as the stationary distribution of the Markov chain described with matrix A by solving the Equation (4).

$$\begin{aligned} \pi A &= \pi \\ \sum_i \pi_i A_{ij} &= \pi_j \end{aligned} \quad (4)$$

With these three elements, the HMM is fully defined. The model is denoted $\lambda = (A, B, \pi)$. A HMM can be graphically depicted by Trellis diagram which is shown in Figure 1. The joint probability of O and Q, which corresponds to the trellis diagram, is described by the Equation

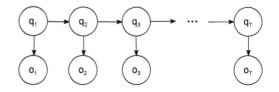

Figure 1: Trellis diagram of a HMM.

(5). By means of the above notation, it can be formally described as in the Equation (6).

$$P(o_1, \ldots, o_T, q_1, \ldots, q_T) = P(q_1)P(o_1|q_1)\prod_{k=2}^{T} P(q_k|q_{k-1})P(o_k|q_k) \quad (5)$$

$$P(o_1, \ldots, o_T, q_1, \ldots, q_T) = \pi_{q_1} b_{q_1, o_1} \prod_{k=2}^{T} a_{q_{k-1}, q_k} b_{q_k, o_k} \quad (6)$$

3.2 Clustering approaches

Hidden Markov models are often used in cluster analysis of sequences [1, 9, 18]. Clustering sequences is more complex task than clustering feature vectors since infinite sequences are not in a Euclidean space and sufficiently long finite sequences are in a high-dimensional Euclidean spaces. Although there exist approaches how to measure distance between two sequences (Levenshtein distance, Hamming distance, longest common subsequence, etc.), however, they may not be always meaningful. It may be more reasonable to learn a HMM for each sequence and cluster the HMMs. A HMM is the random process that produces the sequence.

Due to the fact that HMMs' parameters lie on a nonlinear manifold, application of the k-means algorithm would not succeed [3]. In addition, parameters of a particular generative model are not unique, therefore, a permutation of states may correspond to the same model [3]. It means that different sequences may be generated by the same HMM.

There are already a few approaches to the cluster analysis by means of HMMs. One of them uses the spectral clustering with Bhattacharyya divergence [9]. Another commonly used dissimilarity measure in spectral clustering of HMMs is the Kullback-Leibler divergence [10, 21, 24].

The approach called variational hierarchical expectation maximization (VHEM) [3] is also based on spectral clustering. It directly uses the probability distributions of HMMs instead of constructing an initial embedding and besides clustering, it generates new HMMs. The newly generated HMMs are representatives of each cluster.

A disadvantage of all the mentioned methods is the assumption that observations are normally distributed and can be described using the Gaussian mixture model. A distance measure between two HMMs with normally distributed observations can be computed in polynomial time. However, that assumption can be too restrictive for many real-life applications.

Dissimilarity measures of HMMs The definition of a distance between two HMMs is challenging since HMM consists of a Markov chain and a joint distribution of observations. In [5], the authors considered two distance measures applicable to HMMs λ and λ'. The first of them is a normalized Euclidean distance of the corresponding matrices B, B',

$$d_{ec}(\lambda,\lambda') = \sqrt{\frac{1}{N}\sum_{i=1}^{N}\sum_{k=1}^{M}||b_{ik}-b'_{ik}||^2}, \qquad (7)$$

where N denotes a number of states and M denotes a number of observations. The number of states of both models has to be identical $N = N'$. The second distance proposed in [5] is defined by

$$d_{mec}(\lambda,\lambda') = \sqrt{\frac{1}{N}\sum_{i=1}^{N}\min_j\sum_{k=1}^{M}||b_{ik}-b'_{jk}||^2}. \qquad (8)$$

A disadvantage of the considered distances is that they ignore the Markov chain. Therefore, there exist HMMs λ and λ' the distance between which is zero although the generated probability distributions P_λ and P'_λ are different. Consequently, both distance measures are not metrics, but only pseudometrics [11]. Although the distances ignore the Markov chain, it is agreed that the observation probability distribution matrix B is, in most cases, a more sensitive set of parameters related to the closeness of HMMs then the initial distribution vector π or the state transitions matrix A [10].

Another distance between HMMs λ, λ' is the Kullback-Leibler divergence (KL divergence)

$$d_{KL}(\lambda,\lambda') = \int_O \frac{1}{G(O)}\log\frac{P(O|\lambda)}{P(O|\lambda')}P(O|\lambda)dO, \qquad (9)$$

where $G(O)$ is a function weighting the length of the sequence O. Two kinds of such weighting functions are commonly used. The function $G(O)$ is equal to the length of sequence if we measure the divergence between two HMMs that generate equally long sequences. It is equal to expected value of lenghts of sequences if we measure the divergence between two HMMs which generate various long sequences.

An analytic solution for integral in the Equation (9) exists for HMMs with Gaussian distributed observations [8], otherwise it can be calculated numerically. The time complexity of the numerical computation grows exponentially with the length of the sequence. Since we want to use it for long sequences we use an aproximation described in [5]. We assume to have an ordered set of output sequences $F = \{O_1,...,O_L\}$. Any sequence O could became l-th member

of set with a probability proportional to $P(O|\lambda)$. Using Viterbi algorithm, the most likely sequence Q_{opt} of states can be computed by $P(Q_{\text{opt}},O|\lambda) = max_Q P(Q,O|\lambda)$. This leads to the KL divergence.

$$d_{\text{Vit}}(\lambda,\lambda') = \int_O \frac{1}{G(O)}\log\frac{P(Q_{\text{opt}},O|\lambda)}{P(Q'_{\text{opt}},O|\lambda')}P(O|\lambda)dO \quad (10)$$

We assume that:

- The most probable sequences of both hidden Markov models are equal for both HMMs. The assumption is reasonable if two HMMs are not too dissimiliar.

- The Markov chain is ergodic. A Markov chain is called ergodic if there is a nonzero probability to get from any state q to any other state q' (not necessarily in one move). A Markov chain with an ergodic subset (in particular, an ergodic Markov chain) generates sufficient long sequence.

With these assumptions, the KL divergence can be computed using following equation

$$d_{Vit}(\lambda,\lambda') = \frac{1}{G(O)}\log\frac{P(Q_l,O|\lambda)}{P(Q_l,O|\lambda')}P(O|\lambda)+\varepsilon, \quad (11)$$

where ε is an approximation error [5]. According to Subsection 3.1, the equation can be rewritten using the notation of HMMs as it is shown in the Equation (12).

$$d_{Vit}(\lambda,\lambda') - \varepsilon = \frac{1}{G(O)}\sum_{t=1}^{T-1}\left(\log a_{y_t,y_{t+1}} - \log a'_{y_t,y_{t+1}}\right)+$$
$$\frac{1}{G(O)}\sum_{t=1}^{T}\left(\log b_{y_t,x_t} - \log b'_{y_t,x_t}\right)$$
$$(12)$$

If a sequence O is long enough, the law of large number allows us to approximate Equation (12) as (13) [5].

$$d_{Vit}(\lambda,\lambda') \approx \widetilde{\delta}_{Vit} = \sum_{i,j}a_{ij}\pi_i\left(\log a_{ij} - \log a'_{ij}\right)+$$
$$\sum_{i,k}b_{ik}\pi_i\left(\log b_{ij} - \log b'_{ij}\right)$$
$$(13)$$

A disadvantage of the KL divergence is that it is not symmetric.

The Bhattacharyya divergence is also a commonly used metric for HMMs. For two probability distributions f and g, it is defined by the Equation (14). Similarly to the KL divergence, it can be easily computed if HMM has normally distributed observations [7]. Differently to the KL divergence, the Bhattacharyya divergence is symmetric.

$$d_B(f,g) = -\ln(\int \sqrt{f(x)g(x)}dx) \qquad (14)$$

Using a chosen dissimilarity measure, a dissimilarity matrix can be created and used for clustering, in particular, in hierarchical and spectral clustering algorithms.

Spectral clustering uses similarities between objects represented as a weighted graph. There are three ways how to create such a graph:

1. **The ε-neighborhood graph.** In this way, all pairs of points with distances smaller than ε are connected. The graph is often considered as unweighted because its edges are based on the dichotomous property of distances at most ε.

2. **k-nearest neighbor graphs.** In this way, the goal is to connect vertex v_i with vertex v_j if v_j is among the k nearest neighbors of v_i. This way is usually used in image segmentation where each pixel has its neighbourhood defined by 4 or 8 pixels.

3. **The fully connected graph.** This way means connecting all points the pairwise similarity of which is positive. This construction is usually chosen if the similarity function itself already encodes mainly local neighborhoods. An example of such a similarity function is the Gaussian similarity function ($s(x_i, x_j) = e^{-\frac{\|x_i - x_j\|^2}{2\sigma^2}}$). The parameter σ controls the width of the neighbourhood.

Spectral clustering can be performed by three different algorithms [19]:

1. Unnormalized spectral clustering

2. Normalized spectral clustering according to Shi and Malik

3. Normalized spectral clustering according to Ng, Jordan, and Weiss

4 Proposed approach

This article focuses on behavioral modeling and analysis of animals that live in a closed environment. This simplifies the abstraction of the behavior since the number of possible actions of animals in a closed environment is limited. The proposed approach has been illustrated on a herd of cows containing one hundred of individuals.

The transition and emission matrices of the hidden Markov model are estimated using a sequence of states and sequence of observable values, therefore a set of possible states and a set of possible observable variable values have to be predefined. Each element of the sequence describes one minute of animal's behavior.

Five possible states that represent actions which an animal can do are defined. These states are denoted $S1, S2, S3, S4, S5$. An animal is considered to be in the state $S5$ if it is not in any of the states $S1$-$S4$. States S1, S2, S3 and S4 correspond to eating, drinking, resting and being milked.

Two observable variables are calculated for each state except the state $S5$:

1. the duration of the last occurrence of the state,

2. the time elapsed since the last occurrence of the state.

These eight variables are discretized using binning by equal frequency into four or five bins. The ninth observable variable represents a daytime which is discretized into six blocks of four hours. The Cartesian product of the value sets of observable variables contains, after discretization, 1,500,000 combinations of values.

To avoid zero probabilities in the emission and transition matrices, empirical transition and emission matrices averaged over all models of respective animal are used as initial estimates. Zero probabilities in those initial estimates are replaced with small probabilities estimated as one over the number of elements in the matrix.

Since the assumption of normally distributed observations is in our case not valid, we use an approximation of the Kullback-Leibler divergence, recalled in Subsection 3.2, as the similarity measure for HMM clustering. Using this approximation, a distance matrix D for the set of HMMs constructed for the individual anamals is computed, i.e., $D_{i,j}$ represents the KL divergence of the j-th from the i-th most likely sequence ($D_{i,j} = d_{\text{Vit}}(\lambda_i, \lambda_j)$). The properties of the KL divergence imply that the matrix is real valued, non-symmetric and its diagonal has zero values.

Hierarchical and spectral clustering were applied to cluster the models. A parameter of hierarchical clustering is the kind of linkage. Since HMMs are not points in an Euclidean space, the single, average or complete linkage can be used. An optimal number of clusters can be determined by the domain expert from the dendogram of the hierarchical clustering.

For the spectral clustering, a fully connected graph based on the Gaussian similarity function is used as the similarity graph. Estimation of the parameter sigma of the similarity function is based on the optimization of balance of clusters.

The results of clustering were subsequently analysed using descriptive characteristics (e.g., age and weight of the animal) that were not among the observable variables.

5 Experimental results

The experiment is devided into two parts, behavioral modeling and clustering of the models. Section 5.1 describes results of the modeling using HMMs and Section 5.2 presents the results of clustering.

5.1 Hidden Markov modeling

The dataset that consists of ten consecutive days was split into train and test sets in a ratio 9:1. Parameters of a model were estimated with data of nine consecutive days and the model was evaluated with data of the tenth day. For each

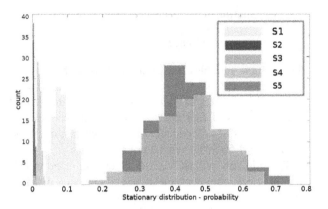

Figure 2: For each animal a stationary distribution of its Markov chain is calculated from a sequence of 14400 measurements. Values of these distributions are visualized for each state separately in a distribution.

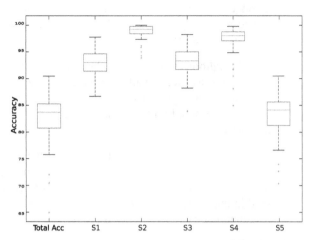

Figure 3: Accuracy of Viterbi's sequence.

animal, transitions and emissions matrices were estimated using the Baum–Welch algorithm.

Hidden Markov models were evaluated in two different ways, visually by a domain expert and using the Viterbi's sequence. The domain expert checks if the real animals' behavior is consistent with the stationary distribution of the resulting Markov chain, which describes the behavior to which the Markov chain converges. Consequently, the stationary distribution describes how much time an animal spends doing some activity in comparison with all activities.

Stationary distributions were computed for each animal separately. A histogram of the probabilities of individual states in the stationary distributions is shown in Figure 2.

Probabilities of the stationary distributions averaged over all animals are in Table 1.

State	Average probability
S1	8.5%
S2	0.4%
S3	44.8%
S4	1.8%
S5	44.5%

Table 1: Average stationary distribution.

The second way of evaluation is using the Viterbi's sequence. The Viterbi's sequence determines the most likely sequence of states given a sequence of observations and is denoted $v_1 v_2 .... v_T$. To get an accuracy of the prediction of a sequence of states, the real sequences of states are element-wise compared with the Viterbi's sequences. The accuracy is calculated as number of elements that do not differ divided by length of sequence. It was calculated separately for each state as well as for whole sequence.

The total accuracy was calculated as

$$\text{Acc} = \frac{|\{i : v_i = q_i\}|}{T} \qquad (15)$$

and an accuracy of a state s was calculated as

$$\text{Acc}_s = \frac{|\{i : v_i = q_i, q_i = s\}|}{|\{j : q_j = s\}|}. \qquad (16)$$

Resulting models are able to predict animals' actions with an average accuracy of 83.86%. It can be seen that the state S5 has the worst accuracy from all states. It is caused by a delay. A model can relatively precisely detect that an action has started but the detection of a termination of the action is delayed. It causes that the state S5 has worse accuracy than other states. Figure 3 visualizes the results of evaluation of the Viterbi's sequence.

5.2 Clustering

In this subsection, we discuss results and evaluation of the cluster analysis. The visualisation of a distance matrix is shown in Figure 4. A color of the point i,j represents distance between i-th animal's model and j-th animal's model. The lighter the color is the less similar the models are. The distance matrix is used by both clustering methods.

Linkages of hierarchical clustering can be visualized by dendrograms. Dendrogram is used to visually estimate an optimal number of clusters. The dendrogram of a complete linkage is shown in Figure 5. According to it, animals can be assigned into several approximately equally sized clusters.

The evaluation of clustering results is a difficult task since there are no references for validation. However, clusters can be validated by a domain expert based on descriptive characteristics related to animals (e.g., age, weight). These characteristics were not used for modeling, thus,

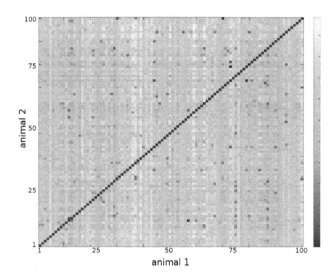

Figure 4: Kullback-Leibler divergence based distance matrix between estimated models. A color of the point i,j represents distance between i-th animal's model and j-th animal's model.

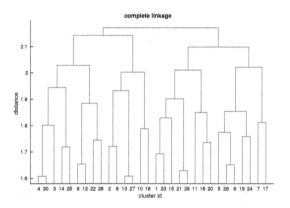

Figure 5: The dendrogram for a complete linkage.

they can not influence the clustering. Figures 6, 7 and 8 show results of the spectral clustering according to Shi and Malik with a fully connected similarity graph with sigma equal to 0.65. In the figures can be seen that there are differences in descriptive statistics of such characteristic between individual clusters. For example, animals assigned to cluster 1 have significantly higher values of the characteristic than animals of other clusters. It indicates that the clustering is reasonable and meaningful.

6 Conclusion

Hidden Markov models are proved to be applicable to modeling of animal behavior represented as a sequence of states. According to their evaluation, the model is able to predict animals' actions with an average accuracy of

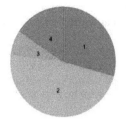

Figure 6: Proportions of four clusters, which were created using spectral clustering according to Shi and Malik.

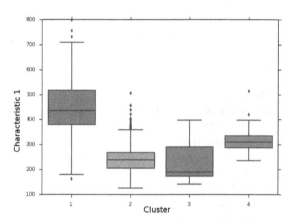

Figure 7: Boxplots of unobserved descriptive characteristic showing differences between four clusters.

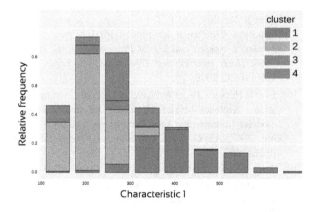

Figure 8: Distribution of unobserved descriptive characteristic showing differences between four clusters.

83.86%. Furthermore, the stationary distributions of the resulting models were validated by a domain expert. Cluster analysis was performed by classical clustering algorithms using the approximation of KL divergence. The clustering produces meaningful results and clusters animals into interpretable groups

Prediction can be further improved with better definition of states. In particular, the state S5 can be divided into more disjoint states. This may positively influence results of the clustering. Moreover, different modeling approaches commonly used for modeling sequences, such as dynamic Bayesian networks, conditional random fields, are intended to be researched, as well as their clustering possibilities.

References

[1] Jonathan Alon, Stan Sclaroff, George Kollios, and Vladimir Pavlovic. Discovering clusters in motion time-series data. In *Computer Vision and Pattern Recognition, 2003. Proceedings. 2003 IEEE Computer Society Conference on*, volume 1, pages I–375. IEEE, 2003.

[2] Longbing Cao and Philip S Yu. *Behavior computing*. Springer, London, 2012.

[3] Emanuele Coviello, Gert R Lanckriet, and Antoni B Chan. The variational hierarchical EM algorithm for clustering hidden Markov models. In *Advances in neural information processing systems*, pages 404–412, 2012.

[4] Qi Dai, Xiao-Qing Liu, Tian-Ming Wang, and Damir Vukicevic. Linear regression model of dna sequences and its application. *Journal of Computational Chemistry*, 28(8):1434–1445, 2007.

[5] Markus Falkhausen, Herbert Reininger, and Dietrich Wolf. Calculation of distance measures between hidden Markov models. In *In Proc. Eurospeech*, pages 1487–1490, 1995.

[6] Y. Guo, G. Poulton, P. Corke, G. J. Bishop-Hurley, T. Wark, and D. L. Swain. Using accelerometer, high sample rate GPS and magnetometer data to develop a cattle movement and behaviour model. *Ecological Modelling*, 220(17):2068–2075, 2009.

[7] John R Hershey and Peder A Olsen. Variational Bhattacharyya divergence for hidden Markov models. In *Acoustics, Speech and Signal Processing, 2008. ICASSP 2008. IEEE International Conference on*, pages 4557–4560. IEEE, 2008.

[8] John R Hershey, Peder A Olsen, and Steven J Rennie. Variational Kullback-Leibler divergence for hidden Markov models. In *Automatic Speech Recognition & Understanding, 2007. ASRU. IEEE Workshop on*, pages 323–328. IEEE, 2007.

[9] Tony Jebara, Yingbo Song, and Kapil Thadani. Spectral clustering and embedding with hidden Markov models. In *Machine Learning: ECML 2007*, pages 164–175. Springer, 2007.

[10] Biing-Hwang Fred Juang and Lawrence R Rabiner. A probabilistic distance measure for hidden Markov models. *AT&T technical journal*, 64(2):391–408, 1985.

[11] John L. Kelley. *General Topology (Graduate Texts in Mathematics)*. Springer, 1975.

[12] John D. Lafferty, Andrew McCallum, and Fernando C. N. Pereira. Conditional random fields: Probabilistic models for segmenting and labeling sequence data. pages 282–289, 2001.

[13] Sang Wan Lee, Yong Soo Kim, and Zeungnam Bien. A nonsupervised learning framework of human behavior patterns based on sequential actions. *IEEE Transactions on Knowledge and Data Engineering*, vol. 22(issue 4):479–492, 2010.

[14] Maja Matetić, Slobodan Ribarić, and Ivo Ipšić. Qualitative modelling and analysis of animal behaviour. *Applied Intelligence*, vol. 21(issue 1):25–44, 2004.

[15] Bill O'Brien, John Dooley, and Thomas J Brazil. Rf power amplifier behavioral modeling using a globally recurrent neural network. In *Microwave Symposium Digest, 2006. IEEE MTT-S International*, pages 1089–1092. IEEE, 2006.

[16] Vladimir Pavlović, James M Rehg, Tat-Jen Cham, and Kevin P Murphy. A dynamic Bayesian network approach to figure tracking using learned dynamic models. In *Computer Vision, 1999. The Proceedings of the Seventh IEEE International Conference on*, volume 1, pages 94–101. IEEE, 1999.

[17] Amy L. Sliva. *Scalable techniques for behavioral analysis and forecasting*. 2011.

[18] Padhraic Smyth et al. Clustering sequences with hidden Markov models. *Advances in neural information processing systems*, pages 648–654, 1997.

[19] Ulrike Von Luxburg. A tutorial on spectral clustering. *Statistics and computing*, 17(4):395–416, 2007.

[20] Nelleke d. Weerd, Frank v. Langevelde, Herman v. Oeveren, Bart A. Nolet, Andrea Kölzsch, Herbert H. T. Prins, and W. F. Boer. Deriving animal behaviour from high-frequency GPS: Tracking cows in open and forested habitat. *PLoS One*, 10(6), 06 2015.

[21] Jie Yin and Qiang Yang. Integrating hidden Markov models and spectral analysis for sensory time series clustering. In *Data Mining, Fifth IEEE International Conference on*, pages 8–pp. IEEE, 2005.

[22] S.-X. Zhang. *Structured Support Vector Machines for Speech Recognition*. PhD thesis, Cambridge University, March 2014.

[23] Shi Zhong. Semi-supervised sequence classification with HMMs. In Valerie Barr and Zdravko Markov, editors, *FLAIRS Conference*, pages 568–574. AAAI Press, 2004.

[24] Shi Zhong and Joydeep Ghosh. A unified framework for model-based clustering. *The Journal of Machine Learning Research*, 4:1001–1037, 2003.

ITAT 2016 Proceedings, pp. 179–186
ISBN 978-1537016740, © 2016 O. Trunda, R. Brunetto

Fitness landscape analysis of hyper-heuristic transforms for the vertex cover problem

Otakar Trunda and Robert Brunetto

Charles University in Prague, Faculty of Mathematics and Physics
Malostranské náměstí 25, Praha, Czech Republic
otakar.trunda@mff.cuni.cz, robert@brunetto.cz

Abstract: Hyper-heuristics have recently proved efficient in several areas of combinatorial search and optimization, especially scheduling. The basic idea of hyper-heuristics is based on searching for search-strategy. Instead of traversing the solution-space, the hyper-heuristic traverses the space of algorithms to find or construct an algorithm best suited for the given problem instance. The observed efficiency of hyper-heuristics is not yet fully explained on the theoretical level. The leading hypothesis suggests that the fitness landscape of the algorithm-space is more favorable to local search techniques than the original space.

In this paper, we analyse properties of fitness landscapes of the problem of minimal vertex cover. We focus on properties that are related to efficiency of metaheuristics such as locality and fitness-distance correlation. We compare properties of the original space and the algorithm space trying to verify the hypothesis explaining hyper-heuristics performance. Our analysis shows that the hyper-heuristic-space really has some more favorable properties than the original space.

1 Introduction

Hyper-heuristics are becoming more and more popular in the field of combinatorial search and optimization. They transfer the search process from the space of *candidate solutions* to a space of *algorithms that create candidate solutions*. Such approach combines metaheuristic techniques with algorithm selection and proved to be efficient on many domains [2]. Several theoretical results about hyper-heuristics have been established. For example: given a set of low-level algorithms, the hyper-heuristic combination of them can outperform each of those individuals on *all* domains. *"The hyper-heuristic lunch is free [8]."* However, the efficiency and inefficiency of hyper-heuristics on some domains is not yet fully understood.

In this paper, we explore the hypothesis, that the efficiency of hyper-heuristics is caused by the fact that the space of algorithms is easier to explore for local search techniques than the original space. We use fitness landscape analysis to compare properties of hyper-heuristic space with the original space and to determine which one is more suitable for local search. We work with the vertex cover problem, as an example of a well-established and hard optimization problem.

In the next section, we provide some basic background on the vertex cover problem, fitness landscape analysis techniques and hyper-heuristics. The third section presents our design of a hyper-heuristic for the vertex cover. In the fourth section, we then define the spaces we analyse and the results of the analyses are given in the fifth section. The paper is concluded by a discussion about the results and possible future work.

2 Background

2.1 Vertex cover problem

An undirected graph G is a tuple $G = (V, E)$, where $V = \{v_1, v_2, \ldots, v_n\}$, $E = \{e_1, e_2, \ldots, e_m\}$, such that $\forall e_i \in E, e_i = \{a_i, b_i\}, a_i, b_i \in V, a_i \neq b_i$ (no loops) and $\forall e_i, e_j \in E, i \neq j \implies e_i \neq e_j$ (no multiple edges). A set $S \subseteq V$ is a vertex cover in G iff $\forall e_i \in E, \exists s_j \in S$, s. t. $s_j \in e_i$.

An undirected vertex-labelled graph G is an undirected graph together with a cost function $c : V \mapsto \mathbb{R}^+$ that assigns positive costs to vertices. Given an undirected vertex-labelled graph $G = (V, E)$, the minimal vertex cover problem deals with finding a set $S \subseteq V$ minimizing $\sum_{s_i \in S} c(s_i)$ under the condition that S is a vertex cover in G. From now on, by *graph* we will always mean undirected vertex-labelled graph.

We use several other standard graph notions: for $v_i \in V$, by $\Gamma(v_i)$ we denote the neighborhood of v_i i. e. the set of all vertices that are connected to v_i by an edge. $\Gamma(v_i) = \{v_j \in V \mid \exists e_i \in E, e = (v_i, v_j)\}$. By $deg(v_i)$ we denote the degree of vertex. $deg(v_i) = |\Gamma(v_i)|$. A vertex v is called *leaf* if it's degree is 1. A graph is called *regular*, if all its vertices have the same degree.

We forbid loops in the graph as they don't present any new challenge to the problem. Vertices with loops always have to be in the vertex cover, so by a linear preprocessing (removing all loopy vertices), we can reduce the problem with loops to an equivalent problem without loops.

We forbid multiple edges between the same pair of vertices as well. We could simply leave multiple edges in the graph as they have no effect on the set of vertex covers nor on the optimality of the solutions, but it would change degrees of vertices which might lead our search algorithms astray.

Many real-life optimization problems from transportation, scheduling and operations research can be directly reduced to vertex cover. As for the complexity of the problem, the vertex cover is a well-known NP-complete problem, a 2-approximation algorithm exists, and using parametrized complexity, the best known optimal algorithm for the unweighted version runs in time $O(kn + 1.274^k)$, where n is the number of vertices and k is the size of an optimal vertex cover [3]. In practical applications, heuristics are typically used [1].

2.2 Fitness landscape analysis

In the theory of local search algorithms, like evolutionary algorithms, hill-climbing, tabu-search and so on, the fitness landscape analysis is used to assess efficiency of the algorithm on a given problem. The theory of fitness landscapes can also be helpful when designing new metaheuristic algorithm for a specific problem [9, 10].

A fitness landscape of an optimization problem is a set M together with a function $f : M \mapsto \mathbb{R}$ and a distance measure $d : M \times M \to \mathbb{R}^+$. M denotes the set of all candidate solutions, f is the fitness function which tells us how good the candidate solution is, and d measures distance between candidate solutions. We work with combinatorial problems, so the set M will be discrete and finite.

In Figure 1, there is an example of a fitness landscape of a small instance of the Travelling Salesman Problem [11]. The tree in the upper part enumerates the set of all permutations which constitutes the set M. Beneath it, there is a graph of the fitness function for each point of M (the length of a tour corresponding to each permutation). The points of M are arranged linearly by their lexicographical order which induces the distance measure and structure. The marked point corresponds to the solution shown in Figure 2 which is a local optimum.

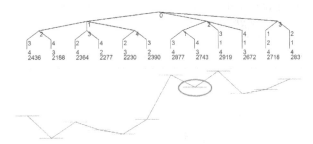

Figure 1: Example of a fitness landscape of a small TSP

The measure d is typically not given explicitly, but instead it is derived from the *search operators* that the algorithm uses. (For example a mutation operator used by genetic algorithms.) Formally: a unary search operator p is a map $p : M \mapsto 2^M$, where $p(m)$ is the set of all possible modifications of m - i.e. the set of possible results of the operator. When applying the operator p to a point $m \in M$, the algorithm replaces m by one of the points from $p(m)$. The point can be selected randomly, or by some criterion, e.g. minimum, in case of greedy operators. The algorithm repeatedly applies operators to move from one candidate solution to another.

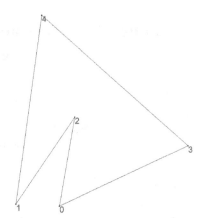

Figure 2: One of the solutions of the TSP example

The role of the distance measure is to introduce a structure to the set M. For the purposes of analysis, it is especially important to define neighborhoods of points. For $m_i \in M$, we denote the neighborhood of m_i as $N(m_i)$. It is a set of all points from M that are *close to* m_i.

If d is given explicitly, then N can be defined as $N(m_i) = \{m_j \in M \mid d(m_i, m_j) \leq \varepsilon\}$. Typically ε is taken to be 1. In the much more common case when we are given the set of search operators P instead of d, the neighborhood is defined as $N_P(m_i) = \{m_j \in M \mid \exists p \in P, m_j \in p(m_i)\}$, i.e. the set of all solutions reachable from m_i by an application of a single operator. The operators can also induce a distance measure as $d_P(m_i, m_j) = $ *minimum number of applications of operators from P that allow moving from m_i to m_j*. Formally:

1. $d_P(m_i, m_i) = 0$

2. $d_P(m_i, m_j) = (\min_{m_k \in N_P(m_i)} d(m_k, m_j)) + 1$

In the following text, we will use a few simple notions from function analysis and theory of search. Given a function $f : M \mapsto \mathbb{R}^+$, that we want to minimize, we say:

- $x^* \in M$ is an optimal solution (or global optimum) iff $\forall m \in M : f(x^*) \leq f(m)$

- $x \in M$ is a local optimum iff $\forall m \in N(x) : f(x) \leq f(m)$

- if x is not an optimal solution, then the escape distance of x is $ed(x) = \min_{\{m \in M \mid f(m) < f(x)\}} d(x, m) = $ distance to the nearest point with strictly lower fitness value

Fitness landscape analysis studies properties of fitness landscapes that are related to performance of local search algorithms. For example, smooth and globally convex function with a single local optimum is much easier to deal with than highly rugged function with many local optima. Several methods for analyzing fitness landscapes have been developed:

- Size of M: smaller $|M|$ leads to higher performance and vice versa

- Number of local optima: many local-search algorithms are attracted to local optima. The higher number of local optima therefore slows down the convergence to global optimum.

- Average size of neighborhood: large neighborhood decreases the number of local optima, but dramatically increases time that the algorithm needs to traverse the space, and operators with large range of values are close to random search. It is therefore important to keep the neighborhoods small.

  For example, if all points of M are neighbors, then there are no local optima except the global ones. On the other hand, if neighborhoods are empty, i.e., no pair of points are neighbors, then every point is a local optimum. There is therefore a trade-off between size of neighborhoods and number of local optima.

- Fitness-distance correlation (FDC): even with only one local optimum, the algorithm might not be able to find it if it is surrounded by points with high fitness values. It is therefore important that the optimal solutions are surrounded by low-fitness valued points and are far from high-valued points. FDC measures how the distance between points corresponds to difference between their fitness values. Ideally, there should be a strong positive correlation – i.e. the further from the nearest global optimum the point is, the higher fitness value it should have.

  Formally, the FDC is computed as: $FDC = \frac{c_{fd}}{\rho(f)\rho(d_{opt})}$, where c_{fd} is a covariance of f and d_{opt}, $c_{fd} = \frac{1}{|M|}\sum_{i=1}^{|M|}(f(m_i)-\overline{f})(d_{m_i,opt}-\overline{d_{opt}})$, $\overline{f}$ is average fitness value over the whole M, $d_{m_i,opt}$ is a distance between m_i and the nearest optimal solution, and $\overline{d_{opt}}$ is the average of $d_{m_i,opt}$ over the whole M. $\rho(f)$ and $\rho(d_{opt})$ are standard deviations of f and d_{opt} respectively.

  FDC is in range $[-1,1]$. In the ideal case, where $f(m_i)=d_{m_i,opt}$, the FDC = 1, for a random function, the FDC is close to 0 and FDC = -1 means that the optimal solution is "hidden" among high-valued points.

- Ruggedness: rugged function is opposite to smooth - it is erratic, with large differences in fitness values between nearby points. Ruggedness is computed as $R = \frac{\overline{f(x)f(x)_{d(x,y)=1}}-(\overline{f})^2}{\overline{f^2}-(\overline{f})^2}$. Where *overline* denotes average over all values [7]. R is always in $[-1,1]$, value of 1 indicates constant function, 0 means that values of neighbouring points are independent and -1 indicates that the neighbouring points have opposite values (i.e. every point is a local extreme). Note that higher ruggedness coefficient actually denotes more smooth function which is favorable for local search.

- Average escape distance: low escape distance allows the algorithm to quickly find a point with better fitness value. Ideally the $ed(m)$ should be constant for each $m \in M$. We only compute average of $ed(m)$ over local optima since for points which aren't locally optimal, the escape distance is always 1.

The landscape-analysis techniques have to traverse the whole search-space of the problem multiple times. As such search-spaces are typically very large, the analysis can only be done on small instances. There are techniques that allow to estimate some properties even in large spaces by sampling, but we won't be using those here.

Note that our main purpose here is not to actually *solve* large instances of vertex cover, but rather to verify the hypothesis, that hyper-heuristic spaces might have very different properties and might be much more favorable for local search techniques than the original space.

2.3 Hyper-heuristics

Hyper-heuristics represent a new approach to search and optimization which combines metaheuristics, automated parameter tuning, algorithm selection and genetic programming. Nowadays, the algorithm selection approaches are becoming more and more popular in combinatorial optimization, as it is clear that no single algorithm can outperform every other on all domains, and therefore, the most suitable algorithm has to be selected for the problem at hand [4, 5].

Hyper-heuristics try to build an algorithm suited for given task by combining so called *low-level algorithms* during the search. A pool of simple algorithms is given and the hyper-heuristic combines them into more complex units. The combination procedure is often based on some kind of evolutionary computation and the quality of resulting units is measured by how well they can solve the original task. The approach was especially successful in the area of scheduling and it is now applied to many other kinds of problems [2].

Instead of searching the *solution space* directly, hyper-heuristics search the *algorithm space*. The approach is based on an assumption that *similar algorithms will find solutions of similar quality (not necessarily close to each other)* which implies that the algorithm space has some favorable properties: high locality, i.e., elements close to each other have similar evaluation, and low number of local extrema. See figure 3. On spaces with those properties, optimization metaheuristics can find good solutions quickly. Of course, such improvements come for a price: evaluating an element from the algorithm space takes much more time because it involves searching for a solution in the solution space.

Consider the following example: we want to color a graph with the fewest colors possible. Using a genetic algorithm, we could come up with a metaheuristic that will work on the set of all possible assignments of color to vertices a the fitness function will penalize violations (connected vertices having the same color) and high number

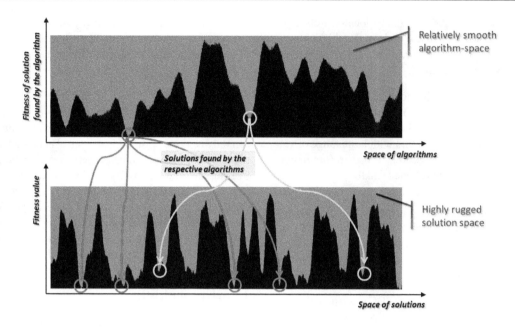

Figure 3: The hypothesized schema of a hyper-heuristic transformation

of color used. Such algorithm might converge to globally optimal solution, but it would take a long time.

We could also use a greedy algorithm which works as follows: picks a vertex from a graph according to some criterion and colors it by the lowest color possible, according to the colors of its neighbours. Then it picks another vertex and so on until the graph is colored. The greedy algorithm is very fast, but in most cases it wont converge to global optimum.

There are several vertex-picking criteria, for example:

- Largest degree (L) - picks a vertex with the largest number of neighbours

- Saturation degree (S) - picks a vertex who's neighbours are colored with the largest number of different colors

- Incidence degree (I) - picks a vertex with the largest number of colored neighbours

Based on these three low-level greedy algorithms, a hyper-heuristic would search a space of all combinations of them (the algorithm space). On a graph with 5 vertices, the algorithm space would consist of all sequences of length 4 containing symbols L, S and I. To evaluate the point from the algorithm space, the hyper-heuristic would use the algorithm to find a solution, then evaluates the solution by the original fitness function and uses the value to evaluate the algorithm. For example a point *ILS* (from the algorithm space) is evaluated as follows:

1. Select a vertex based on the I criterion and color it with the lowest possible color

2. Select a vertex based on the L criterion and color it

3. Select a vertex based on the S criterion and color it

4. Color the last vertex

5. Compute the total number of colors used and use it as the fitness value of the point (ILS)

The hyper-heuristic might also be based on an evolutionary algorithm, which would in this case work on the algorithm space. This is popularly summarized as *Heuristics select moves, hyper-heuristics select heuristics*. The hyper-heuristic might be able to find an optimal solution, and more importantly, it might be able to find high-quality solutions much faster than the former approach.

3 Hyper-heuristic for minimal vertex cover

We have designed a hyper-heuristic for the vertex cover in the similar manner as in the example mentioned earlier. We used a pool of simple greedy algorithms and the hyper-heuristic combines them in order to solve the problem. The low-level algorithms work sequentially as described in Algorithm 1.

Algorithm 1 Greedy vertex cover

1: $S \leftarrow \emptyset$
2: **while** G contains some edge **do**
3:     $v \leftarrow$ select vertex according to some criterion
4:     $S \leftarrow S \cup \{v\}$
5:     remove v from the graph (with incident edges)
6: **return** S

As the vertex-selection criteria, we use the following:

- Leightest (W) : selects the vertex with minimal weight (cost)

- Deg (G) : selects the vertex with maximal degree

- Sub (S) : selects the vertex v with maximal [(sum of costs of neighbors) - cost of v] i.e. selected = $argmax_{v \in V} \left(\sum_{\{w \in \Gamma(v)\}} c(w) - c(v) \right)$

- WDeg (G) : selects the vertex with minimal *weight / degree*. Selected = $argmin_{v \in V} \left(c(v) / deg(v) \right)$

- Div (D) : selects the vertex v with minimal ratio of cost of v and sum of costs of neighbors. Formally selected = $argmin_{v \in V} \left(c(v) / \sum_{\{w \in \Gamma(v)\}} c(w) \right)$

- Leaf (L) : selects the vertex v with minimal difference between cost of v and (sum of costs of neighbors of v that are leaves), e.i. selected = $argmin_{v \in V} (c(v) - \sum_{\{w \in \Gamma(v) \mid w \text{ is a leaf}\}} c(w))$

- Neig (N) : selects the vertex with maximal sum of costs of neighbors

- Next (X) : selects the vertex which is the next in order after the vertex selected by (W) (we used this as an example of non-greedy, chaotic algorithm)

We break ties simply by the ordinal numbers of vertices, i.e., if more than one vertex achieve the optimal value of the criterion, we select among then the one with the lowest number.

The space of algorithms consists of all sequences of letters W,G,S,D,L (corresponding to selection criteria) of a fixed length. The i-th symbol in the sequence determines the criterion by which the i-th vertex is selected. If a valid vertex cover is found before all symbols are used, the rest of the sequence is ignored. In much more frequent case when we have already traversed the whole sequence but there are still edges in the graph, we use two strategies: (i) start over and read symbols from the beginning of the sequence (*repeat* strategy) and (ii) use the last symbol in the sequence for as long as there are edges in the graph (*last* strategy).

4   Analysis of the fitness landscapes

The hyper-heuristic can be viewed as a transformation of the search space. We will now describe properties of the original and transformed spaces. We use the notation of fitness landscapes as defined earlier.

4.1   Original space

- M: set of all vertex covers (not necessarily minimal in inclusion)

- f: total weight of the vertex cover - sum of costs of all vertices in the cover

- d: distance between vertex covers is measured as the number of elements on which the two covers differ. Formally: $S_1, S_2 \subseteq V$: $d(S_1, S_2) = |\{S_1 \setminus S_2\} \cup \{S_2 \setminus S_1\}|$

The distance measure is related to the search operators *add vertex* and *remove vertex*. One application of such operator creates a solution within distance of 1 from the original point.

4.2   Hyper-heuristic space

- M: set of all fixed-length sequences of symbols corresponding to low-level heuristics

- f: total weight of the vertex cover found by the application of the sequence

- d: distance between sequences is measured by the *Levenshtein distance* which is the minimal number of operations *add symbol*, *remove symbol* and *replace symbol* needed to transform the first sequence into the second.

This distance measure is intuitively related to search operators *add symbol*, *remove symbol* and *replace symbol*.

We distinguish the hyper-spaces by the set of low-level algorithms that are used. We do not always use all the algorithms, partially because of the high computational cost and partially because on some kinds of graphs, the criteria degenerate. For example, on a uniformly-weighted graph, the algorithm *Neig* will work exactly the same as *Degree* so its not worth using both of them. Furthermore, we would like to be able to asses performance of single algorithms, pairs, 3-tuples, 4-tuples and so on.

We work with these types of spaces: original space (denoted *Cover*), hyper-space with a specific set of low-level algorithms L and a fixed length of sequences k (denoted $H_{L,k}$). We distinguish two alternatives as mentioned earlier: (i) a space, where during the evaluation, the sequence is applied repeatedly from the beginning until a valid cover is found (denoted $H_{L,k}^{repeat}$), and (ii) a space, where during the evaluation, after reaching the end of sequence, the last symbol is applied repeatedly until a valid cover is found (denoted $H_{L,k}^{last}$).

5   Experiments

We generated a set of graphs, constructed the corresponding spaces and computed fitness landscape metrics for those spaces. We used graphs of various sizes, densities and types. For each type of graphs, we generated about $30 \sim 40$ instances and average the results.

We used graphs of sizes $n = 16 \sim 45$ vertices (not all values from the range were used). The densities were 0.1, 0.2, 0.3, 0.4, 0.5 and 0.7. The density of c means that there were $\frac{c}{2} \cdot n \cdot (n-1)$ edges in the graph. We used two policies to add edges - uniformly randomly (select random pair of vertices and add an edge until the desired number of edges is reached) and regularly (adds edges more likely to vertices with low degrees to create a near-regular graph). Weights of vertices are integers taken uniformly from ranges $(50 \sim 50)$, $(50 \sim 60)$, $(50 \sim 100)$ and $(50 \sim 1000)$.

In total, we generated over 24 000 graphs, roughly half of them were near-regular and half of them used the uniform edge distribution. For each graph, we constructed the vertex covers-space and 20 hyper-spaces (for various combinations of parameters - $H_{L,k}^{last}$ and $H_{L,k}^{repeat}$ with different sets L). The experiments run on 11 computers with 8 cores each for 20 hours on each.

We present graphs comparing various metrics between spaces. On x-axis, there is the number of vertices in the graph, y-axis shows values of the particular metric. We plot several color-distinguished series in the same graph, each series represents one space. The space is described in the legend by an enumeration of low-level algorithms used. Exclamation mark at the end denotes the *last* strategy; no mark means that the *repeat* strategy is used. The word *cover* denotes the original space of all vertex covers.

We use a normalization so that different columns are of a similar magnitude and can be depicted in the same graph. Instead of plotting *criterion*, we plot *criterion / number of vertices - number of vertices*. With this normalization, values related to different number of vertices are not directly comparable, but values related to the same number of vertices are, which is good enough for our purposes. With this normalization, we plot *weight of the cover divided among each vertex*.

We plot averages over all generated graphs grouped into categories by number of vertices. We tried to distinguish the results further by edge-generation policy (regular graphs vs. random graphs), edge-density and width distribution. In most cases, such further distinguishing didn't provide any new information - the results were very similar in each of the smaller categories.

***Last* vs. *repeat* strategy** First, we have tried to compare the two ways of evaluating the sequences - repeat the whole sequence from the beginning and repeating only the last symbol, i.e. the spaces $H_{L,k}^{repeat}$ and $H_{L,k}^{last}$. We believe that different algorithms should be used in the beginning of the search and different one at the end, so the space $H_{L,k}^{last}$ should contain better solutions. We measure the value of the global optimum in each space. The graph is shown in Figure 4. $H_{L,k}^{last}$ is slightly better than $H_{L,k}^{repeat}$ for all L.

Solution quality in spaces Hyper-spaces doesn't contain all the vertex covers, they only contain some of them. For example, the set of *all* vertices is a valid vertex cover, but it is never generated by any algorithm sequence. On the other hand, some vertex covers might be generated by many different sequences of algorithms. To ease the search, the hyper-space should contain an algorithm that can generate an optimal solution, there should be a large number of different sequences that generate high-quality solutions and very few or none sequences that generate low-quality solutions.

To assess the quality of solutions generated by points in the hyper-space, we created a histogram of quality of all solutions from original and hyper-space. It is depicted

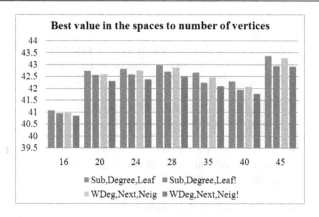

Figure 4: Best solutions in $H_{L,k}^{repeat}$ and $H_{L,k}^{last}$

in Figure 5. Red columns come from the original space and yellow ones come from one of the hyper-spaces. The hyper-space is smaller in size, so the total volume of yellow is smaller. Solutions in the original space seem to follow normal distribution, while in the hyper-space, most of the points generate near-to-optimal solutions or near-to-average solutions. The behavior can be explained as follows: high-quality solutions are generated due to greediness of the selection criteria and average-quality solutions are generated since their number in the original space is very high.

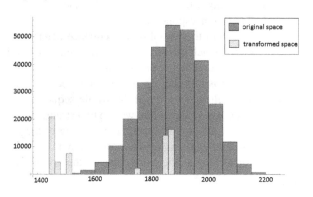

Figure 5: Histogram of distribution of solutions based on their quality in the two spaces.

We also monitor the average value of solutions in each space. Results are shown in Figure 6. All three hyper-spaces show significantly lower average value than the original space. (I.e. even a blind random search should provide better solutions in the hyper-space then in the original space.)

Combination of algorithms We test the hypothesis, that the combination of low-level algorithms can out-perform each of the individual algorithms. In Figure 7 there is the quality of an optimal solution in several hyper-spaces. *Min* denotes the best solution that can by found by repeated application of just one low-level algorithm. Other colors correspond to combinations. For all graph size, qual-

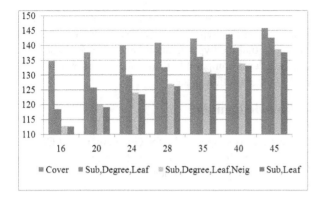

Figure 6: Average quality of solutions in spaces

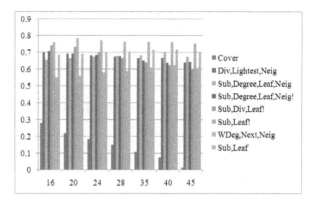

Figure 8: FDC of spaces

ity of optimal solution is better for most combinations of low-level algorithms. This result supports the hypothesis and suggests that the hyper-heuristic might be worth using even with its overhead (evaluating points in hyper-space is costly). TODO in most cases, however cover je lepsi nez H-H takze transformation vede ke ztrate optimalniho reseni.

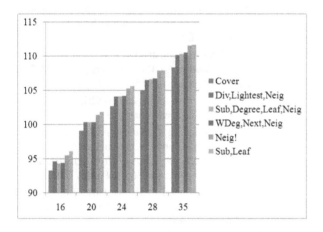

Figure 7: Best solutions of single algorithms and combinations

Fitness-distance correlation Figure 8 shows the FDC for several spaces. In the original space, FDC decreases with the number of vertices, while in the original space it stays high regardless of the size of the graph. (Note that higher FDC is better for local search algorithms.) This graph is shown without normalization, as the FDC is naturally in $[-1, 1]$. The rest of graphs are also without normalization since it's not needed.

Ruggedness In Figure 9 there is the ruggedness of our spaces. Most of hyper-spaces have higher ruggedness that the original space which is again better for local search algorithms. The ruggedness seem to be independent on the size of the graph.

Escape distance Figure 10 shows the average escape distance (ED) of some of our spaces. The ED is systematically lower in all hyper-spaces. The difference might not

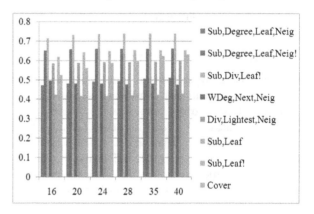

Figure 9: Ruggedness of spaces

be large, but note that the amount of work needed to escape the local minimum is *(number of neighbors)^{ED}*, so any savings in the exponent are significant.

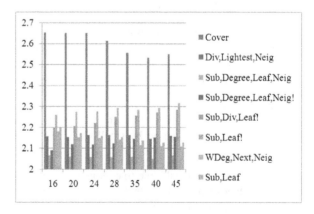

Figure 10: Escape distance from local optima

Number of local optima The graph 11 shows frequency of local minima in our spaces (i.e. the number of local minima over all nodes). The result is much better in the original space than in the hyper-spaces. This is partially caused by the fact that hyper-spaces contain many points that have the same fitness value and we define local minima as non-strict - i.e. points on plateaus are all considered local minima.

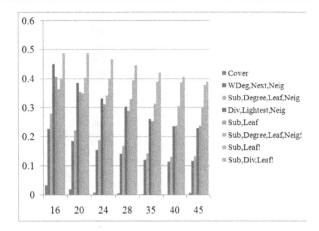

Figure 11: Frequency of local optima

6 Conclusions and future work

We presented a hyper-heuristic transformation for the vertex cover problem and constructed several variants of hyper-heuristic spaces using a set of greedy algorithms. We measured several important features of the original space and the hyper-spaces and by comparing them we have experimentally verified the hyper-heuristic-hypothesis that tries to explain the efficiency of hyper-heuristics in practise by properties of hyper-space. Our results can be summarized as follows:

1. Combination of greedy algorithms is in most cases much better that using single algorithm all the time

2. Only small part of the original space can be generated from the hyper-space. Most of high-quality solutions can be generated, but sometimes we loose the optimal solution by the transformation

3. The transformation improves fitness-distance correlation, escape distance and average solution quality. It has some positive effect on ruggedness as well, but it increases the frequency of local optima in the space.

4. There were no significant differences between various types of graphs, e.g. regular vs. random. We believe that this is caused by small size of our test graphs.

As future work, we would like to continue the analysis using more landscape analysis techniques, such as *neutrality* [6], *decomposability* etc. Also, we would like to add more low-level algorithms into the pool, especially less-greedy ones. Greediness of the algorithms causes that only a very small portion of vertex covers are reachable from the hyper-space. In some cases, more than 50% of all algorithms in the space generated the same vertex cover. Such small range of unique fitness values then creates large plateaus, which contribute to an illusion of high locality and fine ruggedness. It is also responsible for the large number of local extrema that we observed in the hyper-spaces.

It would also be beneficial to actually run some search algorithm on the hyper-space (for some large instances) and prove that the hyper-heuristic really works in practice and is at least comparable to metaheuristics working directly in the solution space.

Acknowledgement

The research is supported by the Grant Agency of Charles University under contract no. 390214 and it is also supported by SVV project number 260 104. We would like to thank the anonymous reviewers for their useful comments and suggestions.

References

[1] Eric Angel, Romain Campigotto, and Christian Laforest. Implementation and Comparison of Heuristics for the Vertex Cover Problem on Huge Graphs. In *11th International Symposium, SEA 2012*, volume 7276 of *Lecture Notes in Computer Science*, pages 39–50, Bordeaux, France, June 2012.

[2] E. K. Burke, M. Gendreau, M. Hyde, G. Kendall, G. Ochoa, E. Ozcan, and R. Qu. Hyper-heuristics: a survey of the state of the art. *Journal of the Operational Research Society*, 64(12):1695–1724, Dec 2013.

[3] Jianer Chen, Iyad A. Kanj, and Ge Xia. *Improved Parameterized Upper Bounds for Vertex Cover*, pages 238–249. Springer Berlin Heidelberg, Berlin, Heidelberg, 2006.

[4] Youssef Hamadi, Eric Monfroy, and Frédéric Saubion. *Autonomous search.* Springer-Verlag, 2012.

[5] R. Kumar, S. K. Singh, and V. Kumar. A heuristic approach for search engine selection in meta-search engine. In *Computing, Communication Automation (ICCCA), 2015 International Conference on*, pages 865–869, May 2015.

[6] Marie-Eléonore Marmion, Clarisse Dhaenens, Laetitia Jourdan, Arnaud Liefooghe, and Sébastien Vérel. On the neutrality of flowshop scheduling fitness landscapes. *CoRR*, abs/1207.4629, 2012.

[7] Peter Merz and Bernd Freisleben. Fitness landscapes, memetic algorithms, and greedy operators for graph bipartitioning. *Evol. Comput.*, 8(1):61–91, March 2000.

[8] Riccardo Poli and Mario Graff. *Genetic Programming: 12th European Conference, EuroGP 2009 Tübingen, Germany, April 15-17, 2009 Proceedings*, chapter There Is a Free Lunch for Hyper-Heuristics, Genetic Programming and Computer Scientists, pages 195–207. Springer Berlin Heidelberg, Berlin, Heidelberg, 2009.

[9] Franz Rothlauf. *Representations for genetic and evolutionary algorithms (2. ed.).* Springer, 2006.

[10] Franz Rothlauf. *Design of Modern Heuristics.* Natural Computing Series. Springer, 2011.

[11] Mohammad-H Tayarani-N. and Adam Prügel-Bennett. An analysis of the fitness landscape of travelling salesman problem. *Evolutionary Computation*, 24(2):347–384, Jun 2015.

ITAT 2016 Proceedings, pp. 187–194
ISBN 978-1537016740, © 2016 P. Vidnerová, R. Neruda

Vulnerability of machine learning models to adversarial examples

Petra Vidnerová, Roman Neruda

Institute of Computer Science, Academy of Sciences of the Czech Republic
petra@cs.cas.cz

Abstract: We propose a genetic algorithm for generating adversarial examples for machine learning models. Such approach is able to find adversarial examples without the access to model's parameters. Different models are tested, including both deep and shallow neural networks architectures. We show that RBF networks and SVMs with Gaussian kernels tend to be rather robust and not prone to misclassification of adversarial examples.

1 Introduction

Deep networks and convolutional neural networks enjoy high interest nowadays. They have become the state-of-art methods in many fields of machine learning, and have been applied to various problems, including image recognition, speech recognition, and natural language processing [5].

In [12] a counter-intuitive property of deep networks is described. It relates to the stability of a neural network with respect to small perturbation of their inputs. The paper shows that applying an imperceptible non-random perturbation to an input image, it is possible to arbitrarily change the network prediction. These perturbations are found by optimizing the input to maximize the prediction error. Such perturbed examples are known as *adversarial examples*. On some datasets, such as ImageNet, the adversarial examples were so close to the original examples that the differences were indistinguishable to the human eye.

Paper [4] suggests that it is the linear behaviour in high-dimensional spaces what is sufficient to cause adversarial examples (for example, a linear classifier exhibits this behaviour too). They designed a fast method of generating adversarial examples (adding small vector in the direction of the sign of the derivation) and showed that adding these examples to the training set further improves the generalization of the model. In [4], in addition, the authors state that adversarial examples are relatively robust, and they generalize between neural networks with varied number of layers, activations, or trained on different subsets of the training data. In other words, if we use one neural network to generate a set of adversarial examples, these examples are also misclassified by another neural network even when it was trained with different hyperparameters, or when it was trained on a different set of examples. Another results of fooling deep and convolutional networks can be found in [10].

This paper examines a vulnerability to adversarial examples throughout variety of machine learning methods.

We propose a genetic algorithm for generating adversarial examples. Though the evolution is slower than techniques described in [12, 4], it enables us to obtain adversarial examples even without the access to model's weights. The only thing we need is to be able to query the network to classify a given example. From this point of view, the misclassification of adversarial examples represent a security flaw.

This paper is organized as follows. Section 2 brings a brief overview of machine learning models considered in this paper. Section 3 describes the proposed genetic algorithm. Section 4 describes the results of our experiments. Finally, Section 5 concludes our paper.

2 Deep and Shallow Architectures

2.1 Deep and Convolutional Networks

Deep neural networks are feedforward neural networks with multiple hidden layers between the input and output layer. The layers typically have different units depending on the task at hand. Among the units, there are traditional perceptrons, where each unit (neuron) realizes a nonlinear function, such as the *sigmoid* function: $y(z) = tanh(z)$ or $y(z) = \frac{1}{1+e^{-z}}$. Another alternative to the perceptron is the rectified linear unit (*ReLU*): $y(z) = max(0, z)$. Like the sigmoid neurons, rectified linear units can be used to compute any function, and they can be trained using algorithms such as back-propagation and stochastic gradient descent.

Convolutional layers contain the so called *convolutional units* that take advantage of the grid-like structure of the inputs, such as in the case of 2-D bitmap images, time series, etc. Convolutional units perform a simple discrete convolution operation, which – for 2-D data – can be represented by a matrix multiplication. Usually, to deal with large data (such as large images), the convolution is applied multiple times by sliding a small window over the data. The convolutional units are typically used to extract some features from the data, and they are often used together with the so-called *max pooling* layers that perform an input reduction by selecting one of many inputs, typically the one with maximal value. Thus, the overall architecture of a deep network for image classification tasks resembles a pyramid with smaller number of units in higher layers of the networks.

For the output layer, mainly for classification tasks, the *softmax* function: $y(z)_j = \frac{e^{z_j}}{\sum_{k=1}^{K} e^{z_k}}$ is often used. It has the advantage that the output values can be interpreted as probabilities of individual classes.

Networks with at least one convolutional layer are called *convolutional neural networks (CNN)*, while networks with all hidden layers consisting of perceptrons are called *multi-layer perceptrons (MLP)*.

2.2 RBF networks and Kernel Methods

The history of radial basis function (RBF) networks can be traced back to the 1980s, particularly to the study of interpolation problems in numerical analysis [8]. The RBF network [3] is a feedforward network with one hidden layer realizing the basis functions and linear output layer. It represents an alternative to classical models, such as multi-layer perceptrons. There is variety of learning methods for RBF networks [9].

In 1990s, a family of machine learning algorithms, known as kernel methods, became very popular. They have been applied to a number of real-world problems, and they are still considered to be state-of-the-art methods in various domains [14].

Based on theoretical results on kernel approximation, the popular support vector machine (SVM) [2, 13] algorithm was developed. Its architecture is similar to RBF – one hidden layer of kernel units and a linear output layer. The learning algorithm is different, based on search for a separating hyperplane with the highest margin. Common kernel functions used for SVM learning are linear $\langle x, x' \rangle$, polynomial $(\gamma \langle x, x' \rangle + r)^d$, Gaussian $\exp(-\gamma |x - x'|^2)$, and sigmoid $\tanh(\gamma \langle x, x' \rangle + r)$.

Recently, due to popularity of deep architectures, such models with only one hidden layer are often referred to as *shallow models*.

3 Genetic Algorithms

To obtain an adversarial example for the trained machine learning model (such as a neural network), we need to optimize the input image with respect to network output. For this task we employ genetic algorithms (GA). GA represent a robust optimization method working with the whole population of feasible solutions [7]. The population evolves using operators of selection, mutation, and crossover. Both the machine learning model and the target output are fixed during the optimization.

Each individual represents one possible input vector, i.e. one image encoded as a vector of pixel values:

$$I = \{i_1, i_2, \ldots, i_N\},$$

where $i_i \in <0, 1>$ are levels of grey, and N is the size of a flatten image. (For the sake of simplicity, we consider only greyscale images in this paper, but it can be seen that the same principle can be used for RGB images as well.)

The crossover operator performs a classical two-point crossover. The mutation introduces a small change to some pixels. With the probability p_{mutate_pixel} each pixel is changed:

$$i_i = i_i + r,$$

where r is drawn from Gaussian distribution. As a selection, the tournament selection with tournament size 3 is used.

The fitness function should reflect the following two criteria:

1. the individual should resemble the target image

2. if we evaluate the individual by our machine learning model, we aim to obtain a prescribed target output (i.e., misclassify it).

Thus, in our case, a fitness function is defined as: $f(I) = -(0.5 * cdist(I, target\_image) + 0.5 * cdist(model(I), target\_answer))$, where $cdist$ is a Euclidean distance.

4 Experimental Results

The goal of our experiments is to test various machine learning models and their vulnerability to adversarial examples.

4.1 Overview of models

As a representative of deep models we use two deep architectures – an MLP network with rectified linear units (ReLU), and a CNN. The MLP used in our experiments consist of three fully connected layers. Two hidden layers have 512 ReLUs each, using dropout; the output layer has 10 softmax units. The CNN has two convolutional layers with 32 filters and ReLUs each, a max pooling layer, a fully connected layer of 128 ReLUs, and a fully connected output softmax layer. In addition to these two models, we also used an ensemble of 10 MLPs. All models were trained using the KERAS library [1].

Shallow networks in our experiments are represented by an RBF network with 1000 Gaussian units, and SVM models with Gaussian kernel (SVM-gauss), polynomial kernel of grade 2 and 4 (SVM-poly2 and SVM-poly4), sigmoidal kernel (SVM-sigmoid), and linear kernel (SVM-linear). SVMs were trained using the SCIKIT library [11], Grid search and crossvalidation techniques were used to tune hyper-parameters. For RBF networks, we used our own implementation. Overview of train and test accuracies can be found in Tab. 1.

4.2 Experimental setup

The well known MNIST data set [6] was used. It contains 70 000 images of hand written digits, 28×28 pixel each. 60 000 are used for training, 10 000 for testing. The genetic algorithm was run with 50 individuals, for 10 000

	RBF	MLP	CNN	SVM-gauss	SVM-poly2	SVM-poly4	SVM-sigmoid	SVM-linear
Train	0.96	1.00	1.00	0.99	1.00	0.99	0.87	0.95
Test	0.96	0.98	0.99	0.98	0.98	0.98	0.88	0.94

Table 1: Overview of accuracies on train and test sets.

generations, with crossover probability set to 0.6, and mutation probability set to 0.1. The GA was run 9 times for each model to find adversarial examples that resemble 9 different images (training samples from the beginning of training set). All images were optimized to be classified as zero.

4.3 Results

Figures 1 and 2 show two selected cases from our set of experiments. For example, the first set of images shows a particular image of digit five from the training set, and best evolved individuals from the corresponding runs of GA for individual models.

In Tables 2–5, the outputs of individual models are listed. In Tab. 2 and 4, we show output vectors for training sample of digit five and four, respectively. In Tab. 3 and 5, we show output vectors for adversarial examples from Fig. 1 and 2, respectively.

For this case, the adversarial examples were found for MLP, CNN, ensemble of MLPs, SVM-poly2, and SVM-sigmoid. For RBF network, SVM-gauss, SVM-poly4, and SVM-linear, the GA was not able to find image that resembles the digit 5 and at the same time it is classified as zero.

If we look on a vulnerability of individual models over all 9 GA runs we can conclude the following:

- MLP, CNN, ensemble of MLPs, and SVM-sigmoid were always misclassifying the best individuals;

- RBF network, SVM-gauss, and SVM-linear; never misclassified, i.e. the genetic algorithm was not able to find adversarial example for these models;

- SVM-poly2 and SVM-poly4 were resistant to finding adversarial examples in 2 and 5 cases, respectively.

Fig. 3 and 4 deal with the generalization of adversarial examples over different models. For each adversarial example the figure lists the output vectors of all models. In the case of a digit 3, the adversarial example evolved for MLP is also misclassified by an ensemble of MLPs, and vice versa. Both examples are misclassified by SVM-sigmoid. However, adversarial example for the SVM-sigmoid is misclassified only by the SVM-linear model. Adversarial example for SVM-poly2 is misclassified also with other SVMs, except the SVM-gauss model.

In general, it often happens that adversarial example evolved for one model is misclassified by some of the other models (see Tab. 6 and 7). There are some general trends:

- adversarial example evolved for CNN was never misclassified by other models, and CNN never misclassified other adversarial examples than those evolved for the CNN;

- adversarial examples evolved for MLP are misclassified also by ensemble of MLPs (all cases except two) and adversarial examples evolved for ensemble of MLPs are misclassified by MLP (all cases);

- adversarial examples evolved for the SVM-sigmoid model are misclassified by SVM-linear (all cases except two);

- adversarial examples for the SVM-poly2 model are often (6 cases) misclassified by other SVMs (SVM-poly4, SVM-sigmoid, SVM-linear), and in 4 cases also by the SVM-gauss. In three cases it was also misclassified by MLP and ensemble of MLPs, in one case, the adversarial example for SVM-poly2 is misclassified by all models but CNN (however, this example is quite noisy);

- adversarial example for the SVM-poly4 model is in two cases misclassified by all models but CNN, in different case it is misclassified by all but the CNN and RBF models, and in one case by all but CNN, RBF, and SVM-gauss models;

- RBF network, SVM-gauss, and SVM-linear were resistant to adversarial examples by genetic algorithm, however they sometimes misclassify adversarial examples of other models. These examples are already quite noisy, however by human they would still be classified correctly.

5 Conclusion

We proposed a genetic algorithm for generating adversarial examples for machine learning models. Our experiment show that many machine models suffer from vulnerability to adversarial examples, i.e. examples designed to be misclassified. Some models are quite resistant to such behaviour, namely models with local units – RBF networks and SVMs with Gaussian kernels. It seems that it is the local behaviour of units that prevents the models from being fooled.

Adversarial examples evolved for one model are often misclassified also by some of other models, as was elaborated in the experiments.

Acknowledgements

This work was partially supported by the Czech Grant Agency grant 15-18108S, and institutional support of the Institute of Computer Science RVO 67985807.

	0	1	2	3	4	5	6	7	8	9
RBF	0.04	-0.07	0.08	0.24	-0.04	**0.73**	-0.04	0.21	0.03	-0.18
MLP	0.00	0.00	0.00	0.00	0.00	**1.00**	0.00	0.00	0.00	0.00
CNN	0.00	0.00	0.00	0.00	0.00	**1.00**	0.00	0.00	0.00	0.00
ENS	0.00	0.00	0.00	0.00	0.00	**1.00**	0.00	0.00	0.00	0.00
SVM-gauss	0.00	0.00	0.00	0.00	0.00	**1.00**	0.00	0.00	0.00	0.00
SVM-poly2	0.00	0.00	0.00	0.02	0.00	**0.98**	0.00	0.00	0.00	0.00
SVM-poly4	0.00	0.00	0.00	0.02	0.00	**0.98**	0.00	0.00	0.00	0.00
SVM-sigmoid	0.01	0.00	0.03	0.32	0.00	**0.61**	0.00	0.01	0.01	0.01
SVM-linear	0.00	0.00	0.01	0.10	0.00	**0.89**	0.00	0.00	0.00	0.00

Table 2: Evaluation of the target digit five (see Fig. 1) by individual models.

	0	1	2	3	4	5	6	7	8	9
RBF	0.21	-0.05	0.09	0.23	-0.04	**0.51**	-0.05	0.17	0.07	-0.09
MLP	**0.98**	0.00	0.00	0.00	0.00	0.01	0.00	0.00	0.00	0.00
CNN	**0.95**	0.00	0.01	0.01	0.00	0.02	0.00	0.00	0.01	0.00
ENS	**0.98**	0.00	0.01	0.00	0.00	0.01	0.00	0.00	0.00	0.00
SVM-gauss	0.00	0.00	0.01	0.39	0.00	**0.59**	0.00	0.00	0.00	0.00
SVM-poly	**0.88**	0.00	0.02	0.02	0.00	0.07	0.00	0.00	0.00	0.00
SVM-poly4	0.01	0.01	0.14	0.29	0.01	**0.50**	0.01	0.01	0.02	0.01
SVM-sigmoid	**0.82**	0.00	0.03	0.05	0.00	0.08	0.00	0.01	0.01	0.01
SVM-linear	0.02	0.03	0.21	0.21	0.02	**0.33**	0.03	0.04	0.05	0.05

Table 3: Evaluation of adversarial digit five (from Fig. 1) by individual models.

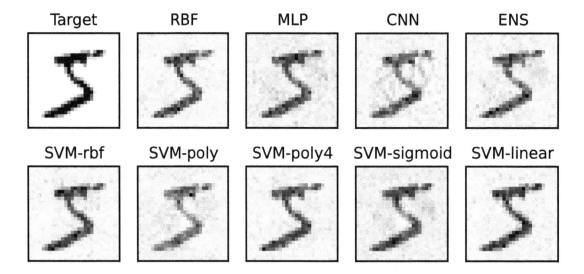

Figure 1: Best individuals evolved for individual models and digit five. The first 'Target' image is the digit from the training set, than follows adversarial examples evolved for individual models.

	0	1	2	3	4	5	6	7	8	9
RBF	-0.06	0.07	0.16	0.06	**0.67**	0.00	0.01	0.15	-0.01	-0.05
MLP	0.00	0.00	0.00	0.00	**1.00**	0.00	0.00	0.00	0.00	0.00
CNN	0.00	0.00	0.00	0.00	**1.00**	0.00	0.00	0.00	0.00	0.00
ENS	0.00	0.00	0.00	0.00	**1.00**	0.00	0.00	0.00	0.00	0.00
SVM-gauss	0.00	0.00	0.00	0.00	**0.99**	0.00	0.00	0.00	0.00	0.00
SVM-poly2	0.00	0.00	0.00	0.00	**0.97**	0.00	0.00	0.01	0.00	0.00
SVM-poly4	0.00	0.00	0.00	0.01	**0.96**	0.00	0.00	0.01	0.00	0.00
SVM-sigmoid	0.00	0.00	0.01	0.02	**0.94**	0.00	0.00	0.01	0.00	0.01
SVM-linear	0.00	0.01	0.05	0.04	**0.84**	0.00	0.01	0.04	0.00	0.02

Table 4: Evaluation of the target digit four (see Fig. 2) by individual models.

	0	1	2	3	4	5	6	7	8	9
RBF	0.06	0.08	0.14	0.08	**0.49**	-0.01	0.03	0.14	0.02	0.02
MLP	**0.96**	0.00	0.01	0.00	0.02	0.00	0.00	0.01	0.00	0.01
CNN	**0.89**	0.00	0.02	0.00	0.05	0.00	0.00	0.01	0.02	0.00
ENS	**0.96**	0.00	0.01	0.00	0.02	0.00	0.00	0.00	0.00	0.01
SVM-gauss	0.01	0.01	0.07	0.12	**0.50**	0.03	0.01	0.06	0.09	0.08
SVM-poly	**0.75**	0.00	0.03	0.01	0.09	0.00	0.01	0.04	0.03	0.04
SVM-poly4	**0.71**	0.01	0.04	0.01	0.11	0.02	0.02	0.04	0.02	0.02
SVM-sigmoid	**0.84**	0.00	0.02	0.03	0.03	0.02	0.01	0.01	0.00	0.03
SVM-linear	0.02	0.02	0.18	0.18	**0.26**	0.03	0.05	0.11	0.03	0.11

Table 5: Evaluation of adversarial digit four (from Fig. 2) by individual models.

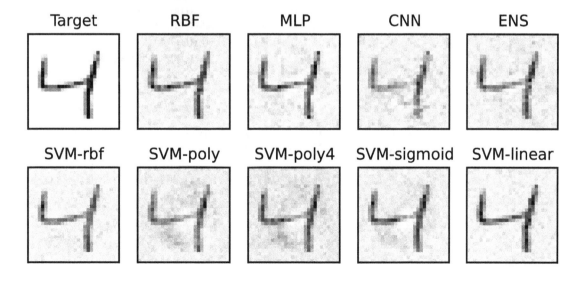

Figure 2: Best individuals evolved for individual models and digit four. The first 'Target' image is the digit from the training set, than follows adversarial examples evolved for individual models.

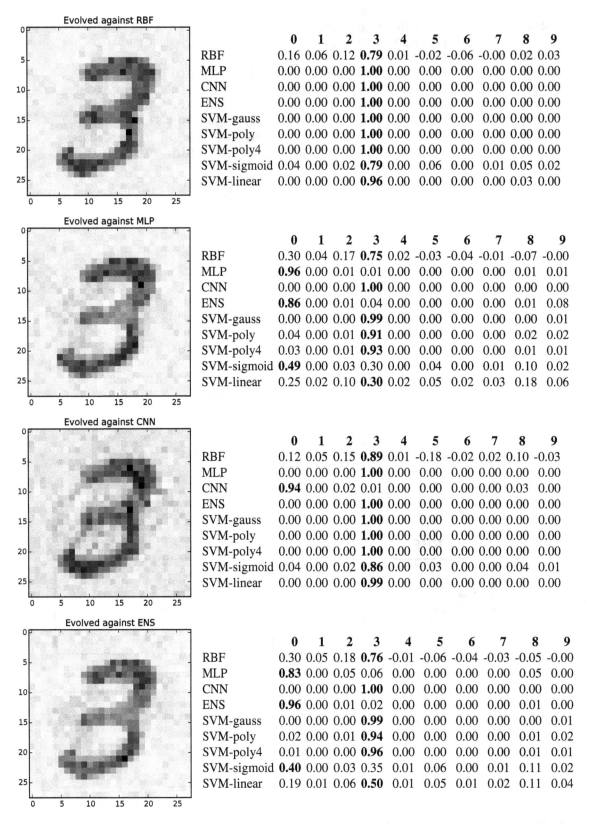

Evolved against RBF

	0	1	2	3	4	5	6	7	8	9
RBF	0.16	0.06	0.12	**0.79**	0.01	-0.02	-0.06	-0.00	0.02	0.03
MLP	0.00	0.00	0.00	**1.00**	0.00	0.00	0.00	0.00	0.00	0.00
CNN	0.00	0.00	0.00	**1.00**	0.00	0.00	0.00	0.00	0.00	0.00
ENS	0.00	0.00	0.00	**1.00**	0.00	0.00	0.00	0.00	0.00	0.00
SVM-gauss	0.00	0.00	0.00	**1.00**	0.00	0.00	0.00	0.00	0.00	0.00
SVM-poly	0.00	0.00	0.00	**1.00**	0.00	0.00	0.00	0.00	0.00	0.00
SVM-poly4	0.00	0.00	0.00	**1.00**	0.00	0.00	0.00	0.00	0.00	0.00
SVM-sigmoid	0.04	0.00	0.02	**0.79**	0.00	0.06	0.00	0.01	0.05	0.02
SVM-linear	0.00	0.00	0.00	**0.96**	0.00	0.00	0.00	0.00	0.03	0.00

Evolved against MLP

	0	1	2	3	4	5	6	7	8	9
RBF	0.30	0.04	0.17	**0.75**	0.02	-0.03	-0.04	-0.01	-0.07	-0.00
MLP	**0.96**	0.00	0.01	0.01	0.00	0.00	0.00	0.00	0.01	0.01
CNN	0.00	0.00	0.00	**1.00**	0.00	0.00	0.00	0.00	0.00	0.00
ENS	**0.86**	0.00	0.01	0.04	0.00	0.00	0.00	0.00	0.01	0.08
SVM-gauss	0.00	0.00	0.00	**0.99**	0.00	0.00	0.00	0.00	0.00	0.01
SVM-poly	0.04	0.00	0.01	**0.91**	0.00	0.00	0.00	0.00	0.02	0.02
SVM-poly4	0.03	0.00	0.01	**0.93**	0.00	0.00	0.00	0.00	0.01	0.01
SVM-sigmoid	**0.49**	0.00	0.03	0.30	0.00	0.04	0.00	0.01	0.10	0.02
SVM-linear	0.25	0.02	0.10	**0.30**	0.02	0.05	0.02	0.03	0.18	0.06

Evolved against CNN

	0	1	2	3	4	5	6	7	8	9
RBF	0.12	0.05	0.15	**0.89**	0.01	-0.18	-0.02	0.02	0.10	-0.03
MLP	0.00	0.00	0.00	**1.00**	0.00	0.00	0.00	0.00	0.00	0.00
CNN	**0.94**	0.00	0.02	0.01	0.00	0.00	0.00	0.00	0.03	0.00
ENS	0.00	0.00	0.00	**1.00**	0.00	0.00	0.00	0.00	0.00	0.00
SVM-gauss	0.00	0.00	0.00	**1.00**	0.00	0.00	0.00	0.00	0.00	0.00
SVM-poly	0.00	0.00	0.00	**1.00**	0.00	0.00	0.00	0.00	0.00	0.00
SVM-poly4	0.00	0.00	0.00	**1.00**	0.00	0.00	0.00	0.00	0.00	0.00
SVM-sigmoid	0.04	0.00	0.02	**0.86**	0.00	0.03	0.00	0.00	0.04	0.01
SVM-linear	0.00	0.00	0.00	**0.99**	0.00	0.00	0.00	0.00	0.00	0.00

Evolved against ENS

	0	1	2	3	4	5	6	7	8	9
RBF	0.30	0.05	0.18	**0.76**	-0.01	-0.06	-0.04	-0.03	-0.05	-0.00
MLP	**0.83**	0.00	0.05	0.06	0.00	0.00	0.00	0.00	0.05	0.00
CNN	0.00	0.00	0.00	**1.00**	0.00	0.00	0.00	0.00	0.00	0.00
ENS	**0.96**	0.00	0.01	0.02	0.00	0.00	0.00	0.00	0.01	0.00
SVM-gauss	0.00	0.00	0.00	**0.99**	0.00	0.00	0.00	0.00	0.00	0.01
SVM-poly	0.02	0.00	0.01	**0.94**	0.00	0.00	0.00	0.00	0.01	0.02
SVM-poly4	0.01	0.00	0.00	**0.96**	0.00	0.00	0.00	0.00	0.01	0.01
SVM-sigmoid	**0.40**	0.00	0.03	0.35	0.01	0.06	0.00	0.01	0.11	0.02
SVM-linear	0.19	0.01	0.06	**0.50**	0.01	0.05	0.01	0.02	0.11	0.04

Figure 3: Model outputs for individual adversarial examples.

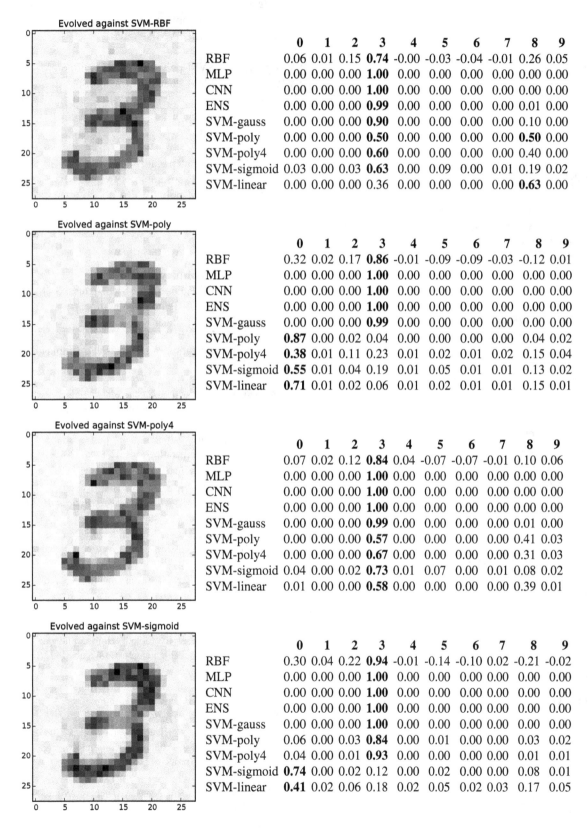

Figure 4: Model outputs for individual adversarial examples.

Evolved for	Also misclassified by
Example 1:	*digit 5*
MLP	—
ensemble	MLP
CNN	—
SVM-poly2	SVM-poly4, SMV-sigmoid, SVM-linear
SVM-sigmoid	—
Example 3:	*digit 4*
MLP	ensemble
ensemble	MLP
CNN	—
SVM-poly2	ensemble, MLP, SVM-gauss, SVM-poly4, SVM-sigmoid, SVM-linear
SVM-poly4	RBF, ensemble, MLP, SVM-gauss, SVM-poly4, SVM-sigmoid, SVM-linear
SVM-sigmoid	SVM-linear
Example 4:	*digit 1*
MLP	ensemble
ensemble	MLP
CNN	—
SVM-poly2	SVM-gauss, SVM-poly4, SVM-sigmoid, SVM-linear
SVM-sigmoid	SVM-linear
Example 5:	*digit 9*
MLP	ensemble
ensemble	MLP
CNN	—
SVM-poly2	ensemble, MLP, SVM-poly2 SVM-poly4, SVM-sigmoid, SVM-linear
SVM-poly4	all except CNN
SVM-sigmoid	SVM-linear
Example 6:	*digit 2*
MLP	—
ensemble	MLP
CNN	—
SVM-poly4	MLP, ensemble, SVM-poly2, SVM-sigmoid, SVM-linear
SVM-sigmoid	SVM-linear
Example 7:	*digit 1*
MLP	ensemble
ensemble	MLP
CNN	—
SVM-sigmoid	—

Table 6: Generalization of adversarial examples.

Evolved for	Also misclassified by
Example 8:	*digit 3*
MLP	ensemble, SVM-sigmoid
ensemble	MLP, SVM-sigmoid
CNN	—
SVM-poly2	SVM-poly4, SVM-sigmoid, SVM-linear
SVM-sigmoid	SVM-linear
Example 9:	*digit 1*
MLP	ensemble
ensemble	MLP
CNN	—
SVM-poly2	all except CNN
SVM-sigmoid	MLP, ensemble, SVM-gauss, SVM-poly2, SVM-poly4, SVM-linear
Example 10:	*digit 4*
MLP	ensemble
ensemble	MLP
CNN	—
SVM-poly2	SVM-poly4, SVM-linear
SVM-poly4	MLP, ensemble, SVM-gauss, SVM-poly2, SVM-sigmoid, SVM-linear
SVM-sigmoid	SVM-linear

Table 7: Generalization of adversarial examples.

References

[1] François Chollet. Keras. https://github.com/fchollet/keras, 2015.

[2] C. Cortes and V. Vapnik. Support-vector networks. *Machine Learning*, 20(3):273–297, 1995.

[3] F. Girosi, M. Jones, and T. Poggio. Regularization theory and Neural Networks architectures. *Neural Computation*, 2:219–269, 7 1995.

[4] Ian J. Goodfellow, Jonathon Shlens, and Christian Szegedy. Explaining and harnessing adversarial examples, 2014. arXiv:1412.6572.

[5] Yoshua Bengio Ian Goodfellow and Aaron Courville. Deep learning. Book in preparation for MIT Press, 2016.

[6] Yann LeCun and Corinna Cortes. The mnist database of handwritten digits, 2012.

[7] M. Mitchell. *An Introduction to Genetic Algorithms*. MIT Press, Cambridge, MA, 1996.

[8] J. Moody and C. Darken. Fast learning in networks of locally-tuned processing units. *Neural Computation*, 1:289–303, 1989.

[9] R. Neruda and P. Kudová. Learning methods for radial basis functions networks. *Future Generation Computer Systems*, 21:1131–1142, 2005.

[10] Anh Mai Nguyen, Jason Yosinski, and Jeff Clune. Deep neural networks are easily fooled: High confidence predictions for unrecognizable images. *CoRR*, abs/1412.1897, 2014.

[11] F. Pedregosa et al. Scikit-learn: Machine learning in Python. *Journal of Machine Learning Research*, 12:2825–2830, 2011.

[12] Christian Szegedy, Wojciech Zaremba, Ilya Sutskever, Joan Bruna, Dumitru Erhan, Ian Goodfellow, and Rob Fergus. Intriguing properties of neural networks, 2013. arXiv:1312.6199.

[13] V. N. Vapnik. *Statistical Learning Theory*. Wiley, New-York, 1998.

[14] J. P. Vert, K. Tsuda, and B. Scholkopf. A primer on kernel methods. *Kernel Methods in Computational Biology*, pages 35–70, 2004.

Workshop on Algorithmic and Structural Aspects of Complex Networks and Applications (WASACNA 2016)

The network science is an interdisciplinary, very active research area that blends rigorous theory and experiments in analyzing structure and behavior of real-world complex networks. Computer simulations are often an inseparable part of such research. Thus, the design, implementation and evaluation of efficient or advisable algorithms play its important role in the network science.

The Workshop on Algorithmic and Structural Aspects of Complex Networks and Applications (WASACNA 2016) follows a similar event from two years ago, WAACNA 2014, held in Jasná and collocated with ITAT 2014. The objectives of this year's workshop are to provide a forum on current trends of the mentioned research and present contributions directly connected to applications addressing real-world problems. Besides well-established topics (e.g. the utilization of networks in transportation, the community detection in complex networks), this year's contributions also include emerging areas, such as the analysis of eye-tracking data via networks, network application in genealogy or medicine.

All submissions were evaluated according to their originality, quality, and relevance with respect to the main research topic of the workshop. Each submission was reviewed by at least two reviewers. Thereafter, 5 regular papers were accepted by Program Committee members out of 8 contributions. Apart from the regular contributed talks, the workshop included the invited presentation by Ľuboš Buzna. All regular papers and also the extended abstract of the invited presentation are included in the proceedings of the workshop. Some submissions which have not been chosen as regular papers are published separately as abstracts.

The Program Committee members are grateful to all the authors who submitted their papers for consideration and to all additional reviewers who assisted the Program Committee in the evaluation process. The committee wish to thank also the ITAT Program Committee chair Broňa Brejová and all the members of the Organizing Committee. The conference management system EasyChair was used to handle the submissions and to assist with the management of referee reports during the evaluation process.

Martin Nehéz and Marek Lelovský
Slovak University of Technology in Bratislava, Slovak Republic
Workshop organizers

Program Committee

Naďa Krivoňáková, Slovak University of Technology in Bratislava
Marek Lelovský, Slovak University of Technology in Bratislava
Martin Nehéz (chair), Slovak University of Technology in Bratislava
Soňa Pavlíková, Slovak University of Technology in Bratislava
Imrich Vrťo, Slovak Academy of Sciences

ITAT 2016 Proceedings, pp. 197–199
ISBN 978-1537016740, © 2016 Ľ. Buzna

Equitable Distribution of Scarce Resources in Transportation Networks (Invited Talk)

Ľuboš Buzna[1,2]

[1] Faculty of Management Science and Informatics, Department of Mathematical Methods and Operations Research,
University of Žilina, Univerzitná 8215/1, 010 26 Žilina, Slovakia
Lubos.Buzna@fri.uniza.sk,
home page: http:frdsa.uniza.sk/~buzna
[2] ERA Chair in Intelligent Transport Systems, University Science Park,
University of Žilina, Univerzitná 8215/1, 010 26 Žilina, Slovakia
home page: http://www.erachair.uniza.sk/

1 Introduction

Problem of fair allocation of scarce resources appears in many applications on networks. The basic dilemma is between how much of importance to attribute to individual outcomes and to what extent to prioritize the value of the aggregate outcome. High values of the aggregate outcome are often associated with situations when some individual actors receive no or very little allocation. Conversely, equitable distributions may lead to very low aggregate outcome and thus very low efficiency of the system. In this contribution, we describe the basic optimization framework, alpha-fairness [1], that allow for trading off the degree of equality for the overall efficiency of the system by capturing the utilities of individual actors by the utility function:

$$U_j(f_j, \alpha) = \begin{cases} \frac{f_j^{1-\alpha}}{1-\alpha} & \text{for } \alpha \geq 0,\ \alpha \neq 1 \\ \log(f_j) & \text{for } \alpha = 1, \end{cases} \quad (1)$$

where $j = 1, \ldots, R$ is the group of actors and f_j is an allocation assigned to the actor j. Then, the aggregate utility $U(\alpha) = \sum_{j=1}^{R} U_j(f_j, \alpha)$ is maximized under the constraints that allocations to all actors are feasible. Value $\alpha \geq 0$ is a parameter. When $\alpha = 0$, we maximize the aggregate utility, obtaining solution known in the literature as utilitarian solution, system optimum or in the context of flow problems it is known as maximum flow. If $\alpha \to \infty$ we obtain equitable solution, known as max-min fairness. Here, the allocation to the actors with the minimum allocation is maximized first, and once these "poor" actors receive the largest possible allocation, the process repeats iteratively for the next more well-off actors. For the intermediate values of α we obtain trade-off solutions. Among them, probably the most prominent is the proportionally fair solution [1] obtained for $\alpha = 1$. This framework can be easily applied in environments where all the limitations can be expressed by the set of linear equalities and convex inequalities. Thus, in cases when the convex optimization can be utilized as a basic solving technique. We illustrate the broad applicability of alpha-fairness by briefly introducing three applications.

2 Application 1: Resilience of Natural Gas Networks During Conflicts, Crises and Disruptions

Human conflict, geopolitical crises, and natural disasters can turn large parts of energy distribution networks offline. Europe's current gas supply network is historically largely dependent on deliveries from Russia and North Africa, creating vulnerabilities to social and political instabilities. During crises, less delivery means greater congestion, as the pipeline network is used in ways it has not been designed for. Thus, an approach that can distribute limited capacities among affected countries and cities is needed. Combining three spatial data layers (see Figure 1), gas import and gas export data with a proportionally fair congestion control flow model we created a model of the European gas pipeline network and we analysed large set of crises scenarios [2].

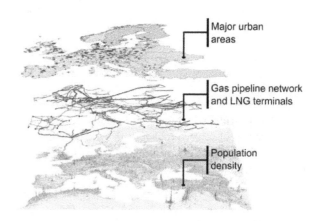

Figure 1: Spatial data involved in the analysis: population density (source: Landscan 2012); gas pipeline network (source: Platts 2011) and major urban areas (sources: European Environment Agency and Natural Earth) [2].

3 Application 2: Design of Public Service Systems

This application is motivated by problems faced by public authorities when locating facilities, such as schools, branch offices and ambulance, police or fire stations to serve spatially distributed population. These systems are typically operated from public money and they should account for equitable access of customers to services (see Figure 2).

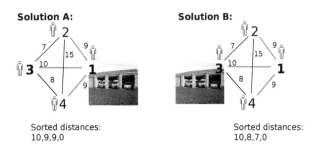

Figure 2: Schematic illustrating a road network connecting four customers that are supposed to be served by one facility that is to be located in one of the network nodes. Customers access the facility over the shortest paths. Location of the facility in node 1 results in the following descendingly sorted vector of distances between customers and the closet located facility $s_1 = (10, 9, 9, 0)$ while locating the facility in node 3 results in $s_2 = (10, 8, 7, 0)$. Solution s_2 is lexicographically smaller (it has smaller value of the first non equal element) than s_1 and thus it is more favourable [3].

This problem can be formulated as discrete location problem. We explain how the concept of max-min fairness generalizes in a discrete space to the lexicographic minmax concept. Previous approaches to the lexicographic minimax facility location problem, result in a specific form of the mathematical model that is supposed to be solved by a general purpose solver. This limits the size of solvable problems to approximately 900 customers and 900 candidate facility locations. Building on the concept of unique classes of distances, we proposed approximation algorithm providing high quality equitable solutions for large instances of solved problems [3]. We used the resulting algorithm to perform extensive study using the well-known benchmarks and two new large benchmarks derived from the real-world data.

4 Application 3: Coordination of EVs Charging in the Distribution Networks

With the possible uptake of electric vehicles in the near future, we are likely to observe overloading in the local distribution networks more frequently. Such development suggests that a congestion management protocol will be a crucial component of the future technological innovations in low voltage networks. An important property of a suitable network capacity management protocol is to balance the network efficiency and fairness requirements.

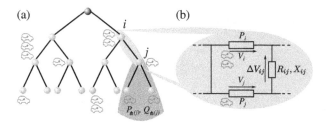

Figure 3: (a) We analyse tree-like distribution network while modelling each network edge as the circuit shown in panel (b). Electric vehicles choose a charging node with uniform probability, and plug-in to the node until fully charged, as illustrated by the electric vehicle icons on the network. Network edge (i, j) has impedance $Z_{ij} = R_{ij} + iX_{ij}$. Vehicles consume real power only, but network edges have both active (real) and reactive (imaginary) power losses [4].

We explored the onset of congestion by analysing the critical arrival rate, i.e. the largest possible vehicle arrival rate that can still be fully satisfied by the network for two basic control strategies: the proportional fairness and the maximum flow [4]. By numerical simulations on realistic networks (see Figure 3) we showed that proportional fairness leads not only to more equitable distribution of power allocations, but it can also serve slightly larger arrival rate of vehicles. For the simplified setup, where the power allocations are dependent on the occupation of network nodes, but they are independent of the exact number of vehicles, we validated the numerical results, by analysing the critical arrival rate on a network with two edges, where the optimal power allocations can be calculated analytically.

Acknowledgement

This lecture was supported by the research grants VEGA 1/0463/16 "Economically efficient charging infrastructure deployment for electric vehicles in smart cities and communities", APVV-15-0179 "Reliability of emergency systems on infrastructure with uncertain functionality of critical elements" and it was facilitated by the FP 7 project ERAdiate [621386]"Enhancing Research and innovation dimensions of the University of Zilina in Intelligent Transport Systems".

References

[1] Luss, H.: Equitable Resources Allocation: Models, Algorithms and Applications. John Wiley & Sons, New York, NY, USA, (2012)

[2] Carvalho, R., Buzna, Ľ., Bono, F., Masera, M., Arrowsmith, D. K., Helbing, D.: Resilience of Natural Gas Networks during Conflicts, Crises and Disruptions. PLoS ONE **9**(3), (2014), e90265

[3] Buzna, L., Koháni, M., Janáček: An Approximation Algorithm for the Facility Location Problem with Lexicographic Minimax Objective, Journal of Applied Mathematics. **2014** (2014) 562373

[4] Carvalho, R., Buzna, Ľ., Gibbens, R., Kelly, F.: Critical behaviour in charging of electric vehicles. New J. Phys. **17**, (2015) 095001.

ITAT 2016 Proceedings, pp. 200–205
ISBN 978-1537016740, © 2016 J. Coroničová Hurajová, T. Madaras

Revising the Newman-Girvan algorithm

Jana Coroničová Hurajová[1]* Tomáš Madaras[2]

[1] The Faculty of Business Economics with seat in Košice,
The University of Economics in Bratislava,
Tajovského 13, 041 30 Košice, Slovakia
jana.coronicova.hurajova@euke.sk

[2] The Faculty of Sciences,
P.J. Šafárik University in Košice,
Jesenná 5, 040 01 Košice, Slovakia,
tomas.madaras@upjs.sk
WWW home page: umv.science.upjs.sk

Abstract: One of the common approaches for the community detection in complex networks is the Girvan-Newman algorithm [5] which is based on repeated deletion of edges having the maximum edge betweenness centrality. Although widely used, it may result in different dendrograms of hierarchies of communities if there are several edges eligible for removal (see [6]) thus leaving an ambiguous formation of network subgroups. We will present possible ways to overcome these issues using, instead of edge betweenness computation for single edges, the group edge betweenness for subsets of edges to be subjects of removal.

1 Introduction

One of fundamental analyses performed in the exploration of complex networks concerns the detection of their community structure, which means to find, within a graph representing the network, certain clusters of vertices which are, at one side, sparsely interconnected and, on the other side, they have dense in-cluster links by many edges. The vertices within a cluster show a kind of similarities and form functionally compact units. As there is no general definition of cluster, there are many ways to obtain collections of network communities; a comprehensive overview of contemporary state-of-art in this area can be found in [3].

Among the approaches that determine the graph communities by breaking it into smaller parts, an important role plays the Girvan-Newman algorithm described first in [5]. It is based on successive deletion of edges which have the maximum *edge betweenness centrality* which is the quantity measuring the frequency of appearance of an edge on geodesic paths in a graph. Formally, it is defined as the sum $B(e) = \sum\limits_{u,v \in V(G)} \dfrac{\sigma_{u,v}(e)}{\sigma_{u,v}}$ where $\sigma_{u,v}$ is the number of shortest $u - v$-paths and $\sigma_{u,v}(e)$ is the number of shortest $u - v$-paths which contain the edge e. Interpreting

the edge betweenness as an amount of information flow being propagated through a link between actors of a complex network (and assuming that the information exchange takes place mainly on shortest paths), one may argue that distinct communities within a network are mutually connected (and, hence, communicating) with relatively few edges whose edge betweenness is higher than of those ones between the actors of the same community. When deleting those edges, the network tends to simplify, eventually breaking into smaller subnetworks (note, however, that after each deletion, edge betweenness centralities of the resulting network shall be recalculated again). Thus, we obtain a sequence of graphs starting from the original one and ending with an edgeless graph, along with the sequence of partitions the vertex set (the initial partition is the whole set, the final one consists of isolated vertices); when two consecutive graphs differ in their connected components, we record the splitting (refining) of the partition of the predecessing graph. In this way, the sequence of partitions forms a dendrogram showing the hierarchy of communities within the graph (the choice of the appropriate level describing, in the best way, the community structure of the graph, is a matter of external decision and does not follow from algorithm).

Despite the elegancy of Girvan and Newman approach and the popularity of their algorithm, an attention recently turns to other methods, mainly due to the fact that they are quicker (the Girvan-Newman algorithm has, in general, the complexity $O(m^2 \cdot n)$, thus can be effectively used on graphs up to $n \sim 10000$, see [3]). Furthermore, it seems that many implementations of community detection algorithms which are based on recursive edge deletion do not make difference when equivalent edges (for example, with the same edge betweenness) are considered for deletion. This issue was adressed in [6] where it was demonstrated how the random deletion of different edges with the same maximum edge betweenness centrality results in different hierarchies of partitions, when used on the wheel graph W_6. A possible obvious suggestion to remove all such edges at once (as discussed, for example, in [1] in the connection with possible speeding up the

*Research supported by the project for young teachers, researchers and PhD. students No. I-16-104-00

original Girvan-Newman algorithm) would, however, individualize all the vertices (thus producing no reasonable hierarchy) – even at the very beginning of the process – of edge transitive graphs, and, more generally, of so called edge betweenness-uniform graphs (that is, the graphs whose edges have the same value of edge betweenness centrality). Such graphs are not so rare: in [4], it was shown that each strongly regular graph (that is, an n-vertex k-regular graph with the property that any pair of its adjacent vertices has λ common neighbours, and any pair of its nonadjacent vertices has μ common neighbours, for certain n, k, λ, μ) is edge betweenness-uniform; since it is also known that, for particular n, k, λ, μ, the number of nonisomorphic strongly regular graphs is at least exponential in terms of number of vertices (see [2]). We tested all edge betweenness-uniform graphs on 3–10 vertices (their list was published first in [6]) for communities using the procedures FindGraphCommunities[...,Method -> "Centrality"] (to obtain the list of sets of vertices forming communities) and CommunityGraphPlot[...] (to visualize communities within a graph) of Wolfram Mathematica, or using the procedure IGCommunitiesEdgeBetweenness[...] from the Wolfram Mathematica third-party package IgraphM (see [7]). The results for graphs on 3–9 vertices are shown in Figure 1 (the brown clusters correspond to graph communities based on partitioning by FindGraphCommunities[...,Method -> "Centrality"] procedure, the yellow clusters to the ones based on IGCommunitiesEdgeBetweenness procedure); one can see that, on some graphs, the community structure is different although the underlying algorithm should be the same (the most remarkable difference can be observed on the blue-highlighted 9-vertex graph of Figure 2 obtained from two 6-cycles by identifying the corresponding vertices of their maximum independent sets). Also, for many of these graphs it seems that they have no community structure (as both built-in and IGraphM community finding procedure aggregate all vertices into a single cluster); hence, when being processed by algorithm of [1], one would have only two possibilities for communities: either the whole vertex set or the partition consisting of singletons (and the more reasonable choice would be the single community). Nevertheless, our results show that there are also edge betweenness-uniform graphs for which both procedures (as well as other community detection methods, like modularity maximization) return non-trivial community structure which, however, cannot be obtained by the algorithm of [1].

2 The revised Newman-Girvan algorithm

In order to overcome – at least, on theoretical basis – the problem to decide which edge has to be removed if there are several ones with the same maximal edge betweenness, we will utilize the concept of *group edge betweenness* which is defined, for a subset A of edge set of a graph

G, as the sum $B(A) = \sum\limits_{u,v \in V(G)} \dfrac{\sigma_{u,v}(A)}{\sigma_{u,v}}$ where $\sigma_{u,v}(A)$ is the number of shortest $u - v$-paths which contain at least one edge from A. Note that if $|A| = 1$ then we obtain the standard edge betweenness as in [5]. The revised Newman-Girvan algorithm on a graph G then proceeds as follows: starting with $G_0 = G$, a sequence $\{G_i\}_{i=0}^k$ (where G_k is edgeless graph) is constructed in such a way that, if there appears, during the computation of edge betweennesses of G_i, a set M_i of $m_i \geq 2$ edges all of them having the maximum betweenness among the edges of G_i, then determine the smallest ℓ_i such that there is unique subset $\widehat{E}_i \subseteq M_i$ of ℓ_i edges with the property that the group edge betweenness centrality of $\widehat{E}_i$ is the maximal among all subsets of M_i consisting of ℓ_i edges (note that $\ell_i \leq m_i$, thus it is well defined). The graph G_{i+1} is then obtained from G_i by removing all edges from $\widehat{E}_i$; if G_{i+1} has more components than G_i, the vertex sets of its components forms the new level in hierarchy of partitions of $V(G)$. The pseudocode for this process is given in Algorithm 1; the used notation follows the common standards of graph theory, the particular specialized symbols are $b_0(G)$ (the zeroth Betti number of G, that is, the number of its connected components), $\langle V_i \rangle$ (the subgraph of G induced by the set $V_i \subseteq V(G)$) and $G \setminus E_i$ (the subgraph of G obtained by deleting all edges of E_i).

We have implemented the key elements of the algorithm in Wolfram Mathematica 10 along with the algorithm for edge group betweenness calculation. Since the latter algorithm is – according to our knowledge – not yet known to have effective implementation, we used the straightforward approach which determines, for each pair u, v of vertices of a graph G, all shortest $u - v$-paths (in Wolfram language, this can be done by calling procedure FindPath[G, u, v, GraphDistance[G, u, v], All] and then checks how many of them passes through an edge of the given edge group. Our implementation of the edge group betweenness algorithm – when being called on a single edge – is also useful as an alternative for built-in Wolfram Mathematica procedure EdgeBetweennessCentrality[..] which returns numerical approximations (although with high precision) of edge betweenness centralities whereas our version returns exact values in the form of fractions.

Let us note that our approach may lead, in particular cases, to much worse performance of the corresponding algorithm when compared with the original Newman-Girvan algorithm; this is caused mainly by large number of subsets of edges with the same maximum edge betweenness which have to be checked to select the unique one with the maximum group edge betweenness. This is, however, the trade-off for getting rid of uncertainties in edge removal.

To show the difference of behaviour of our algorithm in comparison with the original one or the one of [1], consider the graph of Figure 3. It contains

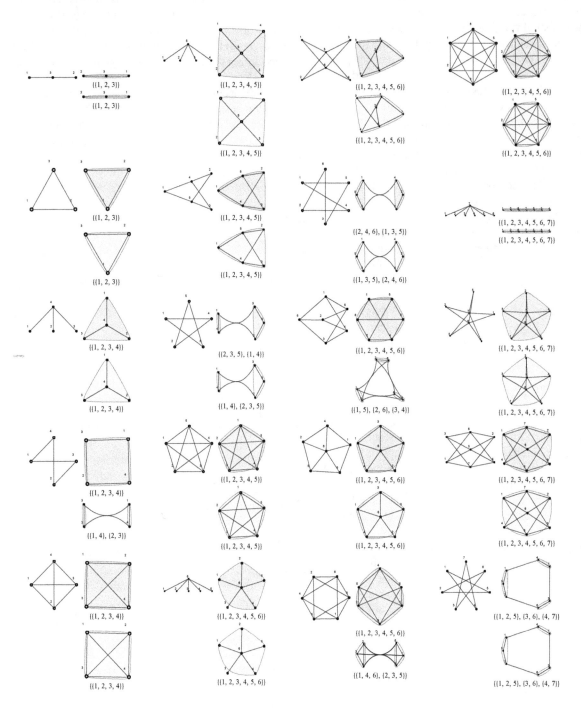

Figure 1: The communities in edge betweenness-uniform graphs detected on basis of edge betweenness

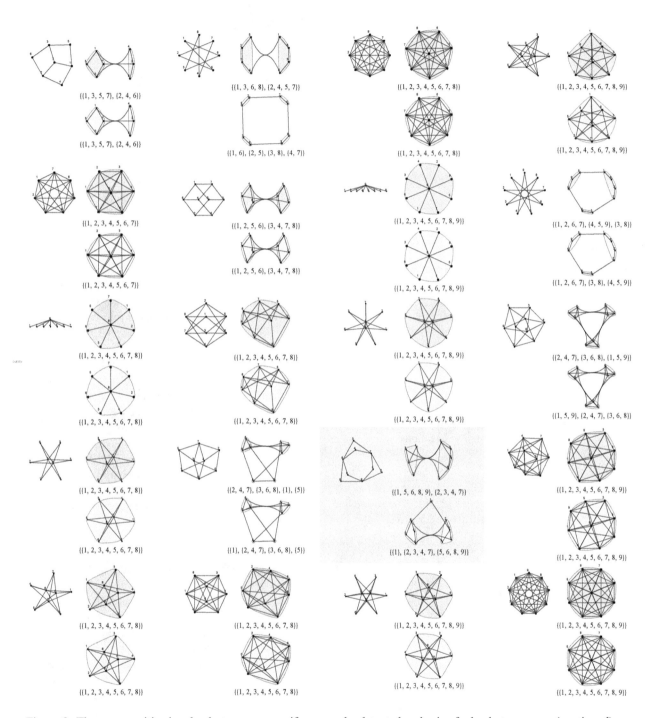

Figure 2: The communities in edge betweenness-uniform graphs detected on basis of edge betweenness (continued)

```
RevisedNewmanGirvan(G)
```
Data: a graph G
Result: the hierarchy of nested partitions of $V(G)$
$G_0 := G$;
$P_0 := \{V(G)\}$;
$i := 0$;
$c := 0$;
while $E(G_i) \neq \emptyset$ **do**
$\quad S_i := \{B(e) : e \in E(G_i)\}$;
$\quad mx := \max S_i$;
$\quad M_i := \{e \in E(G_i) : B(e) = mx\}$;
$\quad \widehat{E}_i := M_i$;
$\quad \ell_i := 1$;
$\quad$ **while** $|\widehat{E}_i| > 1$ **do**
$\quad\quad \ell_i := \ell_i + 1$;
$\quad\quad U_{\ell_i} := \{B(A) : A \subset M_i \wedge |A| = \ell_i\}$;
$\quad\quad gmx := \max U_{\ell_i}$;
$\quad\quad \widehat{E}_i := \{A \subset M_i : |A| = \ell_i \wedge B(A) = gmx\}$;
$\quad$ **end**
$\quad G_{i+1} := G_i \setminus \widehat{E}_i$;
$\quad$ **if** $b_0(G_{i+1}) > b_0(G_i)$ **then**
$\quad\quad c := c + 1$;
$\quad\quad P_c := \{V_1, \dots, V_{r_c} :$
$\quad\quad \langle V_1 \rangle, \dots, \langle V_{r_c} \rangle$ are connected components of $G_{i+1}\}$
$\quad\quad$;
$\quad$ **end**
$\quad i := i + 1$;
end
return $\{P_i : i = 0, \dots, c\}$

Algorithm 1: The group edge-centrality based Newman-Girvan algorithm for community detection.

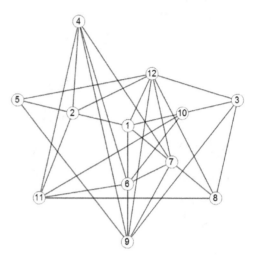

Figure 3: The example of a graph where revised Newman-Girvan algorithm behaves differently than the original one or the one of [1]

five edges with the maximum edge betweenness, namely $\{8,11\}, \{6,9\}, \{3,10\}, \{3,9\}$ and $\{2,11\}$. Now, these five edges form ten 2-element subsets with group edge betweenness centralities $\frac{52}{3}, \frac{52}{3}, \frac{52}{3}, \frac{49}{3}, \frac{52}{3}, \frac{49}{3}, \frac{52}{3}, 16, \frac{52}{3}, \frac{52}{3}$, and ten 3-element subsets with group edge betweenness centralities $26, 25, 25, \frac{74}{3}, 25, 25, \frac{71}{3}, 26, 25, \frac{74}{3}$; we see that, among these subsets, the uniqueness with respect to the maximum group edge betweenness is not preserved. But, for five 4-element subsets of $\{\{8,11\}, \{6,9\}, \{3,10\}, \{3,9\}, \{2,11\}\}$, the group edge betweenness centralities are $\frac{97}{3}, \frac{101}{3}, \frac{98}{3}, \frac{97}{3}, \frac{97}{3}$, thus there is unique 4-element subset – the set $\{\{8,11\}, \{6,9\}, \{3,10\}, \{2,11\}\}$ – reaching the maximum value $\frac{101}{3}$. Hence, the edges of this 4-element set are removed, and the sequence of single edge removals continues with $\{1,12\}, \{6,7\}, \{4,9\}$ after which there are detected two edges ($\{4,7\}$ and $\{1,7\}$) with the same highest edge betweenness. After they are removed, the edge removal continues with $\{2,12\}$ and then with $\{2,5\}$ where the graph splits, for the first time, into two components with vertex sets $\{1,2,4,6,10,11\}$ and $\{3,5,7,8,9,12\}$.

On the other hand, when the algorithm of

[1] is used on the same graph, first, five edges $\{8,11\}, \{6,9\}, \{3,10\}, \{3,9\}, \{2,11\}$ are removed at once, followed by sequential removals of $\{3,12\}, \{7,8\}$ and $\{8,12\}$ where the graph splits into two components, one of them being the single edge $\{3,8\}$. Therefore, we see that the hierarchies of nested partitions produced by our algorithm and the one of [1] differ already at the highest level. In addition, a particular run of the original Newman-Girvan algorithm (using random selection of an edge from the set of several edges with the same maximum edge betweenness) on this graph may produce yet another hierarchy: if the edge $\{3,9\}$ is removed first, then the edges $\{3,12\}, \{3,8\}$ and $\{3,10\}$ are removed sequentially, thereby separating the single vertex 3 from the rest of the graph.

Note also that the existence of unique set of edges which have to be removed depends heavily also on the edge automorphism group Aut^* of a graph. It is easy to see that, for any edge automorphism φ of a graph G and any $A \subset E(G)$, $B(A) = B(\varphi(A))$ holds; consequently, if $Aut^*(G)$ is nontrivial and the edge automorphisms do not fix A, then there are several different subsets of edges with the same group edge betweenness as A. Thus the uniqueness of the edge subset of particular size with the maximal group edge betweenness cannot be guaranteed for graphs possessing a lot of symmetries. Some particularly bad examples occur among edge betweenness uniform graphs – in the wheel W_6, among all sets of edges of cardinality $i \leq 9$, there are always at least two distinct sets whose group edge betweenness is maximal among all i-sets, hence, the unique maximum group edge betweenness set coincides with the whole edge set of W_6, and the revised Newman-Girvan algorithm breaks the vertex set of W_6 into six singletons.

Unfortunately, similar issues may appear also in real networks. We illustrate this on the example of the network of Zachary karate club [8] shown at Figure 4.

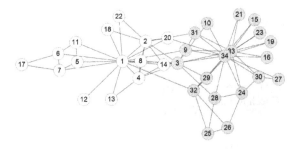

Figure 4: The Zachary karate club network

The standard Newman-Girvan algorithm removes the edges with the maximum edge betweenness in the order $\{32,1\}, \{3,1\}, \{9,1\}, \{34,14\}, \{34,20\}, \{33,3\}, \{31,2\}, \{3,2\}, \{4,3\}$ after which two edges with the same maximum edge betweenness are detected, namely $\{14,3\}$ and $\{8,3\}$. After their simultaneous removal, the graph splits into two components and the sequence of removed edges continues with $\{34,10\}, \{34,28\}, \{10,3\}$ after which again two maximum betweenness edges, $\{7,1\}$ and $\{6,1\}$, are detected; their removal yields another pair of edges with the same maximum edge betweenness, namely $\{1,5\}$ and $\{1,11\}$. The sequence of single edge removals continues with edges $\{34,32\}, \{33,32\}, \{34,29\}, \{26,24\}, \{28,24\}, \{9,3\}$ followed by simultaneous removal of $\{34,27\}$ and $\{1,12\}$, then by single removals of $\{30,27\}, \{13,1\}, \{13,4\}$. Now here appears the situation when the graph contains even 10 edges of maximum edge betweenness, namely $\{34,23\}, \{34,21\}, \{34,19\}, \{34,16\}, \{34,15\}, \{33,23\}, \{33,21\}, \{33,19\}, \{33,16\}$ and $\{33,15\}$ (which are all contained in the same star-like connected component). However, the computation of group edge betweenness for subsets of this edge set reveals that the whole set has to be removed as there are always many proper subsets of smaller sizes having the same maximum group edge betweenness (this is most likely also caused by symmetries of that particular connected component). Hence, for the network of Zachary karate club, the revised algorithm just confirms that the order of edge removal as obtained by the version of Newman-Girvan algorithm from [1] is probably optimal; nevertheless, it would be interesting to find an example of real network where the revised algorithm would lead to different sequence of removed edges, or even a different hierarchy of graph communities.

An area where the revised Newman-Girvan algorithm would apply concerns the looking for "null models", that is, the graphs without community structure (see [3], pages 90–91). Based on the above considerations, we propose to take, for such graphs, the ones which are edge betweenness-uniform, have trivial edge automorphism group and, moreover, for each i which is less than the number of edges, there are always at least two sets consisting of i edges such that their group edge betweenness

is the maximal among all i-subsets. For these graphs, the hierarchy of communities produced by our revised algorithm collapses into singletons although their trivial automorphism group should prevent easy replication of subsets of edges with high group edge betweenness. At the moment, no infinite family of such graphs is known; nevertheless, we believe that the candidate graphs might be found among strongly regular graphs, where are known examples with trivial vertex automorphism group, and, possibly, also ones having trivial edge automorphism group.

References

[1] Despalatović, L., Vojković, T., Vukičević: Community structure in networks: Girvan-Newman algorithm improvement. MIPRO, Opatija, Croatia, May 26-30, 2014, 997–1002.

[2] Fon-der-Flaass, D.G.: New prolific constructions of strongly regular graphs. Adv. Geom. **2** (2002) 301—306

[3] Fortunato, S.: Community detection in graphs. arXiv:0906.0612 [physics.soc-ph]

[4] Gago, S., Coroničová Hurajová, J., Madaras, T.: Betweenness centrality in graphs. In: Quantitative graph theory: mathematical foundations and applications (Dehmer, M. and Emmert-Streib, F., eds.), CRC Press, 2015

[5] Girvan, M., Newman, M. E. J.: Community structure in social and biological networks. Proc. Natl. Acad. Sci. USA **99** (2002) 7821—7826

[6] Coroničová Hurajová, J., Madaras, T.: The edge betweenness centrality – theory and applications. Journal of innovations and applied statistics **5 (1)** (2015) 20–29

[7] https://github.com/szhorvat/IGraphM

[8] Zachary, W. W.: An information flow model for conflict and fission in small groups. Journal of Anthropological Research **33 (4)** (1977) 452—473

ITAT 2016 Proceedings, pp. 206–211
ISBN 978-1537016740, © 2016 J. Doležalová, S. Popelka

The use of simple graphs and cliques
for analysis of cartographic eye-tracking data

Jitka Dolezalova

Department of Geoinformatics, Palacký University Olomouc
17. listopadu 50, Olomouc, Czech Republic

Stanislav Popelka

Department of Geoinformatics, Palacký University Olomouc

Abstract. *Usability testing with the use of eye-tracking technology is now emerging. Measuring point of gaze is employed in different fields of research and helps to solve real world problems. One of these areas is cartography. In addition to traditional methods of analyses of eye-tracking data, as attention maps and gaze plots are, a more sophisticated method exists – scanpath comparison.*

Many different approaches to scanpath comparison exist. One of the most frequently used is String Edit Distance, where the gaze trajectories are replaced by the sequences of visited Areas of Interest. In cartography, these Areas of Interest could be marked around specific parts of maps – map composition elements. We have developed an online tool called ScanGraph which output is visualized as a simple graph, and similar groups of sequences are displayed as cliques of this graph. ScanGraph uses modified Levenshtein distance and Needleman-Wunsch algorithms for calculating the similarities between sequences of visited Areas of Interest. Cliques in the graph are sought with the use of the exhaustive algorithm.

ScanGraph functionality is presented in the example of cartographic study dealing with uncertainty in maps. Stimuli in the study contained several visualization methods of uncertainty and eye-tracking experiment with 40 respondents was performed. With the use of ScanGraph, groups of participants with similar strategy were identified.

1 Introduction

Eye-tracking is one of the most precise and objective methods of usability studies. The term usability is defined by ISO 9241-11 as "the effectiveness, efficiency, and satisfaction, with which specified users achieve specified goals in particular environments". To be able to derive qualitative or quantitative measures of the user attitudes to the product, many evaluation methods exists: focus group studies, interview, direct observation, think-aloud protocol, screen capturing and eye-tracking [1]. Each of the methods for studying usability has its advantages and disadvantages. Methods of focus groups and interview use a direct contact with the user. They are based on a targeted questioning and recording of discussions and reactions of individuals or groups of respondents to a particular product. A very important method of usability assessment is Think-aloud. Participants verbally describe the process of particular task solving and also their feelings [2]. In the above methods, the problem is the fact that participants are not aware of all processes, and not all processes can be simply expressed in words. The information that respondents communicate during an interview or fill in the questionnaire may not correspond to reality, although respondents believe their answers [3]. Cognitive load of the respondent during a think-aloud method can be so large that it affects his interaction with the map. In contrast, during eye-movement recording, the cognitive load associated with self-reporting is eliminated. Eye-tracking can be considered an objective method because recording eye movements does not rely on

self-reporting [4]. A combination of different methods is used very often (i.e. [5] or [6]).

Hammoud and Mulligan [7] state that the beginning of the scientific study of eye movement begun at the end of the 19th century, when many methods for measuring eye movements were developed. Some of these methods were based on a mechanical transmission of the position information of the eye [8], others use study of photographs [9]. Most of the modern eye-trackers work on the principle of non-contact recording of the pupil and corneal reflection [10]. Eye-tracker is usually located below the monitor displaying studied stimuli. This unit incorporates one or more infrared light that shines in the direction of the user. The apparatus also includes a camera that captures the user's eyes. The center of the pupil and the reflection of infrared light is found by image recognition. From the relative positions of these two points, the device calculates the direction of view (Point of Regard).

Eye-tracking is used in many areas. The most common are psychological studies, medicine, HCI (Human-Computer Interaction), marketing, usability studies and also cartography.

Although the eye-tracking was firstly used for the evaluation of maps and cartographic works in the late 50s of the 20th century [11], it is increasingly used in the last ten to fifteen years. The reason is the decreasing cost of equipment and the development of computer technology, which allows faster and more efficient analysis of the measured data. The eye-tracking in cartography can be used for evaluation of map portals [5], meteorological maps [12], for analysis of text labels on the map [13] or 3D visualization in cartography [14].

In most of the studies, measured data were evaluated with the use of statistical analysis of eye-tracking metrics. For visualization of the data mostly only basic visualization methods such as Scanpath or Heatmaps were used. In some cases, the most sophisticated method of analysis is needed.

The example of this sophisticated method is Scanpath Comparison. This method can be used in the situation when the similarity between different participants' strategy is investigated. The beginning of the interest about distinctive scanning pattern can be found in the study of Noton and Stark [15], who reported a qualitative similarity in eye-movements when people viewed line drawings on multiple occasions. The scanpath consists of sequences of alternating saccades and fixations that repeat themselves when a respondent is viewing stimuli. Scanpath comparison methods can be divided into six groups (String Edit Distance, ScanMatch, Sample-based measures, Linear distance, MultiMatch and Cross-recurrence quantification analysis). The comparison of these methods is described in [16]. One of the most frequently used methods is String Edit Distance, which is used to measure the dissimilarity of character strings. For the use of String Edit Distance, the grid or Areas of Interest (AOI) have to be marked in the stimulus. The gaze trajectory (scanpath) is then replaced by a character string representing the sequence of fixations with characters for AOIs they hit. Only 10 percent of the scanpath duration is taken up by the collective duration of saccadic eye-movements. Fixations took 90 percent of the total viewing period [17].

2   Methods

ScanGraph is a web application developed by authors of the paper. Its purpose is to analyse similarities between sequences of visited Areas of Interest from eye-tracking data. It is designed to load data directly from open-source application OGAMA [18], so no additional data preparation is needed. The motivation for the creation of the application was the lack of any other tool which will allow finding groups of participants with a similar strategy of stimuli observation based on the given degree of similarity. The interface of ScanGraph is displayed in Figure 1. The application is freely available at www.eyetracking.upol.cz/scangraph. More information about the use of the application is available in [19] and needed principles are described below.

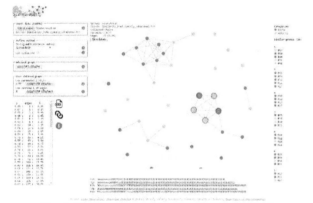

Fig. 1. The interface of the ScanGraph application.

Let $D: \Sigma^* \times \Sigma^* \rightarrow \mathbb{R}$ be a distance function measuring the distance between two given sequences (words) $a, b \in \Sigma^*$. We require D to have these properties:

$D(a, a) = 0$ (reflexivity)
$D(a, b) = D(b, a)$ (symmetry)
$D(a, b) + D(b, c) \geq D(a, c)$ (triangle inequality)

ScanGraph uses two distance functions based on a Levenshtein distance and Needleman-Wunsch algorithm.

Levenshtein distance is named after the Russian scientist Vladimir Levenshtein [20]. Levenshtein distance between two strings $a = a_1, a_2, ..., a_{|a|}$; $b = b_1, b_2, ..., b_{|b|}$ of the length $|a|$ and $|b|$ (let us denote $Lev(a, b)$) is the number of deletions, insertions, or substitutions needed to transform source string into target string. Hence, $Lev(a, b) = 0$ if and only if the strings are equal and $Lev(a, b) = \max\{|a|, |b|\}$ if and only if there is any correspondence between the strings. The value of Levenshtein distance is increasing with larger differences between the strings. The modified Levenshtein distance function $Lev'(a, b)$ used by the ScanGraph is defined by this equation:

$$Lev'(a, b) = 1 - \frac{Lev(a, b)}{\max\{|a|, |b|\}}. \tag{1}$$

The other used metric of sequence alignment is called Needleman-Wunsch algorithm [21] with its scoring system.

The Needleman-Wunsch algorithm (let us denote its value $NW(a, b)$) searches for concordant elements between two strings $a = a_1, a_2, ..., a_{|a|}$; $b = b_1, b_2, ..., b_{|b|}$ of the length $|a|$ and $|b|$. The basic scoring system used for our needs is given by Match reward equal to 1, Gap cost equal 0 and Mismatch penalty equal to -1. Hence, $NW(a, b) = \min\{|a|, |b|\}$, when a is a subset of b or b is a subset of a. The value of $NW(a, b)$ is increasing with the similarity between the strings.

The modified Needleman-Wunsch algorithms $NW'(a, b)$ used by the ScanGraph is defined by this equation:

$$NW'(a, b) = \frac{NW(a, b)}{\max\{|a|, |b|\}}. \tag{2}$$

The values of $Lev'(a, b), NW'(a, b) \in \langle 0, 1 \rangle$ express the degree of similarity. The higher the value, the greater similarity. The matrix $M = (m_{ij})$ formed by these values is constructed. The user sets a value, which represents the minimal desired degree of similarity. This value is called the parameter and is denoted as p. Hence, the adjacency matrix $A = (a_{ij})$ of the graph G is created from the matrix M according to this relation:

$$a_{ij} = \begin{cases} 1, \text{if } p \geq m_{ij} \\ 0, \text{otherwise}. \end{cases} \tag{3}$$

Groups of sequences with a degree of similarity higher or equal to the desired parameter are equivalent to cliques in the given graph G.

ScanGraph seeks the cliques as submatrices $S = (s_{ij})$ order m of the adjacency matrix A order n, $m \leq n$, where $s_{ij} = 1, \forall i, j \in 1, ..., m$, and there doesn't exist any matrix $S' \supset S$ with the same condition.

Maximal clique problem is NP- complete problem [22]. Hence, the algorithm doesn't run in a polynomial time. When the computing time is too long, the greedy heuristic is used.

3   Example case study

Analysis of recorded eye-tracking data using ScanGraph can be employed in every case, where it is appropriate to compare different groups of respondents. Despite the fact that ScanGraph is quite new, it was used for several case studies yet. Analysis of differences between cartographers and non-cartographers observing different map compositions was performed in [19]. Differences between males and females during searching for point symbol in a map were found in [23]. Snopková [24] analysed differences of map reading between people with normal vision and with colour-blind participants. Apparently, ScanGraph can also be used in other fields of research (not only cartography). Pulkrtová [25] used it in her psychological thesis dealing with the different perception of red colour by males and females. Hájková [26] used

ScanGraph in the study at Department of Physiotherapy, University Hospital Olomouc with patients after brain stroke. She compared the control group with two groups of patients with different types of stroke.

In this paper, possibilities of Scangraph will be presented on the example of cartographic study dealing with the uncertainty visualization of maps. Uncertainty is seen as vagueness, randomness of conditions or result of particular processes and phenomena. The concept of uncertainty is also quite often used to describe little certainty about a particular phenomenon in maps [27]. Many approaches and methods of uncertainty visualization have been developed based for example on Bertin's theory of graphic variables and combining both static and dynamic elements of visualization [28].

The case study uses data from master thesis [29]. In this thesis, sets of cartographic symbols for visualization of an uncertainty of point, lines and areas were created. Point symbols have been set up according to the study of [30]. These symbols were placed into maps, and these maps were used as stimuli for the eye-tracking experiment and online questionnaire. The aim of the thesis was to find which visualizations are the most comprehensible for the map reader. The experiment was conducted with 40 participants. Twenty of them were students of cartography, twenty of them were respondents with no education in cartography. In the thesis, eye-tracking metrics (Trial Duration, Gaze Length) and accuracy of answers were compared to all stimuli. Total of 27 maps with point symbols were used in the experiment. Thirteen of them were depicting the single phenomenon; eight were representing the combination of more phenomenon. The last six maps were showing the spatial and temporal uncertainty separately.

In the beginning, user observation of stimulus BK07 was analysed. In this case, the map contained 16 point symbols representing the possible occurrence of three animal species (wild boar, hare, and fox) with different level of uncertainty. The task was to find the most probable locality, where it is possible to found each animal. The legend for all three species was located on the right side of the stimulus. The left part contained an orthophoto map with point symbols. Areas of Interest were marked around the map field and each part of the legend (see Figure 2).

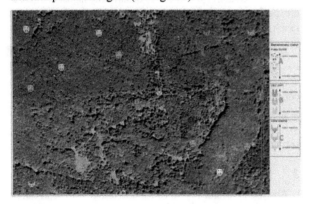

Fig. 2. Areas of Interest marked in the stimulus BK07.

Gaze data were converted to the strings of characters according to the position of fixations in marked Areas of Interest in OGAMA software [18]. The process of conversion is displayed in Figure 3. From the scanpaths (left side of Figure 3), the character strings are generated. For the analysis, collapsed strings (with no consecutive characters - right part of Figure 3) will be used.

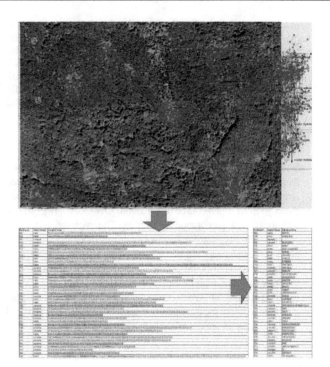

Fig. 3. The process of conversion of the scanpaths to the character strings and their collapsed variant.

In the ScanGraph interface, modified Levenshtein computation method was selected. As is mentioned above, collapsed data were used for analysis. The parameter (see above for more information) was set up to $p = 0.8$ (representing the similarity at least 80%). Six non-trivial cliques were found in the resulting graph (see Figure 4).

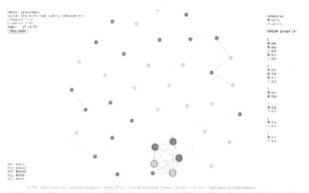

Fig. 4. The result of the ScanGraph for stimulus BK07 and parameter $p = 0.8$.

The largest clique contained five sequences (participants). Three of them were cartographers; two belonged to the group of non-cartographers. The strategy of these participants can be described as an ideal one. All of them started in the center of the screen (AOI D). Then they moved their gaze to all parts of the legend (AOI A, B, and C) and then they moved back to the map field (AOI D) and sought for the correct answer. Participants P13 and P17 made an additional fixation in the AOI A after looking into AOI B.

In the clique with four participants, the situation was similar. In this case, all sequences were "DABCD" The only exception was participant P20, who performed an additional fixation in AOI B at the end of stimulus observation.

The rest of displayed non-trivial cliques contained only two participants. All of these participants omitted AOI C during their view of the stimulus. The AOI C was marked around the last part of the legend (representing the possible occurrence of the fox). Because all legends looked similar, these participants decided not to look into the last part.

The rest of participants from the experiment were isolated nodes. That means that their sequence of visited Areas of Interest was not similar to any other sequence (according to parameter $p = 0.8$). An example of these sequences can be participant P29 with sequence "DABADADADADA BDBCBDAD", P30 with sequence DAD, or P43, who spent the whole observation time in the map field (sequence "D"). All these three participants belonged to the group of non-cartographers.

With the use of ScanGraph, we were able to find quickly the group of participants, who observed the stimuli in a similar way. After examination of the particular sequences, it was discovered that this sequence was the "ideal one".

The second analysed map from the experiment was stimulus C03. The map, in this case, depicted the possible occurrence of the fox. Unlike of the previous stimuli, spatial and temporal uncertainty was displayed with two different map symbols. The task of respondents was to find a place, where is the most probable possibility (both spatial and temporal) to found a fox. Areas of Interest were again marked in the stimuli (see Figure 5). AOI A represented the correct answer. AOI B was marked around the symbol of the fox, which also served as a map title (recorded incidence of foxes). Other two AOIs were marked around two parts of the legend (spatial uncertainty - AOI C and temporal uncertainty - AOI D). The last AOI (E) was marked around the map field (except the correct answer location).

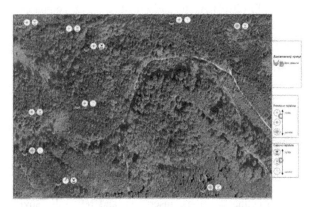

Fig. 5. Areas of Interest marked in the stimulus C03.

The same settings of ScanGraph as in the previous example was used, only the parameter value was set up to $p = 0.7$. This example contained more AOIs, so the lower similarity between sequences can be assumed. When we tried to use the same value of the parameter as in the previous example ($p = 0.8$), only one clique containing two participants was found. Resulting graph can be seen in Figure 6.

Total of 13 non-trivial cliques were found in the output of ScanGraph. Interesting is the comparison between two cliques containing three participants. The first one is a clique

with participants P14, P22, and P27. All of them belonged to the group of cartographers. The second clique with participants P16, P29 and P43 is highlighted in Figure 6. All these participants were non-cartographers. The difference between these cliques lies in the fact, that none of the non-cartographers observed the AOI B marked around the map title. Students of cartography are taught to pay attention to the map title. Similar behaviour was found in another study comparing respondents' reading of different map compositions [31]. Non-cartographers were almost entirely omitting the map title during a free-viewing task.

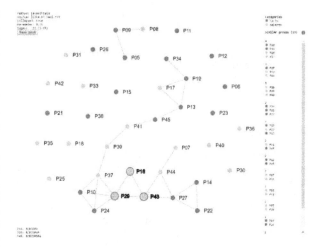

Fig. 6. The result of the ScanGraph for stimulus C03 and parameter $p = 0.7$.

4 Possibilities

Our primary goal was to enhance the outputs of the eyePatterns by a new method of finding groups with similar strategy. After discovering the inaccuracies of eyePatterns, we decided to create the application for the whole process of scanpath similarity calculation. From that reason we started with algorithms included in eyePatterns.

The algorithms were originally developed for the different purposes, like biometrics or linguistics. Because of that ScanGraph uses a modified metrics, more suitable for analysing of eye-tracking data.

But our aim is to develop an even better metrics for eye-tracking data, at least to data with a certain character. Next step is to verify the suitability of Δ-similarity algorithm. In contrast with already used Needleman-Wunsch modified algorithm, it takes into account the length of both compared sequences.

Δ-similarity is a function $\Sigma^* \times \Sigma^* \to \langle 0,1 \rangle$, such that

$$(\forall a, b \in \Sigma^*) \ \Delta(a,b) = \frac{2 \cdot |LCS(a,b)|}{|a| + |b|},$$

where LCS means the longest common subsequence.

The longest common subsequence $LCS(a, b)$ of sequences (words) a, b is the sequence c with maximal length $|c| = n$ such that there exist $k_1, \dots, k_n$ and $l_1, \dots, l_n$ such that $\forall i, j : i < j \implies k_i < k_j \wedge l_i < l_j$ and $\forall i \leq n : a_{k_i} = b_{l_i} = c_i$.

The second possible algorithm, called Damerau–Levenshtein distance [32] is an enhancement of Levenshtein distance algorithm. In addition, it calculates with transitions.

The Damerau–Levenshtein distance $DL(a, b)$ is a distance between two sequences a, b, given by counting the minimum number of operations needed to transform one string into the other, where an operation is defined as an insertion, deletion, or substitution of a single character, or a transposition of two adjacent characters. For example $LD(CA, ABC) = 2$ against $Lev(CA, ABC) = 3$.

The final selection of the used metric will depend on the character of data and distribution of AOI within the stimuli.

Unless the calculation uses the exhaustive algorithm it finds an optimal solution with all non-trivial cliques in the given graph. The computational time of the exhaustive algorithm is $O(2^n)$. When the time exceeds the tolerable limit, greedy heuristic algorithm is used. The reliability of the results is arguable. For the purposes of eye-tracking data analyses, the higher value of similarity (hence lower number of edges) is investigated. Moreover, the Bron and Kerbosch algorithm [33] for maximal clique problem will be tested and compared to the currently used algorithm.

5 Conclusion

The paper describes the newly developed tool for the analysis of eye-movement data. Eye-movements are represented as sequences of fixations recorded in Areas of Interest marked in the stimuli. The application uses modified Levenshtein distance and Needleman-Wunsch algorithms and visualize the result in the form of a simple graph. Groups of participants with similar strategy are represented as cliques of this graph. The paper describes the principles of the computations. The functionality of the application is presented in the example of cartographic case study dealing with map uncertainty visualization.

The tool is called ScanGraph and is freely available at www.eyetracking.upol.cz/scangraph.

Acknowledgment

We would like to thank Michal Kučera, who's data were used for the case study. This paper was supported by projects of Operational Program Education for Competitiveness – European Social Fund (projects CZ.1.07/2.3.00/20.0170), of the Ministry of Education, Youth and Sports of the Czech Republic and the student project IGA_PrF_2016_008 of the Palacky University.

References

[1] Li, X., Çöltekin, A., Kraak, M.-J. (2010) Visual exploration of eye movement data using the space-time-cube. In Geographic Information Science. Springer, pp. 295-309.

[2] Dykes, J., Maceachren, A. M., Kraak, M.-J. (2005) Exploring geovisualization. Elsevier, 710 p.

[3] Coltekin, A., Heil, B., Garlandini, S., Fabrikant, S. I. (2009) Evaluating the effectiveness of interactive map interface designs: a case study integrating usability metrics with eye-movement analysis. Cartography and Geographic Information Science, 36(1), pp. 5-17.

[4] Goldberg, J. H., Kotval, X. P. (1999) Computer interface evaluation using eye movements: methods and constructs. International Journal of Industrial Ergonomics, 24(6), pp. 631-645.

[5] Alacam, Ö., Dalci, M. (2009) A usability study of WebMaps with eye tracking tool: the effects of iconic representation of information. In Human-Computer interaction. New trends. Springer, pp. 12-21.

[6] Cutrell, E., Guan, Z. (2007) What are you looking for?: an eye-tracking study of information usage in web search. In Proceedings of the Proceedings of the SIGCHI conference on Human factors in computing systems, ACM, pp. 407-416.

[7] Hammoud, R. I., Mulligan, J. B. (2008) Introduction to Eye Monitoring. In Passive Eye Monitoring. Springer, pp. 1-19.

[8] Delabarre, E. B. (1898) A method of recording eye-movements. The American Journal of Psychology, 9(4), pp. 572-574.

[9] Dodge, R., Cline, T. S. (1901) The angle velocity of eye movements. Psychological Review, 8(2), pp. 145-157.

[10] Holmqvist, K., Nyström, M., Andersson, R., Dewhurst, R., Jarodzka, H., Van De Weijer, J. (2011) Eye tracking: A comprehensive guide to methods and measures. Oxford University Press, 537 p.

[11] Enoch, J. M. (1959) Effect of the size of a complex display upon visual search. JOSA, 49(3), pp. 280-285.

[12] Fabrikant, S. I., Hespanha, S. R., Hegarty, M. (2010) Cognitively inspired and perceptually salient graphic displays for efficient spatial inference making. Annals of the Association of american Geographers, 100(1), pp. 13-29.

[13] Ooms, K., De Maeyer, P., Fack, V. (2015) Listen to the Map User: Cognition, Memory, and Expertise. The Cartographic Journal.

[14] Popelka, S., Dedkova, P. Extinct village 3D visualization and its evaluation with eye-movement recording. 2014. Lecture Notes in Computer Science (including subseries Lecture Notes in Artificial Intelligence and Lecture Notes in Bioinformatics).

[15] Noton, D., Stark, L. (1971) Scanpaths in saccadic eye movements while viewing and recognizing patterns. Vision Research, 9//, 11(9), pp. 928-929.

[16] Anderson, N. C., Anderson, F., Kingstone, A., Bischof, W. F. (2014) A comparison of scanpath comparison methods. Behavior research methods, pp. 1-16.

[17] Bahill, A. T., Stark, L. (1979) The trajectories of saccadic eye movements. Scientific American, 240(1), pp. 108-117.

[18] Voßkühler, A., Nordmeier, V., Kuchinke, L., Jacobs, A. M. (2008) OGAMA (Open Gaze and Mouse Analyzer): open-source software designed to analyze eye and mouse movements in slideshow study designs. Behavior research methods, 40(4), pp. 1150-1162.

[19] Dolezalova, J., Popelka, S. (2016) ScanGraph: A Novel Scanpath Comparison Method Using Visualization of Graph Cliques. Journal of Eye Movement Research, In print.

[20] Levenshtein, V. I. (1966) Binary codes capable of correcting deletions, insertions, and reversals. Soviet physics doklady, 10(8), pp. 707-710.

[21] Needleman, S. B., Wunsch, C. D. (1970) A general method applicable to the search for similarities in the amino acid sequence of two proteins. Journal of molecular biology, 48(3), pp. 443-453.

[22] Gross, J. L., Yellen, J. (2005) Graph theory and its applications. CRC press.

[23] Dolezalova, J., Popelka, S. (2016) Evaluation of user strategy on 2D and 3D city maps based on novel scanpath comparison method and graph visualization. In Proceedings of the ISPRS 2016, Prague.

[24] Snopková, D. (2016) Tvorba a užití map osobami se sníženou schopností rozpoznání barev. Brno, Masaryk University.

[25] Pulkrtová, T. (2016) Vliv červené barvy na vnímání atraktivity žen. Brno, Masaryk University.

[26] Hájková, M. (2016) Eye tracking vyšetření predilekce očních pohybů u pacientů po cévní mozkové příhodě. Olomouc, Palacký University Olomouc.

[27] Brus, J. (2013) Uncertainty vs. spatial data quality visualisations: a case study on ecotones. International Multidisciplinary Scientific GeoConference: SGEM: Surveying Geology & mining Ecology Management, 1, pp. 1017.

[28] Kubíček, P., Šašinka, Č., Stachoň, Z. (2012) UNCERTAINTY VISUALIZATION TESTING. In Proceedings of the Proceedings of the 4th conference on Cartography and GIS, Sofia, T. BANDROVA, M. KONEČNÝ, G. ZHELEZOV eds., Bulgarian Cartographic Association, pp. 247-256.

[29] Kučera, M. (2016) Uživatelské testování a optimalizace vizualizací nejistoty prostorových dat. Olomouc, Palacký University Olomouc 64 p.

[30] Maceachren, A. M., Roth, R. E., O'brien, J., Li, B., Swingley, D., Gahegan, M. (2012) Visual semiotics & uncertainty visualization: An empirical study. Visualization and Computer Graphics, IEEE Transactions on, 18(12), pp. 2496-2505.

[31] Brychtova, A., Popelka, S., Dobesova, Z. (2012) Eye - Tracking methods for investigation of cartographic principles. In Proceedings of the 12th International Multidisciplinary Scientific GeoConference and EXPO, Varna, pp. 1041-1048.

[32] Damerau, F. J. (1964) A technique for computer detection and correction of spelling errors. Communications of the ACM, 7(3), pp. 171-176.

[33] Bron, C., Kerbosch, J. (1973) Algorithm 457: finding all cliques of an undirected graph. Communications of the ACM, 16(9), pp. 575-577.

ITAT 2016 Proceedings, pp. 212–217
ISBN 978-1537016740, © 2016 A. Jursa

Fast algorithm for finding maximum clique in scale-free networks

Andrej Jursa

Department of Applied Informatics, Faculty of Mathematics, Physics and Informatics, Comenius University in Bratislava
andrej.jursa@fmph.uniba.sk

Abstract: The maximum clique problem in graph theory concerns finding the largest subset of vertices in which all vertices are connected with an edge. Computation of such subset is a well-known NP-hard problem and there exist many algorithms to solve it. For our purposes we created an algorithm specially targeted for solving this problem in scale-free networks, where many significant search improvements may be introduced. We use the general purpose algorithm developed by Östergård in 2002 as subroutine for our new algorithm. We improved the search process by initial heuristic. Firstly we compute preliminary clique size and then reduce the graph by k-core decomposition of this size. Subsequently, we employ greedy algorithm for coloring of chosen vertex as well as its neighbors. Our algorithm is able to solve maximum clique problem for arbitrary graphs, but together with these and some other, less significant pruning techniques, the overall algorithm performs exceptionally well on scale-free networks, which was tested on many real graphs as well as randomly generated graphs.

1 Introduction

For our study of functional brain networks we needed an algorithm to solve maximum clique problem in these graphs to compare networks of three classes of participants. We realize that using a general purpose algorithm for this task may lead to very long computation times. According to the scale-free structure of functional brain networks we can implement several pruning techniques to make the search process faster. Functional brain networks we have data for are simple undirected graphs. Off course there exists randomized or heuristic algorithms like [3] or [5] which can give solution quickly, but for our study we needed algorithm which can give us exact solution in shortest possible time. Our algorithm we have created is based on exact algorithm created by Östergård and described in [4].

Undirected graph is combinatorial structure which we can denote as $G = (V, E)$, where V is set of vertices and E is set of edges or pairs of vertices. We can say that two vertices are adjacent, if there is edge between them. The number of edges which are connecting vertex v with other vertices is denoted as degree k of vertex v (we are denoting this as $deg(v) = k$). For vertex v we can get his open set of neighbors $N(v) = \{u | u \in V \land (u, v) \in E\}$ or close set of neighbors $N[v] = N(v) \cup \{v\}$.

Simple graph does not have loops from - to the same

vertices, does not have multiple edges between the same pair of vertices and does not have weighted edges. Our algorithm is targeted to solve maximum clique problem for simple undirected graphs. For simple undirected graph we can compute density of that graph as $D = \frac{2|E|}{|V|(|V|-1)}$.

A clique in simple undirected graph is a subset of vertices $V' \subseteq V$ so that $\forall v \in V', \forall u \in V' : u \neq v \implies (v, u) \in E$. The maximum clique is largest clique in undirected simple graph. The size of maximum clique is also called clique number of graph G and can be denoted as $\omega(G)$.

Scale-free networks are simple undirected graphs whose degree distribution asymptotically follows power law. There is no specific scale in degree distribution. Fraction $P(k)$ of vertices having degree equal to k scales for large values of k as $P(k) \sim k^{-\gamma}$, where γ is typically in range $2 < \gamma < 3$. For given graph G we can compute degree distribution. It can be done by counting how many vertices in G have particular degree. We can visualize this distribution for scale-free networks in a log-log plot (it can be seen on figure 1 in part (a)).

The k-core decomposition of the graph G forms an induced subgraph H, where all vertices have the degree at least k. When we compute k-core decomposition from the scale-free network, we can remove large amount of vertices with the degree lower than k. In the diagram in (b) part of figure 1 the red area represents all vertices removed from scale-free network due to k-core decomposition. By computing new k-core decomposition each time we know new size of clique, we can reduce search space for next iteration of searching.

2 Östergård's algorithm

The original algorithm is processing graphs vertices from the highest index to the lowest one. During this process it also maintains array called $c[i]$, where i is the index of already processed vertex. It stores value of *max* in the array $c[i]$ after vertex i and his neighborhood is processed. This algorithm is using subroutine CLIQUE for branching over neighbors of the initial vertex. To get this neighbors it is using sets defined as $S_i = \{v_i, v_{i+1}, v_{i+2}, \ldots, v_{|V|}\}$, where i is an index of starting vertex.

In algorithm 1 one can see pseudo-code of this original algorithm. At line 8 there is condition for number of vertices remaining in set U with respect of current clique *size*. If this condition holds, algorithm is unable to find clique with size higher than *max*, so it can return from subroutine. Also similar test is introduced at line 11. In this

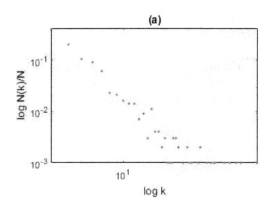
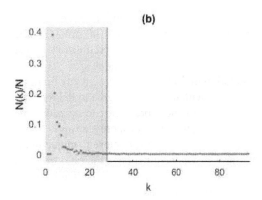

Figure 1: Scale-free network degree distribution in log-log plot (a) and vertices potentially removed by k-core decomposition, where $k = 0.3 \cdot deg_{max}(G)$ (b).

case it is testing if previous search from vertex with index i have founded clique size hight enough that with respect to current clique *size* algorithm can find clique higher than *max*. If this condition does not hold, it will return from subroutine as well.

This algorithm can be used for arbitrary simple undirected graph and it will find maximum clique size. The values of array c behaves following: $c[i] = c[i+1]$ if algorithm does not find new, higher, clique size, otherwise $c[i] = c[i+1] + 1$.

3 Our algorithm

Our solution is using original Östergård's algorithm[1] [4] as a subroutine. Our algorithm is following the same principles as the original one by processing vertices from the highest index to the lowest. In the whole process of searching for maximum clique size we have global variable named *max* which contains currently known maximum size of clique found in the process.

Our algorithm is split in two phases. In the first phase, which is called initialization phase, the algorithm is using heuristic function to find preliminary clique size. This process may return clique size close to maximum clique size[2]. The preliminary size returned by heuristic is set into variable *max*. When the initialization phase know this value the algorithm reduces the search space of graph by computing *max*-core decomposition[3]. At the end of this phase it computes new isomorphic graph, where all vertices are indexed again from 1 to $|V_k|$ but also the vertex degree is raising with indexes[4]. The $V_k \subseteq V$ is the set of vertices of the graphs k-core decomposition.

First step of the initialization phase is to compute preliminary clique size by heuristic function. Similar method

---

[1]Östergård's subroutine CLIQUE is used in our algorithm.

[2]But there is also chance for returning very small size compared to maximum clique size in graph.

[3]It is k-core decomposition of graph, where $k = max$.

[4]Vertex with index 1 have minimum degree in a graph and vertex with index $|V_k|$ have maximum degree in a graph.

Algorithm 1 Östergård's original algorithm.
Input: Simple undirected graph G.
Output: Clique number $\omega(G)$ in global variable *max*.

```
 1: procedure CLIQUE(U, size)
 2:     if |U| = 0 then
 3:         if size > max then
 4:             max ← size
 5:             found ← true
 6:         return
 7:     while U ≠ ∅ do
 8:         if size + |U| ≤ max then
 9:             return              ▷ Nothing better can be found.
10:         i ← min{j|v_j ∈ U}
11:         if size + c[i] ≤ max then
12:             return              ▷ Nothing better can be found.
13:         U ← U \ {v_i}
14:         CLIQUE(U ∩ N(v_i), size + 1)
15:         if found = true then
16:             return              ▷ Higher clique size was found,
    return to main loop.
17: procedure MAIN
18:     max ← 0
19:     for i ← |V| downto 1 do
20:         found ← false
21:         CLIQUE(S_i ∩ N(v_i), 1)
22:         c[i] ← max               ▷ Store clique size for next
    iteration, this is used for pruning.
```

was used in [2] and [5] but our heuristic function is slightly different. First it needs to determine the threshold value of the degree (line 11 of algorithm 2) and then for each vertex in the graph which have the degree equal or higher than the threshold it runs iterative process to find clique, as it is described on algorithm 2. After several experiments on the scale-free networks we have decides that the good value for this threshold is 0.95 times maximum degree in the graph G. This will enable the heuristic function to run tests for large number of vertices with almost maximum degree in graph but not for all vertices in graph, so the heuristic have good chance to find the preliminary clique size very close to the real maximum clique size.

Heuristic iteration of finding clique is a greedy function which adds vertices with maximum degree to the forming clique and when there is no more vertex to be added the clique is found. Repeating this for more starting vertices this process can find clique size very close to clique number of input graph G. On the other hand the ratio between clique size of graph G and size found by the heuristic can be also close to zero in some cases.

Algorithm 2 Preliminary clique size heuristic function.

Input: Simple undirected graph G.
Output: Preliminary clique size in graph G.

1: **function** CLIQUEHEURISTICSTARTINVERTEX$(G, i, lastMax)$
2: 　　$Clique \leftarrow \{v_i\}, Nb \leftarrow N(v_i)$ ▷ Initialize clique and neighbor sets.
3: 　　**while true do**
4: 　　　　**if** $|Clique| + |Nb| \leq lastMax$ **then** ▷ Higher clique size can not be found.
5: 　　　　　　**return** $lastMax$
6: 　　　　**if** $|Nb| = 0$ **then** ▷ All possible vertices are processed.
7: 　　　　　　**return** $|Clique|$
8: 　　　　$j \leftarrow$ index of vertex $w_j \in Nb$ which have maximum degree
9: 　　　　$Clique \leftarrow Clique \cup \{v_j\}, Nb \leftarrow Nb \cap N(v_j)$ ▷ Update clique and neighbor sets.
10: **function** CLIQUEHEURISTIC(G)
11: 　　$deg_{threshold} \leftarrow \lfloor 0.95 \cdot \max \{deg(u) | u \in G_S\} \rfloor$
12: 　　$heurMax \leftarrow 0$
13: 　　**for** $i \leftarrow 1$ **to** $|V|$ **do**
14: 　　　　**if** $deg(v_i) \geq deg_{threshold}$ **then**
15: 　　　　　　$max \leftarrow$ CLIQUEHEURISTICSTARTINVERTEX$(G, i, heurMax)$
16: 　　**return** $heurMax$

After heuristic search is completed the algorithm knows preliminary size of the clique and it saves it to the variable *max*. For next phase it is necessary to compute *max*-core decomposition which removes possibly large amount of vertices and effectively reduces search space[5]. Because algorithm is processing vertices by their indices from higher to lower we run renumbering procedure on new *max*-core decomposition so that vertices will be sorted by their degree. This sorting can improve search process because it allows to skip several vertices with higher degrees whose neighbor sets are smaller or equal to the current *max*.

The process of computing k-core decomposition is very simple iterative deletion of vertices which degree is lower than k and it is described on the algorithm 3. In this algo-

rithm $V(G)$ denotes the set of vertices V belonging to the graph G.

Algorithm 3 k-core decomposition of graph G.

Input: Simple undirected graph G, desired value k.
Output: k-core decomposition of graph G.

1: **function** COMPUTEKCORE(G, k)
2: 　　$G_{k\text{-}core} \leftarrow G$
3: 　　**repeat**
4: 　　　　$G_{tmp} \leftarrow G_{k\text{-}core}$
5: 　　　　**for all** $v \in G_{k\text{-}core}$ **do**
6: 　　　　　　**if** $deg(v) < k$ **then**
7: 　　　　　　　　$V(G_{k\text{-}core}) \leftarrow V(G_{k\text{-}core}) \setminus \{v\}$
8: 　　**until** $|V(G_{tmp})| \neq |V(G_{k\text{-}core})|$ ▷ If there is no change in graph then the k-core decomposition is finished.
9: 　　**return** $G_{k\text{-}core}$

After completion of the initialization phase the main search phase follows. The algorithm works with two nested loops, first is iterating over last k-core decomposition (line 7 in algorithm 4) and starting the second loop. Here is the algorithm processing vertices from higher index to lower (inside last computed k-core decomposition, line 8 in algorithm 4). For each vertex v_i is testing number of colors needed to color vertices from $N[v_i]$ which forms induced subgraph. If this number of colors is higher than currently know *max*, there can be clique with higher size than *max*.

To obtain neighbors set of vertex v_i new metric is introduced. We call it internal degree and it is defined in equation 1.

$$deg_v(u) = \left| \{w | w \in N[v] \wedge (u, w) \in E\} \right| \qquad (1)$$

In the search process our algorithm will processes each vertex only once. This is guaranteed by checking the array c (line 10) from the Östergård's algorithm. If this array is already set for the given index, then we know that the vertex with this index was processed before.

In the main loop, where the algorithm is iterating through all unprocessed vertices, it is running greedy function for coloring[6]. Result of this coloring function is suboptimal number of minimum colors needed to color vertex and it neighborhood, which can be performed quickly. It gives us a good information whether it is promising to find better clique size when the algorithm starts branching from this vertex. The process of coloring vertex v and it neighborhood $N_v = \{v\} \cup \{u | u \in N(v) \wedge deg(u) \geq max \wedge \arg u > \arg v\}$ is described in algorithm 5.

---

[5]In some cases heuristic can find maximum clique size and *max*-core decomposition can be empty.

---

[6]This function is similar to one mentioned in [2] but in our implementation this is performed in the process of selecting vertices for branching not before the whole process.

Algorithm 4 Algorithm for finding maximum clique in scale-free networks.

Input: Simple undirected graph G.

Output: Clique number $\omega(G)$ in global variable max.

1: **function** SORTGRAPHBYDEGREEASCENDING(G)
2:     **return** new G_I isomorphic graph, where vertex with maximum degree have maximum index
3: **procedure** MAIN
4:     $max \leftarrow$ CLIQUEHEURISTIC(G)
5:     $G_{max\text{-}core} \leftarrow$ SORTGRAPHBYDEGREEASCENDING(COMPUTEKCORE(G, max))
6:     $lastMax \leftarrow max$
7:     **while true do**
8:         **for** $i \leftarrow$ maximum index in $G_{max\text{-}core}$ **downto** minimum index in $G_{max\text{-}core}$ **do**
9:             $found \leftarrow$ **false**
10:             **if** $c[i]$ is already set **then**   ▷ Vertex v_i has been already processed.
11:                 **continue**
12:             **if** GETMINCOLORS($G_{max\text{-}core}, i, max$) $> max$ **then**
13:                 $N_{v_i} \leftarrow \left\{ u \middle| u \in S_i \cap N(v_i) \wedge deg_{v_i}(u) \geq max \right\}$
14:                 CLIQUE($N_{v_i}, 1$)
15:                 $c[i] \leftarrow max$
16:                 **if** $found =$ **true then**
17:                     **return**
18:         **if** $lastMax = max$ **then**   ▷ All vertices are processed and there is no better solution.
19:             **break**
20:         **else**
21:             $lastMax \leftarrow max$
22:             $G_{max\text{-}core} \leftarrow$ COMPUTEKCORE(G, max)

4 Results and testing

Our algorithm is able to solve maximum clique problem, as well as Östergård's algorithm, for all sorts of simple undirected graphs. But for all graphs with scale-free property it is our algorithm able to do so much faster. Most useful improvement here is the heuristic function which finds preliminary clique size in initialization phase, with subsequent k-core decomposition throughout whole process of searching. By decomposition the algorithm is able to reduce the graph size by removing vertices which can not be part of a maximum clique. Also degree distribution after each decomposition step is changing from original (asymptotically following power law) to linear looking one. When the final clique is found[7] and last computation of max-core decomposition the remaining vertices does not forms scale-free network anymore and they must be processed all to confirm found clique number. It is also possible that the last max-core decomposition will return

---

[7]The one representing one of maximum cliques in graph.

Algorithm 5 Greedy algorithm used to find minimum colors needed to color vertex i and it's neighbors.

Input: Simple undirected graph G, index of vertex i.

Output: Suboptimal number of minimum colors needed to color v_i and it immediate neighborhood.

1: **function** GETMINCOLORS($G, i, minDegree$)
2:     $colors \leftarrow 1$, $colorMap[v_i] \leftarrow 1$
3:     $Neighbors \leftarrow \{u | u \in N(v_i) \wedge deg(u) \geq minDegree \wedge \arg u > i\}$
4:     $AllNodes \leftarrow Neighbors \cup \{v_i\}$
5:     **for all** $u \in Neighbors$ **do** ▷ Iterate over neighbors u of vertex v_i.
6:         $N_u \leftarrow N(u) \cap AllNodes$ ▷ Assemble set of neighbors of u within neighbors of v_i.
7:         $minColor \leftarrow 1$, $UsedColors \leftarrow \{\}$
8:         **for all** $w \in N_u$ **do** ▷ Iterate over all neighbors w of vertex u ...
9:             **if** $colorMap[w] \neq$ **null then**   ▷ ... and collect all colors already used.
10:                 $UsedColors \leftarrow UsedColors \cup \{colorMap[w]\}$
11:         **for** $color \leftarrow 1$ **to** $colors + 1$ **do**
12:             **if** $color \notin UsedColors$ **then** ▷ New unused minimum color is found.
13:                 $minColor \leftarrow color$
14:                 **break**
15:         $colorMap[u] \leftarrow minColor$
16:         $colors \leftarrow \max(colors, minColor)$ ▷ Remember the highest color number used.
17:     **return** $colors$

empty graph, this means immediate finish of the algorithm without additional need to confirm found clique number.

In the search phase an additional pruning techniques were introduced. First was computation of minimum colors needed to color starting vertex and his neighborhood. This is greedy function so it can not compute optimal solution, but approximative solution is good to decide if processing of neighbors of the starting vertex is promising to find higher clique size. Second pruning here is neighbors node selection by testing their internal degree (according to equation (1)). Because connections outside neighborhood of the starting vertex does not contribute any vertex to the clique that we look for inside this neighborhood, we may omit these vertices when we deciding if vertex from neighborhood have to be added to the set of neighbors used for branching. This can reduce search space for each starting vertex and speed up the algorithm.

We have tested our algorithm on our FMRi data of functional brain networks as well as on simple undirected graphs from the database which can be found on https://snap.stanford.edu/data/[8] and on some graphs from DIMACS dataset. We also generated some test-

---

[8]Stanford dataset and FMRi functional brain networks represents real world graphs.

ing graphs using Bernoulli graph distribution, Barabáshi-Albert graph distribution [1] and Watts–Strogatz graph distribution [6]. Our implementation is written in Java and all tests were preformed on computer with Inter core i7 4790K@4.0GHz processor with 16GB of RAM. Running process of our algorithm have heap size of 12GB.

Table 1 contains some results from test runs. The graph name is represented by G, D is the density of edges inside graph G. $|V|$ and $|E|$ represents the sizes of vertices and edges set of graph G. Preliminary size of clique is denoted here as s_p while maximum clique size is denoted as clique number of graph $\omega(G)$. There is also ratio between s_p and $\omega(G)$ which represents how close the initialization phase heuristic search was to the real maximum clique in the given graph. Also times are displayed here, the „Time of phase 1" is time needed to compute preliminary clique size[9] and „Time of phase 2" is time needed to complete iterative branching of search phase.

The graph „C125.9" is from DIMACS dataset. It is the smallest one from DIMACS and it does not represent the scale-free network. It is random graph with edge probability of 0.9, with 125 vertices and 6963 edges. It takes 1637 seconds for our algorithm to process this graph. This is clear demonstration that our algorithm is able to find a maximum clique in an arbitrary undirected graph, but the time to process it is not better than the time needed by Östergård's algorithm[10]. Also graphs called „BG_n_p" are random graph, generated by Bernoulli graph distribution, where n is number of vertices and $\frac{p}{100}$ is probability of edge between two vertices. The time needed to solve these graphs is exponentially rising with number of vertices (the probability of edge is the same for both of them).

The graph called „facebook", as well as „as-skitter", „Email-Enron", „CA-AstroPh", „CA-CondMat" and „CA-HepPh" represent scale-free networks from Stanford snap datasets. One may see that the „facebook" graph have higher density than other graphs from dataset and the time needed to compute the maximum clique is around 379 seconds for just 4039 vertices and 88234 edges. On the other hand graph „as-skitter" with has 1696415 vertices and 11095298 edges, and very low density is processed in only 99 seconds. Initialization phases heuristic time for this graph is 28.6 seconds due to the large amount of vertices. We may say that number of vertices and the edges density is the key factor of the algorithm speed. Graph „CA-HepPh" is an example of a graph, where heuristic function finds maximum clique size and resulting k-core decomposition forms an empty graph. We also tested some randomly generated graphs by Barabási-Albert graph distribution. These graphs are „BA_n_k", where n is number of vertices and each new vertex is con-

nected with k edges. These graphs was also solved quite fast and initial heuristic have found preliminary clique sizes very close to graphs clique numbers.

Graphs „awith_*", „awout_*" and „young_*" represents FMRi functional brain networks for adult participants with Alzheimer disease, without this disease and young participants without disease. All are scale-free networks having from 5400 to 8200 vertices. Here we can also see that the key factor is a density of edges and the number of vertices. We can see that some graphs were processed under one second by our algorithm. We also tested the performance of the original Östergård's algorithm on these graphs, which needs tens of minutes or several hours to process them.

Last dataset of graphs are named „WS_n_p_k", these are random graphs generated using Watts–Strogatz graph distribution, where n is number of vertices, $\frac{p}{100}$ is rewiring probability starting from $2k$-regular graphs. One can see that our algorithm is also performing well on small-world networks even it was not designed for this type of graphs. Results of heuristic here is also very close to final graph clique numbers.

For our scale-free brain functional networks or other graphs with scale-free property our algorithm gives us exact results much faster than the Östergård's one. That means we are able to analyze scale-free graphs for our purposes very quickly.

References

[1] ALBERT, R., AND BARABÁSI, A.-L. Statistical mechanics of complex networks. *Reviews of Modern Physics 74* (Jan. 2002), 47–97.

[2] EBLEN, J. D., PHILLIPS, C. A., ROGERS, G. L., AND LANGSTON, M. A. The maximum clique enumeration problem: Algorithms, applications and implementations. In *Proceedings of the 7th International Conference on Bioinformatics Research and Applications* (Berlin, Heidelberg, 2011), ISBRA'11, Springer-Verlag, pp. 306–319.

[3] NEHÉZ, M. Analysis of the randomized algorithm for clique problems. In *Proceedings of the 15th Conference on Applied Mathematics APLIMAT 2016* (Bratislava, Slovak Republic, Feb. 2016), SUT Publishing, pp. 867–875.

[4] ÖSTERGÅRD, P. R. J. A fast algorithm for the maximum clique problem. *Discrete Appl. Math. 120*, 1-3 (Aug. 2002), 197–207.

[5] PATTABIRAMAN, B., PATWARY, M. M. A., GEBREMEDHIN, A. H., LIAO, W., AND CHOUDHARY, A. N. Fast algorithms for the maximum clique problem on massive sparse graphs. *CoRR abs/1209.5818* (2012).

[6] WATTS, D. J., AND STROGATZ, S. H. Collective dynamics of 'small-world' networks. *Nature 393*, 6684 (1998), 409–10.

---

[9]Graph loading and construction as well as post heuristic renumbering of graph and k-core decomposition is not included in this time.

[10]Actually by using additional techniques like k-core decomposition and others which are not included in Östergård's algorithm, the run time of our algorithm for graphs of these types is higher than time needed by original algorithm.

G	$|V|$	$|E|$	D	Preliminary size (s_p)	Time of phase 1	$\omega(G)$	$s_p/\omega(G)$ ratio	Time of phase 2
C125.9	125	6963	0.8984516129	32	0.016	34	0.94118	1636.768
BG_500_40	500	49820	0.3993587174	9	0.031	11	0.81818	21.386
BG_1000_40	1000	199909	0.4002182182	11	0.169	12	0.91667	2031.105
facebook	4039	88234	0.0108199635	7	0.068	69	0.10145	378.944
as-skitter	1696415	11095298	0.0000077109	37	28.609	67	0.55224	98.769
Email-Enron	36692	183831	0.0002730976	17	0.177	20	0.85000	1.974
CA-AstroPh	18771	198050	0.0011242248	23	0.202	57	0.40351	0.934
CA-CondMat	23133	93439	0.0003492312	4	0.142	26	0.15385	0.297
CA-HepPh	12006	118489	0,0016441731	239	0.097	239	1.00000	0.068
BA_300_20	300	5790	0.1290969900	20	0.003	21	0.95238	0.008
BA_1000_20	1000	19790	0.0396196196	17	0.019	21	0.80952	0.071
BA_10000_20	10000	199790	0.0039961996	20	0.191	21	0.95238	0.430
BA_100000_20	100000	1999790	0.0003999620	20	3.249	21	0.95238	7.786
BA_250000_50	250000	12498725	0.0003999608	51	25.653	51	1.00000	25.013
awith_09	7558	102091	0.0035748773	23	0.078	29	0.79310	0.884
awith_37	6218	73880	0.0038223046	33	0.058	36	0.91667	0.324
awith_02	7529	66494	0.0023463649	28	0.077	41	0.68293	0.302
awith_40	5677	17200	0.0010675720	11	0.018	12	0.91667	0.012
awout_13	7416	139482	0.0050730283	62	0.116	68	0.91176	31.105
awout_14	6849	172969	0.0073757698	80	0.149	94	0.85106	12.116
awout_04	8000	183940	0.0057488436	45	0.152	55	0.81818	4.518
awout_15	5439	20276	0.0013710523	36	0.017	38	0.94737	0.014
young_26	8183	211232	0.0063098303	103	0.192	124	0.83065	335.649
young_17	7553	134565	0.0047182467	84	0.091	94	0.89362	40.639
young_16	7032	131887	0.0053350197	88	0.102	108	0.81481	18.437
young_34	7131	93643	0.0036835396	66	0.069	89	0.74157	0.884
WS_500_25_50	500	25000	0.2004008016	13	0.011	16	0.81250	1.345
WS_500_40_50	500	25000	0.2004008016	9	0.012	11	0.81818	0.892
WS_5000_25_50	5000	250000	0.0200040008	13	0.165	16	0.81250	13.091
WS_5000_40_50	5000	250000	0.0200040008	8	0.172	11	0.72727	8.630
WS_10000_25_50	10000	500000	0.0100010001	14	0.405	16	0.87500	25.030
WS_10000_40_50	10000	500000	0.0100010001	9	0.485	12	0.75000	15.354

Table 1: Results of test runs of our algorithm for different datasets. Times are in seconds.

ITAT 2016 Proceedings, pp. 218–225
ISBN 978-1537016740, © 2016 R. Mařík

On Large Genealogical Graph Layouts

Radek Mařík

Department of Telecommunication Engineering, Faculty of Electrical Engineering
Czech Technical University in Prague
Technicka 2, Dejvice, Prague CZ-166 27, Czech Republic, EU,
Radek.Marik@fel.cvut.cz,
WWW home page: https://comtel.fel.cvut.cz/en/users/marikr

Abstract: Classical ancestor trees, descendant trees, Hourglass charts, and their visual variants such as node-link diagrams or fan charts are suitable for assessment of people's relationships when one is focused on a particular person (the so-called main person) and his/her direct ancestors and descendants. Such tree-based representations miss a broader context of relationships and do not allow quick assessment of several interlinked families together. We propose utilization of directed acyclic graph visualizations with constraints specified by layers and ordering of groups of nodes within layers. The computed constraints can be mapped, at least partially, into the DOT language property directives used by the Graphviz toolbox. We demonstrate achievements on datasets containing 1600 people (a private family tree collection) and 3000 people (an Egyptology database of officials from 4th, 5th, and 6th dynasty).

1 Introduction

Although it is more than 55 years since Tutte introduced barycentric embedding, research of graph visualization techniques remains a highly active field attracting a lot of attention [1, 2, 3]. Graph visualization can help to form an overview of relational patterns and detect data structure much faster than data in a tabular form. The form in which the graph is presented has a significant impact on how the graph is understood and the time that is necessary to achieve this. Nodes placed close to one another might be interpreted by the user as a true relationship whether or not this relationship exists [4, 3]. Working with genealogical graphs is no exception in this sense.

Tree based drawing methods of genealogical graphs have been among the standard techniques for centuries. Ancestor trees, descendant trees and Hourglass charts [5] belong to a set of traditional tools implemented by a majority of freeware, shareware, or commercial tools, for example Gramps [6] or MyHeritage [7]. These tools provide a clear description of a situation when the user needs to investigate direct ancestors and/or descendants of a given person (often the so-called main or center person). The main person is placed into the root of the tree. Thus, the generation of the main person consists of only one person and the size of other generations grows exponentially with a branching factor often over 2. Therefore, the graphical

representation results in a triangular shape. Such a classical node-link tree representation wastes about one half of the drawing area. There are other more space-efficient representations such as fan charts or H-charts [8, 9, 10, 11]. As any pure tree representation enables any ordering of node predecessors/successors, it is possible to specify the type of ordering, such as children ordered by their birth dates. It is also possible to extend any such tree representation with additional nodes that can be attached as single nodes to any tree node (in the Gramps tool [6] this type of graph is called a Relationship Graph). In this way a tree with direct ancestors/descendants can cover, for example, spouses/partners. Therefore, tree representations can be laid out in such a way that family members are grouped together. The obvious drawback of the pure tree representations is that selecting a different main person leads to a different graph that must be rendered again.

However, the situation with family members grouping changes significantly if the assumptions of one main person and direct ancestors/descendants are dropped. In a number of cases it is highly beneficial if the entire network of families or at least a significant part can be displayed in one layout. Then we face issues with challenges linked with edge crossing and preferences on node clustering [12, 13, 14]. The genealogical tools often do not provide such specialized visualizations. At present it is possible to use methods dedicated to a general graph layout. Hierarchical layouts are suitable for genealogical directed graphs, for example, implemented and provided by tools such as dot.exe (DOT) in Graphviz package [15] or yEd [16]. Unfortunately, these tools, and others we are aware of, do not support any kind of constraints that would allow the setting of node cluster preferences. Based on our own experience and observations made during our cooperation with Egyptologists, the researchers prefer grouping based on families.

Fig 1 depicts Nyankhkhnum's and Khnumhotep's family reconstructed from the database of the Egyptian officials [17]. In this case, the layout was produced using the yEd tool. Although it is possible to improve such a layout manually, one cannot waste time redoing the layout for all database families whenever the database is updated.

It is possible to group children or their parents (but not both). Unfortunately, directed hierarchical drawing methods such as the very good one implemented as dot.exe [18] results in layouts with mixed generations

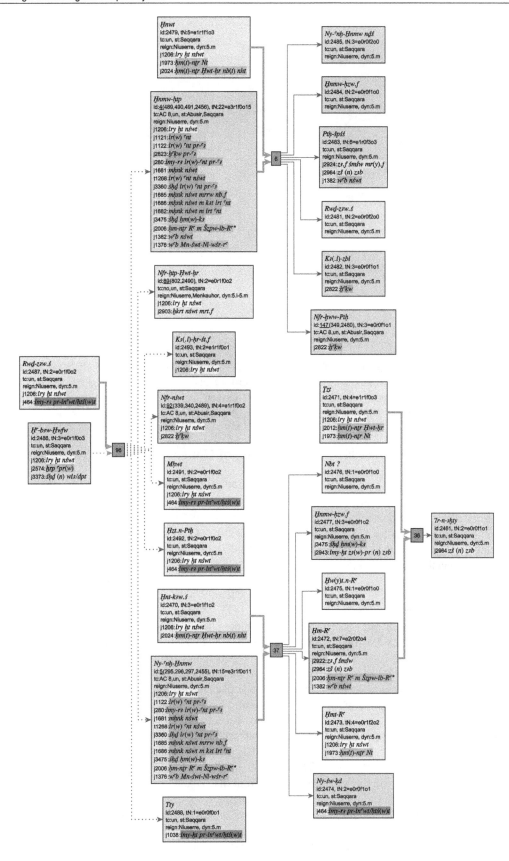

Figure 1: A family tree component presented using a tree layout which is illustrative of Nyankhkhnum's and Khnumhotep's family. The people rectangles contain additional information such as their titles.

Figure 2: A sample private family tree consisting of 1671 people as rendered using the DOT tool without any further constraints. Colored rectangles represent people (reddish women, blueish men). Ovals capture their marriages. Although the visualization seems to be correct, there are many cases when people are moved into different generation layers and many children from different families are mixed. The quality of the picture is decreased to keep family privacy.

and groups mixing several families. Such layouts are difficult to read and comprehend. We are not aware of any method that would enable the definition and use of the necessary constraints. In this paper we focus on several principles that allow the determination of such constraints and how such constraints can be managed. At least partially, the proposed constraints can be mapped to additional graph specifications that result in the DOT algorithm producing the required layout.

More specifically, we focus on two most critical aspects discussed in [13] and dealing particularly with the first two steps of the approach proposed in [18]: 1/ determination of generations (layers, node ranks), and 2/ enforcing family grouping based on propagation of children and marriage orders through generations. We propose several approaches for handling such aspects and we provide efficient algorithmic solutions for them. Of course, one can consider other aspects as well. In this paper we focused only on these two.

The rest of the paper is organized in the following way. In the next section we provide an algorithm that allows setting ranks of nodes for an acyclic graph representing a traditional representation of family tree using marriage nodes. In the next section we design a method that allows propagation of children and parent ordering across generations (ranks). Finally, we discuss some results achieved if the constraints are mapped into DOT language and tested on datasets with thousands of nodes.

2   Ranking of Genealogical Graph Nodes

Even a DOT graph specification does not contain any constraints on node layers. Its implementation ranks nodes as proposed by many authors [13, 18]. In many situations the result layout is produced as required, see Fig 2. Unfortunately, the general criterion used in the DOT implementation leads to node placement breaking generation layering as it is usual and expected in genealogical graphs, i.e. children of one family at the same level and similarly their parents. The DOT language enables the specification that a subset of nodes shares the same rank. The majority of algorithms computing ranks are derived from the topological order computation ($O(n)$ time complexity) [19] and select one of many possible solutions that satisfy layer intervals of node placements. In this section we present an algorithm, using which the ranks of nodes can be determined for any genealogical graph. A genealogical graph is an acyclic bipartite directed graph $G(V_P, V_M, E)$ with two sorts of nodes, people V_P and marriages/partnerships V_M. The edges E are directed from parent nodes to marriage nodes and from marriage nodes to children nodes. Without loss of generality we can assume that the index of the generation layer of parents (also denoted as ranks) is lower than the index of their marriage node, and further that the index of the marriage node is lower than the index of children nodes.

In the following algorithm we assume that the processed graph is directed and acyclic. Classical algorithms start from a single node, the only one with no predecessors. Generally, a genealogical graph can consist of several nodes without predecessors and several nodes without successors. Let us use a convention that generation layers are identified by numbers $\lambda(v)$ and successors have higher levels. Each node is assigned an interval of generation levels at which the node can appear with regard to a base level. The following proposed algorithm uses two simple passes through a graph. Each node is assigned the highest possible level with respect to the current highest base level of successors during the first pass.

$$\lambda_1(v) = \begin{cases} \max_{(v,w) \in E} \lambda_1(w) - 1 & \text{if } v \text{ has successors} \\ 0 & \text{otherwise} \end{cases}$$

Thus, the node(s) with the lowest level can be determined. A generation level for each node is set as the maximum level of the node predecessor levels increased by one during the second pass. The second pass starts from the nodes with the lowest level.

$$\lambda_2(v) = \begin{cases} 0 & \text{if } v \text{ has the lowest level} \\ \lambda_2(w) - 1 & \text{if } w \text{ has predecessors} \\ & \text{partially processed} \\ & (v,w) \in E \text{ and} \\ & \lambda_2(v) \text{ is not assigned} \\ \min_{(w,v) \in E} \lambda_2(w) + 1 & \text{if } v \text{ has all predecessors} \\ & \text{processed} \end{cases}$$

Each node is visited twice during each pass using depth first search (DFS) using an explicit LIFO queue. The first visit ensures that all successors/predecessors are processed already. When the node is visited again, its level is determined as minimum/maximum of successors/predecessors levels. As children from a single marriage have only one common predecessor, the marriage node, they share the same generation level. However, parent nodes can be assigned to different levels. Nevertheless, the algorithm guarantees that parents linked to a marriage node always have a lower layer number than the marriage node and children attached to the marriage node have higher layer numbers than the marriage node. Any layout with nodes placed in layers following, for example, increasing generation levels always has the same direction of all edges. The edge layout direction cannot be reverted ever as it might occur in methods based on a general optimization criterion such as the one used in the DOT.

The algorithm uses two DFS passes with linear complexity. Therefore, the time complexity is $O(N)$, where N is the number of graph nodes. Two arrays are used for the maintenance of minimum and maximum levels for each node. A DFS pass requires an implicit or explicit stack. Different implementations of the stack, a graph representation, and the related DFS implementation can result in different space requirements ranging from the maximum depth of the acyclic graph (its diameter) to the number of all nodes. The length of the queue in our implementation is constrained by $O(d * b)$, where d is the maximum depth of the graph and b is the maximum branching factor. Both d and b parameters do not cross value 15 in the majority of cases (the maximum number of generations, the maximum number of children/partners). Thus, the space complexity is again in the range of $O(N)$.

3 Same Generation Nodes Ordering

Using the state of art of graph layout techniques such as those implemented in Graphviz [18] leads to results that are almost acceptable, however, with some drawbacks. Assuming that a genealogical graph is layered according to the generation levels determined by the algorithm proposed in the previous section, the main complaint stems from mixing of children/partners from different families. When several families linked through a partnership relationship are visualized, one can cluster either children or partners, but generally not both. For example, Relationship graph visualization implemented in the DOT creates subgraphs of partners. Siblings from different families can be mixed.

In this section we support the approach when siblings of one family are clustered tightly while partnerships/parents might be mixed. The obvious reason behind this variant is that the number of children is much higher than 2, often reaching values over 10. Thus, an injected edge crossing because of mixed parents is much lower than when it occurs when children are mixed, and families can be identified easily by a number of parallel edges leading from marriage nodes to children nodes.

The problem of a layout design might then be reduced to a determination of the order of people belonging to one generation. We propose that children belonging to a single family are ordered by their birth dates. Subtrees of the child descendants, including descendant marriage nodes, hold this order. In the opposite direction, i.e. from a marriage node to its spouses, the order of spouses can be determined according to birthdates of spouses. There might be cases when two or more people from two or more different families create partnerships. In such situations we cannot insist on the order of marriage nodes as the order requirements might be contradictory, for example, in the case of two families both with two children that creates two marriages in the opposite order of their birthdates. We would need other constraints to resolve them. In this paper we provide only a simple solution based on a random order of families. As these cases are not common, the resulting edge crossing is acceptable. A more sophisticated solution would create three sets of marriage nodes. The middle set, consisting of nodes representing marriages of children from both families and determining the order of families, in a way minimizes edge crossing. The other two side sets of marriages can follow the order of the two families and the order of their children. Nevertheless, the general situation with more than one marriage involving two and more families is rather complex and is considered beyond the scope of this paper. We denote the defined order of children and spouses as basic order subsequences.

The proposed solution is based on a propagation of basic order subsequences from lower levels of generations to higher ones, and similarly in the opposite direction. A linear graph composed of a disjoint sequences of nodes belonging to a given generation layer is maintained. That means, at a particular step of the algorithm, the set of nodes belonging to the processed generation layer is decomposed into a set of linear sequences. Each sequence determines an order of its nodes that is kept unchanged. In each propagation step, the nodes of a sequence in one generation layer are projected into their successor/predecessor nodes in the next/previous generation layer. The resulting sequence is fused from sequences already defined in the next/previous generation layer. In fact, any contradictory order requirements leading to loops must be dropped. We are aware that more sophisticated techniques of such requirements dropping can be implemented and can lead to better layouts. Nevertheless, our present basic solution uses a strategy adding additional order constraints in a step by step manner. If a requirement would create a loop, it is dropped.

As the genealogical graph is assumed to be acyclic and connected, the shortest trail linking any two nodes can be found. Any triple of nodes spouse-marriage-spouse or child-marriage-child defines the order of the two nodes. As any two nodes in a given generation layer can be ordered, a single sequence of totally ordered nodes in each single layer can be created. In other words, basic order subsequences fully specify a topological order of all nodes in the graph. Of course, different layouts can be achieved if we select a different dropping criterion of redundant order requirements.

Let us describe a propagation technique using just subsequence structures. Initially, the sequence of siblings based on their birthdates belonging to a family is computed for each family with children. Similarly, a sequence of marriage nodes is created for spouses with multiple marriages. Then the process iterates from lower to higher generations. In each iteration all edges of sequences from the lower generation are propagated to edges linking the related sequences in the higher generation.

It is obvious that the critical operation is the mapping from nodes to sequences and linking of sequences. There are several possible solutions. Firstly, a given generation layer of nodes can be represented as a directed graph. Whenever we need the first or the last node of a sequence to which a given belongs we can find it through a path against or along the direction of edges, respectively. As sequences get longer, the processing time of this operation grows exponentially. Secondly, it is possible to maintain a mapping from each node to its sequence first and last nodes. Initially, each node references itself as the first and the last node of a primitive sequence consisting of the node itself. Whenever two sequences are merged, all its node references of the first and the last nodes must be updated. At present, our implementation uses this approach. We do not perceive any performance issues if used on graphs with several thousands of nodes. Thirdly, as merging of sequences can be considered as a union of two sets, the very efficient union-find algorithm can be used. Furthermore, we would need to maintain a reference to the first and last nodes for each such union sequence representative node. We will describe this efficient method further in this section.

A special treatment must be paid to linking of sequences. It is very easy to create a loop, for example, if there are two families, one with two boys and one with two daughters, and they create two families when the older boy is married with the younger daughter and the younger boy is married with the older daughter. In such a case we have contradictory requirements for the order of marriage nodes of young couples. If all such order requirements are propagated, a loop in the order sequences is created. At present we propagate an order requirement only if it does not create a loop. Loops can be created over a merged sequence or over the input sequences. All possibilities must be checked and avoided.

An actual efficient implementation of the propagation method is not complicated, and it is rather simple using a union-find technique and a binary tree. A sequence of nodes is projected into the other sequence through order edges linking subsequent nodes in the source layer. The resulting destination sequence of nodes must be decomposed into subsequences already existing in the destination layer. We can employ a combination of two techniques, the union-find method with its fast searching for a subsequence (set) representing node and a binary tree structure that is able to represent a subsequence as the preorder of its leaves and to accomplish two subsequences merging by adding a new binary tree root referencing the tree roots of subsequences as its children ($O(1)$ time). In other words, the union-find structure maps the graph layer nodes into their current maximum subsequence tree roots ($O(\alpha|V|)$, where α is inverse Ackermann function [19]) and the selected binary tree roots are then merged. Thus, processing of any graph node can be performed in almost constant time. The algorithm must make three passes through all layers of the genealogical graph, i.e. each constraint must be propagated fully in both directions. Thus, the overall asymptotic amortized time complexity is $O(1 + \varepsilon)$. It should be noted that subsequence merging using a binary tree does not suffer from possibilities of creating loops as each graph node is referenced just once and the binary tree node always represents a properly oriented subsequence.

4 Implementation, Experiments, and Discussion

We have not attempted to implement a completely new acyclic genealogical graph layout algorithm. We precom-

```
{ edge[style=invis]; node[style=invis]; "p0"->"p1"->"p2"->"p3";}
{ rank = "same"; "p0"; "I1436"; "I1221"; "I1140"; "I1073"; "I1141";}
{ rank = "same"; "p1"; "F0417"; "F0497"; "F0405"; "F0414";}
{ rank = "same"; "p2"; "I1185"; "I1417"; "I1224"; "I1236"; "I1152"; }
{ rank = "same"; "p3"; "F0477"; "F0415"; "F0413"; "F0475"; }
```

Figure 3: A snippet of a graph specification controlling node ranks.

pute the constraints on generation layers and node orders in each generation. These constraints can be mapped into a graph specification of some already implemented tools. In particular, the DOT specification implemented by Graphviz tools enables such extensions.

Constraints on generation layering can be mapped easily to rank directives of the DOT language. A special node is created for each generation layer. The several additional subgraphs are generated. The first subgraph determines the sequence of generation layers using special generation nodes. Both nodes and edges can be set with the attribute style=invis so that these nodes and edges are not shown in the generated drawing although they control the layout. Then, other unnamed subgraphs are generated for each generation layer with the attribute rank=''same'' as a list of node identifiers belonging to that generation prepended with the node identifier of the given generation layer. A snippet of such an additional DOT specification is shown in Fig 3. The snippet also demonstrates how generations of people with node identifiers starting with "I" are interleaved with generations of marriages nodes starting with "F".

We selected two datasets for an evaluation of the proposed constraints contribution. The first dataset consists of 1671 people of the author's private family relationship genealogical graph. The set is created as a merge of several family trees ranging over 14 generations with the first records dated the year 1647. The second dataset consists of 3057 people of the database created by Egyptologists [17]. The database covers high rank officials from the 4th, 5th, and 6th dynasties and their families. One can reconstruct over 160 families with up to 6 generations. The database has been filled over ten years. Generated graphs covering more families help greatly Egyptologists to assess quickly investigated social phenomena.

The graph of the entire private family database was depicted on Fig 2. The layout was generated by DOT tool when the graph specification contains only a description of nodes representing people and marriages and genealogical edges (links between partners and their marriages, links between marriages and children). Although the overall appearance of the graph seems to be correct, there are serious deficiencies. Some parts of generations were moved upwards or downwards. Thus, the generations are mixed. In many cases, members of different families are mixed or some children are placed with a different family even if it causes obviously more edge crossing or longer edges.

When the constraints on generation layers are specified, the DOT tool might create a layout holding the rank specifications as depicted on Fig 4. One can spot immediately families as ovals followed by several rectangles. Not only family members are close to each other, but also their partial family trees are close, too. Unfortunately, one can also identify heavy crossing among spouses from several families with more children on the right side of the graph. There is always a marriage couple linking two large families together. An appropriate constraint avoiding such phenomena was proposed earlier in this paper. However, it must be properly combined with the computation of the constraints for children order and marriage order. Also, the solution must deal with a set of families that might be linked in a pairwise manner. At present, we are experimenting with several techniques to propose their best combination.

Experiments with families of the Egyptian database did not exhibit any breaking of these specifications as the families are quite simple and not larger than 50 family members.

A layout generated using the constraints proposed in this paper only without any further influence of the DOT tool is shown in Fig 5. The ranks of nodes were placed uniformly in a horizontal direction while their nodes were placed uniformly in a vertical direction. The nodes were linked with straight-lined edges. The layout is created very quickly (below 0.5 second with a Python script on DELL XPS 13 using an Intel i7 2GHz processor.

Nevertheless, there are also other issues connected with the DOT tool. The DOT tool takes the proposed order of nodes only as initial advice that does not need to be followed. Thus, if the DOT implemented criterion produces stronger values, it can break the specified node order and the layout can be again very confusing. For example, several ranks might be merged to save space if a generation layer is sparse. One might link children of a family with directive subgraph, but there is no specification on how ranking and subgraph specifications are combined and how they worked together. We performed a number of experiments with such more complex combinations with rather unpleasant results. We are not aware of any other tool that would allow a specification of a graph where one part controls the layout and the other part is presented, i.e. only coordinate positions of nodes are computed and edges are routed.

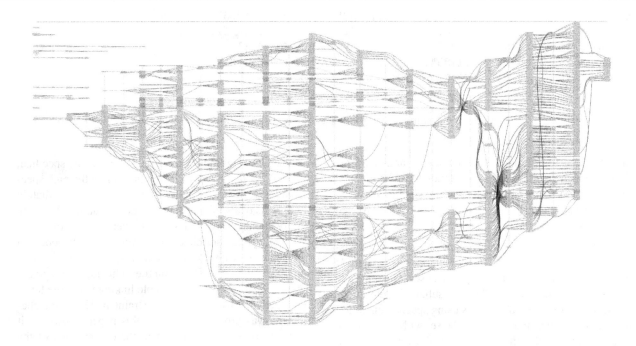

Figure 4: A visualization of the sample private family tree consisting of 1671 people if it is rendered using the DOT tool with the constraints on node ranks and their order within their ranks. Green edges control the layout. The top sequence of nodes defines ranking/generations. The quality of the picture is decreased to keep family privacy.

5   Conclusion

In this work we proposed two simple constraints on node order with regard to their ranks and to their order in ranks. The constraints produce graph layouts that are more acceptable for the user if they deal with large family trees combining several trees into a single acyclic graph. In fact, the constraints result in a fully specified topological arrangement of the graph nodes in plane. The constraints can be computed very efficiently. The experiments demonstrate clearly a significant improvement in graph comprehension and indicate that the results provided by the present state of the art tools are quite far from the optimum layout, at least for special sorts of graphs such as genealogical ones.

The proposed constraints do not cover properly a situation when more families with many children and a larger number of their mutual marriages are involved. Some hints on a better treatment were provided, but the search for their best combination is the current subject of our research. The proposed approach performs well if genealogical data resembles a composition of structures similar to trees with occasional crossovers of large families with many children.

Acknowledgement

Sponsored by the project for GAČR, No. 16-072105: Complex network methods applied to ancient Egypt data in the Old Kingdom (2700–2180 BC).

References

[1] W. T. Tutte, "Convex representations of graphs," *Proceedings of the London Mathematical Society, Third Series*, no. 10, pp. 304–320, 1960.

[2] ——, "How to draw a graph," *Proceedings of the London Mathematical Society, Third Series*, no. 13, pp. 743–768, 1960.

[3] H. Gibson, J. Faith, and P. Vickers, "A survey of two-dimensional graph layout techniques for information visualisation," *Information Visualization*, vol. 12, no. 3-4, pp. 324–357, 2013. [Online]. Available: http://ivi.sagepub.com/content/12/3-4/324.abstract

[4] C. McGrath, J. Blythe, and D. Krackhardt, "Seeing groups in graph layouts," *Connections*, vol. 19, no. 2, pp. 22–29, 1996.

[5] K. Keller, P. Reddy, and S. Sachdeva. (2010) Family tree visualization. Course project report. http://vis.berkeley.edu/courses/cs294-10-sp10/wiki/images/f/f2/Family_Tree_Visualization_-_Final_Paper.pdf. University of Berkeley. Accessed: 5.6.2016.

[6] (2016) Gramps. genealogical research software. https://gramps-project.org/. Accessed: 5.6.2016.

[7] (2016) Myheritage. https://www.myheritage.cz. Accessed: 5.6.2016.

[8] C. Tuttle, L. G. Nonato, and C. Silva, "Pedvis: A structured, space-efficient technique for pedigree visualization," *IEEE Transactions on Visualization and Computer Graphics*, vol. 16, no. 6, pp. 1063–1072, Nov 2010.

[9] V. Yoghourdjian, T. Dwyer, G. Gange, S. Kieffer, K. Klein, and K. Marriott, "High-quality ultra-compact grid layout of grouped networks," *IEEE Transactions on Visualization*

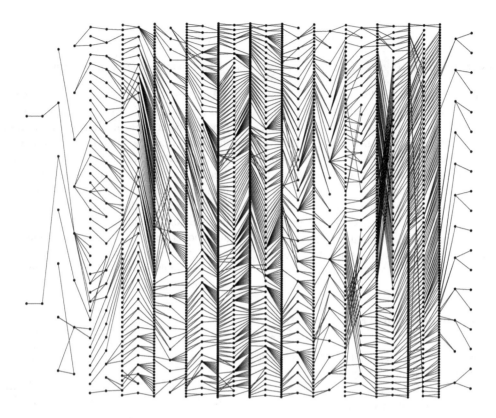

Figure 5: A visualization of the sample private family tree created from the rank and node order constraints proposed in this contribution only. An ideal layout would result in edges creating "waves" only. The heavy edge crossing on the right side is caused by the too simple local dropping of contradictory order requirements.

and Computer Graphics, vol. 22, no. 1, pp. 339–348, Jan 2016.

[10] R. Ball and D. Cook, "A family-centric genealogy visualization paradigm," in *14th Annual Family History Technology Workshop*, Provo, Utah, 2014.

[11] S. Kieffer, T. Dwyer, K. Marriott, and M. Wybrow, "Hola: Human-like orthogonal network layout," *IEEE Transactions on Visualization and Computer Graphics*, vol. 22, no. 1, pp. 349–358, Jan 2016.

[12] J. N. Warfield, "Crossing theory and hierarchy mapping," *IEEE Transactions on Systems, Man, and Cybernetics*, vol. 7, no. 7, pp. 505–523, July 1977.

[13] K. Sugiyama, S. Tagawa, and M. Toda, "Methods for visual understanding of hierarchical system structures," *IEEE Transactions on Systems, Man, and Cybernetics*, vol. 11, no. 2, pp. 109–125, Feb 1981.

[14] K. Sugiyama and K. Misue, "Visualization of structural information: automatic drawing of compound digraphs," *IEEE Transactions on Systems, Man, and Cybernetics*, vol. 21, no. 4, pp. 876–892, Jul 1991.

[15] (2016) Graphviz - graph visualization software. www.graphviz.org. Accessed: 5.6.2016.

[16] (2016) yed graph editor. http://www.yworks.com/products/yed. yWorks. Accessed: 5.6.2016.

[17] V. Dulíková, "The reign of king Nyuserre and its impact on the development of the Egyptian state. A multiplier effect period during the Old Kingdom." Ph.D. dissertation, Charles University in Prague, Faculty of Arts, Czech Institute of Egyptology, 2016.

[18] E. R. Gansner, E. Koutsofios, S. C. North, and K. phong Vo, "A technique for drawing directed graphs," *IEEE Transactions nn Software Engineering*, vol. 19, no. 3, pp. 214–230, 1993.

[19] T. H. Cormen, C. E. Leiserson, R. L. Rivest, and C. Stein, *Introduction to Algorithms, Third Edition*, 3rd ed. The MIT Press, 2009.

ITAT 2016 Proceedings, pp. 226–231
ISBN 978-1537016740, © 2016 M. Markošová

Dynamic model of functional brain networks

Mária Markošová

Faculty of Mathematics, Physics and Informatics, Department of Applied Informatics, Comenius University, Bratislava

Abstract: Functional brain networks are networks created with a help of fMRI measurements of the in vivo brain activity [3], [4]. I elaborated a dataset, which contains functional brain networks of young participants, healthy elderly participants and elderly participants with diagnosed Alzheimer disease. All networks were measured at the three different correlation thresholds.

In this paper I present a data driven mathematical model of functional brain networks. It is based on the threshold related shape of the degree distribution. The model is numerically simulated and results of the simulation are compared to the real dataset.

1 Functional brain networks

Functional Magnetic Resonance Imaging (fMRI) is a technique for gaining high resolution images of neural activity in the brain [3], [4]). FMRI images are captured in a series of two dimensional slices, with each slice representing a cross section of the brain less than 10 mm thick. A single slice is comprised of a rectangular grid of discrete 3D regions ($3 \times 3 \times 10$ mm) known as voxels (volumetric pixels). A full 3D image of the brain is achieved by combining these slices together. fMRI is an ideal technique for deriving functional connectivity. One can ask to which extend spatially distinct regions of the brain exhibit similar behavior over time. By modeling this functional connectivity as a network, we can explore the ways in which regions of the brain interact, and use techniques from the graph theory to evaluate the topological characteristics of these functional networks of interaction.

In this paper I used the brain fMRI data collected by Buckner [1], (data set no. 2-2000-118W from the fMRI Data Center: http://www.fmridc.org). The participants were divided into three groups: healthy young (HY) participants, healthy elderly (HE) participants and elderly participants with diagnosed Alzheimer disease (AD) (AE group). Structural and functional MRI data were acquired from 41 subjects in total. The HY group had 14 subjects (9 females/5 males) with the mean age 21.1 years (SD 2.0). The HE had 15 subjects (9 females/6 males) of the mean age 75.1 years (SD 6.9). The AE group had 12 subjects (7 females/5 males) of the mean age 77.1 years (SD 5.3). There was no statistically significant difference in the mean age of the latter two groups.

The standardized data were then used in [3], [4] to create functional brain networks for each participant in all three groups. These data were further elaborated by me.

Functional brain networks, contrary to the structural neuronal brain networks, are temporal networks. Certain type of the functional brain network exists only during that time, when the brain is involved in the cognitive task and reflects the functional cooperation of different brain areas. Since the smallest unit of the measured fMRI signal is an integrated signal of the neurons contained in one voxel, voxels are thus natural candidates for the nodes of the functional brain network. If the two voxels functionally cooperate (based on the underlying physical connectivity), the measured signal is highly correlated over time. To measure the amount of the signal correlation, the Pearson correlation coefficient is calculated for all the voxel pairs:

$$r(i,j) = \qquad\qquad (1)$$

$$\frac{<V(i,t)V(j,t)> - <V(i,t)><V(j,t)>}{(<V(i,t)^2> - <V(i,t)>^2)^{\frac{1}{2}}(<V(j,t)^2> - <V(j,t)>^2)^{\frac{1}{2}}}$$

where $r(i,j)$ is the correlation coefficient, $V(m,t)$ is the measured activity in the m-th voxel at time t, and $<.>$ denotes the time averages. A link between the voxel pair (nodes) is established, if $|r(i,j)| > \theta$, where θ is a prescribed correlation threshold. It is opted for an absolute value of correlation, that is both strongly positively and strongly negatively correlated voxels are included in the functional network, because the functional interaction between neurons can be either positive (excitatory) or negative (inhibitory). In any case, by nature, such created networks are unweighted and undirected, because correlation is a symmetric function. That means, that the node degree is simply a number of the closest neighbors.

Simple measures, that characterize the network in general are averages: such as average degree, density, average shortest path, average clustering coefficient, etc. Usually, these simple measures are not sufficient and one have to rely on distributions, such as degree distribution for example, to acquire more detailed network properties.

2 Data analysis

In this section I complete a basic network analysis of the measured data, already done and published by [3], [4]. The networks are constructed with respect to the three different correlation thresholds, namely $\theta_1 = 0.819398$, $\theta_2 = 0.899876$ and $\theta_3 = 0.962249$. McCarthy et al. [3], [4] have calculated average properties, i.e. number of nodes, density, degree, clustering coefficient, path length, local and global efficiency, small world index, assortativity for all classes of functional networks. These values were compared across each of the three groups, in order to find differences related to the age and the presence of AD. I concentrated my attention to the degree distributions in all three groups of participants at each of the three thresholds. The reason is, that the dynamical functional brain network model is based on this.

First, the whole brain networks of the healthy young (HY) participants are described. Then I mention also the other participant groups. At the beginning I have to state, that network is scale free if it has a power law degree distribution (4). .

For the lowest correlation threshold $\theta_1 = 0.819398$ one can see in Fig. 1, that the degree distribution does not have a power law character. Thus, the functional brain networks are not scale free and the tail of the distributions is not long enough to estimate the power law scaling exponents correctly.

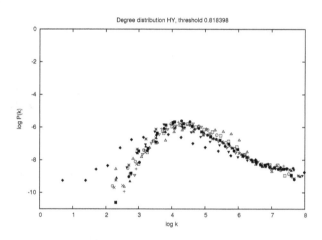

Figure 1: HY group. Degree distribution for the functional brain networks at the lowest threshold $\theta_1 = 0.819398$.

For the correlation threshold $\theta_2 = 0.899876$ the degree distribution reveals more pronounced power law tail , with the average scaling exponent $\gamma^2_{HY} = -1.14$ (see Fig.2). The scaling exponent is calculated as an average of all scaling exponents of all distributions for the threshold in question.

The situation changes dramatically for the highest correlation threshold $\theta_3 = 0.962249$. The functional brain networks now have a well defined scale free structure, reflected in the power law degree distribution with the average scaling exponent $\gamma = -1.36$ (see Fig.3) with the individual differences in the interval $[-1.7812, -0.9346]$.

The same statistical distributions as for the previous group were analyzed for the HE group of participants. For the lowest correlation threshold θ_1 the degree distribution shows similar features as in the group of the healthy young participants, with the exception, that the individual differences are more pronounced.

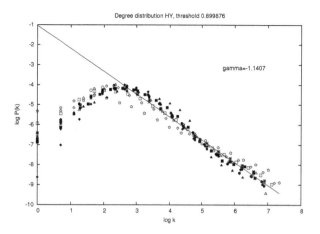

Figure 2: HY group. Degree distribution for the functional brain networks at the middle threshold $\theta_2 = 0.899876$.

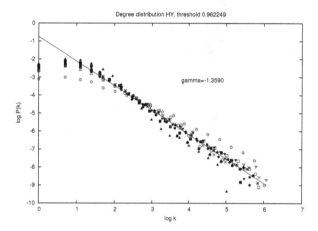

Figure 3: HY group. Degree distribution for the functional brain networks at the highest threshold $\theta_3 = 0.962249$.

For the medium threshold θ_2 the degree distribution reveals more pronounced tail in the log–log plot and shows more variability in individuals then the similar degree distribution of the HY group. Statistical analysis of the networks generated for the highest threshold θ_3 shows that the degree distribution seems to be scale free, but with more individual differences than in the HY group. Average scaling exponent is $\gamma_{HE} = -1.3609$ and all individual scaling exponents are in the interval $[-2.0396, -1.0500]$.

We have also analyzed the functional brain networks of the elderly people with diagnosed mild or very mild Alzheimer disease (AE group) for all of the three thresholds. In comparison to the first two groups, namely HY and HE, we have noticed greater individual differences. Even for the highest threshold not all of the networks are scale free.

For the θ_1 correlation threshold, the networks are not scale free, There are more pronounced power law tails of the degree distributions at the θ_2 correlation threshold and the average scaling exponent is $\gamma_2 = -0.8641$. Four (out

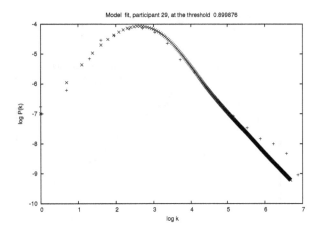

Figure 4: HY group. The best fit of the model at the θ_2 threshold. Parameters: $a = 1.3957$, $b = 0.0013$, $a_1 = 3.7477$, $b_1 = 243,1351$.

of 12) individual distributions do not have the power law tail at all for this threshold.

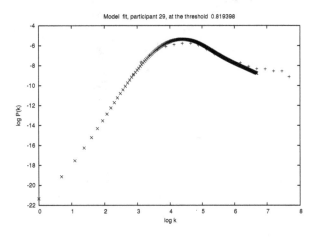

Figure 5: HY group. The best fit of the model at the θ_1 threshold. Parameters: $a = 12.2377$, $b = 1.7657$, $a_1 = 14.4403$, $b_1 = 888,3863$.

At the highest threshold (θ_3), the degree distribution of the majority of networks has a power law character. The exception is one outlier. The average scaling exponent is $\gamma_3 = -1.3429$ (interval $[-2.1867, -0.8046]$.)

3 Model of the functional brain networks

There are only a few papers, which attempt to model the dynamics of functional brain networks. For example Portillo and Gleiser [5] developed an adaptive complex network model, where different anatomical regions in the brain are represented by microscopic units, dynamical nodes. They start from a small random network, which grows by the addition of the new nodes with fixed number of connections. The newcomers are linked at random, but

then the connections are adaptively rewired according to coherence. The state of the system is calculated at each iteration, and the evolution of nodes is given by the dynamical equation describing a set of non-linear phase oscillators. The global and local rewiring process depends on the current state. Gleiser and Spoormaker later adapted this model to model the hierarchical structure in the functional brain networks [2]. A different principle to model functional brain networks has been used by Vértes and others [6]. They proposed a model incorporating the factor of economy governing a link establishment. The topology of functional brain networks emerges from the two competitive factors: a distance penalty based on the cost of maintaining long range connections and a topological term favoring links between brain regions sharing similar input.

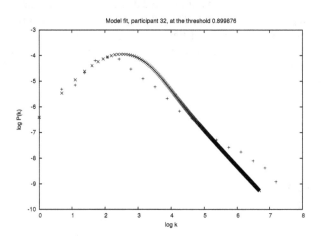

Figure 6: HY group. The worst fit of the model at the θ_2 threshold. Parameters: $a = 1.8655$, $b = 0.0000$, $a_1 = 3.6148$, $b_1 = 528,5197$.

In this paper I follow a different principle. Similar picture, as with changing the correlation threshold in our analysis, is described in Scholz et al. [7] for the noisy scale free networks. The authors started from a network with pure scale free degree distribution. Then, after fixing the number of nodes to N_0, and also the initial number of edges to L_0, this network is disturbed by some type of noise: i.e. random link removal, random link exchange and random link addition. The authors have studied, how the degree distribution drifts from the power law character with increasing the noise (randomness) in the network.

I observed the same pattern, namely, that the lowering of the correlation threshold is analogical to increasing the probability of addition of random links in the functional networks, which in turn causes, that the degree distribution is not power law any more. The situation can be described as follows: To utilize a view of coming nodes at each time unit, common in the growing network models, I relate time and threshold. One starts at the highest threshold θ_3 (time $t_0 = 0$), where the network is scale free having N_0 nodes, L_0 edges and the power law degree distribution. Then the threshold is lowered as the time flows. New nodes and edges are added to the network by both – a preferential and random linking. We suppose, that the threshold discrete and infinitesimal "jumps" can be accommodated in such a way, that only one new node and on average the same number of new edges appear per iteration. Each new node brings a_1 new edges, which are linked preferentially and a edges which are linked randomly. The total amount of edges brought by one node in each time step is therefore $a + a_1$. Simultaneously another process takes place. As the threshold decreases (time flows), some correlations between the couples of nodes already present in the network become significant. Therefore new edges are distributed randomly (b) and preferentially (b_1), respectively, among the nodes being already in the network.

Thus, unlike in the model of Scholz et al [7], the network grows in the number of nodes and edges as well. Because the network at the highest threshold, which corresponds to time t_0, is scale free, it is supposed, that the real correlations between voxels construct scale free structure, which is, as the threshold lowers (time grows), disturbed by the accidental correlations (links). These correlations are caused either by the real influence between the two voxels or by an accidental resemblance of the two measured signals. As we know from the theory of growing networks, scale free degree distribution is created by the preferential attachment [8].

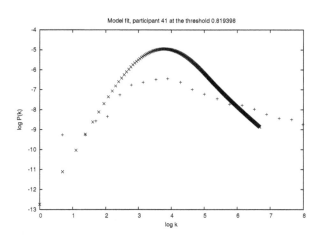

Figure 7: HY group. The worst fit of the model at the θ_1 threshold. Parameters: $a = 6.8756$, $b = 0.0600$, $a_1 = 6.9720$, $b_1 = 824,4624$.

The equation describing the above mentioned dynamical processes in the model is:

$$P(k,t+1) = p_{k,k-1}(t)P(k-1,t) + (1 - p_{k+1,k}(t))P(k,t) \tag{2}$$

In (2) the transition term $p_{k,k-1}(t)$ reads:

$$p_{k,k-1}(t) = \frac{a + 2b}{N_0 + t} + \frac{(a_1 + 2b_1)(k-1)}{2L_0 + A(t)}, \tag{3}$$

where $A(t) = 2(a + b + a_1 + b_1)t$.

In (2, 3) $P(k,t)$ is the normalized number of nodes having the degree k at the time (threshold) t. In (3) N_0, L_0 denote initial number of nodes and edges, a, b are the number of randomly added edges per iteration, where a is the number of edges fetched by a new-coming node and b is the number of edges added between an older network nodes. Similarly a_1, b_1 denote the number of edges by which a new node links preferentially (a_1) to the network and b_1 is the number of edges linking older nodes preferentially. The transition term $p_{k+1,k}(t)$ describes, how the number of nodes having the degree k changes due to the above mentioned dynamical processes. The first term of the equation (2) is a gain term and the second one is a loss term. In the model, it is neglected what happens with the other links, the attention is payed to the fact how the link addition affects the degree k (2, 3) .

4   Results of numerical simulations

The model (3) have been simulated numerically. Each simulation have been attempted for all functional brain networks for all the three groups of participants and compared to the data at the thresholds θ_2 and θ_1. The best, and the worst fits for the HY group of participants and for each threshold are presented here at figs 4 - 7 together with the best fits for the HE and AE groups (figs 8 - 11). The networks, which were excluded, and the reasons why they were excluded, are to be explained later.

First the experimental data have been used to find the parameters c and γ in the power law distributions at the highest threshold θ_3 (4). This threshold, in the threshold – time view, corresponds to the initial time $t_0 = 0$, i.e.:

$$P(k) = ck^\gamma \tag{4}$$

Both parameters c and γ are derived from the data. The power law distribution function at the highest threshold has been normalized by the constant n (based on the data) calculated from the equation

$$n = \int_1^\infty P(k)dk. \tag{5}$$

and it has been checked whether the sum of all probabilities of the initial distribution is close to one after the normalization. The networks, for which the integral (5) does not converge (in a case $-1.0 < \gamma < 0.0$) were excluded. Here γ is a scaling exponent of the power law degree distribution (4) at the highest threshold.

In the numerical simulations I first applied the model to model the transition between the two highest correlation thresholds, namely θ_3. and θ_2 of the functional brain networks. Each model has been iterated $N_2 - N_0$ times (because at each time unit only one node appears) for the defined set of parameters a, a_1, b, b_1. N_0, N_2 denote the number of nodes at the initial time (threshold θ_3) and at the time t_2 corresponding to the lower correlation threshold θ_2. These numbers of nodes I have from the data. In

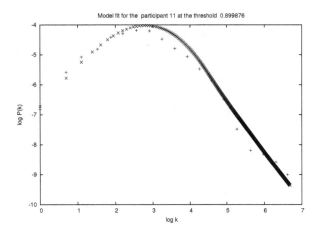

Figure 8: HE group. The best fit of the model at the θ_2 threshold. Parameters: $a = 2.6028$, $b = 0.0000$, $a_1 = 2.5687$, $b_1 = 313,4685$.

each time step (a discrete small threshold change) a fixed number of edges is added, namely $\frac{(L_2-L_0)}{(N_2-N_0)}$, where L_2 is the number of network edges gained from the measured data at the threshold θ_2 and L_0 is the initial number of edges. To find the best set of parameters a, b, a_1, b_1 we used the hill climbing algorithm, in which the mean square error between the measured and simulated datasets has been calculated. From the best fit parameters in the current simulation fifteen new sets of parameters have been derived by slight perturbations of the currently best fit parameter set. This is a standard procedure in the hill climbing algorithm. The hill climbing algorithm has been iterated 800 times .

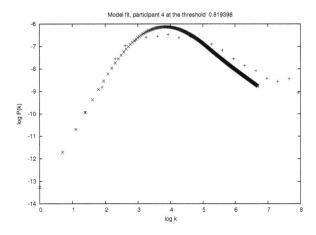

Figure 9: HE group. The best fit of the model at the θ_1 threshold. Parameters: $a = 9.3095$, $b = 1.7183$, $a_1 = 12.3784$, $b_1 = 3167,9538$.

Second, I do the same job as before to model the data at the threshold θ_1. The only difference is, that the hill climbing algorithm has been iterated $N_1 - N_0$ times, where N_1 is the number of nodes at the lowest threshold θ_1 . Also the number of edges added in each threshold jump (time step)

is different, namely $\frac{(L_1-L_0)}{(N_1-N_0)}$, where L_1 is the number of edges in the functional brain network created at the lowest threshold θ_1. N_1, N_0, L_1, L_0 are estimated from the data.

Because of the lack of place I present here the more complete results for the HY group only. The best fits in this group at the thresholds θ_2, θ_1 are seen at figs (4, 5). The worst fits for the HY group at the threshold θ_2 , θ_1 are depicted at figs (6, 7). The best fits for the HE and AE groups are presented at figs 8 - 11. The comparison of the groups is described in the discussion.

5   Summary and discussion

In this paper functional brain networks created at the three different correlation thresholds were analyzed. The networks have been measured in a three different groups of participants, namely the HY (healthy young), HE (healthy elderly) and AE (elderly with the Alzheimer disease) group.

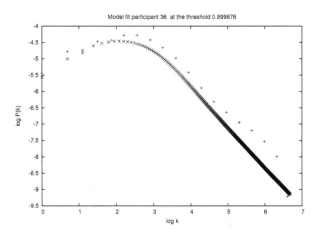

Figure 10: AE group. The best fit of the model at the θ_2 threshold. Parameters: $a = 0.1516$, $b = 0.0000$, $a_1 = 2.0920$, $b_1 = 228,0264$.

As a first steps a check at which threshold the networks are scale free and how they change with the threshold changes is performed. For this reason the degree distribution for each participant at each correlation threshold has been created and looked for the power law tails. It has been found found that:

- In general, the degree distributions of the functional brain networks changes with the threshold. At the highest threshold θ_3 the degree distributions are scale free with well developed power law tail (fig. 3). As the threshold decreases, the degree distributions are changing and the power law tails are less pronounced. That means, that the network looses its scale free structure (figs. 1, 2).

- There are significant intergroup differences in the degree distributions at each threshold. For example, at the highest threshold, the power law tails are less pronounced in the AE group in comparison to the HY and HE group. In one case there is no power law tail at all in the AE group.

- There are also individual differences in the functional brain network degree distributions in each group at each threshold. These individual differences are most significant in the AE group. The HY group exhibits the most coherent behavior. In this group my dynamical model is most successful in fitting the data correctly.

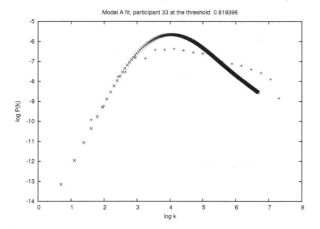

Figure 11: AE group. The best fit of the model at the θ_1 threshold. Parameters: $a = 8.2092$, $b = 0.0000$, $a_1 = 15.5483$, $b_1 = 1232, 3125$.

The reason of these studies was to get an insight into the in group and inter group differences in order to create an appropriate mathematical model. The overall picture was very similar to the one produced by the model of the noisy scale free network with randomly added edges Scholz et al [7].

As a second step a model of the functional brain networks has been suggested. Its detailed description is in the previous section. The model describes the dynamical processes which occur in the growing noisy, initially scale free, network. The noise in the model is due to the random distribution of a constant number of edges among a nodes being already in network. On the other hand, the preferentially distributed edges among the nodes already in network, support the scale free structure. The network also grows by the node addition, each node brings a constant number of a new edges, which are distributed either randomly or preferentially.

Due to the fact, that the original data in the HY group were the least noisy and exhibit the greatest coherence of behavior, the model gives the best results for this group. The measured data in the other groups (HE, AE) were rather noisy which influenced also preprocessing and network creation itself [3] [4]. The model gives less accurate

fits in these groups, although they are qualitatively in an accordance with the data.

In conclusion, I would like to point out, that the same model accounts for the data from the HY, HE and AE individuals. This means that there might be a universal principle how the brain dynamically organizes its functional networks regardless of the age and/or onset of a neurodegenerative disease. This is a prediction arising from the model, which however needs further testing. For example the model could be enriched by taking into account a fact, that only one edge can be added at a time step to a certain node. The others should be added elsewhere. If such model will perform better, it is possible to test another one, allowing two, three... edges to be added in one time step to the same node. This is, however, left for further studies.

Regardless brain functional network, I think, that the mathematical model of growing noisy scale free network can be interesting itself as well. There might be another situations in reality to which such model can be applied.

I would like to thank prof. Beňušková for careful reading of this text. I am also grateful to doc. Rudolf for many discussions.

References

[1] Buckner, R. L., Snyder, A. Z., Sanders, A. L., Raichle, M. E., and Morris, J. C. Functional Brain Imaging of Young, Nondemented, and Demented Older Adults. Journal of Cognitive Neuroscience, 12 (Supplement 2), 24-34, (2000).

[2] Gleiser, P. M., Spoormake,r V. I., Modeling hierarchical structure in functional brain network, Philos. Trans. A Math. Phys. Eng. Sci 368 (1933), pp 5633-44, (2010)

[3] McCarthy P., Benuskova L., Franz E. A. Functional network analysis of aging and Alzheimer disease: Results. Technical Report OUCS-2013-12, University of Otago, New Zealand, (2013).

[4] McCarthy P., Benuskova L., Franz E.A. The age-related posterior-anterior shift as revealed by voxelwise analysis of functional brain networks. Frontiers in Aging Neuroscience. 6:301. doi: 10.3389/fnagi.2014.00301, (2014)

[5] Portillo, I. J. G., Gleise,r P. M, An adaptive complex network model for brain functional networks, PLoS One 4 (9), pp 1-8, (2009) .

[6] Vértes, P. E., Alexander - Bloch, A. F., Gogtay N., Giedd, J. N., Rapoport, J. L., Bullmore, E. T., Simple models of human brain functional networks, Proc. Natl. Acad. Sci. USA 109 (15), pp. 5868-73, (2012)

[7] Scholz, J., Dejori, M., Stetter, M., Greiner, M., Noisy scale free networks, Physica A 350 (2-4), pp 622 -642, (2005)

[8] A. L. Barabási, R. Albert, mergence of scaling in random networks, Science 286, 3616 (1999)

ITAT 2016 Proceedings, p. 232
ISBN 978-1537016740, © 2016 D. Bernát

On the Mean Value of Domination Number of Random Regular Graphs
(Presentation Abstract)

Dušan Bernát

Slovak University of Technology in Bratislava
Faculty of Informatics and Information Technologies
Ilkovičova 2, 842 16 Bratislava, Slovak Republic
dusan.bernat@stuba.sk

This short note presents an outline of simulation results for the size of minimum dominating set (MDS) of random graphs with a toroidal base graph. Particularly the base graph under consideration is 2-dimensional 1-fold torus, which can be imagined as a grid with an extra edges connecting two opposite border vertices (both vertical and horizontal). This is a 4-regular graph and in this case the mean value of MDS size of random torus obtained by simulations appears to be well approximated by a weighted sum of Bernstein polynomials.

Let $G = (V, E)$ be a simple graph of order $N = |V|$. Subset $D \subseteq V$ is called a *dominating set* of vertices if every vertex $v \in V$ is either in D or is adjacent to some vertex in D. Formally, $\forall v \in V - D, N(v) \cap D \neq \emptyset$, where $N(v)$ is an *open neighbourhood* of vertex v, $N(v) = \{u | (u, v) \in E\}$. Cardinality of the minimum over all dominating sets for given graph G is called a *domination number*, denoted $\gamma(G)$. Though it is easy to find some dominating set for a graph, finding the minimum dominating set is known to be an NP-hard problem [1]. Obtaining MDS or its cardinality takes exponential time with respect to the graph order. Moreover, some results show that it is not possible to achieve constant approximation ratio for this problem [2].

By a *random graph* $\mathbf{G} = (G, p)$ we mean a graph obtained from the base graph G by selecting each edge independently with equal probability of p. The question of concern here is what is the average domination number of multiple realisations of $\mathbf{G}$ for some fixed base graph and how does it change with changing probability parameter p. Recent work by M. Nehéz [3] provides upper and lower bounds for random tori which are in good accordance with the simulation results.

We performed several simulations where random 2-dimensional tori were generated with probability parameter p ranging from zero to one with the step 0.01 and domination number was computed by the use of integer linear programming methods. It is noteworthy that mean value of the domination number as a function of p can be approximated by a simple formula comprising p and parameter D. Here D denotes the number of neighbours of a graph vertex. For the case of 2-dimensional tori used in our simulations the value of $D = 4$. But we conjecture that the formula holds for any D-regular graph.

Present simulation results confirmed the formula for the 4-regular 2-dimensional torus with the maximum absolute difference up to 3.5%. Results for the 2-regular circle (1-dimensional torus) had absolute difference between simulation and computed result at most 1.4%. Perhaps this can be further improved by taking more simulation runs or the higher order of the graph. Future work will be aimed at other D-regular graphs, as well as the theoretical support of these simulation based results.

Acknowledgements. This work was supported by Slovak Science Grant Agency VEGA, project no. 1/0616/14.

References

[1] T.W. Haynes, S.T. Hedetniemi, P.J. Slater: Fundamentals of Domination in Graphs. Marcel Dekker, New York 1998.

[2] M.R. Garey, D.S. Johnson: Computers and Intractability, A Guide to the Theory of NP-Completeness. W.H. Freeman and Company, New York, 1979.

[3] M. Nehéz: personal communication (2016-07-11). To appear in WASACNA 2016.

ITAT 2016 Proceedings, p. 233
ISBN 978-1537016740, © 2016 M. Nehéz

On Some Combinatorial Properties of Random 2-Dimensional Tori
(Presentation Abstract)

Martin Nehéz

Institute of Information Engineering, Automation and Mathematics,
Faculty of Chemical and Food Technology, Slovak University of Technology in Bratislava
Radlinského 9, 812 37 Bratislava, Slovak Republic
martin.nehez@stuba.sk

Two-dimensional grids are typical instances of planar graphs often used as underlaying topologies in various industrial applications such as VLSI circuits, interconnection networks for parallel architectures, etc. Two-dimensional tori represents 4-regular graphs with a similar structure as grids. In this paper, we consider random tori, i.e. random graphs, denoted by $\mathbf{G}(T_{\sqrt{n} \times \sqrt{n}}, p)$, obtained from a base graph by independently removing each edge with a constant probability. The probability space $\mathbf{G}(T_{\sqrt{n} \times \sqrt{n}}, p)$ is a modification of the well-known Erdös-Rényi random graph model where the base graph is an n-node 2-dimensional torus.

The domination number of a graph G, denoted $\gamma(G)$, is the minimum size of a dominating set of vertices in G. The problem of determining the exact value of domination number for grids is rather complicated and was fully solved only recently in [1] and there are not many results on invariants of random tori.

In this paper, we examine the asymptotic bounds on the domination number for random tori $\mathbf{G}(T_{\sqrt{n} \times \sqrt{n}}, p)$. Our proof is based on the second moment method adopted from probability theory. It follows that the expected number of vertices with a given degree k (for $k = 0, \ldots, 4$) can be expressed, in random tori, by the Bernstein polynomial $b_{k,4}(p)$. Main results are formulated in terms of lower and upper bounds on the asymptotic value of γ for random tori. The general upper bound is complemented by the piecewise-defined lower bound depending on four subintervals of a unit interval. The limit cases for $p \to 0$ and $p \to 1$ are in good correspondence with the trivial value of γ for $p = 0$ and with the result [1], respectively.

Acknowledgement

This research is supported by the Ministry of Education, Science, Research and Sport of the Slovak Republic under the grant KEGA 047STU-4/2016.

References

[1] D. Gonçalves, A. Pinlou, M. Rao, S. Thomassé: The Domination Number of Grids. SIAM J. Discrete Math. **25**(3), (2011) pp. 1443–1453

[2] T. W. Haynes, S. T. Hedetniemi, P. J. Slater: Fundamentals of Domination in Graphs. Marcel Dekker, Inc., New York (1998)

[3] S. Janson, T. Łuczak, A. Ruciński: Random Graphs. Wiley-Interscience Publication (2000)

[4] E. M. Palmer: Graphical Evolution. John Wiley & Sons, Inc., New York (1985)

ITAT 2016 Proceedings, p. 234
ISBN 978-1537016740, © 2016 M. Nehéz, J. Kožíková

Toward Fast Computation of Proteomic Parsimony via Bipartite Graphs (Presentation Abstract)

Martin Nehéz, and Júlia Kožíková

Institute of Information Engineering, Automation and Mathematics,
Faculty of Chemical and Food Technology, Slovak University of Technology in Bratislava
Radlinského 9, 812 37 Bratislava, Slovak Republic
martin.nehez@stuba.sk

We address the problem of proteins identification for a cell or tissue. One of the methods used for this purpose is based on assembling peptides and analyzing the peptide–protein relationships [3]. Such relationships are represented by bipartite graphs and, subsequently, the original problem is reduced to finding a dominating set in a given peptide–protein graph. However, the minimum dominating set problem is an NP-hard even for bipartite graphs [1]. Thus, inventing of a fast algorithm for the mentioned task is of great significance. In our overview, various approaches which would lead to solve the above problem are discussed. As we take the general version of the problem into account, some of the algorithms examined in [2] would compute satisfactory solutions. At last, directions for the future research are also mentioned.

Acknowledgement

This research is supported by the Ministry of Education, Science, Research and Sport of the Slovak Republic under the grant KEGA 047STU-4/2016.

References

[1] Liedloff, M.: Finding a dominating set on bipartite graphs. Information Processing Letters (2008), **107**, pp. 154–157.

[2] Nehéz, M., Bernát, D., Klaučo, M.: Comparison of algorithms for near-optimal dominating sets computation in real-world networks. In Proc. of the 16th Int. Conference on Computer Systems and Technologies, ACM New York (2015), pp. 199–206.

[3] Zhang, B., Chambers, M.C., Tabb, D.L.: Proteomic Parsimony through Bipartite Graph Analysis Improves Accuracy and Transparency. J. Proteome Research (2007), **6** (9), pp. 3549–3557.

Algorithmic Aspects of Finding Semigroups of Partial Automorphisms of Combinatorial Structures (AAFSPACS 2016)

The problem of the time complexity of determining the full automorphism group of a combinatorial structure (for example a graph) is one of the well-known unsettled algorithmic problems with numerous practical implications in a number of fields. The relevance of this topic was well documented by the immense interest exhibited by the research community with regard to the recent breakthrough of Laszlo Babai who announced the discovery of a quasipolynomial time algorithm for graphs. The focus of our workshop will be on an extension of the automorphism group problem to that of inverse semigroup problem. The full inverse semigroup of partial automorphisms of a combinatorial structure is a much richer algebraical structure that contains the automorphism group of the combinatorial object as a subgroup. Furthermore, the inverse semigroup of partial automorphisms contains much more detailed local information about the underlying object. Thus, the problem of determining the full inverse semigroup of partial automorphisms of a combinatorial structure is at least as hard as the corresponding automorphism group problem.

In our workshop, we focus on algorithmic problems related to determining the inverse semigroup of a combinatorial structure as well as related problems of finding structures with a given inverse semigroup, and applications of inverse semigroups to constructing objects with a prescribed relation between their local and global properties.

Presenters at his workshop submitted only abstracts, no full-length papers were solicited.

This workshop is sponsored by the VEGA 1/0577/14 grant aimed at investigating the relations between Semigroup Theory and Combinatorics.

Tatiana Jajcayová
Róbert Jajcay
Comenius University in Bratislava, Slovakia
Workshop organizers

ITAT 2016 Proceedings, p. 236
ISBN 978-1537016740, © 2016 O. Grošek

Semigroups in Cryptography
(Presentation Abstract)

Otokar Grošek

Slovak University of Technology, Bratislava, Slovakia
otokar.grosek@stuba.sk

In our talk we will discuss the appearance of semigroups in this very fruitful research area. We will start our discussion with a semigroup structure of S_{pq}, i.e. the multiplicative semigroup (mod pq), following by other semigroups for which the Global Euler Fermat Theorem is known. Then we will switch our attention to a 'very simple' congruence $ax \equiv b$ (mod n), and its relation to the idempotent structure of $\mathscr{Z}_n$. Finally we will mention some other applications of Semigroup theory in cryptography.

ITAT 2016 Proceedings, pp. 237–240
ISBN 978-1537016740, © 2016 O. Gutik

ITAT

On the Group of Automorphisms of the Brandt λ^0-Extension of a Monoid With Zero
(Presentation Abstract)

Oleg Gutik

Faculty of Mechanics and Mathematics, Ivan Franko National University of Lviv, Universytetska 1, Lviv, 79000, UKRAINE,
o_gutik@franko.lviv.ua, ovgutik@yahoo.com,
WWW home page: http://prima.lnu.edu.ua/faculty/mechmat/Departments/Topology/Gutik_mine.html

Abstract: The group of automorphisms of the Brandt λ^0-extension $B_\lambda^0(S)$ of an arbitrary monoid S with zero is described. In particular we show that the group of automorphisms $\mathbf{Aut}(B_\lambda^0(S))$ of $B_\lambda^0(S)$ is isomorphic to a homomorphic image of the group defines on the Cartesian product $\mathscr{S}_\lambda \times \mathbf{Aut}(S) \times H_1^\lambda$ with the following binary operation:

$$[\varphi, h, u] \cdot [\varphi', h', u'] = [\varphi\varphi', hh', \varphi u' \cdot uh'],$$

where $\mathscr{S}_\lambda$ is the group of all bijections of the cardinal λ, $\mathbf{Aut}(S)$ is the group of all automorphisms of the semigroup S and H_1^λ is the direct λ-power of the group of units H_1 of the monoid S.

1 Introduction and preliminaries

Further we shall follow the terminology of [2, 21].

Given a semigroup S, we shall denote the set of idempotents of S by $E(S)$. A semigroup S with the adjoined unit (identity) [zero] will be denoted by S^1 [S^0] (cf. [2]). Next, we shall denote the unit (identity) and the zero of a semigroup S by 1_S and 0_S, respectively. Given a subset A of a semigroup S, we shall denote by $A^* = A \setminus \{0_S\}$.

If S is a semigroup, then we shall denote the subset of idempotents in S by $E(S)$. If $E(S)$ is closed under multiplication in S and we shall refer to $E(S)$ a *band* (or the *band of S*). If the band $E(S)$ is a non-empty subset of S, then the semigroup operation on S determines the following partial order $\leqslant$ on $E(S)$: $e \leqslant f$ if and only if $ef = fe = e$. This order is called the *natural partial order* on $E(S)$.

If $h\colon S \to T$ is a homomorphism (or a map) from a semigroup S into a semigroup T and if $s \in S$, then we denote the image of s under h by $(s)h$.

Let S be a semigroup with zero and λ a cardinal $\geqslant 1$. We define the semigroup operation on the set $B_\lambda(S) = (\lambda \times S \times \lambda) \cup \{0\}$ as follows:

$$(\alpha, a, \beta) \cdot (\gamma, b, \delta) = \begin{cases} (\alpha, ab, \delta), & \text{if } \beta = \gamma; \\ 0, & \text{if } \beta \neq \gamma, \end{cases}$$

and $(\alpha, a, \beta) \cdot 0 = 0 \cdot (\alpha, a, \beta) = 0 \cdot 0 = 0$, for all $\alpha, \beta, \gamma, \delta \in \lambda$ and $a, b \in S$. If $S = S^1$ then the semigroup $B_\lambda(S)$ is called the *Brandt λ-extension of the semigroup S* [4]. Obviously, if S has zero then $\mathscr{J} = \{0\} \cup \{(\alpha, 0_S, \beta) \colon 0_S$ is the zero

of $S\}$ is an ideal of $B_\lambda(S)$. We put $B_\lambda^0(S) = B_\lambda(S)/\mathscr{J}$ and the semigroup $B_\lambda^0(S)$ is called the *Brandt λ^0-extension of the semigroup S with zero* [8].

If $\mathscr{I}$ is a trivial semigroup (i.e. $\mathscr{I}$ contains only one element), then we denote the semigroup $\mathscr{I}$ with the adjoined zero by $\mathscr{I}^0$. Obviously, for any $\lambda \geqslant 2$, the Brandt λ^0-extension of the semigroup $\mathscr{I}^0$ is isomorphic to the semigroup of $\lambda \times \lambda$-matrix units and any Brandt λ^0-extension of a semigroup with zero which also contains a non-zero idempotent contains the semigroup of $\lambda \times \lambda$-matrix units. We shall denote the semigroup of $\lambda \times \lambda$-matrix units by B_λ. The 2×2-matrix semigroup with adjoined identity B_2^1 plays an impotent role in Graph Theory and its called the *Perkins semigroup*. In the paper [20] Perkins showed that the semigroup B_2^1 is not finitely based. More details on the word problem of the Perkins semigroup via different graphs may be found in the works of Kitaev and his coauthors (see [17, 18]).

We always consider the Brandt λ^0-extension only of a monoid with zero. Obviously, for any monoid S with zero we have $B_1^0(S) = S$. Note that every Brandt λ-extension of a group G is isomorphic to the Brandt λ^0-extension of the group G^0 with adjoined zero. The Brandt λ^0-extension of the group with adjoined zero is called a *Brandt semigroup* [2, 21]. A semigroup S is a Brandt semigroup if and only if S is a completely 0-simple inverse semigroup [1, 19] (cf. also [21, Theorem II.3.5]). We shall say that the Brandt λ^0-extension $B_\lambda^0(S)$ of a semigroup S is *finite* if the cardinal λ is finite.

In the paper [14] Gutik and Repovš established homomorphisms of the Brandt λ^0-extensions of monoids with zeros. They also described a category whose objects are ingredients in the constructions of the Brandt λ^0-extensions of monoids with zeros. Here they introduced finite, compact topological Brandt λ^0-extensions of topological semigroups and countably compact topological Brandt λ^0-extensions of topological inverse semigroups in the class of topological inverse semigroups, and established the structure of such extensions and non-trivial continuous homomorphisms between such topological Brandt λ^0-extensions of topological monoids with zero. There they also described a category whose objects are ingredients in the constructions of finite (compact, countably compact) topological Brandt λ^0-extensions of topological monoids with zeros. These investigations were continued in [10] and [9], where established countably compact topological Brandt λ^0-extensions of topological monoids with zeros and pseudocompact topological Brandt λ^0-extensions of semitopological monoids with zeros their corresponding categories. Some other topological aspects of topologizations, embeddings and completions of the semigroup of $\lambda \times \lambda$-matrix units and Brandt λ^0-extensions as semitopological and topological semigroups were studied in [3, 5, 7, 11, 12, 13, 15, 16].

In this paper we describe the group of automorphisms of the Brandt λ^0-extension $B_\lambda^0(S)$ of an arbitrary monoid S with zero.

2 Automorphisms of the Brandt λ^0-extension of a monoid with zero

We observe that if $f: S \to S$ is an automorphism of the semigroup S without zero then it is obvious that the map $\widehat{f}: S^0 \to S^0$ defined by the formula

$$(s)\widehat{f} = \begin{cases} (s)f, & \text{if } s \neq 0_S; \\ 0_S, & \text{if } s = 0_S, \end{cases}$$

is an automorphism of the semigroup S^0 with adjoined zero 0_S. Also the automorphism $f: S \to S$ of the semigroup S can be extended to an automorphism $f_B: B_\lambda^0(S) \to B_\lambda^0(S)$ of the Brandt λ^0-extension $B_\lambda^0(S)$ of the semigroup S by the formulae:

$$(\alpha, s, \beta)f_B = (\alpha, (s)f, \beta), \quad \text{for all } \alpha, \beta \in \lambda$$

and $(0)f_B = 0$. We remark that so determined extended automorphism is not unique.

The following theorem describes all automorphisms of the Brandt λ^0-extension $B_\lambda^0(S)$ of a monoid S.

Theorem 1. *Let $\lambda \geqslant 1$ be cardinal and let $B_\lambda^0(S)$ be the Brandt λ^0-extension of monoid S with zero. Let $h: S \to S$ be an automorphism and suppose that $\varphi: \lambda \to \lambda$ is a bijective map. Let H_1 be the group of units of S and $u: \lambda \to H_1$ a map. Then the map $\sigma: B_\lambda^0(S) \to B_\lambda^0(S)$ defined by the formulae*

$$\begin{aligned} ((\alpha, s, \beta))\sigma = &((\alpha)\varphi, (\alpha)u \cdot (s)h \cdot ((\beta)u)^{-1}, (\beta)\varphi) \\ &\text{and} \quad (0)\sigma = 0, \end{aligned} \tag{1}$$

is an automorphism of the semigroup $B_\lambda^0(S)$. Moreover, every automorphism of $B_\lambda^0(S)$ can be constructed in this manner.

Proof. A simple verification shows that σ is an automorphism of the semigroup $B_\lambda^0(S)$.

Let $\sigma: B_\lambda^0(S) \to B_\lambda^0(S)$ be an isomorphism. We fix an arbitrary $\alpha \in \lambda$.

Since $\sigma: B_\lambda^0(S) \to B_\lambda^0(S)$ is the automorphism and the idempotent $(\alpha, 1_S, \alpha)$ is maximal with the respect to the

natural partial order on $E(B_\lambda^0(S))$, Proposition 3.2 of [14] implies that $((\alpha, 1_S, \alpha))\sigma = (\alpha', 1_S, \alpha')$ for some $\alpha' \in \lambda$.

Since $(\beta, 1_S, \alpha)(\alpha, 1_S, \alpha) = (\beta, 1_S, \alpha)$ for any $\beta \in \lambda$, we have that

$$((\beta, 1_S, \alpha))\sigma = ((\beta, 1_S, \alpha))\sigma \cdot (\alpha', 1_S, \alpha'),$$

and hence

$$((\beta, 1_S, \alpha))\sigma = ((\beta)\varphi, (\beta)u, \alpha'),$$

for some $(\beta)\varphi \in \lambda$ and $(\beta)u \in S$. Similarly, we get that

$$((\alpha, 1_S, \beta))\sigma = (\alpha', (\beta)v, (\beta)\psi),$$

for some $(\beta)\psi \in \lambda$ and $(\beta)v \in S$. Since $(\alpha, 1_S, \beta)(\beta, 1_S, \alpha) = (\alpha, 1_S, \alpha)$, we have that

$$\begin{aligned} (\alpha', 1_S, \alpha') &= ((\alpha, 1_S, \alpha))\sigma = \\ &= (\alpha', (\beta)v, (\beta)\psi) \cdot ((\beta)\varphi, (\beta)u, \alpha') = \\ &= (\alpha', (\beta)v \cdot (\beta)u, \alpha'), \end{aligned}$$

and hence $(\beta)\varphi = (\beta)\psi = \beta' \in \lambda$ and $(\beta)v \cdot (\beta)u = 1_S$. Similarly, since $(\beta, 1_S, \alpha) \cdot (\alpha, 1_S, \beta) = (\beta, 1_S, \beta)$, we see that the element

$$\begin{aligned} ((\beta, 1_S, \beta))\sigma &= ((\beta, 1_S, \alpha)(\alpha, 1_S, \beta))\sigma = \\ &= (\beta', (\beta)v \cdot (\beta)u, \beta') \end{aligned}$$

is a maximal idempotent of the subsemigroup $S_{\beta', \beta'}$ of $B_\lambda^0(S)$, and hence we have that $(\beta)v \cdot (\beta)u = 1_S$. This implies that the elements $(\beta)v$ and $(\beta)u$ are mutually invertible in H_1, and hence $(\beta)v = ((\beta)u)^{-1}$.

If $(\gamma)\varphi = (\delta)\varphi$ for $\gamma, \delta \in \lambda$ then

$$\begin{aligned} 0 \neq (\alpha', 1_S, (\gamma)\varphi) \cdot ((\delta)\varphi, 1_S, \alpha') = \\ = ((\alpha, 1_S, \gamma))\sigma \cdot ((\delta, 1_S, \alpha))\sigma, \end{aligned}$$

and since σ is an automorphism, we have that

$$(\alpha, 1_S, \gamma) \cdot (\delta, 1_S, \alpha) \neq 0$$

and hence $\gamma = \delta$. Thus $\varphi: \lambda \to \lambda$ is a bijective map.

Therefore for $s \in S \setminus \{0_S\}$ we have

$$\begin{aligned} ((\gamma, s, \delta))\sigma &= ((\gamma, 1_S, \alpha) \cdot (\alpha, s, \alpha) \cdot (\alpha, 1_S, \delta))\sigma = \\ &= ((\gamma, 1_S, \alpha))\sigma \cdot ((\alpha, s, \alpha))\sigma \cdot ((\alpha, 1_S, \delta))\sigma = \\ &= ((\gamma)\varphi, (\gamma)u, \alpha') \cdot (\alpha', (s)h, \alpha') \cdot (\alpha', ((\delta)u)^{-1}, (\delta)\varphi) = \\ &= ((\gamma)\varphi, (\gamma)u \cdot (s)h \cdot ((\delta)u)^{-1}, (\delta)\varphi). \end{aligned}$$

Also, since 0 is zero of the semigroup $B_\lambda^0(S)$ we conclude that $(0)\sigma = 0$. $\qquad\square$

Theorem 1 implies the following corollary:

Corollary 1. *Let $\lambda \geqslant 1$ be cardinal and let $B_\lambda(G)$ be the Brandt semigroup. Let $h: G \to G$ be an automorphism and suppose that $\varphi: \lambda \to \lambda$ is a bijective map. Let $u: \lambda \to G$*

be a map. Then the map $\sigma\colon B_\lambda(G) \to B_\lambda(G)$ defined by the formulae

$$((\alpha,s,\beta))\sigma = ((\alpha)\varphi, (\alpha)u \cdot (s)h \cdot ((\beta)u)^{-1}, (\beta)\varphi)$$
$$and \quad (0)\sigma = 0,$$

is an automorphism of the Brandt semigroup $B_\lambda(G)$. Moreover, every automorphism of $B_\lambda(G)$ can be constructed in this manner.

Also, we observe that Corollary 1 implies the following well known statement:

Corollary 2. Let $\lambda \geqslant 1$ be cardinal and $\varphi\colon \lambda \to \lambda$ a bijective map. Then the map $\sigma\colon B_\lambda \to B_\lambda$ defined by the formulae

$$((\alpha,\beta))\sigma = ((\alpha)\varphi, (\beta)\varphi) \quad and \quad (0)\sigma = 0,$$

is an automorphism of the semigroup of $\lambda \times \lambda$-matrix units B_λ. Moreover, every automorphism of B_λ can be constructed in this manner.

The following example implies that the condition that semigroup S contains the identity is essential.

Example 1. Let λ be any cardinal $\geqslant 2$. Let S be the zero-semigroup of cardinality $\geqslant 3$ and 0_S is zero of S. It is easily to see that every bijective map $\sigma\colon B^0_\lambda(S) \to B^0_\lambda(S)$ such that $(0)\sigma = 0$ is an automorphism of the Brandt λ^0-extension of S.

Remark. By Theorem 1 we have that every automorphism $\sigma\colon B^0_\lambda(S) \to B^0_\lambda(S)$ of the Brandt λ^0-extension of an arbitrary monoid S with zero identifies with the ordered triple $[\varphi, h, u]$, where $h\colon S \to S$ is an automorphism of S, $\varphi\colon \lambda \to \lambda$ is a bijective map and $u\colon \lambda \to H_1$ is a map, where H_1 is the group of units of S.

Lemma 1. Let $\lambda \geqslant 1$ be cardinal, S be a monoid with zero and let $B^0_\lambda(S)$ be the Brandt λ^0-extension of S. Then the composition of arbitrary automorphisms $\sigma = [\varphi, h, u]$ and $\sigma' = [\varphi', h', u']$ of the Brandt λ^0-extension of S defines in the following way:

$$[\varphi, h, u] \cdot [\varphi', h', u'] = [\varphi\varphi', hh', \varphi u' \cdot uh'].$$

Proof. By Theorem 1 for every $(\alpha, s, \beta) \in B^0_\lambda(S)$ we have that

$$(\alpha,s,\beta)(\sigma\sigma') = ((\alpha)\varphi, (\alpha)u \cdot (s)h \cdot ((\beta)u)^{-1}, (\beta)\varphi)\,\sigma' =$$
$$= \big(((\alpha)\varphi)\varphi', ((\alpha)\varphi)u' \cdot ((\alpha)u \cdot (s)h \cdot ((\beta)u)^{-1})\,h' \cdot$$
$$\cdot \big(((\beta)\varphi)u'\big)^{-1}, ((\beta)\varphi)\varphi'\big) =$$

and since h' is an automorphism of the monoid S we get that this is equal to

$$= \big(((\alpha)\varphi)\varphi', ((\alpha)\varphi)u' \cdot ((\alpha)u)\,h' \cdot ((s)h)\,h' \cdot$$
$$\cdot \big(((\beta)u)h'\big)^{-1} \cdot \big(((\beta)\varphi)u'\big)^{-1}, ((\beta)\varphi)\varphi'\big) =$$
$$= \big((\alpha)(\varphi\varphi'), (\alpha)(\varphi u' \cdot uh') \cdot ((s)h)\,h' \cdot$$
$$\cdot (\beta)\big(\varphi u' \cdot uh'\big)^{-1}, (\beta)(\varphi\varphi')\big).$$

This completes the proof of the requested equality. $\square$

Theorem 2. Let $\lambda \geqslant 1$ be cardinal, S be a monoid with zero and let $B^0_\lambda(S)$ be the Brandt λ^0-extension of S. Then the group of automorphisms $\mathbf{Aut}(B^0_\lambda(S))$ of $B^0_\lambda(S)$ is isomorphic to a homomorphic image of the group defines on the Cartesian product $\mathscr{S}_\lambda \times \mathbf{Aut}(S) \times H_1^\lambda$ with the following binary operation:

$$[\varphi, h, u] \cdot [\varphi', h', u'] = [\varphi\varphi', hh', \varphi u' \cdot uh'], \qquad (2)$$

where $\mathscr{S}_\lambda$ is the group of all bijections of the cardinal λ, $\mathbf{Aut}(S)$ is the group of all automorphisms of the semigroup S and H_1^λ is the direct λ-power of the group of units H_1 of the monoid S. Moreover, the inverse element of $[\varphi, h, u]$ in the group $\mathbf{Aut}(B^0_\lambda(S))$ is defined by the formula:

$$[\varphi, h, u]^{-1} = \big[\varphi^{-1}, h^{-1}, \varphi^{-1}u^{-1}h^{-1}\big].$$

Proof. First, we show that the binary operation defined by formula (2) is associative. Let $[\varphi, h, u]$, $[\varphi', h', u']$ and $[\varphi'', h'', u'']$ be arbitrary elements of the Cartesian product $\mathscr{S}_\lambda \times \mathbf{Aut}(S) \times H_1^\lambda$. Then we have that

$$\big([\varphi, h, u] \cdot [\varphi', h', u']\big) \cdot [\varphi'', h'', u''] =$$
$$= [\varphi\varphi', hh', \varphi u' \cdot uh'] \cdot [\varphi'', h'', u''] =$$
$$= [\varphi\varphi'\varphi'', hh'h'', \varphi\varphi'u'' \cdot (\varphi u' \cdot uh')h''] =$$
$$= [\varphi\varphi'\varphi'', hh'h'', \varphi\varphi'u'' \cdot \varphi u'h'' \cdot uh'h'']$$

and

$$[\varphi, h, u] \cdot \big([\varphi', h', u'] \cdot [\varphi'', h'', u'']\big) =$$
$$= [\varphi, h, u] \cdot [\varphi'\varphi'', h'h'', \varphi'u'' \cdot u'h''] =$$
$$= [\varphi\varphi'\varphi'', hh'h'', \varphi(\varphi'u'' \cdot u'h'') \cdot uh'h''] =$$
$$= [\varphi\varphi'\varphi'', hh'h'', \varphi\varphi'u'' \cdot \varphi u'h'' \cdot uh'h''],$$

and hence so defined operation is associative.

Theorem 1 implies that formula (1) determines a map $\mathfrak{F}$ from the Cartesian product $\mathscr{S}_\lambda \times \mathbf{Aut}(S) \times H_1^\lambda$ onto the group of automorphisms $\mathbf{Aut}(B^0_\lambda(S))$ of the Brandt λ^0-extension $B^0_\lambda(S)$ of the monoid S, and hence the associativity of binary operation (2) implies that the map $\mathfrak{F}$ is a homomorphism from $\mathscr{S}_\lambda \times \mathbf{Aut}(S) \times H_1^\lambda$ onto the group $\mathbf{Aut}(B^0_\lambda(S))$.

Next we show that $[1_{\mathscr{S}_\lambda}, 1_{\mathbf{Aut}(S)}, 1_{H_1^\lambda}]$ is a unit element with the respect to the binary operation (2), where $1_{\mathscr{S}_\lambda}$, $1_{\mathbf{Aut}(S)}$ and $1_{H_1^\lambda}$ are units of the groups $\mathscr{S}_\lambda$, $\mathbf{Aut}(S)$ and H_1^λ, respectively. Then we have that

$$[\varphi, h, u] \cdot \big[1_{\mathscr{S}_\lambda}, 1_{\mathbf{Aut}(S)}, 1_{H_1^\lambda}\big] =$$
$$= \big[\varphi 1_{\mathscr{S}_\lambda}, h 1_{\mathbf{Aut}(S)}, \varphi 1_{H_1^\lambda} \cdot u 1_{\mathbf{Aut}(S)}\big] =$$
$$= \big[\varphi, h, \varphi 1_{H_1^\lambda} \cdot u 1_{\mathbf{Aut}(S)}\big] =$$
$$= \big[\varphi, h, 1_{H_1^\lambda} \cdot u\big] =$$
$$= [\varphi, h, u]$$

and

$$\big[1_{\mathscr{S}_\lambda}, 1_{\mathbf{Aut}(S)}, 1_{H_1^\lambda}\big] \cdot [\varphi, h, u] =$$
$$= \big[1_{\mathscr{S}_\lambda}\varphi, 1_{\mathbf{Aut}(S)}h, 1_{\mathscr{S}_\lambda}u \cdot 1_{H_1^\lambda}h\big] =$$
$$= [\varphi, h, u],$$

because every automorphism $h \in \mathbf{Aut}(S)$ acts on the group H_1^λ by the natural way as a restriction of global automorphism of the semigroup S on every factor, and hence we get that $1_{H_1^\lambda} h = 1_{H_1^\lambda}$.

Also, similar arguments imply that

$$[\varphi, h, u] \cdot [\varphi, h, u]^{-1} = [\varphi, h, u] \cdot [\varphi^{-1}, h^{-1}, \varphi^{-1} u^{-1} h^{-1}] =$$
$$= [\varphi\varphi^{-1}, hh^{-1}, (\varphi\varphi^{-1}) u^{-1} h^{-1} \cdot uh^{-1}] =$$
$$= [\varphi\varphi^{-1}, hh^{-1}, (1_{\mathscr{S}_\lambda}) u^{-1} h^{-1} \cdot uh^{-1}] =$$
$$= [\varphi\varphi^{-1}, hh^{-1}, u^{-1} h^{-1} \cdot uh^{-1}] =$$
$$= [1_{\mathscr{S}_\lambda}, 1_{\mathbf{Aut}(S)}, 1_{H_1^\lambda}]$$

and

$$[\varphi, h, u]^{-1} \cdot [\varphi, h, u] = [\varphi^{-1}, h^{-1}, \varphi^{-1} u^{-1} h^{-1}] \cdot [\varphi, h, u] =$$
$$= [\varphi^{-1}\varphi, h^{-1}h, \varphi^{-1} u \cdot \varphi^{-1} u^{-1} h^{-1} h] =$$
$$= [\varphi^{-1}\varphi, h^{-1}h, \varphi^{-1} u \cdot \varphi^{-1} u^{-1}] =$$
$$= [1_{\mathscr{S}_\lambda}, 1_{\mathbf{Aut}(S)}, 1_{H_1^\lambda}].$$

This implies that the elements $[\varphi^{-1}, h^{-1}, \varphi^{-1} u^{-1} h^{-1}]$ and $[\varphi, h, u]$ are invertible in $\mathscr{S}_\lambda \times \mathbf{Aut}(S) \times H_1^\lambda$, and hence the set $\mathscr{S}_\lambda \times \mathbf{Aut}(S) \times H_1^\lambda$ with the binary operation (2) is a group.

Let $\mathbf{Id} \colon B_\lambda^0(S) \to B_\lambda^0(S)$ be the identity automorphism of the semigroup $B_\lambda^0(S)$. Then by Theorem 1 there exist some automorphism $h \colon S \to S$, a bijective map $\varphi \colon \lambda \to \lambda$ and a map $u \colon \lambda \to H_1$ into the group H_1 of units of S such that

$$(\alpha, s, \beta) = (\alpha, s, \beta)\mathbf{Id} =$$
$$= ((\alpha)\varphi, (\alpha)u \cdot (s)h \cdot ((\beta)u)^{-1}, (\beta)\varphi),$$

for all $\alpha, \beta \in \lambda$ and $s \in S^*$. Since $\mathbf{Id} \colon B_\lambda^0(S) \to B_\lambda^0(S)$ is the identity automorphism we conclude that $(\alpha)\varphi = \alpha$ for every $\alpha \in \lambda$. Also, for every $s \in S^*$ we get that $s = (\alpha)u \cdot (s)h \cdot ((\beta)u)^{-1}$ for all $\alpha, \beta \in \lambda$, and hence we obtain that

$$1_S = (\alpha)u \cdot (1_S)h \cdot ((\beta)u)^{-1} = (\alpha)u \cdot ((\beta)u)^{-1}$$

for all $\alpha, \beta \in \lambda$. This implies that $(\alpha)u = (\beta)u = \widetilde{u}$ is a fixed element of the group H_1 for all $\alpha, \beta \in \lambda$.

We define

$$\ker N = \Big\{ [\varphi, h, \widetilde{u}] \in \mathscr{S}_\lambda \times \mathbf{Aut}(S) \times H_1^\lambda :$$
$$\varphi \colon \lambda \to \lambda \text{ is an idemtity map,}$$
$$\widetilde{u}(s)h\widetilde{u}^{-1} = s \text{ for any } s \in S \Big\}.$$

It is obvious that the equality $\widetilde{u}(s)h\widetilde{u}^{-1} = s$ implies that $(s)h = \widetilde{u}^{-1} s \widetilde{u}$ for all $s \in S$. The previous arguments implies that $[\varphi, h, \widetilde{u}] \in \ker N$ if and only if $[\varphi, h, \widetilde{u}]\mathfrak{F}$ is the unit of the group $\mathbf{Aut}(B_\lambda^0(S))$, and hence $\ker N$ is a normal subgroup of $\mathscr{S}_\lambda \times \mathbf{Aut}(S) \times H_1^\lambda$. This implies that the quotient group $(\mathscr{S}_\lambda \times \mathbf{Aut}(S) \times H_1^\lambda)/\ker N$ is isomorphic to the group $\mathbf{Aut}(B_\lambda^0(S))$. $\qquad\square$

References

[1] A. H. Clifford, *Matrix representations of completely simple semigroups*, Amer. J. Math. **64** (1942), 327–342.

[2] A. H. Clifford and G. B. Preston, *The Algebraic Theory of Semigroups*, Vols. I and II, Amer. Math. Soc. Surveys 7, Providence, R.I., 1961 and 1967.

[3] S. Bardyla and O. Gutik, *On a semitopological polycyclic monoid*, Algebra Discr. Math. **21**:2 (2016), 163–183.

[4] O. V. Gutik, *On Howie semigroup*, Mat. Metody Phis.-Mekh. Polya. **42**:4 (1999), 127–132 (in Ukrainian).

[5] O. Gutik, *On closures in semitopological inverse semigroups with continuous inversion*, Algebra Discr. Math. **18**:1 (2014), 59–85.

[6] O. V. Gutik and K. P. Pavlyk, *Topological Brandt λ-extensions of absolutely H-closed topological inverse semigroups*, Visnyk Lviv Univ., Ser. Mekh.-Math. **61** (2003), 98–105.

[7] O. V. Gutik and K. P. Pavlyk, *On topological semigroups of matrix units*, Semigroup Forum **71**:3 (2005), 389–400.

[8] O. V. Gutik and K. P. Pavlyk, *On Brandt λ^0-extensions of semigroups with zero*, Mat. Metody Phis.-Mekh. Polya. **49**:3 (2006), 26–40.

[9] O. Gutik and K. Pavlyk, *On pseudocompact topological Brandt λ^0-extensions of semitopological monoids*, Topological Algebra Appl. **1** (2013), 60–79.

[10] O. Gutik, K. Pavlyk, and A. Reiter, *Topological semigroups of matrix units and countably compact Brandt λ^0-extensions*, Mat. Stud. **32**:2 (2009), 115–131.

[11] O. V. Gutik, K. P. Pavlyk, and A. R. Reiter, *On topological Brandt semigroups*, Mat. Metody Fiz.-Mekh. Polya **54**:2 (2011), 7–16 (in Ukrainian); English version in: J. Math. Sci. **184**:1 (2012), 1–11.

[12] O. V. Gutik and O. Ravsky, *On feebly compact inverse primitive (semi)topological semigroups*, Mat. Stud. **44**:1 (2015), 3–26.

[13] O. V. Gutik and O. V. Ravsky, *Pseudocompactness, products and Brandt λ^0-extensions of semitopological monoids*, Mat. Metody Fiz.-Mekh. Polya **58**:2 (2015), 20–37.

[14] O. Gutik and D. Repovš, *On Brandt λ^0-extensions of monoids with zero*, Semigroup Forum **80**:1 (2010), 8–32.

[15] J. Jamalzadeh and Gh. Rezaei, *Countably compact topological semigroups versus Brandt extensions and paragroups*, Algebras Groups Geom. **27**:2 (2010), 219–228.

[16] J. Jamalzadeh and Gh. Rezaei, *Brandt extensions and primitive topologically periodic inverse topological semigroups*, Bull. Iran. Math. Soc. **39**:1 (2013), 87–95.

[17] S. Kitaev and V. Lozin, *Words and Graphs*, Monographs in Theor. Comput. Sc. An EATCS Series. Springer, 2015.

[18] S. Kitaev and S. Seif, *Word problem of the Perkins semigroup via directed acyclic graphs*, Order **25**:3 (2008), 177–194.

[19] W. D. Munn, *Matrix representations of semigroups*, Proc. Cambridge Phil. Soc. **53** (1957), 5–12.

[20] P. Perkins, *Bases for equational theories of semigroups*, J. Algebra **11**:2 (1969), 298–314.

[21] M. Petrich, *Inverse Semigroups*, John Wiley & Sons, New York, 1984.

ITAT 2016 Proceedings, p. 241
ISBN 978-1537016740, © 2016 T. Jajcayová

The Word Problem in Free Inverse Monoids
(Presentation Abstract)

Tatiana Jajcayová

Comenius University, Bratislava, Slovakia
tatiana.jajcayova@fmph.uniba.sk

In our presentation, we will address some algorithmic questions (the Word Problem, for instance) concerning presentations of inverse monoids by considering automata rising from these presentations. The automata considered are in general infinite, but in specific cases we are able to detect so called finite core that encodes the important information about the automaton in a 'finite' subgraph. We introduce certain classes of HNN-extensions for which we were able to provide an iterative procedure for building these automata, and to show that in some cases this procedure yields an effective construction, and thus provides a solution for the word problem. We analyze conditions under which the procedure is effective and show that, in particular, the word problem is decidable for HNN-extensions of free inverse monoids.

ITAT 2016 Proceedings, p. 242
ISBN 978-1537016740, © 2016 R. Jajcay

Inverse Semigroups of Partial Automorphisms of Graphs
(Presentation Abstract)

Robert Jajcay

Comenius University, Bratislava, Slovakia
robert.jajcay@fmph.uniba.sk

The concept of an automorphism group of a combinatorial structure is a fundamental concept in both Combinatorics and Group Theory. Finding the automorphism group of a specific structure is a notoriously hard problem whose general complexity has not been resolved but it is believed to be exponential. Finding the full inverse semigroup of partial automorphisms of a combinatorial structure is at least as hard as finding its automorphism group, but detailed knowledge of this semigroup holds promise of 'local' information lost in the automorphism group. In our talk, we will focus on specific problems from graph theory that appear to be particularly suited for using inverse semigroups of partial automorphisms. These problems include problems from extremal graph theory, namely the Cage and Degree/Diameter Problems, as well as the Graph Reconstruction Problem and the related problem of pseudo-similar vertices.

ITAT 2016 Proceedings, p. 243
ISBN 978-1537016740, © 2016 L. Márki

The Theory of Morita Equivalence of Semigroups
(Presentation Abstract)

László Márki

MTA Rényi Institute, Budapest, Hungary
marki.laszlo@renyi.mta.hu

Seen from a different angle, transformation semigroups are the same as semigroup actions on sets, which are usually called acts by semigroup theorists. All actions of a semigroup S form a category $S-act$, which has several interesting subcategories like that of unitary actions ('unitary' can be defined in several ways). Two semigroups are called Morita equivalent if the categories of their unitary actions (in the simplest case) are equivalent. The notion of Morita equivalence originates in rings with identity; for monoids it has turned out to be of little interest because it coincides with isomorphism in too many cases. On the other hand, it yields a rich theory if instead of requiring the presence of an identity element in the semigroup we require the presence of 'local units', as shown by works of Lawson, Laan and Márki. Recent investigations of Laan and Márki deal with the case when even the requirement of local units is weakened. Tensor product is the main tool in these investigations.

ITAT 2016 Proceedings, p. 244
ISBN 978-1537016740, © 2016 E. Rodaro

Decidability vs Undecidability of the Word Problem in HNN-Extensions of Inverse Semigroups
(Presentation Abstract)

Emanuele Rodaro

Politecnico di Milano, Milan, Italy
emanuele.rodaro@gmail.com

The solvability of the word problem for Yamamura's HNN-extensions $[S; A_1, A_2; \varphi]$ has been proved in some particular cases. However, we show that, contrary to the group case, the word problem for $[S; A_1 A_2; \varphi]$ is undecidable even if we consider S to have finite $\mathscr{R}$-classes, A_1 and A_2 to be free inverse subsemigroups of finite rank and with zero, and φ, φ^{-1} to be computable.

ITAT 2016 Proceedings, p. 245
ISBN 978-1537016740, © 2016 N. Szakács

Inverse Monoids and Immersions of 2-Complexes
(Presentation Abstract)

Nóra Szakács

University of Szeged, Szeged, Hungary
szakacsn@math.u-szeged.hu

It is well known that under mild restrictions on a connected topological space X, the connected covers of X may be classified via conjugacy classes of subgroups of the fundamental group of X. This also gives rise to the theory of Deck transformations — the action of the fundamental group of a space on its universal cover. Margolis and Meakin have extended these results to study immersions between 1-dimensional CW-complexes, that is, graphs, which Meakin and the speaker have generalized to 2-dimensional CW-complexes. An immersion $f : D \mapsto C$ between CW-complexes is a cellular map such that each point y in D has a neighborhood U that is mapped homeomorphically onto $f(U)$ by f. In order to classify immersions into a 2-dimensional CW-complex C, we need to replace the fundamental group of C by an appropriate inverse monoid. We show how conjugacy classes of the closed inverse submonoids of this inverse monoid may be used to classify connected immersions into the complex.

ITAT 2016 Proceedings, p. 246
ISBN 978-1537016740, © 2016 M. B. Szendrei

On Products of Inverse Semigroups
(Presentation Abstract)

Mária B. Szendrei

Bolyai Institute, University of Szeged, Hungary

A fundamental construction of permutation groups is forming wreath product which appears in a number of ways in combinatorics.

In the talk we introduce a wreath product of inverse semigroups of partial bijections which generalizes this construction. Moreover, we define a product of semidirect type for arbitrary inverse semigroups where the action involved is a strong partial action by partial automorphisms. Finally, we discuss how these products relate to each other, and to former constructions (λ-wreath product and Houghton wreath product) which play important role in the structure theory of inverse semigroups.

Index